D0071951

Introduction to Medieval Europe, 300–1550

'An awe-inspiring and magisterial survey of twelve centuries of Medieval History. Written with verve and flair but never patronizing or too simplifying, it provides an up-to-date synthesis of recent scholarship on the Middle Ages by two outstanding Dutch medievalists.'
Elizabeth van Houts,
Emmanuel College, University of Cambridge

'The best medieval history textbook I have ever read.'
William H. TeBrake, *University of Maine*

The Middle Ages evoke images of towers and castles where minstrels perform courtly love songs and stout-hearted knights challenge one another in honourable fashion at tournaments. These are typical of the clichés that cloud our view of a long, complex and varied period of European history brought vividly to life in this comprehensive textbook. Medieval Europe was a world that, by modern standards, was technologically underdeveloped, poor, unjust and extremely violent. It was also a world dominated by figures of almost mythical proportions such as Saint Augustine and Charlemagne, Dante Alighieri and Thomas Aquinas, Frederick Barbarossa and Joan of Arc. *Introduction to Medieval Europe* surveys the years between 300 and 1550, and covers themes as diverse as barbarian migrations, the growth of cities, kingship, religious reform and renewal, the Crusades, commerce, the

Black Death, and the intellectual and cultural life of the Middle Ages. It shows the driving forces behind the formation of medieval society and the directions in which it developed and changed.

This inspiring textbook:

- provides a clear and stimulating survey account of medieval history over more than a thousand years;
- covers all the main issues and themes within a clear interpretive framework;
- includes illustrated, focused case studies in each chapter to assist learning, covering topics such as Roman Law, architecture, taxation, advances in medicine, the indulgence trade in the Church and a merchant's manual;
- gives wide geographical coverage and is richly illustrated with over a hundred photos, engravings, maps, tables and figures;
- is written by two leaders in their field with the most up-to-date research and reading.

Wim Blockmans is Professor of Medieval History at the University of Leiden and is Rector of the Netherlands Institute of Advanced Study in Humanities and Social Sciences.

Peter Hoppenbrouwers is Professor of Medieval History at the University of Amsterdam.

Introduction to Medieval Europe, 300–1550

Wim Blockmans and
Peter Hoppenbrouwers

Translated by Isola van den Hoven

Routledge
Taylor & Francis Group

LONDON AND NEW YORK

First published in 2002 in the Dutch language as 'Eeuwen des
Onderscheids: Een geschiedenis van middeleeuws Europa' by
Prometheus

English translation, 'Introduction to Medieval Europe: Age of
Discretion', first published 2007
by Routledge
2 Park Square, Milton Park, Abingdon, Oxon OX14 4RN

Simultaneously published in the USA and Canada
by Routledge
270 Madison Ave, New York, NY 10016

*Routledge is an imprint of the Taylor & Francis Group, an informa
business*

Publication has been made possible with the financial support from the
Foundation for the Production and Translation of Dutch Literature.

'Eeuwen des Onderscheids: Een geschiedenis van middeleeuws
Europa' © 2002 by Prometheus, Amsterdam

'Introduction to Medieval Europe: Age of Discretion' English translation
© 2007 Routledge

Typeset in Garamond and Univers by
Keystroke, 28 High Street, Tettenhall, Wolverhampton
Printed and bound in Great Britain by
The Cromwell Press, Trowbridge, Wiltshire

British Library Cataloguing in Publication Data
A catalogue record for this book is available from the British Library

Library of Congress Cataloging in Publication Data
Blockmans, Willem Pieter.
[Eeuwen des onderscheids. English]
Introduction to medieval Europe, 300–1550 : age of discretion / Wim
Blockmans and Peter Hoppenbrouwers ; translated by Isola van den
Hoven.
p. cm.
Includes bibliographical references and index.
1. Middle Ages–History. 2. Europe–History–476–1492. 3. Civilization,
Medieval. I. Hoppenbrouwers, P. C. M. II. Title.
D117.B5413 2007
940.1–dc22
                        2006029744

ISBN10: 0–415–34698–3 ISBN13: 978–0–415–34698–6 (hbk)
ISBN10: 0–415–34699–1 ISBN13: 978–0–415–34699–3 (pbk)

Contents

Illustrations

MAPS

TABLES

UNNUMBERED PLATES AND FIGURES

Boxes

Illustration acknowledgements

MAPS

Illustration section with kind permission of An Delva. Drawn and supplied by kind permission of P. Hoppenbrouwers.

PLATES

1.1 World map, Ms D'Orville 77, f. 100 r. © The Bodleian Library, University of Oxford.

2.1 'Tabula Peutingeriana', Cod. 324, Segm. IV. © Austrian National Library Picture Archives, Vienna.

2.2 Interior of Hagia Sophia, Constantinople. © Bridgeman Art Library, London.
Unnumbered plate of Suebe skull (Osterby skull). © Archaeological Museum, Schloss Gottorf, Schleswig-Holstein.
Unnumbered plate of ivory panel at Monza, © Monza Cathedral, Monza

4.1 Mater Ecclesiae. Ms. Barb. Lat. 952, fragment 1 b/c. © Vatican Library, Rome.
Unnumbered plate of Jellinge rune stones and church. Redrawn by P. Hoppenbrouwers.

4.2 Shrine of the St Patrick bell. © National Museum of Ireland, Dublin.

4.3 Dome of the Rock on the Temple Mount in Jerusalem. © Bridgeman Art Library, London.

5.1 Gold treasure from the grave of a Frisian lord. © Rijksmuseum van Oudheden, Leiden.
Unnumbered plate in the Lord of the Rings box, showing burial with master and slave from Stengrade, Denmark, from p. 55 *The Vikings*, by Else Roesdahl, translated by Susan M. Margeson and Kirsten Williams, Allen Lane, 1991, Penguin Books 1992, © Else Roesdahl 1987. This translation © Susan M. Margeson and Kirsten Williams, 1991.
Unnumbered plate showing three gold bracteates. © National Museum of Denmark.

5.2 Haithabu harbour reconstruction. © Archaeology Museum at Christian Albrechts University, Kiel. Photo from Hildegarde Elsner, Wikinger Museum, Haithabu.

6.1 Lombard royal crown. Photo: Raffaello Bra. Courtesy cathedral at Monza.

6.2 Statuette of Charlemagne from the Louvre Museum. Originally treasure from the cathedral at Metz. Photo © Jean-Gilles Berizzi/© RMN/Réunion des Musées Nationaux, Musée du Louvre.

6.3 Throne at Aachen. Archiv für Kunst und Geschichte. Photo © AKG Images, Berlin.

6.4 Map of England and Scotland. Ms 16, fv.v. © Masters and Fellows of Corpus Christi College, Cambridge.

6.5 Moorish castle, Obidos, Portugal. Photo © Rui Cunha.

6.6 (a) and (b). Öseberg ship in Museum of Cultural History, University of Oslo, Norway. Photo © Wim Blockmans.

7.1 (a) Ard and (b) Mould-board ploughs and both depicted in (c) Bayeux Tapestry. (a) and (b) courtesy Groningen Institute for Archaeology, Groningen; (c) 1995; Bayeux Tapestry, the Prisoner scene 2 (border detail), 108.1. © Musuem Service, Reading Borough Council. All rights reserved. Photo © Bridgeman Art Library, JF115611.

7.2 Ivory chess game. Louvre Museum. Photo © Daniel Arnaudet/ RMN – Paris.

7.3 Bamberg Knight, 5-B10-E1-67. © AKG Images, Berlin.

8.1 Coronation of Henry the Lion. © Herzog August Bibliothek, Wolfenbüttel, Germany. Unnumbered plate showing the Emperor Constantine. Sainte Chapelle, Paris.

8.2 Cluny abbey. © Bibliotheque Nationale de France.

8.3 Vézelay door. XIR 68512. Photo © Bridgeman Art Library, London.

8.4 Fresco of St Francis by Giotto. © 1990. Photo SCALA, Florence 2007.

8.5 Montségur. Photo ©Toulouse-Editions d'Art Larrey. Unnumbered plate showing St Hubert's key, St Servaas, Maastricht.

9.1 Power symbols of the Holy Roman Empire (a) SK XIII.1 (Reichskrone); (b) SK XIII.17 (Mauritiusschwert); (c) SK XIII.2 (Reichsapfel) © Historical Museum, Vienna.

9.2 Coronation ritual of Henry VI. Ms Petrus de Eboli, Liber ad honorem Augusti, Cod. 120 II, f. 105 recto. © Bürgerbibliothek, Bern.

9.3 Martyrdom of Thomas Becket. Ms Harley 5102, f. 32. © British Library.

9.4 Rheims cathedral. Photo © An Delva, Ghent.

10.1 Krak des Chevaliers (a) and (b). Photo © Wim Blockmans.

10.2 Images of Tartars. Ms 16, f. 167r. © Corpus Christi College, Cambridge.

10.3 The drapery market, Bologna. From the Medieval Civic Museum, Bologna. Ms 93, f.1. Photo © Alinari Archives.

10.4 Portolan Map. Ms Douce 390, ff. 4v–5. © Bodleian Library, University of Oxford.

10.5 Two scenes in a counting house. Ms Add. 27695, f. 8. © British Library, London.

11.1 Lorenzetti fresco of the Palazzo Pubblico in Siena. Photo © 1990 SCALA, Florence 2007.

11.2 View of Zürich, © Swiss National Museum, Zürich. Unnumbered plate showing 'Wounds man' from the surgical manual, *Surgical Treatment for Blows, Stab and Gunshot Wounds*. From Shipperges, p. 115.

12.1 A medieval library. © Bridgeman Art Library, London.

12.2 Aristotle Lectures. Ms 72, f. 1r. © Ghent University Library.

13.1 Pest procession. Duc de Berry archive, Musée Condé , Paris. ff. 71v–72r. Photo © Bridgeman Art Library. Unnumbered plate showing triumph of death fresco, fourteenth century. Photo © 1990 SCALA, Florence, 2007.

13.2 Chess game with death. © BPK (Bildarchiv Preussischer Kulterbesitz), Berlin, 2006

13.3 Danse macabre (a) and (b). © Artaud Frère, Rue de la Métalurgie, 44470 Carquefou-Nantes, France.

13.4 Poor relief, Bruges. Photo: Dienst Stedelijke Musea, Bruges.

14.1 Royal body as an allegory of the state. French miniature from the Avis aus Roys, *c.* 1369. Ms. 456, f. 5. © Pierpont Morgan Library, New York.

14.2 Monstrelet, Chronique: Battle of Agincourt. © Leiden University Library, Ms. VGGF2, fol. 124v.

14.3 Opening of the English Parliament, April 1523. The Royal Collection, Windsor Castle. © 2005, Her Majesty Queen Elizabeth II.

15.1 Holy sacraments, Van der Weyden. Inv. nr 393. © Koninklijk Museum, Antwerp.

15.2 Pulpit by Michelozzo on the outside wall of the Cathedral of Santo Stefano at Prato. © Alinari Archives.

15.3 Purgatory. Musée Condé, Chantilly, France. Les très riches heures du duc de Berry. f. 113v. Photo © Bridgeman Art Library.

15.4 Thomas a Kempis. Cod. 1576. f. 9 ro. © Austrian National Library, Vienna.

15.5 House altar. © Koninklijk Museum, Antwerp.

CHAPTER 1

Concepts and interpretive frameworks

An observer in the early years of the twenty-first century trying to make sense of the Middle Ages must overcome a degree of culture shock and discard a number of concepts that seem perfectly natural to his or her own situation. Try to imagine a Europe in which:

- the limits of the continent have not yet been explored entirely;
- the living environment of most people is local, at most regional;
- the territories of countries that still exist under their medieval names were then often quite different to those of the present day;
- Christianity informs practically every aspect of daily life;
- Europe is far less developed than a number of cultural spheres, in particular the Mediterranean Muslim world.

When the step to this other world has been taken, it is possible to realize that the European Middle Ages still show a fundamental connection to our own times. Medieval culture is not entirely unrelated to ours, as is that of the Aztecs, for example. On the contrary, there has been expansion and progress in Europe in numerous fields ever since the seventh or eighth century. At the same time, acceleration, delays and also periods of decline can be discerned, as well as certain qualitative transitions such as urbanization and colonization. The foundations of modern-day Europe, even of much of the modern-day world, lie in the European Middle Ages: the spread of Christianity, the establishment of areas sharing a common language, the formation of territorial states with seeds of national consciousness, the urbanization of particular regions, the renewed development of rational-empirical scientific thought,

the creation of political structures based on representation and the expansion of commercial networks.

In other words, the dynamism, the continuous and sustained growth undergone by the world population

Plate 1.1 In this map the world is divided into five equatorial zones. It is often thought that in the Middle Ages people saw the world as a flat plane, yet surviving texts show that it was commonly described as a sphere. Medieval rulers then held an orb, not a disc, in their hands as a symbol of power. Map of the world from Macrobius, *Commentary to the 'Somnium Scipionis'*, South Germany, *c.* 1000

and the world economy in the last few centuries, had its starting-point in the period and region central to this book. Other spheres of culture underwent growth and expansion, too, even to other continents. As far as general economic and cultural development was concerned Europe lagged behind until the eighteenth century, particularly in comparison with China. But Europe gradually struggled out of this position and imposed its own model of development on the rest of the world. The formation of a mentality and an economic system that allowed this to happen stems from conditions that were created in the Middle Ages, the centuries of distinction, the centuries in which Europe grew up.

THE TERMS 'MIDDLE AGES', 'HUMANISM', 'RENAISSANCE' AND 'REFORMATION'

Nowadays, the term 'medieval', with 'feudal' used as a regular alternative, often represents something backward and barbaric. The Middle Ages are all too easily presented as obscure (the Dark Ages), in contrast to the periods before and after, which would have been so much more splendid. How did such a view come about?

Beginning in Italy during the fourteenth century, poets and scholars who considered themselves humanists variously expressed the belief that they were at the threshold of a new era of intellectual brilliance that would stand out sharply against the darkness of preceding centuries. The term *tenebrae* (mists) came from the pen of Francesco Petrarch (1304–1374), the famous poet who inspired such passionate admiration for Roman Antiquity; he used the word to refer to the time following Antiquity. After Petrarch, others spoke of *media tempestas, media aetas, media tempora*, the interim period. All these terms have a decidedly negative connotation. The Middle Ages was for them nothing but an unfortunate and uninteresting period of decay between Antiquity and the new golden age epitomized in the humanist scholars themselves.

The expression *medium aevum* was given official status in 1678 when Du Cange published his two-volume *Glossarium* of Latin words used in the Middle Ages that deviated from the classical meaning. Ten

years later Christophorus Cellarius presented the first history of the Middle Ages under the title, *Historia Medii Aevi*, which covered the period from Emperor Constantine the Great (306–337) to the Fall of Constantinople (1453).

Since 'Middle Ages' is a humanist construct, the success of the concept is no doubt connected to the strong development of the system of Latin schools and grammar schools for secondary education. This was where humanistic ideas fully came into their own, since the study of the classical languages formed the basis of the curriculum. It was hoped that through the study of the biographies of famous men and of the history of ancient culture, including poetry and rhetoric, new generations would be elevated to the idealized image of the heroes of Antiquity. Until well into the nineteenth century Latin remained the language of university education, so that every intellectual was immersed in the bath of Antiquity.

In Catholic countries in particular there was renewed interest in the Middle Ages from the seventeenth century onwards, which was reflected in the institutions specifically established to study the period. In the Protestant world, however, the Middle Ages were rather disregarded as an academic subject, so that emphasis instead could be placed on all the good that had been achieved since the Reformation. The religious divisions between thinkers thus perpetuated for ideological reasons the dividing line in history that the humanists had drawn out of scholarly motives.

During the nineteenth century ideologies again played an important part in the view of the past. If, in the period of classicism, the medieval cathedrals and monasteries had been allowed to fall into disrepair or even destroyed on purpose, as happened during the French Revolution, from the 1820s it again became fashionable to build in the Gothic style, even improving upon the medieval builders. In literature, Romantic authors like Sir Walter Scott, Heinrich Heine and Victor Hugo seized eagerly upon medieval stories to present the greatness of a medieval past, in contrast to the rationalism of the Enlightenment and the French revolutionaries. Into this past were projected conservative values such as kingship, Church and nobility, or civic freedom and national character, depending on what was required. The highest stone towers built in

Europe in the nineteenth century were those of the Gothic Revival cathedrals in Ulm and Cologne. The Houses of Parliament in London and Budapest are neogothic gems, as is the town hall of Munich. The past was thus coloured according to the preferences of the following centuries. Having first been maligned, the Middle Ages – or the image constructed of them – were now extolled.

In the course of the nineteenth century historical studies developed into a scholarly discipline. As more university professorships were introduced accepting the demarcation lines of humanism, the Renaissance and the Reformation, and as more learned societies, publications and journals focused on the times before or after these periods, such a division of the historical process was everywhere accepted as a fact. Jacob Burckhardt's *Die Kultur der Renaissance in Italien*, which appeared in 1860, played a key role. The phenomenal success of this book can be explained by the elegance with which the author formulated the historical myth imposed upon everyone who had enjoyed more than just an elementary education: the myth that a few generations of Italian intellectuals and artists had – through a truly cultural revolution – freed Europe from the stifling bonds of a society that was collectively oriented and in which every aspect of life on earth was focused on life after death.

'Renaissance' literally means 'rebirth', and that rebirth refers to the resurgence of ancient ideas and ideals. In modern usage it can refer to the resurgence of just about anything, from the renewed study of ancient texts to a harking back to the language of classical forms in architecture and the visual arts. Compared with this loaded concept of 'Renaissance', 'humanism' seems more neutral and therefore easier to deal with. Strictly speaking, humanism refers to a philological procedure consisting of two parts: on the one hand, of attempts to unearth more ancient texts by intensive research in libraries and through the translation of Greek authors into Latin; and on the other, of philological efforts to establish versions of those texts that resemble the originals as closely as possible. In addition to this, however, humanism has a more general and certainly vaguer meaning – that of an intellectual search more focused on mankind and of greater interest in the human individual and their intentions and emotions.

Burckhardt concentrated chiefly on this second meaning and raised one subjective observation about Italian culture in the late Middle Ages – the increased appreciation for individual human achievement – making it a key element in the process of revolutionary change that he detected. The renowned Dutch historian Johan Huizinga has already shown in his *Waning of the Middle Ages* (1919) how dangerous that is. He had no difficulty in tracing any number of 'typically medieval' cultural expressions in the fifteenth century. In his view they revealed a nostalgia for the past, rather than an aversion to it. The unique and revolutionary nature of the Italian Renaissance was undermined by other critics who pointed to a number of 'renaissances before the Renaissance'. The most important were the Carolingian Renaissance and the twelfth-century Renaissance. As concepts of periodization in the study of medieval history they have become as generally accepted as has Burckhardt's Italian Renaissance.

As for the religious Reformation, we shall demonstrate that from a theological and institutional point of view the Reformation of the first half of the sixteenth century follows on naturally from a long series of reform movements that began in the eleventh century. Its defining function is thus as debatable as that of the terms 'Renaissance' and 'humanism'. Nevertheless, the educational establishment in Protestant countries subsequently promoted the Middle Ages in stark contrast to later times, in order to stress its singularity.

PERIODS AND TYPES OF SOCIETY

Now that we know where the essentially functional term 'Middle Ages' comes from, and why it has remained in use, the question arises of whether there is any point in our continuing to use it. Is the definition more than just a self-glorification of humanistic scholars perpetuated by the education system?

We are not referring to the sterile question of whether historical periods that have been distinguished for the sake of didactic convenience should be finely demarcated with symbolically valued data. It will always be the case that radical transformations take place gradually, so that remnants of old structures co-exist with all sorts of new phenomena for a fairly long time. Moreover, changes do not take place everywhere at the same time; a distinction should thus be made between the time and speed of the change according also to its geographical location. From this assessment, then, we have opted for a periodization in which emphasis is placed on transitions rather than sharp breaks, on processes of far-reaching change within which elements of the old society exist alongside the new.

An even more fundamental question is on the basis of what criteria do we distinguish periods. What are the factors that cause such far-reaching social changes that all aspects of society are affected by them? There is no doubt that the process of industrialization signified the beginning of transformations in every field of individual and collective existence. In the case of the transition from the Roman Empire to the early Middle Ages, not only did sweeping constitutional and religious changes occur but at the same time there was also a fundamental transformation of social patterns and the economic order. It should be noted here that this break was only found in the Western Roman Empire. The Eastern Roman Empire continued to exist until 1453 – although considerably reduced. Of course it underwent a metamorphosis with the collapse of the western part, and from the beginning of the eleventh century it suffered a dramatic loss of power and territory, but it did continue to exist. Thus we come to the conclusion that the Middle Ages, as a generally accepted period in world history, have a purely Western European basis. But what of the developments between the fifth and eighteenth centuries? Is there not an equally fundamental swing to be observed somewhere within that period? And where should it then be situated?

All historians agree that in Western Europe the beginning of the process of urbanization, the renewed growth of towns and the commercialization of the economy connected to it, signalled a fundamental change throughout society. It is clear that it was only possible for more people to move to the growing towns because enough food was produced in the country to keep them alive, without their own labour being necessary. A new form of society was created in those towns, with its own lifestyle, mentality and values. An extensive network of commercial relationships, overseas trading posts and genuine colonies emerged from the larger coastal towns. The transcontinental expansion that started in Spain and Portugal in the fifteenth century was an immediate continuation of a development that the Italians had set in motion some centuries earlier around the Mediterranean and the Black Sea.

There was no question of sustained economic growth in Western Europe before about 1750. On a world scale the differences in development were as yet limited. With periodization in mind, two questions arise:

1 Did the changes in every field (economic, social, political and religious) that took place after the tenth century signify a transformation so sweeping that an essentially new type of society was created?
2 Did developments in all these spheres ('modern' state-formation, Renaissance, Reformation and overseas colonization) from the fifteenth century again signify a transformation, or were they no more than an accelerated continuation and extension of trends that had started some 500 years earlier?

There have been diverse answers to these questions. Medievalists apply a clear distinction between the almost exclusively agrarian early Middle Ages and the more urbanized and commercialized late Middle Ages, with the tenth to eleventh centuries as the turning point. Given that the evolution developed from a very low starting level it occurred extremely slowly, and the spread of innovations over the continent took hundreds of years. Precisely because this spread of innovations was so gradual, it is important to be aware of the considerable differences in development that existed between the various regions of Europe at any one time. The dynamism was earliest and strongest in the South and the West, whence it spread slowly over the remaining parts of the continent. While a highly developed urban society functioned in North and central Italy in the year 1200, societies of primitive farmers, and in some places even nomads, still existed in large areas of Scandinavia and in central and Eastern Europe. The interaction between societies at such different levels of development was itself another factor in the continuing dynamism.

Neither chronology nor the type of society alone provides an adequate interpretative framework for the examination of these great historical developments.

Both dimensions reveal the complex interactions leading to the evolution of societies. What is essential is that differences in the level of development can lead to dynamism, and that during a given period of time one specific type of society gains the ascendancy. Then what is known as '*die Ungleichzeitigkeit des Gleichzeitigen*' in recent German historiography comes into being: the situation where societies at different levels of development exist alongside each other at the same time.

There is thus some point to the demarcation of a period lasting from the fourth century to the sixteenth on other than humanistic grounds, but only when the demarcation contributes to our ability to discern far-reaching social transformations. Among such transformations we can mention the following:

- the weakening and disappearance of the Roman Empire, with its centralized imperial bureaucracy, its homogeneous administrative structure centred on *civitates*, and its subordinate system of production and distribution;
- relatively large-scale migration of multi-ethnic barbarian groups, followed by the formation of proto-national 'regnal communities' (Reynolds) in the West;
- enlargement of agricultural production within the framework of various types of local lordship, which preconditioned long-term population growth, and
- urbanization on a wide scale, supported by commercialization and economic expansion, partly along capitalist lines;
- the virtual disappearance of slavery, and eventually also of other forms of unfree personal status (although not everywhere), which from the late Middle Ages onwards allowed the emergence of the commoner, the free man in possession of basic rights in towns, villages and states, the backbone of society;
- the evolution of barbarian kingdoms into dynastic monarchies and a wide variety of other types of pre-modern state;
- the rationalization and partial secularization of the world-view and the view of mankind;
- the development of a new spirituality, also among the great masses of the faithful;

- successive revolutionary changes in written communication in the twelfth and fifteenth centuries.

After the sixteenth century there were quantitative but not qualitative changes in these transformations. The distinction between the late Middle Ages and new (or early modern) history does not then rest on fundamental differences according to type of society, or on radical breaks in social developments. Major processes, such as urbanization and the secularization of the world-view, ran a continuous course from the eleventh century to the end of the *ancien régime*, or even until now. Much of what is new, 'modern', in the early modern period goes back to the later Middle Ages.

To sum up: in this book we use the term 'Middle Ages' simply because it is generally accepted, for reasons of pragmatism and not of principle. We shall examine the period from the fourth to the sixteenth centuries, with special attention for the structural changes taking place at that time. We consider the changes occurring between the fourth and tenth or twelfth centuries to be of a more fundamental nature than those of the sixteenth century.

REGIONAL DIVERSITY

Unlike North America or central Asia only in the eastern part of Europe were there extensive, easily accessible and homogeneous regions stretching over thousands of kilometres. Geographical variety is a natural phenomenon that has most certainly contributed to the long survival of widely differing cultural niches. Even in the twentieth century, despite the strongly homogenizing effects of Church and state institutions, the transport revolution and the mass media, we can identify a multitude of regional cultures that are apparent in their own organization of material life, in their own customs and concepts and in their own languages or dialects. With the current trend towards globalization it is not easy for us to realize that until the eighteenth century the horizon of most Europeans did not extend beyond the place where they lived or the region where they were born. This does not mean that nobody ever travelled or that there was no mobility, or that there were no large-scale migrations; it was just that these were relatively uncommon. Normally, people remained for the most part tied to a particular area; this naturally resulted in considerable differences in economic development and cultural outlook.

Major coordinating, intellectual, constitutional or religious constructions such as the Church, kingship and state, with which we are nowadays familiar, or which a highly developed elite devised at the time, were far removed from everyday experience at the local and regional level. This was certainly a hindrance to the efforts at unification made by the higher political authorities. For us as historians, the same local diversity and changeability make it extremely problematic to write a comprehensive cultural history of the Middle Ages that would cover all of Europe over more than a thousand years. This has not prevented us, however, from clarifying important cultural phenomena in the successive political, socio-economic, and religious chapters that are the backbone of this book. In that respect, culture, in its broadest sense of those variegated channels through which people give symbolic meaning to existence, has been provided for.

WHICH EUROPE?

The term 'Middle Ages', then, only has meaning in a European context. Yet the geographically defined continent of Europe does not provide the most appropriate spatial framework for our considerations. For the clerical literate elite the demarcation lay naturally at the frontiers of Christianity. As a result of missionary work Iceland was part of the Christian European culture from the tenth century, and contacts with the East Slavonic principalities increased, but the Urals and the Arctic Circle were still far away. We shall have to assume expansive core areas that in some way or other asserted their superiority, often through conquest but also through peaceful cultural transfer. This means that we shall have to stress those developments that, more than others, have induced long-lasting effects in a wide context.

Seen in this light there can be no doubt about the head start enjoyed by the Mediterranean world. Even after the decline of the Roman Empire, the losses caused by the barbarian invasions and the disruption that may at first have been created by the Arab conquests, there was still considerably more wealth and potential for development available in southern Europe than in northern Europe. These were nourished by the sustained economic and cultural exchanges that were springing up between Christians and Muslims in Iberia, Sicily and southern Italy. By presenting the Mediterranean area as an economic and cultural zone of contact and transit we prevent medieval Europe from turning in on itself, so to speak.

From the thirteenth century onwards more and more Europeans crossed the frontiers of the continent of Europe. Overland journeys were made all over Asia to examine the possibilities for direct commercial links with China and India and, of course, for the further propagation of the Catholic faith. In 1291 two Genoese brothers by the name of Vivaldi sailed through the Straits of Gibraltar, 'westwards to India'. It is not known whether they found America, or indeed any other part of the world, for nothing more was heard of them. But their brave initiative sprang from a tremendous drive for expansion, which their fellow townsman, Christopher Columbus, would emulate with greater success, though with resources not much technically improved, 201 years later.

A comparable expansive core lay at the other extreme of the continent – that of the Vikings. The head start that early medieval Scandinavia had acquired in a number of respects compared to eastern and north-west Europe resulted in remarkable journeys of discovery to all corners of the world, in commercial ties with Byzantium and central Asia, and in the settlement of its people in Iceland, Greenland, North America, Russia, Britain, Ireland and Normandy. From the eleventh century, however, the expansion stagnated. Its demographic potential was apparently exhausted, and its technical advantage had been matched. The northern (and later Norman) elements were assimilated into the diverse receiving cultures without leaving any dominant trace. By contrast, the Mediterranean expansion that, viewed economically, continued until the sixteenth century, and in the field of the arts even longer, shows that it was based on far firmer foundations. Viking society consisted of peasants and chieftains who now and then went overseas in small groups; the difference from free burghers in large towns is striking.

The Europe that we shall study, therefore, corresponds only partially with the geographical concept of the continent. On the one hand we see large areas on its western, northern and, in particular, eastern peripheries that were only late and superficially integrated into the developments in the south and west (Christianization, urban growth, commercialization, consolidation of states). On the other hand, we can only understand the dynamism emanating from southern Europe by seeing it in relation to the head start achieved by regions outside Europe, the Byzantine and Arab worlds, which in their turn were connected with the Far East.

FROM SCARCITY TO HEGEMONY

No clairvoyant making a prediction in 1400 about which part of the world would dominate in the future would ever have mentioned Europe. The continent had just lost one-third of its population through a succession of plague epidemics; its religious leaders were involved in a painful schism; the Ottoman Turks were trampling over the remains of the Byzantine Empire in the Balkans; the kings in the West were at war with each other and exhausting their resources; peasants and townspeople were rising up in great numbers against the lords who oppressed them.

The clairvoyant would more probably have named the Mongol conqueror Timur Lenk (Tamerlane) as the future world leader. In the preceding years, Timur had established his iron authority over the enormous region stretching from the Caucasus to the Indus. He had conquered great cities like Baghdad, Edessa, Isphahan, Ankara, Damascus and Delhi. Perhaps our clairvoyant would have foretold the sudden death of this despot in 1405, putting an end to the Mongol terror. The seer may well have considered the flourishing dynasties in the Muslim sultanates of Granada, Egypt and Tunis, but he would have hesitated, for they were quarrelling among themselves and were thus not very stable, despite the glories of their courts and mosques.

It would have been impossible for him to ignore the thousand-year Chinese Empire. Did it not encompass an area as large as all Europe, cities with a million inhabitants, a very productive agriculture and a highly developed administrative system? The Chinese had for centuries surpassed the Europeans with their technical and organizational capacities; long before 1300 they already had iron tempered with coke, gunpowder, the ship's compass, and paper money issued in the emperor's name. They undertook journeys of discovery and commercial expeditions along the coast of India as far as East Africa. There was busy shipping in the China Sea and the Bay of Bengal; large numbers of Chinese traders dealing in high-quality goods were established in foreign ports. If there were ever to be a dominant world power it would have to be China – that is what any sensible person must have thought in 1400. Yet things turned out differently: eventually, between 1000 and 1800, Europe moved from its backward position to the forefront.

In what way was Europe different from its eminent precursors? The distinction lies in the strong drive for expansion to other parts of the world. First and foremost, Europe gained an essential technical advantage over the rest of the world in the fourteenth century through the development of firearms. Advances in shipbuilding and navigational techniques brought possibilities of sailing the oceans on an unprecedented scale. The key question, then, is how this technical lead was managed once it had been achieved.

The most important difference between Europe, China and all the other highly developed regions of the world lies in the fact that there was no unitary authoritative structure in Europe. At the beginning of the fifteenth century Chinese voyages of discovery along the coast of East Africa could easily have meant that not Vasco da Gama but a Chinese admiral would be the first to sail round the Cape of Good Hope and discover new oceans. But in 1434 the imperial court decreed that no more exploratory expeditions should be undertaken. The capital had just been moved to Beijing so that the threat from the Mongols in the north could be better resisted. The capital's food supply was ensured by the completion of the Great Canal, some 1,500 kilometres in length, which was opened in 1411 and connected the old capital Hang Chow with Tientsin near Beijing. This achievement required a gigantic undertaking by a state that could establish priorities in its territory and for a population that was as large as Europe's.

No single European body had at its disposal the possibilities of organizing such an enormous concentration of resources to implement state decisions or completely suppress commercial initiatives. There would always be another leader ready to venture an experiment. The hundreds of autonomous principalities, prince bishoprics, city-states, republics and peasant cantons, all of which governed small parts of Europe, found themselves in a constant state of rivalry, and often at full-blown war. Moreover, no single political unit was able to establish its authority permanently. Despite all the resulting devastation, the attempts to expand the means of exercising power were a stimulus to innovation. The Chinese Empire, on the other hand, was mainly occupied in preserving its internal stability and avoiding every innovation. Imperial rule was not restricted to the political sphere. It also controlled religion and the economy, so that it resembled a totalitarian system.

In Europe, by contrast, the religious and political spheres became more clearly separated in the later Middle Ages. Before then popes and emperors had struggled in vain to achieve supremacy, thus only proving that a truly universal European power did not exist. A relatively autonomous third power appeared in some regions during the Middle Ages – that of the towns. Towns in Europe, unlike those in other parts of the world, enjoyed an administrative and legal autonomy that expanded as the town grew and the local ruler became weaker. This enabled commercial and industrial enterprise to expand without insurmountable restrictions being imposed by Church or political governments. They often threw up obstacles and tried to take as large a share as possible of the profits from trade. If they went too far, however, the capital would take flight to a safer place where it could then grow further.

In this way the segmentation of power over a variety of political units and an independent Church created the unique situation that gave rise to capitalism. This largely autonomous method of organizing production and trade is aimed primarily at making as large a profit as possible, through the subordination of other motives – political, ethical and religious. It grew into a dynamic market system that was not limited to a particular area of authority but everywhere seized the opportunity to pursue profits. This exercise of power in the political, legal, religious and economic field gave entrepreneurs in Europe chances that elsewhere were often frustrated by authoritarian religious and secular rulers. And for the same reasons Europe was more open to foreign innovations than any other culture.

FURTHER READING

Encyclopedias, thematic surveys, debates

Linehan, Peter and Janet Nelson (eds) (2001), *The Medieval World* (London: Routledge).

Little, Lester K. and Barbara H. Rosenwein (eds) (1998), *Debating the Middle Ages. Issues and Readings* (Oxford: Blackwell).

Routledge Encyclopedias of the Middle Ages, 13 vols to date (2006) (London and New York: Routledge).

Strayer, Joseph (gen. ed.) (1982–2004), *Dictionary of the Middle Ages*, 13 vols (with Supplement) (New York: Charles Scribner's Sons).

Vauchez, André, Barrie Dobson and Michael Lapidge (eds) (2000–2001), *Encyclopedia of the Middle Ages*, 2 vols (Cambridge: James Clarke).

Multi-volume textbooks

Abulafia, David *et al.* (eds) (1995–2005), *The New Cambridge Medieval History*, 7 vols (Cambridge: Cambridge University Press).

Modern historiography

Partner, Nancy (ed.) (2005), *Writing Medieval History* (London: Hodder Arnold).

Guides, atlases

Jotischky, Andrew *et al.* (2005), *The Penguin Historical Atlas of the Medieval World* (London: Penguin).

Mackay, Angus (with David Ditchburn) (1997), *Atlas of Medieval Europe* (London and New York: Routledge).

McKitterick, Rosamond (2004), *Atlas of the Medieval World* (Oxford: Oxford University Press).

(Printed) source books

Anderson, Roberta and Dominic Bellenger (2003), *Medieval Worlds: A Sourcebook* (London and New York: Routledge).

Geary, Patrick (ed.) (1991), *Readings in Medieval History*, 2nd edn (Peterborough, Ontario: Broadview Press).

Readings in Medieval Civilizations and Cultures, 11 vols to date (2006) (Peterborough, Ontario: Broadview Press).

Speed, Peter (ed.) (1996–1997), *Those Who Fought, Those Who Worked, Those Who Prayed. Three Anthologies of Medieval Sources*, 3 vols (New York: Italica Press).

Sub-periods

EARLY MIDDLE AGES

Collins, Roger (1991), *Early Medieval Europe, 300–1000* (Basingstoke and London: Macmillan Press).

McKitterick, Rosamond (ed.) (2001), *The Early Middle Ages: Europe 400–1000* (Oxford: Oxford University Press) [Short Oxford History of Europe].

Smith, Julia M.H. (2005), *Europe after Rome. A New Cultural History 500–1000* (Oxford and New York: Oxford University Press).

CENTRAL MIDDLE AGES

Barber, Malcolm (2004), *The Two Cities. Medieval Europe 1050–1320*, 2nd edn (London and New York: Routledge).

Jordan, William Chester (2001), *Europe in the High Middle Ages* (London and New York: Allen Lane/ Penguin Group).

Mundy, John H. (1991), *Europe in the High Middle Ages 1150–1309*, 2nd edn (London and New York: Longman).

Power, Daniel (ed.) (2006), *The Central Middle Ages* (Oxford and New York: Oxford University Press) [Short Oxford History of Europe].

LATE MIDDLE AGES

Brady, Thomas A. Jr., Heiko A. Oberman and James D. Tracy (eds) (1994), *Handbook of European History, 1400–1600. Late Middle Ages, Renaissance and Reformation* (Leiden: E.J. Brill).

Waley, Daniel and Peter Denley (2001), *Later Medieval Europe 1250–1520*, 3rd edn (Harlow: Longman).

CHAPTER 2

The Roman legacy

After his coronation as emperor in Bologna in 1530, and especially during his entrances into Italian cities, including Rome in 1536, Charles V showed himself as the perfect reincarnation of an ancient emperor. For both his ethics and his appearance, Marcus Aurelius served as his model. Copies of his equestrian statue were put in several places and even Charles's hair and clothing, on coins, medals, medallions and statues, were exact copies of the classical model. Of course the artists adopted the Renaissance style prevailing at the time. In this Charles testified to the typically medieval fascination for classical culture. The Roman civilization, far more so than the Greek, continued to be the ideal for rulers throughout the Middle Ages – and long afterwards. Every ruler who felt in any way superior to his rivals – from the barbarian kings through Charlemagne, Frederick II, Charles V, Napoleon and Mussolini, right up to Bokassa who had himself crowned emperor of the central African Republic in 1977 – adorned himself with the symbols of the Roman emperors. A major part of Rome's cultural heritage continued to function for those who had reached a certain level of development. In the eleven centuries following the symbolic deposition of the last Western Roman emperor in 476, Roman history, its form of government, law, architecture, language, science and literature continued to exert a compelling force on the imagination and activities of the upper strata of society in the West.

DISINTEGRATION OF THE EMPIRE

The structure of government

Of course, what most appealed to the imagination was imperial authority itself: sovereign power over an immeasurable area encompassing numerous ethnic groups. Not since then has Europe had an integrated state structure on the scale of the Roman one, although attempts in that direction have been made with a certain regularity, and for short periods extensive conquests have taken place. What was essential was that the Roman Empire formed a unit that could function for hundreds of years, based as it was on a solid economic organization, an impressive infrastructure and highly developed systems of law and government. The ambitious scale of the organization was visible in the enormous defence system built by the Empire to repulse barbarian attacks. A line of defensive towers and garrison towns formed the *limes*, the boundary along the Rhine, the Danube and the North Sea. In 122 Emperor Hadrian built his famous wall, which stretches for 117 kilometres between Newcastle upon Tyne and Carlisle. In the fourth century an army of between 300,000 and 400,000 men was mobilized to protect the borders. European kingdoms did not manage to raise an army of such a size until the seventeenth century. In the military structure that took shape under Diocletian, *duces* were the commanders of border troops. The term *comitatus* originally meant 'escort of the emperor', but in time came to refer to the mobile field army with a heavily armed cavalry. Both terms were used in later centuries: *dux*, or duke, was a person with authority over an important region, not infrequently on the borders of a kingdom; and from *comitatus* derived the function of *comes*, or count, the king's representative in an administrative district.

The military organization, which was the basis of the conquests that gave the Roman Empire its extensive territory, of necessity continued to form the core of its unity, because the pressure from the surrounding peoples was great. An extensive network of well-built paved roads formed the backbone of the Empire. Their purpose was primarily administrative and military: to ensure communications between the main towns and the borders. The total length of the Roman road system is estimated at between 80,000 and 100,000 kilometres. There were milestones, halts, stop-overs and hostelries at regular intervals. Until the eighteenth century these roads remained the longest and best line of overland communications in Europe. Many stretches remained in use for centuries because no government authority appeared to be able to produce anything to equal the Roman system, and certainly not over such vast distances.

A coherent vision of the administrative structure of the Empire lay behind this system of roads. A map of the world has come down to us from the fourth century, spanning the world from Britain to India (see

Plate 2.1 'All roads lead to Rome'. Detail from the Peutinger Table, a copy of a third-century Roman map of roads and watercourses, named after the humanist Conrad Peutinger. A number of recognizable points are visible on the map, especially towns and watercourses

Plate 2.1). It shows exactly how the roads ran and the distances between the towns. This map reflects both the cohesiveness and the internal hierarchy of the empire. It was possible to govern this Empire only because abstract concepts concerning administration and law were widely accepted. In 292 Emperor Diocletian introduced a reorganization under which the Empire was divided into prefectures, dioceses and approximately one hundred provinces. Each province was subdivided into *civitates*, a term that was applied to their principal towns and which in many later languages became their main word for a town: *città, cité, ciudad, city*. The street map of the typical town in the provinces reflected the systematic and methodical nature of the design: a square layout with streets in a chessboard pattern, axes from the gates to the central square, the forum, where a basilica, a public building with law courts and temples gave expression to the enduring values of the Empire.

Afterwards in Europe these organizational principles disappeared almost entirely, and only ruins and the layout of town centres still recalled the glories long past. So great is the contrast that it is impossible to avoid asking why that which was achieved between the first century BC and the fifth century AD could not be repeated later on the same scale: a lasting, large-scale, clear administrative hierarchy with its material expression in urban patterns, architectural forms, an economic order, a state religion and a system of communications. All the cities and states that have been created since then have lacked that vision of unity, that scale, that order, that abstraction and rationality. When cities emerged later they took on irregular, diverse but globally concentric forms, resembling configurations from nature (crystals, leaves). States appeared and disappeared in all shapes and sizes yet without any compelling, mutually hierarchic relationships. Roads were no longer maintained, and when, from the thirteenth century, intensive road-building was again undertaken it was on a remarkably modest scale. Europe's present-day network of motorways still shows the seams and gaps of the individual states that originally conceived and built them.

In contrast to the Roman Empire modern Europe has grown from below, out of many small and individual units. It was not conceived from above. Fundamental to this difference is that Roman supremacy was won from a single, central region, with Rome as its capital. As its territory expanded methods of administration and concepts of law were developed and refined. Rome was a republic when it made its greatest conquests. This meant that territorial gains belonged to the Republic and not to the conquering general and his family. Generals could certainly achieve great fame through their conquests: they could hold a triumphal procession, and a triumphal arch or a commemorative column would be erected for some, but the new territory nevertheless belonged not to them but to the state. In medieval and early modern Europe it was the princely dynasties that established the larger political units, but even in the nineteenth century they were still thinking basically in terms of their own private patrimonies: for them, lands were possessions to be used as security or inherited, divided and consolidated within the family.

The memory of the past glory of the Roman Empire, and the yearning for it, nevertheless remained profound. It was more than just an idealized picture: in spite of all the disruptions and social differences a sense of continuity emanated from its structures. Moreover, Roman models were frequently used in matters of administration and law.

The Catholic Church was certainly the most important heir to the Roman Empire. It grew up inside the Empire, at first in conflict with those in power. When Christianity was recognized in 311 the persecution of the Christians came to an end and the highest authorities became closely connected to the new religion. The Church structure was expanded in the Roman administrative centres, and during the Council of Nicaea, in 325, the Church took over from the Empire the division into four administrative levels. The patriarchs with seats in Antioch, Alexandria, Rome and Constantinople, together with the Patriarch of Jerusalem, exercised extensive powers over a large area; metropolitans supervised a number of bishoprics, and the bishops were responsible for the parish priests. The terms 'diocese' and *civitas* for a bishop's see and its capital recall their Roman origin; *epi-scopus*, derived from the Greek (over-seer, bishop), explains the function. During the early Middle Ages this function was by far the most important in the Church hierarchy.

The first bishops, Church Fathers and saints belonged to the Roman senatorial class: they possessed the material wealth and the intellectual training necessary for building the new framework. Ambrose, bishop of Milan; Zeno, bishop of Verona; Symmachus, bishop of Turin; Martin, bishop of Tours, and the saintly Melanie (whose ownership of sixty *villae* (estates) enabled her to buy 8,000 slaves their freedom, so the story goes) are among the founders of the Church who came from the Roman aristocracy. The earliest Church, like the Empire, was a hierarchy established in the towns: its leaders belonged to the old elites whose culture they fostered in many respects: the language, scientific knowledge, administrative ideas, the universalistic ideal. The latter meant that authority stretched beyond geographical, ethnic and cultural borders. It was also centralized, so that every authority at a local or regional level was dependent on the central power base, the imperial government.

When Christianity became the official state religion between 381 and 391–392, and other religions were forbidden, Emperor Theodosius nonetheless chose a number of important officials who, with their families, remained faithful to the old cult. In this way he demonstrated his independence from the Catholic Church. The Church could develop within the already existing structures of the Empire, which it had to accept as an independent reality. From its origins in a breakaway movement from Judaism, recognized by the Romans as a religion, the Christian Church evolved into a mainstay of the established order, one of the last binding elements of the Late Empire. The Christian emperors, following ancient tradition, continued to act as head of both Church and state. In Byzantium this situation never changed, but when the emperors in the West disappeared the popes could fill the vacuum.

In spite of its formal independence from the highest secular power, the Church in the West nevertheless took over many concepts from the Roman Empire. Concepts such as hierarchy in administrative levels, territoriality of authority and the concept of office itself were linked with the administrative structure. All of these were abstract ideas for which the barbarian peoples of the fourth and fifth centuries were ill prepared, but which had gradually been given content and a theoretical basis during the Roman Republic. One of the most studied texts of the Middle Ages, *De Officiis*, by Cicero (106–43 BC), the lawyer, orator and political philosopher, had office and duty as its main themes.

According to Cicero, an office has duties attached to it that are defined independently of the holder, and the holder should satisfy the criteria laid down beforehand. The selection for office should follow a well-defined procedure and a person who does not live up to expectations should be removed from office in accordance with existing procedures. The expected purpose pertaining to the office remains, regardless of how it is performed. In return for his services the office-holder receives a fixed salary. The Church borrowed important elements of Cicero's concept of office for its priests and dignitaries. It is true that limits were no longer set for the length of time an office could be held, and the possibility of payment in money largely disappeared. When, from the fourth century, the state apparatus became increasingly susceptible to corruption and personal empowerment, the Church still carried on the Roman tradition to some extent.

Officialdom implied literacy, an art the Church alone kept alive for centuries in a world based on oral tradition. The Church also continued to use Latin, both for liturgy and administrative matters. This enabled it to function effectively as a universal organization that recruited its staff from Africa, Asia and from Ireland to Estonia. Its priests could be deployed anywhere regardless of their place of origin, and could provide services for temporal lords in all corners of the world. Until the twelfth century on the European continent Latin was the only written administrative language in the whole of Christian Europe, and only clerics could master it. There is no doubt that this universal administrative monopoly contributed substantially to European rulers being gradually imbued with certain Christian-inspired values.

This was equally true of written law. The complexity of Roman society resulted in a highly developed system of laws that survived in the codifications established under Emperor Theodosius II (*c.* 440) and, the most famous, the Corpus Iuris Civilis under Justinian (*c.* 530). These codifications collected and systematized the legislation, procedural law and jurisprudence that had taken shape and acquired validity over the course of many centuries.

The Roman legal system provided a refined intellectual framework that, from the twelfth century onwards, became one of the foundations of university training for jurists in Western Europe. In this way

it once again – and increasingly – determined the thinking of administrators and lawyers. In addition, the Church saw further developments in canon law. As a legal doctrine the whole body of Church law owed much to the Roman legal system.

Thus the Church took responsibility for the preservation of classical culture, largely because the Church itself was an important relic of that culture. Clerics copied and studied the works of Christian and non-Christian writers. A learned Latin culture continued to exist in the microcosm of the Church while it virtually disappeared in the world outside. The barbarians in the north belonged to a radically different culture in which a magical world-view, personality of power, the spoken word and the ritualization of government and justice held sway. While they were acquiring a dominant position the Church continued to defend the superiority of its authority. It did so naturally enough on the basis of its role as representative of the divine will. In addition, it made use of all the instruments coming from a higher culture that were indispensable for the conservation of public authority: the art of writing, a universal language, professionalism in administration and written law, and a stable organization with fixed territorial divisions. Long before any king had thought of it, popes such as Gelasius I (492–496) issued decrees that testified to a coherent vision of unity. In the midst of a world where everything had become uncertain the Church represented fixed values, often perceived as higher values.

A state economy

During the Late Empire the state had a large stake in the economy. It intervened deeply in production relationships in order to ensure sufficient tax revenues to realize its own objectives. This meant maintaining an immense army on the borders, paying an extensive civil service and providing the towns with basic foodstuffs at prices affordable even to the poorest. The produce from state domains was applied to these ends. Roads, harbours, warehouses and canals were built primarily for military and administrative purposes. For a long time the state rewarded its veterans with a plot of land in the provinces on the periphery.

The enthusiasm of shipmasters and tradesmen to work for the government waned in the fourth and fifth centuries as the army grew in size, while the state's revenues decreased. On the one hand, the increasing pressure on the borders made it necessary to spend more of the revenues on defending the borders and on land for some of the barbarians and for buying off others; on the other hand, the lack of security on the land caused agricultural production to fall, and the flow of tax revenues into the state coffers from these abandoned regions dried up. Larger sums were needed for army pay, but resentment at the growing tax burden increased. A temporary solution was to devalue the currency, but that led to more and more transactions being made in kind, and money became scarce. Provisioning the towns grew more difficult as the state distribution system became disrupted.

The Late Empire took stringent measures to tackle its enormous economic problems. After 332 *coloni* (farmers owning their land, or tenants) and *mancipia* (slaves) were hereditarily bound to the land they worked. This was clearly intended to counter the labour shortage, but at the same time it limited the farmers' personal liberty. Compulsory measures were also introduced for tradesmen. The state compelled sons to follow the professions of their fathers, apparently because it had become financially unattractive to do so. In the towns, purchasing power collapsed as members of the aristocracy preferred to retire to their estates. There they were able to supervise production directly and were certain of their means of subsistence. In about 400 the state established its own system for the production and distribution of essential goods. Imperial textile factories set previously free craftsmen to work in a regime of forced labour. Emperor Majorian (457–461) even tried to prohibit girls under 14 from entering a convent and to force widows to remarry within five years, under penalty of confiscation of half their possessions. He hoped in this way to combat the alarming drop in population. All these compulsory measures show that the economic and fiscal system upon which the Empire rested was caving in.

'Imperial overstretch' is a term commonly used to illustrate the tendency of great empires to expand beyond the limits of their control. This is surely what happened to the Roman Empire: safeguarding the borders brought an exceptionally heavy fiscal burden and an enormous amount of government intervention in the economy. The establishment of its own production and distribution systems dislocated the market and required a growing number of officials and compulsory measures. The state thus stifled economic initiative and the basis for the Empire subsided.

Ruralization

If the Empire was founded on an urban society and good communications, during the fourth and fifth centuries these characteristics disappeared. The flow of currency dried up until only bronze coins remained, and these went no further than the place or region where they were minted. Gold and silver pieces circulated less as coinage but increasingly as gifts between the elites. Army units were forced to use tax revenues in kind from the immediate surroundings to provision themselves. The state machinery that had directed a considerable share of the flow of goods and services collapsed. Trade that the state had arranged in distant areas came to a standstill; towns lost their attraction as centres of consumption.

The period from the fourth to the sixth centuries saw a substantial decrease in the total population. Figures for the time can be no more than indicative estimates simply because representative statistical sources are not available. Yet numbers of between forty and fifty million inhabitants for Western Europe during the second century have been mentioned, as opposed to no more than thirty million at the end of the fifth. In particular the populations of the towns and garrisons fell. This alone was enough to reduce the demand in trade: once public services fell away, as well as the safety (guaranteed by the Empire) and the wealth of the elites who lived on state incomes, the urban market disappeared. All together, the urban population during the Empire is estimated to have been 10 to 20 per cent of the total. At that time most Roman towns had between 3,000 and 10,000 inhabitants, and only a few major cities, such as Lyons and Trier, contained up to 50,000. Rome itself was, of course, the exception. After the fifth century only a skeleton of all these towns remained in the West. Especially, places where bishops took residence survived – thanks to religious and administrative functions.

One consequence must have been that agricultural production, and certainly the acreage under cultivation, dropped. Countless records of abandoned fields testify to this. No later than the fifth century great agricultural estates, *latifundia*, encompassing hundreds of hectares, formed the heart of society in the (former) Western Roman Empire. The old senatorial class had used its political clout to obtain fiscal privileges for itself. Senatorial estates enjoyed a status of immunity, where the power of the state could not reach. The great landowners, with their large numbers of dependent peasants, could defend themselves better in times of uncertainty than ordinary, self-employed individuals. They assumed military styles, their central buildings became fortresses, and in this way they were able to organize an armed defence against roving gangs. Lack of safety and an increasing tax burden persuaded many originally free smallholders to place themselves under the protection of a neighbouring landowner. Sometimes this happened by way of a formal transaction known as *precaria* (literally meaning 'request'), in which the peasant relinquished his land and paid a fee in recognition to the landlord. In return he retained the right to use the land. Many others acquired the status of *colonus*, which tied them to the land the landowner allowed them to work in exchange for part of the produce and often also specified services.

In this way large landowners usurped the dwindling powers of the state by taking the law into their own hands and by strengthening their position of power through patronage over weaker individuals. In this relationship a powerful man offered his protection to the vulnerable. These people could do little else than give up their property and, eventually, their freedom. In the absence of state authority the man in power could very largely determine how much pressure he would exercise on his potential dependants. So we can see how economic and social relationships were created out of the ruins of the Late Empire, which would become characteristic features of the early Middle Ages.

THE EASTERN ROMAN EMPIRE

Byzantium was the Greek name for the unassuming town on the Bosporus that Emperor Constantine the Great (306–337) enlarged to be his capital. A variety of factors played a part in his choice: first, of course,

its strategic location on the boundary between two continents; next, the growing demographic, and probably economic, weight of the eastern part of the Roman Empire; and, finally, the emperor's desire to distance himself – literally – from an Italian senatorial class that was by no means docile: it clung stubbornly to the old Roman gods, for example, while Constantine tried to put Christianity on an equal footing in the Empire.

BOX 2.1 THE ROMAN LAW

The actual work on Justinian's codification was carried out by a special commission consisting of jurists attached to the imperial court or to one of the two most renowned schools of law in the Empire, at Beirut and Constantinople. The work was completed within a surprisingly short time. In its entirety it was known as the Corpus Iuris Civilis (Body of Civil Law), but in fact it was made up of three very different parts. The Codex Iustinianus contains all the imperial edicts from Hadrian (117–134) until the year 533. This part was intended to replace older, less complete compilations such as the Codex Theodosianus, which dated from about 440. A separate part, the Novellae constitutiones, known as 'Novellae', with additions from after 533, appeared later. The largest part of the Corpus is formed by the Digesta (*Pandectès* in Greek), an extensive selection of legal commentaries by 39 well-known Roman lawyers from the Roman imperial age. The last part, although more modest in size, was perhaps the most influential. It is called 'Institutiones' and was intended as a manual for law students or as a reference book for practising lawyers. Institutiones looks most like a statute book, a systematic survey of rules of law, which actually are concerned solely with private law. The speed with which a codification of laws of such high quality was compiled is proof that the government apparatus of the Eastern Empire set great store by a legal training. From the late Middle Ages onwards the Corpus Iuris Civilis would be a major influence on legal concepts and the administration of justice in the West.

As far as private law was concerned Roman law offered many ways of enabling individuals to secure property rights, dispose of possessions by testament, to enter freely into contracts, and by which the rights of women and minors were protected. The Codex Iustinianus recognized the statute of the legal person through which collectivities (*universitates* in Latin) such as guilds and local communities were able to assert their rights. Civil and criminal procedures were laid down precisely, so that individual litigants could appeal to them, even against the power of the state. On the other hand, during the compilation many centuries-old provisions were revised in the light of the new relationships in the Eastern Empire where the emperor and his officials exerted sovereign powers in legislation, the administration of justice, government, tax law and the conduct of war. In Justinian's Corpus Iuris Civilis we find the principles that 'the ruler is not bound by the law' and that 'what pleases the ruler has the force of law', to which later monarchs with absolutist tendencies like to refer.

The emperors of the fourth century did everything possible to give Byzantium – or Constantinople ('Constantine's town') as it was soon called – some of the aura of Rome. Constantine and his son Constantius II (337–361) started an ambitious programme of construction in which monumental Christian buildings had a central place right from the beginning, but at the same time the public amenities that were so characteristic of Roman urban culture – forums, baths, theatres, racecourses – were enlarged and improved. The ceremonial heart of the city lay directly on the Bosporus: it was formed by the great imperial palace, the racecourse (Hippodrome), the first Hagia Sophia – the church dedicated to 'holy wisdom' or the Holy Ghost – the most important government building (the Silention, the basilica of silence) and the forum of Constantine. There was also a separate Byzantine senate. The population increase was phenomenal between the fourth and sixth centuries, in sharp contrast to the decline in the city of Rome at the same time. While Rome must have had some 800,000 inhabitants

in about 400, by the middle of the sixth century there were no more than 30,000. Constantinople had by then grown into a metropolis of about half a million people. This number dropped later, and Constantinople was never as large as Rome had been during the Empire, but throughout the Middle Ages it remained by far the largest city in Europe.

Justinian

After 476 the Eastern Roman emperors laid claim to the recovery and restoration of the Empire, *renovatio imperii*, from Byzantium and with authority over Rome. The man who really gave shape to this was Justinian (527–565). His policy of renewal had four cornerstones: the recovery of the regions that had been lost; the clarification and codification of Roman law; an economic policy based on the support of the military apparatus; and the establishment of religious unity. In the beginning this policy proved to be very successful, but in about 550 it started to go wrong and the gulf between ideal and reality widened.

Justinian tackled the wars of reconquest shrewdly. In order to avoid a war on two fronts he first of all negotiated a long-term truce with the Persians, the most formidable of the enemies of the Eastern Roman Empire. Then an expeditionary force attacked the lands of the Vandals in North Africa. It soon met with success, but the Byzantine presence there would prove as short-lived as that of the Vandals. In 647 the Muslim advance placed the region around Tripoli under Arab rule. By 670 the whole of North Africa was in Arab hands.

Later the Byzantines managed to gain a firm foothold on the east coast of Spain, but Justinian underestimated the strength of the kingdom of the Ostrogoths in Italy. The attack began in 535. It ended in two exhausting wars of attrition that together would last for almost twenty years and plunge Italy into acute misery. The Ostrogoths used not only force but also international diplomacy. The finest example was when the Ostrogothic king, Vitigis, persuaded the Persian shah to declare war on the Byzantines so that the second front, which Justinian had so feared, became reality. To make matters worse, the greater part of the territorial gains were nullified through a new barbarian confederation, that of the Lombards, which invaded the peninsula shortly after Justinian died.

In the long run the Byzantines would retain some lands in Italy, but not very many. They included two old imperial residences: Rome and Ravenna. The first city would never fall into barbarian hands; the second not for a very long time. Ravenna became the seat of the Byzantine governor, the exarch, who was only driven out by the Lombards in the middle of the eighth century. With the advantage of hindsight Justinian's attempts to restore Roman rule in the West by military means can only be seen as a failure.

The second cornerstone of the imperial restoration, the clarification and codification of Roman law, which Justinian ordered soon after he began his long reign, was far more successful and lasted considerably longer. According to the concepts of late Antiquity it was no longer the 'people of Rome', represented by the Senate, but the emperor, who was considered to be the only source of justice and law, and this gradually assumed the quality of a divine mandate. Since, for Christian Roman emperors too, justice had to be anchored in what Justinian called the 'honourable authority of tradition', the codification of Roman law into the Corpus Iuris Civilis made him more than just a virtuous emperor who took seriously his responsibility to dispense justice. This selfsame administrative act linked him directly with the deep-rooted foundations of Roman authority. Yet the Corpus Iuris Civilis proved to be less useful for the application of justice in the Eastern Roman Empire, for which it was intended, because fewer and fewer people, intellectuals included, spoke or wrote Latin. For a long time lawyers and jurists had to make do with Greek extracts from the *Corpus*. Not until the end of the ninth century did a more-or-less complete Greek translation appear, on behalf of the state, to which a large number of legal texts from previous centuries were appended.

The third aspect of Justinian's *renovatio imperii*, the wars of conquest, the vast building projects, the grain supply for the metropolis of Constantinople – all proved extremely expensive, making the tax burden under his rule very heavy. In 541 the Mediterranean region was struck by an epidemic of bubonic plague, the first of its kind in Europe. In the East the Persians, the arch-enemy, pushed forward. The North had to face more barbarian invasions when two new nomadic confederations from the steppes entered the Danube valley from the Ukraine: first the Avars, later the

Bulgars. They imposed tribute upon various Slavic peoples. In their efforts to escape from this iron yoke groups of Slavs then made their way into the Balkans and Greece, where they settled permanently. In the West the conquests made in Italy and Spain were to a large extent undone by the Lombards and Visigoths. Justinian's ambitions, in the fourth place, likewise appealed to a long Roman tradition, the interweaving of state affairs and religion, and the view that the emperor was also the religious leader. Since Constantine, this meant that it was the emperor's duty to lead the Christian Church and to defend it from internal and external enemies. In this way the expedition against the Vandals was consciously promoted as a holy war against heretics, because although the Vandals had converted to Christianity they were followers of Arianism, which had been decreed a heresy. Within the Empire, Justinian battled even more fiercely than his predecessors, but with as little success, against Monophysitism, another heretical current with

Plate 2.2 Interior view showing the imperial gallery in the Hagia Sophia in Constantinople, built in the sixth century by order of Emperor Justinian

a growing following in Syria and Egypt. To crown his solidarity with the Christian religion and the Byzantine Church, and as the expression of his primacy there, Justinian had the Hagia Sophia, situated right next to the imperial palace, transformed into the largest and most majestic church in Christendom.

Towards the end of Justinian's reign there were visible changes in the emperor cult. In the Late Roman Empire the emperors had been given a semi-divine status and the emperor's person had become the subject of veneration. In the second half of the sixth century the emperor was worshipped less, and God more and more. Icons (painted images of the saints) and relics (physical remains of the saints) were used to come closer to God. The emperors then adopted this new trend and had their portraits painted and their images sent to highly placed administrators, asking them to give the icons a prominent place in public ceremonial areas.

Implosion and consolidation

The Byzantine attempts to hold off the external threats met with varying degrees of success. The rule of Emperor Heraclius I (610–641) can be called tragic in that respect. Less than ten years after a spectacular victory against the Persians in 627, the Byzantines suffered a humiliating defeat at the hands of the Arabs (636). Syria and Palestine were lost for ever, and Egypt followed shortly after Heraclius' death.

The demographic crisis and the loss of territory had serious consequences for the Byzantine economy and society, and for the administrative and military organization of the Empire. During the seventh century the Byzantine economy showed clear signs of contraction. In the West the most vital framework of the economy and society of late Antiquity, the small town (*civitas*), was thoroughly disrupted in the early Middle Ages, and the same happened in the East. Another, no less far-reaching, consequence of the territorial shrinkage, in particular, lay in the social and cultural sphere. Although the rulers and people of the Byzantine Empire persisted in referring to themselves as 'Romaioi' (Romans), and Arabs and Turks similarly still spoke of 'Rum', the Empire was rapidly becoming Hellenized. And from a religious point of view it became increasingly separate from Western Christianity.

Under Heraclius and Constans II (641–668), his grandson and successor, a number of important reforms in taxation, military organization and imperial bureaucracy were implemented. In rural areas responsibility for the payment of taxes came to rest directly on the farming communities and their leaders. The new taxes were paid mostly in gold coin. In this way the vital monetary link between the subjects/taxpayers on one hand, and (professional) soldiers and public servants on the other, could remain intact. Army and bureaucracy were drastically reduced in the centuries after Justinian: the total number of soldiers available for recruitment, some 150,000 men under Justinian, dropped to an estimated 80,000 in about 740, when the Empire had a population of about seven million; in Constantinople the central civil service of 2,500 at the beginning of the sixth century fell to just 600 in the eighth century.

In this waning situation, and under the ever-present threat to the Empire from Arabs, Slavs and Bulgars, either Heraclius or Constans II completely remodelled the army. The core of the Byzantine army was still a popular army of semi-professionals, recruited on a voluntary basis. Now, a new division was made in four large army corps or *themes*, all of which were stationed in Asia Minor, the largest and richest region that the Byzantine Empire still possessed. A fifth *theme* was similar to a marine corps and was based on naval units in the Aegean Sea.

New *themes* were established to protect the remaining Byzantine regions in the western part of the Mediterranean Sea (parts of Italy, Sicily, Sardinia and the Balearic Islands). The continuing threat from the Arabs, who from 717 to 718 laid siege to Constantinople itself, and from domestic conspiracies against the emperor, persuaded Constantine V (741–775) to create six new, elite corps of really professional soldiers, known as *tagmata*, which were better paid and more closely linked to the emperor. They consisted of 18,000 men – on paper anyway – relatively many of them cavalry. This meant that in times of crisis the emperor was much better prepared. Very soon, however, a new danger loomed on the horizon: the *tagmata* commanders in fact determined who would become emperor. The solution to this problem was the formation, in the course of the ninth century, of an imperial bodyguard of hand-picked men, some of them barbarians. Before the year 1000 the *theme* armies, in their old form, had had their day. After that, in newly conquered regions, purely military districts were established with their own, continuously active troops, whose *strategoi* (commanders) were directly responsible to the emperor. These new-style *themes*, however, were considerably smaller than the old.

Also about the middle of the seventh century the imperial bureaucracy was drastically restructured. A limited number of specialized departments or *sekreta* were set up. The two most important were certainly the *strategikon* (military affairs) and the *genikon* (tax department), which is not surprising since about 60 per cent of the estimated state budgets were spent on the army. At the head of the entire civil bureaucracy was the *sakellarios* (chancellor), who would become a very powerful figure in Byzantine politics.

Renewed expansion

Renewed wide-scale territorial expansion would not take place until the tenth century, although there were smaller successes earlier, such as the reconquest, soon after 800, of the western part of the Peloponnese, whose inhabitants had been mainly Slav for more than two centuries. Some of them were deported and replaced by indigenous Greeks. Civil war and foreign adversaries precluded any further expansion in the area. In the ninth century it was the Bulgarian khans in particular who kept the Byzantines fully occupied. After the power of the Avars collapsed in about 800 (see Chapter 6), the Bulgarian kingdom continued to expand steadily westwards until at its largest it encompassed not only modern Bulgaria but also all of Macedonia and major parts of present-day Serbia and Albania. The emperors in Constantinople could then do little to stop them.

It was not until the end of the ninth century that the tide began to turn: although most of Sicily had fallen to the Muslims, the Byzantine position was strengthened in mainland Italy and Anatolia. The major conquests that followed in the tenth century were in part made possible by the weakening of Byzantium's traditional enemies (notably the Muslim rulers in the Middle East), and in part the result of reasonable political stability in Byzantium itself. An effective balance was found between hereditary monarchy and army intervention in matters of state, an almost unavoidable feature of a relatively centralized state that made high demands on the army. This balance meant that the highest military commanders showed restraint in 'correcting' weak emperors or filling power vacuums, notably created when an emperor died before his son had attained his majority; but at the same time they kept a finger on the pulse. This turned the court into a shadow world where behind the fairy-tale scene the air was thick with plots and the protagonists regularly disappeared into the wings.

Throughout the tenth century there were really only two emperors: Constantine VII (913–959) and his grandson Basil II (963–1025). The former reigned first under the regency of the Patriarch of Constantinople, and then under that of his mother, the courtesan Zoë 'of the coal-black eyes' (*Karbonopsina*), and finally, for nearly twenty-five years, he had to put up with the career general Romanus Lekapenos as co-emperor beside him. To distinguish him from Lekapenos, Constantine was given the surname Porphyrogenitus ('he who was born to the purple' – the purple of the imperial childbed), meaning that he was the lawful hereditary monarch. Under Basil II the generals Phocas and Tzimisces forced their way one after the other – and after the latter had had the former liquidated – into the role of co-emperor.

These arrangements had a good and a bad side. Lekapenos, Phocas and Tzimisces were all very capable soldiers who, thanks to their position, could pursue their military ambitions. Lekapenos put heavy pressure on the Bulgarian Empire, which had flourished remarkably under the powerful khan Symeon (893–927) and his successors. Phocas annexed Cilicia (the south-eastern corner of Asia Minor), Armenia and the islands of Crete and Cyprus, and through his conquest of Antioch acquired a bridgehead in northern Syria. Tzimisces chased the Russians out of Bulgaria, started to occupy Bulgarian Thrace and reduced the Arab emirates of Aleppo and Mosul in the north of Mesopotamia to Byzantine vassal states. The downside of the generals' high-handed actions was that rivalry and self-interest all too easily resulted in internal squabbles. This is what happened after the death of Tzimisces in 976. Thirteen years of civil war followed, which only came to an end when the young Basil II managed finally to take control. The alliance that Basil made with Vladimir, the Russian ruler of Kiev, was of particular importance in this struggle for power.

On the military front Basil scored many successes. He completed the conquest of Bulgaria, with a cruelty that exceeded even the norms of the time, earning him the sobriquet 'the slayer of the Bulgars'. The small Christian kingdoms to the south of the Caucasus, such as Georgia, were brought under Byzantine rule more or less by force. And, lastly, Basil strengthened the Byzantine presence in southern Italy. Only his efforts to recover Sicily from the Muslims came to nothing.

The renewed Byzantine expansion was accompanied by the strengthening of the army. The tactical importance of the cavalry was growing unmistakably in the Islamic world as well as in the West. Cavalry units were more heavily armed and were given more important offensive duties, while the infantry was trained to protect the cavalry from counter-attack by taking up a square formation on the battlefield. These army reforms went hand in hand with legislation on recruitment and costs. Basil introduced the principle of subsidiary fiscal solidarity. This meant that larger landowners were obliged to take on the fiscal responsibilities (not the land) of small farmers in the same village who were in financial difficulties. Should the land still fall to the treasury despite all this, then it was leased rather than sold. The maintenance costs of the heavily armed cavalrymen, who had to have more than one horse each at their disposal and who needed costly weapons and equipment, were apportioned over certain pieces of land. The owners of that land were then jointly responsible for the maintenance of one cavalryman. In this way the army remained a public organization, and for the time being the situation was avoided whereby local and regional rulers sprang up as autonomously operating warlords, as happened in many places in the West during the tenth and eleventh centuries.

When Basil II died in 1025 Byzantium was once again a major power. The Empire was certainly twice as large as it had been in the eighth century. Basil reigned supreme from the Straits of Messina to the east coast of the Black Sea. The rapid expansion had obvious disadvantages. The vast territory was characterized by equally large geophysical and ethnic differences and was therefore not easy to control. In the extensive periphery the seeds of ethnic or religious separatism were always present. But above all it became increasingly difficult to guarantee that power was shared out principally through the court in Constantinople. A growing number of matters were arranged on the initiative of the powerful and wealthy families of Asia Minor with their own clienteles.

FURTHER READING

Bowersock, G.W., Peter Brown and Oleg Grabar (eds) (1999), *Late Antiquity. A Guide to the Postclassical World* (Cambridge, Mass.: Belknap Press of Harvard University Press).

Brown, Peter (1971), *The World of Late Antiquity. From Marcus Aurelius to Muhammad* (London: Thames & Hudson).

Cameron, Averil (1993), *The Mediterranean World in Late Antiquity A.D. 395–600* (London and New York: Routledge).

—— (2005), *The Later Roman Empire* (Cambridge, Mass. and London: Harvard University Press).

Haldon, John F. (1990), *Byzantium in the Seventh Century. The Transformation of a Culture*, 2nd edn (Cambridge: Cambridge University Press).

—— (1999), *Warfare, State and Society in the Byzantine World 565–1204* (London: UCL Press).

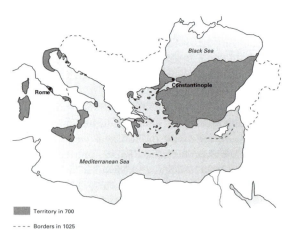

Black Sea

Constantinople

Rome

Mediterranean Sea

▬ Territory in 700

- - - - Borders in 1025

Map 2.1 The Byzantine Empire in about 700 and shortly after 1000

Jones, A.H.M. (1964), *The Later Roman Empire 284–602. A Social, Economic and Administrative Survey*, 4 vols (Oxford: Blackwell Publishers).

Kaegi, Walter E. Jr. (1992), *Byzantium and the Early Islamic Conquests* (Cambridge: Cambridge University Press).

—— (2003), *Heraclius, Emperor of Byzantium* (Cambridge: Cambridge University Press).

Kelly, Christopher (2004), *Ruling the Later Roman Empire* (Boston, Mass.: Belknap Press of Harvard University Press).

Moorhead, John (1994), *Justinian* (London: Longman).

Potter, David S. (2004), *The Roman Empire at Bay, AD 180–395* (London and New York: Routledge).

Salzman, Michelle Renee (2002), *The Making of a Christian Aristocracy: Social and Religious Change in the Western Roman Empire* (Cambridge, Mass. and London: Harvard University Press).

Stein, Peter (1999), *Roman Law in European History* (Cambridge: Cambridge University Press).

Stephenson, Paul (2003), *The Legend of Basil the Bulgar-Slayer* (Cambridge: Cambridge University Press).

Treadgold, Warren T. (1995), *Byzantium and Its Army, 284–1081* (Stanford, Calif.: Stanford University Press).

—— (1997), *A History of the Byzantine State and Society* (Stanford, Calif.: Stanford University Press).

Ward-Perkins, Bryan (2005), *The Fall of the Roman Empire and the End of Civilization* (Oxford: Oxford University Press).

Whittow, Mark (1996), *The Making of Orthodox Byzantium, 600–1025* (Houndmills and London: Macmillan Press).

Williams, Stephen and Gerard Friell (1999), *The Rome That Did Not Fall. The Survival of the East in the Fifth Century* (London: Routledge).

CHAPTER 3

The migration period

The suggestive term, 'the wandering of peoples' – a literal translation of the German stock term *Völkerwanderung* – always brings to mind an image of massive invasions of wild, barbaric tribes who, in a very short time, overran and brought down the highly cultured and powerful Roman Empire. In fact this name for the period between *c.* 400 and *c.* 600 is an unfortunate legacy from the Romantic historians of the eighteenth and nineteenth centuries, who in turn had adopted without question the stereotyped view of barbarians that existed in late Antiquity. This makes both parts of the term 'the wandering of peoples' rather problematic. What should 'peoples' mean in this connection? And what exactly were the 'wanderings'?

WAITING FOR THE BARBARIANS

For those who lived outside the borders of the Empire the Romans used a Greek word, 'barbarian', originally applied to everybody who did not speak Greek. These barbarians were looked upon with a mixture of fear, admiration and scorn. Prudentius, the early fourth-century Spanish Christian poet, believed that the difference between Romans and barbarians was as great as that between humans and 'four-footed animals'. Other descriptions of barbarians were built on negative stereotypes. Germans, for example, the vague term for the barbarians from across the Rhine, were long-haired and reddish-blond, they stank and drank, were always looking for a fight and they could not be trusted. And most frightening of all, there were hordes of them. On the other hand, the Romans had great admiration for the Germans' courage and fighting spirit. They were happy to recruit Germans into the army and many a Roman general showed off with a bodyguard of strangely clad barbarians from the north.

The creation of a watershed between civilized Romans and uncivilized barbarians had above all an ideological purpose. It had little to do with reality. The Roman Empire had never been a hermetically sealed world, even in its heyday. The impressive barrier of border fortresses, walls and heavily guarded caravan routes was not intended to keep the barbarians out at any cost, but rather to control the very intensive border traffic. Moreover, the continual expansion of the Empire had resulted in the admission and incorporation of large foreign populations. They gradually became Romanized, but never lost their ethnic diversity. The Roman Empire was an effervescent melting pot of cultures, with a large barbarian component. Moreover, the Romans did not have an immeasurable technological advantage over the surrounding barbarian society, either in the primary, mainly agricultural, production or in the weapon technology that was so important for the balance of power. More than anything, the Romans owed their dominant position to their superior organizational skills.

Roman writers did their best to bring some order into the barbarian masses which surrounded them on every side. They grouped them neatly into *nationes* (singular *natio*) and *gentes* (singular *gens*). Both these Latin words suggest that the barbarian groups were seen as descent societies, because *natio* – as Isidore of Seville explained in the sixth century – is derived from the verb *nasci*, to be born, and *gens* from *gignere*, to beget. These writers seldom undertook any ethnographical research on which to base this sort of assumption. Most of them had never travelled through the regions they described. They relied on hearsay or on what other 'geographers' had reported.

To modern historians looking back at the migration period a basic division between sedentary and nomadic barbarian peoples immediately leaps to the eye. In the densely forested plains and mountain chains to the north and north-east of the Roman Empire there were barbarians in farming communities, peasants normally living in small villages controlled by native warrior aristocracies. It should be made clear that the rough tripartition of these northern and north-eastern barbarians into Celts, Germans and Slavs, which is often made in modern literature, is not a borrowing from ancient ethnographers. It is based on philological research into 'barbarian' linguistic remnants from European prehistory. In the eighteenth century it was determined that the languages spoken in the northern barbarian world stemmed from three main groups or major linguistic families. Then, rather precipitately, archaeologists turned these linguistic families into 'cultures', which does not make much sense scientifically. Apart from that, the cultural recognition of Celts, Germans and Slavs has led to less harmless claims. The equating of Germany with linguistic Germania, the vast region where Germanic languages were spoken, or had once been spoken, provided German nationalism with dangerous 'historical' claims to *Lebensraum* far beyond the German borders. The perceived pan-Celtic and pan-Slav cultures have been similarly exploited for nationalistic purposes.

Even now there is discussion about the location of the primordial areas where Celtic, Germanic and Slav languages were spoken, as well as the nature and speed of their geographical spread and the rationale behind it. Some of these north and north-eastern barbarian peoples must have moved over large distances, just as later stories about them suggest. For instance, the Goths would have been in close contact with, if not migrated from, South Scandinavia in various stages to the lower Danube area and the adjacent parts of Ukraine, where they lived in late Antiquity. Most modern historians and archaeologists are prepared to accept that these tales of wandering reflect some basic historical reality, but all underline that its time-frame must have extended over many centuries and would have constantly changed the ethnic composition and cultural identity of the Goths.

The non-sedentary barbarians, who influenced the history of late Antiquity and the early Middle Ages in Europe to an extent that should not be underestimated, can be divided into two main categories: nomads from the steppes and desert nomads. They wandered with their vast droves of horses, sheep and camels over the endless steppes of Eurasia and the deserts of North Africa, Arabia and Syria. Such pastoral economies could only exist through regular contact with agricultural communities to exchange livestock, hides and wool for grain and other produce from the land.

These contacts between nomads and agricultural communities always formed a potential threat to the latter. This was linked to two structural features of nomadic groups. In the first place, the relatively specialized pastoral economy caused the nomads to be more dependent on the farmers than vice versa. Because of their limited contact with the sedentary world and the extreme fluctuation of earnings from their cattle the nomads had irregular incomes, and bottlenecks could easily occur in their supply of food, arms and other primary necessities. This compelled them, it seems, to a forceful exploitation of sedentary groups, in the form of either predatory raids or demands for tribute that looked like extortion. With the accumulation of sufficient wealth and integration with subjected groups, the conditions were right for some form of political centralization in which the nomads became more or less sedentary, and the pastoral component of their economies became more closely linked to the form of agriculture practised by the peoples over whom they ruled.

Nomads often succeeded in a lengthy exploitation of the sedentary groups thanks to – and this is the second feature – their great mobility and competence in the martial arts. The steppe nomads were superb horsemen, and their archers were without equal. Their wanderings through inhospitable natural environments made them tough and sharpened their powers of endurance. Life in small groups created a sense of solidarity among them but at the same time formed, with the constant threats from outside, the breeding ground for a culture of violence. When they set aside their mutual enmities the nomad groupings could rapidly unite into great, multi-ethnic confederations forming redoubtable fighting machines in times of war.

The threat they posed to western Europe was always limited. West of the Carpathians there are simply not the open spaces essential for both a peaceful nomadic existence and a real 'Mongolian storm'. The only region that in any way met the geographical requirements was the Carpathian basin, coinciding approximately with present-day Hungary. As far back as classical Antiquity, this situation enabled ever-new groups of steppe nomads originating from central Asia to maintain from there, on the very borders of the Roman Empire, a plunder economy for shorter or longer periods. At the time of the great migrations we see first the Huns and the Alans (*c.* 400), later the Avars (*c.* 550) and Bulgars (*c.* 680), and finally the Magyars and Cumans or Kipchaq Turks (from *c.* 890) make their way into the Carpathian basin. With the exception of the Alans, who came from the Iranian plateau, all these peoples were of non-Indo-European, Ural-Altaic origin.

Of the desert nomads, or Bedouin, it was the Arabs who had the greatest influence on medieval history. In late Antiquity they wandered with their flocks of camels and sheep through an area stretching far to the north of the Arabian peninsula. The area included the whole of the desert-like centre of the 'fertile crescent'. It brought the Arabs into the sphere of influence of the Romans and Persians, where they came into contact with highly developed agricultural communities. There were, of course, forms of sedentary agriculture on the peninsula of Arabia itself, particularly in oases. These oases, especially if situated on important caravan routes, sometimes grew into marketplaces almost resembling towns. They attracted specialized craftsmen and merchants. Thus, in the case of the early Arabic world, the label 'nomadic' covers a society of considerable complexity.

Tribes, peoples and ethnogeneses

Barbarian groups in the times of these migrations are usually referred to in the literature as tribes or peoples. This is a loose translation of ancient terms such as the Latin *nationes*, *gentes* and *populi* or Greek *ethnoi*. The problem is that what classical writers meant by *nationes* or *gentes* does not fully coincide with the purely classificatory meaning that the modern social sciences give to 'tribe' or 'people'. However, we must make a choice between them and we have opted for modern terminology. Now, in anthropology the word 'tribe' refers to a certain stage of political organization. Tribes are small communities of no more than a few thousand people that may be segmented (for example, living in

different settlements), but within which there is not yet an economic basis for domination by an elite. Tribes are therefore predominantly egalitarian societies. As far as we are able to tell, most barbarian groups at the time of the migrations did not correspond to this definition, and for this reason we reject the designation 'tribe'.

With the word 'people', the situation is rather more complicated. In common parlance 'people' has two meanings: ethnic group and nation. An ethnic group is an enduring community clearly defined by its own culture. An essential feature is that its members are conscious of their ethnic identity. This consciousness is expressed in its own proper name or ethnonym, and in the awareness of a shared past (real or not) and a common destiny. A nation is either an ethnic group that has given political meaning and content to its identity, or a multi-ethnic political community that consciously presents itself as one people.

There are many pitfalls to research into ethnic groups in the (distant) past, which makes it extremely difficult to consider barbarian groups from the time of the migrations as such. First, ethnic groups are only comprehensible to archaeologists, historians and linguists in so far as their doings have materialized in objects, texts and linguistic remnants. Moreover, as the story of the 'Suevian knot' shows (see Box 3.1), it is not always simple to establish to what extent and under which circumstances such remnants 'produced' ethnic meaning. It is clear from this that an unusual hairstyle can just as well be a social or political statement as an ethnic one.

Furthermore, most of the written information about barbarians comes from Roman or Greek writers. The supposedly ethnic features of barbarian groups are, therefore, largely attributed from outside. What we miss is a look from inside. And third, exceptional circumstances can intensify the dynamics of ethnic groups, and above all politicize ethnic sentiments. This is exactly what happened regularly during the period of the migrations: ethnic groups (or parts of them) joined together into large multi-ethnic alliances for particular purposes.

If such multi-ethnic confederations lasted long enough they could grow into new peoples, each with its own, new identity, which for a more or less significant part was grafted on to the culture of the dominant

BOX 3.1 HAIRSTYLE AS AN ETHNIC MARKER? THE SUEVIAN KNOT

Classical writers were often definite in attributing typical external features to certain barbarian 'peoples', as the following fragment from chapter 38 of Tacitus' *Germania* shows:

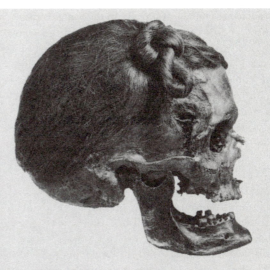

> Now I shall speak of the Suevi. They do not form one people as the Chatti or the Tencteri do. It is rather the name for the inhabitants of more than half of Germania, and they should be distinguished in a series of independent tribes, each one with its own name. Nevertheless they are often all classed together as 'Suevi'.
>
> A peculiarity of the Suevi is that they comb their hair to the side and bind it together in a knot. In this way the Suevi distinguish themselves from other Germans, and the free men from the slaves. Other peoples also wear their hair in this way, perhaps because they feel related to the Suevi or perhaps, as is often the case, simply because they like this fashion. But this hairstyle is unusual except among the Suevi, and is generally found only among young people. The Suevi, on the other hand, even those of advanced age, comb their unruly hair back and then make the knot on the crown of the head. The nobles dress their hair even more artfully.

Images of barbarian warriors on triumphal columns and the discovery of a skull with the hair preserved in a peat bog in Schleswig-Holstein confirm the accuracy of Tacitus' description. Yet the specialists hesitate to see a Suevian in every description, image or discovery of a head with a hair-knot. Tacitus' text gives reason enough for such caution. Historical-ethnographic research reinforces this. It teaches us that clothing, tattoos and hairstyles were sometimes intended as ethnic distinctions, but they may also indicate age, social status or political persuasion or, trivially enough, may just have been in fashion at the time. All these functions, then, are also subject to changes in time and geographical space. So it may very well be that the hairstyle that was perhaps typical for the Suevi of the first century later spread to other barbarian groupings outside the Roman Empire or even – why not? – to the Romans themselves. There are striking examples of the 'barbarian look' being adopted in the Roman Empire. In the fifth and sixth centuries it was fashionable for young men in Constantinople to wear their hair in the Persian or Hunnish mode: the hair was shaved high at the front and allowed to hang in thin strands to below the shoulder at the back. It is doubtful whether all Persians and Huns wore their hair in this way. The Greek Priscus, who for some years was close to Attila, left a reliable description of the infamous king of the Huns. According to Priscus, Attila wore his hair short, more in the style of the Romans.

The passage from *Germania* was borrowed from the German translation of Wilhelm Harendza (Munich, 1964). For the discussion on hairstyle as an ethnic marker at the time of the peoples' migrations see Walter Pohl, 'Telling the difference: signs of ethnic identity' in *Strategies of Distinction. The Construction of Ethnic Communities, 300–800*, Walter Pohl and Helmut Reimitz (eds) (Leiden, 1998), pp. 17–69.

– often name-giving – group within the confederation. It presupposes that elements of that culture were consciously perpetuated by a 'tradition-carrying (aristocratic) kernel' over a long period of time. This must have happened time and again during the slow migration movements that various barbarian peoples, as we saw, had made in prehistory. Now similar processes of ethnogenesis took place in a much accelerated form, although still taking decades rather than years to be completed. The classic example is presented by the Tervingian Goths: in about 375 they left their homelands in the Crimea and on the lower Danube, were admitted into the Roman Empire, and then after repeated moves established their own, semi-autonomous kingdom in the region around Toulouse. During the fifty years or so this alternation of moving and settling took, the ethnic composition of the group changed constantly – but it continued to being called 'Gothic'. The new 'people' that was thus shaped round an 'authentic' Gothic core eventually adopted a new name in confirmation of its own identity: the Visigoths (literally, 'brave Goths'). However, some historians think such an interpretation goes way too far, and refuse to view the Tervingians who crossed the Danube in 375 as in any way the same group as the Visigoths who settled in Aquitaine in 416. For them, the preservation of the 'Gothic' label alone is not enough to assume any real cultural continuity.

MIGRATIONS

Backgrounds: push and pull factors

The traditional historical view of the 'Germanic Invasions' dates from writers of late Antiquity who systematically painted the flow of barbarians into the Empire in stark and sombre tones. They were fond of using marine metaphors: 'angry waves' of merciless Goths, Vandals, Huns and what have you pounding the borders of the once-so-powerful Empire that, alas, was finally swamped by these barbarian hordes. This negative note has survived remarkably intact in modern historiography. The dramatic effect is heightened by squeezing together onto one geographical map, in a wild jumble of arrows, movements, each of which often took decades – and sometimes even longer – and which

added together, stretched on for more than two centuries. The final result most resembles tank divisions advancing on a modern battlefield.

In actual fact various types of movement were behind the peoples' migrations, of which large-scale attacks on the Roman Empire by barbarian confederations was just one. At the other extreme was the gradual infiltration, sanctioned or not by the Roman authorities, of border areas inside the Empire by barbarian peasant-colonists. Any number of hybrid and transitional forms could be found between these two extremes. One common denominator was the formation of barbarian mercenary armies, inside or outside the borders of the empire, which were brought in to defend the border or to combat internal enemies.

Precedents for all these movements can easily be found in the earlier history of the Roman Empire, in the turbulent third century in particular, when on several occasions armies of Goths, Alamans and Franks penetrated deep into the south. That the migrations did not then begin is only due to the lack of political will on the part of the governing establishment to admit sizeable barbarian groups into the Empire and give them far-reaching political autonomy. The imperial authority made a strong recovery and transformed that lack of will into an active policy of forcing the invaders out.

This does not alter the fact that barbarian involvement in the Roman world of late Antiquity increased. It can be attributed to various causes, which can somewhat schematically be reduced to push and pull factors. The latter were linked mainly to developments inside the Roman military organization, the former to socio-economic and political circumstances on the barbarian side of the northern border of the Empire known as the *limes*.

By the time of Julius Caesar the Romans were already making considerable use of barbarian auxiliary troops for their military operations. The barbarization of the Roman armies was to accelerate further during the Late Empire for two reasons. First, towards the end of the third century the Romans switched to a new 'Grand Strategy'. They chose no longer to defend the Empire at its frontiers with entire legions stretched along the whole length of the border. The new plan was to distinguish between lightly armed border troops (*limitanei, ripenses*) and mobile intervention armies (*comitatenses*), stationed in large garrison towns a good distance from the *limes*. The biggest advantage was a greatly improved utilization of the main armies' radius of action. The disadvantage was that the border could be easily penetrated, and certainly by small raiding parties. The Romans tried to overcome the problem by forming human buffer zones where groups of barbarians were allowed to extend their settlements outside the borders into the thinly populated demilitarized zone inside the *limes*. In exchange, the barbarians had to defend these areas as Roman allies. This happened on a small scale until about half way through the fourth century. After that, agreements were made regularly with sizeable groups who formally submitted but were then allowed to remain together, and who thereafter often assumed a large degree of autonomy. The first of these *foedera* (literally meaning 'treaties', singular form is *foedus*) was entered into with the Salian Franks soon after 340. They were given permission to settle in the Betuwe, in the lower Rhine area, but in the following centuries in fact colonized what is now Brabant and Flanders. Similar agreements were made with many other barbarian groups. At a later stage *foedus* came simply to mean a mercenary's contract. There was no formal submission and no connection with border defence. Moreover, these new-style *foedera* entitled the barbarians to payment. In order to secure this payment, even in the periods when there was no work for their warriors, the leaders of the barbarian mercenary groups tried to obtain a high Roman military rank. One warlord who operated from his own power base in this way in the later years of the Western Empire was Childeric, the father of the Frankish king Clovis. Childeric called himself *rex* (king), but in addition bore the Roman rank of *magister* (general).

The growing importance of *foedera* for maintaining Roman order was not an isolated phenomenon, and that brings us to our second point. The increase in the size of the army under Diocletian (284–305) and his successors in a period of demographic stagnation ensured a rapid rise in the number of foreign soldiers in the regular legions. A logical result was that barbarian leaders advanced to the top of the Roman military command structure. In the western part of the Empire after the death of Theodosius (379–395) the real power was often in the hands of barbarian commanders such as the Vandal, Stilicho, (see Box 3.2) and the Skyr, Odoacer. In 476 Odoacer deposed the last emperor of the West in a palace revolution and had himself proclaimed 'king of the (barbarian) peoples' (*rex gentium*) of Italy. In the East the Alan, Aspar, was commander-in-chief between 431 and 471, making him one of the most powerful men in Constantinople.

Antipathy to the barbarians was greater in the East than in the West. The growing barbarization of the legions and the *foederati* policy met with fierce opposition, especially from the upper echelons of the civil administration into which far fewer barbarians had penetrated. Senator Synesius of Cyrene called it 'folly to use wolves as watchdogs'. He called Emperor Arcadius, who had hired the wolves, 'a jellyfish', a slimy, spineless creature.

BOX 3.2 A VANDAL SAVES ROME FLAVIUS STILICHO (*C.* 365–408)

The ivory diptych in the cathedral treasure of Monza shows Flavius Stilicho (*c.* 365–408), in military dress, with his wife Serena and their son Eucherius on his left. The panel was made in 396, or shortly afterwards, on the occasion of the appointment of the minor Eucherius to a high public office.

Stilicho was the son of a Vandal king, and was therefore always called *semibarbarus* (half-barbarian). Under Emperor Theodosius he made a

brilliant military career, which ended in his appointment as commander-in-chief (*magister utriusque militiae*) of the Roman legions in the West. Stilicho was a prop and stay to Theodosius. His wife Serena was a niece of Theodosius, who had adopted her as his daughter and entrusted his youngest son, Honorius, to her care. Before this Theodosius had 'recommended' (*commendati*) to Stilicho both Honorius and his older brother Arcadius, who would succeed him as emperors of the western and eastern parts of the Empire respectively. This is why Arcadius and Honorius are depicted on Stilicho's shield. Stilicho allied himself even more closely to the imperial family by marrying his daughter Maria to Honorius, while it was also his intention to marry his son Eucherius to Honorius' sister Galla Placidia; this marriage never took place, however. Through all these alliances Stilicho felt not only connected to the imperial family by right and reason, he clearly also cherished dynastic ambitions: his son Eucherius would be emperor, and preferably over a united Roman Empire. Moreover, Stilicho always pressed for the integration of barbarians in the Roman army and in Roman life.

From the imperial palace in Ravenna Stilicho played a tragic key role in a crucial episode in Roman history: the (in hindsight) definitive division between the Eastern Empire and Western Empire, exactly what he had wanted to avoid at all costs. Yet the matter was in his own hands. Originally, Stilicho refused to transfer the provinces of Illyria and Africa from the Western to the Eastern Empire. Arcadius then sent Alaric and his Gothic army to Italy. Stilicho defeated Alaric a number of times, and it remains a mystery why he allowed the Gothic army to remain intact. Second, the large-scale invasion of Italy by a group of Goths under Radagaïs obliged Stilicho to pull his troops out of Gaul in 406. Although Radagaïs' army was crushed at Fiesole, Gaul was weakened militarily and the great coalition of Vandals, Suevi and Alans, which had crossed over the frozen Rhine near Mainz towards the end of 406, could thrust deep into Gaul without meeting much opposition. Both events seriously weakened the Roman grip on the West.

Vague plans to re-unite both parts of the Empire after the death of Arcadius in 408 led to Stilicho's downfall, because Honorius suspected Stilicho of wanting to put his own son, Eucherius, on the throne in Constantinople. The rebellion of a Roman army, which had been brought together in Pavia in the summer of 408 in preparation for an expedition to Gaul, brought discredit on Stilicho. He sought refuge in Ravenna where he and his followers were brutally murdered on Honorius' orders.

Claudian, an Egyptian-born poet and protégé of Stilicho's wife Serena, sang the praises of Stilicho in countless panegyrics. He gave Stilicho his image as saviour of Rome: 'restituit Stilico cunctos tibi, Roma, triumphos' (Stilicho has given all your triumphs back to you, Rome), runs one of his verses. After the death of Claudian in 404 Stilicho had a collection made of all the poems eulogising himself; they were an important means of propaganda for the general.

Literature: Santo Mazzarino, *Stilicone. La crisi imperiale dopo Teodosio* (Rome, 1942). Alan Cameron, *Claudian. Poetry and Propaganda at the Court of Honorius* (Oxford, 1970). *Illustration*: Cameron, *see* opposite title page.

The criticism was not entirely undeserved because the *foederati* policy tempted new groups of barbarians to make incursions, and their leaders rather resembled the genie in the bottle: once they were called in they were difficult to control. Very often little more could be done than try to employ one group of barbarian mercenaries to tackle another. This is why modern historians are divided in their assessment of the rulers in Rome, Ravenna and Constantinople and their policy towards the barbarian invaders. Some admire the cunning and ability of emperors like Honorius and Zeno and generals like Stilicho and Aetius to get new groups of barbarians to do their dirty work for them and avoid dangerous military confrontations. Others assert that this policy, at least in the western part of the Empire, led to Rome's interests being bargained away, often to a state of downright anarchy.

The major push factor behind the swelling flow of barbarians into the Empire can be traced back in the long run to the enormous difference in economic strength, and thus in wealth and prosperity, between the Roman Empire and the barbarian world of North and central Europe in particular. The people on the other side of the *limes* took advantage of Rome's riches in varying degrees. This situation sharpened social differences and led to the formation of a military aristocracy with private armies and often-violent competition between barbarian peoples and confederations. The clever Romans then used divide-and-rule diplomacy and quickly changed alliances. Political unrest in the most densely populated area of the *limes*, the upper and middle Rhine and the upper and middle Danube, was thus fed gradually over the centuries. It resulted in a regular regrouping of the barbarian confederations outside the borders of the Empire, in a growing migration pressure, and often in violent raids too. The 'ritual dump' of the Angles near Thorsbjerg in the south of present-day Denmark provides grim evidence of the endemic raiding and warfare in the northern border regions of the Roman Empire. Archaeologists found only the remains of sacrificial animals and pottery in the lowest layers, while the upper layers, in addition to coins, contained mostly weapons and pieces of equipment, some of it Roman. The peat bogs of Jutland and Schleswig-Holstein have yielded similar finds, including spears and swords, which turned up by the hundreds. They show better than anything else how in the first century AD a society of peaceful farmers increasingly became a society geared to war.

This tendency was further promoted by the nature of political organization in barbarian society. We have already stated that the northern barbarian groups who played a significant part in the migration period were not tribes in the anthropological sense of the word. But what were they then? They were at least one rung higher on the ladder of forms of political organization. We use the term *chiefdoms*. Chiefdoms are characterized by the formation of local elites, in this case warrior aristocracies, who are able to use force when necessary to defend their position of power. To achieve this they must have at their disposal armed followers and allies whose loyalty can be ensured through material favours. This again presupposes a steady supply of either war booty or agricultural surpluses that will reach the hands of the leaders and will be converted into prestige goods (weapons, jewels, horses) valued by their warriors or allies. The regular fabrication of prestige goods requires a certain amount of economic specialization (craftsmanship, trade). Finally, social inequality in chiefdom societies was often sanctioned by religion.

Roman sources use the term *comitatus* to refer to the armed retinue of the barbarian warlords, but the modern German translation *Gefolgschaft* is more popular. In the *Gefolgschaft* the status of follower was a rare and desirable position. Barbarian chiefs recruited their followers on the basis of physical strength and skill with weapons. The rise of *Gefolgschaften* fits perfectly in the process of the militarization of the northern barbarian world described above. All of this did not make the *Gefolgschaften* Wagnerian fighting machines, however. Indeed, the very opposite is evident in the report of the battle between a large barbarian confederation and the legions of the co-Emperor Julian near present-day Strasbourg in 357. The Alaman Chnodomarius was the most important barbarian 'king' (rex). Accompanied by his *comitatus* of 200 warriors, who had sworn to be true until death, he plunged into battle. But when the bloated Chnodomarius fell from his horse and was unable to get up, his followers promptly called it a day and surrendered. Their leader spent his last days in luxurious exile in Rome; his warriors were probably absorbed into Roman legions, as so often happened.

Chronology

The event heralding the symbolic beginning of the great migrations, however, had nothing to do with the developments in the zone of contact between Romans and barbarians; this event was the appearance of the Huns in the western steppes of central Asia. The terror sown by these Altaic nomads in the lands round the Black Sea caused a large group of Goths to take flight. In 376 this group was granted permission to cross the Danube, but the Roman authorities failed to receive the vast stream of refugees in a humane way. The Goths revolted, and an Eastern Roman army led by Emperor Valens was cut to pieces near Adrianople in 378. The Goths were then given the status of *foederati* and allocated territory in what is now Serbia. But they were still not satisfied. Under the command of a strong new leader, Alaric, they rose up again and attacked Thrace shortly after 390. During the first decade of the fifth century Alaric went through Italy twice as a *foederatus* of the Eastern Roman emperor who wanted to bring an end to Stilicho's power in the West. Alaric never managed to threaten Ravenna, the Western Roman imperial capital, but in 410 he succeeded in taking and plundering Rome itself, the eternal city, an event that came as a bombshell at the time. He died soon afterwards in southern Italy. His successor turned round immediately and led his Goths out of Italy into Gaul.

At that time chaos reigned in Gaul. Possibly in the wake of the westward shift of the Huns into the Hungarian plain, which shattered the balance of power between the Germanic poeples living there, a huge barbarian confederation of Vandals, Suevi and Alans crossed over the frozen Rhine on the last day of 406. Over the next three years they moved slowly southwards. A large force crossed the Pyrenees at the end of 409. The commander of the Roman forces in Britain tried to capitalize on the chaotic situation and seize power in Gaul. It is not unlikely that in the circumstances Emperor Honorius managed to direct the Goths to South Gaul to help restore order. In any case, a new *foederati* contract was concluded in 418 under which the Goths were allotted part of the province of Aquitania. A kingdom was formed, with Toulouse as its capital. The empire of the Goths – or Visigoths as they were often called after that – extended in the course of the fifth century over the largest part of Gaul south of the Loire and over the whole of the Iberian peninsula.

At the same time as the (Visi)goths arrived in Aquitania the Roman legions departed from Spain. The vacuum left behind gave the invaders the opportunity to establish themselves there as the new rulers. That led to continual struggles between Vandals, Alans, Suevi and Visigoths. In 429, according to their own estimates, 80,000 Vandals – men, women and children – crossed the narrow strait between Spain and Morocco. Having arrived as *foederati* of a rebel general, within ten years they ruled as lord and master in North Africa. The power of this hundred-year Vandal empire was concentrated in the old Punic capital, Carthage, close to modern Tunis.

Of all the migrations, these 'epic journeys' of the Goths and Vandals still form the episodes that most fire the imagination. We know far less about other similar migrations, those of the Burgundians, for example. In the first quarter of the fifth century they created – possibly as *foederati* – a legendary kingdom along the middle Rhine, near to where Mainz and Worms are situated. Apparently this was soon seen as a threat to Roman authority because other *foederati* were sent to deal with them, first the Visigoths then the Huns. The confrontation between Huns and Burgundians must have left a deep impression on their contemporaries for it may have provided the source material for one of the great medieval epic texts, the *Nibelungenlied*, which was first written down in Lower Austria in about 1200. With their power in the middle Rhine area broken, the Burgundians started drifting again. In the framework of new *foederati* agreements Flavius Aetius, the commander of the Roman legions in the West, in 440 gave them permission to settle in the middle Rhône region and around Lake Geneva. From there they took control of the low, north-western part of present-day Switzerland, so that they eventually ruled over an area stretching from Basle in the north to Avignon in the south. In 534 'Burgundy' was conquered by the Franks and added to the Merovingian kingdoms.

During all this time Burgundy bordered on the lands of the Alamans in the north. The Alamans, together with the Franks, provide a good example of northern barbarians who, again often within the framework of *foederati* agreements, had extended their original territories inside the borders of the Empire without ever having made a 'journey' or wandering, at least not en masse. As far as the Franks and Alamans were concerned it was more a matter of a gradual shift, which cannot be precisely followed and which coincided with peasant settlement. By the end of the migration period the Alamans were named as the inhabitants of the upper Rhine area and the adjoining part of modern South Germany. The Salian Franks had by then extended their territory as far as present-day northern France.

The migrations of North German and South Scandinavian barbarians to England form a middle way between outright invasion and the colonization of a neighbouring region. The real settlement of these groups dates from the beginning of the fifth century when the Romans withdrew their regular troops from England and left the defence against barbarians from Ireland and Scotland, including the Picts, in the hands of the Angles, Saxons, Jutes and Frisians from the continental North Sea coastal areas, who for that purpose were, again, formally given the status of *foederati*.

A completely new phase in the history of the migrations was ushered in when, in 476, there was no appointment of a separate emperor for the western part of the Empire. For the moment, it confirmed the fiction of a Roman Empire again undivided. Certainly the emperors in Constantinople made use of the barbarians to turn this fiction into reality and to restore effective Roman authority in the West, beginning with Italy and Rome itself. After the new Rome – Constantinople – had been repeatedly threatened in the eighth decade of the fifth century by rebellious troops under the command of the Ostrogoths, Emperor Zeno had cleverly persuaded the Ostrogothic leader, Theoderic, to undertake a campaign of conquest in Italy where Odoacer was still in control. Theoderic's mission was successful, and he established a government that lasted from 493 to 526, not only in Italy but later also in Slovenia, Provence and even for a while in Spain.

Although Theoderic did his utmost to make it look as if the emperor in Constantinople had delegated royal authority to him, his *de facto* independence and the growing power of the Ostrogoths made further Byzantine intervention in Italy inevitable. This resulted, after 535, in the Gothic wars. As usual, barbarian *foederati* were employed, among them the Langobards, or Lombards. Yet the major invasion of Italy by the Lombards in 568 was not the result of a direct order or request from the emperor in Constantinople. The background to the incursion remains something of a mystery but was connected with the appearance of the Avars in the Carpathian basin. The Lombards, whose homelands were in that area, had apparently concluded a treaty of non-aggression with the Avars, only to then begin a war against the Gepids, at that time the most powerful people in the area. It is possible that as a consequence of this treaty the Lombards departed for Italy en masse immediately after their total victory over the Gepids.

Within a few years the Lombards had subjected large parts of Italy, though not all the territories adjoined each other. In fact three centres of power were created: in the north Friuli and the Po Valley (which would be called Lombardy after the Lombards), with Pavia as the royal seat; in the Apennines, the 'dukedoms' or vicegerencies of Spoleto and Beneventum. These two dukedoms were almost always as good as independent of the kings in Pavia, yet were never recognized as kingdoms. The Byzantines lost a lot of land, but managed to retain important bases both along the coast (Venice, Ravenna, Naples and Rome) and inland (Sicily, Apulia and Calabria).

The final phase of the period of migrations began shortly after the Lombard invasion in Italy and was similarly connected to the expansion of the power of the Avars and the weak defence of the European part of the Byzantine Empire. In about 570 Slavic-speaking groups under the control of the Avars from the region of the lower Danube attacked Greece and the Balkans. Originally marauding raids, these incursions continued at frequent intervals for about fifty years and gradually acquired the nature of aggressive migrations with the aim of permanent settlement. The Slavs were given every opportunity for this since the Byzantines had long neglected the Danube border while they were entangled in exhausting wars against the Persians in the East. In the circumstances the emperors could do little but accept the situation and implement a policy of accommodation. This included sending missionaries to the Slav communities in Byzantine territory. Later, Byzantine policies became far more aggressive, leading to a series of wars of submission and the deportation of large groups of Slavs to the interior of Asia Minor.

Owing to the differing forms of the migrations here discussed, there was much variety in the nature of the settlement of the barbarian groups. The only common factor is that everywhere the newcomers were small minorities – even in what is now England, over which a different view has long been held. At times the invading barbarians formed such a small group that they could not immediately hold effective control over the territory they claimed to have subjected. They entrenched themselves in central strongholds, from which in the early years they tried to terrorize the native landowners. We are most familiar with this pattern of settlement in the empire of the Vandals in North Africa. One variant of this pattern could only take place in areas where the Roman tax system was still intact, as it was in Ostrogothic Italy at the beginning of the sixth century. There, for quite some time, the barbarians received tax payments in kind, usually grain, just as regular soldiers of the Roman legions had done in the past. However, this system was always a temporary arrangement that sooner or later turned into occupation of land.

In other cases colonization was the principal motive behind barbarian 'invasions' right from the beginning. We must not then hazard too high a guess at the numbers concerned. In the first half of the sixth century perhaps 10 per cent of the inhabitants of the northern part of Gaul were Franks; in the southern part, which did not fall into Frankish hands until later, and where there were many more towns, it was at most 2 per cent.

THE BARBARIAN KINGDOMS

Barbarian kingship

In the western part of the Roman Empire the new barbarian rulers everywhere formed kingdoms, and kingship thus became the dominant form of government in medieval Europe. The question is whether the barbarians merely implanted this form of rule that they had enjoyed from time immemorial, or whether it was a new construction that, partly under the influence of Roman ideas, gradually received its definitive form. The latter is the most plausible. Only the Goths in the Black Sea region may have had stable, territorially extensive kingdoms before their arrival in the Roman Empire.

The Roman contribution to the 'production' of barbarian kingdoms in the migration period cannot be underestimated. Barbarian leaders looked up to the Romans and saw Roman recognition as a clear legitimization of their own power. Some even tried to link themselves with the imperial family through marriage. Barbarian kings such as Theoderic, Sigismund

of Burgundia and Clovis continually showed that in their own perception they were part of the Roman order. Although boasting on descending from an age-old Gothic royal family, the Amals, Theoderic repeatedly called his Italian kingdom *res publica Romana* (a Roman state) and condescendingly addressed his fellow-princes as barbarians. Sigismund spoke of himself as a 'soldier of the emperor'. After his victories over the Visigoths in 507 and 508 Clovis held triumphal feasts at which, following old Roman custom, he dressed in purple. A century and a half later the Visigothic king of Spain, Recceswinth (653–672), seems consciously to have modelled himself on his great idol, the emperor Justinian.

The Romans, for their part, did much to keep the barbarian leaders as friends, according them titles of honour (*patricius*) or high military rank (*magister*) and alluding to their illustrious ancestry: the Franks, like the Romans themselves, would have been of Trojan origin; after the fall of Troy and years of wandering they had arrived at the Rhine. Of course, this is all nonsense, and nowadays it is generally thought that embellishing the barbarians with this sort of myth about their origins was part of Roman diplomacy.

Most barbarian kingdoms in the West immediately acquired a Christian patina, in addition to a Roman one. Kings were gladly seen as shepherds to whom their people were entrusted as a flock of sheep. The most important duty of the king was to protect his subjects from the sins endangering the eternal salvation of their souls. Unlike the clergy, who shared this main task, the king could – even had to – act firmly if necessary. Of course the king himself had to be the very model of Christian virtue, a true *princeps religiosus* (religious prince).

In barbarian kingship two tendencies can be discerned, from the beginning, in the customs concerning the succession: one is a tendency to hereditary succession and the formation of a dynasty, and the other to election by the most important aristocrats. Neither principle was applied in its purest form; there was always a mixture. It is true that one kingdom tended more to the first and another to the second, but the preference was not invariable. The Visigoths mostly held to the electoral basis, the Angles and Saxons in England, the Franks, and actually the Lombards as well, to that of hereditary succession through one family. In the case of hereditary succession the agreement of the most important people involved (father, queen mother if the father was already dead, uncles and the most important aristocrats) was essential if one was to ascend to the throne, and certainly if one was to remain there.

The view that kingdoms could be divided up was never entertained either. A reign was shared on occasion, for example between father and son, or between two brothers, but mostly that did not lead to a division of the territory. The Merovingian Franks form an exception in this respect. Between the sixth and the eighth centuries there were normally two or three kingdoms side by side, which were considered by their kings – often brothers – to be personal possessions. Other barbarian kings, the Visigoths in Spain for example, did not do that; they made a distinction, borrowed from Roman law, between the private fortune of the king and the public wealth of the kingdom.

The barbarian kingdoms in the West

Whoever would have compared, in about 500, a map of Europe with another one of about 200, could not have failed to be impressed at the successes achieved by the barbarians. Where once the Romans held sway from the Irish Sea in the north-west to the mouth of the Danube in the south-east, barbarian kingdoms had now been established throughout western and southern Europe. The most extensive of these kingdoms was without doubt that of the Visigoths. At the end of the fifth century their power stretched from the Loire in the north and the Rhône in the east to the southernmost tip of the Iberian peninsula. Only after the Visigoths had been forced to give up the greater part of South Gaul after their crushing defeat by Clovis near Vouillé in 507 did they really manage to consolidate their control over the whole of the Iberian peninsula. Apart from the military successes of King Leovigild (569–586) this was mainly due to the conversion of Reccared (586–601), Leovigild's son, from Arianism (a heretical persuasion within early Christianity) to Catholicism. These two factors caused the process of political, social and cultural integration between the descendants of the barbarian invaders and of the native Ibero-Roman population to gain momentum. In 711 the Gothic kingdom in Spain came to an abrupt and radical end.

A large Muslim army under the command of Tariq ibn Zeyad ('Gibraltar' comes from *djebel al'Tariq*, 'Tariq's mountain') crossed over from Morocco and crushed the Spaniards near Jerez de la Frontera. Within a few years the greater part of the peninsula was in Arab hands.

The kingdoms of the Burgundians in the Rhône valley and Savoy, of the Vandals in North Africa and of the Ostrogoths in Italy were even more short-lived. The first was conquered by the Franks in 534, as we have already seen. The second was recovered by the emperor in Constantinople after a brief campaign in 533, more than a hundred years after the Vandal confederation had crossed into North Africa. This region owed its enormous importance in Antiquity to its grain production. Together with the rich agricultural lands of modern Tunisia a large fleet of transport ships had also fallen to the Vandals, and they used these to extend their supremacy over all the major islands of the western Mediterranean. Various Eastern Roman emperors tried to drive the Vandals out of North Africa in the second half of the fifth century, but they never succeeded. Yet the Vandal kingdom was very weak

‖‖‖ Kingdom of the Ostrogoths	⠿ Kingdom of the Burgurdians
⑊⑊ Kingdom of the Visigoths	⫽⫽ Kingdom of the Franks
▦ Kingdom of the Suevi	▓ Kingdoms of the Anglo-Saxons
▓ Kingdom of the Vandals	═ Kingdom of Provence (507–536 Ostrogothic, 536 Frankish)

Map 3.1 Barbarian kingdoms in the West, *c*. 525

internally. At the time of the conquest many Roman landowners had been killed or driven out, and the Vandals never managed to repair this vital link between the primary economy and the ruling upper layer of society (which they had now become). In the major coastal towns they formed a small elite, which did not mix with the rural population and had too little direct involvement with economic and social life.

Quite a lot is known about the government of the Ostrogoths over Italy thanks to the *Variae*, a collection of state papers, edited by Cassiodorus, a son of the Roman governor of Sicily and Calabria in the later years of Odoacer's rule. Cassiodorus held the important post of chancellor a number of times under Theoderic the Great (493–526) and his immediate successors. From the *Variae* it appears that Theoderic did his utmost to operate a dictatorial government over Italy, closely modelled on the Roman pattern. The cooperation of the Roman aristocracy, tried and tested in classical officialdom, was essential in this. In return, Theoderic protected Italy by taking the two open land approaches to the peninsula – West Pannonia (modern Slovenia) in the east and Provence in the west. Theoderic's kingdom collapsed soon after he died: this was mainly due to the aspirations of Justinian, the Eastern Roman emperor, to return Italy to the Roman Empire. The two devastating Gothic wars (535–552), which he waged for this purpose, proved a disaster for Italy.

In recent years historians have taken a more positive view of the kingdom – or kingdoms – of the Lombards in Italy that continued to exist until the final Frankish conquest of 774. The Lombards used to be considered as wild barbarians who had scarcely any contact with (Roman) civilization. The conquest of Italy would have been one of extreme violence and there would never have been any real integration with the indigenous population, partly because the Lombards remained stubbornly Arian. It has now become clear, however, that this biased picture is based on contemporary sources that were very hostile to the Lombards. The popes, for example, felt threatened by them, and in diplomatic documents constantly referred to them in derogatory terms such as 'the greatest criminals' or 'the stinking Lombards'. In fact the Lombards did merge with the Italian population. Arianism was never an insurmountable obstacle – not all Lombards were Arians. A visible proof of the successful integration can

be seen in the spread of Lombardic names, while, on the other hand, Lombard as a spoken language rapidly gave way to proto-Italian. There is admiration for the legislative activities of the Lombard kings: they reflect the desire of the new rulers to enlarge the legal security of their subjects, much after the example of the ancient Romans. Lombard law, which betrays remarkably little influence of Roman law, nevertheless had a wide reach. Finally, the Lombards were able to maintain an urban society in North Italy even though they did not have an urban background themselves. Northern Italy was governed from the urban centres of the old *civitates*, where the Lombard elite also settled. Official governors with the title of 'duke' were appointed in the larger towns. In Friuli and Lombardy these were supported by the 'gastalds', whose task it was to oversee the royal domains and public revenue. The establishment of such a position probably became necessary when, shortly after the invasions, it was decided that the dukes could keep for themselves half the public revenues (mostly the proceeds from taxes) destined for the king. This provision made the office of duke very profitable: small wonder that it soon became hereditary. Another consequence was that *civitates* with their own duke enjoyed a large degree of independence.

The observer of 500 would have found the rapid fall of the kingdom of the Ostrogoths no less astonishing than the rapid rise of the *regnum Francorum*, the kingdom of the Franks. Not much of that was visible as yet. There were indeed various Frankish warlords between Cologne and Paris who assumed the title of 'king', but their power did not stretch far. Among them was Clovis, the son of Childeric, whose power base was in Tournai, but who often operated far beyond and in the service of the Romans. After Childeric's death in 481, Clovis extended his power in the north of Gaul, but his major successes came later in life. In 507 he defeated the Visigoths, as we have seen. At a stroke he now possessed Aquitania, almost the entire south-west corner of Gaul. Then followed merciless campaigns in which he eliminated a number of rival Frankish kingdoms in the Rhineland, including that of the Ripuarian Franks around Cologne. The kingdom of the Burgundians was annexed under Clovis's successors. Other neighbours were forced to accept some form of dependence. This led sometimes to the formation of real Frankish satellite kingdoms, such as that of the Alamans (on the upper

Rhine), the Bavarii (cf. Bavaria) and the Thuringi (cf. Thuringia). This was accompanied by the appointment of a Frankish or a native duke or governor. Sometimes the dependence was limited to the payment of annual tribute as a sort of recognition of the Frankish overlord. The (continental) Saxons and the Lombards were apparently obliged to pay this tribute for some time. In other regions, such as Brittany, Gascony (the French Basque country) and Frisia (the North Sea coastal fringes of the present-day Netherlands and Germany) short phases of strong Frankish influence alternated with longer periods of virtual autonomy. In these latter periods it often happened that the originally Frankish line of dukes increasingly identified with the 'people' over which they had been appointed to rule. The most striking example of this are the Agilolfings, a house of probably Frankish origin, which held the hereditary dukedom (governorship) over the Bavarians and which was increasingly seen as an exponent of the Bavarian struggle for independence. In the early Middle Ages the Agilolfings enjoyed almost royal standing and were closely related to the most important dynasty of Lombard kings.

The attitude of the Franks was ambivalent, especially towards the peoples whose homelands were situated in north or north-east Francia (the usual umbrella term for the Frankish kingdoms), such as the Westphalians and Saxons. This is understandable, because on the one hand these groups formed a threat to the power of the Franks while, on the other, they functioned as a sort of human buffer zone between Francia and the Slavic Wends, and as a human reservoir for the formation of East Frankish armies.

The picture that we have of Great Britain in about 500 is very diffuse. The groups of Angles and Saxons who had come to England as *foederati* at the beginning of the fifth century had settled there permanently and interbred with the Romano-British population. The invaders were so dominant that they were able to impose their own language. Even so, large parts of Great Britain remained outside the reach of the Anglo-Saxon settlement: Cornwall (until the ninth century), Wales and Scotland thus kept their Celtic language and their own character. In the part of England under the control of the continental barbarians many small 'kingdoms' (or chiefdoms?) were

created, which were constantly at war with each other. They eventually grew into seven larger units: Essex, Sussex and Wessex – the kingdoms of the East, South and West Saxons respectively – Kent, East Anglia, Mercia and Northumbria. Of these seven, Mercia – which we must place in the Midlands – was by and large the most important during the early Middle Ages. This meant that for longer periods some or all of the six other kingdoms recognized the supremacy of Mercia, at least in name. Northumbria and Wessex also had a similar position, although for a shorter period. The best-known king of Mercia is Offa (757–796), whose name lives on in the new coins he had minted, in the customary laws (*dooms*) that he had collected and recorded, and in the impressive earthwork (Offa's Dyke) that he apparently had built, either as a defence or simply as a marker, on the border between Mercia and Wales, for a distance of more than 110 kilometres. Offa maintained regular diplomatic contacts with the court of Charlemagne, which indicates that Anglo-Saxon England was by no means isolated from the Continent. There are further proofs of this. One is the epic poem *Beowulf*, which probably acquired its definitive form in Offa's Mercia but which tells the story of events that took place in South Scandinavia in the sixth century – something that seemed to fascinate the Anglo-Saxons centuries after their arrival from the same region. Not long before, in the early eighth century, they had already 'rediscovered' their supposed kinship with the continental Saxons.

Segregation or integration?

It has long been thought that in their newly settled kingdoms the barbarian invaders, who everywhere formed numerically small minorities, did all in their power to keep themselves separate from the native population in order to limit the number of people that could share in the advantages of the newly won position. Segregation could have happened in three ways: by forbidding mixed marriages, by introducing the principle of legal personality and by consciously adhering to Arianism, a heretical movement inside Christianity. In recent times there has been serious doubt not only about the feasibility of implementing strict segregation on an ethnic and religious basis but also about the will of the barbarian kings to remain separate. Theoderic, king of the Goths, may once again serve as an example. His subjects were divided in two groups, *Romani* and *Goti*. This originally ethnic distinction quite soon acquired a functional character: *Romani* came to mean 'civilians' and *Goti* 'military'. The ethnic background was no longer important, nor was the religious preference. Important secular and Church leaders and advisors were recruited from both groups.

Of the methods of segregation mentioned, legal personality – the principle of treating each ethnic group or social category within a political unity according to its own law – is the most problematic. The impression is that barbarian rulers were in principle never in favour of legal segregation, but that in the beginning they had to accept it in practice because those seeking justice appealed to their own traditional legal rules, the barbarians to their customary law, the Romans to written Roman law. So, if requested, the king had to provide both. The problem gradually faded as the different population groups increasingly mixed. This mixing could only have been prevented by a rigid enforcement of a ban on mixed marriages. Such a ban did exist in Visigothic Spain in the first half of the sixth century, but it was only in that place and at that time, and the background is obscure. In Spain the opposition between Arians and Catholics remained real and sharp the longest – until 589. In other barbarian kingdoms it either did not exist at all (in Frankish Gaul since Clovis) or it did not run along the dividing line between barbarian newcomers and native populations (in Ostrogothic Italy), or it was insignificant. The Lombard rulers in Italy, for example, never made an issue of religious convictions.

All in all, the evidence for a consciously sought segregation is meagre. Only for a short time after gaining power in a particular region was segregation sometimes an option, but this was dictated by the barbarian leaders' desire to guarantee rewards for their warriors and to put matters on a permanent basis, and not by a deliberate policy of apartheid. Ethnic sentiments were only played to in specific circumstances. Justinian's wars of reconquest, in particular, caused the barbarian kings to turn away from 'Roman' and 'Catholic' and begin to present themselves as Arian barbarians (Goths, Vandals). The Gothic wars in Italy prove that such a politicization of ethnicity was not deeply rooted. For average Italians the loyalty attaching to where they lived or to their social position weighed far more heavily than the feeling of being 'Roman' or 'Gothic': they changed sides as it suited them.

On the other hand, the evidence for integration is stronger and more plentiful. Archaeologically seen, it is everywhere difficult to distinguish between barbarian invaders and native populations soon after the arrival of the former, which points to a rapid acculturation. Also, the barbarians abandoned their own language rapidly and easily almost everywhere: the Avars and the Bulgarians exchanging their Altaic-Mongolian languages for Slavic ones; the Visigoths and Suevi in Spain, the Burgundians in Savoy and Provence, the Franks in Gaul and the Lombards in Italy giving up their Germanic languages for regional Romance languages. Only the invaders in England, the Franks in the Rhine area of the modern Netherlands, Flanders and a part of northern France, the Alamans in the upper Rhine area and lower Switzerland, the Britons in Brittany and the Magyars in Hungary, immigrants all, succeeded in making their language the dominant one in regions that were once for some length of time part of the Roman Empire. In the Alps interesting mixing zones emerged, where two languages continued to exist side by side. The durability of this form of integration can be seen in the fact that the linguistic boundaries of Europe today essentially date back to those outlined above.

Proto-nation formation

Outside Italy integration between barbarian minorities and indigenous majorities contributed to the creation of a new consciousness of supra-local solidarity, of the idea that natives and newcomers together formed one people. Where this consciousness was strongly politicized – which in this context means a close link with kingship – we can talk of proto-nation formation. Visigothic Spain is an early example of this: here, in seventh-century literary and legal sources, *rex, gens et patria Gothorum* becomes the standard formula to refer to the 'king, people and homeland of the Spaniards', regardless of their ethnic origins. Some decades later 'Hispani' replaced the word 'Gothi' for Spaniards. 'Gothi' was then again used to refer to the barbarians who conquered Spain in a past that was almost mythical even at that time. The depth of this consciousness of solidarity among the Spanish is shown in a curious little historical work about the Visigothic king Wamba, written by Julian, bishop of Toledo. In 673 Wamba harshly put down a revolt in 'Gaul', the area round Narbonne north of the Pyrenees, which at that time was still part of the Visigothic Empire. In his account Julian enlarges upon the enmity of the Spaniards towards their Gallic fellow-citizens, who clearly did not belong to Spain.

In other barbarian kingdoms the name of the invaders persisted as a proto-national point of reference, as in Burgundia and Francia, the kingdoms of the Burgundians and Franks, and eventually also in Anglia, the collective name for the kingdoms of the Anglo-Saxons in England. At the same time, Burgundians, Franks and Angles became the usual names for all the inhabitants, whether their origin was barbarian-allochthonic or autochthonic. The formation of the new names, 'Franks' and 'Angles', was even linked to the conscious presentation of the Franks and Angles as a chosen 'people', or even 'race' – meaning a large pseudo-family with a shared past, its own identity, and a common destiny within the framework of Christian salvation history.

When considering proto-nation formation in the early Middle Ages we must, of course, expel any notion of modern national consciousness, which is why we use the word 'proto'. We just do not know how deep the feelings described amongst the peoples of these societies ran. Neither did the barbarian kings possess the military or communications facilities to control fully and continuously the enormous regions over which their power extended in name; for this reason, whether they liked it or not, they had to accept a large degree of local and regional autonomy. The formation of barbarian kingdoms in the early Middle Ages therefore reveals all sorts of centrifugal forces at work, as well as centripetal forces. Which of the two would prevail depended finally on the length, geographical range, the extent of suppression and the zeal of the domination. Should the last two weaken then the opportunity arose to break with the trend towards acculturation and to strengthen old traditions. One place where this occurred was in Frankish Gaul, south of the Loire. But modern Romania provides the most remarkable evidence of this: the Latin language persisted in isolated mountain villages in the Carpathians, which were left undisturbed by the rapidly changing rulers in the region (Byzantines, Avars, Bulgars and Slavic groups).

THE ARAB CONQUESTS

At about the same time as the Lombards entered Italy and groups of Slavs swarmed over the Balkans, Muhammad (c. 570–632) was born in Mecca on the west of the Arabian peninsula. What we know of him we know solely from the Arabic tradition, which was only written down a century later and is far from unprejudiced and cannot be verified through other sources. According to the tradition, in later life Muhammad had visions in which God (Allah) revealed his will to him. On Allah's orders Muhammad spread the revelation and became Allah's Prophet. This caused tension in Mecca and Muhammad and his followers fled northwards to Medina, an event that marks the beginning of the Islamic era (622). Seven years later he returned to Mecca and assumed power. Support for him grew rapidly all over south and west Arabia. Under his first successors (caliphs) the authority of Mecca expanded with incredible speed. It was first directed at the north and east of the Arabian peninsula and the neighbouring desert regions between the 'fertile crescent' where many Arab Bedouin roamed. In the year 637 the Byzantines and Persians suffered humiliating defeats at the Yarmuk river (south of Damascus) and al-Qaddisya (near Kufa on the Euphrates) respectively. This opened the way for the Arab conquest of present-day Syria and Iraq. A few years later the Byzantines were easily driven out of Egypt. Raids and expeditions into Iran and North Africa were undertaken from these new bases. Within a hundred years of Muhammad's death, Arab power stretched from Spain in the west to Samarkand and the Indus delta in the east. Shortly after 660 its centre was moved from Mecca to Damascus, the seat of the caliphs of the Umayyad family. This move was of enormous importance for Arabic culture, which was now exposed to considerable Syrian and Persian influence.

This rapid Arab expansion, however, was not without its problems. Some of these were caused by questions of succession, but most related to the control of this enormous area that the Arab armies had conquered. As the Arab population was small there could be no question of all the conquered territory being occupied, and thus, if they did not return home, the Arab warriors established themselves in towns and villages as a ruling upper class. In that respect the Arab conquests resembled those of the northern barbarians in some parts of Europe. But there are also substantial differences. The Arabs exposed themselves to social and cultural integration far more slowly than the barbarians in the West. Initially, the Arabs did not impose their religion, Islam, on the conquered populations. They strove rather to retain their ethnic purity, and in all probability for a long time succeeded in this. In contrast, the Arabs learnt a lot about administration from the Byzantines and Persians. No barbarian kingdom in the West could approach the highly developed administrative system of the Arabs.

In order to support themselves the Arab soldier-immigrants in the conquered regions of the Middle East received an allowance from the taxes that the subjected peoples had to raise. The amount of the allowance depended on the status of the recipient, which was in part determined by genealogical proximity to the Prophet and by the contribution made in military campaigns. In the long term, the maintenance of such a system, which presupposes an impressive bureaucracy, caused serious friction among the Arab recipients and between the Arab upper class and the indigenous population. The inequality in the fiscal treatment of Arab and non-Arab Muslims was a particular cause of tension. Arabs were not required to pay taxes although they were obliged to give alms (Arabic: *sadaqa*), officially for the poor. Non-Arab converts paid a heavy land- and poll-tax, and in that respect were treated no differently from those who had not converted. This situation was ended at the beginning of the eighth century when Arab and non-Arab Muslims were treated alike for tax purposes, which greatly encouraged conversion to Islam. But the Arab upper class continued to monopolize military and administrative power, and this finally became unacceptable to the native elites. Abu-Abbas al-Saffah, scion of another house of Mecca that was related to the Prophet, took advantage of this disaffection to stir up rebellion against the Umayyads in the north-east of Iran. The rising was successful and led to the establishment of the caliphate of the Abbasids, who had a

new capital built on the Tigris – Baghdad – that would grow into one of the largest cities in the world.

The Abbasids pursued a rigorous policy of centralization, which led to even more bureaucracy. The policy stood or fell by the effectiveness of the means of exercising power that the caliphs had at their disposal, in particular the military support from the Iranians who had helped the Abbasids gain control. Regional separatism lay dormant everywhere. At the beginning of the ninth century things started to go wrong and a long period of civil war and revolts broke out. One consequence was that the Sawad, the fertile southern part of Mesopotamia where Baghdad itself was situated, fell into serious economic decline, threatening the caliphs' most important source of income. Some caliphs tried to turn the tide by taking reformative measures. Al-Mutasim (833–842) was the first to experiment with armies composed of non-Arab warriors from distant border territories (Turks, Armenians, Kurds, Berbers). This was the beginning of what was to be a long tradition in the Islamic world, where the nucleus of the army consisted increasingly of non-Arab elite corps; and it would not be long before the commanders of these corps became part of the ruling elite. As in medieval Europe this development was connected to the professionalization of the conduct of war and the growing importance of the cavalry. Turkish nomads and Berber Bedouin were particularly sought after because they were excellent, tough horsemen. During the tenth century the Arabic system of 'mamelukes' (slaves) came into being: mounted soldiers of non-free status were placed in moderate-sized companies under their own commander, who paid them and whom they had to obey. This created a strong *esprit-de-corps*, in which homosexual relationships often played a part.

A second measure intended to deal with the crisis was the issue of what is known as *iqta*. These were contracts in which the state revenues (taxes, domain produce, etc.) within a certain area were lent for a short period to a person of high standing, who during that period exercised both civil and military authority in that area. In exchange, the holder of the *iqta* had to pay the troops, if he held a military command. This *iqta* system has sometimes been compared to the feudal–vassal relationships that developed in Western Europe at about the same time, but the differences

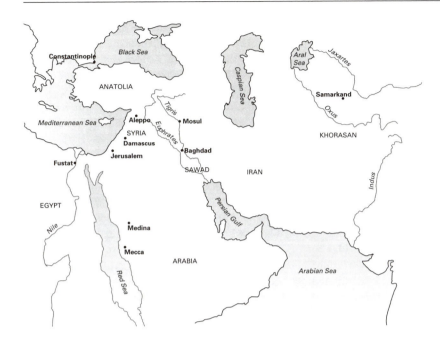

Map 3.2 The Islamic world of the Middle East

outnumber the similarities. In particular, the element of homage was absent in the *iqta*.

After the first quarter of the tenth century not much authority remained to the caliph of Baghdad. His military commander-in-chief was now in charge and took the title *amir al-umara* (literally meaning 'leader of leaders'). From the second half of the tenth century this position was practically monopolized by the Buyids, a family originating south of the Caspian Sea but which had created its own kingdom in west and central Iran. The Buyids probably encouraged the Islamic Shi'ite tradition (see Chapter 4), thus lending valuable support to the development of Shi'itism into a real force within the Islamic faith. This led to a sharpening of religious differences in Iraq, because the caliphs tended to take the side of the Sunnis.

The fact that the Buyids were able to create their own kingdom was symptomatic of the collapse of the united Arabic empire – which in fact already had a precedent in 750 when the last of the Umayyads fled from Damascus to Spain, where the dynasty would remain in power for many centuries without paying much heed to Baghdad. In the tenth century numerous small kingdoms in the Middle East, which were still

more or less loyal to the caliph, worked themselves loose from Baghdad. It is better not to use the terms 'the Arab empire' or 'the Arab world' to describe the situation at this time: 'Islamic' is preferable, because the Arabs no longer had to impose themselves on the vast area that they had once conquered. They had created a sense of unity and solidarity, from then on Islam was the unifying force.

In the border area of the north, in particular, political fragmentation resulted in a serious weakening of the military; the small kingdoms of Armenian and Kurd rulers bore the brunt respectively of renewed Byzantine aggression and of Turkish nomads who at the beginning of the eleventh century left their Kazach steppes and pushed into eastern Iraq by way of Azerbaijan. On the other hand, the regionalism brought opportunities for the formation of strong, new cores, as the rise of the Fatimids shows. The Fatimids were the descendants of a Syrian leader from the Ismaili Shi'ite sect, who had proclaimed himself an imam shortly before 900. Soon afterwards he fled to Ifriqya (approximately modern-day Tunisia) where the Ismaili movement had more followers than in Syria. With the support of the Kutama Berbers, who wanted nothing to do with the Arab elite, the Fatimids seized power and proclaimed themselves caliphs. Since the Umayyad ruler in Spain had reacted by doing the same, from that point on there were three caliphs. From Ifriqya the Fatimids extended their power through attacks on the Maghreb and Egypt. They conquered Egypt in 969, where they built a new capital, al-Qahira (Cairo, which literally means 'the victorious').

From Egypt the Fatimids finally advanced on Palestine and their homeland Syria. By then it had become evident that they must strengthen the military basis of their power; this they did chiefly through the Mameluke system. The Fatimids remained in power until the middle of the eleventh century in spite of some eccentric caliphs. Among them was al-Hakim (996–1021), a dangerous psychopath whose reign of terror lasted for 25 years. His name was always uttered with loathing in the West, for in 1009 he plundered Jerusalem and destroyed the Holy Sepulchre.

The strength of the Fatimids lay in their enormous prestige; because of it the succession never formed a problem. Unlike the Abbasids they allowed family members to share the power as little as possible, so that the caliph would never suffer competition from his family. They also had a tolerant attitude towards religion, never attempting to make Egypt a Shi'ite state. Finally, Egypt enjoyed great prosperity under the Fatimids. Cairo became an important transit market for trade between the Indian and African worlds on the one hand and the Mediterranean world on the other. The Azhar mosque, the building of which started shortly after 969, soon developed into a great centre of learning. By the eleventh century Baghdad was no longer the beating heart of the Islamic world: Cairo had taken its place.

FURTHER READING

Amory, Patrick (1997), *People and Identity in Ostrogothic Italy, 489–554* (Cambridge: Cambridge University Press).

Blair, Peter Hunter (2003), *An Introduction to Anglo-Saxon England* (Cambridge: Cambridge University Press).

Christie, Neil (1995), *The Lombards* (Oxford: Blackwell Publishers).

Crone, Patricia (1987), *Meccan Trade and the Rise of Islam* (Princeton, N.J.: Princeton University Press).

—— (2004), *God's Rule: Government and Islam. Six Hundred Years of Medieval Islamic Political Thought* (New York: Columbia University Press).

Curta, Florin (ed.) (2005), *Borders, Barriers, and Ethnogenesis. Frontiers in Late Antiquity and the Middle Ages* (Turnhout: Brepols).

Ferrill, Arther (1986), *The Fall of the Roman Empire: the Military Explanation* (London: Thames & Hudson).

Geary, Patrick J. (2002), *The Myth of Nations. The Medieval Origins of Europe* (Princeton, N.J. and Oxford: Princeton University Press).

Gillett, Andrew (2003), *Envoys and Political Communication in the Late Antique West, 411–533* (Cambridge: Cambridge University Press).

—— (ed.) (2002), *On Barbarian Identity. Critical Approaches to Ethnicity in the Early Middle Ages* (Turnhout: Brepols).

Goetz, Hans-Werner, Jörg Jarnut and Walter Pohl (eds) (2003), *Regna and Gentes. The Relationship between Late Antiquity and Early Medieval Peoples and Kingdoms in the Transformation of the Roman World* (Leiden and Boston, Mass.: Brill Academic Publishers).

Goffart, Walter (1980), *Barbarians and Romans, AD 418–584: The Techniques of Accommodation* (Princeton, N.J.: Princeton University Press).

—— (1988), *The Narrators of Barbarian History (AD 550–800): Jordanes, Gregory of Tours, Bede, and Paul the Deacon* (Princeton, N.J.: Princeton University Press).

Harries, J. (1994), *Sidonius Apollinaris and the Fall of Rome, A.D. 407–485* (Oxford: Clarendon Press).

Heather, Peter (1996), *The Goths* (Cambridge, Mass. and Oxford: Blackwell).

—— (2005), *The Fall of the Roman Empire: A New History of Rome and the Barbarians* (Oxford: Oxford University Press).

James, Edward (2001), *Britain in the First Millennium* (London and New York: Arnold/Oxford University Press).

Kennedy, Hugh (1986), *The Prophet and the Age of the Caliphates. The Islamic Near East from the Sixth to the Eleventh Century* (London and New York: Longman Group).

—— (2001), *The Armies of the Caliphs. Military and Society in the Early Islamic State* (London and New York: Routledge).

Merrills, Andrew (ed.) (2004), *Vandals, Romans and Berbers. New Perspectives on Late Antique North Africa* (Aldershot: Ashgate).

Moorhead, John (1992), *Theoderic in Italy* (Oxford and New York: Clarendon Press/Oxford University Press).

Murray, Alexander Callander (ed.) (1998), *After Rome's Fall: Narrators and Sources of Early Medieval History. Essays Presented to Walter Goffart* (Toronto: University of Toronto Press).

Noble, Thomas F.X. (ed.) (2006), *From Roman Provinces to Medieval Kingdoms* (London and New York: Routledge).

Pohl, Walter (ed.) (1997), *Kingdoms of the Empire. The Integration of Barbarians in Late Antiquity* (Leiden: Brill Academic Publishers).

—— and Helmut Reimitz (eds) (1998), *Strategies of Distinction. The Construction of Ethnic Communities, 300–800* (Leiden: Brill Academic Publishers).

Rollason, David (2003), *Northumbria, 500–1100: Creation and Destruction of a Kingdom* (Cambridge: Cambridge University Press).

Saunders, John (1978), *A History of Medieval Islam* (London: Routledge).

Sawyer, P., and I.N. Wood (eds) (1977), *Early Medieval Kingship* (Leeds: School of History, University of Leeds).

Tolan, John V. (2002), *Saracens: Islam in the Medieval European Imagination* (New York: Columbia University Press).

Whittaker, C.R. (1994), *Frontiers of the Roman Empire. A Social and Economic Study* (Baltimore, Md. and London: Johns Hopkins University Press)

Wolfram, Herwig (1988), *History of the Goths* (Berkeley: University of California Press)(orig. German, 1979).

—— (2005), *The Roman Empire and Its Germanic Peoples* (Berkeley: University of California Press) (orig. German, 1990).

CHAPTER 4

Christianity and Islam

The establishment of two world religions

THE CHRISTIAN CHURCH IN THE TRANSITION FROM ANTIQUITY TO THE MIDDLE AGES

Late Antiquity was a time of great religious ferment. Many people turned away from the fossilized worship of the innumerable gods of the classical Graeco-Roman and eastern pantheons. They sought contact with the philosophical currents that inclined towards the belief in one divine power, such as Neoplatonism, or with mystical sects that guaranteed personal contact with a humane deity. Those religions that brought a message of individual salvation and rebirth after death were especially popular. That message was – and is – central to the Christian religion. For Christians, Jesus of Nazareth, who had lived in Palestine under the rule of the emperors Augustus and Tiberius, was not only the Messiah (literally meaning 'anointed', *christos* in Greek), the saviour of the people of Israel promised to the Jews, but even the son made flesh of the only God. His resurrection from death on the cross opened, for the faithful, the way to their own victory over death and to eternal salvation. Yet this sort of conviction was by no means unique at the time. What made Christianity so different was its universal appeal and its ethics. The ethics were based on a virtuous commandment to unselfish love of one's neighbour (*caritas*), especially the weaker members of society, for which nothing should be expected in return. The universal appeal of the early Christian Church is expressed in the adjective 'catholic', coming from the Greek word for 'general'. Christianity was thus in principle open to everyone, whatever their sex, origin and legal status, yet for a long time it retained an air of exclusiveness and distinction. This 'catholic' objective had important social consequences, albeit in the long term; in the beginning the early Christian Church showed itself to be no more tolerant than other cults towards either slaves or women. That does not alter the fact that in the Late Empire public opinion probably looked with admiration upon the close-knit solidarity within the Christian community. This reinforced a feeling of moral superiority among the Christians, giving them strength and resolve in times of persecution.

The only other ancient religion with universal pretensions was Judaism. In the struggle for followers Christianity, which was originally a Jewish sect, scored an important victory even before the fourth century when it appropriated the most important collection of Jewish religious texts. These texts, *tanach* in Hebrew, deal with the relationship between Jahweh, the one true God, and the people of Israel. It was translated into Greek during the third century BC and was then known as the *Septuagint*, but we always refer to it as the 'Old Testament'. At the same time a new, supplementary written tradition took shape, built up around the four Gospels, the life and teachings of Jesus of Nazareth, which were written down within a few generations of his death (scholars still disagree about how many). Together with a selection of letters and reports of the activities of his most important followers, the apostles, and with an enigmatic vision of the end of the world, the 'Apocalypse' or 'Revelation' of John of Patmos, the Gospels form the 'New Testament' – in other words, the New Covenant of God with the new Israel, the Christian Church. The claim behind this was clear: God's chosen people were no longer the Jews but the Christians.

The Jews, on the other hand, were harassed by the Roman authorities from the beginning of the third century. This took on more discriminatory forms after Christianity had been officially permitted in 311. Jews were not allowed to marry Christians, for example, nor could they keep Christian slaves. In the early Middle

Ages further anti-Semitism was held in check by an attitude that can best be described as one of repressive, strictly limited toleration. This was based on the ideas of Paul the Apostle and leading Church Fathers such as Augustine and Pope Gregory the Great. They were convinced that through their treatment of Christ the Jews had followed the path of evil, but that they would eventually turn again to God. Until that time came, the Jews who lived among Christians could hold up a negative mirror, so to speak ('this is the wrong way'). Systematic persecution of the Jews was only very sporadic in the early Middle Ages; it occurred in Visigothic Spain in the first half of the seventh century. In the Carolingian Empire the Jews were placed under the direct protection (*tuitio*) of the king.

Whether the Christians would have managed to become the dominant religious group inside the Roman Empire through their own efforts we shall never know. Constantine's mysterious conversion on the eve of the battle of the Milvian Bridge (312) – a year after the Edict of Milan, by which Christianity was officially tolerated – instantly altered everything, however half-hearted it may appear to our eyes. Politically speaking, it was very clever of Constantine to proceed with such caution. He did not want to offend Italy's powerful senatorial elite under any circumstances. So while he favoured the Church on the one hand, on the other he remained openly associated with the old state religion that focused on the worship of the invincible sun god (*Sol Invictus*). The assimilation of this god with Christ can still be seen in our Christmas, for 25 December counted as the birthday of the sun. In the year 321 Constantine also introduced the 'venerable day of the Sun' (Sunday) as a compulsory, weekly day of rest. Outside the Church the emperor never showed himself as a Christian prince. For his entire life Constantine remained *katechumen*, a Christian in preparation. He was only baptized on his deathbed.

The religious sympathies of Constantine's successors also fluctuated; Christianity did not become the state religion until the reign of Theodosius I (379–395). The whole process was not without consequences. The number of Christians rose rapidly in the fourth century: from 10–25 per cent of the total population of the whole Roman Empire in around 300 to an estimated 50 per cent in about 400. The success also had a downside. The once suspect, closed, regularly persecuted sect emerged in the fourth century as an aggressive and triumphalist movement with a militant side and a growing intolerance towards other faiths. The old notion that the seed of Christianity, once sown, fell into good earth, and that all the inhabitants of the Roman Empire opened their hearts eagerly and joyfully to the word of the Gospel, has long been superseded. It was too readily assumed that, in spite of their rich diversity, the non-Christian cults of late Antiquity no longer provided a satisfactory framework for life. This was most certainly not the case. That is why there was massive opposition to Christianity throughout the fourth century. The Christians tried to overcome this opposition using every possible means of persuasion, from kindness to force. The latter could include verbal aggression, intimidation or ridiculing heathen customs, but the Christians did not shrink from using crude physical violence against heathen shrines, including the famous temples of Serapis in Alexandria and of Zeus Marnas in Gaza. Such targeted and humiliating destruction was certainly intended to convince non-Christians that their gods were non-gods. Why otherwise would they allow the violent desecration of their holy places? It was a fairly successful ploy, later enthusiastically copied by missionaries operating in the heathen world of the northern barbarians. But the intolerance did not stop at material damage. Soon after 400 the first heathen martyrs fell: one of them was the Alexandrian philosopher Hypatia, who was stoned to death by the Christians for her Neoplatonist ideas – even though the Christian religion was itself permeated with these same ideas.

The fury of the Christian aggression increased under Theodosius. Action against the heathens was supported by the favouritism openly shown to the Christians, the exclusion of non-Christians from government office and the threat of severe punishment for non-conformists. This inevitably ended in active persecution by state authorities, which reached its miserable nadir in the East in the second half of the sixth century under Emperor Justinian and his successors.

The success of Christianity was further strengthened by three more institutional factors that determined the direction in which the Christian Church would develop in the following centuries: first, the leading role that the emperor and the bishop of Rome (the pope) each demanded for himself; second, the rapidly growing wealth of the Church; and finally, its tight organization in bishoprics, grafted on to the basic units of civil government of late Antiquity, the *civitates*.

The relationship between emperor and pope

According to both Judaeo-Christian and Islamic tradition all legitimate authority derives directly from God, and so the highest office-holder is answerable to God alone. One calls this belief theocratic. In the Latin-Christian Middle Ages the theocratic idea of authority was behind three different perceptions about the relationship between worldly power and spiritual authority. In the 'caesaropapist' perception, which fitted perfectly with the ancient Roman view of emperorship, the highest secular ruler was *ex officio* the head of the Church. In contrast the hierocratic view attributed a universal primacy of authority to the highest spiritual authority on earth, in this case the pope. A compromise was formed by the dualism that considered secular power and spiritual authority as two separate, autonomous spheres.

Constantine and Theodosius, and their successors as emperors of the Roman or Byzantine Empire, always considered themselves the undisputed leaders of the Christian Church. They did not think of themselves as just ordinary, secular people, but as sacral beings, earthly extensions of the divine king in heaven. Their task was thus not only to lead the Church and defend her from external enemies but also to guard the contents of religious doctrine. As early as 314 – two years after his 'conversion' – Constantine had called a council in Arles to pass judgment on the North African Donatists. The beliefs of the barbarian kings in the West in fact did not differ fundamentally from those of the emperor in Constantinople. They too looked upon themselves as *rex et sacerdos* (king and priest), as Christian leaders of the Christian community, who were intermediaries between clergy and people (*mediator cleri et plebes*), and whose authority originated directly from God.

Although the caesaropapist position was also brought up openly for discussion by other bishops, including Ambrose of Milan (374–397), it was the popes as bishops of Rome who quickly took the lead in the matter. At the end of the fifth century Gelasius I (492–496) formulated an apparent compromise, known as the 'doctrine of the two swords'. It connects the underlying idea of a clear division of powers, each of which would operate autonomously in its own sphere – dualism – with the conviction that, in the final analysis, spiritual authority was superior to secular power because 'at the Last Judgment it [would be] the task of the priests to render account for the behaviour of kings'. This addition would give radical popes in the eleventh and twelfth centuries a basis for a hierocratic reinterpretation of the doctrine of the two swords.

In the West the struggle for the highest power in the world had an entirely different, 'more actual' character than in the East. There, the conflict came to a head in an unequal struggle between the emperor and the patriarch of Constantinople; in the West, in a titanic battle between (German) emperor and pope. When the emperor of Constantinople lost effective control over Rome and the surrounding territory at the beginning of the eighth century it also signified the end of his authority over the pope. Three matters further deepened the rift between emperor and pope at the time. First, the Byzantine encroachment on the Roman Church's considerable possessions in southern Italy and Sicily; second, the preference of a number of stubborn emperors for iconoclasm, an obnoxious heresy (see p. 52) in the eyes of the popes; and third, the threat to the interests of the Church of Rome in central Italy from the Lombards, against which the emperor could not offer sufficient protection. For all these reasons the popes went in search of a new ally and protector, and this they found in about 750 in the Franks. First, Pope Zacharias (741–752) recognized the Carolingian mayor of the palace, Pippin the Short, as the lawful successor to the Merovingian kingdoms. A few years later Pippin intervened in Italy in favour of the pope. The most significant, direct result of this was the formal recognition by the Franks of what the popes for some decades had called *res publica Sancti Petri* (literally 'the republic of Saint Peter') and which, for the sake of convenience, we shall call the 'Papal State'. This had for a long time been only vaguely defined, and was actually a conglomerate of lordship rights around the two territorial cores on which the Byzantine Exarchate of Ravenna was originally based – the regions round Rome (Latium) and Ravenna

(Romagna and the Anconan Marches), which were linked to each other by a narrow corridor through the Apennines.

The alliance between the pope and the Carolingians most certainly contributed to the growing alienation between the Church in the East and in the West, although questions of dogma were always the root cause of these schisms. The best-known schisms were those of Photius (866/67) and Michael Cerularius (1054), and are named quite wrongly after the Patriarch of Constantinople involved – as if he were the only guilty party. After every schism the dialogue was renewed. Attempts to reunite the Churches of the East and West very nearly succeeded in 1450, but the Fall of Constantinople three years later put an end to all illusions.

Material wealth. accumulation and distribution

A second factor in the success of the Christian Church was doubtless her enormous wealth, which accumulated rapidly in the centuries following Constantine's conversion. In the Byzantine Empire the Church in its entirety was probably richer than the state as early as the sixth century. The rapid increase in wealth at that time was in part thanks to the appropriation of the riches from pagan shrines, and in part thanks to rich gifts from emperors and prosperous individuals who believed that the uncertain fate of their souls after death would be helped by good works in their lifetime.

With its wealth the Christian Church held a key position in the social redistribution of income through different forms of social charity (care of the poor, the sick, widows and orphans). Its wealth thus gave the Church not only political power but, more especially, moral authority in broad (under)layers of the populations of the great cities of late Antiquity. The *diaconiae* ('deaconries') are a good example; these were established by the popes in Rome and other large cities, such as Ravenna and Naples, when the authority of Byzantium was failing. They were sort of social welfare centres, staffed by monks, where the needy could get bread and a bath.

When we talk about the wealth of the Church we must remember that the Catholic Church as an umbrella association of believers did not have a central

treasury. Its wealth was in the hands of the separate institutions that constituted the Church – bishoprics, parish churches, monasteries, and so forth. The further growth of this institutional capital came from two directions. The most important of these was the ceaseless flow of gifts from members of the aristocracy. They very soon took to building a church or monastery on their own land out of their own pocket, preferably provided with rich altar plate and real relics. They arranged the appointment of a priest or abbot or abbess themselves. And of course they were keen to be buried there, so that after death they would be close to the saint to whom the church in question was dedicated. This phenomenon, which was very widespread in the early Middle Ages, is known as the 'proprietary church system'. Because people of aristocratic origin filled all the important positions in the Church, German histo-

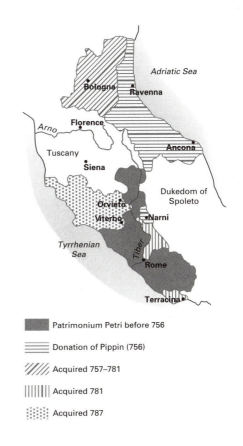

Map 4.1 The beginnings of the Papal State (700–800)

rians refer to the early medieval Church as *Adelskirche*, meaning 'a Church of and mostly for the aristocracy' (Fletcher).

The motives behind the foundation of proprietary churches or monasteries were many and varied. First and foremost, this generous action assured the founders of the salvation of their souls. The possession of a church or a monastery also gave them prestige, and not infrequently it generated income for them. Moreover, the proprietary church system enabled aristocratic families to keep their family property undivided and out of the eager hands of kings.

The wealth of the Church was also fed from below, or rather by the free peasants. This took place through the levying of tithes, a sort of tax on agricultural produce, based on the Old Testament commandment to make a yearly gift of one-tenth of all the yields of the land to God. Exhortations to pay the tithe appear in council resolutions as early as the sixth century, but the tithe only became compulsory in (Christian) Europe generally in the course of the ninth and tenth centuries. At the same time it was given a more specific allocation. Normally one-quarter was for the bishop and the remaining three-quarters went to the maintenance of the (parish) clergy, the local poor and the parish church. Now and then this development encountered fierce opposition, not only from the peasants but also from influential high clerics such as Alcuin of York, Charlemagne's advisor, who in about 800 openly opined that 'it was better to neglect the tithe than to lose the faith'. Alcuin's fears were not ungrounded. The introduction of the tithe undermined the already precarious rural life of the early Middle Ages considerably, especially as most of the tithes did not end up in the hands of the groups for which they were intended. Usually the noble owners of churches and monasteries appropriated the largest share of the tithes connected to them.

CHURCH ORGANIZATION

The clergy and its tasks

Already in late Antiquity, the Christian Church was excellently organized, and this would remain so during the early Middle Ages when public administration shrank so severely that it barely provided reference points beyond the local ones. This gave the Church a comparative advantage that should not be underestimated.

The good organization had its origins in the fact that the Christian Church had a professional, hierarchically organized clergy, *clerus* (literally 'the elected ones'), early on. Its primary task was to lead the 'flock' of believers along the dangerous narrow path to eternal salvation. In the early Middle Ages the clergy had no fewer than eight levels of holy orders: four lower ones, of which that of exorcist (expeller of evil spirits) was surely the oddest, and four higher ones: subdeacon, deacon, priest and bishop. In the higher orders originally only the bishops had doctrinal authority, which means the competence to explain the teachings of the Church. Originally only bishops and priests were allowed to administer the sacraments; the deacons and subdeacons could only assist them.

A person who wanted to enter the clergy first had to shave the crown of his head (tonsure). Then he had a sort of candidate status, during which period he fell directly under the authority of the bishop. Like the ordained clergy, the candidate enjoyed all the privileges belonging to the clerical state. The most important of these were the *privilegium fori* and the *privilegium immunitatis*. The first meant that clerics did not have to obey a summons to a secular court of law and only had to answer for their (criminal) deeds to a Church court. The second brought with it exemption from every fiscal or military obligation in the public domain. Although both privileges dated from the fourth century they were only described with legal precision in the twelfth century, when Church law was finally systematized.

A fundamental task of the higher clergy was, as we have said, the administration of the sacraments. By sacraments we mean the visible signs (*signa*), established by Christ himself, of the personal bond between God and the faithful. Since the twelfth century it has been generally accepted that this sacramental bond signifies the bestowal of God's grace. The number of sacraments was then also fixed at seven. The most important ones are the Eucharist, baptism and confession. Holy matrimony was, and still is, the only sacrament for which no intervention of a priest was/is required.

The Eucharist, meaning 'thanksgiving' and often also called the 'holy mass', is the collective commemoration by a Church community of the last supper that Christ shared with his apostles shortly before his redeeming crucifixion. In time, the mass was sometimes given a utilitarian character when it was offered to ask for a special favour – a good harvest or a fruitful marriage, for example. Baptism was the 'sacrament of initiation' that made a candidate believer a full member of the Christian community and at the same time opened the way for the salvation of the soul. Baptism was consciously presented as a rebirth, where the baptismal waters washed away the new Christian's original sin with which mankind had been burdened since Adam, the first man, had fallen from grace. Because every sin committed after baptism could only be atoned for by very strict penance many aspiring Christians waited to be baptized until they were on their deathbed. In the early Middle Ages the reasoning was reversed and it became customary for babies to be baptized shortly after birth so that the powers of evil could not take hold over them. At first the confession of faith was made by the parents, but for practical reasons it was soon done by sponsors or godparents, usually close relatives of the parents. Sponsors are first mentioned in the sermons of Caesarius of Arles in the first half of the sixth century.

These changes in the sacrament of baptism prompted changes in the way in which the sacrament of penance – better known as the confession – was administered. Every grave sin committed after baptism required expiation through Christ. This was the purpose of confession. It began with the confession of guilt by the sinner, and was followed by forgiveness (absolution) and the imposition of a penalty (penance) by the administrator of the sacrament. In the beginning confession and penance took place in public, and the penalties imposed were extremely heavy. Under the influence of monastic practice public confession was gradually replaced by private, aural confession. Here the confession became something personal between priest and sinner; the repentant, obedient 'son' whispered his sin in the ear of his 'father' confessor; the penance imposed remained secret. Sometime after the eleventh century it also became the task of the father confessor to help the sinner disclose his sins by asking direct questions. This gave the confession the character

of a systematic soul-searching, which had to bring the sinner not only to an admission of his sins but, more importantly, to an understanding of them, and thus to repentance.

Higher-ranking ordained clerics had to be well informed about the complicated rituals and formulas surrounding the sacraments as well as about the Church ceremonies in which they took place. These can be summarized under the term 'liturgy', from the Greek *leitourgia*, meaning 'service'. Priests and bishops also had to be able to explain Bible texts in a discourse or sermon during the service, which meant that higher-ranking clerics had to be better educated than the lower-ranking, although our expectations of their education should not be too high. This is obvious from the complaints made about the level of the clergy at ecclesiastical councils and in programmes for reform. St Boniface, the famous missionary and archbishop of Mainz (674–754), once grumbled about priests in Bavaria who uttered the baptismal formula thus: *baptizo te in nomine patria et filia* ('I baptise you in name: the fatherland and the daughter') instead of the correct *in nomine patris et filii [et spiritus sancti]* ('in the name of the Father, the Son [and the Holy Ghost]').

The overall impression we receive of the early medieval clergy is quite ambiguous, however. On the one hand it was a long time before the high moral demands made of the clergy were taken seriously. In late Antiquity discussion about moral standards centred on the celibacy of the higher-ranking clerics, who, after all, performed sacred acts, and in the view of late Antiquity had therefore to be pure, undefiled by sexuality. Some, like Augustine, wanted to go further and pleaded for the celibacy of the clergy in general. In practice that proved not to be feasible. Even in the deeply Christian Eastern Roman Empire of Justinian, only bishops had to live in celibacy; married men could be ordained as priests, but unmarried priests, once ordained, could not then marry. In the West all the rules were far slacker. It was not until the great movement for reform in the eleventh century that the guidelines were sharpened. Clerical celibacy did then, finally, become the rule in the West; not in the East. Members of the lower clergy in the West were still allowed to marry, but only once.

On the other hand, the shining example of Augustine, who led a communal life with the priests and deacons attached to his cathedral church at Hippo Regius, was followed on a wide scale. The extension of liturgical tasks, with choral prayer in particular, and the gradual Christianization of the countryside required increasing numbers of clerics in higher orders. Many of them lived together in communities or *monasteria* that were set up around cathedrals and other important places of worship, ranging from churches provided with baptisteries and churches where important relics were kept to churches with *hospitia*, shelters for travellers, pilgrims, invalids and otherwise destitute people, attached to them. They were then known as 'canonical clerics', or simply 'canons', because they were deemed to abide strictly by the Church's rules of conduct (*canones*). Yet, their way of life differed from that of monks in several essential points; canons did not take monastic vows and they were allowed to have personal possession. Evidently this created difficulties in differentiating between canons and monks and in distinguishing canonical monasteries from monasteries of monks. This, and the prejudice that many canons lived too unruly lives, gave rise to a reform movement in the Carolingian period which set both objections right (see p. 56).

Church hierarchy: episcopate and diocese

The bishops were undoubtedly the pivot on which the organization of the Church revolved. Their jurisdiction was called a 'diocese' or a 'parish'. In late Antiquity the borders of a diocese usually coincided with those of the *civitas*, the basic unit of Roman civil administration, which should be seen as an urban core with a surrounding (rural) district. Accordingly, the density of bishoprics in the Mediterranean region was far greater than in Western Europe, where *civitates* dating from Roman times were larger and had often disappeared. The popes showed restraint in increasing the number of bishoprics, because the Council of Sardica had decided in 343 that only towns of some importance could be episcopal sees, 'lest the name of a bishop and his authority be taken too lightly' (*ne vilescat nomen episcopi et auctoritas*).

With their great authority the bishops fulfilled a key function in the transition from Antiquity to the Middle Ages in two respects. They represented the Christian Church and its values at the local and regional level and they made an important contribution to secular public administration (see Chapter 6). Bishops were almost always sons of aristocratic families. As dignitaries of the Church they had five important tasks:

1 They guarded orthodoxy and correct religious practice. To that aim, they actively exercised doctrinal authority by preaching, taking part in synods and sometimes by writing scholarly Bible interpretations or treatises on Christian doctrine or morality.

2 Bishops ensured that Church rules and orders were applied correctly and, when necessary, issued new regulations.

3 Bishops ordained clerics and had immediate supervision over the clergy and monasteries in their dioceses.

4 Bishops administered justice: *ratione personae* (because of the [status of the] person) over members of the clergy, and *ratione materiae* (because of the [nature of the] material) over Church affairs, beliefs and Christian morality (including everything related to marriage and sexuality). From late Antiquity officials with the title of 'archdeacon' ('arch' comes from the Greek prefix *archi-*, meaning 'first' or 'most important') took the place of the bishops in their judicial function.

5 Bishops administered the property attached to the bishopric, but were also expected to be generous in the distribution of charity.

Metropolitans and archbishops, patriarchs and pope

The idea that bishops of large towns had a higher status than others was already prevalent in the fourth century. They were called 'metropolitans'. During the seventh and eighth centuries the metropolitan gradually lost in status to the archbishop. Originally this was an honorary title given by popes to bishops with a special, important assignment not without its dangers – that of spreading the Christian faith among the heathen. The first to receive this title was Augustine, not the Church Father and bishop of Hippo but a monk sent from Rome to England in 597 to convert the Anglo-Saxons. He became archbishop of Canterbury. More than a

Plate 4.1 'Mater Ecclesia'. Coloured pen drawing in an 'Exultet' role, a liturgical manuscript that was created in the Benedictine Abbey of Montecassino *c.* 1075–1090

century later the first Anglo-Saxon missionaries on the Continent likewise received the archiepiscopal dignity. Under Charlemagne archbishoprics increasingly began to resemble Church provinces comprising various dioceses.

Another hierarchic layer had been formed above the metropolitans, that of the patriarchs or 'archfathers', the honorary title used during the Council of Nicaea (325) for the bishops of the four most important cities of the Christian Roman Empire – Rome, Constantinople, Antioch and Alexandria; in 451 Jerusalem was added to these. In time, the inevitable struggle for the highest place broke out between the patriarchs of Rome and Constantinople. The patriarch of Rome – the pope – won the struggle with flying colours. Apart from Rome's enormous prestige the victory was mainly due to the special place that the Eternal City occupied in Christian sacred history. Had not Peter, the principal apostle, to whom Christ himself – according to the Gospel of St Matthew (16: 18–19) – had said 'Thou art Peter, and upon this rock [*petros* in Greek means 'stone' or 'rock'] I will build my church', died a martyr's death in Rome? And was it not written in the same text that Christ had given Peter 'the keys of the kingdom of heaven', and that whatever Peter arranged on earth should so prevail in heaven? By now consistently presenting Peter as the first bishop of Rome and themselves as his successors, powerful popes such as Damasus I (366–384) and Leo the Great (440–461) were able to establish the primacy of Rome over the Christian Church. Although Emperor Justin I (518–527) recognized this position officially, it took far longer for the patriarchs of Constantinople to be reconciled to it.

From early on the popes gave credence to their claims by stimulating the worship of Peter's grave in Rome. For a long time there was uncertainty about its exact position, but it was finally located on the Vatican, a low hill on the far side of the Tiber. With financial support from Emperor Constantine the modest burial chapel already in existence was extended into a large basilica, the predecessor of the great St Peter's that we still admire today. Curiously enough, the Vatican did not become the pope's residence. Instead, Constantine had already had a new palace and church built on imperial ground to the east of Rome, far away from the Vatican: the Lateran.

Church parishes

In the early Middle Ages the organization of the Church was not yet crystallized below the level of the bishoprics. In those few cities of any size with a busy Church life, such as Rome, parishes with their own church and their own priests came into existence quite early on. Normally we call these constituent parts of bishoprics 'parishes', although the word *parochia* – as we have already seen – originally meant 'bishopric'. The formation of parishes in the country was a very gradual development, more or less simultaneous with the further expansion of the Christian faith over rural areas (*paganus*, literally meaning 'country-dweller', was for a long time synonymous with 'heathen'). In Gaul, for example, the first country parishes, served by their own permanent, resident priests, came into being in the sixth century. There were thirty-six of these in the old diocese of Auxerre in about 600. It was certainly not until the ninth century that Gaul, by then often referred to as 'Francia', had a cohesive network of country parishes.

Church councils

The Catholic Church was probably the first organization in the West to have a real conference culture, and this, too, contributed to its internal unity. In the early Christian period the bishops regularly met to discuss matters of faith and organization. The tradition became firmly rooted under Constantine and his successors. The emperors themselves convened meetings of bishops on several occasions, which were known as 'synods' or 'councils'. They were often regional meetings, but sometimes the bishops from all over the Empire were invited; this was then called an 'ecumenical council', from the Greek *oikoumenè*, meaning 'the whole (civilized) world'. These ecumenical councils took important decisions both on doctrine and ethics, which had a major influence on the further development of the Church. The Council of Nicaea of 325 saw the establishment of the creed that would acquire an almost constitutional status, with the well-known formulation that the Church was one, holy, catholic and apostolic (*una, sancta, catholica et apostolica*). Nicaea was a town in Asia Minor where initially many such ecumenical councils took place. From the sixth century they were more often held in Constantinople, generally in the imperial palace (*Troullos*). The first general Church council to be held in the papal residence in Rome (the Lateran) was that of 649. This was also the first council convened by the pope and not by the emperor. The second council at Nicaea in 787 was the last attended by bishops from both the East and the West. In 1123 the tradition of ecumenical councils was restored in the West, but then the Greek Church no longer took part.

The custom of regularly calling regional synods was continued in the new barbarian kingdoms in the West after the period of the migrations. It was the kings who organized the meetings and who were committed to executing the decisions reached. Normally, practical matters concerning Church discipline and organization came up for discussion at these regional Church meetings in the West far more often than questions of dogma. In the Carolingian Empire in particular synods were used to enforce reforms of the clergy and the monasteries. Between the Concilium Germanicum of 742, conducted by that 'indefatigable quibbler' Boniface (Dierkens), and the great reforms of 816–817 under the rule of Louis the Pious, it seemed as if a permanent reformation was taking place in the Frankish Church. The two most important targets of these reforms were the monasteries of monks, which

time and again were told that they must adopt the Benedictine Rule, and the canonical clergy, who were also exhorted to follow well-defined rules, preferably in the context of a formal association or 'chapter'. Laypeople did not escape the reforming zeal either. On several occasions new rules relating to marriage and divorce were formulated in about 800. What is particularly striking in all this is that the Carolingians also promulgated measures for Church reform through capitularies, ordinary edicts issued by the secular administration.

RELIGIOUS DOCTRINE, ORTHODOXY AND HETERODOXY

One of the most important tasks of the councils was to decide what exactly Christian doctrine should contain. There was no discussion about the sacred texts on which it should be based. First of all there was the Bible: but how should what was written in the Bible be understood? A contemporary of Jesus himself, a Jewish philosopher by the name of Philo who lived in Alexandria, had indicated that the Bible should be interpreted on three different levels: historical, moral and allegorical. This view was later accepted by the early Christians, but of course it did not make Bible exegesis any easier, if only because for them there were two sets of texts, the Old and the New Testament. Church leaders, who enjoyed an exceptional reputation for explaining the Bible and the will of God expressed in it, were quickly seen as authorities, as a source of religious doctrine. Four of them are known as the great Church Fathers. The saintly bishops of Milan and Hippo Regius (Ambrose and Augustine), and Jerome, were more or less contemporaries, living in about 400. Two centuries separated them from the fourth, the only pope in the illustrious company, Gregory the Great (590–604). Jerome, an Istrian who settled in Palestine, produced a new Latin translation of the Old and New Testaments with the help of Greek and Hebrew text material. This translation is known in the various surviving early medieval editions as the 'Vulgate'. It was to remain the standard Bible text until the end of the Middle Ages.

Besides the Bible and the works of the great Church Fathers the reports (*acta*) and decisions (*canones*) of the ecumenical councils were given the status of authoritative texts early on. Finally, there is the interesting question of the extent to which pronouncements of the pope in Rome had doctrinal authority (in other words, were by definition orthodox). This was not yet the case in the early Middle Ages, as is evident from the infamous condemnation of Honorius I at the sixth ecumenical council, held at Constantinople in 680. In the course of time the pope's competence to create binding rules was generally accepted, although the pope only 'gave law' in reaction to explicit questions put to him. General, anticipatory rulings in the modern sense of the word have traditionally remained the prerogative of ecumenical councils.

Of the four great Church Fathers it was Aurelius Augustinus (354–430) who undoubtedly had the most far-reaching influence on the intellectual culture of the Middle Ages. After the Bible his work – almost 240 tracts and countless letters and sermons – was the most widely read, cited and commented-on text material in the Middle Ages. His most famous works are *Confessiones* (Confessions) and *De civitate Dei* (On the city of God). The former is not so much an autobiography as a uniquely frank account of Augustine's long search for the one true God. One half of *De civitate Dei* is a lengthy theological proof of the superiority of Christianity over both Neoplatonism and the old Roman state religion; the other half tells the story of the Christian spiritual history. As a leitmotiv Augustine uses the image of two cities over which mankind is divided: the earthly city (*civitas terrena*) represents the leaning towards the ungodly world, selfishness, materialism and disdain for God; on the other hand, the city of God (*civitas Dei*) stands for what is good, selfless and spiritual – in short, for the true love of the true God. The first city cannot simply be identified with the secular state or with the heathen world, nor the second with the people of Israel and later the Christian Church. Certainly, when the Church was faced with a great influx of believers after Constantine's conversion, she became by definition a 'mixed body' (*corpus permixtum*). For Augustine, the 'city of God' is thus a city in the making, whose true, legitimate citizens will only emerge triumphantly after the Last Judgment.

The relative openness with which the early medieval Church discussed the content of its doctrine also had its dangers. It exposed all the deep internal differences of opinion that threatened the unity of the Church. The Greek word for heresy, *heresia*, literally means 'choice'; and, indeed, in any religion attempts to formulate dogmas – doctrines that, once accepted, are inviolable – demand that choices be made, and, as a result, the denunciation as heresy of the rejected options. According to Augustine *heretici* (heretics) could therefore never be heathens. Heretics were Christians who resisted the correct dogma, which they ought to know.

Late Antiquity was teeming with heretics. At the beginning of the fifth century Epiphanius, bishop of Cyprus, drew up a list of 80 *heresiai* whom he expressly repudiated. His colleague Philastrius, bishop of Brescia, came to almost twice that number in about the same period! No wonder that quarrels abounded in the early Christian Church – certainly in the East. There existed a long tradition of rational philosophy, borrowed from the Greeks, which attempted to define absolutely everything, including the indefinable.

The pre-eminent example of the indefinable, the subject of passionate discussion in the East, was the nature of God. From the outset Christianity was presented as a monotheistic religion; there was just one God, who in the New Testament is manifest in three forms: Father, Son (Jesus Christ) and Holy Ghost. What exactly was the relationship between the three? Christ was especially difficult to fathom, because according to the Bible he was the word of the Father made 'flesh' – so a human being. Some thought that Christ had just one nature: the Monophysites (*monophysis* means 'one nature') believed this nature to be divine; the Nestorians, on the other hand, believed that it was human. Later, concessions were made to the Monophysites by suggesting that Christ had both natures but just one will (*thelèsis* in Greek). This was then the monotheletic interpretation. Even more complicated was Arianism, a doctrine named after Arius, an Alexandrian priest who lived at the beginning of the fourth century. He recognized the divine nature of Christ, but did not consider him equal to God the Father because the Father had created the Son and must, therefore, have more substance. At the Council of Chalcedon (451), none of these views was accepted as orthodox; orthodoxy was – and is – the dogma of the 'holy trinity', the 'three-in-one': there are three godlike persons, who are essentially equal, but of whom just one – Christ – has two natures, one human and one divine.

What we probably find more attractive nowadays are two heresies about which we know a lot from the writings of Augustine, who fiercely challenged both of them: Donatism, a North African movement, and Pelagianism. In Donatism – the movement was inspired by the priest Donatus – the idea of purity was central. Bishops and priests who had forsaken their faith in the last great persecutions under Diocletian were considered unclean. Sacraments administered by them were of no value. The true Church was a community of untainted people, of saints; the self-appointed Catholic Church was in fact the 'synagogue of Satan'.

Pelagius, a monk from Britain who was popular in intellectual circles in the Rome of about 400, was also of the belief that the true Church consisted only of a spiritual elite. In Pelagius' view this elite was made up of highly motivated believers who consciously refrained from all sin and who gave active meaning to God's commandments, especially that of charity (love of one's fellow-men). Against both Donatists and Pelagians, Augustine always defended the view that the Church derived its sanctity from the intrinsic value of the sacraments, and not from the moral qualities or motivation of its members, whether lay or cleric. The earthly Church must therefore be open for everyone who wanted to believe. The Church was of necessity a reflection of human society in all its imperfections. For Augustine the Church contained 'both the corn and the chaff'. They would only be separated on God's threshing floor at the Last Judgment.

Augustine and Pelagius differed, too, in their view of the scope of man's free will and of divine grace. Pelagius argued that through God's grace every individual was free to choose between good and evil, between 'a new life in Christ' and the rejection thereof – with all the resulting implications. In Augustine's view so much responsibility for mankind went too far. Since the Fall mankind had been tainted with original sin, which baptism washed away only temporarily. When the sick had been healed by a physician, could they not fall sick again? In everyday life every person's will was fettered by selfishness, intemperance and pride. For Augustine divine mercy was not, then, the gift of moral freedom, but liberation from the chains of sinfulness.

An important question, then, is on whom God confers grace, and whether God has made his choice beforehand. On this point Augustine wanted to believe the seemingly impossible: that absolute divine pre-destination and human free will existed side by side. The dogma of an absolute predestination, which preordained many to evil and to eternal damnation, was rejected at the Synod of Orange in 529 as being a 'fatalistic conviction' (*fatalis persuasio*). After that, the belief very subtly expressed by Augustine came to prevail: that in his predestination God has already taken man's individual conduct into account.

Some heterodox beliefs continued to exist because rulers were openly sympathetic to them. Constantine's son and successor, Constantius II (337–361), supported Arianism, whereas Justinian's wife, Theodora, was in favour of Monophysitism. But by far the fullest imperial support was given to the last, great heterodoxy of the early Middle Ages, iconoclasm (the destruction of religious images). Since the end of the sixth century the fast-growing popularity of the devotion to icons and relics in the Byzantine Empire had roused the opposition of conservative Christian communities in Syria and Anatolia, where the making of images of God and the saints was seen as an infringement of the second of the Ten Commandments. This view was reinforced by the enormous success of Islam, which also forbade images of God and the prophets.

The question of devotion to images was one that divided the Byzantine Empire for almost a century and a half, from the beginning of the eighth century to the middle of the ninth. Iconoclasm was orthodox for two rather long periods: the first between 730 and 780 under the rule of the successful Anatolian general, Leo the Isaurian, and his son, Constantine V, 'with-the-shit name' (*Kopronymos*), as his opponents called him; the second between 813 and 843. After that the Byzantines renounced iconoclasm for good. In the medieval West neither iconoclasm nor its counterpart – the Byzantine practice of image worship – ever caught on. Roman opinion has always been that a distinction should be made between the pictorial representation and the person represented. The latter could be worshipped, but not the former. The portrayal of saints had first and foremost a didactic purpose in a world where few people could read and write: 'The written word is for the literate', Pope Gregory the Great once wrote in a letter to the bishop of Marseilles, 'what the image is for the illiterate . . ., for in the image even the ignorant can see what they must imitate.'

Various other heretical doctrines owed their continued existence to their connection with a dormant regional separatism, such as Monophysitism in Armenia, Syria and Egypt (where the Coptic Church originated), Nestorianism in Iran, and Donatism in North Africa.

Sainthood and saints

The early Christian Church owed a significant part of its strength and authority to the fact that it had been regularly persecuted and there had been many martyrs, determined 'witnesses' who had shown their willingness to die for their faith. From the beginning the martyrs had been venerated as saints, and their deaths were annually commemorated at their graves. When Christianity was elevated to become a state religion this veneration only increased. Believers saw the holy martyrs as symbols of already-won victories of the spirit over the body, of courage over fear, and, above all, of life over death. The mortal remains of the martyrs were a means of coming into personal contact with the divine, who might respond by working miracles through his saints. And if the morally perfect part of the earthly existence of the saints could not be exactly imitated it still served as an ethical guideline. When in time it became impossible to build every church over a martyr's grave, the solution was either to venerate the saint through a painted or sculptured image or to distribute the saint in parts. The first martyr to be 'dismantled' in this way was St Stephen, who was stoned to death soon after the crucifixion of Christ in Jerusalem, and whose grave was discovered in 415. Soon there was a buoyant market for relics (the tangible physical remains or personal possessions of a saint), and we know that important monasteries in the Frankish kingdoms, such as those at Saint Riquier, Sens and Chelles, treasured hundreds of relics, all carefully documented, and ranging from scraps of the robe of the Virgin Mary, pieces of Jesus' crib, and all sorts of body parts of any one of the apostles to leftovers of manna from the exodus of the Jewish people out of Egypt.

At the beginning of the fourth century, when the persecutions had come to an end, the question arose of how members of the Christian community should then make their mark in order to be recognized as 'saintly'. The ambitions in this direction of one specific group, the monks, who considered themselves model witnesses of the faith – 'martyr' literally means 'witness' – were never generally accepted. In the end the practice developed in the East was very different from that in the West. In the East a reputation for exceptional virtue was sufficient for a person to be recognized as a saint, social background played no part. In the West, on the other hand, it was mainly abbots, bishops and devout ladies of aristocratic origin to whom this honour fell. It was generously allocated by the local Church communities and bishops, without any authorization from a general council or pope. The strict procedure of canonisation, as it is still practised today, was only fully developed in the pontificate of Gregory IX (1227–1241).

In the course of the early Middle Ages the veneration of saints took on greater significance as Christ was seen increasingly less as man and was more emphatically associated with the highly exalted, awe-inspiring, three-in-one God. In this way the role of saints as mediators between God and ordinary believers grew. Such mediation was seen not just in the area of spiritual support but more especially for the acquisition of material assistance. There were even some rather comical rituals in which images of saints were punished like naughty dolls if they failed to deliver. At other times devout donors did not hesitate to take back their offerings in anger when the hoped-for divine intervention did not take place. Seen from this perspective, early medieval hagiolatry formed a perfect link with the sort of barter relationships that were characteristic for the functioning of aristocratic networks (see Chapter 5).

Real saints had contact with God through visions and showed their special relationship with him by performing miracles, which were all the more convincing when they surpassed the laws of nature. Miracles – or more probably tales of miracles – that proved the omnipotence of the Christian God could be used as propaganda in spreading the faith, even though missionaries realized that it was better not to exaggerate. Adam of Bremen, who wrote a history of the archbishopric of Bremen-Hamburg in the eleventh century, in looking back to the Christianization of the area, dryly observed that heathens too could create the illusion of a wonder. Was not the conversion of a soul to the Christian faith the only miracle that really mattered?

Miracles and visions nevertheless became fixed ingredients in the popular biographies or *vitae* of saints, which were intended primarily for a public of clerics and monks. They were always written in Latin, a language that was spoken and understood by far fewer people the more the Christian community expanded. *Vitae* form an important literary genre with a fairly fixed pattern that was laid down in certain late Antique biographies, the style of which was much admired, such as the life of Martin of Tours as told by Sulpicius Severus. They supplied a model for the literary presentation of saints as inspired, charismatic men and women of God, who led exemplary lives and, if necessary, could bring about God's miraculous intervention. A central point of many of the *vitae* is formed by the conversion (*conversio* literally meaning 'turning round') of the protagonist who, after an originally sinful life, receives a sign from God, repents and thereafter offers his life to the service of God. Compilations of saints' lives were rapidly produced, and bishops and priests could draw upon them when preparing edifying sermons. The *Liber vitae patrum* (Book of lives of the saints), a collection put together by Gregory, bishop of Tours (539–594), enjoyed wide popularity in the early Middle Ages.

MONASTICISM AND THE MONASTIC LIFE

It has been suggested, and not without reason, that in the early Middle Ages it was the monks, not popes and bishops, who were the most important role models in Christianity. The roots of Christian monasticism reach back to the third century at least. At that time there were believers in Egypt and Syria who had completely withdrawn from the world in order to concentrate on the spiritual and the divine, hoping in this way to bring

about their own personal salvation and that of their fellow Christians. Some of these 'monks' did this in solitude (the Greek *monachos* literally means 'living alone'); others gave form to their ideal in small, like-minded communities; still others preferred a middle ground. The second model, which for convenience we will call 'the monastic life', prevailed in the West, although the first form never quite disappeared.

In part the monastic life fitted in with the ancient (Stoic) ideal of achieving wisdom and spiritual freedom by disengaging from material and physical needs. Apart from that it clearly had its own character, linked to Christian values. We have seen above the new interpretation that monks tried to give to the old Christian ideal of martyrdom. Both implied a form of sacrifice. By abandoning the world and worldly things monks considered themselves the only Christians capable of preserving the grace-giving action of the sacraments of the Church – baptism, in particular – during life. Ordinary believers lapsed immediately into new sins. In this respect, early medieval monasticism had by definition an almost Pelagian view.

The growing significance of monasteries and the monastic way of life for early medieval culture and intellectual training also had the effect that monastic ideals and rules became the standard against which all society was measured. In this connection the religious historian, R.A. Markus, has spoken of a gradual 'de-secularization' of western culture as a result of the suffocating influence of the monastic ideals of world renunciation, spiritual contemplation and sexual abstinence.

Originally the Church authorities looked upon monks as neither clerics nor ordinary laypeople. For Augustine, both clerics and monks were servants of God (*servientes Deo*) and therefore deserved the same legal status and treatment. This view led to the convergence of clerics and monks into one 'clerical estate', a tendency that was reinforced when many monks were eventually ordained as clerics and monasteries were often given tasks in the field of spiritual care. The position of women was still complicated; they could not enter the priesthood but were allowed to become nuns or canonesses, at first only when advanced in years, later at marriageable age. Nuns were given a special ordination and enjoyed the same legal privileges as clerics and monks.

In the first centuries of the Middle Ages monasticism was far from being organized and well structured. It embraced a motley collection of stylites, herbivores, obscure sects with strange names such as 'Those who never sleep', as well as communities of more than a thousand members, and all of which were difficult to regulate. For rural people in particular, the monks formed an alternative source of spiritual authority over which the Church had little control. As the communal form gradually began to predominate some sort of order came into being. Specifically the Church tried to provide rules for monastic communities or to grant official authority to those rules already in existence. The foundation of new communities and the appointment of abbots were also made subject to the approval of the bishops.

An extremely large number of monastic rules have survived. In the West especially, these resembled precepts or sets of instructions. Matters such as obedience to the abbot, communal activities such as prayer, eating and fasting and acceptable conduct were described clearly and precisely. But there was great diversity because influences were felt from many directions. In Gaul/Francia, where more than two hundred new monasteries were founded in the seventh century alone, we can distinguish four great monastic traditions side by side. The two oldest date from the time of the migrations: that of Martin, an eccentric who was first a professional soldier, then a monk, and finally bishop of Tours, where he died shortly before 400; and that of Honoratus and Cassianus, founders of monasteries located respectively on the island of Lérins (off the coast near Cannes) and close to Marseilles. It has been said of Honoratus and Cassianus that they 'brought the desert to the town', meaning that they introduced ideas that were borrowed directly from the eastern, ascetic monastic tradition into the urban culture of (southern) Gaul. Its influence was even larger since both were advocates of alternately holding the offices of abbot and bishop.

The third monastic tradition recognizable in Gaul only dates from much later and was linked to another phenomenon that was typical of Irish monasticism: *peregrinatio*, which literally means a 'stay in foreign parts' or 'exile'. Instead of remaining inside the monastic community Irish monks went out into the wider world to preach Christianity and to found new monasteries. In this way they gave tangible form to the metaphor that, for a real Christian, life on earth is no more than a sojourn among strangers, an exile that will only end with the beginning of eternal life. Besides, leaving one's own community voluntarily could be interpreted as choosing social death for the sake of one's faith, thus as a form of martyrdom. On the way the Irish monks founded monastic communities where possible, naturally in remote places that were difficult to reach, like Iona and Lindisfarne, situated respectively on islands off the west coast of Scotland and the east coast of England.

The Irish monks wandered around the continent too. In about 590 Columbanus, a monk from the monastery of Bangor (not far from modern Belfast) arrived in Gaul. In the following years he journeyed through the Vosges and northern Italy, founding abbeys on the way, such as the renowned Luxueil and Bobbio. His immediate involvement in the establishment of other monasteries cannot always be proved, but there is no doubt about the Irish influence on Frankish monasticism. It ensured, amongst other things, that cloistered communities were no longer generally situated in or near urban settlements, but often far away in desolate areas.

Map 4.2 Important Carolingian abbeys

The fourth monastic tradition that was active early in Gaul was that of the Benedictines. They took their name from Benedict of Norcia (*c.* 485–*c.* 560), the founder of three monasteries in Italy, including that of Monte Cassino, high on its ridge between Rome and Naples. The Benedictine Rule is in fact no more than an adaptation of an extensive and rather militaristic monastic rule composed at the beginning of the sixth century by a man whom we only know as 'Magister', the master. Benedict toned it down somewhat. His monks were not allowed personal belongings. They were not permitted to leave the monastery (the rule of *stabilitas loci*, permanency of place [of residence]). They must live chaste lives and had to obey the abbot, the head of the monastic community, unconditionally. Obedience was seen as a religious exercise, an exercise in absolute compliance with God's will, as Christ had complied. This was even harder for the monks and nuns of the early Middle Ages, most of whom came from aristocratic families and were therefore accustomed to command rather than to obey. The abbot was enjoined to observe moderation in asserting his authority and to listen to what his 'brothers' had to say.

In general the Benedictine Rule can be summed up in the double command to 'work and pray' – although that prayer was also called work, the doing of God's work (*opus Dei*). The Master had laid down a strict daily routine, which Benedict refined into a set programme of singing and reading at fixed times (the hours). The other forms of work soon came to imply intellectual work only, studying or writing or teaching.

Benedict's Rule owed its enormous popularity in early medieval monasticism in Western Europe to support from two sides. First, in about 600 Pope Gregory the Great showed himself to be a tireless propagandist of Benedict's life and works. Next, Church reformers, such as Boniface and Chrodegang of Metz, working in the Frankish Empire in the eighth century, pressured monastic communities into following the *regula Benedicti*. The Rule was also introduced fairly generally outside the Frankish Empire. This does not mean that the monasteries that followed the Benedictine Rule in the early Middle Ages as yet formed an 'order' in the sense of a congregation with a coordinating organization. Monastic orders in that sense only came into existence in the eleventh century.

The practice of the monastic rules was a fairly casual affair, for monasteries formed part of the aristocratic world. This meant, for example, that visitors came and went freely, that monasteries often accommodated important guests and their retinues, and that monks and abbots sometimes surrendered cheerfully to worldly pleasures, such as hunting. In the early Middle Ages monasteries were also used as prisons to confine – either temporarily or permanently – important officials who had fallen from favour, unwanted pretenders to a throne, deposed kings or others who might be considered a danger to the state.

SPREADING THE FAITH

Missions and conversion

Christianity is a religion that has always aimed at expansion, at converting others who do not yet share the true faith. This missionary urge is anchored in the Gospels. According to St Matthew, Jesus of Nazareth sent his 12 disciples out as messengers or apostles with the words, 'And as ye go, preach, saying, The kingdom of heaven is at hand' (Matthew 10.7). The task of conversion was thus clearly connected with the expectation that the end of time was close by. Christ added threatening words that cast an ominous shadow over how conversion to Christianity would take place, 'But whosoever shall deny me before men, him will I also deny before my Father who is in heaven'. And, 'Think not that I came to send peace on the earth: I came not to send peace, but the sword'.

Until 311 this missionary zeal was not so urgent. Only later, when Christians were allowed to express their faith openly, did the mission become serious. In the view of Augustine it was explicitly not to be limited to the civilized world of the Roman Empire. The heathen barbarians beyond the borders should also learn to know the Truth. At the same time Augustine was against forceful conversion. A firm hand could only be used to return heretics and schismatics to the bosom of Mother Church: the unbelievers had to be persuaded. This was a progressive voice that in Augustine's time was drowned out by another, which said that Christianity and the barbarian world were irreconcilable. Bishops were appointed to Christian communities outside the *limes* only at their own request. This must have happened in the area of the Goths to the north of the Black Sea and in modern-day Georgia, and also in far-flung regions such as Yemen and Ethiopia.

The best-known example is Ireland, where conversion must have started in about 450 by the semi-legendary St Patrick, who was born in the north of Britannia and was abducted and sold as a slave by Irish marauders when a young boy. After six years he escaped and came into contact with Christianity in Gaul, eventually returning to the 'island at the end of the world' to bring the new faith to his former captors. Whether the story is true or not, in the early Middle Ages the Christian faith and Church organization in Ireland took on their own, fascinating forms, which were closely connected to the numerous clan-kingdoms of Ireland's characteristic social and political structure. The strict ascetic monasticism caught on, and instead of bishoprics it was the monasteries that became the centres of Church life. One consequence of this was that abbots, not bishops, emerged as the real leaders in the early Irish Church. Irish bishops generally remained as monks in the cloisters where they were subject to the authority of the abbots.

Elsewhere, the barbarian invasions caused a temporary retreat of Christianity. We see this in fairly large towns on or close to the *limes*, border forts such as Cologne, Mainz, Trier and Tongeren/Maastricht. As early as the fourth century these were home to a Christian community with its own bishop, but the series of bishops was interrupted for a long period from the beginning of the fifth century. In spite of this, most barbarian invaders converted to Christianity amazingly quickly (the Goths even before 400), although it was often to the unorthodox Arian faith. The fact that Clovis, king of the Franks, converted to Catholicism in about 500 is seen by many, even today, as an example of astonishing political insight, although nothing at all is known about his motives. Clovis may well have realized that it would be impossible to rule Gaul without the support of the Gallo-Roman senatorial elite. This elite was Catholic – anti-Arian – and controlled the allocation of the bishoprics that were so important for the civil administration. On the other hand Clovis' arch-enemies, the Visigoths of Aquitaine, were Arians. A number of other motives have been mentioned:

through Clovis' baptism, his *Heil*, the quasi-magical luck attributed to a successful *Heerkönig* (warlord), was given a new, divine dimension, further strengthened through association with a god who had already often shown himself victorious.

In at least one respect Clovis' conversion to (Catholic) Christianity was tied closely to *Gefolgschafts*-thinking: all warriors/followers were expected to follow the example of the lord/leader. Conversion was not just an individual act of faith, but a collective action within a system of clientage. One variant of this was that individual converts considered that their entire household (*familia*) had been converted. This meant that thousands of slaves and serfs were automatically counted as Christians after the conversion of their aristocratic masters or after they had been handed over to a Church institution. Whatever they or the 'ordinary free Frank' might have thought about Christianity had nothing to do with it. With the baptism of Clovis the Franks had become Catholic – in the eyes of many modern historians too! Excavations of early medieval burial grounds and saints' narratives show how gradual the Christianization of Frankish Gallo-Roman society took hold. In about the middle of the seventh century, some 150 years after Clovis' death, St Amandus was working as a missionary in today's Franco-Belgian border area, right in the heart of the Merovingian Empire.

This pattern of conversion of an elite followed by a far more gradual, general conversion to Christianity was often repeated in the barbarian kingdoms of the early Middle Ages and occupied several centuries. Kings and their aristocratic elites opted for Christianity out of political opportunism when they were in danger of succumbing to hostile, external pressures or when they wanted to make advantageous alliances. Conversion thus began as often with diplomatic negotiations – not infrequently after a defeat on the battlefield – as with the work of missionaries. Anglo-Saxon England presents numerous examples of this. It did not always immediately produce sincere Christians, as the example of Raedwald, king of East Anglia shows. According to the Anglo-Saxon historian and monk, the Venerable Bede (*c.* 673–735), after his conversion Raedwald continued to worship the old gods as well as the Christian God, a double insurance policy often pursued at that time. It made it possible to postpone making a definite choice until one's deathbed, and sometimes the old gods were given the benefit of the doubt. The discovery of what is probably Raedwald's grave at Sutton Hoo has provided dazzling proof of this. As was the custom among many heathen barbarians in the north Raedwald had all his belongings buried with him, a treasure of inconceivable wealth, piled up in a fully rigged wooden ship. No true Christian would have done that, because he lived in the certainty that his body had no further value after death and thus would not need sustenance. A true Christian would have found it more prudent to aid the salvation of his own soul by leaving money or goods to a church, monastery or the poor. We should be careful, however, with such generalizing interpretations; giving burial gifts was common practice in aristocratic circles until the eighth century, and the Church was not against it in principle. Burial gifts were perhaps a reflection of social prestige rather than of conceptions of life after death.

The Christianization of Anglo-Saxon England was not systematically violent, although Pope Gregory the Great, who initiated the mission to England from Rome, was the first to call the unbelievers 'enemies of God'. The missions of conversion from the Frankish Empire on the continent, on the other hand, were accompanied by brute force. In this case the Christianization was undertaken with the conscious aim of expanding Frankish authority. An alarming portent can be found in the *vita* of St Amandus, who followed the Frankish armies of Dagobert I (623–639) into the Basque country and over the Danube into the Slav lands as a missionary. Barely a century later the renewed drive for expansion under the Pippinid or Carolingian mayors of the palace led to a harsh policy of systematic, military subjection and forced conversions. The first victims were the Frisians and Saxons living north and east of the Rhine.

Here the work of conversion was undertaken by Anglo-Saxon monks. Like the Irish they had a missionary zeal and were surely still aware of their ethnic proximity to the inhabitants of the North Sea lands. Willibrord, the 'apostle of the Frisians' (658–739), concentrated on the coastal areas of the northern Netherlands, where, until shortly before 700, Frisian power stretched as far as the old Roman fortified town of Utrecht. He immediately tied his fate as missionary to that of the Pippinids, who wanted to subdue the

Frisians by force of arms. Willibrord sought authorization from the pope, and was appointed archbishop of the Frisians with Utrecht as his seat. Above all, it was this coalition with the Frankish rulers – symbolically expressed in the rededication of the church in Utrecht to St Martin of Tours, the patron saint of the Frankish Empire – that the Frisians could not forgive Willibrord and his followers. They set fire to the newly founded churches at every opportunity, until their resistance was finally broken by Charles Martel.

The conversion of the Saxons followed a similar pattern. The chief initiator was Winfrid, a monk from near Southampton, who is better known as St Boniface. He, too, carried out his missionary work with a papal mandate as well as under the special protection of the Franks. In 745 the pope appointed him archbishop of Mainz, in the area east of the middle Rhine, where he had already been active for years, and where in 744 he had founded the monastery of Fulda on land donated to him by Carloman, son of Charles Martel. The Carolingians sometimes delayed the mission work, however, and as Boniface could do nothing without the military support of the Franks, the mission in Saxony did not progress. How superficially the new faith penetrated becomes apparent from a depressingly long list of 30 superstitions and heathen practices (*superstitiones et paganiae*) that was drawn up in those years by a person close to the archbishop. He eventually had more success in Bavaria. In the end, the tireless Boniface was killed by robbers in 754, at the age of 80, while travelling on official business in Frisia, which was still half-heathen and dangerous.

The recalcitrant Saxons were only really 'converted' when Charlemagne decided to subdue them by military means soon after he became king. Originally this seemed an easy undertaking, because after a couple of campaigns he advanced into the Saxon heartland at the source of the Lippe where he set up the royal residence (*palts*) of Paderborn. After they had been subjected the Saxons promised to convert to Christianity. However, they soon started to rebel, spurred on by a new leader, Widukind. When Widukind was defeated, Charlemagne spared his life on condition that he consented to be baptized. Charlemagne himself stood as godfather at his baptism; this was not out of kindness, but a public gesture to make it clear that Widukind could count on his special protection and would be, at the same time, entirely at the king's 'fatherly' mercy. There are many similar examples, especially in Anglo-Saxon England, where royal godfathers were quite common. Louis the Pious, Charlemagne's son, was godfather at the baptism of the claimant to the Danish throne, Harald Klak, in 826, and the Byzantine emperor Michael III stood godfather to Boris, khan of the Bulgars in 865.

Further rebellions followed in Saxony, and these long hindered the missionary work. For the first time there are signs here that the aristocracy's switch to Christianity did not automatically cause the widespread baptism of the ordinary free people – quite the contrary. The conversion of the elite was apparently seen as an expression of a pro-Frankish policy, and thus as a betrayal of the Saxon cause. Altogether several decades went by before Christianity made much headway in Saxony. It raised the question in Church circles of whether the use of force was expedient in spreading the true faith. Important advisors to Charlemagne, such as Alcuin of York, were adamantly

Plate 4.2 The shrine of the St Patrick Bell dates from about 1100 and is considered one of the finest examples of Irish goldsmiths' work in the Scandinavian style

against it. In his view the acceptance of Christianity must be born of an inner conviction; force and violence were entirely wrong. This standpoint became official Carolingian policy after the subjection of the Avars in the years after 796. The Avars were not converted to Christianity very quickly.

Another strategy often used, and which was applied in Saxony as well as in Bavaria and Carinthia, regions where Christianity had been introduced in the eighth century, was to use native-born missionaries, often the sons of noblemen who had been sent to Francia as hostages. The important monastery of Corvey, on the upper Weser, for example, was founded by Saxon missionaries who had been brought up in the Neustrian abbey of Corbie (Corvey means 'new Corbie'). Another missionary to the Saxons and Frisians, Liudger, was a Frisian who had been educated in Utrecht and York. In 805 he became the first bishop of Münster and was the forefather of a remarkable 'priestly dynasty'. For many generations his descendants held the combined positions of abbot of Werden and bishop of Münster and Halberstadt.

The first attempts to convert Scandinavia to Christianity date from the reign of Louis the Pious, who sent missionaries to Denmark and Sweden. The newly established double archbishopric of Hamburg-Bremen was the base of operations, but the campaign soon foundered. This is not surprising as it was precisely at this time that the Vikings set out on their marauding expeditions in western Europe. The earliest missions to the Danes should be seen partly in this context. The Carolingians probably hoped to avert the threat of Viking attacks by intervening in the domestic politics of the Viking kings. It did not bring them much success. It was not until the tenth century that new attempts would be made to bring Christianity to Scandinavia and to those groups of Vikings who had settled in Francia, England and Ireland.

The definitive conversion of Scandinavia itself was driven by the new fervour of the German Empire of the Ottonians. The king of Denmark converted in about 960. In the eleventh century his grandson, Cnut, was already reputed to be the ideal Christian monarch. In Denmark, by far the most powerful of the Scandinavian kingdoms, Christianity survived above all because the kings saw that their conversion to it brought them impressive military and political success, such as the conquest of England. Naturally they attributed this to the good fortune which Christ had brought them, the *gipta Hvítakrists* ('luck of the white Christ') of Old Danish. In Denmark there soon developed a Danish *Adelskirche* with a 'proprietary church system', based entirely on the German model.

Of course, the spread of Christianity in Scandinavia, just as everywhere else in Europe, showed a considerable delay between the conversion of kings and aristocratic elites on the one hand – for Norwegians and Swedes alike dating from about 1000 – and the conversion of the common people on the other. Heathen rituals were held at the great pre-Christian shrine of Uppsala until well into the twelfth century. They did not stop until 1164 when the bishop of Sigtuna moved his seat to Uppsala and was promoted to archbishop. By then Christianity had penetrated into the remotest corners of medieval Europe. The first bishopric in Iceland, Skálaholt, was established at the beginning of the eleventh century. Greenland followed soon after 1125.

That same German fervour that initiated the permanent process of the conversion of Denmark should also be seen behind the Christianization of the Wends, the common collective name for the Slavic-speaking peoples east of the Elbe. This did not happen under the guidance of native kings but rather followed the pattern of the conversion of the Franks and Saxons: a joint missionary offensive with attempts at military subjection. Ironically enough the Saxons – the Ottonians had their home base in Saxony – played an important role in this. The Saxon rulers suffered a major reverse when the Wends rebelled in 983 and Hamburg was reduced to ashes. It would be nearly two centuries before the Wends finally accepted Christianity. A combination of three factors proved to be decisive for the final success: crusade, colonization and the foundation of monasteries. When, in 1147, the aristocracies of Saxony and Denmark appeared unwilling to take part in the second crusade to the Holy Land as long as the heathens were still in their own back yard, so to speak, Pope Eugene III labelled as 'crusades' what in fact were nothing more than marauding raids into Slavonic territory. At the same time the German colonization of thinly populated areas to the east of the Weser, Elbe and Oder got

under way, and the Wendish frontier was studded with monasteries, belonging in particular to the new, highly motivated orders of the Cistercians and Premonstratensians.

From the very beginning the situation in the central Slavonic region was quite different. Unlike the politically divided north, two large territorial principalities, Bohemia and Poland, had been established there quite early on. German influence was strong, but no attempt was made at political and military subjugation. The conversion of the first Bohemian princes is shrouded in legend, but can safely be placed at the beginning of the tenth century: the bishopric of Prague was established before 967. The conversion of Poland was undertaken from Bohemia, a major role being played by the first non-German bishop of Prague, Vojtech-Adalbert. This eccentric character spent more time in Italy than Bohemia, much to the displeasure of his ecclesiastical superior, and perished while preaching among the Prussians, a Baltic people. Just a few years later he was revered as a holy martyr in Gniezno, the centre of the first Polish archbishopric.

During missionary work among the southern Slavonic peoples – which took place from two directions, Salzburg and Aquileia, in the second half of the ninth century – another problem arose: competition from the Byzantine Empire. In the struggle for power that ensued after Charlemagne's destruction of the kingdom of the Avars, two key players, the prince of Moravia and the khan of Bulgaria, tried to gain support – sometimes from the Eastern Franks, sometimes from Constantinople. Religious conversion was always a condition of support. Two Byzantine missionaries, the brothers Cyril and Methodius from Thessaloniki, had the lead on the Eastern Franks in the decades after 860, not only because they spoke the Slav language (the Eastern Frankish missionaries working in the area generally did so too) but also because they were the first to put the spoken Slavonic language into writing. In that way the Bible and other essential liturgical texts could be written in Slavonic. This considerably improved the missionaries' means of communication and contributed to releasing tensions between Bulgaria and Byzantium. The rival Eastern Frankish missionaries found that a Bible in the vernacular bordered on heresy. The quarrel ended in compromise: the pope approved the use of Slavonic as a language of the Church, the Church of Bulgaria came under the authority of the patriarch of Constantinople, and the Church of Moravia and Pannonia (respectively the regions north of Vienna and the western part of modern Hungary) under Rome.

Missionaries from the West did not at once gain from this arrangement because soon after 900 Moravia and Pannonia were overrun by the pagan Magyars. When the Magyars were Christianized the whole story was repeated. The first Magyar rulers to convert were baptized in Constantinople, a logical consequence of the anti-Bulgarian alliance they had made with the Byzantines in about 950. For similar reasons the princes of the Russian Empire of Kiev followed in the wake of the Greek Church. However, it was the German kings who subdued the Magyars in battle, after which Hungary finally came into the Latin-Roman Church. Just as had happened in Norway and Denmark, the appeal of Christianity in Hungary was consciously enlarged by making one of their own kings a saint. In Hungary that happened immediately with the first Catholic Magyar prince, Waik, who received the baptismal name of Stephen and had the odour of saintliness about him throughout his life. He was venerated everywhere very soon after his death in 1038.

Thus by about the middle of the eleventh century, more than eight hundred years after the conversion of Constantine, almost all Europe, or at least its ruling elites, had converted to Christianity. Just two groups of peoples were still unconverted: the Balts (a non-Slavonic-speaking group of peoples that included Prussians, Latvians and Lithuanians) and the (non-Indo-European) Estonians and Finns. Other missionaries followed Adalbert of Prague, but met with equally little success in the inaccessible region of impenetrable forests on the south-eastern shores of the Baltic Sea. Not until well into the fourteenth century could Christianity take root in the Baltic lands, but the laborious attempts at conversion had been given a cruel charter in 1171 with the promulgation of the bull, *Non parum animus noster*. In this bull the pope determined that the struggle against the heathens in the north would forever be on an equal footing with the struggle against the Muslims. In practice it meant that the nobility of Western Europe were licensed to hunt

down the Balts wherever and whenever they wanted. In spite of the successes of the Teutonic Order, however, which extended its violent activities into the Baltic region after 1230, the native rulers did not allow themselves to be completely overwhelmed. Just as everywhere else in medieval Europe earlier, Christianity could not triumph here until the native aristocracy showed themselves prepared, for whatever reasons, to be receptive to the new faith.

Christianization and syncretization

The centuries-long monopoly of Christian historians on the historiography of the Middle Ages created an erroneous picture of the Christianization of Europe, which needs to be adjusted. Not only did everything take place more slowly than is often thought, but also our sources, such as the lists with pagan superstitions mentioned on p. 58, show how imperfectly the new faith spread. In this connection it is useful to make a distinction between delayed social and delayed mental penetration. By the former we mean that Christianity reached the masses later than the elites; by the latter, that the faith of the believers was for a long time superficial and directed towards externals. Internalization required intensive pastoral support, which for a long time was of a dubious quality. The first hesitant attempts to raise the consciousness of ordinary believers date from the Carolingian period and were aimed mainly at moral improvement, less at religious instruction. Similar initiatives were also seen outside the Carolingian Empire, in the England of Alfred the Great (871–899) and the Asturias of Alfonso III (866–910).

One of the first obstacles was that almost all the texts essential for a knowledge of the faith – foremost the Bible – were written in Latin only. In Anglo-Saxon England text material in the vernacular became available only in the second half of the seventh century; in the Carolingian Empire that did not happen until after 800. A famous early example of an edifying text in the vernacular is the *Heliand*, an epic story of the life of Christ in Old High German, which dates from between 825 and 850. Yet the Church continued to use predominantly Latin until the thirteenth century.

No wonder, then, that generations of missionaries, village priests and bishops failed to root out pre-Christian practices. They certainly tried hard enough.

One favoured method was the merciless destruction of cult places, such as the *Irminsul* (literally, 'Pillar of the firmament'), the great holy-tree of the Saxons, which must have stood in a forest near Ober-Marsberg in Westphalia, before Charlemagne had it pulled down in 772. The Church always had a rather ambivalent attitude to the use of force to spread Christianity. The advice that Gregory the Great gave to his missionaries in England in 601 is typical: destroy the images in heathen shrines, but convert the shrines themselves into churches. Pope Boniface IV (608–615), one of Gregory's successors, himself set a good example by rededicating the famous Pantheon in Rome as the church that it still is today: St Maria Rotonda. Countless missionaries and temporal rulers copied the example of the pope, also outside the early Roman Empire, where church density was far lower. The cathedral of Uppsala in Sweden stands on the site of an important pre-Christian shrine, and that of Vilnius in Lithuania had a heathen predecessor that was probably built as late as the first half of the fourteenth century.

The cultic re-use of these holy places proved the superiority of the Christian God, and at the same time it could be seen as a token of respect for the losers. The latter was all the more important because pre-Christian shrines fulfilled a central function in ancestor worship and were, therefore, an essential identity-defining element in local or regional communities. The *vé* at Jelling in Denmark (see Box 4.1) shows how complicated the interpretation of such rededication can be. It is for this reason that in recent years, particularly under the influence of cultural anthropology and comparative religious studies, a history of Christianity approached purely and simply from a Christian perspective is considered to be a pointless exercise. Nowadays, there is a preference for syncretism, the functional fusion of old and new religious representations. The designation

of time – a religiously loaded subject – provides a good example. Throughout Europe the designation of the days and the months are of pre-Christian origin. Only our calendar of years and holidays has been completely Christianized, with certain notable exceptions including the midwinter and midsummer celebrations. The midwinter feast was a barbarian adaptation of the Roman feast of Saturnalia (the feast of Saturn, the god of seed-time), which in turn was of Etruscan origin. The pre-Christian midsummer feast was given a Christian make-over as the feast-day of St John the Baptist (24 June), but it is still abundantly celebrated in its pagan form in unimpeachably Christian countries such as Norway and Sweden.

A second aspect of syncretism relates to the tolerated identification of heathen gods and practices with Christian saints and rites. In Brittany the exceptional devotion to St Anne appears to date directly from the Celtic or even pre-Celtic worship of a 'mother goddess of the earth' called Ane. In the same region, until well into the nineteenth century, mothers of twins directed their prayers to St Gwen Teirbron, a Celtic fertility goddess whose likeness, to the discomfort of many a village priest, was conspicuous for the three prominently displayed breasts. Finally, a certain degree of religious ambiguity was accepted for a long time. Christian Anglo-Saxon kings continued to trace their ancestry back to Woden – until the eighth century when someone hit on the brilliant idea of dropping Woden's divine status and tracing his ancestry back to Adam, the first man. At different locations in Scandinavia soapstone moulds have been found in which both a crucifix and a Thor-hammer could be cast.

Similar processes of syncretism were facilitated because many early medieval Christian practices were soaked in magic. Who cared about the difference

---

BOX 4.1 A PAGAN SHRINE SUPPLANTED: FROM VÉ TO CHURCH IN JELLING

One of the most interesting archaeological sites in Denmark is in the little town of Jelling in Jutland.

In the middle of a large open space are two man-made mounds with a small whitewashed church in the middle between them. In the tenth century Jelling was the residence of at least two kings of Denmark: Gorm the Elder (d. 940) and his son, Harald Bluetooth (*c.* 935–985). The runic inscrip-

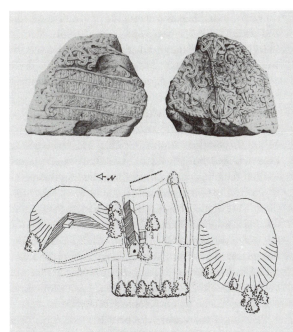

tions on two richly decorated (and once-coloured) granite stones standing near the church attest to this. On the smallest is written: KING GORM PLACED THIS COMMEMORATIVE STONE HERE IN REMEMBRANCE OF HIS WIFE THYRA, THE GRACE OF DENMARK ('Danabod', the oldest reference to Denmark in Denmark itself). The inscription on the larger stone reads: KING HARALD PLACED THIS MONUMENT HERE IN MEMORY OF HIS FATHER GORM AND HIS MOTHER THYRA, THE HARALD WHO UNITED ALL DENMARK AND NORWAY AND WHO MADE THE DANES CHRISTIAN. There is no reason to doubt the veracity of these short statements. We know from another source that Harald Bluetooth's authority stretched over a large part of modern Denmark, and that he moved his permanent residence from Jelling to Roskilde. It has also been established that Harald was baptized by a German missionary called Popo. The decorated figures on the large stone at Jelling depict a Christ triumphant who has defeated (heathen) Evil in the form of two intertwined monsters.

In the first 'national' history of Denmark, the chronicle of Saxo Grammaticus completed in about 1200, it was already assumed that the two mounds at Jelling were indeed the graves of Gorm and Thyra. Archaeological excavations to verify the assumption did not take place until the nineteenth century. Then it was found that one mound contained the remnants of an empty wooden double grave and the other mound . . . nothing at all. At least, that was what was believed for almost a century. Then, in 1941, new excavations brought to light the remains of a platform constructed of wooden posts, which had possibly once served as the base of a watch tower. Even more sensational were the findings from the excavations under the little Romanesque church in Jelling, which must have been built in about 1100. Under the church appeared to be the remains of no fewer than three earlier wooden churches, the oldest of which dates from the time of Harald Bluetooth. A burial chamber was revealed under the choir, containing the skeleton of a man of about 50 years of age. It was concluded from the rather disorderly position of the skeleton that this had been a reburial. It is generally assumed that Gorm's body was moved from his pagan grave in the hill to the Christian church after the conversion of his son Harald. But where is Thyra? This is one of the riddles that Jelling poses. The other relates to the discovery of a large triangular space, bounded by large stones and situated partly under the church and partly under the graveless mound. There is no doubt that this is the remains of a pre-Christian place of worship, or *vé*. Its exact function and its relationship to the burial grounds, which are also pre-Christian, still remain a mystery.

Literature: Johannes Brøndsted, *The Vikings* (Harmondsworth, 1965), pp. 293–297. Leif Ingvorsen, *Jelling in the Viking Age* (Jelling, n.d.); the illustrations were also borrowed from this publication, by permission of Jelling Bogtrykkeris Forlag in Jelling.

between the healing effects of holy relics or of talismans and amulets? Valuable caskets have been excavated in which they were kept side by side. Certainly the parish priest, with whom the majority of believers came into contact, worked in this semi-magical world. Only with the pursuit of the ideals of the eleventh-century Reform movement were the priests forced to follow the Church's moral line; their duties were increasingly limited to administering the sacraments and hearing simple catechisms. Only then did Catholic priests become 'sacramental priests' more than 'magical priests', (A.C. Murray). Even after that, the Church was only partially successful in reaching the masses and impressing upon them her dogmas, moral precepts and rituals. Long after the Middle Ages Argus-eyed priests gazed in puzzlement at the veneration of a holy greyhound near Lyons, of a hunting goddess with bear-claws instead of hands in the Dolomites, bulls offered in sacrifice in Scotland and numerous pilgrimages to holy wells, streams, lakes, trees and forests in Wales and Cornwall, all barely understood witnesses to a world that had gone, but also silent protests against an invader, against a strange religion that had been imposed from outside.

ISLAM

In contrast with the slow spread of Christianity over early medieval Europe, the expansion of Islam, which literally means 'subjection' (to the will of God), seemed to take place with lightning speed. This was due only in part to the actual tenets of the faith, because Christianity and Islam share a number of fundamental similarities. Both have the same Jewish roots. They also share three important dogmas with the Jewish religion: belief in one (male) God, knowledge of whom can only be obtained through revelation; belief in a life after death, after a final judgment where God separates the good from the bad; and the conviction that the profession of the true faith contributes to individual salvation in the life hereafter. And in all three religions faith contains not only metaphysical ideas but also a clear view of life and the world. (Orthodox) Jews and Muslims go furthest in this: for them, all of life – internal and external, private and public – is impregnated with religion, and ethical precepts and courses of

action for individual dealings in the political, economic and social fields are borrowed from religion. Strictly speaking, Islam makes no distinction between secular and spiritual law: Islam has only the *sharia*, the body of regulations for living, never systematically codified and held to be in accordance with God's will. Islam similarly makes no distinction, at least in theory, between secular and spiritual authority. In the early Middle Ages the caliph, as direct successor of the Prophet, was both head of state and leader of the Islamic religious community (*umma* in Arabic; compare with the Christian '*ecclesia*'). The *umma* dwelt in the 'House of the Islam' (*Dar al-Islam* in Arabic) which was rigidly divided from the hostile outside world, the 'House of the War' (*Dar al-Harb*). Thus Islam created for the first time in Arab society a focus of strong loyalty above and beyond the clan or the grouping of kinship. Without this new bond the spectacular Arab conquests would have been inconceivable.

Because of the similarities between Islam, Judaism and Christianity, Jews and Christians – the 'peoples of the Book' as they were often called – were generally tolerated in the Islamic world. There was little pressure to immediate conversion – from that perspective the high-speed spread of Islam in the trail of Arab conquests is as illusory as the Christianization of barbarian Europe. Conversely, medieval Christians did not see Islam as a new religion but as a reprehensible aberration of their own faith. This negative perception later expanded: Islam was not only just a heresy, 'the sect of Muhammad' was now also seen to be a punishment from God, a terrible affliction that, through their own fault, Christians had to suffer in the long progress to the Last Judgment.

From the very beginning Islam had its own book, the Koran (*Qur'an* means 'what has been recited'), the record of Allah's revelation to the Prophet Muhammad. According to the Arab tradition the text of the Koran was laid down in its present, definitive form in about 650. Several of the 114 chapters or *suras* stress that Allah revealed himself to Muhammad in Arabic. For orthodox Muslims this meant until recently that the Koran could only be read, listened to, recited and reproduced in Arabic. This resulted in a wide dissemination of Arabic as a 'higher' language in lands where Arabic was not and is not spoken at all. The Koran was translated into Latin shortly before

1150. Not much later, Peter the Venerable, abbot of the famous Benedictine abbey at Cluny, prided himself on the fact that he had read the Koran, and during the late Middle Ages there was for some time a centre for Koranic studies in Barcelona. Of course, this was not entirely out of purely academic interest but rather under the motto, 'know your enemy so that you can better fight him'.

In addition to the Koran, Islam recognizes various other sources of religious authority. The most important of these form the so-called Hadith texts (Hadith means 'tradition'), a body of sayings and deeds ascribed to the Prophet himself. They were collected and memorized during his lifetime by the 'Companions', the people close to him. Then for centuries they were passed down by word of mouth in unbroken chains (*isnads*) from generation to generation, so that there were eventually tens of thousands of Hadith in circulation. In about 850 two revised compilations were put into writing, quite independently of each other, which since then have become the standard corpus. Taken together the Hadith comprise the *sunnat*

Plate 4.3 The Dome of the Rock on the Temple Mount in Jerusalem, built under Caliph Abd al-Malik and completed in 691–692, contains many Jewish–Christian elements. The interior, with mosaics inspired by Byzantium, has scarcely changed since the seventh century. The exterior, on the other hand, was embellished with majolica tiles by Sultan Suleyman II (1520–1566)

al-Nabi ('customs of the Prophet'), *soenna* for short, whence derives 'Sunni' for those who hold to the *soenna*.

Unlike Catholic Christianity Islam does not have a hierarchic clergy. In principle the establishment of what is true has been made dependent on individual exegesis, and even nowadays competent teachers of the Koran have great social, and often political, influence. On the other hand, the danger of confusion and heterodoxy is inherent in the same principle. Islam has countered that with the formation of a limited number of recognized schools of exegesis, the *madhhab*. The same is true for another important aspect of Islamic religious studies, the *fiqh* (meditation), which deals with the study of Islamic law.

The ethical aspects of Islam are, as we have seen, more rigorously elaborated and more explicitly bound to the notion of God than is Christianity. Some Orientalists, therefore, refer to Islam as 'orthopractical' rather than 'orthodox' (Schimmel). The religious-ethical duties are described simply and precisely. The five so-called 'pillars of the faith' are central: (1) the public confession of the belief in Allah and his Prophet; (2) regular recital of prayers; (3) giving alms for the poor; (4) fasting in the month of Ramadan; and (5) making a pilgrimage to Mecca at least once in a life-time. Among the less precisely described obligations is the jihad, which is not mentioned in the Koran but is described in the Hadith. It is often translated as a 'holy war', but it literally means 'effort', defined as the 'effort to spread the laws of Allah and Islam over the earth'. Force of arms is just one of the instruments through which this duty of effort can be fulfilled. There are also innumerable instructions relating to everyday life. Because this changes with time and differs per culture more enlightened Islamic scholars have advocated that a distinction be made between sacrosanct dogmas and religious precepts on the one hand and adaptable rules for moral living and social intercourse on the other.

Despite its emphasis on tradition, universality, comprehensiveness, and ethical pragmatism Islam has not succeeded in keeping *Dar al-Islam* one and undivided. The most important split dates from the problematical years following the Prophet's death, when a significant minority was in favour of the succession of Ali, a first

cousin of Muhammad who was also married to his daughter, Fatima. Eventually, Ali was made caliph, but the seeds of discord had been sown, and a hard core of malcontents was formed who believed that only Ali and his descendants could be the true heirs to the Prophet. This resulted eventually in the formation of a broad separatist movement, the 'party of Ali', (*shi'at 'Ali* in Arabic), whose adherents were called Shi'ites and which had, and still has, a particularly large following in Iraq and Iran. The Shi'ites do not reject the *soenna*, but they have their own tradition and their own spiritual leader appointed by Allah himself, the Imam, who must be a direct descendant of one of the two sons of Ali. There were more splits within Shi'ism, even before 1500. The so-called 'Twelvers' only recognized the authority of twelve Imams, whose graves (for example, at Nadjaf and Kerbela in Iraq) are most holy objects of pilgrimage and prayer. According to the Twelvers the twelfth Imam, or Mahdi, is immortal. This Muhammad al-Muntazar disappeared around 875 and has lived in hiding ever since. One day he will reveal himself and reclaim his authority over the true Islam, unsullied by Sunni blemishes. A second breakaway movement, the Ismaeli, named after the son of the sixth Imam, Jafar al-Sadiq (*c.* 760), was created by the desert Bedouin of Syria and North Arabia who were dissatisfied with the rule of the Abassids. More branches then broke off from the Ismaeli Shi'ites, including the Fatimids and the Druses, a sect that took root in about 1000 in the Egypt of Caliph al-Hakim; the caliph soon sent its leaders off to Syria.

FURTHER READING

Arnold, John H. (2005), *Belief and Unbelief in Medieval Europe* (London: Hodder Arnold).

Bachrach, David S. (2003), *Religion and the Conduct of War, c.300–1215* (Woodbridge and Rochester, N.Y.: Boydell & Brewer).

Blair, J. and R. Sharpe (eds) (1992), *Pastoral Care before the Parish* (Leicester: Leicester University Press).

Brown, Michelle P. (2003), *The Lindisfarne Gospels: Society, Spirituality and the Scribe* (Toronto and Buffalo, N.Y.: University of Toronto Press).

Brown, Peter (1981), *The Cult of the Saints. Its Rise and Function in Latin Christianity* (Chicago, Ill.

and London: University of Chicago Press/SCM Press).

—— (1995), *Authority and the Sacred. Aspects of the Christianisation of the Roman World* (Cambridge: Cambridge University Press)

—— (1996), *The Rise of Western Christendom. Triumph and Diversity A.D. 200–1000* (Oxford: Blackwell Publishers).

—— (2000), *Augustine of Hippo. A Biography*, revised edition with a new epilogue (Berkeley: University of California Press) (orig. 1967).

Chadwick, Henry (1986), *Augustine* (Oxford and New York: Oxford University Press).

—— (2002), *The Church in Ancient Society: From Galilee to Gregory the Great* (Oxford: Oxford University Press).

Constable, Giles (1964), *Monastic Tithes from Their Origins to the Twelfth Century* (Cambridge: Cambridge University Press).

Dietz, Maribel (2005), *Wandering Monks, Virgins, and Pilgrims: Ascetic Travel in the Mediterranean World, AD 300–800* (University Park, Pa.: Penn State Press).

Dunn, Marilyn (2000), *The Emergence of Monasticism: From the Desert Fathers to the Early Middle Ages* (Oxford and Malden, Mass.: Blackwell).

Esler, Philip F. (ed.) (2004), *The Early Christian World* (London and New York: Routledge).

Fletcher, Richard (1997), *The Conversion of Europe. From Paganism to Christianity 371–1386 A.D.* (London: HarperCollins Publishers).

—— (2003), *The Cross and the Crescent. Christianity and Islam for Muhammad to the Reformation* (New York: Penguin).

Flint, Valerie I.J. (1991), *The Rise of Magic in Early Medieval Europe* (Princeton, N.J.: Princeton University Press).

Geary, Patrick J. (1994), *Living with the Dead in the Middle Ages* (Ithaca, N.Y. and London: Cornell University Press).

Gregg, Robert C. and Dennis E. Groh (1981), *Early Arianism – A View of Salvation* (London and Philadelphia, Pa.: SCM Press/Fortress Press).

Gurevitch, Aron (1988), *Medieval Popular Culture. Problems of Belief and Perception* (Cambridge and Paris: Cambridge University Press/ Editions de la Maison des Sciences de l'Homme).

Hamilton, Bernard (1986), *Religion in the Medieval West* (London: Arnold).

Harrison, Carol (2000), *Augustine: Christian Truth and Fractured Humanity* (Oxford: Oxford University Press).

Hopkins, Keith (1999), *A World Full of Gods: Pagans, Jews and Christians in the Roman Empire* (London: Weidenfeld & Nicolson);

Howard-Johnston, J., P.A. Hayward and R.A. Markus (eds) (1999), *The Cult of Saints in Late Antiquity and the Middle Ages: Essays on the Contribution of Peter Brown* (Oxford: Oxford University Press).

Humphreys, R. Stephen (1991), *Islamic History. A Framework for Inquiry*, 2nd edn (Princeton, N.J.: Princeton University Press).

Jong, Mayke de (1996), *In Samuel's Image. Child Oblation in the Early Medieval West* (Leiden and New York: Brill) (orig. Dutch, 1986).

Lawrence, C.H. (2001), *Medieval Monasticism. Forms of Religious Life in Western Europe in the Middle Ages*, 3rd edn (Harlow: Pearson Education).

Macmullen, Ramsay (1984), *Christianizing the Roman Empire (A.D. 100–400)* (New Haven, Conn. and London: Yale University Press).

—— (1997), *Christianity and Paganism in the Fourth to Eighth Centuries* (New Haven, Conn. and London: Yale University Press).

Markus, R.A. (1990), *The End of Ancient Christianity* (Cambridge: Cambridge University Press).

—— (1997), *Gregory the Great and His World* (Cambridge: Cambridge University Press).

Milis, Ludo J.R. (1992), *Angelic Monks and Earthly Men: Monasticism and its Meaning to Medieval Society* (Woodbridge: Boydell Press).

Montgomery Watt, W. (1985), *Islamic Philosophy and Theology*, 2nd edn (Edinburgh: University Press of Edinburgh).

Moorhead, John (1999), *Ambrose: Church and Society in the Late Roman World* (London: Longman).

—— (2005), *Gregory the Great* (London and New York: Routledge).

Noble, Thomas F.X. (1984), *The Republic of St. Peter. The Birth of the Papal State, 680–825* (Philadelphia, Pa.: University of Pennsylvania Press).

Paxton, Frederick S. (1990), *Christianizing Death: The Creation of a Ritual Process in Early Medieval Europe* (Ithaca, N.Y.: Cornell University Press).

Pelikan, Jaroslav (1975), *The Christian Tradition: A History of the Development of Doctrine. Vol. I. The Emergence of the Catholic Tradition (100–600)* (Chicago, Ill.: University of Chicago Press).

—— (2003), *Credo: Historical and Theological Guide to Creeds and Confessions of Faith in the Christian Tradition* (New Haven, Conn.: Yale University Press).

—— (2005), *Whose Bible Is It? A History of Scriptures Through the Ages* (London: Penguin Group).

Rees, B.R. (1988), *Pelagius, A Reluctant Heretic* (Woodbridge: Boydell Press).

Rosenwein, Barbara H. (1999), *Negotiating Space: Power, Restraint, and Privileges of Immunity in Early Medieval Europe* (Manchester: Manchester University Press).

Rydstrøm-Poulsen, Aage (2002), *The Gracious God:* Gratia *in Augustine and the Twelfth Century* (Copenhagen: Akademisk).

Schimmel, Annemarie (1992), *Islam: An Introduction* (New York: State University of New York Press) (orig. German, 1990).

Schulenberg, Jane Tibbetts (1998), *Forgetful of Their Sex: Female Sanctity and Society, ca. 500–1000* (Chicago, Ill.: Chicago University Press).

Smalley, Beryl (1983), *The Study of the Bible in the Middle Ages*, 3rd edn (Oxford: Blackwell).

Thacker, Alan and Richard Sharpe (eds) (2002), *Local Saints and Local Churches in the Early Medieval West* (Oxford and New York: Oxford University Press).

Tilley, Maureen A. (1997), *The Bible in Christian North Africa: the Donatist World* (Minneapolis, Minn.: Fortress Press).

Ward, Benedicta (1987), *Harlots of the Desert: A Study of Repentance in Early Monastic Sources* (London: Mowbray).

Weaver, Rebecca Harden (1996), *Divine Grace and Human Agency: A Study of the Semi-Pelagian Controversy* (Macon, Ga.: Mercer University Press).

White, S.D. (1988), *Custom, Kinship and Gifts to Saints: the* laudatio parentum *in Western France, 1050–1150* (Chapel Hill and London: University of North Carolina Press).

CHAPTER 5

Society and economy in the early Middle Ages

The turbulence of the migration period and the great epidemics of plague in the sixth century left behind a world that was more empty and desolate than it had been even in the latter years of the Roman Empire. Of course not a lot is known about this time. Pedological (soil) research shows that in many parts of Europe the forests increased during the fifth and sixth centuries. In addition, a large number of archaeological findings point to a sharp fall in population density. For many years the entire period from 500 to 1000 was depicted as a time of demographic stagnation, but that view has been revised. Nowadays, we tend to think in terms of a slow but sure recovery that started in the West at the beginning of the seventh century, or maybe even as early as the sixth century in the new Frankish heartland between the Rhine and the Loire. A cautious estimate suggests that the population of western Europe doubled between 600 and 1000 from about 12 to 24 million.

EARLY MEDIEVAL SOCIETY

Transformation: the aristocracy

This modest demographic and economic recovery certainly did not make the early Middle Ages a pleasant world. The vast majority of the population lived, from our perspective, in shocking conditions and under constant threat of hunger and the brutality of a small but violent elite. However, this elite changed radically in the course of the earlier Middle Ages. At first the barbarian *Gefolgschaft* ('followers') system, with its strong and directly personal ties between the chiefs and their warriors, was still clearly recognizable. Such a structure could only remain intact in its purest form in an almost permanent state of warfare, because only war

could give the warriors a *raison d'être*. And only war could keep in place the system of gift-exchange, which we shall look at on pp. 77–79, and which held a central place in the pattern of social, economic and political relationships within which the elites were able to function. Thus war was an essential feature of the culture and ethos of the early medieval aristocracy. Even in the most advanced political unit of the early Middle Ages, the empire of Charlemagne, the king went campaigning almost every year. On the surface, the core of his army was made up of a collection of *Gefolgschaften* whose leaders, the *magnati* or great men of the empire, were in turn part of the *Gefolgschaft* of the king.

Nevertheless, using the same example, it can be argued that times had changed, at least in the Frankish Empire, and that Charlemagne was more than just a warlord from the time of the migrations. Two things point to this. First, in Charlemagne's campaigns the interests of the state mattered above purely personal or dynastic interests. This is evident from what happened after the Frankish conquest of the 'ring' (the capital) of the Avars in 795, when cartloads of priceless treasures were captured. Charlemagne had these distributed not only among his warriors and foreign allies who had been directly involved, as the rules of the 'gift-economy' required, but also among his ideological pillars: the major institutions of the Church (bishoprics and abbeys) and the main secular office-holders (counts) within his empire.

Second, it was quite impossible for Charlemagne to keep with him everyone who was tied to him in a relationship of personal loyalty, or even to take them all on the same campaign. In other words, the *Gefolgschaft* system in its authentic form – with intimate relations between lord and warriors, who lived with their lord for part of their life, received their arms from him and were immediately rewarded after heroic deeds – had given way in the Carolingian Empire to a new type of relationship, which we call 'vassalage', and which was geared to a larger political and geopolitical scale (see further in Chapter 6).

In the shaping of this relationship the Carolingians, stimulated by the early and rapid integration of the Gallo-Roman nobility and the Frankish warrior elite, were able to elaborate on two late Roman traditions that were to develop into the material cornerstones of a new system of aristocratic patronage: the granting of land and elevation to high position, both secular and ecclesiastical. The earliest reports of warriors being regularly rewarded with formerly imperial, royal or church estates date from the middle of the fifth century to the very beginning of the eighth. They come not from Gaul but from Vandal Africa, Ostrogothic Italy, Visigothic Spain and Anglo-Saxon England. Everywhere in the barbarian kingdoms founded on Roman soil wealth and power were increasingly derived from the possession and exploitation of land; everywhere, warrior aristocrats, like the kings themselves, became large landowners. Only in Visigothic Spain another traditional source of public income that could be accumulated by the ruler and if need be redistributed, the general land tax was kept intact to the end of the kingdom. This having been said, we must not forget that the barbarian world beyond the borders of the former Roman Empire, which was ruled by less-imposing warlords and their warrior retinues, was much more extensive. Here, the often transregional aristocratic networks continued to follow the traditional path for a long time.

This early medieval aristocracy, which we presented first and foremost as warriors and then in a certain sense as large landowners, may now, arguably, be called 'nobility'. The description seems to be primarily a question of definition. It is a fact that the term *nobiles* (nobility) appears rarely in source texts before the twelfth century, and when it does it mainly indicates a moral quality. References to the social elite point variously to prominence (*proceres*, the foremost), wealth (*divites*, the rich), political and military power (*potentes*, the powerful) and freedom-independence (*liberi*). All these qualities were held to be transferable. They were thus seen to be attributes of families rather than of individuals; individual preponderance was determined by the possession of lordship, either as 'senior' over (other) free men or as master of all sorts of dependent people and slaves. If one insists on speaking of 'nobility' in this period, one must realize that it was not a matter of a hermetically closed class, entered exclusively by birth. Aristocratic qualities had to be proven. In that sense, throughout the whole of the Middle Ages nobility was always a question of birth and achievement and lifestyle – in that respect there was no difference between the early and the late Middle Ages.

Demotion: the free fighting men

Among the barbarian groups that had seized control of the largest part of the Empire the non-aristocratic, free, able-bodied men had two important public tasks which in the Roman Empire had been in the hands of professionals: military service and the administration of justice. The former is understandable, given the background of the establishment of barbarian kingdoms in the West, as was outlined in Chapter 3. But for a long time after the migrations some sort of general conscription on a nominally ethnic basis continued to exist in the empires of the Visigoths, Lombards, Franks and Anglo-Saxons. In Lombard Italy it was even the case that until far into the eighth century non-Lombard free men were not called to arms. The armies of the Frankish and Visigothic kingdoms around 600 seem to have been built up of free landowners, all considered to be 'Franks' and 'Goths' respectively, around a core of royal and aristocratic retinues. Already in the course of the seventh century this started to change to the extent that substantial free landowners substituted for just free landowners. It is difficult to imagine that a broadly based royal levy could still function well under the Carolingians. As we have seen, Charlemagne and his predecessors campaigned almost every year against increasingly distant enemies. The campaigns lasted for months and generally took place in the spring or summer, the very time that peasants had better things to think about than attacking other peasants. On top of this the warriors had to provide their own supplies during the campaigns. At the beginning of the ninth century Charlemagne took steps to limit military service for ordinary free men. After that, only those who owned more than a certain amount of land had to join the army in person: free peasants who had less land either took turns at military service or were jointly responsible for equipping a warrior. Alternatively, service could be bought off by paying compensation money, called *haribannus*, which originally must have been a penalty for non-attendance. Only when the empire itself was invaded did the entire able-bodied male population have to take up arms in its defence. A similar system was introduced in Anglo-Saxon England at about the same time.

In time another development came to play a role: the growing importance of the horse in battle. Aristocratic warriors always travelled on horseback, of course, but in battle the animal was of limited value, and when it came to fighting warriors either fought on horseback or dismounted, depending on the circumstances. The tactical significance of the cavalry only grew with the spread of the stirrup, introduced into western Europe by the Avars after 550, and, of even greater importance, the panelled saddle. These innovations enabled a rider to apply momentum and force. Although mounted warfare may not have been uncommon throughout the early medieval period, real frontal cavalry charges are not known from before *c*.1000, and those formed just the onset to the formidable shock combat of mounted knights, armed with couched lances and broadswords, which was so characteristic of battles in the following centuries. In any case it means that, gradually, war was becoming a matter for well-trained specialists, who had to have the resources to devote themselves full-time to the practice of arms and to purchase a number of horses and expensive weapons and armour. With a few exceptions the real military function of the free peasant-warriors came to an end. This development, which took centuries, contributed to the further social demotion of the non-aristocratic free man.

Descriptions of contemporary society show that military specialization formed the main wedge between the aristocracy and ordinary free men in the barbarian kingdoms of the early Middle Ages. In addition to a dichotomic division into *liberi* ('free men', but meaning aristocrats) and *pauperi* ('poor men', but meaning powerless people), a fixed tripartition in 'estates' (*ordines* in Latin) was becoming increasingly evident: there were people who prayed (clerics), people who fought and people who did manual work. There was no

doubt that peasants – free or not – belonged to the third category and no longer to the second. The first text in which this comes to the fore is the Anglo-Saxon translation of Boethius' *De consolatione filosofiae* (The Consolation of Philosophy; 524), made for King Alfred the Great of Wessex (871–899).

We can see a similar development in the administration of justice in the Carolingian Empire. The Franks originally required all free men to attend public legal proceedings and, if asked, to pass judgment – to give a verdict in accordance with the prevailing customary law. As the body of law grew and became more complicated this became a very heavy task and Charlemagne relieved the ordinary free men of this obligation pertaining to their estate. The administration of justice now came into the hands of small, permanent benches of judges known as *scabini* (aldermen) – who, it should be remembered, are not to be confused with the 'aldermen' of the late medieval or early-modern period. As far as we know, the Carolingian *scabini* were always aristocrats and dealt with cases coming from a wide area, usually a whole *pagus* (county).

Developments of this kind are symptomatic of the unstoppable undermining of the public social functions of ordinary free men, in contrast to the growing concentration of both landownership and political and military power in the hands of the aristocracy. The process was further reinforced by another, with an even longer time span: the formation of a broad class of non-free people, the greater number of whom worked the land and can best be referred to as serfs. From the time of the late Empire their numbers swelled in fits and starts from two sources: on the one hand many originally free peasants placed themselves under the protection of aristocratic landowners, either voluntarily or involuntarily; on the other, the position of the slaves was improved, for reasons which we shall discuss.

A similar tendency could be detected beyond the frontiers of what had been the Roman Empire. In Iceland, for example, which had been colonized from Norway in the second half of the ninth century, it is estimated that shortly after that time not more than 3 or 4 per cent of the population consisted of free peasants. Society was entirely dominated by the lords (*gothar*) and their followings of warriors. Almost everybody below them was unfree. Only in Francia south of the Loire and in Catalonia did slavery and non-aristocratic free ownership of land continue to exist side by side in their more or less classical form until the end of the first millennium.

Promotion: the slaves

The idea that slavery did not exist in the 'free' barbarian world is based on a misconception. On the contrary, slavery was an institution that was present everywhere; it matched the Roman variety in its ruthlessness, and simply continued to exist after the collapse of the Empire. Only the best-known form of Roman slavery – the exploitation of vast farms with massive slave labour – had already disappeared in late Antiquity. The interminable petty warfare between the warlords, however, and the yearly campaigns kings undertook against foreign enemies, ensured a constant supply of human cattle in the slave markets of Western Europe. Slaves were just about the only export article of any value in the thriving Christian trade with the Islamic world. In time the region occupied by the still-pagan Slavs was the major source, hence the word 'slave', a dubious honour in naming, in which the Celtic Britons were ahead of the Slavs (in early medieval times 'briton' was another word for 'slave'). The great slave markets then moved eastwards, to towns such as Mainz and Prague, with Venice as their main port of export on the Mediterranean. In addition to these organized manhunts the slave population was replenished by those wretches who through poverty or debt were forced to sell themselves or their children, or who were enslaved as a punishment.

Another misconception is that the early Christian Church spoke out explicitly against the institution of slavery. That, too, is incorrect. The Church Fathers in fact considered slavery to be proof of the great wickedness of those who found themselves in that deplorable situation. Important dignitaries and institutions of the Church themselves possessed large numbers of slaves. The Church clearly was morally ambiguous in the matter, however, and Christianity did indeed contribute to the radical disappearance of slavery from Christian Europe. From the beginning Christianity had welcomed the unfree. Even though slaves were looked upon as second-class Christians who

were not allowed to hold priestly office, for example, they were nonetheless members of the Christian community, fellow Christians and thus fellow men. This sort of reasoning was an enormous advance on the ancient view of slaves as beasts or machines. *Instrumentum vocale*, 'tool-with-a-voice', was a common classical designation for a slave. Following that, Church leaders took over certain Stoic ideas concerning slavery. One of these ideas was that although the institution of slavery may have been unavoidable, that in itself was no reason to treat slaves inhumanely; another, that regularly manumitting slaves contributed to an individual's moral edification. Many abbots, bishops and devout noble women enhanced their saintliness through their efforts to procure the formal liberation of slaves. Finally, from the eighth century onwards, Church leaders started to prohibit outright the sale of Christian slaves to pagans, but the fact that such appeals were repeated time and again during the eighth and ninth centuries creates the impression that they were not very effective.

Within the kingdoms of the Christian West, however, matters were different. In addition to ecclesiastical prohibitions certain socio-cultural and economic factors probably contributed to a relative improvement in the treatment of slaves. In the early Middle Ages, unlike in the heyday of the Roman Empire, many of the slaves living in Latin Christian Europe were indigenous or came from kindred cultures. This reduced the distance between master and slave. Finally, the structural labour shortage in a situation of low population density helped pave the way for the disappearance of ancient forms of slavery. On the one hand the scarcity led to the accelerated spread of labour-saving technology such as water-mills (an invention of the first century before Christ), which relieved slave labour and to some extent made it unnecessary. On the other hand, the landowning elite found it extremely convenient to bring as much as possible of the land on their estates under cultivation and to keep it so. One method of doing this was to give a slave a small plot of land with a small house; in this way the difference between slaves and the other peasants settled on the estate tended to disappear. The new class of serfs grew out of this process of social convergence.

Serfdom, lordship over land and the manorial system

The institution of serfdom is always associated with two other phenomena typical of early medieval Western society: lordship, associated with large landownership, and the manorial system. It is a well-established fact that over time the great landowners acquired far-reaching control over the peasants who were settled on their estates. Among other things, this control could be exercised over the serfs' freedom of movement. Serfs could not leave the estate and settle elsewhere without the permission of the lord of the land. When a serf died the lord took the best part of his movables. The lords also administered justice over their serfs, except in cases of serious crime when they were responsible for handing over the accused to royal courts of law, at least where these functioned. It is difficult to gauge the basis of these rights: they probably had no other than the authority considered as natural to them by those who exercised it in their capacity as aristocrat, landowner and owner of people. In this connection

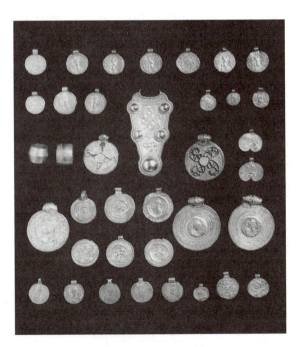

Plate 5.1 The gold treasure found in the grave of a Frisian lord (*c.* 630) consists of gems and jewellery made from coins

German historians speak of 'land-lords' and 'land-lordship' (*Grundherrschaft*). By modern standards private interests and elements of the exercise of public authority were inextricably linked in these seigneurial rights.

The growth of this type of lordship in large parts of early medieval Europe was accompanied by a fundamental change in the way in which agricultural surpluses were transferred to the aristocracy. Marxist historians use the term 'surplus extraction' in this context to demonstrate that in the end the transfer was not left to the free operation of market forces, but was effected under non-economic pressures linked to seigneurial power. How and when surplus extraction occurred can best be explained through a simple diagram (Figure 5.1) of a *peasant*-economy cycle, which was no more than a small-scale agrarian economy, with little specialization and few surpluses. The diagram shows the routes peasant households had to follow to ensure maintaining the capacity of the three classic production factors (land, labour and capital goods), which they applied in combination in order to survive. They managed to do this simply by consuming the greatest part of the products from agriculture and non-agrarian side activities in the form of food for themselves and their livestock, and seed, or in the form of homemade clothing, shoes, housing, tools, household goods and fuel, etc. that they found themselves. The entire right-hand side of the reproduction cycle shown, the commercial side as it were, is not of much significance. The peasants' efforts were directed at just being able to support themselves. In that connection the terms 'subsistence economy' or 'survival economy' are often used.

The diagram shows the four points at which the early medieval lord of land could siphon off a 'surplus': directly, through the services of labour (1) and the supply of part of the physical (agrarian and non-agrarian) produce (2 and 3). Far less surplus flowed off in the form of all manner of cash payments after the sale of products in the market (4). It must be stressed again that the level of dues was not determined by scarcity factors expressed in market prices but solely by arbitrary factors and customary traditions. In this way the actual burden of the peasants' regular charges varied enormously from manor to manor, and even on one and the same manor.

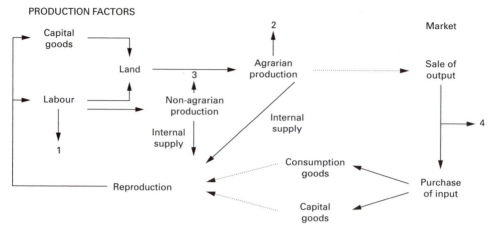

Figure 5.1 Simple reproduction cycle of peasant households

(1, 2, 3 and 4 = points at which surplus could be 'tapped')

In order to let this surplus extraction take place smoothly, in Carolingian times large landownership was organized in a specific way, namely in estates called manors (*villae, curtes* or *villicationes* in Latin). These were properties with a clear administrative centre, known as *sala* (hall) and *curia* (court) or *casa indominicata* (house of the lord), which could be exploited in a number of different ways. In the classic or 'dual' form of this manorial system this happened in a semi-direct way. The arable lands and the meadows of a manor were divided into two parts, which were generally not equal in size and not necessarily adjacent. The part that the lord kept for himself was called the lord's land (*terra indominicata*), the part that was given to peasant farmers in hereditary possession was known as the (peasant) holdings' land (*terra mansionaria*). A considerable part of what was given in return for the possession of these holdings took the form of labour that the serfs who owned a farmstead (*servi casati*) supplied to cultivate the lord's land, often together with serfs who did not have a farmstead (*servi non casati*) and real slaves (*mancipia*) of the lord of the estate.

The plots of land belonging to the serfs varied in size, from about 15–30 hectares. This was less than it seems, because much of the ground lay fallow every year and the actual yields were shockingly low. However, not every farmstead was taxed with the same labour services and dues. A distinction was frequently made between 'free holdings' (*mansi ingenuiles*) and 'unfree holdings' (*mansi serviles*), probably stemming from differences in the legal status of the original peasant owner. Free holdings were generally taxed less heavily than the unfree, but many other aspects are not very clear. Did free or unfree holdings make their successive owners respectively free or unfree, or, conversely, did the legal position of the successive owners change the status of the holding? Such elementary matters are very uncertain, and that makes it difficult to fit the development of serfdom in the early Middle Ages into a general pattern.

Moreover, the classic form of the manorial system, as sketched above, was most certainly not the only one. It was particularly evident in the region between the Rhine and the Loire, where large landownership was often concentrated, making possible the formation of very extensive estates. On the other side of the Rhine, and in Frankish Italy, there were other forms, varying from small estates consisting of demesne lands of modest dimensions to parcelled estates that had no demesne land at all, where the lord's hall served as the collection point for dues in kind from serf holdings that were scattered over a wide area. The manorial system did not penetrate the whole of the Mediterranean area: it certainly existed in Lombard, later Frankish, Italy, but was found far less in Francia south of the Loire and in Catalonia. There, as we have seen, most land-users were small free peasants, while large-scale properties were still often exploited in the classic manner, i.e. exclusively through the use of slave labour. In the Papal States and the Byzantine parts of southern Italy, including Sicily, large landowners from early on preferred indirect exploitation. In that case the land was leased out in hereditary tenure to peasants who were often tied to the land, and who can thus be considered as serfs, but who did not have to provide regular labour services.

We can best understand the operation of the manorial system through what are known as polyptychs, inventory-like descriptions of the possessions of a number of large monasteries made in the Carolingian period, such as the well-known polyptych of Irmino, the abbot of Saint-Germain-des-Prés near Paris (829). This may well colour our view in certain respects (geographical, social), but no better data has survived. Similar Church institutions doubtless also possessed more, often even dozens of manors, preferably spread over different agro-ecological zones, so that they would be self-supporting in wine and wool as well as in grain. Among the lay aristocracy there would certainly have been many smaller landowning lords who had just one manor.

The polyptychs and certain capitularies (royal instructions) suggest that the manorial system with bipartite estates was a typically Carolingian institution, maybe consciously extended by the kings, even if similar arrangements existed elsewhere, as in Anglo-Saxon England.

But regardless of whoever started it, and where, the manorial system in its classic form most certainly contained one new element when compared to the already existing forms of surplus extraction: the binding of peasants who had their own means of production to landowning lords through the imposition of non-commercial labour services. Three general factors explain the necessity behind this form of forced labour. First, the low population density in the early Middle Ages, which made labour a scarce commodity. Second, the imperfect functioning of markets, including a labour market. Finally, the loss of public tax levies in Western Europe, with the exeception of Visigothic Spain, deprived the aristocracy of an alternative source of income. Surplus extraction had of necessity to take place at the agrarian basis.

Evaluations of the manorial system as a whole have varied considerably right up to the present day. The pessimists point in particular to the low yields compared to the relatively high costs of transport and supervision; the optimists, to an interplay between the spread of the manorial system and slow demographic and economic expansion. Indeed, data on the size of families on peasant farms point to population pressure at the beginning of the ninth century. The more than 1,450 peasant families living on the demesnes of Saint-Germain-des-Prés at the beginning of the ninth century consisted of between five and nine members each, depending on the size of their farm. And peasants on the estates of Saint-Victor at Marseilles had on average five or six children who survived the vulnerable early years of life. That is why the reclamation and cultivation of land was generally started from over-populated demesnes. Then the ownership of large estate complexes made risk-spreading and a certain amount of division of labour and specialization, such as wine-growing, possible, and that must have been good for productivity and commercialization. Some estates even expanded into real towns: Liège is a prime example.

BOX 5.1 MASTER AND SLAVE EVEN UNTIL DEATH

In the second decade of the tenth century Ibn Fadhlan, an envoy of the Caliph of Baghdad, made a journey through the Volga region where he came into contact with a group of Vikings (*Rus*). Never had he come across filthier people amongst all of Allah's creatures: 'They do not wash even after they have relieved nature or had sex, nor do they clean themselves after they have eaten'. The tall, fair-haired men were tattooed from head to toe, always carried arms and shamelessly copulated in public with slave-girls. Ibn Fadhlan also witnessed the funeral preparations of a dead chief:

When a chief dies his slaves and servants are asked who is prepared to follow him into death. Whoever volunteers cannot go back on the decision. In this case a woman volunteered. She was treated with much respect while preparations for the cremation went ahead. On the day of the cremation the chief's boat was pulled up on to land and the people walked around it muttering all sorts of words. An old woman who was called the 'Angel of Death' placed a bier covered in rugs and cushions on the boat. She was responsible for all the preparations. The dead body, which had been kept in a burial pit for ten days, was brought out and dressed in splendid robes made especially for the occasion. Then this corpse was stood among the cushions in the tent that had been erected on the ship over the bier. The dead chief was provided with alcoholic drink, food, aromatic herbs and all his arms. Then a dog, two horses, two cows, a cock and a hen were killed and placed on the ship.

The woman who was going to die went to all the tents in the camp and had sex with the owner of each tent, who then said: 'Tell your lord and master that I do this out of affection for him'. Then she completed various rituals. A circle of warriors lifted her up three times above something resembling a door post. The first time she said, 'Look, I see my father and mother'; the second time, 'I see all my dead kinsfolk together'; and the third time, 'I see my master sitting in paradise; it is green and beautiful there, he is surrounded by men and slaves and he is calling me. Lead me to him'. Then she killed a chicken and was taken to the ship where she removed all her jewellery, drained two goblets and sang a song. Finally she was taken to the tent of her dead master, and when she hesitated she was roughly pushed inside by the Angel of Death. Six warriors followed her in and had sex with her. Then she was placed next to her master and killed. Two of the warriors held her feet, two her hands, and two strangled her with a cord, while the Angel of Death stabbed her repeatedly in the breast until

she gave up the ghost. The dead chief's closest relatives set fire to the firewood under the boat. Others threw flaming branches on to the fire and within an hour everything had been burnt. Then they covered the remains with earth and on the hill they put a post with the name of the chief and the name of their king, who dwelt in the fortified place called Kyawh (Kiev).

Ibn Fadhlan's description of the Vikings' barbaric appearance and their customs clearly contains a number of stereotypes from ancient geography. But archaeological finds in Scandinavia have confirmed several of the unlikely-sounding details from the story of the cremation. The graves of men of high status often contain double interments of master and slave, as can be seen in the sketch of the contents of a double grave found near Stengade on the Danish island of Langeland. The left-hand skeleton must be that of the master, the right-hand one that of the slave who, voluntarily or not, followed him in death, because the head of the right-hand skeleton had been severed from the body and the feet had probably been tied together. A long spear had been laid diagonally across both bodies.

Text fragments from Ibn Fadhlan and illustration of the Stengade grave from Else Roesdahl, *The Vikings* (London: Penguin Books 1998), pp. 34, 54–55 and 157; illustration by permission of Penguin Books, London. For a more extensive account of the Ibn Fadhlan fragment see F. Donald Logan, *The Vikings in History* (London, 1983), pps. 197–200.

TRADE AND GIFT-EXCHANGE

Economic life in the early Middle Ages has long been described in terms of decline and decay, or at best of stagnation and inertia. True, a smaller part of the total production reached the market than in late Antiquity. Moreover, owing to the absence of population pressure and tax burden there was not the slightest incentive for intensive land use, and ground productivity was low. On the other hand it can be said that in agriculture, which was by far the largest economic sector, the technological level, in the broadest meaning of the term, increased rather than decreased, and this created the conditions for growth in productivity. We must also try to escape from the almost obsessive fixation on the market economy in our own times. Economic life is conceivable outside the market. Early medieval agriculture had many features of a 'moral economy', an economy where mutual sharing and reciprocity ('you scratch my back, I'll scratch yours') played an important part. Agricultural settlements in the early Middle Ages were so small (between five and ten farms), and so isolated, that mutual cooperation and support were essential conditions for survival. Dealings and transactions in a moral economy are less chaotic and primitive than we tend to think. Reciprocity is only possible when there are clear, socially and culturally rooted norms for division and redistribution.

Another pattern of non-commercial transaction involving reciprocity and redistribution has emerged from the study of long-distance trade in the early Middle Ages, a subject of passionate debate for many decades. This is closely tied to the challenging theory put forward by Henri Pirenne (1862–1935), the Belgian historian, in the 1920s and 1930s, and ever 'a key point of reference' (Wickham). The core of Pirenne's theory is that the migration period left the economic system of late Antiquity, which was centred on the Mediterranean region and linked southern Europe to the Middle East, largely unaffected. To be sure, the establishment of barbarian kingdoms would result in a certain amount of 'degeneration'; but the unity of the Mediterranean world would only be truly disrupted by the Arab conquests from the middle of the seventh century. From then on East and West drifted apart. It forced the Carolingian rulers in the West to create their own institutions, such as feudalism. The importance of long-distance trade declined; its core came to lie in the North Sea basin, in particular in the region between the Seine and the Rhine, where the seed was planted, according to 'the longstanding metanarrative of medieval economic history' (Wickham), for the budding of mercantile capitalism.

Over the years a number of objections to Pirenne's theory have been raised, the most valid being that the Mediterranean region evidently continued to function as an important transit zone after the Arab conquests and that the Muslim world had a substantial share in the recovery of international trade in the eighth century. We would like to approach the Pirenne theory from another angle. Pointers to the circulation of goods and coins need not necessarily be explained as trade, as transactions of a commercial nature. That is not true even for transports of bulk goods, especially grain, to provision the great cities. In the period of the barbarian migrations Rome's grain supply came from Sicily and North Africa where the pope had very extensive domains. Most of it he gave free to the non-aristocratic part of Rome's populace. So there is certainly no question here of commerce, or commodity exchange; it is the continuation of a system of patronage. Much of what we know as 'trade' in the early Middle Ages, when looked at more closely, seems to have fulfilled this support function. In general it only involved relationships within the aristocracy. This also explains why 'trade' did not necessarily take place through towns and urban markets.

A similar interpretation of early medieval transactions of goods owes far more to an anthropological inspiration rather than an economic-historical one. Philip Grierson, the British numismatist, in a criticism of Pirenne's thesis, had already called for such an approach by the end of the 1950s. Grierson was himself inspired by two well-known anthropological studies about the meaning of gift-exchange in 'primitive', non-Western societies, produced respectively by Marcel Mauss and Bronislaw Malinowski. This anthropological view finds that trade should be seen first and foremost as a means of supplying the elite with highly valued, prestige goods that served as gifts, such as weapons, horses, gold and slaves. Unlike ordinary goods (commodities) gifts cannot simply be alienated by the recipient, because the relationship between giver and recipient, as opposed to that between buyer and seller, is not neutral but is characterized by a form of morally decided mutuality: the giving contains the expectancy of a gift in return.

The mutuality can have a like or unlike character. In exchanges based on like mutuality (between allies of equal status, for example) we can speak of reciprocity. In the early Middle Ages not only were prestige goods involved, but also women – aristocratic women, of course. 'Peace-spinsters' (*freothuwebbe*) is one of the terms of respect given them by the poet of the *Beowulf*; it precisely indicates the importance of marriage in maintaining contacts and, in particular, in preserving peaceful relationships between regional rulers. In the case of relationships of unlike mutuality (between chief and warrior, for example) we speak of redistribution; in this connection it means the sharing out of wealth by the lord among members of his clientage. Here, not only were prestige goods involved, but also primary consumer goods; later, land became increasingly involved. In principle a ruler provided for the members of his *Gefolgschaft*. They had the right to eat at his table and to live in his hall. In return, first and foremost, they gave their loyal military support. Both types of circulation are outlined in Figure 5.2.

We can refine Figure 5.2 by taking different contexts into account. It is obviously sensible to make a distinction between the barbarian kingdoms that had been influenced by the traditions of Roman administration and that were also Christian on the one hand, and, on the other, the peripheral areas of Europe that were not yet Christian, such as Scandinavia and Saxony. In the first, the Church was part of the system of gift-exchange and the kings enjoyed a relatively strong, partly centralized position of power. The channels for both the supply and redistribution of the gift-exchange were broader and more intricate there than in the peripheral areas beyond. The kings could exercise force to bind members of the aristocracy to them. To this end the children of powerful aristocrats were often held hostage for indefinite periods of time. Foster-parenting was a less unfriendly alternative, but the effect was the same. At an early stage in Visigothic Spain the kings absorbed warriors of unfree origin into their network to counter the disproportionately large power of certain aristocratic families; this strategy was used much later, from the twelfth century, by the German kings. The networks of the aristocrats were perhaps smaller and less impressive than those of the kings, but the differences were of degree rather than structural.

The schematic representation of the relationships between lords and peasants in Figure 5.2 shows again that the provision of the necessities of life and the allocation of the two most important production

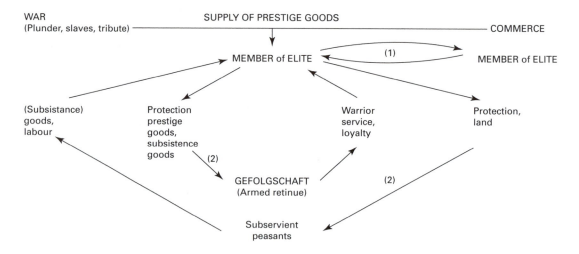

Figure 5. 2 The circulation of prestige goods in an early medieval setting by way of reciprocity (1) and redistribution (2)

factors, land and labour – so actually for the entire primary sector of the economy – were hardly subjected to market forces. On the other hand, the aristocracy had to turn in part to real commerce through specialized middlemen (traders, merchants) for their supply of prestige goods and luxury articles: the spoils of war alone were not enough. This at once meant that such commerce was long-distance trade, because barbarian kings and warriors also valued the exotic products of the East that found their way to the few remaining large markets, such as those of Mainz and Verdun: male and female slaves, costly perfumes and ornaments, pepper and cloves. In addition to this there was a limited amount of trade in raw materials and consumer items for a broader buying public. It would include wool, cloth, leather, skins, earthenware, salt, honey and metal utensils, all of which came from more or less specialized production areas.

Regional trade in small markets only picked up during the seventh century. Several Carolingian kings, including Charles the Bald, granted places market rights (mostly for weekly markets). They must have had a function in the exchange of bulk utilitarian goods. Although this type of trade remains almost invisible in our sources, it is assumed that fairly large amounts of grain and other necessaries were yearly needed for the army and also for feeding the towns. Regional exchange linked up with the larger commerce through the first annual fairs that we know of from the sources. They were held close to important centres of elite consumption, such as the Abbey of Saint-Denis near Paris. The royal courts, although still constantly on the move, were similar poles of attraction, where thousands of people (high placed persons and their retinues) gathered for considerable periods of time to engage in what has been called 'tournaments of value', including all kinds of highly symbolic acts of contract and transaction both between the king and his magnates, and between the terrestrial world of man and the spiritual world of God and his saints.

Trade, insofar as it was not just barter, was supported by a new means of payment, a silver coin minted in the Merovingian Empire from the end of the seventh century. This *denarius*, or penny, was worth one-twelfth of a *solidus*, the standard Roman gold coin. Its introduction was a great success. Within a short time imitations were being made in England and Frisia (they

were known as *sceattas*), and altogether millions of pennies must have been struck during the eighth century. There was no lack of raw material, for the Franks had a rich silver mine at Melle, in the vicinity of Poitiers. The introduction of silver money must be seen partly as a reaction to the continuous flow of gold to the East resulting from a structurally negative balance of payments, which probably had swung round by the early years of Charlemagne's reign, when large quantities of Arab silver coins started to find their way to the West.

The new silver coinage also met the apparent need for a method of payment for small transactions. That the denarius stimulated a certain monetization of the relationships between lords and peasants is evident from some polyptychs. Already in the ninth century the Abbey of Saint-Bertin near Calais, for example, gave the 47 holdings of one of its manors in Poperinge in Flanders in exchange for a payment of money. But this was exceptional. According to the polyptych of Irmino the role of money in the demesnes of Saint-Germain-des-Prés was far more limited at that time. Only a quarter of the obligations of the 'free' holdings (*mansi ingenuiles*) consisted of payments in cash, while, economically seen, this was one of the most progressive regions of early medieval Europe.

Frisians and Vikings

By the beginning of the Middle Ages – even earlier, according to some – the coasts of the North Sea and the Baltic Sea (comprising present-day South Scandinavia, North Germany, the Netherlands and England) formed an extremely dynamic region for migration and trade that grew in significance during the early Middle Ages. This was linked in part to the stable position of the Frankish Empire, with its core in the region between the Seine basin and the Rhine. A growing share of the long-distance trade in luxury articles was directed towards this area. Archaeological finds in southern Scandinavia demonstrate this splendidly. Important commercial contacts with the Black Sea region existed via the Vistula–Dniester route until the beginning of the sixth century. When the Avars and various Slavic groups pushed their way into central Europe this route was closed, and Scandinavian trade moved to the relatively peaceful and powerful northern point of Gaul.

BOX 5.2 LORDS OF RINGS

Rings were an important gift with which lords rewarded their warrior followers in the northern barbarian world. 'Ring-giver' (*beag-gyfa* or *beag-brytta*) was one of the epithets accorded to kings in the Anglo-Saxon epic poem, *Beowulf*. Numerous archaeological finds show that these rings took diverse forms, from thick rings for the finger to slender shoulder and neck rings made of gold or silver. Large quantities of them have often been found together. They were sometimes worn in combination with other jewellery made of precious metals. Typical of the period from the seventh to the eighth centuries was the use of bracteates, wafer-thin plates of gold, silver or bronze that were stamped on one side only. They were often worked together with rings to form one piece of jewellery, as can be seen clearly from this picture of a sixth-century necklace found at Hjørring in North Jutland. The effigy on these bracteates usually represented the heathen god, Woden, whose head was sometimes modelled on that of the emperors on Byzantine coins. Opposite the head of the Woden figure is another man waving a stick. The text of the runic characters on these Hjørring bracteates refers to the respect that the wearer of the ornament is keen to show to the (divine) protector portrayed. It was probably an amulet.

Map 5.1 The world of the Vikings

The Frisians played an important role as intermediaries in the commercial contacts between Scandinavia and the Frankish Empire. At that time their territory stretched from the Weser to the Flemish coast, so that they had control of certain vital traffic routes. With their centuries-old specialization in cattle- and sheep-farming, imposed on them by their environment, the Frisians had a long tradition of sea and river trade. From the middle of the seventh century this was given a new impulse. Frisian traders were the most important middlemen and carriers between the Rhineland, the northern part of the area under Frankish control, North and West England and southern Scandinavia. Major trading stations in the area, such as York and Birka (near modern Stockholm) had Frisian quarters. It is also probable that it was the Frisians who were behind the development of the two most important types of ship of a later period: the hulk, whose round keel made it suitable for the North Sea trade, and the flat-bottomed cog, which was suited to the calmer waters of the Baltic.

Dorestat grew to be the undisputed centre of Frisian commerce: it was a trading settlement established in the seventh century in a bend in the Rhine just south of the old Roman garrison town of Traiectum (Utrecht). Dorestat actually lay in the region of the Frankish Chamavi, but the Frisians were able to bring it into their sphere of influence once they had achieved a certain degree of political unity. Even so, Dorestat was at its largest and most prosperous when it was in Frankish hands. During the long reign of Charlemagne the number of its inhabitants was estimated at a maximum of 2,500. To build its docking facilities and landing stages literally millions of trees must have been cut down in the surrounding woods.

The activities of the Scandinavian Vikings appeal even more to the imagination. Literally, 'Vikings' means something like 'men from the viks (bays, fjords) who do something'. That 'do something' is often translated succinctly as 'engage in trade' but 'to go on a raid' is just as accurate. This is evident from the prose version of *Edda*, the Old Norse collection of myths, made in Iceland by Snorri Sturluson at the beginning of the thirteenth century. There, men who 'do something' do so either *i vikingu* or *i kaupferdum*. The latter obviously means (going) 'on a trading voyage' so the former clearly is 'on a marauding raid'. To the Vikings trading and raiding were part and parcel of each other. This may have something to do with the amoral ideas about the acquisition of wealth that were prevalent among the Scandinavian aristocracy. The accumulation of wealth was, as we have seen, indispensable in the barbarian world for obtaining the prestige essential for leaders to maintain their warrior retinues – and thus their position of power. How they acquired their wealth was unimportant.

That real trade formed an essential part of the proto-historic economy of South Scandinavia is evident from the large number of place-names ending in *-kaupang/-koebing/-køping* (trading post) dating from this legendary period. Most of the coastal areas were unsuitable for arable farming, but they had abundant water, and the vast inland forests provided a variety of products in demand in both the East and West, among them pelts, wax, honey and pitch produced from resin. The most important centres of Viking trade were Haithabu (Hedeby), strategically located on the short-cut through the Schleswig isthmus (by which merchants could save themselves the longer and more dangerous passage round Jutland), Kaupang (in the Oslo Fjord), Birka (mentioned on p. 80) and the island of Gotland. From these centres, groups of Vikings sallied forth as traders, plunderers and, finally, sometimes even as farmer-colonists over the whole of the then-known world.

In this connection it is interesting to note that Danish and Swedish Vikings penetrated the river basins of the Volga, and later, further westwards, of the

Dnieper and the Don. They probably first went along this so-called northern arc soon after 850 as mercenaries in the service of warring Slav groups and steppe nomads, but immediately saw the commercial potential of trade with Byzantium and the Muslim world. They gained control over what has since then been called Russia. Although certain modern-day Russian historians do not like it, the word 'Russian' comes through Finnish from the Old North German *rossmenn* or *rosskarlar*, meaning 'oarsmen' or 'seamen'. The oldest known princes of Novgorod and Kiev had pure Scandinavian names like Igor (from Ingvar) and Oleg (from Helgi). The success of the trade, or what passed for it, with the south is evident from the discovery of hundreds of thousands of *dirhams*, Arab silver coins, found in the soil of north-west Russia. Many of them would have changed hands in the great markets of Bulgar (near the confluence of the Volga and Kama rivers) and Itil (in the Volga delta on the

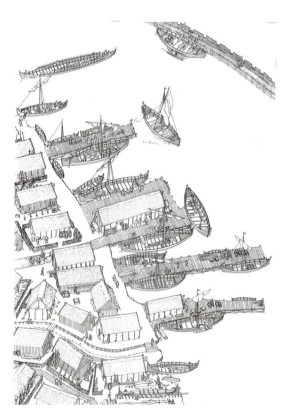

Plate 5.2 Haithabu harbour reconstruction

Caspian Sea) in the steppe empire of the Khazars. This eastern trade of the Russian Vikings dried up fairly suddenly soon after the middle of the tenth century; the reason for this is not so clear.

The picture that emerges of trade in the early Middle Ages is one of a surprising dynamism in an overwhelmingly agrarian economy with a modest degree of commercialization. In this connection Peter Spufford, the monetary historian, once called the enormous expansion of the minting of silver *denarii*, *sceattas* and *dirhams* in the decades round 800 'the false dawn of a money economy'. The ambivalent nature of the circulation of goods (gift-exchange or commercial transaction?) and of the use of coins (prestige object or method of payment?), and the indistinct purpose of 'journeys' (trade or plunder?) make it difficult to form a clear picture for the period before the seventh century. The same is essentially true for the phenomena of market and town in the early Middle Ages. Because of the direct and (almost) exclusive interest of the aristocracy in long-distance trade, such trade was directed more towards 'central persons' than 'central places', as the British archaeologist Richard Hodges once put it. It also means that the few towns that survived were centres of power before anything else, 'public' places linked to the presence – permanent or frequent – of such important persons as kings, dukes, counts or bishops. On the other hand, such other general functions of later medieval towns as concentrated craft production and regional provision were as yet underdeveloped, just as the large trading posts of the period (*emporia* or *wiks/wihs* in contemporary sources), such as Dorestat and Quentovic (near Montreuil), or Hamwic (near Southampton), were not towns in that sense either, or only to a very limited extent. Their main function seems to have been to ensure royal control over the international flows of high-value goods for either military use (weapons) or conspicuous consumption within aristocratic networks. There is even less certainty about the urban status and style of the regional centres of trade we mentioned; in the end, this also remains a matter of definition.

FURTHER READING

Althoff, Gerd (2004), *Family, Friends, and Followers: Political and Social Bonds in Early Medieval Europe* (Cambridge: Cambridge University Press) (orig. German, 1990).

Barford, P.M. (2001), *The Early Slavs. Culture and Society in Early Medieval Eastern Europe* (London: British Museum Press).

Bazelmans, Jos (1999), *By Weapons Made Worthy: Lords, Retainers and Their Relationship in Beowulf* (Amsterdam: Amsterdam University Press).

Bitel, Lisa M. (2002), *Women in Early Medieval Europe, 400–1100* (Cambridge: Cambridge University Press).

Bonnassie, Pierre (1991), *From Slavery to Feudalism in South-Western Europe* (Cambridge: Cambridge University Press).

Christiansen, Eric (2002), *The Norsemen in the Viking Age* (Oxford and Malden, Mass.: Blackwell).

Davies, Wendy and Paul Fouracre (eds) (1986), *The Settlement of Disputes in Early Medieval Europe* (Cambridge: Cambridge University Press).

—— (eds) (1995), *Property and Powers in the Early Middle Ages* (Cambridge: Cambridge University Press).

Duggan, Anne J. (ed.) (2003), *Nobles and Nobility in Medieval Europe* (Rochester, N.Y. and Woodbridge: Boydell & Brewer).

Evans, Stephen S. (1997), *The Lords of Battle: Image and Reality of the 'Comitatus' in Dark-Age Britain* (Woodbridge: Boydell Press).

Halsall, Guy (2003), *Warfare and Society in the Barbarian West, 450–900* (London and New York: Routledge).

Hammer, Carl I. (2002), *A Large-scale Slave Society of the Early Middle Ages: Slaves and Their Families in Early Medieval Bavaria* (Aldershot and Burlington, Vt.: Ashgate).

Havighurst, Alfred F. (ed.) (1976), *The Pirenne Thesis. Analysis, Criticism, and Revision* 3rd edn (Lexington, Mass.: D.C. Heath).

Hedeager, Lotte (1992), *Iron-Age Societies: From Tribe to State in Northern Europe, 500 B.C. to A.D. 700* (Oxford: Blackwell Publishers) (orig. Danish, 1990).

Hodges, Richard (1982), *Dark Age Economics. The*

Origins of Towns and Trade A.D. 600–1000 (London and New York: Duckworth/St Martin's Press).

—— (2000), *Towns and Trade in the Age of Charlemagne* (London: Duckworth).

—— and David B. Whitehouse (1983), *Mohammed, Charlemagne, and the Origins of Europe. Archaeology and the Pirenne Thesis* (London: Duckworth)

—— and William Bowden (eds) (1998), *The Sixth Century. Production, Distribution and Demand* (Leiden: Brill Academic Publishers).

Jong, M. de and F. Theuws (with C. van Rhijn) (eds) (2001), *Topographies of Power in the Early Middle Ages* (Leiden: Brill Academic Publishers).

Logan, F. Donald (1983), *The Vikings in History*, 3rd edn 2005 (London and New York: Routledge).

Marcus, G.J. (1980), *The Conquest of the North Atlantic* (Woodbridge: Boydell Press).

McCormick, Michael (2001), *Origins of the European Economy: Communications and Commerce, AD 300–900* (Cambridge: Cambridge University Press).

Pelteret, David A.E. (1995), *Slavery in Early Mediaeval England: From the Reign of King Alfred until the Twelfth Century* (Woodbridge: Boydell).

Pestell, Tim and Katharina Ulmschneider (eds) (2003), *Markets in Early Medieval Europe: Trading and 'Productive' Sites, 650–850* (Macclesfield: Windgather Press).

Randsborg, Klavs (1991), *The First Millennium AD in Europe and the Mediterranean: An Archaeological Essay* (Cambridge: Cambridge University Press).

Roesdahl, Else (1998), *The Vikings*, 2nd edn (London: Penguin Books).

Verhulst, Adriaan (2002), *The Carolingian Economy* (Cambridge: Cambridge University Press).

Wickham, Chris (2005), *Framing the Early Middle Ages. Europe and the Mediterranean, 400–800* (Oxford: Oxford University Press).

CHAPTER 6

The world of the Franks

THE MEROVINGIANS

The Merovingian dynasty, to which Clovis belonged, monopolized Frankish kingship from the end of the fifth century, but at the same time appears to have considered it as a patrimonial possession to which in principle all male heirs could lay claim. Although this never led to extreme territorial fragmentation, after the death of Clovis in 511 there very seldom was just one king. During the whole of the sixth century there were at times two, three or four Merovingian kingdoms. A change took place when Chlotarius II – one of the rare sole rulers – made his son, Dagobert, under-king in 623, and there were thus once again two kingdoms. One of them consisted of the part of Francia north of the Loire, usually known as Neustria, plus Burgundy, the other of the territory between the Meuse and the Rhine that was known as Austrasia or 'eastern kingdom'. This division was normally upheld. Other territories or *civitates* (local districts), for instance in Aquitaine, were simply divided between the two kings.

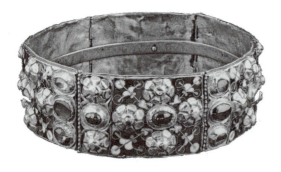

Plate 6.1 Iron crown with semi-precious stones from the fifth-sixth centuries, used for crowning the Lombard Kings. Even Charles V and Napoleon were crowned with it.

The aristocracy always played an important role in Francia, as it did in other barbarian kingdoms. Their influence became stronger during the second half of the seventh century. Amongst other things it is clearly visible in the fact that the highest officials of the Merovingian court – the *maiores domus* ('mayors of the palace') – made their presence increasingly felt. In Austrasia, from the beginning of the seventh century this office was virtually monopolized by members of the Arnulfing or Pippinid dynasty. The basis of their power was formed by their extensive possessions in the Ardennes, a densely forested area where later they would found great abbeys such as Nivelles, Stavelot-Malmédy and Echternach. Shortly before 700 the Pippinids took over the office of mayor of the palace in Neustria as well. Yet their position in the Merovingian kingdoms was far from unassailable. Opposition to them was quite possible, and in 714 after the death of Pippin II the power of the Pippinids was almost broken, not least thanks to the activities of the Frisian 'king' Radbod. The Pippinids, in the person of Charles Martel ('the hammer'), eventually emerged as winners out of this obscure period. He held the office of mayor of the palace in both kingdoms, and the Merovingian kings were no more than puppets under him; but it was his son and successor, Pippin III the Short, who dared to take advantage of the situation and proclaim himself king. Charles Martel had already made the ambitions of the Pippinids perfectly clear. He ruled without a king for the last few years of his mayoralty, and did his utmost to establish Frankish rule over his neighbours to the north, south and east.

How Charles Martel, son of a concubine of Pippin II, succeeded in eliminating the young grandson of Pippin II can only be explained through a combination of coalitions between groups of kindred nobles, leading to frequent battles between the regional warlords.

BOX 6.1 BRUNHILD

Salic law limits inheritance of patrimonial land to male descendants. As a result, women were allowed to inherit only if there were no male heirs, and the same rule applied to royal succession. A fair number of female members of the Merovingian dynasty ended their days in a convent, although occasionally of their own free will, for instance on the death of their spouses. Some of these nuns were deeply unhappy and rebelled; others prayed earnestly for the souls of their loved ones and were generous in their almsgiving. Queen Radegund of Thüringen, who was carried off as booty by Chlotar I in 531 and forced to marry him, willingly exchanged her marriage bed for a convent cell. She made use of her contacts in the outside world to obtain a fragment of the True Cross from the Byzantine emperor Justinian for her community at Poitiers.

Brunhild, daughter of a Visigothic king and married to King Sigebert I of Austrasia (561–575), followed a very different path. The death of her consort was a critical point in her career. She married again, this time the son of King Chilperic I of Neustria, who caused the couple to separate. The Austrasian aristocracy also opposed the intruder. Brunhild had a son, the heir apparent, who was brought up away from his mother's influence. As queen-mother in the midst of a partly hostile nobility she now applied herself to creating her own sphere of influence. In 584 her son Childebert was 15 and was declared of age; now was the time for Brunhild to avenge herself on all those who had previously stood in her way. So strong was her position that she could, and did, have an abbot accused of treason. He was acquitted, but was murdered on his way home. Bishop Egidius of Rheims, who had conspired against her and her son, was banished while the lay plotters were killed.

When Childebert died in 596 Brunhild once again held the powerful position of regent, now for her grandsons, Theodebert II in Austrasia, and Theodoric II in the kingdom of Burgundy, which their father had acquired in 592. As regent, she corresponded with Pope Gregory the Great (590–604) until 602; he asked for her support for Augustine's mission to Kent, and especially for purging the Frankish Church of simony. For her part, Brunhild persuaded the pope to appoint her candidate, Syagrius, bishop of Autun. When Theodebert II turned 15 and of age, the opposition in the Austrasian aristocracy drove Brunhild from court. She sought and found a base with her second grandson. There she expelled some opponents and turned Theodoric against his elder brother, whom she presented as being fathered by a gardener. She even managed to put a stop to Theodoric's proposed marriage to the daughter of a Visigothic king – as Brunhild herself was. She was eager to have her grandson's illegitimate children blessed by Columbanus, the future saint, but he refused and was expelled from the kingdom. She was anxious to remove another woman who might threaten her own position at court. With the help of local factions Brunhild was able to dislodge Bishop Desiderius of Vienne, who had aroused her wrath with his criticism of the king's personal life, and have her men murder him. She had presumably not expected that in doing this she was creating a martyr whose memory would be kept alive by her enemies.

Through her influence in Theoderic's kingdom Brunhild was able to procure the episcopal office for at least four of her supporters, among them Gregory of Tours, the famous chronicler, who never wrote a bad word about her. In 612 she finally persuaded Theoderic to move against his brother. He took Neustria and killed Theodebert and his son, Merovich. Then, as if punished by God, Theoderic died of dysentery. Once again Brunhild arranged the succession by helping Theoderic's eldest son, Sigebert II, to take the throne as the only successor in a reunited kingdom. By passing over Theodebert's second son, Chlotar, Brunhild broke with the Merovingian tradition of dividing the inheritance. Chlotar persuaded the aristocracy to side with him, and Brunhild, Sigebert and his brothers were executed. He accused his great grandmother of having killed ten kings. He may have exaggerated the rank of her victims, but he most certainly underestimated their number. For more than half a century Brunhild had (unofficially) exercised power, both secular and in the Church, out of self-preservation and in defence of her descendants. Her methods differed only in degree from those of other kings and queens of her time, but she survived longer.

Pippin's lawful wife, Plectrude, had tried in vain to eliminate the bastard Martel by imprisoning him. After her two sons had died Plectrude supported her grandchildren, both still minors, and at first managed to have one of them succeed his father as mayor of the palace in Neustria and the other to succeed to the same position in Austrasia. But Charles forced her to hand over his father's treasure chest. Then he even put forward a rival king, and in the end proved to be the strongest. In 719 he drove his most important competitor, Duke Odo of Aquitaine, back beyond the Loire and forced him to hand over King Chilperic. A later chronicler records that Charles then 'kindly allowed him to ascend the royal throne', but only under his control. After Chilperic died in 721 the last kings of the Merovingian dynasty were mere puppets of the mayor of the palace and occupied themselves with the administration of justice and the more ceremonial aspects of power, such as the reception of foreign ambassadors.

The fact that, despite his military strength, Charles Martel did not put aside the Merovingian kings shows that kingship was more than just the supremacy of physical force. Even though kings could be appointed and manipulated by the mayor of the palace, they retained a sacral legitimacy that was passed on through their lineage. But at King Theoderic IV's death in 737, he did not replace him and usurped his position during an interregnum lasting until 743. The territories over which the kings ruled were not precisely defined and changed constantly as a result of inheritance, war and the changing loyalties of regional rulers. Weak and disputed royal power gave lower-ranking rulers – dukes, counts and holders of high office – the chance to align themselves to the party most advantageous for them. Everyone, each at his own level, used power as if it were a patrimonial possession that formed the basis of every activity. In their turn the mayors of the palace also formed their own dynasty; it was originally called the Pippinid dynasty after Pippin I (of Landen), and would later be known as Carolingian, after Charles Martel.

THE ORIGINS OF THE CAROLINGIAN DYNASTY

The defeat of his rivals' armies did not mean that after 721 Charles Martel could exercise power freely over the whole Frankish region. Not only was it business as usual for the intrigues of the high nobility and neighbouring rulers, but in Aquitaine there were threats of Muslim invasions from Spain. The Muslims advanced northwards and pillaged Bordeaux and Poitiers. They were halted near Tours by the Frankish army of Charles Martel, in a battle known in the literature as 'Poitiers 732', but which recent scholarship places a bit further north, near Tours, in 733 or 734. Ian Wood, the scholar who has established this, also suggests that too much importance has been attached to this one battle. Christendom was not saved from extinction at 'Poitiers'.

The Muslim raids gave Charles Martel the chance to set himself up as undisputed ruler of Aquitaine; he was also able to strengthen his hold over Provence and Burgundy. His military successes naturally made a profound impression and brought him many loyal followers and supporters, who offered to enter his service no doubt in the hope of adventure, reward and booty. As victor, he could, moreover, demand tribute from the subjected regions and confiscate land with which to reward his bravest followers. Even church possessions were not spared, which gave him a bad name among later ecclesiastical critics for stealing Church revenues.

Entirely in the style of a Frankish ruler, though still only with the title of mayor of the palace, Charles Martel divided the areas over which he held sway between his two sons before he died in 741. Carloman was given the eastern part, Pippin III the western. There is no reason to suppose that the brothers did not get on with each other at the time, but again there was Grifo, a son of a second wife of Charles Martel, whose claim to a substantial inheritance was not honoured. Frankish custom held that he could not be simply ignored. In short, family rows added to the nobles' pent-up frustrations about the peripheral regions of Aquitaine and Alemannia that Charles Martel had subdued. After several years of violence, Carloman heard the divine call and retired to the Italian monastery of Monte Cassino in 747, entrusting his

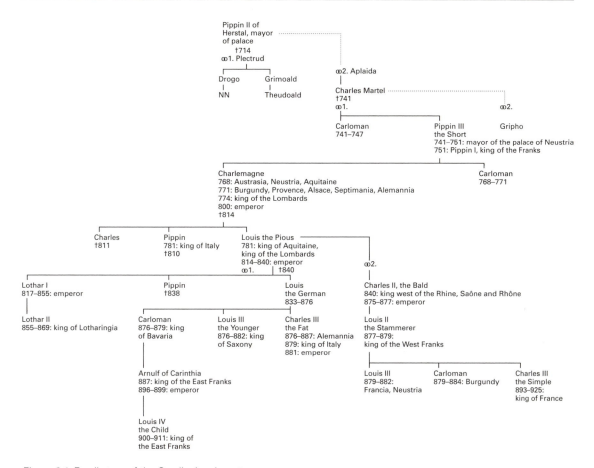

Figure 6.1 Family tree of the Carolingian dynasty

share of the mayoralty, as well as his son, to his brother Pippin.

The combination of military success and powerful rule was probably behind Pippin III's famous question to Pope Zachary in 749 as to 'whether it was good or not that the kings of the Franks should wield no power, as was the case at the time'. The pope, according to a Frankish version of events, agreed that the Franks would be justified in deposing Childeric III and instead making Pippin king. In 754 Pope Zachary's successor, Stephen II, crossed the Alps and anointed Pippin, his wife Bertrada, and their sons Charles and Carloman as the new ruling dynasty of the Franks. In return the pope received protection for the papal territories that formally still belonged to the Byzantine Empire, but which were systematically threatened by the Lombard kings in northern Italy. The theological

estrangement between Rome and Byzantium, and the difficulties that the Eastern Empire itself faced in defending its frontiers against the Muslims and the Avars, had turned the protection given to the papal lands by the *basileus*, the Byzantine emperor, into pure theory.

The anointing of the mayor of the palace, Pippin III, as King Pippin I not only brought an end to the fiction of Merovingian rule after 719 but also recognition of the authority of the Carolingians. Thenceforth they could present themselves as protectors of the Church of Rome, and their power was sanctified and legitimized by the ritual of the anointing with holy oil. With the help of the Church apparatus the Carolingian kings were elevated above the numerous rival dukes and counts who jealously seized upon the kings' every weakness to strengthen their own positions. In retrospect, it made the seizure of ecclesiastical possessions by the mayors of the palace seem reasonable. They had needed these assets to reward their warriors, but in their turn they had given important acquisitions to the Church. The Carolingians would try to disguise the blemish of the bastardy of their descendants and the violent death of several heirs, as well as their *coup d'état*, by allowing their chroniclers to paint as negative a picture as possible of their Merovingian predecessors, and create a most positive image about their own family. This picture is still prevalent in modern historiography.

The Roman Church and the Frankish kings were now dependent on each other in a special relationship of protection in exchange for legitimization. In close cooperation with the kings, Boniface was able to convene church councils that gave a solid framework to the Frankish Church. In view of the role played by the clergy as keepers of written Latin culture this bond lent extra recognition to the classical heritage and an important backing to the expansion of a more institutionalized form of government.

— Frankish Kingdom
||| Conquests by Charlemagne
▦ Papal-'State' (Frankish protectorate)
▦ Remaining Byzantine territories in Italy
    Tributary to the Franks

Map 6.1 Charlemagne's empire

THE CENTURY OF THE CAROLINGIANS

Charles Martel eventually became the founder of a new dynasty of powerful rulers over huge parts of West Europe, who were named after him: Carolingians. In the West Frankish Empire they ruled as kings from 751 to 987, which is a period of almost 250 years. In the East, their rule lasted until 911. However, the century between the emergence of Charles Martel as mayor of the palace in 714 and the death of his grandson, the Emperor Charlemagne, in 814, was characterized by the dynasty's greatest expansion. Like Charles Martel, Pippin the Short had two sons between whom his kingdom was divided on his death in 768: Carloman and Charles. Carloman died three years later after which his family fled to Italy, so that Charles became the sole and undisputed king of the Franks.

The reign of Charles the Great, Charlemagne (768–814), deeply impressed his contemporaries and later generations. Court historians have certainly done much to idealize the life and deeds of their king and emperor, and this idealized representation of

Charlemagne was often recalled in later centuries. Scores of European rulers had complicated genealogies constructed to 'demonstrate' their claims of descent from him. It cannot be denied that Charles's 46-year reign left a profound impact on the history of Europe.

What most characterized his rule was the aggressive, almost continuous waging of war and conquest. He had inherited many challenges from his predecessors, which he tackled with an intense determination. For a start, the popes made repeated calls for protection. In 774 Charlemagne attacked the king of the Lombards, urged on by Pope Hadrian I, who feared the Lombard ruler's threats and encroachment on the papal territories. Charlemagne succeeded in annexing the kingdom of the Lombards and installed Franks and Alamans as colonists and administrators. But the individual character of the region, with its rich, old culture, needed special consideration, and in 781 Charlemagne made it a semi-autonomous kingdom under his infant son, Pippin the Hunchback. In later years this Pippin of Italy conquered the Byzantine territories around Venice and in Istria, which brought him into conflict with the emperor in Constantinople. Because of domestic problems, the latter was unable to maintain his old claims effectively. In 787 the Lombard dukedom of Beneventum, in central and southern Italy, was obliged to pay an annual tribute to the Franks who never really managed to subdue this region but nevertheless extended their sphere of influence. This further weakened the Byzantine position.

As early as 772 a series of cruel wars with a clearly religious dimension was launched against the Saxons; these wars were to last until 804. Frankish victories were followed by Saxon rebellions, leading to bloody reprisals – such as the massacre of 4,500 prisoners at Verden (near Bremen) in 782. Ten years later a new revolt resulted in the massive deportation of Saxons to other parts of the Frankish kingdom, especially Bavaria, after which Frankish and Slav colonists settled in the area. In southern Germania one campaign was directed against the Ba[iu]varii (Bavarians), whose duke, Tassilo, was trying to expand to the south and east. After a rebellion in 757 King Pippin had forced him to a solemn oath of allegiance as a vassal, sworn on many holy relics. In 788 Charlemagne punished the violation of this oath by deposing the duke, who was forced into a monastery, and by incorporating the region into his kingdom. From Bavaria, the Franks pushed on into Pannonia, modern Lower Austria, where the Avars were settled. During successive campaigns in 791, 795 and 796 these people were terrorized and their fabulous treasure in the 'ring', the circular residence of the khan, was seized. Here the Franks established a border region, the Ostmark, the origins of the later dukedom of Austria.

In Gaul expeditions were undertaken into those peripheral regions that had never been completely subjected to the Franks: Brittany, Septimania (the area between Narbonne and the Pyrenees) and Aquitaine. In 781 Charlemagne accorded both Aquitaine and Lombardy the status of separate kingdoms; he gave Aquitaine to his son Louis, as he had given Italy to his son Pippin. A repeat of the alliances between local rulers and Muslim rivals, effected in the 720s, led to the massacre of Charlemagne's rearguard in the Pass of Roncesvalles in 778, mentioned briefly in ninth-century annals, including Einhard's *Life of Charlemagne*, and transformed in the twelfth century into the epic *Chanson de Roland*. Further raids in and after 801 ended in the subjugation of the region around Barcelona and Tarragona as far as the Ebro, where the Spanish March was established.

Charlemagne was undoubtedly a powerful leader who, like his forebears Charles Martel and Pippin the Short, was able to use his personal qualities to bring about the extraordinary expansion of his dynasty's extent of power. There were no major technological advances behind their success. Some writers have indeed argued that the Franks' military superiority can be explained by their heavier armour and the introduction of the stirrup. Others point to the massive confiscations of land and its redistribution, from which many warriors would be rewarded for their efforts and could thus contribute to a large army. Moreover, it has been suggested that the granting of land and the creation of ties of personal dependence became interconnected through what previous generations of historians have called 'feudo-vassalic' ties. All these factors certainly had a part to play, but during the eighth century they did not cause any dramatic changes that might account for the success of the three great Carolingian rulers. By the same token, the disintegration of Charles's enormous empire during the ninth and tenth centuries cannot be explained by the same techno-military or organizational circumstances. So the personal factor must have been decisive: from 714 to 814 three exceptionally strong, probably charismatic, leaders succeeded each other, who were able to inspire great support and whose successes proved to have a great appeal to ambitious warriors. When the spoils of war were shared out Frankish rulers were expected to reward their followers generously; this was possible after a successful campaign when the lands that had been won would be a source of revenue for warriors and officials alike.

Part of the land with which the Carolingians rewarded their warriors came, more or less under pressure, from ecclesiastical resources. The conclusions of the Concilium Germanicum, the Church Council convened by Carloman Snr in 742 or 743, is the earliest text to show that the Carolingians and the Frankish Church had reached a *modus vivendi*, whereby the ruler could indeed request the Church to make land available to the warriors, providing that the rights of the Church were recognized through monetary compensations. Many Church institutions were entitled to a tithe from certain royal estates or other sources of royal income. This *decima regalis* (royal tithe) should not be confused with the ordinary Church tithe (see Chapter 4). The land grants themselves were known as *precariae verbo regis* ('requests [for land] by the king's word'). The land was given as a benefice and fell to those appointed by the king for services rendered.

With their constant wars of aggression and their regular successes Charles Martel, Pippin III and Charlemagne were able to take so much land that they could mobilize exceptionally large armies. As long as there was new land to be shared out, they attracted warriors and thus could muster armies of several thousand men. These were primarily heavily armed horsemen, whose equipment was perfected in the course of the eighth and ninth centuries with the sword, stirrup, panelled saddle and mailcoat. In the area between the Rhine and Meuse, the very heart of the extensive Carolingian domains, there were various iron-ore veins upon which a fine tradition of crafts-manship had been based since Celtic times, and this was important. The mailcoat, the supple combat clothing constructed of small iron rings, appears to have been a Frankish invention; Charlemagne even issued regulations against its export. Of course such a technical advantage cannot be kept secret or exclusive for long – something can always be picked up on the battlefield – and one single factor certainly cannot account for the Frankish superiority.

The heavily armed cavalry would form the core of all Western European armies until the fourteenth century, in contrast to the superiority of the infantry in Antiquity and its renewed importance after 1300. The military value of horsemen was not limited to armies, because in small formations they could show their superiority in speed, arms and strength against peasant folk or irregulars. In an agricultural economy with very low yields, which was characteristic of the early Middle Ages, equipping such warriors and providing for their great horses laid a heavy burden on the scant means available. In those areas where the production of iron was not possible, it had to be purchased with the scarce supply of money or some other surplus. It follows that a very substantial demesne was necessary for the equipment and maintenance of a mounted warrior.

Moreover, the kings could use the authority of their position to call up their free subjects for war. In theory,

Plate 6.2 Ninth-century bronze equestrian statuette of Charlemagne, with imperial crown and imperial globe.

at the end of the eighth century this number amounted to an estimated 100,000 free men who could be mobi-lized. Originally, all ordinary free men may have been subject to military service. In practice this would have meant that because of the vast extent of the Empire and the slowness of communications actual recruitment for war only took place on a regional basis. As we saw in Chapter 5, at the beginning of the ninth century Charlemagne limited full military service to his royal vassals as well as to free men in possession of over four hides (*mansi*) of land. All other ordinary free men had to deliver *adiutorium* ('assistance'); that is to say, contribute to the equipment of warriors. At the same time provisions were issued with regard to the quality of equipment and to the provisioning of armies en route.

PATRIMONY AND STATE

Honour and blood

It is commonplace to say that, in traditional societies, blood relationship is the most universal and obvious means to link people together and arrange them in a hierarchy as well as a potentially supportive network. The degree of kinship, age and gender, which are given by biology, is culturally assessed by custom to determine the importance of everybody's position. In addition to consanguinity, kinship in the wider sense of interrelationship between consanguineal kin groups by affinity or marriage mattered as well. In early medieval society the name of a prestigious forebear would likely be continued by his descendants, and raise their honour.

Honour is the recognition by members of a community of the value given to a person's position. A high rank could be based on descent, fortune or achievements. In the best case these three components coincided. Increasingly, landownership was a condition necessary to equip oneself as a warrior. In martial societies the characteristics needed were bravery, strength and military success. This led to the further enrichment and enlargement of armed retinues who were attracted by fame and a share of the booty. Relatedness, through the right of succession, determined the disposal of land; at the same time it was the first circle inside which warriors could expect to find solidarity. Property and acquired fame were also passed on through blood relationship.

It is understandable, therefore, that the competition for honour, fortune, land and power was played out along the lines of family ties. Because every ruling family had a strong tendency to perpetuate a dominant position by means of inheritance royal kinship co-determined the fate of a king's subjects. If we may believe Gregory of Tours, who wrote in the second half of the sixth century, historical tragedies took place around a monarch's deathbed. Not only the sons but also their mothers and their respective groups of relatives battled for a share of the inheritance, and thus of the kingship. Under the Merovingians and Carolingians, however, territories had become clearly established and designated by their names (e.g. Austrasia, Neustria, Burgundy). These had become the basis for subsequent partitions and heritages. It was a general rule among the Franks that, just as the patrimony was shared between the sons, this had consequences for the succession of kings as well. It is obvious that this rule often resulted in redistributions of regions of control and in violent struggles between brothers.

In many barbarian societies, both sedentary and nomadic, it was families and not individuals who confronted each other in conflicts in which honour or physical integrity were impugned. An insult or injury to a person was taken to heart by the victim's entire family. In the face of offended honour, to a man they felt not only justified but also duty-bound to compensate for the harm done by inflicting commensurate damage on the perpetrator or a member of his family of equal standing. In the most favourable cases this compensation took the form of a payment of money known as *wergeld* (literally: 'man money'). Depending on the status of the victim and the nature of the injury committed, law and custom had established the price for which the injured family could consider themselves compensated. Customary laws from various barbarian kingdoms, codified in the Roman manner in Latin, contain detailed summaries of the recompense allowable for every conceivable level of physical aggression. In the early Frankish kingdoms there were different tariffs for 'Romans' (i.e. natives from Gaul) and Franks; for the Anglo-Saxons the life of a nobleman was set at 1,200 *solidi* (shillings; the name of the ancient standard Roman gold coins) and that of an ordinary free man at 200. For the life of a slave it was the owner who had to be compensated.

When families were unable to reach agreement about the compensation and further acts of revenge took place, the situation often escalated into a feud. In order to preserve their honour, families often fought out these feuds to the last ditch. Only at that point were they prepared to settle the damage to both parties. Once the reconciliation had taken place both families were expected to live in friendship, because they had no reason to reproach each other any longer. Peace then reigned between them; if this peace was broken the king imposed harsh punishments. The ruler did not intervene in the feud itself: to exact revenge was a right of free men, their families were jointly responsible, and injury and recompense were private matters. Even the

Church accepted mitigating circumstances in the case of manslaughter as an act of revenge. For reasons of public order, however, the Carolingian and Anglo-Saxon kings did try to set limits on the involvement of relatives in a blood feud. Nevertheless, it would take many centuries before order could really be enforced on this point.

Vassals and benefices

More importantly, the Carolingian kings, in their relationship with the Frankish aristocracy, consciously intensified the use of non-familial bonds of loyalty and personal dependence. The foremost of these bonds was vassalage. Sources from the Merovingian era mention the term *vassus* (plural, *vassi*) in reference to lower, dependent members of the court. The term was used frequently from the end of the eighth century to the eleventh. It did not have a clearly unambiguous meaning but always referred to free men who were in a relationship of service to a lord or *senior* (seigneur). It was a relationship of mutual dependence: the vassal served and supported the lord, and the lord protected and supported the vassal. As recompense, vassals were often given armour and a share of the spoils of war. Again, two types of overlord in particular were mentioned: church institutions and kings. Between 801 and 813 Charlemagne issued a decree (capitulary) referring to five cases in which a vassal might terminate the allegiance to his lord, from which it is clear that the relationship was tied to conditions for both parties, and that it could be broken. At that time the term *vassi dominici*, meaning the king's vassals, surfaced as a special category of *fideles*, i.e. men who were bound to the king by a special oath.

There are a few accounts, dating from the eighth and ninth centuries, that describe in detail the subjection of a (royal) vassal to his lord. Admittedly, all relate to strongly politically loaded situations where, after a rebellion, amidst great ceremony and before many witnesses, a humiliation was laid upon the subjected person who then had to swear a new oath of allegiance to his victor. In order to be sure that everything would be firmly fixed in the memories of those present, a number of ritual acts took place, including the subjected person kneeling and placing his hands in those of his lord. The oath will have added an extra element of ratification because, according to Frankish custom, it completed a formal reconciliation. This was how Pippin the Short, for example, treated the rebellious Duke Tassilo of Bavaria in 757, who then offered himself to the king in *vassaticum*. However, this is an untypical case and in practice there must have been a variety of forms, just as there was a variety of situations in which oaths of allegiance were sworn or conflicts resolved.

Far more than on vassalic ties, the Carolingians based their power on a far-reaching redistribution of property rights to land, for which ecclesiastical support proved indispensable, because the Church provided an almost inexhaustible reservoir of 'spare' land.

However, while the early medieval Church was by any standard a huge owner of land, this ownership should not be seen in terms of modern undivided and exclusive property right, if only for three reasons. First, much ecclesiastical land was granted for undetermined periods of time, and on various secondary conditions, to all kinds of possessors, ranging from great and powerful lords to small peasants. The longer their possession lasted, the stronger their hold on the land became. Unwritten customary law found that a person who worked a piece of land for a considerable time could not be evicted from it without good reason. So if, for instance, it had been allotted to him for life there was a natural tendency to hand the property over to an heir, unless there were special reasons not to. If the land was in the same hands for more than one lifetime, and if the holder were a free man, then with the consent of the local community it could generally devolve to his children. Second, many, if not most, of the pious people who donated land to the Church did so on condition of usufruct; that is, not only for themselves but also for successive generations. Third, ordinary free peasants, too, sometimes gave the small pieces of land that they owned to the Church in the hope of protecting them from greedy aristocrats. They then asked for the return of their possession, so that they could live on their land and work it for the rest of their lives. The Church consented to this, probably more out of charitable motives than greed. Now, the form in which many such grants of Church land were cast was that of the *precaria* or *beneficium* (benefice), the former literally meaning '[humble] request', the latter referring to the result: a benefice or favour granted. And so it happened that much land that was formally owned by the Church in effect gradually passed into secular hands for a long period of time. Attempts to redress this situation would be a central issue of the Gregorian reform movement of the eleventh century and its struggle for the 'Liberty of the Church' (Chapter 8).

As we are only familiar with transactions of this type to the extent that they were recorded in writing, an art scarcely practised at the time, and have been subsequently preserved, practically all our knowledge of them relates to transfers of land by the Church or the king.

The Frankish kings from the Merovingian dynasty were in the habit of reserving some parts of the royal estates for court officials and counts, who exercised their authority over a particular part of the territory. In that way, grants of land became a compensation for the exercise of the office, simply because in the economy of the early Middle Ages it was the most efficient method of reward. Under the Carolingians, some royal estates were closely associated with specific offices, especially those of counts, and in theory were placed at the disposal of the office-holder only for a limited time. However, in a situation of weak kingship, as was the case in the late ninth and the tenth century, peripheral estates in particular ended up as the hereditary possession of the counts' families, and a temporary circumstance thus developed into a fixed custom and then into far-reaching legal claims.

This development naturally weakened the position of the king with respect to the aristocracy, whose territorial possessions were concentrated regionally. Land may well have become the universal means of exchange, but by its very nature it is an immovable good. In a society with a low level of commercialization, land would therefore have generally belonged to the local ruler or ecclesiastical estate owner, although, especially south of the Loire river, free smallholding maintained its position. Because of the extremely low yields from agriculture in most parts of early medieval western Europe landownership did not form a suitable basis for the centralization of power, unlike in the warmer climate zones around the Mediterranean Sea, in South China and central America, where centralization of power appeared to be possible thanks to higher harvest yields.

But the fact that the Carolingians made systematic use of land grants – be it from appropriated Church estates, from parts of the royal domains or from conquered regions – might explain why, towards the end of the eighth century, the references to *vassi dominici* increased. It means that the two institutions discussed in this section – vassalage and benefice – came together, not yet structurally or in any systematic way, but off and on, when circumstances of which we do not always have knowledge made this suitable or dictated it. This new, feudo-vassalic relationship was used on all levels of the aristocracy, starting with the king, but its essence was always the same: it bound two free men of unequal social rank into a relationship of mutual dependence: each benefited the other and promised to do so. It carried with it mutual fidelity, protection, the agreement about a source of income granted by the higher-ranking or 'senior' in return for the rendering by the lower-ranking of (usually military) services, advice and assistance. Service in exchange for protection had to be coupled with trust on both sides, which meant that both lord and vassal had to be able to count on each other in an emergency.

If it was not unusual in the Carolingian period to give vassals benefices in the form of land, it was only at a much later stage that vassalic relationships might equally well be connected to grants in what now was usually called *feodum* or 'fief', of other assets: offices, lordships, sources of monetary income such as tolls, or even lump sums of money paid out of some treasury. Such alternative feudo-vasallic relationships became widespread only in the eleventh century. Only then did feudo-vasallic relationships develop into a 'feudal system', on which the exercise of 'state' power rested. It was characterized by grants of public administrative offices (in particular those of count, duke and margrave) or lordships to royal vassals, who held them not in any bureaucratic way, but as (hereditary) fiefs from the king. Feudalism in that sense is a form of 'mediation' of state power.

AN INCIPIENT STATE

But was the Carolingian empire a state? The French medievalist Georges Duby quipped that Charlemagne's empire was 'a village chiefdom, stretched to the universe'. For our view of what further happened with this empire, much depends on our appreciation of the effectiveness of Carolingian royal administration, and in particular the ability of counts and dukes, appointed to represent royal authority in each and every corner of the vast territory that the empire enclosed, to really act as public officials and to distinguish between 'public' and 'private' exercise of power. Ironically, one of Duby's major contributions to medieval history, the theory of the 'banal revolution', departs from a rather rosy picture of the Carolingian administrative machinery. We shall return to this point in Chapter 7.

However, nobody would want to deny that a certain amount of institutionalization was necessary to consolidate the military successes. Charles surrounded himself with clerics who, despite his reportedly crude nature, introduced him to some of life's finer aspects. The most prominent of these clerics was the Anglo-Saxon scholar Alcuin, who had been called to Charlemagne's court to teach the king. Alcuin was also one of the advisors who elaborated ideas on Christian kingship and imperial rulership. These were partly based on classical Roman models and partly on the Old Testament. A Christian king was meant to be God's chosen protector of the faith, which allowed him to concern himself with the affairs of the Church and to carry out his own secular political activities in the sign of Christ. The idea of a reborn Roman-Christian empire was made clear to every subject through the new silver *denarii* that Charles had struck after his imperial coronation. On the reverse these pennies bore a cross in or on a classical temple, with the legend CHRISTIANA RELIGIO, and on the obverse the effigy of the emperor draped, just like his illustrious predecessors of late Antiquity, in a toga and wearing a crown of laurels; the circumscription was KAROLUS IMPERATOR AUGUSTUS ('Charles, the august Emperor').

Charlemagne's imperial coronation was actually a repeat at a higher level of the events of 750–751, when Pippin had been anointed king. In 799 Pope Leo III came to Paderborn to ask for Charles's help against a faction of the Roman aristocracy, from whose intrigues he had narrowly escaped. This was Charlemagne's opportunity to invoke the principle that had been formulated for 749: 'he who actually exercises the authority of rex deserves the title of rex'. Had he not, like a true Roman emperor, established his authority over all – or at least many – of the lands of Western Christendom? Was his might not indispensable as protector of the Church? When Charles left for Rome in the autumn of the year 800 to restore the pope to his authority he displayed his effectiveness as protector of the Church, and in this quality proved himself to be the equal to the Byzantine emperor. At the coronation ceremony in Saint-Peter's church on Christmas Day, the pope ensured that he first 'created' the emperor by crowning him, before the acclamation of the Roman people confirmed him in the dignity. By this act a precedent was created that would hold until the end of the Middle Ages.

There is no doubt that the Carolingians took good care of their own propaganda, which resulted in more and more interesting literary and artistic products being produced in their time than in the centuries before or after. These items still guide historians in their interpretations. Among them are the royal annals in which the most important events of each year were recorded, and especially Charlemagne's biography, written by the erudite nobleman, Einhard, counsellor to Charles's son and successor Louis the Pious. Following the model of Suetonius' *Lives* of the first 12 Roman emperors (*c.* 125), Einhard could affirm that 'during his whole reign Charles regarded nothing as more important than to restore . . . the ancient glory of the city of Rome'. The palace chapel in Aachen, with its cupola constructed on an octagonal base, was clearly inspired by a number of architectural models, not least the basilica of San Vitale in the former imperial city of Ravenna and the Lateran Palace in Rome. Marble pillars, capitals and mosaics were brought from Italy to Aachen to lend ancient lustre to the new church. From around 800 onwards, Aachen would become the most important royal residence and the symbolic capital of the reborn empire, a rival – in reality, very small – to Rome. Richly illuminated manuscripts were produced at and for the court of Charlemagne and Louis the Pious. A clear and manageable new style of writing, the Carolingian minuscule, evolved from the Roman script system. With the encouragement of Alcuin and other scholars that he brought from Italy, Ireland, Francia, Saxony and Spain Charlemagne stimulated the study of Latin. Ancient texts were copied and studied with the aim of achieving a more correct understanding of the Christian religion.

Plate 6.3 The imperial throne in Charlemagne's palace chapel at Aachen, built in the years 798–815. The octagonal dome, supported by columns imported from Italy, represented the *translatio imperii* from the Romans to the Franks

The king's palace included his household and some office-holders who were constantly on the move. Even Aachen never developed into the fixed capital of the Carolingian Empire – no more than did any of the later imperial residences, a problem that has left its traces in modern Germany. One of the reasons for this was that the king was always away on military expeditions during the months that were suitable for waging war. Another, that the presence of the king was essential in diverse places in the Empire so that his authority would be respected. A third reason was purely practical: whenever possible, the king and his retinue stayed in one of the more than two hundred palaces in order to make use of the revenues on the spot. In the manorial economy, where there was little traffic, it was simpler to allow these demanding consumers to travel around than to attempt to centralize the harvest yields. The

Latin word *palatium* has given us the word 'palace' and the German *Pfalz*, the central building on a royal domain that was the preferred stopping place of the itinerant king and his court.

One traditional means of exercising power was the oath of allegiance, from 789 on (and then again after an uprising in 792) demanded by the king of all his free male subjects above 12 years of age. In 802 the emperor stipulated that allegiance should be sworn to him 'as a man should swear allegiance to his lord'. In 805 a more exclusive note was heard in the relationship of fidelity: besides swearing allegiance to the emperor, a free man would only be able to swear allegiance to his own lord. Oaths of allegiance were a typical means of exercising power in a society with a limited culture of writing; the bonds of fidelity were direct, personal and mostly unwritten. An oath was sworn with the hand on a holy object, such as a relic or the Scriptures. Breaking an oath provoked divine sanctions along with strong judicial punishment for perjury. In such an extensive empire, the king obviously could no longer administer all these oaths in person, and he was represented by his officials in the various territories. This marks the beginning of the tradition of the oath of office where, in many lands, the formula 'allegiance to the king' still appears.

Alongside this, the chancery, the administrative measures and legislation, the general assembly and the palace school already shaped early forms of state institutions that were separate from the king's person. The Merovingian kings had the greater part of their paperwork carried out by a Church institution at hand, or by the person for whom the document was intended. A chancery of his own enabled the king to complete more written documents without external agency, and even to create an archive to give him closer control of his activities. The Merovingian kings had a chancery with lay notaries, but later scribes were predominantly clerics who were in the direct service of the king/emperor. A particularly important activity of the chancery was to issue numerous capitularies, royal or imperial decrees, split into separate chapters or sections, in which administrative and legislative regulations were promulgated. They often formed the written report of provisions orally agreed and proclaimed by the powerful men of the land at their annual general assembly (the so-called March or May Field; after 755, the meeting took place in May). In that context the spoken word had the power of law. The announcement in everyone's presence voiced the consensus, and at the same time laid the duty on all those present to abide by what had been agreed. It is, therefore, likely that the capitularies served in the first place as a sort of reminder for the chancery and for the *missi dominici*, the emissaries who were sent all over the Empire in the king's name to ensure that the rulings were obeyed.

Strenuous efforts to create a solid state institution in the Roman model were made when it came to the division of the territory and the offices belonging to it. Charles II the Bald used the Codex Theodosianus, as did many other users, including the Church, during the ninth century. Because the Empire was so vast the king/emperor had to delegate his authority. We have already mentioned the foundation in 781 of the kingdoms of Lombardy and Aquitaine, which were held respectively by Pippin and Louis, Charlemagne's younger sons. We have also mentioned the Marches, the border regions with a strong military administration – such as the Spanish and the Eastern March, as well as the Breton, Danish and Friulian. The 400 counts (*comites*) were of paramount importance. The title of count (*comes*) dates from the Late Empire, as does the title of *dux* (duke) that was applied to holders of substantial, strategically situated territories, such as Bavaria.

Counts were basically office-holders whose task it was to represent the king's authority in their region, to administer justice in his name, to lead the general assembly, to summon to war and to ensure that the capitularies were observed. In return, a part of the royal domains in their particular region was placed at their disposal. The majority of counts were Franks, even in regions of a different ethnic composition, apparently because the common background fostered loyalty. The emissary counts and bishops, sent in pairs as inspectors, *missi dominici*, were responsible for checking the counts' activities or related tasks.

The objectification evident in this organization was no doubt a result of the efforts made – under the oft-repeated motto of *renovatio* – to restore the Roman imperium in a Christian form, based on the renewed study of Roman history, law, and literature by the learned clerics of the court. In practice the ambitious project was unmanageable: the material circumstances

of the eighth and ninth centuries simply made it impossible to achieve the results that had still been possible in the fourth century. In this sense we must interpret the capitularies as ordinances through which the king/emperor hoped to change an unmanageable reality, but in fact they were a reflection of that very reality. There are capitularies that decreed that counts could not go out hunting if they had to preside over a court session; must not be drunk while exercising their office; could not accept gifts from parties involved in court cases; were not allowed to blackmail landowners with the threat of taxation or military service, and more. In 810 Charlemagne found it necessary to use a capitulary to denounce drunkenness, lack of piety, desertion resulting in the formation of gangs and banditry; and finally a revealing ordinance from the 62-year-old emperor, 'that the people must obey the emperor's orders promptly'. A fine list of everyday practice.

Among the factors creating unity in the Carolingian Empire, we should again bear in mind the paramount importance of the interdependence with the Church. During the early Middle Ages the Church was the largest highly developed organization in Western Europe, and the only one to have educated staff. The support of the clergy was essential for every ruler at that time, for both technical and ideological reasons: it was the clergy who handed the Carolingians the perfect means to establish a new empire on the Roman model. In Merovingian Gaul there were episcopal domains in *civitates* where bishops had the right to appoint counts, or to hold that office themselves. This was not without its dangers, because the bishops could easily find themselves embroiled in a merciless struggle for power. In the Frankish Empire the autonomous position of the bishops was increasingly felt to be a problem, and under the Carolingians most of the episcopal lordships lost their immunity. But then they had no difficulty in appointing bishops as 'emissary counts'. In short, a practice that was born out of necessity would never disappear in the Middle Ages. Investing holders of high spiritual office with temporal authority was a structural characteristic of the medieval Church. During the tenth and eleventh centuries German kings would make the involvement of bishops in the government of the country a cornerstone of their policy. Episcopal principalities continued to exist in the German Empire until 1806.

Whenever reference is made to a Carolingian state, kingdom or empire, such terms should not be understood anachronistically. In the everyday Germanic and Roman languages there was no word for an abstract concept such as the state. Power relations were linked to a person, concretely and directly. It was not until the reign of Louis the Pious that court scholars found a term that appealed to them in their Latin sources: *res publica* (literally, the public affair). But the concept did not filter through to the reality of the structures of Carolingian government. There are a remarkable number of cases of beheadings of counts accused of high treason, a typically Roman-law concept introduced by the court scholars. Attempts made to establish public institutions were abandoned after a couple of generations. In many respects, the apparatus of state was limited to the court and a few hundred officials who struggled to impose laws in the enormous area stretching from the Ebro to the Oder, and including large parts of Italy. On the basis of a domain economy with a very limited monetary circulation it was a hopeless task to impose a lasting administrative unit on the jumbled diversity of peoples belonging to different cultures and levels of development.

The fiction of a united empire

In 806 Charlemagne made arrangements for his succession. In accordance with Frankish custom he divided the realm between his three sons. Two of them, however, predeceased their father so that the Empire would remain monocratic. While Charlemagne was still alive, he made his only surviving son Louis 'partner in the imperial name', as the Annals of the Frankish Realm specify. He was crowned by his father at Aachen in 813 – an event that might be interpreted as an insult to the pope. However, Pope Stephen came to Francia in 816 to anoint Louis at Rheims. During the early years of his reign, Louis the Pious devoted himself to the protection of Church institutions, from the papacy to the local clergy, in the face of over-powerful secular lords. In 817 he, too, made arrangements for his succession, under which the Empire would again be divided between the three sons that he then had. The emperorship was considered to be an indivisible unit.

His eldest son, Lothar, was therefore proclaimed co-emperor and sole heir to the dignity attached to his father's realm of authority, and in 823 he was anointed and crowned by the pope. The other brothers were given the title of king under the suzerainty of the emperor: Pippin over Aquitaine and Louis over Bavaria, both areas with a strongly developed regional identity. This arrangement may have been intended as a compromise between the customary Frankish law that prescribed division, and efforts to ensure the unity of the Empire. The emperor had very little real power over the (sub-)kingdoms, each of which was allowed a vast amount of autonomy.

Things did not work out as planned. Within four fateful years, between 829 when Louis granted an inheritance portion to his 6-year-old son, Charles (the Bald), born from his second wife Judith, and 833 when the emperor was humiliated and taken prisoner by his elder sons on the Field of Lies near Colmar, the dream of a unified empire meant to embrace and protect a united (Roman) Christendom was shattered. And it did not stop when Louis the Pious died in 840. Lothar's demand for oaths of allegiance to be sworn to his vassals throughout the Empire, following his grandfather's example, stirred up bitter opposition from his surviving brothers, Charles and Louis the German. They defeated the new emperor after a violent struggle, and, at Strasbourg in 842, in the presence of their warriors, they swore solemn oaths of mutual assistance and promised that they would never treat separately with Lothar. These oaths are famous because both kings used the vernacular tongue so that they would be understood by the other's followers: Louis swore in the Roman language (*Romana lingua*), Charles in German (*Theudisca lingua*). Then both groups declared, each in its own tongue, that they would not follow their king if he were to wage an unjustified war against his brother. The ceremony throws an interesting light on the exercise of authority in the middle of the ninth century: personal ties of dependence and fidelity formed the basis of the power structure, between equals as well as between a king and his followers. A publicly sworn oath sealed the bond. In the event that the oath was violated the collective memory of those present formed the touchstone, giving the injured party the right to break the bond of allegiance. Vassals were not tied to their king unconditionally either: the king was required to observe the rules that decided whether a war was justified or not. If it were not, there was no vassal service, and thus no army. It seemed an effective way to prolong peace.

Under the threat of being deposed by a council of bishops and the pressure of his brothers' coalition, Lothar agreed to negotiations. They resulted in the partition of the Empire into three, laid down in the Treaty of Verdun in 843. The brothers divided the means of power as equally as possible between them. They realized that a vassal should hold benefices in only one of the kingdoms so that he would not have a conflict of loyalties should the kings become involved in a dispute. When fixing the boundaries they even tried to take into account the existing bonds of fidelity of the vassals, whose benefices were kept as far as possible inside the kingdom of their own king. One of the problems of this treaty, however, was that the bonds of fidelity did not coincide with the borderlines, showing how much the personal vision of power prevailed above the territorial one. Louis the German was the big winner, being given all the regions east of the Rhine. Charles the Bald received the territories west of the Scheldt, Marne, Saône and Rhône. Lothar, the emperor, kept Italy and the central territories, including both Aachen and Rome. The northern parts would later be called Lotharingia (*Lotharii regnum*, or Lorraine) after his son and namesake, Lothar, who received them after the death of Lothar I in 855. By the same partition Italy went to his eldest brother, while the younger one was given Provence.

The following decades were characterized by short reigns and a rapidly changing composition of territories as a result of repeated divisions of inheritances. In 875 the imperial title, already devalued under Lothar I, fell for just two years to the West Frankish king Charles the Bald. In 881 negotiations with the pope resulted in the recognition of the king of East Francia, Charles the Fat, as emperor. The title would continue to exist in that part of the Empire later known as Germania or Germany, with an interruption in the tenth century, until 1806. So the fiction of the legacy of Rome came to rest upon rulers of a territory that only in its most southerly and westerly extremities had ever been part of the Roman Empire, and which was in many respects less developed than West Francia and in particular the south. The long borders, especially to the east, made it possible to continue to make conquests and exact tribute. Its vast distances, however, made East Francia a region that was difficult to govern internally. Under these circumstances, the substance of the imperial title would change rapidly.

Counts and hereditariness

Although at that point in time the functions of margrave, duke and count were already exercised with a large degree of autonomy and showed a tendency to become hereditary, they were still considered as royal offices. But when the Carolingian conquests reached deadlock and royal authority was further weakened, partly as a result of succession problems, a forceful centrifugal power was set in motion. Dukes, margraves and counts all began to consider their delegated authority to exercise the *bannus* (the royal prerogative to command and rule under penalty of death and loss of property), as well as the lands and *regalia* (royal monopolies) granted to them in benefice, as attachments to their office, as their hereditary possession. Even if they continued to recognize their formal relationship to the king they increasingly went their own way as autonomous rulers over the regions entrusted to them, and in their turn used the granting of land in benefice as a means of committing men, first of all their local agents or viscounts (*vice-comites*), to certain services. There was now no question of a clear and exclusive relationship of loyalty and dependence, which naturally resulted in conflicts and a downward spiral of diminishing grip. In the long term, the only real territorial power in many places was in the form of local, so-called 'banal' lordships (see further in Chapter 7).

There were several ways in which counts, dukes and margraves could try to establish themselves as securely as possible in their positions. They could strengthen their connections with great landowners in the area, perhaps marry a well-off, and if possible, fine-looking local lady, or otherwise marry their offspring into powerful regional families. Such close ties to the regional aristocracy were an essential condition for the effective, long-term exercise of comital or ducal powers. They certainly imply that office-holders of Frankish origin became ever more rooted in the region where they held their office and, conversely, that their loyalty to the distant king diminished. Revolts in several parts of the empire (Bavaria, Saxony, Aquitania) indicate a resistance to Frankish rule by societies that were very conscious of their own identity. The problem of acculturation was thus very real for Frankish counts.

When Charles the Bald travelled to Italy in 877 to have himself crowned emperor he issued a capitulary formally promising the counts who were to accompany him that their sons, provided they were trustworthy, could succeed to them in their office should they happen to die during the journey. This provision, which only applied to West Francia, can be read restrictively as a temporary measure, and a spur to them to join him. The reason behind this measure may have been that Charles was involved in a full-blown row with his son, Louis the Stammerer, and was anxious above all to prevent him appointing his own cronies to high positions when they fell vacant during his, Charles's, absence. The idea that the position of count should become hereditary did not then come entirely out of the blue, and from then on it could be officially discussed. The practice of hereditary office, and of hereditary benefices attached to it, really started during the ninth century and was unstoppable: in the face of such a general trend it was impossible for the king to move forcefully against every usurper. The phenomenon was simply too common, and because not much profit could be expected from such a conflict, few warriors were willing to take part. The king could do little more than accept the reality imposed by material circumstances and human mechanisms for adaptation. In 1037 Emperor Conrad II formally recognized the unhindered possession of fiefs and the right of vassals to pass their fief on to a son or other male heir in Italy. Common practice must have been far ahead of this legislation.

DYNAMIC PERIPHERIES

Britain

The seven kingdoms of the Angles and Saxons followed an evolution that revealed striking similarities and dissimilarities to that of the Frankish Empire. Warrior retinues, feuds, some sort of a manorial economy, and great social inequality could be found on both sides of

the Channel. Now and then Anglo-Saxon kings, just like their Carolingian counterparts, would ask the Church if it could spare a piece of land for a well-loved warrior. One striking difference is that the *dooms*, the Anglo-Saxon laws, were composed in the vernacular, unlike the Frankish capitularies that were formulated exclusively in Latin. Were the linguistic differences in the Frankish Empire bigger than in Britain, and did the Carolingians try to overcome them through the use of Latin? It is also striking that the king of Wessex, Alfred the Great (848/9–899), followed Charlemagne's example and founded a court school. But here translations were made from Latin into the vernacular. In the long term this brought about an indigenous legal tradition in the vernacular that was able to resist the introduction of Roman law, which took place on the continent from the twelfth century onwards.

After 787 the sacral nature of kingship, perhaps on the Carolingian model, was confirmed by the anointing of the king of Mercia by a priest. The king had the right to call up free men for war, but even in the dire emergency of the struggle against the Danes in 878, Alfred the Great could only do this by mobilizing half of the men alternately. On the other hand, the more professional category of warriors in the retinues of powerful men seemed more effective. They shared in the booty, sometimes received a gift or a piece of land in exchange for their services, and their deeds were sung in drinking bouts at court. The most striking contrast between Britain and the continent is that, in 878, the kingdom of Wessex brought the Danish invasions to a halt, and during the first half of the tenth century it succeeded by conquest in the political integration of the seven Anglo-Saxon kingdoms. The Scandinavians who had settled in the north-east of England were allowed so much freedom that they never became a disruptive factor. While the Carolingian drive to conquer led to an imperial overstretch that shrank again as soon as the strong leaders were succeeded by weaker ones, the gradual merging of small kingdoms in England appeared to be permanent. The borders of the former kingdoms remained in the borders of the counties or shires, which in large part were created in the tenth century. At the level of the shires, and of the *hundreds* beneath them, courts of law were established where, under the guidance of royal judges, local notables passed sentence. Under Alfred the Great, Wessex

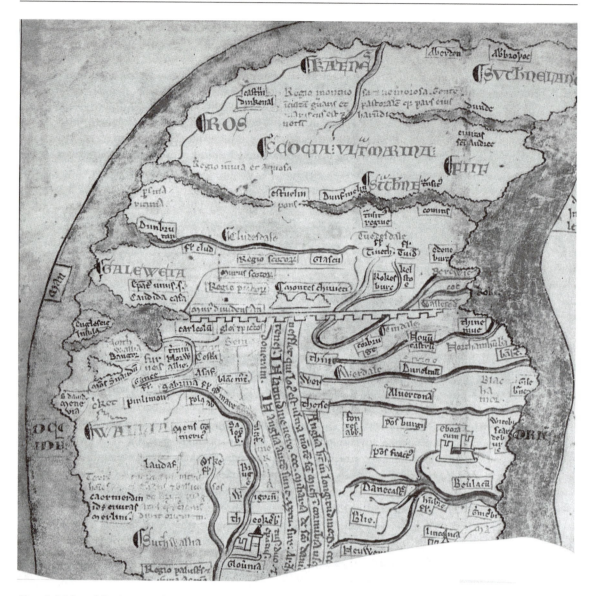

Plate 6.4 Map of England and Scotland in the Historia Major by Matthew Paris, *c.* 1240. Hadrian's wall from Newcastle to Carlisle is clearly recognizable.

was the first kingdom where this took place, and during the following century the system was extended over the whole country. Anglo-Saxon England was thus far ahead of the Continent in matters of administrative and legal organization. Thanks to the strength of the monarchy, there was no usurpation of regalia there, and a distribution of land similar to grants in benefice was a rather limited phenomenon.

Moorish Iberia

Almost immediately after the conquest of Egypt in 642–643 the Arab warriors turned their gaze further westwards. In a little over fifty years the whole of North Africa was under their control. They met very strong opposition because Byzantium had again established its rule in what is now Tunisia, with ancient Carthage as its centre. The region had been intensively colonized by the Romans and had been converted to Christianity long before it was conquered by the Vandals in the fifth century. In 670 the Arabs founded the city of Kairouan at a strategic junction of caravan routes, sufficiently inland to be safe from attack by the Byzantine fleet. Kairouan was the most important administrative centre in the Maghreb, which literally means 'the West'. The great mosque of Kairouan is one of Islam's four holiest places of pilgrimage, together with Mecca, Medina and Jerusalem.

When the Byzantines were finally expelled in 680, the native Berber tribes united in a confederation and offered fierce resistance to the Arab conquerors. Some of the Berbers had been Romanized and lived in towns along the coast, while others were still nomads. In 705 the whole of the Maghreb became the province of Ifriqiya, independent of Egypt. It is possible that reports of confusion in Visigothic Spain led to the crossing of the Straits of Gibraltar by a 7,000-strong army of Islamized Berbers in 711; the invaders had a

rapid victory near Jerez de la Frontera, then advanced on the royal capital at Toledo without meeting any opposition. With reinforcements of 18,000 men from the East, they reached Zaragoza in barely two years. The areas round Barcelona and Narbonne were subdued in 720. Unlike the Arabs in North Africa the Muslims were able to establish their authority in the Iberian peninsula through treaties rather than by force. They made raids over the Pyrenees as far as the Rhône valley, but Islamic fervour was broken when they suffered defeat at the hands of the Frankish leader Charles Martel. In 751 they had to relinquish Narbonne. In the north-east, where Charlemagne had established a 'Spanish March', a number of Frankish districts came into existence, such as the margravates of Barcelona in 801 and Pamplona in 806. The Christian kingdoms of Navarre and Aragon grew out of local resistance, which was directed at Franks and Muslims alike.

The Muslims never established a centralized state in Iberia, which they called *al-Andalus* (Andalucia). They

Plate 6.5 Moorish stronghold and city walls of Obidos, Portugal

used indirect forms of government in the extensive outlying areas, which they controlled only for a short time or in part. In the 'high march', of which Zaragoza was the capital, they made a Visigothic ruler their client. The 'central march', with Toledo, and after 946 Medinaceli, as the capital, was the scene of the most violent struggle against the Christians from the north. The region between the Douro and the Ebro for a long time formed the disputed border area. Extremadura and central Portugal constituted the 'near march', with Mérida as its capital. Military governors maintained authority there. Over the centuries the people of Iberia gradually became Islamized. An eighth of the population was Muslim in the eighth century, a quarter in the ninth, and a third in the tenth. So at no time did the Muslims form a numerical majority; but they certainly enjoyed cultural dominance. Islamic control was only established after much conflict, which is not really all that surprising considering that the immigrant Muslims came from various parts of the Muslim world, with widely varying geographical and cultural backgrounds.

The first wave of conquerors of Iberia came from North Arabia early in the eighth century. They settled chiefly in the towns, and enjoyed a number of privileges that often led to uprisings by the Muslims who had arrived later, sometimes known as 'new Muslims'. These later arrivals from South Arabia, originally peasants, settled in the countryside. Among these 'Arabs' there undoubtedly would have been a large number of other people from the East who had joined the army and rapidly become Arabized. The Berbers from the mountains and deserts of North Africa ended up in central Spain, where they could continue their traditional way of life as cattle herders. Their tribal links remained unchanged for at least three centuries. The region around Valencia and Murcia was farmed by coastal Berbers, using Roman irrigation methods and channels. After the period of conquest, large groups of Berbers again started to immigrate from the end of the tenth century. The Jewish communities, which were particularly important in the towns, welcomed the new Islamic authorities as liberators after the repression they had suffered under the Christian Visigoths. And, of course, there was a shrinking Christian majority who, like the Jews, were also treated with reasonable tolerance by the new rulers. They were allowed to hold religious services, their bishops were respected, they enjoyed a large degree of autonomy, and justice was administered following their own customary law. They had to pay taxes, as *dhimmi* (non-Muslims), in accordance with Islamic law. In the course of time many

BOX 6.2 ST JAMES OF COMPOSTELA

Christian resistance to the Muslims was concentrated in the mountainous north-west of the Iberian peninsula, in Galicia and Asturias, which never came under Islamic rule. The cult of the apostle James became the focus of the Reconquest in Christian Iberia. Although Acts 12:2 tells us that James was buried outside the walls of Jerusalem in the time of King Herod, a Latin Breviarium of the Apostles dating from the late sixth century indicated that James had preached in Spain. In this way Western Christianity did not trace its apostolic origins back to St Peter alone (and thus to Rome), there was also an authentic link with Iberia through St James. This view fitted in perfectly with the efforts of the Visigothic Christians to introduce their own liturgy. During the seventh century numerous altars and churches were dedicated to St James. In the late eighth century Gallic clergy used his cult to give Spain's disorganized Christians something to hold on to. In a liturgical hymn of 785 St James was presented as 'the shining golden head of Spain, our leader and patron saint'. Although a rational explanation has never been given for James's alleged journeys to the north-west corner of Hispania, once to preach and a second time to be reburied, between 818 and 834 a gravestone was indicated as marking the apostle's burial place. Legend has it that a star (*stella*) hung over the grave in a field (*campus*). Since then Santiago de Compostela (*Santiago* is the corrupted Spanish form of 'St James') has been the patron saint of Christian Spaniards and supported them in their centuries-long Reconquest against the Muslims. Santiago quickly became the second most important place of pilgrimage in Christian Europe, after St Peters in Rome.

Christians adapted their way of life, their language and manner of dress – but not their religion – to the dominant Arabic culture: they were called *musta'rib* in Arabic, which is translated as 'Mozarabic'. Christians who converted to Islam, *conversos*, were not treated as equals of the original Muslims, but they were able to climb the social ladder as clients.

The core region of al-Andalus was divided into provinces that stemmed from the dioceses of the Late Roman and Visigothic period. From 716 Córdoba was the seat of the central government. Originally the administration was in the hands of governors serving under the authority of the governor in Kairouan and eventually under the caliph of Baghdad. The fall of the Umayyad dynasty in Baghdad in 750 led to the *de facto* independence of small kingdoms in the Maghreb and Iberia. In 756 Abd ar-Rahman, a descendant of the Umayyads, succeeded in having himself recognized as ruler in Córdoba with the title of emir. After he had suppressed the uprisings of new-Muslims in the mountainous southern provinces, which had been going on for years, Abd ar-Rahman III proclaimed the orthodox caliphate of Córdoba in 929. With this he displayed his legitimacy as a Umayyad, distinct from the Abbasid caliphate in Baghdad and from the heterodoxy of the Fatimids who would establish their own caliphate in Ifriqya and (later) in Egypt.

The Vikings

More than any other group of people in the Middle Ages the Vikings have caught the modern imagination: they are stereotypically portrayed as rough, fair-haired men with two horns on their helmets, roving about in slender, dragon-headed longships. How much this is a myth can be proved by the fact that not a single Viking helmet with horns has ever been found. Many good monks writing chronicles in the age of the Vikings had a much more negative view: to them they were hairy heathens, bent on murder, looting and sacrilege. The *Anglo-Saxon Chronicle* records that in 786 three ships moored off the coast of Dorset, their crew killing the royal sheriff in a fight. There were renewed attacks every year, aimed in particular at the abbeys, whose treasures were stolen and altars desecrated.

In the ninth century it was the same story in countless places along the coasts and rivers of western Europe. Many towns and abbeys there were indeed plundered, and the inhabitants carried off as slaves. Through Viking trade these poor people might end up in Russia and among the Varangians, where they were exchanged for silver and products from the East. Broadly speaking, three sorts of Vikings can be distinguished. Swedes from Stockholm and the island of Gotland sought to expand chiefly along the coasts of the Baltic Sea and into Russia. Norsemen appeared in the mouth of the Loire in 799; in the period 836–841 they turned their fleets towards the Scottish islands, and in 841 Norwegians and Danes landed in Normandy. In 844 they turned up before Lisbon, occupied Cadiz, sailed up the Guadalquivir and pillaged Seville. They were cut to ribbons by the forces of the emir, but new invasions followed in 859, 966 and 971. Between 870 and 930 the Norsemen crossed to Iceland, and in 984 to Greenland and *c.* 1000 to Newfoundland. In 834 the Danes visited the east of England and the rivers of the Low Countries, where they sacked Dorestad. From 855 to 862 the Seine region was the most important objective, from 879 to 892 the area between the Loire and the Rhine, and from 870 to 878 eastern England with Mercia. Einhard, Charlemagne's biographer, wrote at the latest in 826 that the Danish king, Godfred, intended to subject all of Germania, because Frankish actions against the Frisians and Saxons had damaged his sphere of influence. It was most certainly the longest wave of raids and invasions in the West between the sixth and fourteenth centuries.

It is above all archaeological sources that have given us more insight into Viking society. The Vikings were seamen as well as peasants, settled in relatively fertile regions where there was quite a lot of iron ore. They were very skilled in shipbuilding and in making agricultural tools, weapons and other implements. They were very efficient traders as well, as appears from their activities in ports-of-trade such as York, Dublin, Birka, Kaupang and others. The extraordinary propensity of groups of Vikings for expansion is nowadays sometimes put down to rivalry between clan leaders: in order to establish or maintain their authority they had to perform glorious deeds and bring home great booty. In some cases clans also tried to find new places to settle, which would point to the relative overpopulation of their original territory. The meagre resources did not

Plate 6.6 Hull of the large Öseberg burial ship, Oslo, Norway

allow such intensive agricultural production as did more southerly regions.

In spite of what has been suggested in some western chronicles, especially the Annals of the Abbey of St Vaast at Arras and the *Anglo-Saxon Chronicle*, the Vikings were not interested solely in murder, robbery and looting; at the same time they developed commercial ties (see Chapter 5). After 840 they systematically searched for new areas in which to settle, among them Frisia, Northumbria, East Anglia, Ireland and Iceland.

The Franks granted areas of Frisia to the Danes. King Alfred of Wessex and his warships offered some resistance between 870 and 878, but in the end the Danes appropriated two-thirds of his territory. In the region later known as Normandy, Rollo's settlement was recognized by the Frankish king in 911, and Rollo was granted the title of count.

The remarkable success of the Viking invasions can be attributed to the speed with which they made their attacks and then disappeared in their slender boats. The heavy cavalry of the Frankish warriors was not designed for surprise attacks of this sort. It took them a long time to mobilize, and even then they often could do no more than watch from the riverbank or coast while the Viking ships remained out of reach. Only when the Vikings started to spend the winter in sheltered places did they become vulnerable, particularly because their forces were small. Eventually it became clear that the Frankish kings were unable to protect their people, and it was the local lords who offered resistance by building forts along the rivers or fortified bridges. The bridge over the Seine at Pîtres in 864 was a late case in which Charles the Bald took the initiative on one of his royal estates. In this way the invasions helped to accelerate the process of decentralization of power that had already begun.

On the other hand, the protracted Viking contacts in western Europe, though bringing destruction to the existing order, also brought expansion to the commercial activities of the region. Although priests and monks must have found it terrible when their treasures were stolen, from an economic point of view it meant that the precious metals that had long been hoarded were brought back into circulation again as a means of payment in long-distance trade. To finance their defence against the invaders, and to buy time and avoid the expense and risk of full military engagement, the Anglo-Saxon kings introduced a fixed tax in silver coin, 'Danegeld', a land tax levied until 1162, long after Danish kings ruled England in the first half of the eleventh century. Immense quantities of silver were collected: as much as 22 tons in 1018, which would have represented about 42 per cent of the total supply of coins. A large part of this would have come from Frankish sources through trade. This wealth entered into circulation and supported the Vikings' brisk trade with the East. In this way Viking activities in western Europe stimulated the circulation of goods and capital there, and the entry of the region into an intercontinental trading system.

FURTHER READING

Abels, Richard (1998), *Alfred the Great: War, Kingship and Culture in Anglo-Saxon England* (London: Longman).

Barbero, Alessandro (2004), *Charlemagne: Father of a Continent* (Berkeley: University of California Press) (orig. Italian, 2000).

Becher, Matthias (2003), *Charlemagne* (New Haven, Conn.: Yale University Press) (orig. German, 1999).

Collins, Roger (1983), *Early Medieval Spain: Unity in Diversity, 400–1000* (London: Macmillan).

—— (1998), *Charlemagne* (Basingstoke: Macmillan).

Everett, Nicholas (2003), *Literacy in Lombard Italy, c.568–774* (Cambridge: Cambridge University Press).

Fouracre, Paul (2000), *The Age of Charles Martel* (London: Longman).

——, and Richard Gerberding (1996), *Late Merovingian France: History and Historiography, 640–720* (Manchester: Manchester University Press).

Geary, Patrick J. (1988), *Before France and Germany. The Creation and Transformation of the Merovingian World* (New York and Oxford: Oxford University Press).

Glick, Thomas F. (2005), *Islamic and Christian Spain in the Early Middle Ages*, 2nd edn (Leiden: Brill).

Goldberg, Eric J. (2005), *Struggle for Empire: Kingship and Conflict under Louis the German, 817–876* (Ithaca, N.Y.: Cornell University Press).

Innes, Matthew (2000), *State and Society in the Early Middle Ages: The Middle Rhine Valley 400–1000* (Cambridge: Cambridge University Press).

James, Edward (1982), *The Origins of France. From Clovis to the Capetians, 500–1000* (London and Basingstoke: Macmillan).

King, P.D. (1986), *Charlemagne* (London: Methuen).

Loyn, H.R. (1984), *The Governance of Anglo-Saxon England, 500–1087* (London and Stanford, Calif.: Edward Arnold/Stanford University Press).

MacLean, Simon (2003), *Kingship and Politics in the Late Ninth Century: Charles the Fat and the End of the Carolingian Empire* (Cambridge: Cambridge University Press).

McKitterick, Rosamond (1983), *The Frankish Kingdoms under the Carolingians, 751–987* (London and New York: Longman).

—— (1989), *The Carolingians and the Written Word* (Cambridge: Cambridge University Press).

—— (1994), *Carolingian Culture: Emulation and Innovation* (Cambridge: Cambridge University Press).

—— (2004), *History and Meaning in the Carolingian World* (Cambridge: Cambridge University Press).

Nelson, Janet L. (1992), *Charles the Bald* (London: Longman).

Riché, Pierre (1993), *The Carolingians. A Family Who Forged Europe* (Philadelphia, Pa.: University of Pennsylvania Press) (orig. French, 1983).

Reuter, Timothy (1991), *Germany in the Early Middle Ages 800–1056* (London and New York: Longman).

Reynolds, Susan (1994), *Fiefs and Vassals. The Medieval Evidence Reinterpreted* (Oxford: Oxford University Press).

Smyth, Alfred P. (1996), *King Alfred the Great* (Oxford: Oxford University Press).

Stanton, Robert (2002), *The Culture of Translation in Anglo-Saxon England* (Woodbridge and Rochester, N.Y.: Boydell & Brewer).

Story, Joanna (2003), *Carolingian Connections: Anglo-Saxon England and Carolingian Francia, c.750–870* (Aldershot and Burlington, Vt.: Ashgate).

—— (ed.) (2005), *Charlemagne: Empire and Society* (Manchester and New York: Manchester University Press).

Williams, Ann (1999), *Kingship and Government in Pre-Conquest England, c.500–1066* (Basingstoke and New York: Macmillan/St Martin's Press).

Wood, Ian (1994), *The Merovingian Kingdoms 450–751* (London and New York: Longman).

CHAPTER 7

Accelerated growth

The three centuries between about 950 and 1250 were a time of great change in many fields: economic, social, political, religious and cultural. This chapter will first concentrate on three aspects that are closely linked and that are therefore considered as far as possible in relation to each other: population growth, increase in food production and changes to the surplus extraction system. We will be looking at the rural segment of the medieval economy and society; the urban segment will be discussed in Chapter 11. We then examine the drastic changes in the relationship between lords and peasants in this period, and their repercussions for culture and social ideology.

POPULATION GROWTH

The period between 950 and 1250 is usually depicted as one of relatively strong and sustained population growth. But was that really the case? Bold estimates for the whole of continental Europe (including Russia and the Balkans) place the number of inhabitants in the year 1000 at between 30 and 40 million, and by the beginning of the fourteenth century at 70–80 million. This means that the population of Europe more than doubled in the space of three centuries, an increase of 0.25 per cent per year. This figure was confirmed by recent estimates of the population growth in England between 1086 and 1300, which can be relatively well documented. In 1086, the year in which William the Conqueror compiled the *Domesday Book*, the oldest European source in any way resembling a country-wide population statistic, England had between 2.5 and 2.75 million inhabitants: this number rose to between 4 and 4.5 million by 1300, pointing to a growth rate of 0.18 to 0.28 per cent per year.

Certainly, by present-day standards, population growth of this size can hardly be called spectacular and, besides, it probably would not have been much stronger than in the preceding three centuries. As opposed to the model of an explosive growth between about 1000 and 1300, an argument can be made equally well for an alternative model in which population numbers were built up gradually from the seventh century onwards, though with frequent disruptions, until net population increase after *c.* 1000 reached the critical mass necessary to accelerate the processes of commercialization, urbanization and state formation that were so essential for socio-economic and political development.

Even then we should consider the fact that there were large regional differences. Looking at Europe as a whole, a dividing line can be drawn roughly between the south and the west, where the population grew considerably and was relatively densely populated by about 1300, and the north and the east (Scandinavia, Poland, the Baltic region and Russia), where growth lagged behind until the end of the Middle Ages. Demographically speaking, by 1200 the population density of Western Europe was already greatly in excess of that of Eastern Europe.

VOLUME AND NATURE OF AGRICULTURAL PRODUCTION

However meagre the doubling of a population in the space of three centuries may seem to us, it was only possible if food production had also roughly doubled: roughly, because we do not know whether calorie intake remained the same, and we must also make allowances for increasing urbanization. An increase in food production can be achieved in two ways: by a more intensive use of existing agricultural land and by expanding the acreage. The first option was feasible only to a limited extent. In other words, it would not have been possible to double land productivity (the physical yield per unit of surface area) in three centuries, even at the cost of falling labour productivity (the yield per worker deployed). Until long after the Middle Ages an increase of agricultural production primarily meant extending the acreage of arable land – either nearby existing settlements or by colonizing areas far away, even on the frontiers of Latin Christian Europe.

A formidable obstacle to the improvement of soil production was the low level of manuring, mainly due to the lack of integration between arable and pastoral farming. English manorial accounts dating from this period show no relation at all between harvest yields and the extent of livestock grazing. Opportunities to maintain manuring levels by using non-animal fertilizer were seldom taken, one of the exceptions being a wide swathe through northern France where the land was regularly enriched with calcareous marl. A form of green manuring did take place, entirely unintentionally, through the regular but marginal cultivation of legumes (beans, peas); one characteristic of legumes is that they fix atmospheric nitrogen (the most important inorganic fertilizer) in the soil.

Nevertheless, three methods for achieving more intensive soil use are known from that period of expansion. The first and most obvious was to convert grasslands into arable land. The cultivation of grain that can be baked into bread provides between six and seventeen times more calories per unit of surface area than the grazing of cattle. Indeed, some historians believe that agricultural expansion in the high Middle Ages in the first place took the form of extending the cultivation of grain in existing settlements, a process known in German as *Vergetreidung*.

A second possibility lay in pushing back the fallow. In traditional agriculture, farmers never used all their fields at the same time. Experience had taught that after a few years the harvests became smaller, chiefly as a result of the land being overtaken by weeds. So a good part of the farmland was always left fallow. Cattle were then put to graze on this fallow land, in order to eat away the weeds and leave manure. The land was ploughed before it was seeded again. During the period of expansion peasants in different regions of north-west Europe, and first on the great estates of Flanders, northern France and England, switched to an agricultural system with restricted fallow, known as the three-field system. Under this system only about one-third of the farmland was left fallow; a winter cereal (rye or wheat) was grown on another third, and a summer cereal (barley or oats) or legumes on the remainder. Through annual rotation a different third of the land lay fallow every year. After the harvest the stubble was grazed.

A fixed rotation system such as this three-field system did have disadvantages, especially in regions where there were 'open fields', complexes of arable land where the plots of individual peasants were not fenced off separately but where the whole field was enclosed. Open fields encouraged a communal system of usage that deprived peasants of the opportunity to deviate from the fixed crop sequence in order to grow a commercial crop like flax, for example. Because of the increasing importance of these crops in urbanized regions, in the course of the thirteenth century the three-field system began to disappear from open fields – in Flanders for example – during the period of expansion, in favour of a greater flexibility in land use, especially outside the great estates.

Finally, the mould-board plough and horse traction combined two technical inventions that helped to intensify production as well as to extend acreage through land development. On the heavier soils of eastern and north-western Europe the mould-board plough, which was developed in the first millennium, gradually replaced the prehistoric ard, a light plough made entirely of wood (see Plate 7.1). Compared with the ard, the mould-board plough demonstrated three major improvements in construction. First, there are three working parts instead of just one: the coulter (F), a blade projecting vertically downwards from the plough-beam (C) and whose height is adjustable; the ploughshare (E), which was attached asymmetrically at the end of the plough sole, the beam on which the plough rests; and the mould board (G), a wooden plate mounted diagonally on the plough sole (A). Second, two of the parts – coulter and share – were made of iron. Third, the plough-beam was no longer attached directly to the yoke of the draught animals, at least not on the slightly more developed types, but rested on either a sledge-shaped 'foot' or a two-wheeled fore-carriage. This meant that less traction was needed and that the depth of the furrow could be varied with a couple of small adjustments. A mould-board plough with a forecarriage is usually called a wheel plough (Latin: *carruca*). An early picture of one can be seen in the Bayeux Tapestry, the embroidery commissioned by Odo, bishop of Bayeux and half-brother of William the Conqueror, to commemorate the Battle of Hastings. This plough has no mould-board: this may be a mistake on the part of the embroiderer – after all, the peasant walking next to the plough lacks both legs – but coulter, share and forecarriage are clearly recognizable.

The mould-board plough was more sophisticated than the ard: through a combination of a vertical

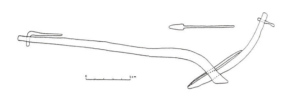

(a) Ard plough

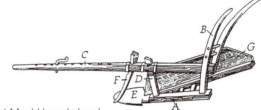
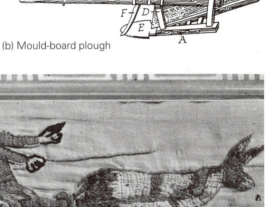

(b) Mould-board plough

(c) Bayeux tapestry

Plate 7.1 Ard (a) and mould-board (b) ploughs. Ploughing, harrowing and sowing as depicted on the border of the Bayeux tapestry (c) (coulter) and horizontal (share) cut, the clods of soil were loosened; the mould-board then turned the soil over. The turning of the soil uprooted the weeds, brought mineral nutrients from the subsoil to the surface, and helped to mix any added manure into the soil. The heavier construction and adjustable iron parts made it possible to till heavy or unstable soil at different depths. When the plough followed a certain set direction it created a pattern of ridges and furrows that ensured good drainage, and thus facilitated the cultivation of winter crops, rye in particular. Finally, a more effective loosening of the soil made crosswise ploughing, which was essential when the ard was used, unnecessary. In this way one ploughing direction was saved. The labour saved was more than compensated for by the fact that mould-board ploughs required more than one person to operate them, particularly when they were drawn by several draught animals. Moreover, the ploughing gang was followed by another gang with a harrow to break up the loosened clods before sowing.

All this can be seen in the Bayeux Tapestry, including also a plough drawn by a mule or a hinny and a harrow by a horse. That brings us to the second agricultural innovation of the Middle Ages: the use of horses instead of oxen as draught animals, in agriculture and elsewhere. The advantages are evident: horses are more manoeuvrable and quicker than oxen and have a more explosive tractive power. There are disadvantages too: oxen are less discriminating in what they eat and less susceptible to sickness, have more stamina, are easier to yoke to agricultural equipment, and, when slaughtered, they provide more and tastier meat. The two major disadvantages would have been overcome precisely during the medieval period of expansion: the problem of fodder, through a strong expansion in the cultivation of oats (which besides being used for horse-feed was also an ingredient in beer); and the harnessing problem, through the combined development of the horse collar (a padded leather collar), girth (belly-band), swingletree (a crossbar to which the traces are attached) and shafts. Through the improved method of harnessing the pressure point sat lower, while the padded collar prevented the draught animal from being choked. In this way the pulling power of horses could be used far more efficiently, which in turn led to the use of heavier, 'cold-blood'

draught horses and heavier-built ploughs and other implements, but also of carts, equipped with a shaft.

Innovations of the sort described above never appear out of thin air, but often are the result of long, intermittent development and adaptation. The oldest archaeological traces of mould-board ploughs and harrows in central and western Europe date from the time of the peoples' migrations, or even earlier. But the types with which we are familiar from the high Middle Ages only resembled their Roman and barbarian prototypes to a limited extent. We must also bear in mind that, as far as technical innovation in the pre-industrial period is concerned, there was often a considerable length of time between the first development and the widespread use of new implements or methods of working. There are two reasons for this. First, technical inventions cannot usually be utilized on their own. They must be applied in a particular technological environment or 'technological complex', as Janken Myrdal puts it. The success of the plough and harrow depended on the availability of two scarce and costly products: horses and iron. In the Carolingian period even large estates possessed only a few iron implements. The situation would have been even worse elsewhere, and probably the vast majority of peasants had only a spade or hoe to till their strips of land. Second, psychological and social factors play a role. Pre-industrial peasants were conservative; their principal survival strategy was the avoidance of risk. Besides, they did not always have a say in the application of expensive tools. We know from the Carolingian polyptychs and the English *Domesday Book* that in the manorial system it was the manor lords who owned the ploughs on their estates.

Even when a technological innovation was introduced and accepted, its use might be lessened if the price ratio between labour and implements changed to the advantage of the former. In Flanders, then in every respect a progressive region, a shift in use could be observed in the thirteenth century from mould-board plough to simple spade; a growing number of peasants had too little land to make the use of the plough cost-effective. Moreover, it has been found that in regions where there was little urbanization, such as Denmark and Scotland, the spade continued to be used as well as the plough. For similar reasons, the ard remained a popular tool for use on lighter soil alongside the mould-board plough in Prussia, Sweden and England.

We are less sure about the effects of technical improvements on the average harvest yields, for example, but there is certainly no question of an agricultural revolution in that respect. From information collected for England, Flanders and Artois we know with reasonable accuracy that the size of the average wheat and rye harvest in about 1300 was between 900 and 1,200 litres gross per hectare; that is to say, before seed for the next year's sowing had been discounted. That is not much, slightly above half the yields achieved in the Netherlands and England in about the middle of the nineteenth century. There was not much change before the seventeenth century.

Gross harvest figures actually tell us very little about the total returns to labour of peasant family businesses unless they are combined with data about the quantities of labour, implements and sowing seed used, as well as about the yields from livestock and non-agrarian activities. The availability of land, which seems very plentiful by current standards, made it relatively simple for peasants to intensify or extend their production depending on their own needs or external pressures; this often happened by allowing part of the land to lie out of crop and to sow seed and cultivate it for a couple of years only when needed. At the other extreme, the intensified use of land in densely populated regions such as the Flemish Scheldt valley and Artois before 1300 led to the cultivation of fodder crops for cattle that were kept in the byre almost year-round. In the same region, for the first time there was a boom in the labour-intensive cultivation of commercial crops, which were used as raw materials in the industries in the towns.

In north-west Europe the need for mould-board-ploughs and horse power increased quickly after the tenth century when the heavy, unstable clay and peat soils were reclaimed rapidly; before then such lands could only be used marginally as hay meadows or summer pasture. This form of reclamation amounted to drainage in combination with dike-building. At first arable farming was certainly possible on the drained peat bog if the land was high enough. After drainage the ground level subsided quickly as a result of the decreased volume and oxidation of the peat bog. This forced peat farmers in low-lying areas, such as the coastal regions of the modern-day Netherlands, to be evermore ingenious in their water management, beginning with the digging of canals and the construction of embankments and sluices and ending with wind-driven watermills to expel the water from completely endiked peat polders into higher-lying channels. This stage was reached in the County of Holland soon after 1400, but the battle against the water was by no means won. The ground level had subsided to such an extent that the peat farmers were forced to give up arable farming and specialize in livestock, or make a living elsewhere.

With their knowledge of drainage and dike-building peasants from Frisia, Holland and Flanders were welcomed as guest labourers (from the Latin *hospites*) when low-lying peat bogs and clay ground were being reclaimed in other parts of Europe. Right at the beginning of the twelfth century they were called in to help with the first phases of the *Ostkolonisation*, the German colonization of the lands east of the Weser, the Elbe, the Oder-Neisse, and later in Prussia east of the Vistula.

The reclamation of peat and clay soils was insignificant on the European scale when compared to the expansion of land for cultivation through forest clearance – the felling of tropical rainforests in our own time is not an exaggerated comparison. Between one-quarter and one-third of all the land that was developed for cultivation between 950 and 1250 must once have been woods and forest. In north-west Europe countless place names ending in -*rode*/-*roth*, -*rade*/-*rath* (see the German verb *roden* which means 'to clear') or -*sart* are reminders of this. Everything seems to indicate, too, that by about the year 1000 there were no longer any vast tracts of virgin forest in West or South Europe. Certainly there were still many woods, but with their numerous clearings of varying size they resembled a cheese with holes in it. Charcoal burners and woodcutters, miners and iron-workers, swineherds, pitch-makers and wax-makers, trappers, hermits and anybody who, for whatever reason, lived cut off from the civilized world shared a marginal and dangerous life there with bears, deer and wolves, animals that were increasingly forced to retreat. It was the peasant colonists who really accelerated the process of deforestation.

There is no indication at all of any ecological concerns. On the contrary, in literary and other texts the picture of the forest as a sinister, dangerous place that should really be eradicated continued to compete with the opposite view (at least as old) of the forest as an unspoiled Arcadia or a place of spiritual contemplation. The best-kept forests were those where kings or other territorial princes vigorously insisted on their royal right to wilderness – their claim to uncultivated land, particularly with an eye to hunting, a favourite pastime. This was why, in England, large complexes of forest survived the expansion phase, although in time it became necessary to enclose them as far as possible to keep the game in and the poachers out. This was not always easy, as we learn from the thirteenth-century folk songs about the legendary outlaw, Robin Hood, and his merry men who hid in Sherwood Forest, one of the large royal woods. Robin Hood is probably a product of the imagination, but the type certainly existed. In about 1280, for example, a search was made for one Geoffrey du Parc who prowled about Feckenham Forest in Worcestershire with a band of some hundred companions, including, sure enough, his own priest.

NEW FORMS OF AUTHORITY

One of the logical consequences of the growing population density during the period of expansion was what French historians have called *encellulement*. By this they mean that in this period people were ordered and grouped into all sorts of bonds of local organization. That happened 'from below', for example, through the formation of local communities (more about this on pp. 125–126), and 'from above' through the establishment of local territorial lordships. It is this last phenomenon that we shall discuss first and most fully.

The 'banal revolution'

The collapse of Charlemagne's empire and the serious weakening of royal power in the individual kingdoms marked the start of a series of radical developments in the history of Western Europe. As we have already indicated in Chapter 6, this began when important Carolingian administrative positions were, almost naturally, seen by the office-holders (counts, dukes,

margraves) as hereditary dignities. This happened earlier and in a rather more clear-cut form in the West Frankish kingdom than in the East Frankish kingdom. The kings of the Capetian dynasty (996–1328) hardly had a say in anything outside their domains in the Île de France until the end of the twelfth century. Some counties (Flanders, Anjou, Champagne) and dukedoms (Normandy, Burgundy, Aquitaine) acquired royal allure. In Germany, where royal power was restored in all its glory under the Ottonians (919–1024), the hereditary nature of high government office was not yet a general rule, but the trend towards patrimonialization was clearly marked.

In short, in both parts of the old Carolingian Empire, by about the year 1000 the first steps were being made towards the formation of territorial principalities within kingdoms. Ironically enough, the tendency would prove to be irreversible in Germany but not in France. An almost automatic result of the hereditary acquisition of high public offices was that the *bannus*, the royal prerogative to command and rule, that was attached to them came to be seen by the office-holders as a licence to exercise control without the need to justify their actions.

The second step was actually a repeat of the first step but at a lower level of public administration; namely, that of viscounts (*vicarii, capitanei*) who represented the authority of counts, dukes or margraves at the local level. From the end of the tenth century this sort of official, but also any number of local notables who held no administrative position at all, began to assume the royal *bannus* and to exploit it in a high-handed manner over an area that was as large as they were able to control using the threat of force.

This phenomenon, the explosive proliferation of *banal lordships* or local seigneuries, is known as the 'banal revolution' because of its far-reaching consequences. It was a revolution in that the whole of the development we have described led to a far more efficient exploitation of people than previously in the early Middle Ages. Even then, *dominium*, lordship, the personal rule over people, was a fixed attribute of aristocrats. The aristocracy was small, however, and the *dominium* of the aristocrats was more limited than the *bannus* of the kings. It only extended to people with whom they had a personal relationship (in other words to their *familia*), which included not only all members

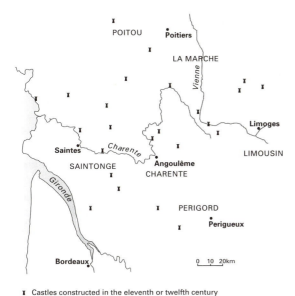

POITOU

Poitiers

LA MARCHE

Vienne

Saintes

Charente

Limoges

LIMOUSIN

SAINTONGE

Angoulême

CHARENTE

Gironde

PERIGORD

Perigueux

Bordeaux

0 10 20km

ꭓ Castles constructed in the eleventh or twelfth century

Map 7.1 Castles of western Aquitaine

Source: A. Debord, 'The Castellan Revolution and the Peace of God in Aquitaine', in Thomas Head and Richard Landes (eds), *The Peace of God: Social Violence and Religious Response in France c. 1000* (Ithaca, N.Y. and London, 1992), p. 137.

of their family and household but also their slaves and all dependent peasants settled on their estates. In this situation large groups of 'ordinary free people' were beyond the direct reach of aristocratic rule. On the other hand, in the early Middle Ages public authority, arising from the royal *bannus*, was generally something far removed from the ordinary free man, because royal power was diffuse and only wielded under particular circumstances in a vaguely defined territory (see Chapter 5). This was to change towards the end of the tenth century. The number of local lordships multiplied rapidly, while at the same time they were put on a different footing. Local leaders seized the exercise of the *bannus*, and thus made strict lordship tangible at local level for everybody who did not belong to the aristocracy or the clergy. From then on it was a question of *nulle terre sans seigneur* ('no land without a lord'), as French jurisprudence puts it so succinctly. Local power no longer rested primarily on the private ownership of large estates, and the peasants settled on them, but on territorial lordship grafted on to the *bannus*.

Of what did this new type of local lordship consist? At its heart was the exercise of justice, including capital and corporal punishment – in other words the trying of serious crimes. This jurisdiction gave the banal lords an excuse to confiscate goods and arrest people arbitrarily, and thus a means of forcing the small, free peasants off their allodial (held in full ownership, free from obligations) property. In addition, it was possible to organize on a local scale what had been impossible to achieve at state level: the levying of general taxes, tallage (often referred to as *tallia* [*taille* in French] or *exactiones* in the sources), or the exacting of other general seigneurial rights that were not infrequently borrowed from the serf statute. Finally, the banal lords managed to impose all sorts of labours and services on their subjects – such as compulsory work in and around their castles – and they exploited costly capital goods, like mills and bakers' ovens, as a monopoly, a practice that earlier was restricted normally to great estates.

Taken together, these rights deriving from banal lordship were called *consuetudines* ('customs'), a euphemism that was soon qualified by the adjective *malae* ('bad'). Banal lordship was often upheld through the use of force, unrestrained and unreasonable even by contemporary standards, against the local peasants. After all, the banal lord was not at war with them, nor involved in a feud with them, nor were they his slaves – all reasons which in the early Middle Ages justified the use of brute force. These were among the reasons why even at the time banal lordship met with unmistakable criticism from clerical circles, however hypocritical this may have been. Ecclesiastical lords and institutions whined, especially when the might of the local banal lords was directed against Church possessions, but often behaved with equal severity and violence against those under their own authority. The clergy never spoke out against the banal order as such. The seigneurs felt no moral compunction at all. Shortly after 1200 the noblemen of Catalonia even demanded from the king of Aragon the right to 'mal-treat' (*male tractare*) their peasant subjects. This would seem to legalize the *malae consuetudines*.

It would have been less easy to establish banal lordships of such a potentially violent nature had not the seigneurs provided themselves with two powerful means of exerting their authority: a castle and a following of well-armed warriors. These castles were not the kind of great protective fortresses built throughout north-west Europe during the ninth and tenth centuries on the orders of kings and counts, near commercial centres such as Dorestat and Middelburg, to offer the people and their property some protection from the Vikings. In the context of banal lordship we are talking about far more modest strongholds. They were not wholly unknown in the Carolingian era, but they spread enormously – they must have numbered thousands – after the middle of the tenth century, quite a time after the last great invasions of Europe by 'barbarian' groups (Vikings, Muslims, Magyars). The primary purpose in building these castles, therefore, could not have been to protect local populations. Only Spain of the Reconquest, embroiled in a struggle to the death with the Moors, formed any sort of exception – both Castile and Catalonia mean 'land of castles'. Elsewhere the principal aim, control of the surrounding area, was less scrupulous and heroic. Castles were erected to keep rival lords out of the region and ambitious territorial princes at a distance, and above all to enable the *bannus* to be exercised as efficiently as possible and under the threat of terror. Importantly, it made no difference whether the castle was the freely held possession of the lord or whether he held it formally in the name of the king, count or duke.

This new type of castle consisted of little more than a motte, a natural or man-made mound, on which was built a wooden or stone tower, the keep (*donjon*), which was several storeys high and could only be entered by a staircase to the first floor. Some castles had a walled space next to the motte, where there was room for outbuildings, stables, etc. In France there was a clear difference between town and countryside. In the few larger urban centres castles were erected within or close to the town itself. If the lord of the town did not live in the castle himself, it was manned by a local official called a castellan. In the countryside, however, most of the castles were situated in relative isolation, far from existing habitation. Only in Italy and southern France was this less often the case. Here, in this period, entirely fortified new settlements were built in many places, with a castle inside. The design of these *castra* or *castelli* included a concentration of habitation and not infrequently a reorganization of the agrarian landscape

adapted to it. The whole phenomenon is known in the literature as *incastellamento*.

All of these new types of castles had a permanent garrison of small contingents of professional soldiers who were in the service of the lord of the castle. The sources often refer to them as *milites castri* ('soldiers of the castle'), the *gregarii equites* ('ordinary horsemen') or *cavalcata* ('cavalry'). They were recruited from the young scions of lesser, local aristocratic families, but sometimes also from among free or even unfree peasants. They were well trained in mounted combat and were mobilized for the defence of the castle and for small-scale, often extremely violent operations in the surrounding area.

Regional differences and feudo-vassalic 'packaging'

The whole idea of the 'banal revolution' has been much disputed during the last two decades. Its opponents stress continuity rather than change, and stress the need to try to find out how core socio-political institutions, such as jurisdiction, actually worked rather than be content with knowing how they functioned by the book. Useful as that may be, we remain convinced with, among others, Chris Wickham, that Western Europe around 1100 was 'structurally distinct' from the world of Charlemagne, and that one key difference consisted in the nature of local lordship. Certainly there was continuity in the quintessentially aristocratic nature of lordship and the exercise of power on every level of society. But the character of aristocratic dominance over people and land changed dramatically when the 'public' order that the Carolingians had succeeded in raising and maintaining – however imperfectly – started to crumble, and not only kings lost control over counts, but counts lost control over local lords as well. By appropriating the king's prerogative to command and forbid, everyone with enough resources, strength or daring could play king on the local level without running the risk of being held accountable to the real king or his officials. To see this point one should keep looking at a multiplicity of indicators instead of hammering away at one issue only, and in addition widen one's scope outside France, the sole case on which the banal revolution argument has rested for too long; one should take into consideration similar phenomena as were observed for France in other parts of the former Carolingian Empire, or even beyond.

For a start, the contrast between France and Germany should not be too strongly stressed. At most, the floodgates burst later in the German Empire than in France – the great uprising against the rule of Henry IV in 1073 is often seen as the fault line. At any rate, at about that time all the symptoms of the formation of autonomous local seigneuries were visible in the German Empire too, especially where, for whatever reason, the evolution towards larger territorial principalities was hampered.

Nevertheless, global differences can be seen between the development of seigneuries in France and the German Empire. More often than in France banal lordships in the German Empire and in the (German) kingdom of Italy evolved directly out of aristocratic large landownership and the lordship rights attached to it, which then grew into a territorial seigneury. Moreover, many banal lordships were rooted in the lay advocacy of ecclesiastical immunities. Such immunities always had a lay advocate to deal with matters concerning weapons or the use of physical violence (such as the administration of corporal and capital punishment), which were considered improper for the clergy. Since lay advocates were without exception powerful aristocrats in the region, the advocacy could easily be the lever for the establishment of a territorial lordship.

It is also true that the establishment of local seigneuries was prevented more often in the German Empire than in France as a result of the active involvement of German territorial princes in the reclamation and colonization of land, and the organization of entirely new settlements created by these developments. The princes arranged the 'public order' all at once, by means of a written charter. The charter not only laid down what the size of the farmsteads should be after the land had been cleared, and how much should be paid to the lord annually for the tenancy, but also how local government and justice should be arranged in the new settlement. This sort of charter gives the impression of a relationship of cooperation and consultation between lord and subjects rather than one of repression and violence.

According to Thomas Bisson, the American medievalist, the tendency to the formation of banal lordships was not limited to the regions within the Carolingian Empire. On its peripheries, the same phenomenon appeared in more or less the same period in the Christian kingdoms of North Spain – but also in England, where there was a long tradition of royal authority and grants to tenants-in-chief (royal vassals) after 1066 never included 'public' offices. Everywhere, first here, then there, there was an enormous proliferation of local lordships based on force, over which neither kings nor the holders of territorial office had any control. Sometimes the development was coincidentally reinforced by political circumstances: examples include the organization in Castile and León of the defence against the renewed aggression of the caliph of Córdoba in the last decades of the tenth century, and in England the period of 'Anarchy' (1135–1154) between the death of Henry I and the coronation of Henry II.

In all this it is essential to bear in mind that the weakening of royal authority through the simultaneous formation of proto-territorial principalities (counties, dukedoms, margravates) next to local banal lordships cannot be labelled simply as 'feudal anarchy', as it used to be. The increasingly systematic use of feudo-vassalic relationships in fact actually helped prevent long-term anarchy. The relationships are to be found at every level: in the long run, counts, dukes and margraves, whether in France or in Germany, and however autonomously they may have operated, all became vassals of the king and, ultimately, recognized to hold their counties, dukedoms and margravates in fief from him. In turn these counts, dukes and margraves were able to compel many banal lords into a feudal bond – or back into one – while the banal lords themselves entered into feudo-vassalic relationships with their *milites*. The ramifications of this multi-layered network in about the middle of the twelfth century are evident in a survey that the count of Champagne had made in 1172 of all the vassals and their fiefs in his county, possibly with the intention of demanding *ligesse* (preferential fealty) from them all. This survey, known as the *Feoda Campanie*, contains the names of no fewer than 1,900 'lords' and 'knights'.

If feudo-vassalic relationships contributed to an early control over banal lordships, these lordships only really disappeared when central, territorial and quasi-sovereign authority was restored, either at the level of kingdoms – as in England in 1154 – or at the level of counties, dukedoms and margravates. It meant that kings or other territorial princes made strenuous efforts to monopolize and centralize those core responsibilities – administration of justice, use of force, public administration, legislation – that nowadays are recognized as 'public' ones. The removal of autonomous seigneuries fitted into the framework of these efforts. When things did not succeed immediately, banal lords were at least forced into a feudal relationship. In this way the possession of a lordship was politicized and became part of the mechanism for distributing political power. Particularly in the later medieval German Empire, territorial princes gave seigneurial rights of their own accord, especially over villages, in fief. This is sometimes called '(low) jurisdictional lordship', because it generally included only limited exercise of justice and local government, and there was no question of real autonomy. The position and the jurisdiction of such 'jurisdictional lords' is in no way comparable to that of the banal lords of a far earlier period.

Changes in the surplus extraction. Adjustments in the demesne economy

The establishment of banal lordships led to considerable shifts in agrarian surplus extraction; that is, the extent to which, and the way in which, income was transferred from peasants to lords. Before that time the transfer was settled chiefly through obligatory services of labour and the payment of surpluses by serf peasants within the framework of the manorial system and 'land-lordship'. Banal lords, on the other hand, exploited people – whether as serfs or not – in a well-defined territory on the basis of usurped public authority.

This shift was closely connected to the evolution of the manorial system itself, which, during the period of expansion, fell into decline wherever it had been prevalent, except in England. There are a number of deeper-lying reasons for the decline. It is quite possible that financial problems of the aristocracy played a role. With the general increase in population, the aristocracy increased too, and that meant that the inheritances for succeeding generations gradually became smaller. In many regions the relative impoverishment was underlined by the often extravagantly large gifts of land and tithes made to Church institutions. These were probably intended as gifts with a proviso through which the donors retained certain rights, in particular rights of usufruct. However, in their attempts to reduce secular influences on the Church, and with the revival in canon law of the concepts of ownership borrowed from Roman law, abbeys and other ecclesiastical institutions began to look upon gifts as permanent transfers of property. In some areas, too, the ownership of many tithes, an important source of revenue for the aristocracy, was returned to the Church. Falling incomes contrasted with rising costs. These were caused in part by the increased costs of warfare, in part by the re-opening of trade with the Middle East that made countless desirable luxury goods (including spices, silk and ivory) available, so that the aristocratic way of life became more sophisticated but above all more expensive.

Moreover, the disappearance of the classical manorial system from many regions of Europe during the period of expansion can be explained more neutrally by two economic developments. First, rising urbanization simultaneously created demand for agricultural products and offered employment outside agriculture. This partly offset the effects of the second development; namely, the inversion of the land–labour ratio, the scarcity relationship between the production factors of land and labour. As a result of the growth in population, land became scarcer and more expensive, and labour more plentiful and cheaper. This stimulated the conversion of serf labour services into delivery in cash or kind. Serf labour services in the manorial system were, after all, connected to the ownership of a farmstead, and were originally intended to ensure that labour, which was scarce, was kept on the manor. Large landowners who had dispensed entirely with the labour services of serfs when it was no longer labour but land that was scarce, were now faced with a stark choice. They could completely abandon the direct exploitation of their demesnes, and then lease out the *indominicatum* (land held in demesne) in its entirety or in parts on hereditary lease or short-term lease; or they could continue to keep the land in direct use, but now exploit it with the help of paid labourers. During the eleventh and twelfth centuries large landowners all over Europe chose primarily the second option, but in the longer term preference was given to the first alternative. The new monastic orders of Cistercians and Premonstratensians formed an exception. They were able to continue with the direct exploitation of their land by bringing in so-called *conversi*, simple lay brothers who provided the order with cheap labour. England was again somewhat out of step insofar as, from the end of the twelfth century, many lords of manors (secular and ecclesiastical) resisted the switch from serf labour services in order to profit as much as possible from the high grain prices. In England the manorial system was maintained in its classical bipartite form until well into the fourteenth century.

Outside England not only did serf labour services tied to the direct exploitation of the manor disappear but other servile obligations could also be gradually commuted into fixed money payments, like the lord's right to the best of the movable property in a serf's legacy or to compensation for serf daughters who wanted to marry someone from outside the manor. The entire development had three serious consequences. First, over time serfdom lost much of its real significance; in many areas this was translated into the disappearance of the legal status of serfs and the specific customary law attached to it (the whole complex of legal regulations to which serfs were subject). This led to greater social differentiation and geographic mobility in the countryside. Second, the fact that it was possible to commute serf labour and to buy off other servile obligations in regions where there were many manors meant a breakthrough in the commercialization and monetization of the rural economy. Peasants were now compelled to convert either their surpluses or their own labour into money. And third, the manor lords themselves suffered losses insofar as labour services or other servile obligations were converted into cash payments. Rents were fixed once and for all, while the thirteenth century was a century of rapid inflation. The real value of the periodic payments was soon eroded, to the advantage of the paying tenants. At a later stage manor lords tried to counteract this by letting out parts of the demesne over which they still had some control on a short-term lease for a limited number of years. An alternative was the sharecropping or divided lease (French *champart* is derived from the Latin *campi pars*, meaning 'part of the field'), which was most common in certain parts of France and Italy. In this system the owner received a fixed share, usually one-third or one-quarter – but in Italy later one-half also (*mezzadria*) – of the gross yields of the lands he had leased out.

KNIGHTS AND PEASANTS IN THE MEDIEVAL IMAGE OF SOCIETY

The installation of banal lordships or similar forms of control can be seen as the tailpiece of an earlier-discussed, lengthy socio-historical process: the gradual formation of a new style of warrior aristocracy. This was reflected in the earliest examples of the three estates or orders that have survived from the ninth century (see Chapter 5). The theme is much more explicitly discussed in what is perhaps the most important socio-philosophical statement from the period round the year 1000, the *Carmen ad Rothbertum regem* (Song for King Robert), composed by Adalbero, bishop of Laon, in 1027 for the French king Robert the Pious (996–1031). In this work the widely known division of society into three estates ('those who pray, those who fight and those who labour') is contaminated with a division between nobles and 'freemen' on the one hand and serfs on the other. But however society was divided it was the firm belief of the clerical elite that it always had to function organically, as one body: every social group corresponded to a part of the body; the whole only worked well if all the parts were in their own place, performed their own tasks and worked together in harmony when necessary. In this chapter we are going to focus on the 'fighters' and the 'labourers' outlined by Adalbero; 'those who pray' will have their turn in Chapter 8.

Horsemen become knights

One of the most fascinating socio-historical phenomena of all medieval history was the formation of the knighthood from three elements. We have already touched upon the first two: the growing tactical importance of heavily armed cavalry in the course of the early Middle Ages, and, subsequently, the formation of mounted militias by the banal lords. The third element should be seen in part as a clerical reaction to this, but at the same time it had deeper historical roots: the conscious policy of the clergy to represent the aristocracy as fighters in the service of the holy Church, with the king in the forefront, ready to take up arms to defend the social order desired by God.

The first development led to a clear professionalization of the mounted fighter, which was speeded up even further by progressive technological advances in weaponry and equipment: the perfecting of the chain-mail hauberk and of many types of weapons for striking and stabbing, horse armour, nailed horseshoes and the panelled war saddle with its high, wraparound cantle and pommel. In addition to great skill, the result of long training, the fighter on horseback needed a large fortune, and that was why armed horsemen – *milites* in the Latin of the time – were predominantly aristocrats. Already in Carolingian Francia, the recognition of an aristocratic youth as a *miles*, a true (mounted) warrior, by being ceremonially girded with a sword, was closely associated to the idea that it was this act that made men fit to exercise *honor*, public office, as well as to defend the holy Church against its enemies.

But professionalization also implied that physical fitness, talent and assured loyalty all played a part beside birth and wealth in the recruitment of mounted warriors, while specific historical circumstances would also have an influence of course. We have already seen that banal lordships were partly based on small private armies of horsemen who were equipped and maintained at the expense of the lords of the castles. The often denigrating references to these horsemen lead us to surmise that they were not always of noble origins. In the German Empire kings and holders of high office recruited their horsemen from the unfree estate of *ministerials*, especially in the decades round 1100. On the borders of the Reconquest in Castile and Catalonia there arose a class of peasant horsemen, *caballeros villanos*. The cavalry of the communal armies of the free city-states of North and central Italy had from the beginning a mixed noble-bourgeois character. In England, the Norman Conquest of 1066 was of overwhelming importance: here *milites* referred to the mounted fighters in the army of William the Conqueror, often of noble French origin, who became 'tenants' of the 'tenants-in-chief', the secular 'barons' and dignitaries of the Church who had a direct bond with the king (the Anglo-Norman equivalent of the royal vassals on the Continent). In the decades immediately after 1066 the position of these *milites-*

tenants and their enfeoffment with one or more estates (manors) was emphatically connected to their service as mounted fighters.

Through the growing degree of technical and tactical competence demanded of these mounted fighters, through the crucial role they played in the great military operations of the eleventh century, which at the time greatly fired the imagination, and through their increasingly expensive weapons and equipment, the prestige of the *milites* rose almost before their very eyes. What then happened is remarkable: *milites* of high aristocratic birth allowed themselves to be identified with horsemen of more humble origins. Even monarchs present themselves as mounted warriors. William the Conqueror, for example, is depicted in the Bayeux tapestry more often as a horseman among his *milites* than as a monarch on his throne. After Otto II of Germany, who was one of the first kings to have a seal made showing him as a warrior on horseback, many rulers would follow the example. This fusion of high aristocratic, minor noble and non-noble, sometimes even unfree, elements into an elite military corps that in time became difficult to distinguish from the nobility, was coupled with the development of an *esprit de corps*, a new code of honour and behaviour with its own what we now might call 'sub-culture', while entry to the group was formalized in solemn ceremonial, such as being girded with the *cingulum militiae* ('the girdle of the militia'), and the bestowal of the sword – the accolade only dates from the thirteenth century. From then on we no longer speak of horsemen but of knights, and we speak of the knighthood, of the order of knights (*ordo militaris* in Latin) or of chivalry.

Within the knightly code of behaviour traditional values – many would say universal values – such as courage, loyalty and fellowship always remained important. But in addition to that, the construction of a knightly ethos received the support of the Church from the very beginning. For this purpose an old concept was unearthed: that of *miles Christi* or *miles Sancti Petri* ('soldier of Christ' or 'soldier of Saint Peter'). In early Christendom this title of honour was first given to clerics in general and martyrs in particular. In the fifth and sixth centuries it was passed on to the monks, the new body of the Christian elite. Then it was the turn of the bishops, as we can see from a pastoral letter sent by Pope Nicholas I to the bishops of the West

Frankish Empire in 865. The pope forbade the bishops to take part in any more armed conflicts, for they were the *milites Christi* and, as such, should only fight battles of a spiritual nature and exclusively in the service of the pope.

Oddly enough, it was this concept of *miles Christi* that was regenerated in the circles round Pope Gregory VII soon after the middle of the eleventh century, in an attempt to harness the secular *milites* for the Church by propagating, in addition to bravery and fidelity, such Christian virtues as godliness, the defence of the helpless and peace (towards fellow-Christians). The fight against non-Christians, the infidel enemies of the faith in Spain and the Holy Land, provided unprecedented new opportunities for cloaking the *milites* in Christian ideals. Conversely, efforts to make the clerical morality more military and heroic were much in evidence, as was clearly shown in the *Liber ad milites Templi de laude novae militiae* (Book for the Knights of the Temple in Praise of the New Knighthood) written in about 1145 by that Cistercian pillar of the Christian Church, Bernard of Clairvaux. It is a eulogy of the new religious orders of knighthood, which came into being in the Holy Land at the end of the First Crusade to defend the conquered holy places and to protect, if necessary by force, the newly swelling stream of pilgrims.

The oldest of these unique orders was the 'brotherhood of the poor knights of Christ' founded by the French crusader, Hugo de Payns, and recognized in 1128 as the Order of the Temple (the Knights Templar). This was soon followed by the Order of St John of Jerusalem (the Knights Hospitaller, known from the sixteenth century as the Knights of Malta), the Order of the hospital of St Mary of the Germans (the German or Teutonic Order), and a whole series of smaller, less expansive orders in the Baltic area and in Spain and Portugal, where they held huge estates until well into the early modern era. Both clerics and laypeople could join these orders, but only the latter swore an oath of battle; as compensation, in some orders they were not bound to celibacy.

Bernard of Clairvaux found these new spiritual orders of knighthood the highest possible fulfilment of the new ideal of the *militia Christi*. 'Ordinary' knights – Bernard's *milites saeculi* – were not in the same league: in his view they renounced their original chivalric ideals

by paying exaggerated attention to their appearance and their emphasis on outward show. By this outward show Bernard meant the sub-culture that was growing up around the knights and of which diverse matters such as heraldry, clothing, hair style and training formed a part. By the beginning of the twelfth century there was already much hostile criticism of knights' attire in clerical circles. They looked like women, even on the field of battle where they were decked out in gold and silver jewels. Slightly later there were suspicions about the jousts and tournaments, which probably grew out of the knights' training in arms in about 1100 and rapidly developed into excessively popular spectacles. Because participants were frequently killed, the rules of the game were altered, partly under pressure from the Church, which first prohibited tournaments in 1130. When that was not effective, in 1139 the Church denied Christian burial to knights who died during these tournaments; but this measure met with equally little success.

Only the ritual of inauguration could count on the Church's unceasing approval. It was with this ceremony that the Church had the opportunity fully to immerse the candidate-knight, through rites and symbolic acts, in the Christian values that it saw as the foundations of chivalry. Those who aspired to knighthood also swore to protect the Church and clergy. Moreover, the whole ceremony usually took place in a church or chapel, unless a man was dubbed knight on the battlefield.

Courtly culture: new rules for moving in high circles

The new virtues of chivalry were imprinted during the inaugural ceremonial by moral tracts and didactic poems aimed especially at the chivalric lifestyle, but also through completely new literary genres that formed a part of the so-called courtly culture. The term 'courtly' (*courtois* in French) refers to the courts of monarchs and other great princes who set themselves up as the natural leaders of the new order of knights. Central to the knightly etiquette was 'courtliness', a rather vague concept that has been studied principally from the viewpoint of the history of literature. However, it points towards a specific code of behaviour aimed at:

- the regulation of tensions and avoidance of open aggression and feuds, especially between young men whose entire upbringing was focused on the use of force; and
- achieving an important place at court through the acquisition of 'honour'.

In the beginning this code of behaviour was elaborated in a sort of programme of etiquette, most of which is still considered good manners in our western culture, and which was memorized in simple maxims such as the Middle German 'Wirff nit nauch pürschem Sin/die Spaichel über den Tisch hin' ('Never expectorate over the table like a peasant'). Of a rather more elevated nature were the virtues that the ideal knight was expected to possess: loyalty, (moral) purity, moderation, sense of honour, generosity and readiness to help, coupled with physical strength and control, and a certain knowledge of the world. In this list 'honour' – with its counterpart 'dishonour' – was probably the most important. Honour adhered, as it were, to high social status, but could also be acquired by performing honourable deeds. Bravery in battle (*prouesse* in Old French) was of course essential for knights. But courtly culture required that a warlike spirit be directed to a more sublime goal. Honour did not really count if it was not earned in the service of another person, preferably a lady or a great prince, or, better still, the Christian faith. Only then did honour pave the way to high esteem and especially to (courtly) love and personal salvation.

The two most important characteristics of courtly love (*amour courtois* in French) – a term that was forged into one total concept out of different constituent parts by literary historians only in the nineteenth century – are the inversion of the traditional role pattern (in courtly love the man serves a lady, not vice versa) and the moral improvement to which courtly love can lead (courtly love makes the lovers, in particular the man, morally better people). For the improvement to be fully effected the lover should suffer the necessary privations and humiliations and perform deeds of self-sacrifice and valour for his loved one. But all is well that ends well, and he could then savour the true joys of love.

The practice of courtly love must have been a sophisticated, and now and then perhaps naughty, game with its own complicated set of rules. If the literary texts are

Plate 7.2 A man and a woman playing chess in a tent. Ivory back of a hand mirror from the fourteenth century

to be believed, courtly love at the royal courts was attended to in special parlour games, such as 'the law courts of love' and the *jeux partis* ('shared games'), where the various players took turns to defend another viewpoint over leading questions such as 'If your lady makes the spending of a night of love with you depend on her toothless old husband, would you rather have your turn before or after?'

Apart from the fact that such vulgar aspects of courtly love were completely at odds with Christian ethics on marriage and conjugal love, the whole complexity of ideas about courtliness and courtly love formed a 'social Utopia', in the words of Joachim Bumke, that bore little resemblance to the grim reality of everyday life in a medieval castle. This can be well illustrated by the way women were treated. If the idealized, courtly image of the woman was based on (in our eyes) toe-curling clichés such as 'external beauty is the reflection of a pure soul', it speaks volumes about the fundamentally ambivalent attitude towards women held by men from the higher classes in those days – women were by nature inferior, but at the same time could be models of virtue. It is true that, incidentally, aristocratic women rose to great power, especially as queens or queens-regent over underage princes, but even in that latter situation there were always men pulling the strings. More generally, it has been said that the more land and wealth a woman owned, or could claim by right, 'the more likely she was to be controlled and manipulated by male relatives or lords' (Stafford). Even if one is not inclined to follow such a cynical view of medieval society, one would have to admit that medieval women, certainly aristocratic women, did not enjoy anything like modern western personal liberties. During their youth they were kept strictly secluded from men; many noble girls never married and disappeared into a convent; and those who did marry were given in marriage and were completely subject to the husband's authority. In terms of legal autonomy and freedom of action, the best position for women to have was that of a widow beyond the need or age of remarriage.

On top of ingrained convictions of male superiority and natural dominance over women, there was an unvarying double standard in cases of premarital or extramarital relations, and the whole concept of courtly love and the obsessive longing for unattainable women predominant in it has been interpreted as an outlet for the younger sons of noble families who often felt neglected in their inheritance and could never enjoy the prestige of their father or elder brother. They could do little more than hope for a good marriage or good fortune in battle. In anticipation of this they roamed from castle to castle projecting their erotic feelings on the wife or daughter, for example, of the lord they served as *miles*. In the courtly love of these young knights-errant for unattainable women one variant sees a metaphor for the loyalty owed by vassals to their liege lord. Behind the (literary) expressions of courtly love, then, lay the hidden ambitions of the lower echelons of the nobility to win a place through their skill at arms at one of the larger or small courts scattered throughout feudal Europe. In both views courtly love still remained 'essentially a system men created with the dreams of men in mind' (Meg Bogin).

Courtly culture and courtly love found a literary vehicle in three new genres that flourished in the twelfth and thirteenth centuries: the *chansons de geste*, the courtly lyric and the romances of chivalry. Of the *chansons de geste* (literally 'songs of exploits'), epic texts focusing on the deeds of one person, the subject matter of which

is often borrowed from the time of Charlemagne, the oldest group is probably the most interesting from a socio-historical point of view. The chansons belonging to this group, like *Raoul de Cambrai* (written in the last quarter of the twelfth century), paint a revealing picture of the feudal nobility of northern France as they liked to see themselves: extremely violent and preoccupied with problems of loyalty raised by the rapidly spreading feudo-vassalic networks. At the same time these texts betray the new sensitivity, described previously, which at first sight belies the tough mentality of the knights. How could these bloodthirsty lovers of force ever be moved to tears by stories where ladies faint when they hear of the death of their beloved husbands? And yet this is the sort of sentiment sung in the oldest chanson we know, the *Chanson de Roland* (Song of Roland, *c.* 1120), which tells of the heroic death of one of Charlemagne's army leaders in a battle against the Basques.

The second literary genre that came into being at this time – the courtly lyric, sometimes called the poetry of the troubadours – overflows with this new sentimentality. Its origins can in part be found in the Arabic and Mozarabic culture of the Spain of the tenth and eleventh centuries. Not only the themes but also the rhyme schemes and music are of Arabic origin, as is the word 'troubadour' itself, which probably derives from the Arabic *tarraba*, 'to stir up emotions through song'. Other influences include the Christian religious genre of the Marian hymns and the revived intellectual interest in the love poetry of the Roman poet Ovid. Out of this mixture there developed in Provence and the south of France a complex poetry with an exact form and a new world-view. Although crude erotic verse also has a place in the genre, the woman is generally placed on a pedestal, and the love between a man and a woman is elevated to an ideal of moral self-fulfilment, often achieved only after intense inner conflict. During the thirteenth century the troubadours' poetry, which was composed in Occitan (the language spoken in the south of France at the time), became a symbol of the widespread resistance to the efforts both of the king of France, who wanted to tighten his grip on the south, and of the pope, who wanted to stamp out Catharism, which had been condemned as a heresy. The poetry of the troubadours had a profound influence on the courtly lyrics of other regions, including Sicily (and through Sicily on the great Tuscan poets of the thirteenth and fourteenth centuries) and Germany, where in the thirteenth century Walter von der Vogelweide and Ulrich von Liechtenstein were considered most accomplished *Minnesänger* ('love song singers').

Finally, the younger courtly epic, the real romances of chivalry, combined elements from the *chanson de geste* and the poetry of the troubadours. The works in this genre paint a strongly idealized picture of reality and are brimming with erotic and mystical religious symbolism. It is often difficult for today's readers to fathom the deeper meaning, and that makes it awkward to link the contents to the reality of those days. The pioneer in the field was Chrétien de Troyes, who is often called the father of the romance: for his works he drew from a new vein that had been opened in England in the twelfth century, the *matière de Bretagne* ('material from Brittany'), stories about another legendary figure of the early Middle Ages, King Arthur. In Chrétien's works – written in French between about 1150 and 1180 – courtly and religious sentiments and ideals were woven together with a powerful imagination and a feeling for character development. The adventurous life of a knight was now presented as a spiritual quest in a dream landscape that can be interpreted at different levels – the quest for divine grace, the search for his own identity or place in the aristocratic community, etc. Chrétien sees love as a magical power that can break all social conventions but also rise above them to a higher transcendental level of experience. At the same time his views on love were not just romantic and mystic. In *Erec et Enide* Chrétien suggested to his aristocratic audience that only those who had a heart for the political community over which they were appointed were good enough to rule.

Chrétien's arrangement of the material from Brittany served as a model far beyond France and long after the Middle Ages, in both poetry and prose, but always in the vernacular. The German Arthurian romances of Wolfram von Eschenbach and Hartmann von Aue are considered among the most successful versions; the third great German composer of Arthurian romances in the Middle Ages, Gottfried von Strassburg, used another French-language work as a model for his famous *Tristan*. The influence of courtly literature on western literature has been enormous. It introduced the model of romantic love throughout Europe. What started as a stylized game for courtiers in real castles has been watered down over the centuries to become today's sentimental novel.

Tendencies towards classification and separateness

The time when Chrétien de Troyes was writing his great romances also marked the gradual conclusion of a process that had started two centuries earlier. In different parts of Europe this process took other forms and went at different speeds, but everywhere it set two trends in motion:

1 *A tendency towards internal ranking.* Because there were knights of all sorts and qualities, there was a need to mark the differences in their status. This happened in two ways: first, a distinction between knights from the old nobility and knights of non-noble origin continued to be made in the forms of address and in the sequence in which witnesses were listed in documents; second, through the creation of separate ranks for very important knights, such as the rank of banneret, a knight who led his knight-vassals into battle under his own banner. Because bannerets in their turn were vassals of greater lords (kings, princes), vassalage was an important ranking criterion within knighthood – as it was within the nobility.

2 *A tendency to separateness.* Between about 1130 and 1250 the status of knight became hereditary everywhere. This meant that the criterion of achievement – a knight is an accomplished fighter – was gradually replaced by the criterion of birth – a knight is the son of a knight. Because each son of a knight was now automatically included in the knighthood, while he only really entered the *ordo militaris* after he had received the accolade and been granted the title of knight, a sort of candidate status came into existence in the knighthood – that of squire. For financial reasons, many sons of knights remained squires until they were of advanced age, for the ceremony of investiture into the *ordo militaris* was extremely expensive. The status of squire also required the maintenance of a knightly lifestyle that many young men from

knightly families could no longer afford, yet they often continued to enjoy the fiscal and other privileges linked to their knightly origins for a long time. However, nowhere in the late Middle Ages did knighthood become a fully closed estate, dictated by birth alone. Rich townspeople and even wealthy peasants always managed to find a way in, although only in small numbers. Monarchs always retained the right to elevate individuals to the nobility or to the knighthood, which amounted to the same thing.

Otherwise, there were considerable regional differences in the extent and speed with which knighthood and nobility – or aristocracy – merged. The assimilation went furthest in Catalonia, France and the German regions that were strongly influenced by France, such as Hainaut and Holland in the Low Countries, or the kingdom of Aragon in Spain. Here knighthood and nobility fully coincided.

Plate 7.3 Equestrian statue of a knight, symbolizing the miles Christi, in the choir of Bamberg cathedral

The core territories of the German Empire, northern and central Italy and England underwent a rather different development. The merger of nobility and knighthood got started later in the German Empire than in France, and was never fully completed because knighthood was always associated with the non-free estate of *ministerials*. The element of service made the knighthood unattractive for the high nobility, at least, although some knights of *ministerial* origins managed to become recognized as noble, and German kings from Frederick Barbarossa onwards called themselves 'knight'. In the late Middle Ages a person was counted in the lower nobility if he did not rank higher than *Ritter*. The high or 'free' nobility preferred to call themselves *nobilis*, although all high noblemen were also knights. The separateness of the higher nobility was strengthened in the twelfth century by the recognition in feudal law of the 'imperial princes' (*Reichsfürsten*), the approximately one hundred and forty ecclesiastical and secular lords who had a direct feudal tie to the German king. A second characteristic of the knighthood in the German core lands is that the tendency to separateness began relatively early, also in the twelfth century. An important step was taken in the *Constitutio contra incendiarios* (Law against arsonists) that was included in the Imperial Land Peace of 1186. It laid down that thenceforth the children of priests, deacons and peasants could not become knights.

In the *comuni*, the city-states of northern and central Italy, we have seen that from time immemorial the knighthood formed an amalgam of noble and non-noble elements with one aristocratic lifestyle. What was typical of the Italian cities was that these knighthoods did not include all *milites*, because, beside the new meaning of 'knights', *milites* still retained the old, wider meaning of 'riders', and the urban mounted cavalry did not consist solely of members of the nobility/knighthood. The wealthier elements of the ordinary citizenry also had to turn out on horseback in times of war. For example, in the great battle of Montaperti in 1260, when the communal army of Florence was smashed by that of its arch-rival Siena, the Florentine cavalry consisted of 1,650 men (including 100 mercenaries) against more than 14,000 infantry. Only some of these 1,650 were noblemen (*milites de granditia* or *milites nobiles*), the remainder (*milites de popolo* or *milites popolani*) were not. Not until the fourteenth century was the compulsory mobilization of man and horse in great cities like Florence replaced by a monetary payment that was used to recruit mercenaries.

The same thing had happened in England much earlier. Soon after the Norman Conquest, the *milites* or knights formed a fairly sizeable group of between 4,000 and 5,000 men, which would swell during the twelfth century. Their position was then still chiefly defined in feudo-military terms: they were liegemen of crown tenants who had to follow their lords as fully armed horsemen in times of war. This was the basic agreement of their fief, known as the 'knight's fee' ('fee' is derived from *feodum*, a fief). The social status of this group was not particularly high, and the knights of this time were not generally counted as nobility. This changed in the thirteenth century when their numbers began to dwindle to about 3,000. By that time compulsory attendance had long become commutable, for a sum of money known as scutage (from *scutagium*, literally meaning 'shield money'). From that time, too, the *knightly class* should be seen as strictly separate from the *knighthood*. The former included all families who carried the title of knight; the latter included only those who could, or wished to, afford the lifestyle of a knight and who had themselves formally admitted to the *ordo militaris*. Members of both the knightly class and the higher nobility (baronage or peerage) belonged to this *ordo*. In 1200 the English knighthood would have had about 1,500 members. From the thirteenth century on, the knightly class began to be identified with the lower nobility, in later sources usually referred to as the 'gentry'. The gentry would gradually acquire a permanent role in local government and be looked upon as the natural representative of the local community.

Peasants

Around the year 1000, the workers (*laboratores*) of the tripartite scheme of estates were predominantly peasants. The literate, clerical elite viewed them with mixed feelings. In one passage of the *Carmen ad Rothbertum regem*, Adalbero of Laon speaks compassionately of the harsh fate of the serfs; in another, of the 'lazy, misshapen and in every respect contemptible rustic' (*rusticus piger, deformis et undique turpis*). Adalbero's views on this matter were not very original either. From the Carolingian period many small, free peasants, with their essentially 'public' tasks (attendance in the host and courts of law), lost not only their standing but also, as we have seen, their personal freedom. The rise of knighthood and the growth of towns then led to an increasingly negative stereotyping of peasants, which was completely at odds with the vital social function that was invariably allocated to them in the organic view of society, with the Christian ideal of poverty that they represented and with the concern for the violent circumstances in which they were obliged to live. Attitudes towards low-ranking social groups are often ambivalent. They express a mixture of contempt, compassion and fear, and perhaps, too, an unconscious need to rationalize and justify clear social inequalities.

At the centre of this negative stereotype was a sort of 'bestialization', the identification of peasants with beasts, which in some respects can be compared to the ancient and early medieval view of barbarians, infidels (Muslims, Jews) and slaves. A wide range of harmful and harmless vices was then given to that beast image, from wild savagery to madness, stupidity, and 'an extraordinary proclivity for flatulence' (Freedman). They are referred to in a wide variety of works. Learned political tracts from clerical circles spread the notion that peasants were boorish 'barbarians', an 'asinine race', 'half-savages who cannot govern themselves and are therefore doomed to serfdom', found Aegidius Romanus in *De potestate ecclesiastica* ('On the power of the Church') in 1301. Deadly serious historical works thought that peasants were unable to make love, because one could hardly call their animal urge to copulate by such a name (*Li histoire de Julius César*). Peasants were – even then – the butt of countless crude jokes (*fabliaux, Schwanken*) in which their ignorance, filth and violence formed an easy target for merciless ridicule. Legal texts such as the *Usatges de Barcelona* ('Customs of Barcelona') defined peasants as 'beings that possessed no other value than that of being Christian' – and even that was openly doubted sometimes. And in the standard work on courtly love, *De amore* (1185), the author, André the Chaplain, bluntly suggests that the courtly gallantries to which (noble) ladies were entitled were wasted on peasant girls. André advised his (noble, male) readers to mount them without ceremony, a counsel that was repeated in countless variations in another popular and most approriate literary genre of the later Middle Ages: the pastourelle or 'shepherd's song'. Both in courtly literary works in the proper sense, and even more so in parodies, such as Neidhart's poetical praises of country girls (*c.* 1225), courtliness was willingly contrasted with *rusticitas*, lumpish rusticity. Peasant behaviour was non-courtly in every respect, and contrary to everything a knight stood for: honour, skill at love, courage, moderation. Peasants were just cowardly and lecherous yokels with no sense of decorum.

Should peasants now be considered the underdogs of the medieval world only on the basis of their negative treatment in literary and legal works? There are three reasons for a more balanced view. First, there is the impression that the burden of surplus extraction (see p. 117) slowly diminished during the period of expansion. The deeper background to this is that by medieval standards even peasants were not without rights. Local customary law remained strong in rural areas throughout the Middle Ages, and in the long term the strength of certain customs turned out favourably for the peasants as a class – among them was a serf's right to transmit his farm and land to his children, and the custom that once dues had been set they could not be changed. Second, the increasingly open nature of the agricultural economy during the period of expansion offered peasants opportunities to operate on different product and factor markets, although the risks attached were very real. Third, the social position for negotiation and political involvement of peasants was improved considerably by the development of village communities. In the early Middle Ages the inhabitants of country settlements certainly built up collective activities. These activities were expanded and accentuated with the growth of settlements and housing density and the disappearance of the manorial system. All this has already been indicated in a number of areas: open-field farming was not possible without collective decisions on the sequence of crops sown, beginning the harvest, grazing the stubble and preparing the ground. The extensive use of nearby undeveloped land for pasturing cattle, the gathering and chopping of wood, the cutting of clay or peat and the like – all demanded a degree of management and arrangements with neighbouring communities. In low-lying fen and clay areas, permanent settlement depended on the good organization of drainage and dike maintenance. Then the expansion and density of the network of country parishes brought a collective concern for the building and maintenance of parish churches (for which the parishioners were themselves responsible), and coupled to this was the organization of the local poor relief.

All this led to the establishment of a great variety of local institutions, such as neighbourhoods, marks (local organizations for the management of common pasture and woodland), water boards, and foundations for the maintenance of the parish church and poor relief respectively; they all came together in what was called the village community or *community of the vill* (*communitas villae* in Latin). The term is also found in older sources, but it acquired a new connotation in the twelfth and thirteenth centuries: not only did these village communities have a *de facto* legal personality, giving them the competence to act on behalf of the local community, they also started to exercise powers that we consider nowadays to be in the public domain – local government, issuing local regulations or by-laws and imposing fines on offenders. A bench of *jurati* (sworn men) or *scabini* (aldermen) was often elected to exercise these powers, which were not as yet separate; it consisted of resident peasants, and its composition changed periodically. Sometimes there was no bench and it was the assembly of all the villagers together that governed and administered justice. In that case local officials were appointed just to carry out the tasks. The competence of village communities in the administration of justice was often (but not in principle) limited to judging disputes and infringements of local regulations. Serious crimes, for which corporal or capital punishment was laid down, had to be brought before a higher court of law, usually consisting of noblemen. Just like the towns, villages could also acquire privileges granted by charter, so that they became 'liberties'. We know these existed in central Italy, the north of France and the duchy of Brabant. The propagation of 'liberty' in this sort of charter was sometimes coupled with a rather ridiculous appeal to ancient Roman or biblical-Christian traditions, as if villages became republics freed from tyranny overnight, or, like the Jewish people, had left the slavery of Egypt and crossed the Red Sea in search of the Promised Land. In practice, the granted 'liberty' meant little more than that all the villagers were personally free (the denial of serfdom) or that the *malae consuetudines* were eased, and that the local authority could apply its own law and generally had slightly wider powers than ordinary village communities.

This development of village communities with statutory powers did not take place in Scandinavia or England. Sweden was simply too thinly populated. There the *hundare* or *härad* remained the lowest unit of local government, districts that usually comprised a number of villages or parishes and held jointly a law court or *ting*. In England there were indeed communities of the vill, but they were of little significance because of the continued existence of the manor, the English version of the continental *curtis* or *villa*, which was the most important framework of local organization in rural areas; local government and justice was dealt with in the manor court, the law court of the lord of the manor, and by present-day standards was not of a public nature.

Finally, in emergencies, medieval peasants did not shrink from organizing armed resistance to oppressive lords, thus showing themselves to be far less helpless than clerical and courtly literature liked to depict them. From the thirteenth century there are examples of knightly armies being cut to pieces by peasant militias: in 1227 near the village of Ane in the northern Low Countries, in about 1230 during the so-called revolt of the Stedingers on the lower Weser, and in 1315 at the pass near Morgarten in the Swiss Alps. But, as we see from the countless individual and collective lawsuits that they fought in higher courts of law against noble or clerical landowners and which often dealt with everyday matters, such as the use of woods and peat lands, even if there was no physical combat involved medieval peasants were able to hold their own.

FURTHER READING

Arnold, Benjamin (2004), *Power and Property in Medieval Germany: Economic and Social Change, c.900–1300* (Oxford: Oxford University Press).

Astill, Grenville and John Langdon (eds) (1997), *Medieval Farming and Technology. The Impact of Agricultural Change in Northwest Europe* (Leiden: Brill).

Barber, Malcolm (1994), *The New Knighthood. A History of the Order of the Temple* (Cambridge: Cambridge University Press).

Bartlett, Robert (1993), *The Making of Europe. Conquest, Colonization and Cultural Change 950–1350* (London: Allen Lane).

Barton, Richard E. (2004), *Lordship in the County of Maine, c.890–1160* (Woodbridge and Rochester, N.Y.: Boydell & Brewer).

Berkhofer, Robert F., Alan Cooper and Adam J. Kosto (eds) (2005), *The Experience of Power in Medieval Europe, 950–1350* (Aldershot: Ashgate).

Bisson, Thomas N. (1998), *Tormented Voices: Power, Crisis, and Humanity in Rural Catalonia, 1140–1200* (Cambridge, Mass. and London: Harvard University Press).

—— (ed.) (1995), *Cultures of Power: Lordship, Status and Process in Twelfth-Century Europe* (Philadelphia, Pa.: University of Pennsylvania Press).

Bowman, Jeffrey (2004), *Shifting Landmarks: Property, Proof, and Dispute in Catalonia Around the Year 1000* (Ithaca, N.Y.: Cornell University Press).

Brown, Warren C. and Piotr Górecki (eds) (2003), *Conflict in Medieval Europe. Changing Perspectives on Society and Culture* (Aldershot: Ashgate).

Bumke, Joachim (2004), *Courtly Culture: Literature and Society in the High Middle Ages* (London: Duckworth) (orig. German, 1986).

Cheyette, Fredric L. (2001), *Ermengard of Narbonne and the World of the Troubadours* (Ithaca, N.Y.: Cornell University Press).

Coss, Peter (1991), *Lordship, Knighthood and Locality: A Study in English Society, c.1180–c.1280* (Cambridge: Cambridge University Press).

—— (1993), *The Knight in Medieval England 1000–1400* (Stroud: Alan Sutton Publishing).

Crouch, David (2005), *Tournament* (London and New York: Hambledon & London).

Duby, Georges (1974), *The Early Growth of the European Economy. Warriors and Peasants from the Seventh to the Twelfth Century* (London: Weidenfeld & Nicolson) (orig. French, 1973).

Echard, Siân (ed.) (1998), *Arthurian Narrative in the Latin Tradition* (Cambridge: Cambridge University Press).

Freedman, Paul (1999), *Images of the Medieval*

Peasant (Stanford, Calif. and Cambridge: Stanford University Press).

Genicot, Léopold (1990), *Rural Communities in the Medieval West* (Baltimore, Md. and London: Johns Hopkins University Press).

Glick, Thomas F. (1995), *From Muslim Fortress to Christian Castle. Social and Cultural Change in Medieval Spain* (Manchester and New York: Manchester University Press).

Hahn, Thomas (ed.) (2000), *Robin Hood in Popular Culture: Violence, Transgression and Justice* (Woodbridge and Rochester, N.Y.: Boydell & Brewer).

Harvey, Alan (1989), *Economic Expansion in the Byzantine Empire 900–1200* (Cambridge: Cambridge University Press).

Jaeger, C. Stephen (1985), *The Origins of Courtliness: Civilizing Trends and the Formation of Courtly Ideals 923–1210* (Philadelphia, Pa.: University of Pennsylvania Press).

Kaeuper, Richard W. (1999), *Chivalry and Violence in Medieval Europe* (Oxford: Oxford University Press).

Keen, Maurice (1984), *Chivalry* (New Haven, Conn. and London: Yale University Press).

Knight, Stephen (2003), *Robin Hood: A Mythic Biography* (Ithaca, N.Y. and London: Cornell University Press).

Moore, Robert I. (2000), *The First European Revolution, c.970–1215* (Oxford and Malden, Mass.: Blackwell).

Muir, Lynette R. (1985), *Literature and Society in Medieval France: The Mirror and the Image, 1100–1500* (London and New York: Macmillan/St Martin's Press).

Nicholson, Helen (1995), *Templars, Hospitallers and Teutonic Knights. Images of the Military Orders 1128–1291* (Leicester: Leicester University Press).

Philips, J.R.S. (1998) *The Medieval Expansion of Europe*, 2nd edn (Oxford: Oxford University Press).

Poly, Jean-Pierre and Eric Bournazel (1991), *The Feudal Transformation, 900–1200* (New York and London: Holmes & Meier) (orig. French, 1980).

Thompson, Kathleen (2002), *Power and Border Lordship in Medieval France: The County of the Perche, 1000–1226* (Woodbridge and Rochester, N.Y.: Boydell & Brewer).

Williamson, Tom (2003), *Shaping Medieval Landscapes: Settlement, Society, Environment* (Macclesfield: Windgather Press).

CHAPTER 8

Religious renewal and reform, 1000–1250

The western Church of the early Middle Ages in many ways gave the appearance of a house under construction for which architects with differing ideas had drawn up the plans. On the one hand, the monks' ascetic ideology, aimed at renouncing the world, had set a standard for moral values and spiritual ideals that was beyond the reach of ordinary laypeople. Only by association with these perfectly living Christians, through the donation of gifts, could they hope to secure salvation in the next world. This subtle form of indoctrination ensured a phenomenal growth in the wealth of the abbeys. On the other hand, all aspects of the affairs of both Church and clergy were intertwined with secular interests. Countless churches and monasteries belonged to laymen, who were involved in the appointments of bishops and abbots; once they had been appointed, these bishops and abbots were directly involved in the affairs of secular government in all manner of ways.

The Church was to undergo radical change on all these points in the course of the eleventh and twelfth centuries: the monks' moral grip on the Church and society would weaken and be challenged by an alternative spiritual ideal; the worlds of the cleric and layman would diverge far more than in the early Middle Ages; the interference of secular aristocrats, the masters of the world, in ecclesiastical business would be drastically reduced under the motto *libertas Ecclesiae*, 'liberty of the Church', that is to say, freedom from lay interference; the power of the pope would reach a record height; and the ordinary faithful would manifest themselves in large numbers, and prominently in the Church, as bearers of both old Christian traditions and new religious sentiments.

ASPIRATIONS TO REFORM

Throughout its long existence the Catholic Church has always shown a considerable capacity to purge itself. Long before the Reformation frequent demands for reform had been heard. But we must not confuse attempts at reformation with the desire for innovation. Church reform was always aimed at the restoration of old values and relationships that, in the eyes of those in favour of reform, had been lost or were in danger of being lost. But the attempts at reformation that became apparent in the tenth and eleventh centuries differed in one essential respect from earlier offensives, such as those made under Charlemagne and Louis the Pious. They had always been aimed at improving the morals of individuals: of the monks and lay clergy, to begin with, and then of ordinary laypeople too. The reformers of the tenth and eleventh centuries still considered this an important aim, but in addition they proposed drastic alterations to 'the mystical body of Christ', and to the Church as an institution. The first step necessary to do this was to 'clean the Church of all worldly pollution' (Fulton) by curbing the profound secular influence in the Church on all fronts.

Pope versus emperor: the investiture controversy

The reformers' first target was lay investiture, the early medieval practice whereby clerical dignitaries, bishops in particular, after their election by 'clergy and people' and before their consecration by archbishop (or pope), were invested by the king or his representative with the supreme signs of spiritual dignity, a staff and a ring. The king thus had *de facto* control of the appointment of bishops and abbots because they could not exercise their office without the investiture. That was why it was also customary for the king to give his approval to the election.

For those in favour of reform, this practice was a thorn in the flesh because it created the opportunity for the buying and selling of clerical offices, also known as the sin of simony after a certain Simon who had admitted to it according to the Acts of the Apostles. The conflict over lay investiture was exacerbated in the German Empire by two developments. First, German kings since Otto I – or since the recovery of their control of North Italy and their claims to the imperial dignity – had frequently intervened in the election of the pope. Second, the policy of the German kings was to involve bishops in state government. Of course this was not entirely new. We have seen that it was common enough for bishops to represent the secular authority in their dioceses during the early Middle Ages. The Carolingians often brought in bishops and abbots as royal emissaries, *missi dominici*. From the second half of the tenth century the German kings went a step further: originally just occasionally, but then systematically under the princes of the Salian dynasty (1024–1125), bishops were invested with the title of count or duke. They were thus explicitly given secular authority in addition to spiritual authority. These two authorities did not necessarily cover the same territory; a distinction must be made between bishopric or diocese (Church domain) and prince bishopric, the secular domain. Bishops who were invested with a secular office received this in fief and became vassals of the king.

Nothing like this happened in England after 1066. All bishops and abbots of great monasteries became tenants-in-chief of the crown, but they were never appointed to secular offices; their crown fiefs consisted of estates and the rights attached to them. In France the problem of lay investiture did not become as pressing for yet another reason. In some areas (the Midi, Alsace) bishops were frequently invested with the rank of count. And in various important northern French cathedral cities such as Rheims and Laon, on the basis of their rights as count, they acted as lord of the town, or head of the secular government of the town and its surroundings. However, the position of the king simply remained too weak to make the bishops' activities in secular government a cornerstone of royal policies; the king even lacked the right to appoint (arch)bishops

and abbots in many (arch)bishoprics. This precluded the French version of the 'investiture contest' from becoming an exclusive struggle between king and pope.

Ironically enough, the popes' great offensive against secular investiture in Germany was set in motion by the king. It was Henry III (1039–1056) who shortly before 1050 made an end to the abuses to which the Holy See in Rome had fallen victim and who had had his cousin, Bruno of Egisheim, bishop of Toul, elected pope (Leo IX, 1049–1054). Bruno turned out to be the first in a short line of competent German popes under whom papal authority was undoubtedly strengthened. He received strong support from reform-minded elements in the Curia, the papal court. Their two most radical representatives were Humbert, a scholarly monk from the Burgundian abbey of Cluny, whom Leo IX elevated to be cardinal-bishop of Silva Candida, and Hildebrand of Soana, who was also a monk, but a native of Rome. From 1059 onwards Hildebrand was responsible for controlling the papal finances.

The reformers' first success, in 1059, was to revise the procedure for the election of the pope. Until then, the popes, just like ordinary bishops, had been chosen by their diocese's 'clergy and people'. In practice this meant that the quarrelsome Roman aristocracy determined who became pope. The ruling of 1059 placed the choice of pope in the hands of the 'college of cardinals', the collective name for the most important clergy in Rome. Among their number were the cardinal-bishops, the bishops in the immediate vicinity of Rome who had performed liturgical tasks in the basilica of the papal residence, the Lateran, since the eighth century, and the priests and deacons attached to the most important churches in Rome (cardinal-priests and cardinal-deacons). Altogether, there were about fifty cardinals in 1100; later there would be many more of them. However, this did not mean that the election of the pope was safe from secular interference, for many of the cardinals were scions of Rome's noble families. Moreover, as long as the elections were held in public, there remained a danger of outside interference. The year 1216 saw the first conclave, the election in strict seclusion, which is still the custom today. It did not meet with immediate success: the cardinals were shut up for days in a room that was too small and lacked adequate sanitary facilities – an indescribable situation. This unfortunate start meant that the conclave did not become the rule until 1274.

About a century earlier, in 1179, the Third Lateran Council had eliminated another problem, which in fact had been created by the ruling of 1059. Because of the unequal status of the cardinals not every vote carried the same weight, and this led to repeated disagreements about the result. In 1179 it was decided, therefore, that all the cardinals were equal, and that for the election of a new pope a two-thirds majority of the votes would be required.

Cardinal Humbert of Silva Candida is generally seen as the genius behind the ruling of 1059. He died soon afterwards, however, and it was Hildebrand of Soana who would make reformation a cornerstone of papal policy when he himself was elected pope. As Gregory VII (1073–1085) he ensured from the very beginning that there would be no mistaking his intentions. We are familiar with them through a curious document, *Dictatus Papae* ('Papal Statements') of 1075, drawn up by the new pope soon after he took up office. At first glance the *Dictatus* reminds one of a megalomaniac's wish list. Twenty-seven staccato sentences sum up from where the power of the pope should come:

> [The pope] alone may have control over the imperial insignia. That he may remove emperors. That he may be the only one whose feet must be kissed by all rulers. That he cannot be judged by anybody. That the bishop of Rome, if consecrated according to canon law, is undoubtedly sacrosanct through the merits of St Peter.

In fact what we have here is an extreme reinterpretation of the doctrine of the two swords, through which the highest power in the world was granted to the pope without the batting of an eye. The successors of Gregory VII propagated this view with considerable vigour. The change in the *formulae* for the imperial coronation introduced by Pope Innocent III (1198–1216) was particularly significant in this respect. Until then, when the new emperor had been girded with the sword, the next words in the ceremony stated that the emperor had received the sword 'from God' in order to protect the Church. Innocent changed this to 'from the pope'! This made it perfectly clear that the pope had both swords at his disposal. This was not entirely

original. The same idea had already been hinted at in the *Donatio Constantini* ('Donation of Constantine', see Box 8.1). What was new, however, was how unambiguously Pope Gregory now made explicit old radical claims that had always remained more or less veiled, and presented them as the official papal standpoint. The *Dictatus Papae* should then be seen as the blueprint for a new hierocratic world order which was to replace the old caesaropapist order, in which kings considered themselves as head of the Church in their own kingdoms. The fact that this new order was never actually realized in no way lessens the tremendous impact that the papacy, buttressed by this new ideology, had on the twelfth and thirteenth centuries – but on that period only.

It became increasingly obvious that a conflict between the pope and the German king could not be avoided. The struggle came to a head in 1075 when

Plate 8.1 Miniature of the symbolic crowning of Duke Henry the Lion, and his wife Mathilda of England, in the richly decorated *Gospel Book of Henry the Lion*, made by the Benedictine monk Herimann of Helmarshansen abbey from 1175–1178

Henry IV (1056–1106) installed his chaplain Tedald as archbishop of Milan, while a canonical election had already taken place and the candidate-elect had received papal approval. This was the first step towards one of the most memorable events in medieval history. First of all, Gregory not only excommunicated the emperor but also removed him from office. The first had happened before, but never the second. Now it was clear how great the power of the pope had become, even though he did not have a king's army; there was turmoil in the German Empire and Henry's position was seriously threatened. Henry made the best of a bad job by, literally, going to Canossa to ask for the pope's forgiveness, which Gregory could not refuse (Chapter 9). Yet Henry had to pay a high price for this tactical victory: a German king had implicitly recognized that the pope had control over his kingship, and this set a dangerous precedent.

BOX 8.1 THE *DONATIO CONSTANTINI*

One of the most famous documents in medieval history is the so-called *Donatio Constantini* (Donation of Constantine). This document is in the form of a solemn deed of gift, in which, shortly before his definitive departure for Byzantium-Constantinople, Emperor Constantine not only confirmed the primacy of power of the pope in Rome over the Christian Church but also transferred to Pope Silvester I his palace in Rome, all his imperial insignia and all his authority over the western part of the Roman Empire, including the city of Rome and all Italy and the islands of the West. Constantine further confirmed that he had placed the imperial crown on Silvester's head himself, and on that occasion 'as a mark of respect to St Peter' had held the reins of the pope's horse and helped him to dismount, as if he were Silvester's squire.

It is perfectly obvious that Constantine never issued this document; in this sense it is spurious, but the question is whether it is also a *falsum*, a purposeful falsification, because it is not at all clear who (or what group) would have wanted to make it appear real, and above all why. It has often been suggested that there was a connection with the well-known reversal of 754, when Pope Stephen II, under pressure from the Lombard threat, turned away from the emperor of Byzantium and found a new protector in Pippin the Short, ruler of the Franks. This is understandable, because it is generally agreed that the first version of the *Donatio Constantini* must date from the third quarter of the eighth century. Yet none of the sources point to Pippin or any of his successors being familiar with the text of the *Donatio*. Nor is there any indication that its contents played any part in the ideological basis of papal policies in that turbulent time. What is certain is that the *Donatio* was created in clerical circles close to the pope. There are three theories concerning its purpose. One suggests that the text is no more than a frivolous exercise in rhetoric, in which case the *Donatio* is indeed spurious, but not falsified. The second theory argues that the production of the text served a purely local Roman aim: its authors wanted to stress the importance of the great basilica near the papal residence of the Lateran in a period when the

Vatican and the basilica of St Peter threatened to overshadow the Lateran. The supporters of the third theory take an even broader view: the *Donatio* would have been used against the new Frankish allies to support the claim that the popes had secular supremacy over extensive parts of central Italy – a claim that would appear to be successful. With the last aim the text – in a splendid new transcript that was meant to pass for the so-called fourth-century original – was in any case deployed in the diplomatic game for the 'restitution' of Church areas to Pope John XII (955–964) at the time of the arrival of the German King Otto I in Italy.

With the great Gregorian reform movement from the middle of the eleventh century the *Donatio Constantini* became a real ideological pillar in the defence of papal claims to the highest power in the Christian world, despite the repeated oaths of the pope's opponents that the document was 'false'. Even the scientific unmasking of the *Donatio* by the humanists Nicholas of Kues and Lorenzo Valla, who between 1430 and 1440 used other arguments to prove irrefutably that it could not possibly be dated to the beginning of the fourth century, did not prevent various Renaissance popes from appealing to the Donation of Constantine. It is famously referred to in the Treaty of Tordesillas in 1494, where Pope Alexander VI as alleged lord of the western hemisphere divided the New World into a Portuguese and a Castilian sphere of influence.

Literature: P.H.D. Leupen, 'De Donatie van Constantijn. De stand van kennis met betrekking tot een ideologische hoeksteen in de verhouding tussen Kerk en Staat in de eerste Middeleeuwen', in *Feestbundel aangeboden aan Prof.dr.D.P.Blok* [etc.] (Hilversum, 1990), pp. 216–224. H. Fuhrmann, lemma 'Konstantinische Schenkung', in *Lexikon des Mittelalters V* (Munich and Zurich, 1991), cols. 1385–1386. Hartmut Hoffmann, 'Ottonische Fragen', *Deutsches Archiv für Erforschung des Mittelalters 51* (1995), pp. 53–82. *Illustration*: Bust of Emperor Constantine, sixth century; mounted on a choir stall in the Sainte Chapelle in Paris in about 1368.

As for the pope, Canossa allowed him to formulate his ideas concerning the relationship between kings and popes more broadly and more rigidly. In short, they asserted that the king should be obedient (*obediens*), useful (*utilis*) and suitable (*idoneus*), respectively to the pope, for the pope and in the eyes of the pope. In addition, the German king should no longer have the exclusive right to the emperorship in the West. The tone was set for the struggle between the German king/emperor and the pope, each supported by a part of the German and Italian episcopacy. The nadir was reached in the half century between 1076 and 1122. With daggers drawn, emperor and pope used every means available to harm and humiliate the adversary: from appointing or supporting anti-kings or anti-popes to denouncing or demonizing the opponent. Gregory VII, himself called 'the holy devil', regularly identified Henry with Satan and even developed the idea, for that time bizarre, almost heretical, that all secular authority originated with the devil. Henry's son and successor, Henry V (1106–1125), was not unfavourable to the moral aims of the reform movement, but he would not yield an inch on the question of the bishops' investiture, which he considered to be indissolubly linked with his *ius regni* ('right of kingship'). So the battle continued. A compromise was eventually reached at the Concordat of Worms in 1122. The king gave up the investiture insofar as it related to the confirmation of the spiritual office. He was also obliged to guarantee the 'free' election of bishops, meaning that elections would be safeguarded from interference from laypeople. It meant that thenceforth bishops were elected by the most important priests in the bishopric, usually the canons of the cathedral chapter. The king was allowed to retain the right to investiture with the symbols of any secular authority that might be granted to bishops.

In England the king and pope had worked out an accommodation in 1107: in this, the potential (dual) status of bishops was fully recognized and was provided for in a separate investiture. However, all those elected had first to swear an oath of allegiance to the king. In France the kings also abandoned the investiture to high religious office before 1122, but exactly how this happened is not clear. The popes, at any rate, attached great importance to the Concordat of Worms, for the full text of the agreement was put on the walls of the great receiving hall of the Lateran palace, visible to one and all. Of course Worms, and similar arrangements with other princes, did not provide a true solution to the problem of lay intervention in Church affairs. As long as the offices of bishops and abbots remained profitable and their holders had some secular authority or extensive worldly possessions, then princes and the aristocracy would continue to interfere in elections, only no longer overtly and directly.

The half-hearted ruling for secular investiture and the appointment procedures to high ecclesiastical office were the most radical aspects of the reformers' more general efforts to stem lay influence in the Church. Another path was to limit the 'proprietary church system'. This was successful particularly when new churches (often parish churches) were established, and very gradually through the revision of the status of existing churches. The right of appointing a person as the local priest still often lay in the hands of noble lords, but sometimes in those of local communities too, as was the case in the mountain villages of the Alps and Pyrenees and in several places in Italy. Parishioners everywhere now had a say in looking after the church building, and in related matters such as church properties and local poor relief.

Papal claims to the highest authority in the world

Lacking adequate military and (often) also political weapons, the popes were forced to resort to canonical sanctions, diplomatic bravura and ideological propaganda to realize their hierocratic claims. Undoubtedly, the single most formidable as well as ambitious expression of this was the general exhortation to wage 'holy war' against all enemies of the Christian faith in defence of the Church. The first instance was Pope Urban II's famous call for a crusade to free the Holy Sepulchre issued at a council at Clermont in 1095. The overwhelming response showed that the popes had the authority to deploy the new dynamic of the West's aristocracy to achieve the Church's objectives (see Chapter 10). Many more appeals for crusades would follow, until long after the Middle Ages, directed not only against the Muslim masters of Palestine but also in conjunction with the Reconquista of Muslim Spain, with the conversion of the still pagan Baltic area, with the extermination of heresy in the Latin-Christian heartland and, finally, with combating the pope's political enemies in Italy.

The other two most important weapons in the papal arsenal were excommunication and interdict. By excommunication we mean the exclusion of individual disobedient believers from the Christian community; by interdict we mean the suspension of Church services within a certain area. An even heavier penalty was to accuse a person of heresy, which meant that secular rulers could be asked for military support. So it was that, in 1074, Gregory VII asked King Sven Estridsson of Denmark to come and drive the 'heretical' Normans out of South Italy. A similar appeal was made to Count Robert II of Flanders in 1102, this time aimed against Henry IV. In such cases heresy should not, of course, be seen as a deviation from the Church's doctrine, but as a serious disturbance of the world peace that was guaranteed by the Church. In such circumstances it was the sacred duty of the popes to take action.

Bravura formed the basis of papal claims to territorial authority over large areas of Europe. On the basis of the island clause in the *Donatio Constantini*, just before 1100 Urban II laid claim to Corsica, and soon after 1150 Callixtus III bestowed Ireland on the English king, Henry II. Then the popes looked for allies prepared to recognize them as liege lord. That was not always successful. The oldest case is also the best known: the remarkable alliance that Gregory VII made with the Norman lords of southern Italy in 1080, during the second phase of his trial of strength with Henry IV, took the form of a feudo-vassalic bond. Other princely vassals of the pope included the count of Barcelona and the duke of Dalmatia and Croatia. The latter promoted himself to king in 1076 with Gregory's acquiescence. The kings of Aragon and Navarre and the dukes, later kings, of Portugal maintained a peculiar relationship with the pope that was called *patrocinium*, but it is wrong to see a feudal tie in this, although Gregory VII acted as if there were one. Nor did Gregory hesitate to ask William the Conqueror to become his *fidelis* (vassal) in return for the political and spiritual support he had received from the papacy in 1066. Nowadays it is generally believed that William did not fall for this, just as Frederick Barbarossa would not be misled by a sly diplomatic attempt to present him as the pope's vassal in 1157. More than fifty years later, England's King John could not avoid it: he became the vassal of Innocent III in 1213, and acknowledged that he held England and Ireland in fief from him. In exchange, the pope took John's side in the struggle against the defiant barons, and lifted the interdict that had been placed on England in 1208. In the same period the pope also established his formal lordship over the kingdom of Sicily.

As well as being liege lords and patrons, the popes regularly set themselves up as *speculator*, which translates as 'general observer' of what was going on in the world. The position gave them the authority to determine whether a secular lord was suitable (*idoneus*) for his task. This led to the generally accepted custom of asking the pope to act as arbitrator when problems arose – for example, in cases of succession.

The ideology laden ceremonial activities symbolically demonstrating the pope's supremacy over the emperor were more subtle. The best-known of them is the *stratoris officium* ('office of saddle-boy'): it required that in a meeting between the two, a (future) emperor should assist the pope to dismount. Emperor Constantine was reputed to have performed this service for Pope Silvester I, an event that the popes had recorded on a fresco in the St Silvester chapel of one of their churches in Rome just before the middle of the thirteenth century as a warning to the execrable Frederick II.

It goes without saying that the popes' efforts to secure their authority above that of kings and emperors did not remain unopposed. Of all the German kings and emperors most affected by the question, as we have seen, it was Frederick Barbarossa (1152–1190) who once again took up arms against the pope over this and other matters. He was the first emperor to refer consistently to his authority and his empire as the *Holy* Roman Empire (*sacrum imperium (Romanorum)*), something just as holy and God-given as the Holy Church (*sancta ecclesia*). Moreover, not all clerical

circles shared the extreme interpretation of the doctrine of the two swords that was current since Gregory VII. The moderate or dualist view – that the two powers in the world are more or less equal – was laid down in the *Decretum Gratiani* (*c.* 1140), the most authoritative compilation of canon law in the Middle Ages.

THE POPES AS LEADERS OF THE CHURCH

The struggles of the popes with kings and emperors about supremacy in the world should not be seen separately from the gradual strengthening of the papal hold on the Church itself. It was coupled with the expansion of central administrative organs in Rome. The College of Cardinals, known as the Sacred College (*Sacrum Collegium*), developed in the twelfth century into the popes' most important advisory and administrative body. This led in time to changes in the composition of the College. More clergy were admitted from outside Rome, even from outside Italy. This in turn meant that the great secular princes always had supporters among the cardinals. The popes sent the cardinals everywhere as their personal, authorized envoys (*legati a latere*), ensuring that their authority was felt in every corner of Christendom. The real administration was based on the papal Curia. In the beginning there was no division between governmental and administrative tasks – correspondence, the liturgy in the papal churches in Rome, the management of estates, seigneurial rights and other income. From the second half of the twelfth century, departments began to specialize and become separate; jurisdiction and finance were the first.

The popes had, of course, always had some form of supreme judicial authority in the Latin Church, but it was not institutionalized until the twelfth century. The pope had the sacred duty to defend the Catholic faith, and, according to the supporters of reformation, that duty required more vigorous action on the part of the popes than had been customary. The popes began to take on more jurisdiction, while papal judgments were increasingly sought. At first the pope and cardinals dealt with everything themselves in the consistory, as the regular meetings of the pope and Sacred College were called. One official, the chancellor (*cancellarius*), had a key role in these meetings. He heard cases together with the pope and later presented a verdict in accordance with the judgment that had been formulated *in consistorio*. This development led to a growth of legal expertise in the Curia – even though it was too much of the wrong sort, according to the tireless meddler, Bernard of Clairvaux. This leading Cistercian once observed that it was 'the law of Justinian and not of the Lord' that was applied so busily, in reference to papal judgments given under his former pupil Eugene III (1145–1153). The Curia tried to channel the enormous increase in papal jurisdiction in two ways. First, through the formation of specialized law courts: the *Penitentiaria* to try moral questions, and the *Audientia* for other matters. Second, by dealing with cases wherever they occurred. Native clergy, schooled in canon law and with a special mandate, were appointed for this purpose.

The twelfth century also showed a considerable growth in the income of the Church in Rome. There were two separate funds for administration: the *Camera Apostolica* for the papal share and the *Camera Sacri Collegii* for the cardinals' share, which after 1289 was as large as that of the pope. The Camera Apostolica came under the supervision of the papal treasurer (*camerarius*). In this period the papal domains and the (irregular) sums received from secular princes – to finance crusades, amongst other things – still provided the major part of papal revenues. This second source was less dependable, because the pope had few sanctions to extract payment from an unwilling prince. In time, other more regular sources of income would become more important. Under Innocent III the first attempt was made to tax the clergy by means of a three-yearly levy on their income. Further experiments were made along these lines, much to the dismay of some rulers who viewed in horror the flow of clerical income out of their kingdoms.

The easing of the financial situation and the improvements in financial management then contributed to a strengthening of the pope's hold on what, for the sake of simplicity, we earlier called the 'Papal State' (Chapter 4). The whole complexity of properties and vaguely defined seigneurial rights that made up the Papal State was considerably extended in 1102 with a large number of possessions in Tuscany, Emilia and Lombardy belonging to the estate of the reform-minded margravine Matilda of Tuscany, who died childless in that year, bequeathing all her worldly goods to the Church of Rome. From about the middle of the twelfth century the step-by-step consolidation and territorialization of the worldly power of the popes in central Italy can be traced.

The twelfth and thirteenth centuries were also the era of a new series of ecumenical councils rather different in nature from the papal synods of the early Middle Ages. The conventional idea that questions of doctrine could only be decided by a general Church council still existed, but there had not been many of these meetings since the seventh century. This was chiefly due to another tradition, that ecumenical councils should be chaired by the emperor, and there had not been one for a long time, at least not in the West. The short pontificate of Leo IX saw reforms in this area too. He was the first pope to summon an assembly of bishops from different parts of Latin Christendom, and to preside at it without the emperor being present. This gathering was a prelude to a new series of ecumenical councils in the West that were held regularly from the beginning of the twelfth century, and which marked the transition from a defensive to an offensive strategy. The chief aim was no longer to defend the Church from secular influences but to purge the secular world of elements that were unwilling to conform to the Church, her institutions and her morality, and which thus formed a threat to the unity of Christianity. We shall look later at the consequences of this for dissenters. It is important to stress here that the popes began increasingly to behave like kings. They used councils as a magnificent stage to exhibit their personal power and display the unity of the Church. The legislative role of those attending the councils was soon limited to hearing what decrees had been prepared by the pope and his legal experts before giving them their loud and undivided assent: *fiat!, fiat!* ('Let it be! Let it be!').

From 1123 the scene of these new-style Church assemblies was normally the papal residence in Rome, the Lateran, with its great basilica and adjoining palace. The Third and Fourth Lateran Councils, held in 1179 and 1215 and summoned by Alexander III (1159–1181) and Innocent III (1198–1216) respectively, were the high points of these new ecumenical councils. Both produced comprehensive regulations in many areas: the Third in relation to the election of the pope (as we have seen on p. 130), but also in the field of marriage and kinship. In three plenary sessions, with a ten-day break between each, the Fourth Council approved 71 decrees dealing with a number of different matters: how often a good Christian should make his confession, the morals of the clergy, the prohibition on the clergy against taking part in trials by ordeal, the recognition of certain religious groups and the condemnation of others as heretics, and the injunction that Jews should thenceforth wear a yellow badge on their clothes.

The Fourth Council also broke new ground in that it was the first council to which not only bishops but also other clerical and secular dignitaries were invited. This was a sign of self-confidence bordering on arrogance and belief in their own supremacy that had been built up by the popes since Gregory VII, for the invitation was certainly not based on any intention to give the Christian community a say in Church affairs through its 'natural' representatives. The rulers were not asked to take part in the decisions, only to join in the deliberations and chiefly to witness an event that concerned all Christendom. That does not mean that the sessions were all sweetness and light. When the question of whether or not Frederick II should be recognized as emperor was being dealt with, supporters and opponents alike created pandemonium, and the pope himself joined in vehemently.

The pontificate of Innocent III is traditionally considered to be the climax of papal power in the Middle Ages, but in recent years the reasons for this view have changed. Previously, Innocent was admired as an administrator and *Realpolitiker*, for his impressive legislative and managerial activities, his strenuous efforts to consolidate further the Papal State in the making, his successful mobilization of crusader armies, and his skilful manoeuvres in international politics. More recently, Innocent has been seen above all as the embodiment of the exalted aspirations and ideals of a new papacy that was aimed at the spiritual and eventually political leadership of all Christendom. An important means to achieve that aim was the development of the concept of *plenitudo potestatis* ('the fullness of power'), which had already appeared in works of Pope Leo the Great (440–461). Innocent's predecessor, Alexander III, had reintroduced the term to indicate what he saw as the unrestricted and exclusive judicial and administrative power of the pope within the Church. Innocent III went a step further. By linking *plenitudo potestatis* with the well-known passage in St Matthew's Gospel about the power of the keys (Matt. 16:19), he could substantiate the pretension that the authority of the pope was superior to any worldly power whatsoever.

REFORMATION AND RENEWAL IN MONASTIC LIFE

Cluny and the *Ecclesia cluniacensis*

Other attempts at Church reform in the central Middle Ages concentrated on innovations in the monasteries. The cradle of these reforms was Cluny, in the West Frankish duchy of Burgundy. William the Pious, Duke of Aquitaine, founded an abbey there in 910, which within two centuries would become one of the richest ecclesiastical institutions in the West. As early as the second abbot, Odo (927–942), reforms aimed at restoring the Rule of Benedict were carried out. Cluny made special efforts in connection with the command to pray (*ora*). A lengthy liturgy took shape, and Cluny was the first abbey in which praying for the salvation of the dead – not just dead monks and their relations, but also outsiders – became a serious occupation. With this particular aim Odilo (998–1049), Cluny's fifth abbot, introduced a new Church feast, All Souls' Day, celebrated on 2 November. The idea that the souls of the individual dead were painfully cleansed of their earthly sins before the Last Judgment, or were even punished in hell, gathered weight in about 1000. In their cosmic struggle with the forces of the devil, on All Souls' Day the Cluniac monks gathered together in a dazzling ceremony of singing psalms and chorals. A vast cemetery was laid out next to the abbey for those members of the faithful who wished to be buried within striking distance of holy Cluny. The Burgundian abbey prospered from it as gifts flowed in. By about 1150 Cluny, with 300 monks in residence, was far and away the largest monastery in Latin Christendom. Every day hundreds – some say thousands – of poor people crowded through the abbey

Plate 8.2 The imposing buildings of the abbey of Cluny, destroyed during the French Revolution, after a lithograph by Émile Sagot, after 1798

Plate 8.3 Portal of the nave of Saint Mary Magdalene's church at Vézelay, Burgundy, *c.* 1120–1150, point of departure of the First Crusade and an important assembly point for pilgrims

gates in the hope of being given food. Altogether this must have formed an agglomeration comparable, for that time, to a large town.

Cluny owed its special place in the religious landscape of the dynamic tenth century to four other factors. First, the success with which it conveyed its efforts at reformation to numerous other monastic communities, both new and already established. Eventually, at the beginning of the twelfth century, the Cluny circle (*Ecclesia cluniacensis*) numbered more than a thousand houses that were linked to Cluny itself in various ways. Existing abbeys (possibly with their daughter houses or offshoots) kept their own abbot, while new foundations were guided by a prior appointed by the abbot of Cluny. Such diversity means that it can hardly be termed a real religious order. Yet, with a system of visitations or inspections from Cluny itself, the mother abbey's hold on the associated

monasteries was fairly strong. Second, from the end of the tenth century Cluny enjoyed an unusual form of Church exemption. The abbey was exempted from local episcopal supervision and every form of secular authority. It is true that other great medieval cloisters, Bobbio, Saint-Denis and Fulda among them, had enjoyed this exemption before Cluny, but the granting of it to the Burgundian abbey had even more far-reaching consequences when it was extended to all the houses of the *Ecclesia cluniacensis* in 1024: it made Cluny almost a kingdom within a kingdom, and a powerful bulwark in the emancipatory struggle to free ecclesiastical institutions from secular control.

The third factor was that Cluny had a special relationship not only with the pope but also with the principal apostles, Peter and Paul. This came about in 981 through the ceremonial transfer of relics of Peter and Paul from Rome to Burgundy. For pilgrims from the north the road to Cluny could thus be seen as a sort of second-best pilgrimage to Rome. Gifts of land made to Cluny were expressed as gifts to St Peter, so that the (aristocratic) landowners could imagine themselves to be the 'neighbour of St Peter' (Rosenwein). Could there be a more powerful protector? And fourth, Cluny soon developed into a centre of learning and intellectual training. The abbots enjoyed an impressive reputation throughout Christendom. Their advice was highly valued by kings and popes, and they were much in evidence at all great festivities such as the Peace of God gatherings where lay and ecclesiastical lords promised to collaborate in keeping the peace and prevent violence.

Despite its exceptional allure, Cluny was not an isolated phenomenon. The Burgundian and German kingdoms had their own centres of monastic reform, which had no connection with Cluny, such as the Abbey of St Victor at Marseilles and the Abbey of Gorze in Lotharingia. In the core regions of the German Empire the efforts at reformation were concentrated on the richest and best-known Carolingian abbeys: Corvey, Lorsch, Fulda, Prüm, Echternach, Reichenau and Sanct Gallen, and so on. Other great Benedictine abbeys, notably Monte Cassino, the mother of them all, and which enjoyed a flourishing period in the eleventh century, managed to avoid all attempts at reform.

The new orders

Soon, however, serious criticism was levelled at Cluny from within monastic circles. It was directed at the splendour of its festivities, the relative luxury in which the monks lived, and the intensive involvement of many of Cluny's abbots with secular politics, none of which was compatible with the original monastic ideals of renouncing the world, contemplation and austerity. The 'soft' protest led to the establishment of two new monastic communities, both of which stood for a rigorous observance of the Benedictine Rule: La Grande Chartreuse, in the mountains above Grenoble (1084), and Cîteaux, north of Cluny (1098). They were the mother houses of the first two real monastic orders, the Carthusians and the Cistercians. The Cistercians were especially successful. The number of Cistercian houses grew to over three hundred in the first half of the twelfth century, and in the next 50 years to more than five hundred, in the farthest corners of Latin Europe. All the houses remained part of one centrally administered organization. It had a pyramid structure of mother and daughter houses linked to each other. The highest administrative body was the chapter-general; it consisted of the abbots of all the houses and met once every three years. The abbots were chosen by the monks, to whom they were accountable.

Because of the isolated location of their first houses (a consequence of their attempts to live in strict seclusion from the world), the rejection of ownership of land and tithes, and the restoration of the Benedictine order to work (*labora*), the Cistercians – and the same is true of the Premonstratensians whom we shall discuss later – acquired the not entirely correct reputation of being pioneers in cultivation with progressive ideas about agriculture. The Cistercians and Premonstratensians organized their rural estates into compact units of exploitation, outlying farms known as a *grangie*, supervised by a monk living on the farm itself. The agricultural work was mostly carried out by *conversi*, monks of simple birth who had taken monastic vows but had few liturgical duties because they were illiterate, and who were treated more as servants. They are also known as lay brothers because they had not been ordained and were not tonsured.

The explosive increase of Cistercian monasteries in the early stages was chiefly due to the inspirational activities of Bernard of Clairvaux (1090–1153), named after Cîteaux's third sister monastery, which he had founded to the east of Troyes: Clairvaux or Clara Vallis, meaning 'Clear Valley'. Even though he was the leading figure in a rapidly growing order that considered seclusion from the world and strict asceticism of paramount importance, Bernard himself behaved more like a Cluniac abbot seeking constant involvement in what was happening in the world outside. Spirited and committed as he was, he gave synods, councils, popes, kings, fellow abbots and intellectuals the benefit of his advice and admonitions, whether they asked or not. A fervent champion of a hard, and if necessary armed, fight against non-believers, heretics and other dissidents, in which he included all supporters of the new rationalistic approach to theological questions, Bernard was one of the driving forces behind the Church's growing militancy.

The actions of Bernard of Clairvaux were in many respects typical of the militant nature of the Cistercian order, at least in the twelfth century. The pope deployed the Cistercians as 'missionary storm-troops' (Sayers). They took part in crusades and everywhere established themselves on the borders of the non-Christian world, such as the Slavic regions east of the Elbe. Their example inspired the foundation in Spain of the religious orders of the Knights of Calatrava and Alcántara, which followed the Cistercian rule and maintained links with the order of Cîteaux. And it was the Cistercians whom the pope charged with the (non-military) suppression of the heretical Cathars in Languedoc soon after 1200.

The Carthusian order sprang from the hermitic tradition inside Christian monasticism, which underwent a spectacular resurgence in the eleventh and twelfth centuries. Carthusians lived a community life, but the monks spent the greater part of their time in strict segregation, each in his own cell in the closed precincts of the monastery. The initiatives of Robert of Arbrissel and Norbert of Gennep were equally successful. Arbrissel was the son of a village priest from Brittany. In the years round 1100 he roamed the woods and forests of the Loire valley and collected a motley band of followers. He did not want to send anyone away and eventually set up a cloister near Fontevrault, with separate buildings for men and women, for the sick and for prostitutes, which would later attract the special favour of the Angevin kings of England. Norbert of Gennep (1092–1134) was the founder of the order of the Premonstratensians. Dissatisfied with his comfortable life as a canon of the chapter of Xanten in the duchy of Cleves, Norbert retired into the wilderness. His reputation as a preacher of repentance brought him many followers and resulted in the formation of a religious commune in the woods of Coucy, near Prémontré. Norbert ended his life as archbishop of Magdeburg on the German–Slav border, several years after the pope had recognized the Premonstratensians as a new monastic order. Strictly speaking, Premonstratensians are not monks but canons, higher, ordained clergy who live in accordance with a monastic rule, in this case a rule attributed to Saint Augustine. This happened quite often in those days. All over Europe communities of Augustinian or 'Austin' canons sprang up like mushrooms. This created a difference between canons regular and secular canons. The former were clergy living together in a monastery, who held to monastic rule and were not allowed personal possessions; the latter did not live together and were allowed personal possessions. Contrary to the original intentions of their founder, who had visualized a life of active preaching for them, the Premonstratensians soon began to lead a contemplative, cloistered life.

Vita apostolica and the new spirituality

In addition to varied attempts at reform in the eleventh century a new religious sensitivity with two main features presented itself. One was the idea that good Christians must live following the example of Christ and his apostles in the New Testament. This effort towards *nudus nudum Christum sequi* (literally meaning 'to follow naked the naked Christ') – to lead a morally pure and evangelical or 'apostolic' life (*vita apostolica*) stripped of material excesses – linked itself quite naturally with the second feature, spirituality, the search for a personal, intimate relationship of the mind with God, fed by prayer and meditation. The manifestation of the divine with which clergy, monks and ordinary laypeople now identified themselves more than ever before was God the Son, Jesus Christ – and his mother, Mary. Of vital importance in this was that both were

given a different, human image. Christ changed from a distant, sovereign conqueror of death into a 'helpless Saviour' (Southern) suffering unimaginably – but not beyond human empathy – before death; Mary, from a majestic queen of heaven into a caring and grieving mother, whose sorrow was so much aggravated because she had foreknowledge of her son's human fate. Both turned into objects not only of awe and devotion but even more so of compassion and passionate love, becoming, therefore, the path to true inner conversion.

The new religious fervour found its most radical form of expression in groups that wanted to give more than a spiritual and internal moral meaning to the ideal of the apostolic life. They also wanted to live as Christ and his apostles had lived – according to the Gospels, in poverty – and passionately to proclaim the word of God. The earliest of these radical apostolic movements came entirely from lay initiatives in the rapidly growing towns of Lombardy, the Rhine Valley and the southern Low Countries, where concentrations of wealth paradoxically inspired a fascination with absolute poverty. In Lyons it was a cloth merchant, Pierre Valdo, who gave up all his possessions to go and preach. He invested all his money in the translation of the Bible into Provençal, with which he hoped to be able to reach his audience better, but the Bible in the vernacular was also intended as a weapon in the fight against the heretical Cathars. Ironically, the Waldenses (the followers of Valdo) were themselves declared to be heretics in 1184 because of their particular interpretation of the Bible. They shared that fate with the Humiliati (who were later rehabilitated), the collective name for small communities of pious laypeople that had appeared in various towns throughout northern Italy. They lived a celibate and sober life, doing their normal work and preaching in their free time. The Beguine movement, which began in the bishopric of Liège in the same period, was of a rather different nature. Beguines were pious women who lived together in casual communities and supported themselves with their own handiwork. Thanks to the intervention of highly placed admirers of their movement, they were absolved of any suspicion of heresy and received papal recognition, on condition that they held to a monastic rule. The great spread of Beguine communities apparently answered women's needs to lead a spiritual life. The new monastic orders failed to do this because they were based mostly away from towns and were reluctant to set up houses for women.

The mendicant orders

With their critical attitude towards laxity and 'depravity' inside the Church, these new secular movements balanced constantly on the edge of being condemned for heresy by the Church. Seen in that light, the enormous success of the movement of Francis of Assisi (1181–1226) is particularly remarkable. Neither in his background (he was the son of a cloth merchant from the town of Assisi in Umbria) nor in his activities was Francis very different from someone like Valdo. Francis was a layperson, unschooled in the new scholastic tradition, with little Latin, and not very interested in allegorical interpretations of the Bible: he wanted to take the text literally, especially that of the New Testament, and immerse himself in it. For Francis, the ideal of the apostolic life meant above all the *imitatio Christi*, the empathic reliving of Christ's life. Francis went far in this, for shortly before his death his hands and feet bore the stigmata, the wounds of the crucified Christ. In addition, Francis wanted to embrace life as God had created it in all His infinite goodness, both the breathtaking beauty of nature (Francis and his followers were the first to have an eye for natural beauty and respect for flora and fauna) as well as the horrors of sickness and death. Francis also advocated possessing absolutely nothing; he even spoke out against owning a book. Whoever wanted to follow him had to wander with him and beg for food and shelter. Francis himself struggled between the sacred duty to preach the Gospel to the world and a personal inclination towards contemplation and ascetic isolation.

Francis was on good terms with Ugolino, cardinal-bishop of Ostia and later Pope Gregory IX (1227–1241). This was an important connection for the transformation of his movement into a religious order as it assured him of permanent support in the Curia. It led, amongst other things, to a fairly problem-free recognition of the order of the Friars Minor, as the Franciscans soon came to be called; the Second Order, the female branch of the order that was under the resolute leadership of Francis's fellow Assisan and female alter ego Clara of Assisi (they were called the Poor Clares or Clarissines) was similarly recognized.

Plate 8.4 St Francis supports the Church, which has collapsed. Allegorical fresco by Giotto (*c.* 1267–1337) in the upper church of the basilica of Saint Francis at Assisi

The participation of laypeople was arranged in special statutes for a Third Order (tertiaries), intended for sympathizers who wanted to commit themselves to a life spent in the spirit of the Gospel but who lived a normal married life and continued to work as usual. During the fourteenth century the tertiaries, with increasing frequency, would take monastic vows and live in a community. Even before Francis died, the order of the Friars Minor had spread far beyond Italy, and its phenomenal success continued after his death.

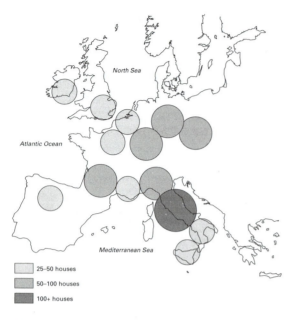

Map 8.1 Density of houses of mendicant orders (Franciscans and Dominicans) in about 1300

By the middle of the fourteenth century the order had some 1,400 houses.

These houses were of course contrary to the founder's aim to have no possessions at all. It is a question that divided minds for a very long time, and proved almost fatal for the survival of the order. It demanded what C.H. Lawrence has called 'heroic gymnastics of conscience' to reconcile the ideal of absolute poverty with the needs of a successful movement eager to spread its message across the world. Two schools of thought were soon evident. The realists, or conventuals, realized that the order needed property and income in order to perform its tasks properly. The other school, the principled or spirituals, wanted to hold on to Francis's ideals. Moreover, they allowed themselves to be led by the unusual philosophy of the Cistercian abbot, Joachim of Fiore, who died in southern Italy in 1202, and who had distilled a new vision of world history from the Bible. Joachim had prophesied that a new era of spiritual purity under the aegis of the Holy Ghost would dawn before Christ's Second Coming, in which the spiritual Franciscans foresaw their own important role. The differences between the two schools dragged on until, in 1318, the General of the order, Michael of Cesena, laid the

matter before Pope John XXII for a definitive ruling. To the dismay of the spirituals the pope issued the bull *Cum inter nonnullos* in 1323, arguing that the view according to which Christ and the apostles had no possessions was heresy. Though this may seem outrageous, the pope no doubt realized that the acceptance of the dogma of apostolic poverty would put a bomb under the Church of Rome in its historically evolved structure.

Just like the Waldenses, the second mendicant order, the Friars Preachers or Dominicans, aimed at challenging the Cathars of southern France from the ideal of evangelical poverty. After his order received papal sanction in 1216, Dominicus Guzman, the Spanish canon who was their founder, preferred another option: no longer to struggle against heretics, but to preach to the ordinary faithful in the vernacular. This meant that the Dominicans had to know their theology and thus had to be well educated. The Dominicans therefore established their own educational system that would allow the best pupils preliminary training, followed by top-quality academic theology studies. In large towns the order set up advanced schools for the study of the arts and theology, an initiative that was rapidly copied by other orders, including the Franciscans.

In other respects, too, the Dominican order was excellently organized. The principal house was in Bologna, and the order's general chapter or assembly often gathered there. The basis of the order was formed by the houses or priories, of which there were nearly 650 in *c.* 1350, usually set up in the poorer quarters of towns and headed by a prior and his *socius* (assessor) – the mendicant orders rejected the lofty position of the abbot of the old Benedictine tradition. The provinces were one level above the local foundations and were governed by provincial chapters, which in turn sent representatives to the general chapter. The whole arrangement in our eyes seems a very democratic one.

The importance of the four mendicant orders – besides the two major orders of the Friars Minor (Franciscans) and the Friars Preachers (Dominicans) there were the Carmelites and the Augustinian hermits – can hardly be overestimated. Their phenomenal success brought about an enormous increase in the religious and moral indoctrination of the laity, above all through the medium of preaching in the vernacular.

BOX 8.2 BUILDING IN THE ROMANESQUE STYLE

The era of the great religious reforms in the eleventh and twelfth centuries was also the period of Romanesque art, a term proposed by modern art and architectural historians that does not go back to any such contemporary expression. The characteristics attributed to the Romanesque style are identified primarily from church architecture and religious sculpture with a further tendency to ascribe Romanesque features to monasteries, castles and utilitarian constructions such as stone bridges, as well as to wall paintings and book illuminations from the same period. This does not make it easy to summarize what exactly 'Romanesque' implies. The problem is magnified by the regional diversity that is so characteristic of political and socio-economic life in the central Middle Ages.

An important starting point is the maxim of Nikolaus Pevsner, the famous architectural historian, that 'technical innovations never make a new style'. By this he meant that we can only speak of a new 'style' if we can discern a specific total concept that is fundamentally different from the prevailing one. As far as church architecture of the eleventh and twelfth centuries is concerned, we could refer then to the emphatic articulation of the interior and the embellishment of the exterior: before, only the inside was considered important, now the outside was given a majestic religious character.

The development of the Romanesque total concept in all its component parts was closely connected to the new and varied functions that churches began to take on from the end of the tenth century. In the great Benedictine monasteries, such as Cluny, a more important role was given to the rich liturgy and choral singing, to which a large lay audience was allowed to listen on feast-days. There was a boom in the worship of relics, meaning that costly reliquaries were given a central, easily accessible place in churches that had to provide room for a massive stream of pilgrims. At the same time the praying for an increasing number of souls required more altars, so that Mass could be said by more priests in the

same church at the same time. In monastery churches this was necessary as more and more monks were ordained priests who had to be in a position to celebrate Mass frequently. In cathedral churches, and possibly in other parish churches in the growing towns, the increasing number of priests attached to one church kept pace with the growth of the parishes and increased spiritual care, but it was also connected to the religious activities of specific groups of laypeople with their own patron saints, such as fraternities. All this meant that there was a greater need for internal spaces that were clearly divided up, and within which there was room for different chapels with their own altars. The exterior provided the opportunity for visual support to sermons, which often were preached in the open air in front of the church's main entrance.

We must fully realize that the Romanesque total concept was not thought up in one place, at one time; it has been (re)constructed in retrospect by art-historical research from the meticulous observation of hundreds of Romanesque churches that are still standing or that are known from illustrations. It is also immediately clear that the Romanesque style, at least in ecclesiastical architecture, is firmly rooted in the past (in particular, in the architecture of Carolingian monastery churches) as it clearly anticipates the later Gothic style (for example, with the first use of pointed arches in ribbed vaults and of support piers or flying buttresses, which were still concealed). What eventually makes a church a Romanesque church is determined by a largest common denominator, which includes the following features:

- the thickness and mass of the walls, essential to providing enough support for the broad and high-rising stone constructions. Light enters chiefly through the small windows of the clerestory in the upper part of the walls of the nave.
- the addition of separate chapels in or around the choir or chancel (the space behind the nave reserved for clerics) or the apse (the semicircular eastern recess behind the main altar). The con-

struction of a choir aisle allowed for unhindered access to the chapels in the apse.

- the further articulation of the crucifix shape of churches by placing a heavy square tower above the crossing where nave and transept meet.
- the further articulation of the division between nave and side aisles by alternating square piers with round columns in the dividing arcade, or by replacing the flat wall between the dividing arcade and clerestory by a second, or even third, row of arches.
- the accentuation of the height of the naves by replacing flat ceilings or traditional truss constructions with semi-cylindrical barrel vaults, made of wood or stone. A further step divides the roof into bays or vaulted segments, and each individual bay is covered by cross vaults that rest on two sides on two piers or columns. At first these were massive vaults of herringbone masonry; after the beginning of the twelfth century, much lighter and more elegant ribbed vaults emerged.
- the articulation and expansion of the functionality of the side aisles through the construction of broad galleries or narrow triforia at the level of the second arcade.
- the articulation of the west front (the main façade) with a decorated portal flanked by two towers.
- a rich ornamentation revealed, for example, in painted ceilings, decorated capitals and carvings on the portals, particularly on the west front. This was the place where biblical stories were told in sculpture, where statues of biblical figures alternated with statues of locally worshipped saints, and sometimes even where reference was made to important events in the 'national' past – such as the west front of Angoulême cathedral, dating from the beginning of the twelfth century, where a passage from the *Chanson de Roland* is carved in stone. The central motif of the carvings on the west front, to which the eyes of the beholder are immediately drawn, is invariably that of the

Last Judgment (and what would happen thereafter).

As we have said, the regional diversity of Romanesque church architecture is very large, and we can draw attention to only a few striking variations. In the building of churches in the West there was a clear preference for the 'long-house' ground plan, which goes back to the great public halls or basilicas of imperial Rome. In the Byzantine world, on the other hand, there was a preference for the 'central building' with domed constructions, for

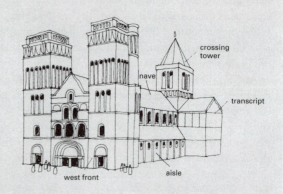

(a) L'Abbaye-aux-Dames at Caen (founded in 1062): the basic form of a large Romanesque church

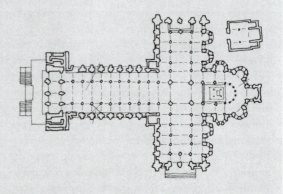

(b) Pilgrims' church of Santiago de Compostela (eleventh to thirteenth centuries)

(c) The ribbed vault

| The Romans constructed simple barrel vaults with coffered ceilings to lower the weight | From there they developed the arched cross vault, which introduced a division of the vault[ing] in bays | The Normans used heavy arched cross vaults of stone, most often in the construction of crypts | One of the weakest parts of the arched cross vault was the rib itself; another problem was supporting the vault while under construction | In the twelfth century the ribbed vault was introduced; while a vault was being constructed, only the ribs needed support | The spaces between the ribs were filled-up with light masonry; consequently, the supporting pillars could be slimmer' |

which late ancient Roman mausoleums were the prototype. Yet there are several Romanesque churches in the West, particularly in Périgord, built to a central plan and with domes. The Saint-Front in Périgueux is a fine example. There are some striking differences, too, between Italian and north-west European churches. The west fronts of many Italian churches have retained the pure form of the late Antique basilica, with its high nave and low side aisles. The façade does not then have the flanking towers, but there is generally a tall bell tower (*campanile*) that is free-standing, or gives the impression of being so. The early Romanesque churches in the German Empire catch the eye with their massive,

closed west fronts, sometimes built out further to a second, west transept with its own apse. They are flanked by rather slender, often round, towers. They often have four or five towers, two flanking the west front, two at the ends of or above the transept and one heavy crossing tower. Many western French and Norman churches have a more 'open' main façade, and the flanking towers rise higher.

Illustrations taken from B. Risebero (adapted by H. Janse), *Architectuur: vijftien eeuwen bouwkunst van de westerse beschaving* (3rd edition, Amsterdam 1981), pp. 49, 51, 55.

It also enabled the Church to respond to the new spiritual sensitivity among the most fervent of the faithful. The downside was that it encouraged intolerance of everyone who did not believe in Christ in accordance with the orthodox views of the Catholic Church. The desire to spread the word of God soon led members of these orders far beyond the borders of Latin Christendom. Among the Franciscans were such famous travellers to Asia as John of Piano Carpi, William of Rubroek and John of Monte Corvino, who visited Mongolia and China in the thirteenth century.

THE FAITHFUL BECOME VISIBLE

God's peace and God's truce

In 1033 it was one thousand years since Christ had died on the cross. To commemorate the event – so wrote the Burgundian monk Rodulfus Glaber (Rudolf the Bald) in his chronicle – large gatherings were organized at various places in Aquitaine where, to the great enthusiasm of the crowds, relics were shown, sermons were preached and truces were concluded with local lords. These events were so popular that they were soon copied in the farthest corners of France and Burgundy. Everywhere the entire populace (*tota multitudo universae plebis*) turned out to listen to their shepherds, miraculous healings took place and invariably there were shouts for 'Peace, peace' – a reference to the movement for 'God's peace' (*Pax Dei*). This came into existence as a result of the unfettered violence that accompanied the establishment of banal lordships in France. Some bishops and abbots, sometimes in cooperation with counts or dukes, then convened synods to establish rules to limit violence. Local lords and their knights (*milites*) were invited from far and wide to swear a solemn oath to observe these rules. Originally the rules were aimed at protecting social groups that were helpless in the face of violence, beginning with the clergy and later extended to include (unmarried) women and children, pilgrims, merchants and other travellers, and finally even 'peasants', who were only once called upon to end their own (counter) violence. We know of some 25 of these peace occasions dating from the first half of the eleventh century. A second, more radical phase forbade acts of violence on specific days and, later, during longer periods of the year, indicated by the Church calendar. This was the *Treuga Dei* ('God's truce'), the oldest of which dates from soon after 1020.

With this movement the Church leaders were in fact trying to take the place of secular rulers. Adalbero of Laon, a fervently royalist bishop, recognized this and fiercely reviled the pretensions of the abbots of Cluny in particular for their takeover of the king's most essential task – maintaining the peace in his kingdom. Adalbero believed that monks should remain inside their cloister walls and lead a life of contemplation. Conversely, kings and other secular princes responded by explicitly proclaiming their own 'peaces', which in the Empire even took on a territorial character (the so-called *Landfrieden*). The ecclesiastical *pax* concept may further have influenced the idea of a normative peace within town walls or in relation to particularly vital objects of public interest such as dikes.

Among the believers

Glaber's chronicle and other texts about the movements for God's peace are actually the first historical documents in which attention is paid to the common faithful. The common people figured in Carolingian writings also, but then only in a non-specific background role. In the eleventh century they made themselves heard, loudly and in an active role. It proves that great progress had been achieved with the internalization of the Christian faith, supported by the steady expansion of spiritual care in an ever-denser network of (rural) parishes. The number of parishes in England, for example, estimated at about two thousand at the end of the eleventh century, would quadruple over the next two centuries.

Not only written texts but other, material, sources too, such as buildings, bear witness to the active involvement of growing numbers of believers. The first really monumental stone churches, catering for a stream of many hundreds if not thousands of faithful, date from the eleventh century. It is no coincidence that the largest lay on the increasingly busy pilgrim routes: Saint-Sernin in Toulouse and the Burgundian showpiece, Sainte-Madeleine in Vézelay, on the main routes to Santiago de Compostela (which had its own impressive church); and in other busy places of pilgrimage: Sainte-Foy in Conques, for example, or Durham Cathedral, built over the grave of St Cuthbert, or in populous and economically successful towns such as Pisa.

The eleventh-century texts reveal strongly divergent aspects of the commitment of the laity. On the one hand they create the impression that the religious enthusiasm of the masses was to a high degree directed, and possibly also abused, by Church authorities. This happened, for example, through adjustments in the liturgy relating to the most important sacramental activities in the Church: the consecration of the bread and wine during the Mass. The lifting of the host and chalice high in the air after consecration, so that the congregation could see, answered the wishes of the laity to be directly involved in one of the great mysteries of the faith. Sometimes holders of high Church office who also had secular powers were able to exploit the military potential of their faithful. After the proclamation of a 'God's peace' they would mobilize religiously inspired people's militias and use their help to break down the power of the banal lords in their territory who were too independent, giving no quarter and, if necessary, using brute force. There are also repeated accounts from this time of the lynching of Jews and heretics.

On the other hand, sources dealing with the traditional elements of the perception of the Christian faith, such as the worship of relics, increasingly reveal manifestations of genuine popular faith. Relic-worship has a magical background: in the relics the believer experiences the saint's physical presence (*praesentia*) and his or her miraculous power (*potentia*). This double experience is felt more intensely the closer the believer comes to the relic. Naturally, this is best achieved when relics are worn on the body, a practice that already existed in the eleventh century. Not everyone could afford to purchase personal relics, however, certainly not the physical remains of important saints. Most believers had to resort to visiting the places where saints were buried or their relics preserved. To achieve optimal physical contact between pilgrims and saints, the tombs and reliquaries, which in pilgrimage churches were usually placed directly behind the main altar, were

made easily accessible so that pilgrims could even clamber over and under them. Some of the faithful were also happy to spend the night close to the reliquary hoping for a dream in which the saint would appear to them and perform a miracle, a form of superstition from as far back as Greek Antiquity. Physical contact with relics or reliquaries was not an essential condition to being able to profit from the miraculous power of the saints. People who were in trouble, wherever they were, could just call upon their favourite saints in a short prayer, and that frequently produced the desired effect – if we may believe the countless stories of miracles that were in circulation.

The sorry state of medical knowledge makes it easy to understand why the faithful looked to the saints for healing their physical or mental ills. It soon led to specializations, traces of which are still visible today: such as St Dympna of Geel in Brabant, a saintly

Plate 8.5 Outside the stronghold of Montségur, situated at an altitude of 1,204 metres south of Carcassonne, more than two hundred Cathars were burned alive in 1244

BOX 8.3 TWICE COPIED AND STILL GENUINE: THE KEY OF ST HUBERT

A finely wrought bronze key, nearly 40 centimetres long, is still kept in the church treasury of Sainte-Croix in Liège. In the late Middle Ages it was believed that the first bishop of Liège, St Hubert (708–727), had received this valuable object from the hands of the pope in Rome. This is certainly not true, as the St Hubert key of Liège was not made until about 1200. What is uncontested, however, is that in Hubert's time the popes in Rome did give keys to important bishops. They were copies of the key to the railings at the entrance to the grave of St Peter (*confessio sancti Petri*) in the crypt of the basilica dedicated to him in Rome. The hilt usually contains a real relic, a fragment of the chains that bound Peter in his prison and which were miraculously broken. The deeper symbolical meaning must be plain: such a 'key of confession' represented the keys of heaven, held by the apostle Peter on the basis of his power to lock and unlock for eternity.

As far as we know, the last time a pope gave a 'key of confession' was in 1079. None of these keys has survived. There are a number of later imitations, including one from Maastricht, the key of St Servatius, the first bishop of Maastricht. The wealthy chapter of St Servatius had this key made in the twelfth century to commemorate the direct connection between the first bishop of Maastricht and the pope in Rome. Quite understandably the bishop of Liège then also wanted a key, for was not

Hubert the legal successor to the bishop of Maastricht, and had he not been appointed bishop by the pope himself, at the behest of an angel, while on a visit to Rome? Whether this imitation imitation-key – complete with chain relic – was also used in the miraculous cure of rabies, as legend has it, is unlikely. The most important place of pilgrimage where St Hubert was worshipped was the monastery in the Ardennes built on the spot where he had repented while out hunting and where Christ had spoken to him, saying: 'You must hunt not deer but souls.' Here, pilgrims could buy small, mass-produced hunting horns and keys. These relics were hung on a cord round the neck and protected the wearer from rabies.

Literature: A.M. Koldeweij, *Der gude Sente Servaes. De Servatiuslegende en de Servatiana: een onderzoek naar de beeldvorming rond een heilige in de middeleeuwen. De geschiedenis van de kerkschat van het Sint-Servaaskapitel te Maastricht, deel I* (Assen-Maastricht, 1985), especially pp. 100–107. Ludo Jongen, *Heiligenlevens in Nederland en Vlaanderen* (Amsterdam, 1988), pp. 148–151.

---

princess of Irish origin who, soon after her grave had been found during reclamation work, enjoyed the reputation of helping in a variety of mental illnesses. This later led to the foundation of madhouses in Geel, the forerunners of the much-talked-about open psychiatric institute that is still located in the village.

Even then, miraculous cures were carefully scrutinized. Official recognition was only given after extensive questioning of both the patient (who might also be put to a test) and witnesses. If a believer was certain that his or her prayer had been heard by a saint,

then the rules of reciprocal exchange came into action, and something had to be done in return to reward the saint and to convince the believer of the miraculous powers of the saint. This quid pro quo came in different forms. It could be a replica of the healed body part, life-size or smaller, and made of wax, silver or gold; or the object that had caused the ill (the pitchfork on to which someone had fallen, the pin that had been swallowed); the aids that the healed person no longer needed (crutches, bandages); or gifts of thanks in cash or in kind (often a quantity of wax or candles), entirely unconnected with the miracle. The most extreme gift was the *deditio*, the dedication of the whole person, who then became the servant (*servus*) or maid-servant (*ancilla*) of the saint. They could always be called upon, in the name of the saint, by the church with which the saint was connected.

The creation of a persecuting society

In another phenomenon re-emerging in the eleventh and twelfth centuries – heresy – the faithful had a double role thrust upon them, that of persecuted and persecutor, of obedient follower and attacker. Here, we do not mean the fight against learned views of Church dogma that were considered incorrect. The word 'heresy' was applied far too often in such cases and the consequences were dire enough for those involved: a ban on teaching, public burning of books, sometimes confinement in a prison or monastery. Heresy, in the sense of a religious community that set itself outside the Church, was of an entirely different character. In the eleventh century heretical groups in this meaning of the word sprang up in many places – first in Champagne, and very soon thereafter through-out the Rhineland, France and England. It is difficult to see any connection between the various dissident groups at this period. The point upon which they were probably most in agreement was their sharp criticism of the corruption and secularization inside the Church, focusing on the secular clergy and their far from apostolic way of life. In that respect the creation of heretical sects and new monastic orders can be seen as two sides of the same coin. There was a fine boundary between canonization and being burnt at the stake so to speak, and for modern observers it is still not clear why some groups (the Franciscans, for example, and later the Humiliati) were recognized and accepted by the Church, while others, notably the Waldenses, were denounced as heretics.

We should not automatically suppose that all the heresies in the West came from the East. The suggestion has been put forward because as early as the eleventh century supporters of heretical groups in Western Europe were called *bulgarelli* ('little Bulgarians', cf. buggers) or *kathari* (from the Greek, 'the pure'). Both terms refer, of course, to dualistic sects in the Byzantine Empire and the Balkans, whose ideas went back to the Manichaeism of late Antiquity. It is very doubtful whether these had any direct connection with kindred spirits in the West before the middle of the twelfth century, although they certainly did after that time. It is more likely that East and West drew on the same gnostic tradition, which apparently was lying dormant.

The Cathars believed that the material world was not created by God but by Satan. Satan was the lord of Genesis; the good God did not reveal Himself until the New Testament, and the physical existence of Christ was only a sham, to mislead Satan. In order to approach the good God, all material things had to be foresworn radically; one had to be cleansed of matter by regular fasting, by not eating meat and by absolute sexual continence. Because this was too difficult to achieve for ordinary people, the Cathars – just like the Manichaeans at the time of Augustine – had two levels of believers: the ordinary *credentes* (believers), who did not follow the strict moral commandments to the letter, and a select elite of *perfecti* (perfect), who did and thus acquired an almost saintly status. Most *credentes* did not become *perfecti* until their deathbed. This was brought about by the administration of the 'sacrament of consolation' (*consolamentum*).

Heresy or not, during the twelfth century Catharism spread unchecked over Languedoc, Provence, Lombardy and Tuscany, regions where in time every settlement of any size had a Cathar community. There was then no question of systematic persecution by Church or civil authorities. This situation changed dramatically at the end of the twelfth century, with the emergence of what the British historian, R.I. Moore, has called 'the persecuting society'. By this he meant that both the Church and the now budding states of the great European kingdoms were beginning to define their own aims and ideologies so precisely that they could identify any conflicting groups or interests much better than before. The content of the Catholic religion had become established through the development of dogmatic theology, the systematization of canon law and the growing number of rules issued. Once it had been determined what was soundly orthodox, and what was not, dissidence could no longer be tolerated; whoever had once been seen as 'erring' was now a 'traitor' or an 'enemy of the faith'. The turning point was reached in about the middle of the twelfth century.

The Church no longer acted reactively, but began an active search for the truth by developing inquisitorial procedures. The pope himself continued to play a steering and controlling role in the whole process, by sending legates, mobilizing the new religious orders (first the Cistercians, later the Dominicans), involving secular military power, issuing anti-heretical decrees and council decisions and, finally, by establishing – under Gregory IX – a special, mobile papal tribunal, the Inquisition, which was intended to counterbalance the laxity of many bishops in persecuting heretics.

The Cathars of southern France were the first to feel the full weight of this coercive machinery, quickly followed by the Jews and marginal groups such as lepers and homosexuals. For the Cathars, it all ended in 1208 with the arrival of a crusader army from the north that used the eradication of heretics as a pretext for land-grabbing, from which the French king eventually emerged as the big winner.

No less appalling was the spectacle of the persecution of the Jews during the build-up to the First Crusade. The connection is obvious: who else but the Jews were responsible for the crucifixion of Christ in the holiest of places that now had to be liberated from the infidel? At a deeper mental level this conviction became mixed with the idea that the Christian community, as the unsullied bearer of Christ's legacy, had to guard its purity and destroy every impurity with fire and sword. With every new crusade to the Holy Land and with every heroic feat of the Reconquest in Spain, the persecutions flared up again. Other factors exacerbated them, such as the growing resentment at the Jews' dominant position in the exchange and credit business, also in connection with the levying of direct taxes by spendthrift kings. Jews could fill this economic niche because in their business dealings with Christians they were not hindered by the Church's prohibition on asking interest on loans.

There are countless other indications from the eleventh and twelfth centuries that a centuries-long latent anti-Semitism had become virulent: Jews were driven off their land or forced to live together in certain quarters of the towns. The earliest accusations of infanticide and cannibalism surfaced more or less simultaneously with the theory of an international Jewish conspiracy. For the first time we hear of anti-Jewish purification rituals, such as stoning Jewish houses or beating Jews at Passover. Jews were forced to wear distinctive clothing. Under a special judicial statute, Jews were directly subject to the authority of the king – which made them an easy prey to exploitation.

All this is evidence that the attitude of negative tolerance, formulated in the days of Augustine, was turning into open discrimination, stigmatization and chronically active persecution. This change in the treatment of the Jews reveals more painfully than anything else that economic expansion, consolidation of the faith, the ideal of service to and the fight for God – in short, everything that was so characteristic of the great period of expansion in medieval history – had a dark, shadowy side.

FURTHER READING

Andrews, Frances (1999), *The Early Humiliati* (Cambridge: Cambridge University Press).

Audrisio, Gabriel (1999), *The Waldensian Dissent: Persecution and Survival, c.1170–c.1570* (Cambridge: Cambridge University Press) (orig. French, 1989).

Barber, Malcolm (1992), *The Two Cities: Medieval Europe, 1050–1320* (London: Routledge).

—— (2000), *The Cathars: Dualist Heretics in Languedoc in the High Middle Ages* (London: Longman).

Barber, Richard (1991), *Pilgrimages* (Woodbridge: Boydell Press).

Bell, Rudolph M. (1985), *Holy Anorexia* (Chicago, Ill.: University of Chicago Press).

Berman, Constance Hoffman (2000), *The Cistercian Evolution: The Invention of a Religious Order in Twelfth-century Europe* (Philadelphia, Pa.: University of Pennsylvania Press).

—— (ed.) (2005), *Medieval Religion: New Approaches* (London and New York: Routledge).

Blumenthal, Uta-Renate (1988), *The Investiture Controversy. Church and Monarchy from the Ninth to the Twelfth century* (Philadelphia, Pa.: University of Pennsylvania Press) (orig. German, 1982).

Brasher, Sally Mayall (2003), *Women of the Humiliati: A Lay Religious Order in Medieval Civic Life* (London and New York: Routledge).

Bredero, Adriaan H. (1971), *Bernard of Clairvaux: Between Cult and History* (Grand Rapids, Mich.: Eerdmans Publishing).

Brooke, Rosalind Beckford and Christopher Brooke (1984), *Popular Religion in the Middle Ages. Western Europe 1000–1300* (London: Thames & Hudson).

Burr, David (1993), *Olivi and Franciscan Poverty: The Origins of the* Usus Pauper *Controversy* (Philadelphia, Pa.: University of Pennsylvania Press).

—— (2001), *The Spiritual Franciscans: From Protest to Persecution in the Century after Saint Francis* (Philadelphia, Pa.: Pennsylvania State University Press).

Bynum, Caroline Walker (1982), *Jesus as Mother: Studies in the Spirituality of the High Middle Ages* (Berkeley: University of California Press).

—— (1987), *Holy Feast and Holy Fast: The Religious Significance of Food to Medieval Women* (Berkeley: University of California Press).

Cameron, Euan (2000), *Waldenses: Rejections of Holy Church in Medieval Europe* (Oxford: Blackwell).

Carville, Geraldine (2003), *The Impact of the Cistercians on the Landscape of Ireland 1142–1541* (Ashford: KB Publications).

Chenu, M.-D. (repr. 1998), *Nature, Man and Society in the Twelfth Century* (Toronto: University of Toronto Press) (orig. English edn, 1968).

Cohen, Mark R. (1994), *Under Crescent and Cross. The Jews in the Middle Ages* (Princeton, N.J.: Princeton University Press).

Constable, Giles (1995), *Three Studies in Medieval Religious and Social Thought: The Interpretation of Mary and Martha, the Ideal of the Imitation of Christ, the Orders of Society* (Cambridge: Cambridge University Press).

—— (1996), *The Reformation of the Twelfth Century* (Cambridge: Cambridge University Press).

Cowdrey, H.E.J. (1970), *The Cluniacs and the Gregorian Reform* (Oxford: Clarendon Press).

—— (1998), *Pope Gregory VII, 1073–1085* (Oxford: Clarendon Press).

Finucane, R.C. (1977), *Miracles and Pilgrims. Popular Beliefs in Medieval England* (London: Dent).

Frugoni, Chiara (1998), *Francis of Assisi: A Life* (London: Continuum International Publishers Group) (orig. Italian, 1995).

Fulton, Rachel (2002), *From Judgment to Passion: Devotion to Christ and the Virgin Mary, 800–1200* (New York and Chichester: Columbia University Press).

Geary, Patrick J. (1978), Furta Sacra: *Thefts of Relics in the Central Middle Ages* (Princeton, N.J.: Princeton University Press).

Head, Thomas and Richard Landes (eds) (1992), *The Peace of God: Social Violence and Religious Response in France around the Year 1000* (Ithaca, N.Y. and London: Cornell University Press).

Hiscock, Nigel (ed.) (2003), *The White Mantle of Churches: Architecture, Liturgy and Art Around the Millennium* (Turnhout: Brepols).

Hugo, William R. (1996), *Studying the Life of St Francis of Assisi: A Beginner's Workbook* (Quincy: Franciscan Press).

Hunter, Ian, John Christian Laursen and Cary J. Nederman (eds) (2005), *Heresy in Transition: Transforming Ideas of Heresy in Medieval and Early Modern Europe* (Aldershot: Ashgate).

Iogna-Prat, Dominique (2002), *Order and Exclusion: Cluny and Christendom Face Heresy, Judaism, and Islam (1000–1150)* (Ithaca, N.Y. and London: Cornell University Press) (orig. French, 1998).

Kieckhefer, Richard (1989), *Magic in the Middle Ages* (Cambridge: Cambridge University Press).

Kienzle, Beverly Mayne (2001), *Cistercians, Heresy and Crusade in Occitania, 1145–1229: Preaching in the Lord's Vineyard* (York: York Medieval Press).

Lambert, Malcolm (1992), *Medieval Heresy. Popular Movements from the Gregorian Reform to the Reformation*, 2nd edn (Oxford: Blackwell).

Landes, Richard, Andrew Gow and David C. Van Meter (eds) (2003), *The Apocalyptic Year 1000: Religious Expectation and Social Change, 950–1050* (Oxford and New York: Oxford University Press).

Lawrence, C.H. (1994), *The Friars: The Impact of the Early Mendicant Movement on Western Society* (London and New York: Longman).

Le Goff, Jacques (1986), *The Birth of Purgatory* (Chicago, Ill.: University of Chicago Press) (orig. French, 1981).

—— (2003), *Saint Francis of Assisi* (London and New York: Routledge) (orig. French, 1999).

Lekai, Louis J. (1977), *The Cistercians: Ideals and Reality* (Kent, O.: Kent State University Press).

Lerner, Robert E. (2001), *The Feast of Saint Abraham: Medieval Millenarians and the Jews* (Philadelphia, Pa.: Pennsylvania State University Press).

Little, Lester K. (1978), *Religious Poverty and the Profit Economy in Medieval Europe* (Ithaca, N.Y. and London: Cornell University Press/P. Elek).

Moore, R.I. (1987), *The Formation of a Persecuting Society: Power and Deviance in Western Europe, 950–1250* (Oxford: Blackwell).

Morris, Colin (1972), *The Discovery of the Individual 1050–1200* (London: SPCK for the Church Historical Society).

—— (1989), *The Papal Monarchy. The Western Church from 1050–1250* (Oxford: Clarendon Press).

Nyberg, Tore (2000), *Monasticism in North-Western Europe, 800–1200* (Aldershot and Burlington, Vt.: Ashgate).

Pegg, Mark Gregory (2005), *The Corruption of Angels: The Great Inquisition of 1245–1246* (Princeton, N.J.: Princeton University Press).

Pelikan, Jaroslav (1980), *The Christian Tradition: A History of the Development of Doctrine. Vol. III. The Growth of Medieval Theology (600–1300)* (Chicago, Ill.: University of Chicago Press).

Robinson, I.S. (1990), *The Papacy 1073–1198: Continuity and Innovation* (Cambridge: Cambridge University Press).

Rosenwein, Barbara H. (1982), *Rhinoceros Bound: Cluny in the Tenth Century* (Philadelphia, Pa.: University of Pennsylvania Press).

—— (1989), *To be the Neighbor of Saint Peter. The Social Meaning of Cluny's Property, 909–1049* (Ithaca, N.Y. and London: Cornell University Press).

Rudolph, Conrad (2004), *Pilgrimage to the End of the World: The Road to Santiago de Compostela* (Chicago, Ill.: University of Chicago Press).

Sayers, Jane (1994), *Innocent III: Leader of Europe 1198–1216* (London: Longman).

Spoto, Donald (2003), *Reluctant Saint: The Life of Francis of Assisi* (New York: Penguin).

Stow, Kenneth R. (1992), *Alienated Minority. The Jews of Medieval Latin Europe* (Cambridge, Mass. and London: Harvard University Press).

Sumption, Jonathan (2003), *The Age of Pilgrimage: The Medieval Journey to God* (Mahwah, N.J.: Hidden Spring).

Taylor, Claire (2005), *Heresy in Medieval France: Dualism in Aquitaine and the Agenais, 1000–1249* (Woodbridge and Rochester, N.Y.: Boydell & Brewer).

Tellenbach, Gert (1993), *The Church in Western Europe from the Tenth to the Early Twelfth Century* (Cambridge: Cambridge University Press) (orig. German, 1988).

Vauchez, André (1993), *Spirtuality in the Medieval West* (Kalamazoo, Mich.: Cistercian Publications) (orig. French, 1975).

—— and Daniel Ethan Bornstein (eds) (1996), *The Laity in the Middle Ages: Religious Beliefs and Devotional Practices* (Chicago, Ill.: University of Notre Dame Press).

Ward, B. (1982), *Miracles and the Medieval Mind: Theory, Record and Event 1000–1215* (Philadelphia, Pa.: University of Pennsylvania Press).

Waugh, Scott L. and Pieter Diehl (eds) (1996), *Christendom and Its Discontents: Exclusion, Persecution and Rebellion, 1000–1500* (Cambridge: Cambridge University Press).

Webb, Diana (1999), *Pilgrims and Pilgrimage in the Medieval West* (London and New York: I.B. Tauris).

—— (2002), *Medieval European Pilgrimage, c.700–c.1500* (Basingstoke: Palgrave).

Weinstein, Donald and Rudolph M. Bell (1982), *Saints and Society: The Two Worlds of Western Christendom, 1000–1700* (Chicago, Ill.: University of Chicago Press).

Wolf, Kenneth Baxter (2003), *The Poverty of Riches: St. Francis of Assisi Reconsidered* (Oxford and New York: Oxford University Press).

CHAPTER 9

Early kingdoms and territorial principalities, 900–1200

The unified structure that Charlemagne's rapid conquests had imposed on the vast reaches of his empire in the end seemed to penetrate far less deeply into society than he must have hoped. From the tenth century new political units, which can best be described as early dynastic states, came into being throughout Europe, both in what once was Charlemagne's empire and beyond. The monarchy remained the main paragon even if, as we shall see, by no means all early states that emerged would turn into kingdoms. At their core was the princely dynasty: the dynasty 'made' the territories, united them and divided them through conquest, marriage, inheritance and negotiation. Around the dynasty hovered a mobile court of vassals and important clerics with whom the prince had to practise a constant balancing act, because each one of them controlled a considerable share of the means of exercising power in the area. The princes were constantly on the move because their power was only respected when they were present, visible and often even tangible. The institutions of the dynastic state were still modest, at the central level often not permanent in time and place. This meant that the institutions of the Church, which had been permanent for centuries, retained a substantial interest in secular affairs too. The consolidation of territorial powers was made possible by more stable relations at the local level in the form of seigneuries, through economic growth and because invasions and migrations had come to a halt.

THE IMPERIAL DREAM

East Frankish and West Frankish kingdoms

Europe today is characterized by a multiplicity of states, strongly divergent in size and internal structure, but all of them firmly rooted in a medieval past. Besides the main nation-states, autonomous principalities like Liechtenstein, Andorra, San Marino and Monaco are also still in existence, while the two self-declared heirs to the West and East Roman Empire – the Habsburg and the Russian empires respectively – survived until 1917/18. The same holds for a third supranational state that extended over most of the former Asian and African provinces of the late Roman Empire: the Ottoman Sultanate. From the early fourteenth century it had gradually established itself in the region of Byzantium by conquest, and early in the sixteenth century it advanced deeply into Hungary (Battle of Mohács, 1526), where it entered into a centuries-long struggle with the Habsburg dynasty.

We shall first examine the German Empire at greater length. There are specific reasons for this: state power developed there relatively early on; the Empire covered an immense area and could therefore exert deep influence on neighbouring regions and, through its central position, it actually 'touched' the greater part of Europe. In addition, the Empire had a unique and extremely complex structure in which state power developed at the level of the Empire as well as at the level of territorial principalities. In this sense the German situation illustrates many problems that also appeared elsewhere in other constellations. In addition, during the late Middle Ages many towns that were in fact fairly independent, developed – sometimes separately and sometimes in alliances – to become

Plate 9.1 Power symbols of the Holy Roman Empire

constitutional units within the Empire. Some results of this unique form of institutionalization are still clearly visible today.

It must be remembered that in the tenth century the regions east of the Rhine and north of the Danube were considerably less developed than southern and western Europe. They had largely missed the effects of Roman colonization, as the low density of population, towns, bishops' sees and paved roads, among other things, made clear. Partly as a result of this, the heart of the Carolingian Empire had been more to the west, between the Loire and the Rhine. Ironically, therefore, Charlemagne's enormous empire was eventually prolonged in its least developed and least Christian eastern parts.

Naturally the continuous availability of powerful leaders played a critical part in the expansion of early dynastic states. King Henry I (919–936) was the first to break with the Frankish tradition of dividing the patrimony, which had earlier meant, at least intentionally, that the territory was shared among all the able sons of the ruler. Even if this had never occurred in the West Frankish and East Frankish kingdoms since the Verdun treaty of 843, this was a coincidence; besides, division had always remained an issue with regard to the central kingdom. But now there was a break: henceforward, in the East Frankish kingdom,

younger sons could still share in the inheritance, but the kingdom became indivisible. The *regnum Teutonicorum*, the 'kingdom of the Teutons/Germans' (the expression was first used in a Salzburg chronicle referring to the king's election in 919), was thus distinct from the patrimonial possessions of the ruling dynasty. Henry I established a strong royal dynasty, known as the Saxon or Ottonian dynasty (919–1024). It was succeeded by two royal lines that ensured a powerful continuity: the closely related Salian (1024–1125) and Hohenstaufen (1132–1254) dynasties.

Ultimately the German kings succeeded earlier than their West Frankish counterparts in putting an end to the centrifugal forces after the Carolingian expansion. But their early bid for renewed centralized power was reversed exactly at the juncture where the luck of the French kings took a turn for the better. In this way the historical development of what we may call France and Germany by the end of the tenth century was intertwined for centuries in a succession of two complex opposing movements. It was one of the most fateful developments in European political history.

The establishment of the German kingdom

After the Carolingian dynasty died out in 911, Henry, the duke of the Saxons, nicknamed 'the Fowler', was elected king in 919 because of his activities in the struggles against Norsemen, Slavs and Magyars. The Bavarian duke also had been elected at the same time, however, and it was two years before he relinquished his claims in exchange for far-reaching autonomy in his own duchy. While the unity of the German kingship was thus ensured, at the same time its limitations were established through the counterweight that the duchies could apply at any time.

By that time the East Frankish kingdom consisted of four duchies that had a partly ethnic basis: from north to south these were Saxony, Franconia (Frankenland), Swabia, and Bavaria. In 925, Henry I took advantage of the western kingdom's weakness to incorporate the former kingdom of Lotharingia/ Lorraine definitively as the fifth duchy in his eastern kingdom. The German Empire thus gained considerable lands in the West. It has sometimes been assumed that the need to defend territories against the Magyars and Slavs led to the formation of these 'tribal duchies'. If this were true, the duchies certainly did not cover the entire East Frankish territory: the Frisians and Alamans did not form separate duchies, neither did the populations of the lower and middle Rhineland. The Thuringians did have their 'tribal duchy' until 908 but were then caught up in the Saxons' expansion eastwards. On the other hand, Lorraine as a duchy did not have in any way a 'tribal' character.

On two occasions during the long reign of Henry's son, the powerful Otto I (936–973), certain dukedoms, collaborating with the archbishop of Mainz, formed coalitions with a view to thwart him. Thanks to his military superiority, Otto was able to escape from these perilous situations: he forced those rebels who had survived the battle into humiliating submission, and then either banished them or gave them positions elsewhere. In the face of these counterforces, the ruling king tried to guarantee the continuity of his dynasty by appointing a son as successor and having him elected and crowned during his own lifetime. Henry I had already done so in 929. Otto I did the same with his son Otto II (973–983), whom he

had elected in 961 and crowned German king (by then Otto I was already emperor) in Aachen, and crowned co-emperor in 967. During the 11-year minority of Otto III (983/994–1002), consequent upon the premature death of Otto II, the widows of the two previous emperors, Adelheid and Theophanu, and Archbishop Willigis of Mainz together held the regency for the child king. This proved a wise move, for the duke of Bavaria again had himself elected king. Appointment and election during the predecessor's lifetime were essential to ensure the continuity of the dynasty when faced with rival dukes and frustrated relatives. This so eroded the tradition of the election that it became little more than a ritual preceded by painstaking negotiation and horse-trading. The most important princes of the Empire – the archbishops from the Rhine cities and the dukes – nevertheless succeeded in maintaining the principle of electing the king.

Only when there was no son as heir did other contenders have any chance. This was the case when Otto III died without issue at the age of 22. Three candidates came forward, each supported by his own people. One candidate was murdered, and the winner from Bavaria, Henry II (1002–1024), never gained real authority in Saxony, even though he was of the same, originally Saxon, lineage as his four predecessors. When Henry also died childless, the line died out and there was an entirely open election for a new king. Under the decisive influence of the archbishop of Mainz, the smooth transfer of power to the Salian dynasty showed, with the election of the Duke of Swabia as Conrad II (1024–1039), that by this time the German kingship was anchored firmly. After the kingdom of Burgundy had been annexed in 1034, the western border of the Empire came to lie along the line of the Rhône, Saône, Meuse and Scheldt.

Family ties were an essential instrument in consolidating royal power, even though they frequently concealed seeds of jealousy, between brothers and half-brothers first, and later wives. Otto I made his brother, Henry, duke of Bavaria, his eldest son, Liudolf, duke of Swabia, and two of his brothers, as well as his son-in-law, duke of Lorraine; he married daughters off to both Louis IV of West Francia and his rival and successor Hugh Capet; he invested his youngest brother with the dignities of the archbishopric of Cologne and of the duchy of Lorraine at the same time; and he procured the archbishopric of Mainz for his son Willigis. The two archbishops played a key role in the political construction of the Empire. Such constructions, of course, did not stop the beneficiaries from seeing that their own best interests lay in extending their position of personal power rather than in loyalty to their royal benefactor.

The German Empire, certainly after the extension of the *regnum Teutonicorum* with the kingdoms of Italy (see p. 161) and Burgundy, had a richly diverse population including Germanic-, Romance- and Slavonic-speaking peoples. The regions of northern Italy managed to keep their identity distinct under German domination. Ties to other Romance-speaking regions remained very loose, as was also the case with the north-western territories on the outskirts of the Empire, later to be known as the Low Countries. Within the German-speaking areas the difference between north and south caused just as many problems of communication as with other western languages. Nonetheless, after the beginning of the tenth century the confrontation of the German peoples with the foreign-speaking Magyars and Slavs was clearly sharper than with Scandinavians, who spoke Germanic languages. The Empire constructed a border zone stretching from the Baltic to the Mediterranean and along the Danube. Reinforced 'Marches' (colonized frontier regions) – the Elbe Marches, the Eastern March, Styrian March, Carinthia, Krajina and the Marches of Verona and Friuli – were intended to hold back the Magyars and Slavs, and also to contain the outposts of Byzantium. This did not in any way impede the cultural integration of the western Slavic and German populations.

The German monarchy held its own during the tenth century by constantly fighting rivals inside the Empire and intrusive or recalcitrant peoples and rulers outside. Its heavily armed cavalry supplied the military impact that was more highly developed than that of the surrounding peoples (Slavs, Magyars, Danes). Between the Elbe and the Oder there was constant fighting, with varying outcomes.

The imperial Church

One essential factor that explains the ascendancy of the German Empire in Europe lies in the fact that the kings based their authority on that of the Church, which they linked very closely with their empire. For that reason, we can speak of the 'imperial Church' (*Reichskirche* in German). To start with, bishops and abbots had the duty to support the king in times of war by equipping heavily armed cavalrymen (*loricati*), paid for from the revenues of their extensive possessions. A recruitment list of 982 shows that the prelates were responsible for the costs of between two-thirds and three-quarters of the *loricati* in the imperial army. Second, as we saw in Chapter 8, about the same time the kings started to invest archbishops and bishops with secular power by appointing them to counties or duchies as a counterpoise to the intransigence of dukes or other secular office-holders. Because of priestly celibacy, bishops could not pass secular offices to their heirs. As a consequence many German archbishops and bishops simultaneously exercised secular and spiritual power in districts that did not always overlap.

Finally, at court, the kings surrounded themselves with highly educated clerics who were entrusted with the most important office of chancellor and other central positions. Then, at the king's instigation, they were invested with Church dignities such as that of archbishop, bishop or abbot so that they could fulfil their duties to the Empire at the expense of the Church patrimony, and contribute to its supra-regional integration. Under Henry III (1039–1056) more than half the German bishops were drawn from the royal court chapel. The chapters attached to episcopal churches also started to function as locations for an extensive network of educated confidants and relations of the king, who himself held the dignity of canon.

For the time being the imperial Church was very helpful to the German kings – and after 962, the emperors as well – who were Christendom's greatest protectors and who actively supported the spread of Christianity. The archiepiscopal see of Magdeburg, established in 967 on the initiative of Otto I, served as an advance German mission station against the Slavic pagans. The systematic approach to missionary work among the Slavic and Magyar peoples led to military conflicts, which strengthened both the cooperation between Church and Empire in combating non-Christians and the solidarity among the peoples of the Empire. Otto's decisive victory over the Magyars at the Lechfeld near Augsburg in 955 was the result of the joint efforts of Saxons, Franks, Alamans, Swabians, Bavarians, Lotharingians and Bohemians, who shortly before this challenge were fully occupied in fighting among themselves.

The construction of monumental cathedrals flourished as a result of direct royal initiative. Otto I showed his fondness for the church he founded at Magdeburg. Henry II built the cathedral in Bamberg, where the chapter school developed into an important intellectual centre with a valuable library. Conrad II built the cathedral at Speyer, in whose crypt many members of the royal dynasty were buried. In the architectural concept characteristic of these Ottonian and Salian structures the west façade was as strongly emphasized as the eastward-facing choir. The symmetry of spiritual and secular power was expressed by two towers of equal height on either side. A throne room was built for the king over the west portal, from which lofty position he was able to hear the mass.

Restoration of the emperorship

The intervention of Otto I in conflicts in Italy caused a crucial twist in the relationship between Empire and Church. Otto was married to Adelheid, the widow of a claimant to the Italian crown, but naturally he also appealed to the Carolingian tradition. Encouraged by local rivalries, as well as by the ambitions of his son Liudolf and of Berengar II of Ivrea, margrave of Friuli (d. 966), Otto led a great army over the Alps in 951. After a successful siege of the old capital of Pavia he had himself elected 'king of the Franks and Lombards', the title Charlemagne had assumed nearly two centuries earlier. The long struggle between the old noble Roman families of the Crescentii and Tusculani led the threatened pope, John XII, who had been 'called' to the highest office at the age of 17, to turn to Otto for protection and to offer him the imperial crown in exchange, exactly as had happened in 800. At Candlemas (2 February) 962 the victorious Otto (whose appearance with his armies was enough to put his enemies to flight), together with the pope, made a triumphant entry into the holy city. The latter

anointed the king and his consort and crowned him emperor 'amidst the applause of the people of Rome'. According to Carolingian tradition the Romans then pledged him their allegiance.

Immediately after Otto's departure the pope whom he had restored to office made a pact with his enemies: Otto turned round and drove the pope out of Rome. He called a synod to remove John and elect his own candidate – another layman – as Pope Leo VIII. The emperor made it clear that thenceforth no pope could be elected or installed without his previous approval. The papacy was now at a low ebb: theologically speaking it did not amount to much, and politically it had become entirely dependent on the emperorship, which itself cherished universal Christian ambitions. These were evident in Otto's activities in southern Italy, where he received homage in Capua, Beneventum and Salerno, and in the campaigns he mounted in Apulia and Calabria, which brought him into the centuries-old Byzantine sphere of influence. It resulted in the marriage in 972 of Otto (II), the heir and successor, to the Byzantine princess Theophanu.

For the German kingship, this renewed link to the Carolingian imperial tradition meant that the position of hegemony it had won in Europe was underpinned by a prestigious ideology of supremacy. At the same time, the papacy was raised for a little while above the level of local rivalries. Now, under Otto III, with the election of his former tutor, the learned Gerbert of Aurillac (999–1003), the *cathedra Petri* received an intellectual boost. Gerbert chose the significant name of Silvester (II), as a token of his affinity with Silvester I (314–335), the bishop of Rome at the time of Emperor Constantine. In the short term, the close links between popes and emperors confirmed the emperors' hold on the imperial Church. In the long term, the reassessment of the papacy held the seeds of inevitable conflict over areas of competences. Moreover, the orientation of the German emperors towards Italy, in addition to their expansion eastwards, demanded considerable military efforts that in time placed an enormous burden on the Empire's resources without producing lasting results. Otto I stayed in Italy from 966 to 972. In the north his position was never really in danger, thanks to capable and trustworthy deputies. The risk for his successors would be greater: after suffering a humiliating defeat at the hands of the Saracens in South Italy in 982, Otto II was immediately faced with grave problems in Germany. It is no exaggeration to say that from Otto I (936–973) to Frederick II (1212–1250) the German kings' fascination with the imperial crown weakened their position of power both in Germany and Italy because in the end they lacked the means to give substance and meaning to the emperorship and were not even able to stop the centrifugal forces it aroused everywhere.

Empire and priesthood

All the German kings from Otto I to Frederick II made the journey south across the Alps at some point in their reign to have themselves invested and crowned as emperor by the pope in the Basilica of St Peter in Rome. By the anointing, the highest religious authority in the West thus bestowed a sacral legitimacy on the emperor's power. The *imperium*, imperial power, consisted of the crowns of Germany, Italy and Burgundy. In addition, the emperors considered themselves to be the highest (suzerain) lords over the kingdoms of Hungary, Poland, Bohemia and Lombardy, and the principalities of Capua, Salerno and Beneventum in southern Italy. For the German kings the link with the Carolingian – and thus the Roman – imperial tradition meant a huge confirmation of their legitimacy. Since 751, the popes had granted the Carolingian kings the ancient title of 'patricius Romanorum', protector of the Romans, which gave them the right to intervene in the turmoil of local factions in Rome. The inspired young emperor, Otto III, had a residence built for himself on the Palatine, the hill in Rome with the ruins of ancient imperial palaces, where he established a household on the Byzantine model.

Yet the German hegemony over Italy was never very significant in practice. Whenever a German king travelled through the land with his army he could usually extract some formal recognition here or there and enforce certain ordinances. Long-lasting control evaded him, however, so that the local and regional powers were always able to regain the upper hand as soon as he left for the north. Resistance to him was often very real. In 1037 Conrad II stood powerless before the closed gates of Milan; in 1047 Henry III laid siege to Beneventum in vain.

In Rome itself the emperors never made any real headway. The rival patrician families asked the Germans for help if it suited them, but the northerners were certainly not popular there. The first German pope, whom Otto III had caused to be elected in 996, Gregory V (996–999), and who had crowned him emperor on Whit Sunday, was driven out by an antipope as soon as Otto had departed. When the emperor returned to Rome in the winter of 997 he had to use force to retake the city. He humiliated the antipope by forcing him to ride through the city facing backwards on a donkey, and he had the patrician Crescentius hanged upside-down. Small wonder, then, that Otto and Silvester II (999–1003), 'his' (second) pope, were driven out of the eternal city in 1002. Both died soon afterwards in miserable circumstances. Now it was again the counts of Tusculum who held the Church territories in central Italy and who for fifty years appointed popes from among members of their family.

It was only under Bishop Bruno of Toul, who was known as Leo IX (1049–1054), that the papal dignity entered a new phase. He, too, was appointed by the emperor, but he belonged to the Burgundian-Lotharingian movement for Church reform that strongly resisted secular influences on the Church (see Chapter 8). The relationship between pope and emperor would always be a sensitive one. The most radical problem was, of course, the dividing line between Church and world, a delicate question that persisted into the twentieth century. In the mind of the deeply religious Henry III there was no discrepancy between the appointment of his chancellor as pope in 1055 and the ideas on reformation. He also considered his own anointed position as sacred. He was the last emperor who was able to appoint his own confidants as popes who were accepted throughout Christendom, and for this he consciously chose two supporters of reform. For the religious legitimation of the emperorship and for the whole system of the imperial Church, however, this movement for the internal purification of the Church contained irreconcilable contradictions. The imperial Church represented such a large-scale involvement of the Church in the apparatus of state, such a close personal and material interlacement, that they could not simply be disentangled without damaging the foundations of the whole Empire.

The battle on two fronts of the Salian House

During a whole century, from 1024 to 1125, four successive German kings belonged to the Salian dynasty, who, as dukes of Swabia, had their home base in south-west Germany. The first three, Conrad II (1024–1039), Henry III (1039–1056), and Henry IV (1056–1106), secured the succession by their eldest sons by having them elected and crowned in Aachen during their own lifetime. Henry V (1106–1125), however, died without heirs, which left the way open for the most important ecclesiastical and secular princes to strengthen their role as electors for at least two reigns. The election of Conrad III of Hohenstaufen, duke of Franconia, in 1138 soon introduced another dynasty of dukes from south-west Germany as the main challengers for a near-hereditary kingship, lasting until 1254. The Hohenstaufen were heavily contested by the Guelph (Welf) family, which dominated the duchies of Saxony and Bavaria, and whose kinsman Otto IV was brought to a much-disputed throne from 1198 until 1218.

The Salian kings had to defend their position towards the regional aristocracy, for whom any sign of royal weakness triggered opposition or even open revolt. Conrad II and Henry III strove to strengthen their own power *vis-à-vis* the Church as well as the magnates. Conrad did so by concentrating and expanding imperial domains, the administration of which he entrusted to a class of noblemen of unfree origin, the so-called ministerials. Henry III submitted Bohemia in 1040 and strengthened the south-eastern border by the creation of the imperial borough of Nuremberg as the main centre of a belt of fortified margravates. He died at the age of 39, leaving his son of six, already crowned, under the protection of the pope.

Henry III was strongly committed to the reform of the Church. In Rome, he made use of his authority as 'patricius' to defend the 'liberty of the Church' against the manipulations of the local aristocratic families. The reasons for this search for 'liberty' was obvious, if one considers that between 1045 and the election of Pope Gregory VII (1073–1085) in 1073, no less than 12 popes had claimed Saint Peter's chair, six of whom were deposed by a council. In Germany, however, ecclesiastical and secular powers were so profoundly

entangled that any application of the same principles would have led to a fatal disruption of the political system. This was exactly the reason why the German kings after Henry III were met with so much greater obstinacy than other kings in Latin Christendom, who were equally accustomed to appointing prelates. Besides, in no other country were the secular rights in the hands of bishops and abbots so extensive as in Germany.

The reign of Henry IV was certainly one of the most dramatic ones of the Middle Ages. During the nine years of his minority, secular and ecclesiastical princes had mainly taken care of their own territorial interests. Also Saxony grew into a nearly permanent hotbed of opposition against Henry's rule, and in particular during the great revolt of 1073–1075. The Saxon magnates reacted against the construction of fortresses in the eastern parts of the duchy, where ministerials instead of their own kinsmen had been appointed as wardens. They would continue to provide the core of aristocratic resistance against the king at any moment when a papal ban put him in a delicate position. Henry's appointments, in 1075, of the archbishop of Milan, the most important city of imperial Italy, and of the bishops of two towns within the papal sphere of influence, Spoleto and Fermo, provoked a fierce reaction from the dogmatic Pope Gregory VII, threatening the king with excommunication. In the next year, German and Lombard bishops' synods refuted obedience to the pope, which in turn led to Henry's excommunication and deposition by the pope. In October 1076 an assembly of German princes, unbound by the pope of their oath of fealty to the king, forced Henry to full compliance, since they made their allegiance to him dependent on his full submission leading to the lifting of his ban before next February. They further decided to submit all disputes between the king and the princes to a court of arbitration, to be chaired by the pope in person. Some of the princes already reflected on the eventuality of electing another king. Two factors concurred to this most dramatic and innovative positioning: first, in a world through and through Christian it was completely unthinkable for ecclesiastical and lay magnates to obey a king banned from the Church; second, many princes were happy enough for other, political reasons to seize any opportunity to weaken the king. Henry's response was as quick as it was daring. In the beginning of 1077, in the depth of winter, he crossed the 2,000-metre (6,500-feet) high Alpine pass of Mont Cenis to ask the pope's pardon publicly in order to deprive his adversaries' actions of legitimacy. For this he had literally to put on the penitential sackcloth and stand in the snow before the walls of Canossa, a stronghold in Tuscany, where Gregory was staying in the company of his faithful ally Mathilda, margravine of Tuscany. Whether or not the gesture was sincere, Gregory could not refuse forgiveness, and so there was no war against Henry. It reduced his opponents to a small minority of bishops and princes. They elected three successive anti-kings, but their influence remained marginal – the pope's open support notwithstanding.

The further conflicts between Henry and the successive popes feature truly heroic episodes, due to the protagonists' obstinate characters. In 1080, Gregory excommunicated and deposed Henry again, and even prophesized his imminent death or decay. However, it was not Henry but the anti-king Rudolph of Swabia who died that same year. Henry retaliated with a synod that deposed Gregory along the rules of canon law, and elected an antipope. In 1081 to 1084, Henry felt strong enough to make a journey through Italy, where he took Rome, drove Gregory into exile, and had himself crowned emperor in the Saint Peter's basilica by the antipope. The whole contest evidently weakened the positions of both protagonists who had overplayed their hands and thus lost legitimacy. The German kings lost their direct control over papal elections, and the struggle between pope and king/emperor provoked schisms in scores of bishoprics. As a consequence, the imperial Church lost a good deal of its efficacy as a pillar of state power. The German princes generally gained autonomy during the contest, while the communes in bishop's cities equally strengthened their influence. Nevertheless, Henry could achieve the election and coronation of his eldest son Conrad in 1087. He then presided over a synod of bishops and aristocrats who proclaimed God's peace in the whole empire. Doing this, he adopted an ecclesiastical instrument to consolidate his secular power. Remarkably, he repeated the issuing of a territorial peace for four years in the Empire (*Reichslandfriede*) in 1103, explicitly including Jews. They had been victims of heavy pogroms in several imperial cities under the impression

of years of food scarcity and the chaotic start of the First Crusade.

Henry's long reign was marked by even more turbulence. The conflict with the papacy was not restricted to the investiture contest (Chapter 8), it was acerbated by the struggle for power over central Italy, where the popes had territorial interests. Pope Urban II (1088–1099) tried to undermine imperial ambitions by supporting an anti-imperial party. In 1089 he arranged the marriage of his staunch supporter, Mathilda, the widowed heiress of the margravate of Tuscany, with the much younger heir of the influential oppositional Guelph family. They even lured Henry's eldest son, King Conrad, into their camp, and had him crowned king of Italy in Milan in 1093. Under these circumstances, the first urban league was created against the emperor, including the Lombard towns of Milan, Cremona, Piacenza and Lodi. As a consequence, Henry deposed Conrad and had his younger son, Henry, elected and crowned in 1099. In spite of the territorial peace, young Henry revolted against his father, finding support with the pope, and with many bishops and princes; 52 of them elected and inaugurated him as king, leaving his father to die in captivity. During his reign, Henry V (1106–1125) still had to face the same problems as his father: opposition of the Saxon aristocracy, rivalry with the pope over Tuscany, the investiture contest, excommunication and deposition. However, the ecclesiastical sanctions had lost much of their impact. In 1121, after years of struggle, a peace committee of 24 princes, 12 of each side, forced emperor and pope to come to terms with regard to the issue of lay investiture. Its result was the Concordat of Worms of 1122.

The Mediterranean ambitions of the Hohenstaufen

The election of Frederick Barbarossa as German king in 1152 marked the dawn of a century in which two impressive emperors of the Hohenstaufen dynasty, Frederick I (1152–1190), and his grandson Frederick II (1212–1250), dazzled Europe. Their aspirations stretched as far as the Holy Land where they went on crusade. They wanted to rule not only Lombardy but also Tuscany and all South Italy, including Sicily and Sardinia. This brought them repeatedly into conflict with the papacy. They maintained close, often tense, relations with the Byzantine emperors and the kings of Castile, France and England. The universal scale of their ambitions and the consolidation of the western kingdoms led to a period of genuine European diplomacy. In addition to styling himself consequently as 'king of the Romans' (*rex Romanorum*), a title frequently but not consistently used by all German kings since the end of the tenth century to express their exclusive claim on the Roman emperorship, Frederick, after his coronation as emperor, was the first to upgrade his imperial authority to 'sacred' (*sacrum imperium*).

To ensure his election and then to stabilize his position Frederick Barbarossa had to make far-reaching concessions as soon as he assumed power. Most important was his policy towards the inheritance of Henry the Proud, from the rival and extremely powerful Guelph dynasty, who had succeeded in laying his hands on both the duchies of Bavaria and Saxony. Barbarossa for the time being opted for appeasement, not confrontation. He confirmed Henry the Proud's son, Henry the Lion, in both duchies, so that the whole of the north and east of the Empire remained in Guelph hands. Although in 1180, after a deep conflict, Barbarossa deprived Henry the Lion of his ducal dignities, this did not break Guelph power, because Henry remained in possession of his family's rich estates and lordships in the Harz mountains and around Brunswick. However, Saxony and Bavaria were now again enfeoffed to different dukes. Besides, Bavaria was reduced in size by the separation of the margravate of Austria, which was itself elevated to the status of a dukedom in favour of the Babenberg dynasty. At the same time, Barbarossa did all that he could to strengthen the *Hausmacht* of the Hohenstaufen, which was concentrated of old in the duchy of Swabia. Through marriage, Barbarossa sought to extend his power over the German free county of Burgundy, the Franche-Comté in French, so that the influence of the Hohenstaufen now stretched over the entire south-west of the Empire. An entire new avenue to the extension of Hohenstaufen power was opened when Barbarossa's eldest son Henry was married to the heiress to the kingdom of Sicily, which comprised all of South Italy (see pp. 163–164). By the time Henry ascended the throne as Henry VI (1190–1197) he could claim to be king over a territory stretching from the marshes of

Plate 9.2 Scenes from the coronation of the emperor, Henry VI, by Pope Celestine III in 1191 in Rome. Coloured ink drawings from the manuscript of Peter of Eboli's *De rebus Siculis carmen*, c. 1200

Holstein in the north to the beaches of Sicily in the south.

After Henry's premature death, the struggle between the Hohenstaufens and Guelphs flared up again during the minority of Frederick II, which would last from 1197 to 1212. Both sides had their own candidate crowned King of the Romans: the Hohenstaufen, backed by the French king, chose young Frederick's uncle, Duke Philip of Swabia; the Guelphs, supported by Richard the Lionheart of England, Henry the Lion's son Otto of Brunswick who, as count of Poitou, was Richard's vassal. When Otto – who had succeeded Philip on his death in 1208 as Otto IV – began to reinforce his authority over Italy, he was excommunicated by Innocent III. It was the beginning of a complex international tug of war which increasingly came to be seen as an extension of the bitter Anglo-French conflict at the time and which only ended in 1214 on the battlefield of Bouvines (see p. 168). Once again, the Hohenstaufen prevailed, and Henry VI's son Frederick was generally recognized as the king of Germany, Italy and Sicily.

Because of his long stays in Italy Frederick II allowed Germany to be ruled by regents, often archbishops. As prince-bishops they were invested with secular power over bishoprics and seemed as eager as any secular prince to extend their own territory. The regency of Henry VII, Frederick's eldest son and King of the Romans, did not meet with much success either. In 1235 Frederick sentenced him to life-long imprisonment for treason, where he committed suicide. The emperor behaved like a foreigner in Germany, and of course his contemporaries noticed this. 'Many camels

and dromedaries, Saracens and Ethiopians who could perform diverse tricks, with apes and leopards' were found in his retinue. His efforts to modernize justice and administration along the lines of the professional and centralized Sicilian model with which he was very familiar failed in Germany, simply because the necessary resources were not available and local customary law would not allow them.

Finally, in 1220 Frederick II yielded to the demands of bishops, archbishops and abbots, invested with secular powers, in matters of their territorial policies, relinquishing, for example, imperial mint and toll sites in the areas of their authority. The spiritual princes acted in this as a close-knit group, very different from the subservient imperial Church of previous centuries. Eleven years later, in 1231, in the *Statutum in favorem principum* ('Statute in favour of the princes'), by and large the same freedom from royal interference was

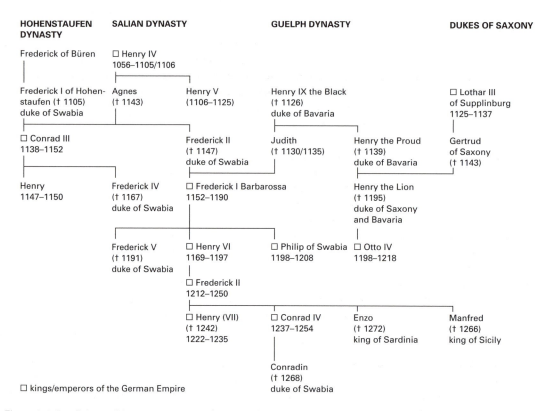

Figure 9.1 Family tree of the emperors and kings of the German Empire, showing changes in dynasties during the twelfth and thirteenth centuries

granted to all office-holders, among others, in their attempts to curb the pursuit of autonomy of countless new towns. From that moment on we can rightly term the dukes, margraves, counts and prince-bishops of Germany 'territorial princes'. It was the outcome of a dramatic struggle for power, in which the German kings had to make continual efforts to stabilize and pacify the conflicting powers north of the Alps, because their attention was focused mainly on Italy. Frederick I spent ten of the first 25 years of his reign in Italy. Frederick II went to Germany for the first time, and still had to learn German, when he was elected King of the Romans as an 18-year-old. After that he still spent the greater part of his life in the south.

Italy

In Lombardy the emperors were faced with rapidly growing and autonomous towns. Milan, the largest of them, took the leadership of a league of Lombard towns. Frederick I managed to force the league into submission in 1158 and, in a diet held at Roncaglia immediately afterwards, issued a manifesto for a centralized government. He tried to establish the rights of the crown, *regalia*, precisely, both in matters of jurisdiction and for receiving revenues. With his coherent and rationally thought-out legislation, Frederick I, for the first time in the Middle Ages, joined the tradition of the Roman emperors. He had the assistance of lawyers from Italian towns, in particular from Bologna, where specialists in the study of Roman and canon law had been settled for some decades. They formed the basis of what is considered to be the oldest university in Europe.

Milan did not give in so easily. Together with Brescia and Piacenza, the town resisted, thereby enjoying the warm support of the pope, who in his own lands was similarly bothered by the assertive emperor. Two parties formed, one supporting the emperor, which was joined by Cremona and Pavia, Milan's rivals, and one supporting the pope. In 1162 Barbarossa's army laid Milan to waste, but Emperor Manuel I of Byzantium offered ample financial help for its reconstruction. He, too, feared the expansion of his western counterpart's authority in Italy. He formed a new alliance against Frederick with Venice, Byzantium's old ally; Verona, Padua and Vicenza

joined in. In 1183, despite all his efforts, Frederick was forced to grant Milan and the other members of the Lombard League substantial jurisdictional autonomy and competences in the areas surrounding them.

The factual stalemate between Frederick I and the Lombard League paved the way for the remarkably independent development of the towns of northern and central Italy. After Frederick's death, imperial power faced periods of weakness and was constantly faced with rivalry from other monarchs and the fierce opposition of cities, communes and noblemen both in Italy and in the Empire. The combination of the crown of Sicily with the ambition to control northern and central Italy and Germany as well, simply proved unrealistic. On the other hand, urban growth was nowhere as dramatic as in northern and central Italy. By the end of the thirteenth century Milan, Venice and Florence had at least 100,000 inhabitants, and 20 other cities had over 20,000. The highest concentration was to be found on two axes in the Po valley, from Milan to Venice and from Milan to Bologna, and in Tuscany in the Arno valley. The major cities in Lombardy, Tuscany and the Romagna dominated their environment (*contado* in Italian) and created city-states with a surface of 2,000 to 3,000 square kilometres; Milan and Bologna even controlled contado's of over 4,000 square kilometres. In the twelfth century most of these city-states were ruled by small councils in which both the old landed nobilities and the wealthy merchant families were represented. Increasingly, they were torn apart by party strife between adherents and adversaries of either emperor or pope. The imperial party became generally known as the Ghibellines, a corruption of Waiblingen, an important stronghold of the Hohenstaufen in Swabia. Their opponents rallied under the name of Guelphs, corrupted from the German Welfen, the Hohenstaufen's most obstinate enemies and in Italy, from the rule of Frederick II onwards, the rallying point for anti-imperial sentiments, usually in favour of the pope.

Frederick I made a brilliant move in 1184 when he betrothed his eldest son, Henry VI, King of the Romans, to the 11-year-older Costanza, daughter of King Roger II of Sicily. At the time William II, her cousin, was king, but the fact that he was still childless after five years of marriage had not escaped Frederick. William died in 1189, and Henry was entitled to call himself king of Sicily on behalf of his wife. He was crowned emperor in 1191 but was unable to take Sicily until 1194, helped then by a curious stroke of luck. No less a person than Richard the Lionheart of England had been taken prisoner in Austria at the end of 1192. He had been shipwrecked on his way home from the Third Crusade and had continued his journey overland in disguise. Since Richard was on the side of the Guelphs, Henry VI only released his prisoner after two years' captivity and payment of an extraordinarily high ransom. In addition, Richard was obliged to ask for the return of his kingdom in fief out of the emperor's hands in exchange for an annual rent. The pope may have guaranteed crusaders indulgence for their sins, but things could sometimes go very wrong in this world.

Emperor Henry VI died in 1197, leaving his 3-year-old son Frederick as king of Sicily. Pope Innocent III, a very learned theologian and canonist, acted as his guardian as liege lord of the kingdom of Sicily. The young Frederick enjoyed a broad education, learnt Italian, Arabic, Greek and Latin and showed a particular interest in the natural sciences. The Arab presence in Sicily gave him access to the latest scientific knowledge. In 1211 young Frederick, already heir to the crown of Sicily since his father's death, was elected King of the Romans; in 1220 he was crowned emperor.

Emperor and pope

The struggle between the emperor and the towns of Lombardy once again intensified when Frederick II accused the Milanese of heresy. Attacking heresy had been a priority of the Church since the Fourth Lateran Council of 1215, and the secular rulers had to move against heresy too. In 1238 Frederick went to war with Milan, which was as usual supported by the pope, while the emperor had the help of a number of other towns in the Po valley. His army contained thousands of Saracens, settled at Lucera in Apulia by him. Again the emperor had the victory, but no definitive result. While the war was raging, the pope excommunicated Frederick on two occasions, and both protagonists organized a vigorous propaganda campaign among other princes. One of the 16 complaints made against the emperor was the following:

'The emperor has described as idiots everyone who believed that God could be born of a virgin, because nobody can see the light of day unless he was conceived in the union of a man and woman. According to him man should not believe anything that he cannot prove through the power of his intellect and nature.'

At first, the excommunication of the emperor had few consequences. Even in 1245, when Innocent IV, who had fled to Lyons, had a council resolve to depose Frederick II, the kings of England and France remained neutral. Not many German bishops put in an appearance at Lyons, but the three Rhine archbishops (Cologne, Trier and Mainz) now switched allegiance to appoint rival kings, among them Count William II of Holland (1247–1256). His authority did not extend beyond the Lower Rhine region.

Innocent IV went to extreme lengths, instructing the clergy, the mendicant friars in particular, to preach a crusade against the emperor rather than against Palestine. In response, Frederick's criticisms of the clergy echoed the arguments of various heterodoxies of the period:

In truth, the enormous incomes with which they enrich themselves through their exploitation of many kingdoms, make them mad. . . . It is therefore necessary to return the clergy of all ranks, especially the highest, to the condition of the original Church, imitating the humility of the Lord in apostolic conduct. . . . Therefore you and all princes must direct all your efforts, together with us, to ensure that they lay aside all excesses and, content with moderate possessions, serve God.

The sudden death of the emperor in 1250, and the short lives of his successors, quickly put an end to the hopeless controversy. Both parties were losers: the popes had to accept that their traditional spiritual weapons (anathema, excommunication, dissolution of loyalty vows), and even the secular ones (enfeoffment and deposition), were no longer of great consequence – unlike in the eleventh century. States were by now based on a tighter organization. Moreover, it was abundantly clear that popes and other princes of the

Church were occupied with worldly politics. The ambitions of the Gregorian reformation to set the clergy above the lay world failed because of this renewed secularization.

After 1190 there was confusion about German kingship. The growing fixation of the Hohenstaufen on Italy, with Sicily already half immersed in other cultures, had alienated them from the German reality. After the death of William II of Holland in 1256 the office of king was exercised only in theory by Richard of Cornwall, a brother of Henry III of England, while another group of princes elected King Alfonso of Castile, who never even set foot in Germany. This period was known as the Interregnum; it did not come to an end until 1273 when Rudolf of Habsburg was elected King of the Romans. He was unable to curb the freedom of the imperial cities or the territorial princes, or even of the peasant communities of the Swiss valleys under direct Habsburg control, who started their push to autonomy immediately after Rudolf's death in 1291. All these new types of territorial principalities would continue to call the shots until 1872, even if from 1438 to 1918 the Habsburg family provided the emperors.

Vassal states in central Europe?

Seen from the double perspective of Christianization and pacification it is understandable that the Empire and the papacy worked hard to establish Christian kingdoms on the exposed eastern flank of Christendom. Already in Charlemagne's days the eastern border of the Frankish world had functioned much like the frontier of the late Roman Empire: it fostered the concentration and consolidation of power *outside the border* in the hands of the strongest and cleverest local and regional Slav leaders. In the ninth century the first powerful early Slav state had emerged in the area that is now Slovakia: the Principality of Great Moravia. It reached its zenith and greatest extent in the 870s, but was destroyed by the Magyars in 906. Soon it would dawn upon the Slav world that the East Franks or Germans, and not the Magyars, would be the adversary to reckon with. From 960, under the leadership of Prince Mieszko, a strong alliance had formed east of the Oder in reaction to the growing pressure of the German margraves. Mieszko was

obliged to recognize the hegemony of the German Empire and pay tribute. When he was baptized in 966, however, the German oppressors lost the excuse of conversion to Christianity and had to accept the development of a native Polish monarchy and recognize Mieszko as an ally. In 992 he sought the more detached protection of Rome by 'offering Poland to Saint Peter'. The foundation of the archbishopric of Gniezno in the year 1000 was a joint initiative of Emperor Otto III and Pope Silvester II. Mieszko's successor, Boleslaw, was able to maintain his position so successfully that he had himself crowned king in 1025 without the involvement of the newly elected German king, Conrad II (1024–39). Mieszko II, on the other hand, paid tribute to Conrad in 1030, but Polish royal power crumbled soon afterwards. In the twelfth century the emperors forced the dukes of Polish lands into vassalage.

In Bohemia, the Germans found greater internal cohesion. As early as the beginning of the tenth century, the house of Przemyslid gained control. While tensions were mounting between emperor and pope, in 1085 Henry IV granted the royal dignity to Bohemia, with the status of imperial vassal to the Przemyslid dynasty. The fateful implication of all this was that vast extents of Slav land – and large Slavonic-speaking populations – were taken up in the German Empire as feudal principalities: in addition to the Przemyslid kingdom of Bohemia, which by this time included Moravia, also the former Polish duchies of Pomerania ('Pommern' in German) and Silesia.

In Hungary, Otto III and Silvester II had crowned Stephen (997–1038, the later saint) king in 1001 and established the central bishop's see in Esztergom. The Arpad dynasty, which seized power in 1046, shook off its original dependence on the Empire, challenged the still-active pagan opposition and kept the Magyars under control in the vast lowland plain that was protected on the north and east by the Carpathians. From there Croatia was annexed in about 1100 and, between 1120 and 1150, Bosnia also came under the protection of Hungary. The new kingdom thus acquired access to the Adriatic Sea, to which it would cling for centuries. Further to the south, Serbia struggled out of Byzantine grasp in the second half of the twelfth century. It was recognized as an independent kingdom in 1217, and in the further course of the thirteenth century would expand remarkably in the direction of both Macedonia and Bosnia.

The emergence, with German support, of the three Christian kingdoms in the border zone between the Slavonic- and German-speaking worlds – Poland, Bohemia and Hungary – was without doubt of enormous significance for the future. The names and status of those kingdoms have remained a reference point for the political activities of states throughout all the uncertainties of history, right up to the present day.

FRANCE: THE CONCENTRIC MODEL

The West Frankish Carolingians did not have a strong power base during the tenth century. They found themselves up against territorial princes and feudal lords who, assured of their strongholds and the surrounding land, entered into alliances with anyone who could offer them any prospect of expanding their power. Nowhere was the crumbling of royal power so complete. Even after Adalbero, archbishop of Rheims, managed to persuade the most important vassals to remove the last, weak Carolingian from the kingship and in 987 engineered the election of the count of Paris, Hugh Capet, of the powerful family of the Robertians, there was little change except that the title of king was retained. The influence of the Capetians was limited to the Île-de-France where, with the assent of the local potentates, they were able to exercise authority. It was not until much later, from the twelfth century, that it became apparent that the Capetian dynasty was in a position slowly to recover some degree of central power. The direct rule of the French crown gradually expanded in a concentric movement in every direction. In the long term, the gradual expansion from a powerful centre in France would make possible the effective government of a considerable territory.

In comparison with Germany, and also, as we shall see, with England and the Spanish kingdoms, the monarchy developed very late in France, actually not until the end of the twelfth century. Under Louis VI (1108–1137) and Louis VII (1137–1180) the region over which the kings could wield their power directly extended no further than the Paris basin and southwards to Sens, Orléans and Bourges. They could mobilize an army there of between 300 and 400 knights, which would be enlarged by the greater numbers of infantry raised by the lands of the independent lordships and royal abbeys. This central region was surrounded by territorial principalities, however, which in theory were held in fief from the crown but where in the preceding centuries powerful princely dynasties had in fact built up their own little autonomous monarchic states. The duchy of Normandy alone had more than a quarter of the resources of the entire kingdom at its disposal, and after 1066 even more when the dukes had become kings of England. The county of Champagne profited from the proceeds of its annual fairs. The Flemish towns underwent a phenomenal growth: in 1128 Louis VI was forced to accept their choice of candidate as count. The later count of Flanders, Philip of Alsace (1157–1191), was a prince of European stature who took part in the second and third crusades, in the latter on an equal footing with Emperor Frederick I Barbarossa and kings Richard of England and Philip II Augustus of France. Besides contending with the territorial princes, the French kings had to assert their claims against the feudal lords who used all means possible to defend their *châtellenies* (literally, 'castle areas'). After a fierce struggle this aristocracy was gradually curbed, becoming loyal vassals in a pyramid of vassal relationships that became the backbone of state polity.

Sometimes small events, including those in an emotional sphere, have large consequences. After 15 years of marriage, which produced two daughters, Louis VII reached the conclusion that his wife, Eleanor of Aquitaine (1122–1204), was too closely related to him to continue living with him in accordance with the rules of the Church. The real reason, of course, was the lack of a son. Salic law stated that the French crown could only be inherited through the male line, so the marriage was annulled. The king in due course took as his wife a daughter of the house of Champagne, who after ten tantalizing years did indeed bear him a son, Philip II. Through this dynastic link the county of Champagne fell to the French crown in 1285. On the other hand, the union of northern and southern France, which had seemed imminent on the marriage of Louis and Eleanor in 1137, was postponed for many decades. In its stead came an east–west split.

Eleanor did not sit still. Within a month of her divorce she married the king's arch-rival, Henry

BOX 9.1 POPULAR SOVEREIGNTY IN FLANDERS, 1128

In medieval Europe recognition of a monarch or a prince of similar rank by the most prominent among his subjects was required, but at the same time conditional: representatives were invited to swear an oath of loyalty as vassals or pseudo-vassals (e.g. towns). This implied that the assent could be withheld or revoked, just as in a feudal contract. An early example of such an action is described in a remarkable Flemish chronicle covering the few years before and up to 1128. After the murder of Count Charles the Good, William Clito of Normandy, a grandson of William the Conqueror, had been inaugurated as the new count in 1127 under condition that he showed respect for the privileges of the land and particularly for those of the rapidly growing cities. Within a year he had violated so many stipulations that citizens rebelled in Saint-Omer and Lille, and a broad movement of opposition arose. In Ghent, the citizens had the following request addressed in their name to the count by a sympathetic nobleman, in the wording of the count's chancery clerk Galbert of Bruges:

'Lord count, if you had wished to deal justly with our citizens, your burghers, and with us as their friends, you would not have imposed evil exactions upon us and acted with hostility toward us but, on the contrary, you would have defended us from our enemies and treated us honourably. But now you have acted contrary to law and in your own person you have broken the oaths that we swore in your name concerning the remission of the toll, the maintenance of peace and the other rights which the men of this land obtained from the counts of the land, your good predecessors . . . and from yourself; you have violated your faith and done injury to ours since we took the oath to this effect together with you. . . . Let your court, if you please, be summoned at Ypres, which is located in the middle of your land, and let the barons from both sides, and our peers and all the responsible [*sapientiores*] men among the clergy and people, come together in peace and without arms, and let them judge, quietly and after due consideration, without guile or evil intent. If in their opinion you can keep the countship in the future without violating the honour of the land, I agree that you should keep it. But if, in fact, you are unworthy of keeping it, that is, lawless and faithless, a deceiver and perjurer, give up the countship, relinquish it to us so that we can entrust it to someone suitable and with rightful claims to it. For we are the mediators between the king of France and you to guarantee that you undertake nothing important in the county without regard for the honour of the land and our counsel.'

This remarkably clear and early pronouncement of the principles of constitutional government under the control of the representatives of the three estates emanates from the feudal notions of contract: a vassal had the right of resistance if he was wrongly treated. The argument introduced the widening of this concept to all citizens; it was grounded on their mutually sworn fealty on the basis of law. The count, however, refused the proposal, rejected the homage previously done to him by the spokesman and challenged him to combat. His reaction refuted the notion of the countship as a public office subject to judgment by the 'wisest' representatives from the three estates, united in his council. The proposed meeting of the broad *curia*, the count's court, was never held, and arms finally decided in favour of the citizens. During the remainder of the twelfth century, successive counts did not repeat the same mistakes, but granted new privileges to the cities; no mention is to be found of any effective assembly of the kind announced in 1128.

Source fragment taken from *Galbert of Bruges, The Murder of Charles the Good, Count of Flanders*, ed. J.B. Ross (New York and London, 1967), ch. 95.

Plantagenet, count of Anjou (1151–1189) and at that moment the most important contender for the English crown, which indeed came to him in 1154, when he became King Henry II. Since Henry's titles, besides that of king of England, included duke of Normandy, count of Anjou, Maine and Poitou, while Eleanor retained her ducal right to Aquitaine (which at that time included all of Auvergne), the new royal pair ruled over one (connected) third of French territory. This power complex, which is usually called the Angevin Empire ('empire of Anjou'), was much larger in France alone than the area ruled directly by the French king. Both Henry and Eleanor were powerful personalities and art lovers. Eleanor bore her second husband eight children, four of them sons.

The Capetian monarchy was not to become dominant until the next generation. The personal qualities of Philip II Augustus (1180–1223) – he earned the imperial soubriquet after his annexation of Normandy – made a decisive contribution to this. There was no one more able who could make use of the chances offered by his rivals' failings. In 1180 he acquired the towns of Arras and Saint-Omer through a dowry. At that time these large, wealthy industrial towns belonged to Flanders, which stretched even further south. In 1185 after a military confrontation with Philip of Alsace, the count of Flanders, the king succeeded in taking the entire southern part of his lands, which came to form the county of Artois. In addition, he acquired Picardy (the area around Amiens) and the county of Vermandois (the area around Péronne). Consequently, the income of the French crown increased by 46 per cent during the first 20 years of King Philip's reign.

But this was just the beginning. The next confrontation was about linking Paris with the North Sea, which in fact meant control of Normandy, the prize possession of the Plantagenet kings of England. After incessant intriguing to stir discontent within the Plantagenet family, Philip Augustus used the violations of feudal law made by Henry II's youngest son and new king of England, John Lackland (1199–1216), as an excuse to censure him as his vassal (in Aquitaine). After a month-long siege of the stronghold of Château-Gaillard, strategically built on a rock on the Seine, French troops seized Normandy and the lands along the Loire in 1204. After Normandy the

other Plantagenet territories north of the Vienne river followed one by one: Anjou, Touraine, Maine and part of Poitou. John's efforts to break the power of the French by forming a coalition with Flanders and Otto IV, the Guelph emperor, failed dismally at the great Battle of Bouvines (1214). In the end, only Aquitaine remained English, albeit, as before, in fief from the French king. Here lay the basic elements for the long-lasting personal union of England and Aquitaine, though to some also a bone of contention, inevitably leading to new war.

The tide had now definitely turned in favour of Philip Augustus. For the first time a French king had a marked preponderance over all crown vassals, both in military and financial terms. Crown income had easily doubled between 1180 and 1220, and whereas King Philip could boast of receiving over 130,000 pounds a year at the end of his reign, his wealthiest vassals, the count of Flanders and the duke of Burgundy, had to be satisfied with about 30,000 pounds.

And that was not all. In the preceding years, King Philip had also profited from Innocent III's witch-hunt against the Cathars in southern France and Aragon, who had been accused of heresy. Simon of Montfort led large numbers of barons from northern France in the Albigensian Crusade (so named after the town of Albi) in 1208. Count Raymond of Toulouse, who was openly sympathetic towards the Cathars and had therefore been excommunicated, defended himself with the aid of the king of Aragon, Peter II. Their troops were defeated in 1213 at the Battle of Muret, where Peter himself, less than a year earlier one of Christendom's great heroes on the field of Las Navas de Tolosa, was now slain as a heretic. For a while, the county of Toulouse was held by Simon of Montfort. In 1229, Raymond's son, another Raymond, was forced to surrender the eastern part of the region, with the towns of Beaucaire and Carcassone, to the French crown. Furthermore his daughter and heiress was given in marriage to a younger son of King Louis VIII (1223–1226), which assured that the county of Toulouse would eventually fall into Capetian hands. Aragon now had no further role to play north of the Pyrenees, and France started to annex Languedoc. Fifty years after 1180 the area under the direct control of the French crown had been quadrupled in the north, west and south. Only after the Hundred Years War

(1337–1453), and especially in the period 1463–1532, the French monarchy would continue to expand its territory in every direction through the systematic annexation of previously autonomous principalities, such as Brittany in the west, and the Dauphiné, Provence, and Franche-Comté east of the Saône-Rhône-line, which for centuries had formed the frontier between France and the German Empire.

A parallel development to this territorial expansion of French royal power, which would not stop until well into the eighteenth century, was the centralization of government. In this respect the reign of Philip II Augustus was also a turning point. In domestic government, he systematically replaced the great vassals in his council with members of more modest origins but with greater technical expertise. He brought in the Order of the Templars to take care of his treasury and also to finance the annexation of Normandy. His most drastic innovation, however, was the introduction after 1190 of regional officials, known as *baillis* in the north and *sénéchaux* in the south, an innovation we shall discuss further (see p. 181).

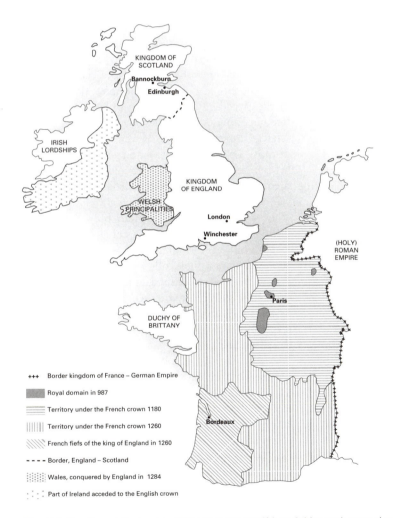

Map 9.1 Creation of England and France in the twelfth and thirteenth centuries

THE MAKING OF ENGLAND

Shortly after the year 1000 the House of Alfred of Wessex, which had ruled over England for more than a century, had to make way for the Danish king Sven Forkbeard, who in 1013 invaded and conquered the country with a large expeditionary force. His son, King Cnut the Great (1014–1035), then ruled over Denmark and Norway as well as England. He based his strong position of authority on his recognition by the thegns, the local Anglo-Saxon aristocrats. Cnut was succeeded by two of his sons, but after a few years, with the accession of Edward the Confessor (1042–1066), the House of Alfred the Great was again on the throne. Through Emma, Edward's mother, many noblemen from her native Normandy gained influence in England. A number of earls were opposed to this. They found a leader in Harold, the earl of Wessex, who was proclaimed king when Edward died. He had to defend his position against his own brother, who sought help from Cnut's relatives. Harald Hardrada, king of Norway, brought a great army against Harold, but was defeated near York. In the meantime, William, duke of Normandy, had crossed the English Channel with a large crowd of warriors eager for booty, to fight for his family's claims. In the famous Battle of Hastings, in September 1066, William's mounted knights defeated the English thegns and housecarls, who had chosen to fight on foot, and Harold was killed. This marked a turning point in English history. William the Conqueror (1066–1087), as he is known in English historiography, consolidated his victory on the battlefield by setting in motion a revolutionary change in landownership that went unparalleled in medieval history. In the five years after Hastings the native Anglo-Scandinavian landowning aristocracy was virtually wiped out and replaced by a new, Norman, landed elite. Whether one should describe the new property relations as feudo-vassalic is a matter of lengthy debate. The Norman landowners, as well as the landowning abbeys and bishoprics, were all called 'tenants', '[land]holders'. It is equally clear that, except for the king himself, all these 'tenants' held their land 'from' someone; that is to say, from either the king or a king's tenant. This implies that landholding was in some way conditional, and in the early years after the Conquest the most important condition was evidently military service. At a later stage military service could be redeemed, and especially land held from the king came to be burdened with tax-like payments that often are reminiscent of feudal obligations, such as 'aid' and 'relief'. Other feudo-vassalic features were the obligation for heirs to tenures to do homage and swear allegiance (superior fidelity) to the king. Whether this turns royal tenants (also called 'tenants-in-chief') and their sub-tenants (most of them knights) into 'vassals' and their tenures into 'fiefs' (a quite common word in English sources after 1066), is a matter of definition and convenience. Some modern authors have no problem at all with speaking of a 'feudal hierarchy', whereas others are more cautious.

From another point of view, landowning was connected to lordship. Most of the land taken over by the Normans was organized in (usually) bipartite estates, called manors, after the Norman word 'manoir', which made owners of tenures at the same time lords of manors wielding limited rights of lordship over the free and unfree (serf) families that were settled on their estates. Important lay lords were commonly styled 'barons'. The sum total of a baron's tenures were called his 'honour'. A baronial honour could amount to hundreds of manors and also include boroughs, but that was rare. Over the course of the first century after the Conquest the greatest barons were provided with the title of earl – the English equivalent of the continental 'count', but, at least after 1066, without the latter's connotation of a public office.

Another way to consolidate the Conquest was the erection of strongholds on the Norman model within major English boroughs (towns). Early examples are the Tower of London and the Norman castles of York, Rochester and Durham.

Finally, the Norman kings consolidated their vulnerable position as foreign conquerors by building a strong, centralized system of government. They used the Anglo-Saxon tradition as a basis to do this. The counties, or shires, which still exist today within practically the same boundaries, date from that time, as do the hundreds into which they were divided and the sheriffs appointed by the king to each shire. These sheriffs had fiscal, military and judicial responsibilities. Unlike the continental counts from the Carolingian Empire, sheriffs were not recompensed for their services with lands given in fief, neither did their office itself ever become a fiefdom, for that matter. Through a hierarchically constructed system of councils that met to discuss certain matters, the *gemot* of the shire and the hundred court, the English crown had been able to create a central royal administration. After 1066 the Norman kings succeeded in maintaining and even reinforcing this structure. At first, it stood parallel to similar institutions in the 'feudal' organization of the land, such as manor and honor courts, but soon the royal administration started effectively to impinge upon them. For all such reasons, and because of the fact that, after 1066, all holders of tenures and public offices pledged allegiance to the king, the continental development towards far-reaching independent principalities did not take place in England. Compared to the situation in Germany, Italy and France, English lords were kept under the increasingly stricter control of the crown. A certain amount of autonomy was only allowed to the barons in the regions bordering Scotland and Wales, for strategic reasons.

When the Conqueror passed away in 1087, the 'restyling' of the governance of England, as just outlined, was still very much in the making. Its outlines clearly appear from the 'Domesday Book', the famous 'description of all England' that the Conqueror ordered to be made in 1086 to get a better view of the assets of his kingdom and their distribution among the aristocracy and the Church.

After the Conqueror's death, his work was vigorously pursued by his sons William II Rufus (1087–1100) and Henry I (1100–1135), especially the latter. Henry I, whose sobriquet 'Beauclerc' refers to the general idea that he was 'well served by his clercs', is seen as an astute, even if inflexible and cruel statesman, who determined the path that English key administrative institutions were going to follow; these are discussed in more detail on pp. 180–181. However, much of Henry's work was undone or set back when he died in 1135 with only a daughter alive, the empress-widow Mathilda ('Maud') who claimed the throne, promised to her by her father, against the opposition of a Norman party led by a grandson of the Conqueror in the female line, Stephen, the count of Blois. England was now plunged into a civil war, the Anarchy, which lasted for 14 years (1139–1153) and ended in Stephen's recognition of Mathilda's son by

second marriage, Henry Plantagenet, count of Anjou, as sole rightful heir to the English throne.

As a king, Henry II (1154–1189), whose marriage to Eleanor of Aquitaine and subsequent formation of the Angevin Empire have already been discussed (p. 168), made a profound impression. Henry was a forceful personality, an indefatigable traveler through his own realm, who must be given credit for reversing some of the vicious tendencies that were set in motion during the Anarchy, in particular the development of hereditary offices and autonomous local lordships. Even Henry II could not prevent baronies, earldoms, and knights' fees from becoming hereditary, but he succeeded with respect to the key royal offices of sheriff and justiciar. From that perspective, the governance of England would always remain half-feudal at the most. However, Henry's long reign was tainted by two other long-standing issues: the repeated rebellions of his sons and the conflict with the archbishop of Canterbury, Thomas Becket. The reasons behind the former were partly purely coincidental: Henry just happened to have a number of capable sons who all grew up to maturity and then asked their father for a stake in the wielding of power. Henry met these demands by having his oldest son crowned king, while the second one was appointed duke of Aquitaine and the third one was married to the heiress of Brittany. His youngest son's (the late arrival John) lack of land was compensated for with the promise of the kingdom of Ireland, yet to be conquered – a first attack was launched in 1171/72, with little success. But Henry was not disposed to give any one of his sons a real say in any matter that would diminish his own authority. Feelings of discontent, even hatred, about this were stirred up by other players in the field, like their mother, Queen Eleanor, or the cunning King Philip of France. The Becket affair only added to the troubles.

In the twelfth century it often happened that a bishop held the highest administrative office in a kingdom or principality – that of chancellor. The chancellor of Emperor Frederick Barbarossa became archbishop of Cologne in 1159; the chancellor of King Louis VII of France was at the same time bishop of Soissons (between 1159 and 1172). So it was not unusual when, in 1162, Henry II engineered the appointment of his chancellor, Thomas Becket, as archbishop of

Canterbury. He most certainly intended to combine the two functions in one person so that he would be able to control the highest authority over the Church in England through his trusted servant.

Becket was of modest origins, although not poor – his father was a London merchant of Norman descent – and he had studied for shorter periods of time in Paris, Bologna and Auxerre. He successively became clerk to the archbishop of Canterbury and archdeacon of Canterbury cathedral. In December 1154, the then archbishop, impressed by Becket's personal qualities, recommended him to the newly crowned king for the post of chancellor. Becket would have been at least 35 at the time; Henry just 21.

The king and his chancellor became firm friends. Thomas was a meticulous and loyal servant to the king, even when his master's claims conflicted with the English bishops' efforts to fend off secular influence over the monasteries. The chancellor made himself particularly unpopular with the bishops and abbots by his relentless demand for scutage for the royal campaigns, a special tax in lieu of military service by knights from Church domains. At the same time he readily accepted the rewards of *custodia*, the interim supervision of vacant bishoprics, and the incomes tied to them. With his newly acquired wealth the chancellor enjoyed an exuberant lifestyle that attracted the attention of his contemporaries. In particular, the enthusiasm with which he headed the king's military operations in France astonished many people.

With his encouragement of Thomas's appointment as archbishop of Canterbury, Henry must have expected that the energy and decisiveness of his faithful servant would help him to solve certain tricky questions in his relationships with the Church. In particular, the king was annoyed with ecclesiastical courts' claims to exclusive jurisdiction over all clergy and all Church lands, even when criminal matters were involved. But just as Thomas had served his new master unswervingly when he had been made chancellor, in his position as archbishop he would devote himself wholeheartedly to the defence of the liberties of the Church. In the spirit of church reform, he now tried to resist secular influences, although he was hindered in this by his status as tenant-in-chief for the Canterbury church lands.

According to one of his modern biographers, Frank Barlow (1986), Thomas behaved like a 'typical parvenu' in this matter, trying to make the very most of the independent and powerful position that he had acquired. He prosecuted important noblemen in the king's service for their moral failings. He resisted secular judgments on the clergy. As archbishop he opposed a royal land tax that he had defended as chancellor. He demanded total obedience from other bishops. Since some of them were better theologians than he was, and his greed made him generally unpopular, within a few months Thomas found himself in conflict with both the English Church and the king.

The king put Thomas on the spot during a meeting of the magnates of the kingdom – the high clergy, barons and holders of royal office – at Clarendon in January 1164. He made Thomas, and after him the other bishops, swear in good faith to observe the laws and customs of the realm. Once these had been put down in writing in the *Constitutions of Clarendon*, they proved to be formulated entirely to suit the king, and Thomas immediately revoked them. He appealed to the pope, which of course took a long time. In November of that year he felt that he had so little support from his bishops and was so threatened by the king and his entourage that he had no other course than to flee to the Continent.

Six years of exile in French monasteries followed. In the abbey church of Vézelay, where St Bernard had called for the Second Crusade, Thomas pronounced a ban against the *Constitutions of Clarendon*, in particular against the articles attacking the rights of the Church. He excommunicated eight people for furthering 'royal tyranny' and appropriating property belonging to the church of Canterbury. Pope Alexander III gradually put more pressure on Henry and his supporters among the English prelates to effect a reconciliation with Becket. This made it possible for Becket at last to return to England in December 1170, but his tactless actions soon brought matters to a head. His intransigence roused opposition everywhere, and once again Henry's wrath was enflamed.

Four of Henry's knights took matters into their own hands and rode to Canterbury on December 29, where they murdered the archbishop after an argument in the cathedral. Soon the dead archbishop was revered as a martyr. Miracles were attributed to him, pilgrims flocked to his grave. In 1172 he was canonized. Under threat of a papal interdict Henry was forced to admit

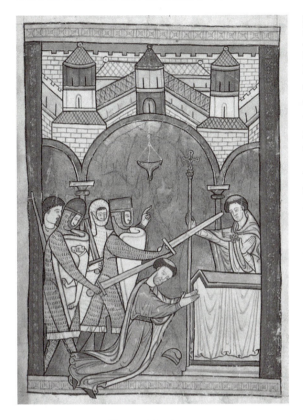

Plate 9.3 Murder of Thomas Becket

that he was the cause of Thomas's cruel death and to retract the laws that were so disadvantageous to the Church. He also promised to go on a crusade for three years. This, of course, he did not do, but in 1174 he did do penance at Thomas's grave in Canterbury, where the prelates and monks gave him hundreds of strokes with a whip.

The conflict between Henry and Thomas typifies the tensions between the Church that was reforming itself and the growing power of the state. The character of the individuals also influenced the course of events. With a little more flexibility and tact, the pope and king reached a compromise, in 1176, on the same issues on which Thomas Becket had refused to give way.

Like the Conqueror, Henry II was succeeded by two of his sons: first Richard I (1189–1199), then John (1199–1216). At first sight there are similarities. For instance, it is tempting to pair Richard with Rufus and John with Henry I: the first two both dashing knights, the second two both calculating schemers. At a closer look, all four of them – not just Beauclerc – were 'well served' by bureaucratic counsellors, capable of taking care of all kinds of problems of government and finance that dashing chivalry and dark plotting created. These new bureaucrats were often men of obscure origins, who were 'raised from the dust' to the pinnacle of power, particularly in the holding of the office of chief justiciar, which, from the reign of Henry I onwards, became the most important position in the royal bureaucracy.

It is also thanks to them that the monarchy survived profound political and financial crises, such as the capture and ransoming of Richard Lionheart in the period 1192 to 1194, the loss of Normandy in 1204, and the interdict placed on England in 1208. In the end, only King John had any limitations imposed on his powers by his barons. Years of war with France over his overseas possessions made him increase his demands on the feudal obligations of the royal tenants and other subjects. Not only did he by far exceed what was commonly felt as fair and in accordance with the law and custom, he moreover lost his battles, and gave up ancestral territory – Normandy – in which many English barons owned large estates. John's utter failure to turn the tide against Philip of France, while putting the screws on his barons, finally led to open rebellion in the spring of 1215. To save his kingdom, the king had to give in, and he did so in a remarkable document: Magna Carta (see Box 9.2).

IBERIA

Among the oldest of Europe's expansive kingdoms were those on the Iberian Peninsula. In the tenth century the emirate of Córdoba – in 929 elevated to caliphate – had emerged as a major power in southern Europe. Its economic and cultural development was far ahead of that of Catholic Europe. In the irrigated regions of Andalusia, and along the east coast of Spain, there was widespread market gardening and agriculture, with a great variety of products: cane sugar, various spices, cotton, linen, grain, rice, wine, dates and some semi-tropical fruits were even exported. State

BOX 9.2 'NO TAXATION WITHOUT CONSENT' IN MAGNA CARTA, 1215

The stretching to the limit of feudal obligation included longer service, farther from home, greater levies on fiefs, unlawful appropriation by the crown. These were the abuses formulated by the barons in the course of years and issued by the royal chancery as a charter containing no less than 63 articles known as the Magna Carta of 1215. Although this document certainly did not emanate from a representative assembly, since the barons could speak only in their own name as the king's tenants, many of its articles were nevertheless referred to later as a constitutional act announcing essential principles to be kept in respect for many centuries.

'[12] No scutage or aid is to be levied in our realm except by the common counsel of our realm, unless it is for the ransom of our person, the knighting of our eldest son or the first marriage of our eldest daughter; and for these only a reasonable aid is to be levied. Aids from the city of London are to be treated likewise.
[14] To obtain the common counsel of the realm about the assessing of an aid (except in the three cases aforesaid) or of a scutage, we [King John] will cause to be summoned the archbishops, bishops, abbots, earls and greater barons individually by our letters; and we shall also have summoned generally through our sheriffs and bailiffs all those who hold

of us in chief, for a fixed date, namely after the expiry of at least forty days and to a fixed place; and in all letters of such summons we will specify the reason for the summons. . . .
[15] We will not in future grant any one the right to take an aid from his free men, except for ransoming his person, for making his eldest son a knight and for once marrying his eldest daughter, and for these only a reasonable aid shall be levied.
[16] No one shall be compelled to do greater service for a knight's fee or for any other free holding than is due from it.'

The separate mention of the city of London in article 13 can only be understood as referring to an independent status on a par with the tenants-in-chief, not as the representation of the commune. Notwithstanding Pope Innocent's – who was John's nominal liege – declaration of Magna Carta to be null and void, Henry III reissued an abbreviated version on his accession to the throne in 1216. Certain legal principles as embodied in some of the articles of the Magna Carta, such as the ban on arresting, holding, dispossessing, or outlawing any free person 'save by the lawful judgement of his peers or by the law of the land', are held of value until the present day.

Source fragment taken from H. Rothwell (ed.), *English Historical Documents, Vol. III (1189–1327)*, (London 1975), pp. 316–324.

revenue rose from 300,000 to 500,000 dirhams between 750 and 930. In the tenth century Córdoba grew into a metropolis of more than half a million inhabitants, 3,000 mosques and 300 bath-houses. Only Constantinople and Baghdad – and a century later, Cairo – were of a similar size. Elsewhere in Europe, the thinly spread towns of the time had just a few hundred, certainly no more than a few thousand, inhabitants. The enormous size of the Mediterranean towns was only made possible through the intensive agriculture and extensive trade in the region. Commercial relations with the Byzantine Empire were generally good, and contacts – varying from plunder to

trade – were also maintained with the Latin-Christian regions around the Mediterranean Sea. The Islamic world provided a vast market stretching from Persia to Portugal. Trade brought products like silk and spices from the Far East to Arab markets. These products formed the basis of advances in pharmacology in which Arab doctors, building on the knowledge of their Greek predecessors, invented preparations containing gum, sugar, musk, nutmeg, cloves, and so forth, which were combined in syrups and elixirs (both words come from Arabic).

There was a constant supply of gold and slaves from inland Africa to the Islamic regions. Trade and plunder also brought slaves from Europe. In the eighth century Arab traders used techniques that would be taken over by the Latin-Christian world only centuries later: association, credit, money transfers and payment by cheque (from the Persian word *sakh*), and capital reinvestment. In the towns of al-Andalus – the Arabic name for Spain – the different ethnic and religious communities lived in separate neighbourhoods but had close contact with each other. Craftsmen of luxury goods specialized in leather-working, arms-making, the production of glass, paper and ceramics, and silk-, textile- and carpet-weaving.

The court (*alcázar*) at Córdoba was a prominent centre of culture. Caliph al-Hakam II (961–967) collected a library of 400,000 manuscripts. Even if that number may be exaggerated it stood in marked contrast with the largest libraries in Western Christendom, those of the popes in Avignon and the Sorbonne library, neither of which contained more than 2,000 volumes. Caliph al-Hakam also enlarged the Mezquita, the great mosque of Córdoba, and placed magnificent Byzantine mosaics in its *mihrab*, the prayer wall facing Mecca.

From the middle of the tenth century, in the multicultural environments of the great Spanish towns – Sicilian and South Italian, too – there was great activity in the translation of works by Greek and Arab scholars. The Spanish March was at the forefront in this. By the second half of the tenth century, monks at the Benedictine abbey of Ripoll were already translating texts on geometry, astronomy and the construction of instruments. Gerbert of Aurillac, later Pope Silvester II (999–1003), acquired much of his advanced scientific knowledge during his visit to the region and contacts with Ripoll between 967 and 969. It was Silvester who introduced Arabic numerals to the West. In this way Latin Christendom had broad access to knowledge from Antiquity, supplemented with Arabic learning.

In the course of the eighth century the Arab language and Islam – the latter used the former exclusively – came to dominate in the conquered areas. Through them the diversity of peoples and political regimes jelled, without really eliminating the disparities between the different population groups. In the tenth and eleventh centuries, the growing homogenization of Arabic culture in al-Andalus led to an exodus of Mozarabs (Arabized Christians) to the Christian king-

doms in the north, which began to adopt a more aggressive attitude. Military expeditions caused the two cultures to grow apart, both stressing their individual character more strongly. Homogenization and integration exacerbated the polarization on either side of the border zone. Yet, during the eleventh and twelfth centuries, in the towns and at the courts of al-Andalus, cultural activity flourished, highly refined and many-sided. It included sophisticated architecture, various branches of science – astronomy, medicine, pharmacology, botany (botanical gardens were established in Córdoba and Toledo) – jurisprudence, theology and philosophy. The royal courts vied with each other in cultural matters: troubadours' poetry sprang up, emotional, profane – even libertine – and dealing with the liberated position of women. Love, battle and nostalgia were themes later to be adopted by the courtly lyrics of Western Europe. The puritanical regimes of the Almoravids and Almohads were a reaction to this.

At the beginning of the eleventh century, the caliphate of Córdoba lapsed into anarchy as a result of crises in the succession, and in 1031, some years after a Berber army had taken its capital, it was even formally abolished. It crumbled into a number of small kingdoms grouped according to ethnic origins, known as *taifas* (from the Arabic *muluk al-tawa'if*, meaning 'party kings'). The rivalry between the regional Islamic rulers played into the hands of the Christians. King Alfonso VI of León and Castile succeeded in advancing deep into the south and laying a heavy tribute on the Muslims. After the fall of Toledo, in 1085, the princes of Seville, Badajoz and Malaga asked the help of Yusuf bin Tasfin, the leader of the Berber tribes from Mauretania that had united under strictly puritanical, Islamic principles. They called themselves *al-murabitun*, 'warriors living together in a ribat (house)', whence the word 'Almoravid'. In the preceding years, they had united large parts of Morocco, founded Marrakesh in 1070, and, moving eastwards, taken Tlemcen, Oran, Algiers and Ceuta. Between 1086 and 1114 Yusuf and his son and heir, Ali, eliminated all the *taifa* rulers and then marched north towards Zaragoza and Barcelona. The Muslims of al-Andalus were again united under one power, the heart of which lay in the western Maghreb.

In 1098 the caliph of Baghdad recognized Yusuf as emir. A new ruler, Yusuf needed religious legitimacy, which he only received because he seemed to be able to guarantee the defence of Islam. The Almoravid government was originally based on strict moral principles, which were at odds with the Hispano-Arabic tradition. This worsened the relationship with the Christians, who became more militant, and, in 1125/26, Alfonso I of Aragon led a Christian army as far as Malaga. Despite the struggles, cultural adaptations and interchange took place on a large scale – an example of this can be seen in the architecture of North Africa.

When Almoravid rule in Morocco came to an end in 1147 the regional princes of al-Andalus again seized power for themselves. In the meantime, rival groups of Berber tribes had united in a religious programme that embraced the jihad, the holy war, first of all against the Almoravids. They were known as *al-muwahhidun* [cf. 'mujahedin'], Almohads, professing the oneness of God. This did not deter them from taking the lives of thousands of people among those who did not share their beliefs. Their leader, Abd al-Mu'min, called himself caliph. His first operation in Andalusia, in 1147, was particularly brutal, yet part of the population recognized him. In 1172 Abu Ya'qub Yusuf added all of al-Andalus to the Almohad kingdom. A vast Christian coalition that Pope Innocent III pronounced to be a crusade finished off this regime in a battle near Las Navas de Tolosa, on the southern slopes of the Sierra Morena, in 1212. This was a turning point for Islam in the Iberian peninsula: the Muslims managed to survive only in the south. Protected by its mountain ranges the kingdom of Granada attracted large numbers of the Islamic population, so that it became very densely populated. Granada held its own against the Christians – who now in their turn were divided among themselves – but was forced to pay tribute to Castile. The benevolent natural environment made Andalusia very prosperous, and a lively trade with North Africa and Italy ensued.

In spite of the territorial losses suffered by the Muslims during the twelfth century, in the following centuries their region still continued to be a cradle for the transfer of culture for which Christian Europe is deeply indebted. Europeans, unfortunately, have tended to see things from another viewpoint and to look upon every small parcel of land regained from Islam as progress. From that point of view, southward expansion of the Christian kingdoms, on the pretext of crusades called for by the popes since 1063, took place along three parallel axes from north to south. After military victories, the count of Portugal proclaimed himself king in 1137, a title later confirmed by the popes in recognition of the region's role in the Reconquest. In 1147 Lisbon fell into Christian hands. The rest of the Reconquest took place in fits and starts; crusaders from north-west Europe, and from Provence in particular, sometimes sent reinforcements. The lands of the Alentejo and Algarve were for the most part taken over by the religious chivalric orders, which ensured both the conquest and the exploitation that followed. Faro was reached in 1249.

In the central kingdoms of León and Castile, which were united under a personal union in 1230, the Christian advance similarly took place in phases. Toledo was taken in 1085, but it was not until 1236 that Córdoba fell, and Seville in 1247; then there was stagnation for another two centuries. On the east coast the centuries-long struggle against the Muslims brought about the union of the individual regions: the March or county of Barcelona, the kingdoms of Aragon, Mallorca, Valencia, Murcia and various overseas settlements of merchants from Barcelona. The integration of Christian Iberia thus took place from north to south, but it enabled the kingdoms of Portugal, Castile-León and Aragon to advance with, and not infrequently against, each other. This can be seen in the linguistic boundaries that came into being in parallel with the three axes of expansion right across the area of the Reconquest: Portuguese, Castilian and Catalan.

One problem of the southward expansion resulted from the shortage of peasants to work the conquered land. The land retaken by the Christians was so thinly populated that Muslims were treated tolerantly in order to keep agriculture going. They were allowed to keep their property, self-rule and religious practices. The proverb *quien tiene moro tiene oro* ('he who has a Moor has gold') dates from this time. In the valley of the Ebro and the kingdom of Valencia, these *mudéjares* even formed a majority. This made it necessary to give attractive privileges to the Christian communities in towns and villages, and in the long term this seriously limited the authority of the kings in the country areas.

Map 9.2 The *Reconquista* (Reconquest) in the thirteenth century

THE INSTITUTIONALIZATION OF THE STATE

The dynamics of monarchy

The preceding paragraphs attempted to show the circumstances in which the new European monarchies emerged. It was noticeable that from the tenth to the thirteenth centuries the foundations were laid of a whole series of monarchies that still exist today within essentially the same territories and with more or less the same names. The first great kingdoms largely determined the future destiny of Europe, because they were important units that combined forces and fought out conflicts. Some of the kingdoms considered above were absorbed into larger political units much later – think, for example, of the royal wedding that permanently united the kingdoms of Castile-León and Aragon, England's union with Wales, Scotland and Northern Ireland or the merging of the Balkan kingdoms. On the other hand, some larger entities fell apart into a myriad of smaller states, as happened to the medieval German Empire. In any case, in more recent times the original units have often turned out to be the frameworks within which their peoples want to be

identified. Most medieval territorial principalities re-emerged in the twentieth century as 'new' states or as regions claiming some measure of political autonomy, if not complete sovereignty.

We can distinguish certain common features in the circumstances under which the earliest monarchies were established. The first and most general is the significant contribution of the Church and Christianity to the growth of the early monarchies, particularly on the Roman Catholic side but also on the Greek Orthodox side. Only the Scandinavian and Norman expansions do not seem to have been linked primarily to a drive for conversion to Christianity. All other kingdoms were given an explicit missionary assignment when they were recognized by the Church. Three circumstances explain this connection. In the first place, the process of Christianization in Europe in about the year 1000 had still not gone far, and large regions of pagans or followers of other religions lay open to the universalistic and exclusivist Christian Church. In matters of faith, there was still a lot to be done in Western Europe, but the Church called actively on resolute warriors to make every effort to spread the true faith, in the face of the considerable presence of entire nations of Muslims, Slavs, Balts and still-pagan Scandinavian. Second, it should be remembered that during the early and high Middle Ages the Church was the only institution that could keep the cultural standards of the Roman Empire in place all over the Continent. In the midst of feudal rivalries and migratory movements, the Church remained the only institution boasting a long tradition that claimed to be universal, and so to stand above parties and the variety of legal systems and languages, and whose personnel were qualified by superior intellectual training. Third, ambitious warriors were glad to array themselves in the sacramental dignity that the Church could offer them in exchange for services rendered. It enabled them to rise above their rivals and made their position of power invulnerable to their neighbours, except the clergy. The kings and aristocracy thus strengthened their position through their cooperation with the clergy. Similarly, the Almoravid and Almohad offensives in Spain were propelled by religious puritanism originating in Morocco.

In the second place, we can distinguish the 'primary' establishment of kingdoms as the result of autonomous development within the society involved from a situation where a 'secondary' development took place, and kingship was rather imposed or encouraged by outside forces. Frankish expansion, and with it the formation of the East and West Frankish empires (the kingdoms of Germany and France), appears primarily to have originated from within. On the other hand, Anglo-Norman kingship developed as the product of invasion and conquest. In turn, however, it became expansionist and tried to force its rule for centuries upon western France, Wales, Scotland and Ireland. Islamic regimes in Iberia obviously had been imposed by external forces. Although the Spanish Reconquest was stimulated by the popes, and the crusades also attracted warriors from more northern lands, the core of the movement for expansion southwards originated in Christian society in northern Iberia and southern France. Finally, Serbian expansion in the thirteenth century can also be called autonomous.

As a derivative form of development of the second type we would indicate the creation, transformation or disappearance of a kingdom or principality under pressure from one or more others. Poland and Bohemia were created in this way by the German Empire and the papacy. Christian kingdoms were formed from Magyar and Bulgarian khanates. Analogous developments can be seen in Norway and Sweden under Danish impulses, in the Marches in the south-eastern part of the German Empire, and in Sicily. From the very beginning, this distinction indicated a difference in dynamics: it is clear that the autonomously formed monarchies had more human and material resources at their disposal, enabling them to set in motion developments elsewhere. To formulate this issue sharply: early monarchies could develop through the strife between elites within a given society, or by imposition from abroad. Both forms have different implications for the stability of a kingship.

A third general characteristic is found only in the autonomous processes of formation. Pre-eminently in the development of the German Empire, France and England, it can be said that the size, concentrated situation and production capacity of domains directly linked to the dynasty were trump cards vital for the growth of the power of the monarchy. The Carolingians had very extensive and productive domains that formed the basis of their activities. The

Ottonians had their *Hausmacht* in Saxony, which included extensive public rights; this was enlarged with the Carolingian inheritance and through conquest and confiscation into a substantial royal domain, spread throughout the imperial territories. The rise of the Capetians was closely linked to the concentrated location of their possessions in the most fertile and most accessible part of the region. In this region, the kings held a direct control over the exercise of public authority in its various forms, which provided them with both power and revenue. William the Conqueror, on the other hand, made sure that the manors of his tenants-in-chief were spread in the furthest corners of the newly conquered land, enabling him to keep both the territory and his men under control.

The fourth general characteristic of the early monarchies is that they were concerned essentially with territorial developments. Kings had plenty of fertile land at their disposal, which provided them with the indispensable wealth to conquer even more land. Overseas connections came into being following a different logic than that of the principalities. In the period under discussion – the tenth and eleventh centuries – Danish and Norman expansion, which moved overseas in the Viking tradition, eventually also focused on the occupation of land for sedentary exploitation after a phase in which the plundering of outsiders had been their chief form of enrichment.

When the demarcation lines between the kingdoms were provisionally and globally drawn in about 1200, some peripheral areas were left over. These consisted of small, but here and there intensively structured areas, situated on the coasts or in the tangents of major spheres of influence. Italy met both criteria: pope and emperor, Byzantium, the Muslims and the Normans – all contributed towards keeping that highly developed and sea-oriented region divided. To a lesser extent the same was true of the coastal regions of Catalonia with their maritime expansion zone, the Low Countries, the areas along the south coast of the Baltic, and the Balkans. A certain logic for the development of these regions must then be sought in two directions: on the one hand, the threat, and at the same time the relative autonomy, provided by their borders with the great empires and, on the other, their different structures. Rulers could influence many things, but not everything. They could establish their control far less easily over coastal areas, which drew their strength from their maritime connections, than over fairly homogeneous land masses.

The more extensive their possessions became, the more people rulers had to employ to secure their control and their incomes. The scale and diversity of such organization made a civil service increasingly necessary. The feudal landowners directed all their attention and activities towards retaining and expanding their patrimonium as far as possible. Families used deliberate strategies of marriage and inheritance to achieve that aim. These were the soft methods of obtaining more property, and thus more power, that were unhesitatingly backed up by force if any dispute arose. The emerging territorial rulers, the kings and emperors of the tenth to the thirteenth centuries, were in fact no more than the winners of the all-against-all struggle for control of the scarce surpluses from a still barely productive agricultural economy. Even when they had reached a position of supremacy, they were still heavily dependent on the good management of their far-flung domains.

Kingship becomes an office

Medieval kings and emperors had every reason to add lustre and persuasiveness to their position by assuring themselves of the support of the clergy. Making their function sacred helped to prop up their often shaky position. The clergy in turn not only provided kingship with its ideological justification, they also put strong emphasis on propagating the Christian faith in secular government. Laboriously and gradually, from the late tenth century, the clergy managed to impose with more success than before Christian values on the conduct of the princes and feudal lords. This was expressed in the following prayer at the coronation ceremony of Otto I in 962 in Mainz:

> Lord . . . enrich the king who stands here with his army with your abundant blessings, make him strong and stable on his royal throne. Appear to him as you did to Moses in the burning bush, to Joshua in battle, to Gideon in his camp, and to Samuel in the temple: fill him with the constellation of your blessing, replenish him with the dew

of your wisdom which was given to the blessed David in his psalms, and which his son Solomon received from heaven through your goodness. Be his armour against his enemies, his helmet against disaster, his restraint in the days of prosperity, his eternal shield of protection: make his peoples remain faithful to him, and the mighty keep the peace; may they reject greed in neighbourly love, proclaim justice and defend the truth. May all of the people be filled with your eternal blessing so that they will be joyous in victory and in peace.

God was thus very directly involved in maintaining Otto's supremacy, which in the eyes of his contemporaries must have given him an exalted and powerful position. After the dual process of election as German king and papal approval of his elevation as emperor, and the anointing belonging to the rites of both coronations (respectively by the archbishop of Mainz in Charlemagne's church in Aachen and by the pope at St Peter's in Rome), the imperial function acquired a sacral character. Its visible emblems, the royal and imperial insignia, specifically the sacred lance, were viewed as venerable relics. From the second half of the eleventh century, when energetic and scholarly popes led the Church, they therefore tried to restrict the position, especially when it interfered in Church matters.

During the eleventh century great kings of recently Christianized nations, such as Olaf of Norway (d. 1030), Stephen of Hungary (d. 1038) and Cnut IV of Denmark (d. 1086), were looked upon as saints because of the miracles they would have performed in person. They asserted that they had been given their authority by the grace of God, so that no one could tamper with it without incurring God's wrath. The Church supported the sacralization of princes in the hope of their help and protection. It could also discredit a ruler by denying or depriving him of that blessing. The Church's movement for peace was imitated by rulers who saw it as a means of curbing turbulent lords who constantly undermined their authority. God's peace thus became the peace of kings and counts. On several occasions in 1043, the German king, Henry III (1039–1056), called upon his subjects from the pulpit to put an end to the feuding of the nobility, to forgive each other and to keep the peace.

His successors repeatedly proclaimed territorial and imperial peace treaties. In the German Empire, the land peaces imposed and guaranteed by the territorial princes within their own jurisdictions gradually became more effective than any royal proclamation. In their turn, they could control the lesser lords. Once again the example of the Church had worked in the secular structures.

Making kingship into an office, rather than a charismatic dignity, was of course not brought about solely by the views expressed by the clergy. Their ideas did no more than substantiate an evolution that, from a purely organizational point of view, must have been inevitable. Through the extension of their lands, the most successful contenders in the power struggle to stabilize the territorial gains were forced to create a structure of government. Pacification was their first concern, above all the suppression of potential internal resistance from rivals or other subjects. In this way they could also assume the aura of someone serving not merely a private interest but the public good, in the knowledge that the Church would support them. The spiritual counsellors and court officials close to them would have encouraged them in this, just like those who shared the renewed interest in Roman law had done since the twelfth century.

Servants of the state

Until the late Middle Ages the government of the German Empire was based above all on personal relationships, which from the twelfth century were increasingly formalized in feudal ties. Germany has been described as an 'aristocracy with a monarch at the top'. In contrast with this the Italian territories were typified as a 'monarchy based on independent communities, nobles and churches, with formally delegated laws of dominion at their disposal' (Haverkamp). As we have seen, monarchic power became rather theoretical in northern and central Italy from the late twelfth century onwards. The landed nobility remained the dominant class in Germany until the nineteenth century, and kings had as little chance to develop as burghers or peasants had. The expansionist movement in the east, along the Baltic coasts and into Italy, absorbed the capacity for growth that elsewhere would lead to new social and political relationships.

The *ministerials* (literally: 'men in service') formed an estate of unfree men who could own fiefs but could not pass them on as a hereditary right. From the middle of the twelfth century, the German kings burdened them with specific functions and offices for which they received a living in the form of a domain from the 'king's estate'. These tasks often included the guardianship of a castle, but increasingly also other positions in the king's service, at court, in the imperial army and as legal officials in the imperial towns. The churches and principalities started to appoint ministerials too. In the thick of the investiture struggle, when his vassals had deserted him, Henry IV found significant support for his army among the ministerials of the empire. This might have grown into an estate of civil servants, which could have strengthened the administrative centre of the Empire as happened in France. The discontinuity and gradual weakening of the kingship, however, brought any such development to a standstill. The ministerials, of course, were focused on rising in society; in the German context this was easier to achieve as lesser nobles in the feudal framework than as government pen-pushers. When Frederick II introduced a civil servant class in his modern state in South Italy and Sicily, therefore, he did not choose Germans, like so many popes and bishops appointed by earlier emperors in Italy, but well-educated Sicilians.

There is a marked contrast between developments in the German Empire and in England. England was tightly organized before the Norman conquest, but the new rulers strengthened the system of government even further with the aim of enabling the foreign minority to keep control by the introduction of a system of quasi-feudal landholding tied to military service, which has already been discussed. Just as happened elsewhere, central institutions in Anglo-Norman England were created from the royal court council (*curia regis*) through the increasing reach of their competences, specialization and then division into independent organs. Everywhere, this sort of functional differentiation first took place in the technical field, in matters of jurisprudence and finances. It is possible that, in late Anglo-Saxon times, there was already a central accounting office before which the royal receivers were held accountable. In the twelfth century it evolved into a real financial department, called the 'Exchequer'. Certainly of Anglo-Saxon origin was the office of sheriff ('shire reeve'), who acted as the king's representative on the level of shires, the English equivalent to continental counties. The Normans strengthened this office and turned sheriffs into almost modern civil servants, in the sense that they carried out a reversible mandate that was not hereditary and for which they were held accountable. The only 'modern' element lacking was a salary.

But the most far-reaching extension of royal control was in the field of law and justice. Over the course of the twelfth century there came into existence, by fits and starts, a 'Common Law', which can best be equated to 'the king's law'. It was dispensed by itinerant royal justices, who heard all kinds of pleas, both criminal and civil, but also handled all other royal business in their 'eyre' or circuit. Royal interference went furthest in the field of criminal law, because, from the start, the Norman kings quite understandably were devoted to the general maintenance of 'the king's peace', and keen on prosecuting all breaches of it. In the trying of criminal offences the royal justices were initially led either by private accusations or by *ex officio* pleas of royal prosecutors. From the time of Henry I onwards criminal pleas were more and more dependent on the sworn declarations of 'juries of presentment', local jurors who gave testimony over felonies or statements about the reputation of notorious suspects. In this way, the English kings succeeded at a relatively early date in monopolizing to a large extent the prosecution of crime – at least of all grave crime. In the sphere of civil law, because of the nature of cases, which were largely questions of right and possession, royal, 'common' justice was only available for free men, who are estimated to have constituted no more than one-third of the population at the time. In civil law suits – usually called 'common pleas' – the accession to royal courts of justice was assured by the use of royal writs or written commands ordering that pleas be heard before a royal official; the use of sworn local informants as 'juries' was introduced in this sphere as well. By the end of the twelfth century a central court for civil law suits was instituted: the Bench or Court of Common Pleas, residing at Westminster.

By feeding an 'ideology of royal-dominated justice' (Hudson) the English Common Law indeed became gradually really 'common'; that is to say, applicable to all the king's subjects. This process came at the expense of enormous diversity of local customary law, which would remain so characteristic for other parts of medieval and early-modern Europe.

Obviously modernization of officialdom was only possible in those areas where the economy was sufficiently monetized. The first really modern-type officials were probably appointed in Flanders by count Philip of Alsace, who in 1170 started to appoint bailiffs (*baillis* in French), who were salaried and dismissable at will. Their main tasks were to maintain the count's prerogatives, organize the administration of justice following the principles of objective examination of the facts, and collect the revenues for the count. At the same time the count ordered the rationalization of criminal law in all the large towns. The count's liege, King Philip Augustus of France, followed the example; the earliest known royal *baillis* are from around 1190. Their position was somewhere between that of the receivers on the desmesnes (*prévôts*) and the royal council (*curia*), so that a clear hierarchy was established. Unlike the *prévôts*, they would no longer lease their office nor hold it in fief, but they received a salary out of the revenues it was their task to collect and were bound to the king through an oath of office (itself a relic of the oral feudal tradition). It was their task to accept homage of royal vassals in the king's name, watch over the administration of the king's justice and tax collection, and on the king's orders summon the crown vassals for military service.

Philip Augustus's grandson, Louis IX (1226–1270), put an end to the itinerant character of the baillis' service. In 1254 he created officially demarcated districts, called *baillages*. From that moment on a great deal of money was spent on fortifying castles, where the baillis lived, and on strategically situated towns within their jurisdiction. King Louis also appointed the first baillis in the south of the kingdom, where they were called *sénéchaux*; their districts *sénéchaussées*.

In all this there was a marked contrast with the German situation. The Empire, which had led the way in the tenth and eleventh centuries, now became set in its traditional structures – which would remain until 1806. In England and France, on the other hand, the first steps were taken towards replacing the old feudal system with a modern, bureaucratic system of government.

A show of strength in Gothic style

A real innovation, which would introduce a new artistic form all over Europe, came from the north, from the Paris basin. Cathedrals heralding a completely new architectural concept were built in a series of cities all over the French crown domains during the twelfth and thirteenth centuries. This concept was later also adapted to civic architecture. To a rather limited extent, it finally reached the Mediterranean lands where it was given its name: Gothic, the style of the Goths, meaning the 'barbarians' north of the Alps and Pyrenees.

In the abbey church of Saint-Denis, north of Paris, where the French kings were buried and valuable relics were kept, Abbot Suger was irritated in the 1120s by the continual jostling of the faithful. He believed that an abundance of light was necessary to honour God

fittingly. In order to give the faithful the chance to get near the relics, he designed a passage behind the main altar, around which a series of chapels in a circle enabled many priests to read the Mass. This ambulatory was consecrated in 1144. It gave extraordinary lustre to the French monarchy, which was engaged in enlarging its power over the territorial princes.

The new concept was introduced into cathedrals built in the wide vicinity of Paris. Much larger windows were cut into the formerly sombre, massive walls. Buttresses and flying buttresses strengthened the exterior walls to provide the stability necessary for the ever-taller buildings. The weight of the roofs was spread geometrically over a large number of abutments through the construction of pointed arches. Work began on the cathedral of Sens in 1133, Noyon in 1151, Laon in 1160 and Paris's Notre-Dame in 1163. At this time of feverish building there was intense competition to create the most spectacular project. The walls became lighter, broken up by windows and recesses. Gothic was characterized by an upward thrust, soaring towards God. The walls were built ever higher: the central nave in Paris was 32.8 metres (107.6 feet) high; 30 years later, in 1194, Chartres reached 36.55 metres (119.9 feet); Rheims measured 37.95 metres (124.5 feet) in 1212 and Amiens 42.3 (138.8 feet) in 1221. The record was achieved in Beauvais, where building began in 1247 and 48 metres (157.5 feet) was reached. This was beyond the limit of technical ingenuity and the roof collapsed in 1284.

Meanwhile, the glories of Gothic had spread to neighbouring countries, each of which had its own variant on the basic concept. In English Gothic, the vaulting was flatter and lower but with more lines in it; in the coastal areas of the Low Countries, and later in the regions round the Baltic Sea, the style was adapted by the use of bricks. In time the decorative elements were very profuse, and the term 'flamboyant Gothic' was used. Milan, extravagantly decorated, considerably wider and proportionately lower than the French models, is one of the rare examples of an entirely Gothic cathedral in Italy. Nevertheless, countless Gothic stylistic elements were very popular. From Trondheim in Norway to as far south as Sicily, Gothic spread as the dominating architectural style until well

Plate 9.4 Rheims cathedral

into the sixteenth century; it also determined the design of furniture and decorative objects.

How could this new concept come into being in the Paris basin, and spread so widely and so rapidly? As far as the architects were concerned, it must be remembered that from the eleventh century onwards education in cathedral schools – those of Chartres, Paris and Rheims, for example – was increasingly associated with the knowledge of mathematics and geometry borrowed from the Arabs. It was this knowledge that enabled architects to make accurate studies of the distribution of weight in their plans. Very detailed plans of the west front of Strasbourg cathedral, drawn on parchment and dating from 1275, have been preserved; for Rheims, we still have some dating from as early as 1250. On a floor in York Minster there are drawings for a glass window dating from about 1395.

The fact that the Gothic could spread so successfully owes much to the prestige that the French kings, who were so eager to expand, lent to cathedral-building in the twelfth and thirteenth centuries. And not only kings: without the strong financial support of the burghers in the rapidly growing towns the immense building projects would never have been realized. There was competition between the towns for the finest and most daring project. In a technical sense, the style was spread through the mobility of the master builders, who were organized into lodges or guilds and moved from one building yard to another. There was competition among them as well, and pupils sometimes developed their masters' designs further in other places. The demonstrative example of the kings caught on: burghers saw it as a means of expressing the worth of their town, and other leaders did not lag behind. The rivalry was now centred on the height of the towers: Strasbourg broke the medieval record in 1420 with its 142 metres (466 feet). The planned second tower, however, was never completed, nor were several other ambitious projects. Some of them, such as the cathedrals of Cologne and Ulm, were not finished until the nineteenth century.

In both form and content, Gothic was a purely medieval creation. Its primary function was to make divine worship as glorious as possible. Other functions came later: the prestige of a monarchy and of the burghers. With that in view the same style was adapted for palaces and purely civic buildings such as town halls, market halls and private residences. In later times, Gothic was so closely identified with the Middle Ages that in the nineteenth century, the Romantic period, those who dreamed of a dominant place for the Church and a corporative class society once again recognized themselves in the style. Neogothic signified a conscious ideological choice through a re-creation of one of the most authentic creations of the Middle Ages.

FURTHER READING

Abulafia, David (1988), *Frederick II. Medieval Emperor* (London: Allen Lane/Penguin Press).

Adams, Jonathan and Katherine Holman (eds) (2004), *Scandinavia and Europe, 800–1350: Contact, Conflict, and Coexistence* (Turnhout: Brepols).

Althoff, Gerd (2003), *Otto III* (University Park, Pa.: Penn State Press) (orig. German, 1996).

Arnold, Benjamin (1997) *Medieval Germany, 500–1300. A Political Interpretation* (Basingstoke and London: Macmillan).

Bagge, Sverre (2002), *Kings, Politics, and the Right Order of the World in German Historiography, c.950–1150* (Leiden: Brill).

Baldwin, John W. (1986), *The Government of Philip Augustus. Foundations of French Royal Power in the Middle Ages* (Berkeley and London: University of California Press).

Barber, Richard (2001), *Henry Plantagenet: A Biography of Henry II of England*, 2nd edn (Rochester, N.Y.: Boydell & Brewer).

Frank Barlow, *Thomas Becket* (London, 1986).

—— (2000), *William Rufus*, 2nd edn (New Haven, Conn. and London: Yale University Press).

—— (2003), *The Godwins: Rise and Fall of a Noble Dynasty* (London: Longman).

Bartlett, Robert (2000), *England under the Norman and Angevin kings, 1075–1225* (Oxford: Oxford University Press).

Berend, Nora (2001), *At the Gate of Christendom: Jews, Muslims and 'Pagans' in Medieval Hungary, c.1000–c.1300* (Cambridge: Cambridge University Press).

Berkhofer, Robert F. III (2004), *Day of Reckoning: Power and Accountability in Medieval France* (Philadelphia, Pa.: Pennsylvania State University Press).

Bernardt, John W. (2002), *Itinerant Kingship and Royal Monasteries in Early Medieval Germany, c.936–1075*, 2nd edn (Cambridge: Cambridge University Press).

Bertelli, Sergio (2001), *The King's Body: Sacred Rituals of Power in Medieval and Early Modern Europe* (University Park, Pa.: Penn State Press) (orig. Italian, 1990)

Bisson, Thomas N. (1991), *The Medieval Crown of Aragon: A Short History* (Oxford: Clarendon).

Bradbury, Jim (1998), *Philip Augustus, King of France, 1180–1223* (London: Longman).

Breay, Claire (2002), *Magna Carta: Manuscripts and Myths* (London: British Library).

Bridgeford, Andrew (2004), *1066: The Hidden History in the Bayeux Tapestry* (London: Fourth Estate).

Brown, Reginald Allen (2000), *The Normans and the Norman Conquest* (Woodbridge: Boydell).

Bull, Marcus (ed.) (2003), *France in the Central Middle Ages, 900–1200* (Oxford: Oxford University Press).

Catlos, Brian A. (2004), *The Victors and the Vanquished: Christians and Muslims of Catalonia and Aragon, 1050–1300* (Cambridge: Cambridge University Press).

Chibnall, Marjorie (1984), *The World of Orderic Vitalis: Norman Monks and Norman Knights* (Oxford: Clarendon).

—— (1986), *Anglo-Norman England 1066–1166* (Oxford: Blackwell).

—— (1999), *The Debate on the Norman Conquest* (Manchester and New York: Manchester University Press).

Clanchy, M.T. (1983), *England and Its Rulers 1066–1272* (Oxford: Blackwell).

—— (1993), *From Memory to Written Record: England 1066–1307*, 2nd edn (Oxford: Blackwell).

Crouch, David (1986), *The Beaumont Twins. The Roots and Branches of Power in the Twelfth Century* (Cambridge: Cambridge University Press).

—— (1990), *William Marshal: Court, Career and Chivalry in the Angevin Empire, 1147–1219* (London and New York: Longman).

—— (2000), *The Reign of King Stephen, 1135–1154* (Harlow: Longman).

Danziger, Danny and John Gillingham (2004), *1215: The Year of Magna Carta* (New York: Touchstone).

Davies, R.R. (1990), *Domination and Conquest: The Experience of Ireland, Scotland and Wales 1100–1300* (Cambridge: Cambridge University Press).

—— (2000), *The First English Empire: Power and Identities in the British Isles, 1093–1343* (Oxford: Oxford University Press).

Douglas, David C. (1964), *William the Conqueror: The Norman Impact upon England* (London: Eyre & Spottiswoode).

Duby, Georges (1990), *The Legend of Bouvines: War, Religion and Culture in the Middle Ages* (Berkeley: University of California Press) (orig. French, 1973).

Duggan, Anne (2004), *Thomas Becket* (London: Arnold).

Dunbabin, Jean (1998), *Charles of Anjou: Power, Kingship and State-making in Thirteenth-century Europe* (London: Longman).

—— (2000), *France in the Making, 843–1180*, 2nd edn (Oxford: Oxford University Press).

Foote, David (2004), *Lordship, Reform, and the Development of Civil Society in Medieval Italy: The Bishopric of Orvieto, 1100–1250* (Chicago, Ill.: University of Notre Dame Press).

Frame, Robin (1995), *The Political Development of the British Isles, 1100–1400* (Oxford: Oxford University Press).

Fuhrmann, Horst (1986), *Germany in the High Middle Ages, c.1050–1200* (Cambridge: Cambridge University Press).

Gillingham, John (1999), *Richard I* (New Haven, Conn. and London: Yale University Press).

Gorecki, Piotr (1993), *Economy, Society and Lordship in Medieval Poland, 1100–1250* (New York: Holmes & Meier).

Graham-Leigh, Elaine (2005), *The Southern French Nobility and the Albigensian Crusade* (Woodbridge and Rochester, N.Y.: Boydell & Brewer).

Green, Judith (1989), *The Government of England under Henry I* (Cambridge: Cambridge University Press).

—— (1997), *The Aristocracy of Norman England* (Cambridge: Cambridge University Press).

Hagger, Mark S. (2001), *The Fortunes of a Norman Family: The De Verduns in England, Ireland and Wales, 1066–1316* (Dublin and Portland, Oreg.: Four Courts Press).

Hallam, E.M. (1980), *Capetian France 737–1328* (London and New York: Longman).

Higham, N.J. (2002), *King Arthur: Myth-Making and History* (London and New York: Routledge).

Holt, J.C. (1992), *Magna Carta*, 2nd edn (Cambridge: Cambridge University Press).

Howard, Ian (2003), *Swein Forkbeard's Invasions and the Danish Conquest of England, 991–1017* (Woodbridge and Rochester, N.Y.: Boydell & Brewer).

Hudson, John (1996), *The Formation of the English Common Law: Law and Society in England from the Norman Conquest to Magna Carta* (London: Longman).

Hyde, J.K. (1973), *Society and Politics in Medieval Italy: The Evolution of Civil Life 1000–1350* (London and Basingstoke: Macmillan).

Ingham, Patricia Clare (2001), *Sovereign Fantasies. Arthurian Romance and the Making of Britain* (Philadelphia: University of Pennsylvania Press).

Jones, Philip (1997), *The Italian City-State: From Commune to Signoria* (Oxford: Clarendon).

Klaniczay, Gábor (2002), *Holy Rulers and Blessed Princesses. Dynastic Cults in Medieval Central Europe* (Cambridge: Cambridge University Press) (orig. Hungarian, 2000).

Kosto, Adam J. (2001), *Making Agreements in Medieval Catalonia: Power, Order and the Written Word, 1000–1200* (Cambridge: Cambridge University Press).

Lawson, M.K. (2004), *Cnut*, 2nd edn (London: Longman).

Le Patourel, J. (1976), *The Norman Empire* (Oxford: Clarendon).

Leyser, K.J. (1982), *Medieval Germany and Its Neighbours, 900–1250* (London: Hambledon Press).

—— (1994), *Communications and Power in Medieval Europe*, 2 vols (London and Rio Grande: Hambledon Press).

MacKay, A. (1977) *Spain in the Middle Ages. From Frontier to Empire, 1000–1500* (London and Basingstoke: Macmillan).

Munz, Peter (1969), *Frederick Barbarossa: A Study in Medieval Politics* (Ithaca, N.Y.: Cornell University Press).

O'Callaghan, Joseph F. (1998), *Alfonso X, the Cortes and Government in Medieval Spain* (Aldershot: Ashgate) (Variorum Collected Studies).

—— (2003), *Reconquest and Crusade in Medieval Spain* (Philadelphia, Pa.: University of Pennsylvania Press).

Prestwich, Michael (2005), *Plantagenet England, 1225–1360* (New York and Oxford: Oxford University Press).

Rady, Martyn (2001), *Nobility, Land and Service in Medieval Hungary* (Basingstoke: Palgrave Macmillan).

Reilly, Bernard F. (1993), *The Medieval Spains* (Cambridge: Cambridge University Press).

Reynolds, Susan (1997), *Kingdoms and Communities in Western Europe 900–1300*, 2nd edn (Oxford: Clarendon Press).

Robinson, I.S. (1999), *Henry IV of Germany, 1056–1106* (Cambridge: Cambridge University Press).

Tabacco, Giovanni (1989), *The Struggle for Power in Medieval Italy. Structures of Political Rule* (Cambridge: Cambridge University Press) (orig. Italian, 1974).

Thomas, Hugh M. (2003), *The English and the Normans: Ethnic Hostility, Assimilation and Identity, 1066–c.1220* (Oxford and New York: Oxford University Press).

Turner, Ralph V. (2005), *King John: England's Evil King?* (Stroud: Tempus Publishing).

—— and Richard R. Heiser (2000), *The Reign of Richard Lionheart: Ruler of the Angevin Empire, 1189–1199* (Harlow: Pearson Education).

Waley, Daniel (1989), *The Italian City Republics*, 3rd edn (London: Longman).

Warren, W.L. (1973), *Henry II* (Berkeley: University of California Press).

—— (1987) *The Governance of Norman and Angevin England, 1086–1272* (Stanford, Calif. and London: Stanford University Press).

—— (19982), *King John*, 2nd edn (New Haven, Conn. and London: Yale University Press).

Weinfurter, Stefan (1999), *The Salian Century: Main Currents in an Age of Transition* (Philadelphia, Pa.: University of Pennsylvania Press) (orig. German, 1991).

Wilson, David MacKenzie (2004), *The Bayeux Tapestry*, 2nd edn (London: Thames & Hudson).

CHAPTER 10

Weakening centres of power in the East and the beginnings of European expansion

THE WEST BECOMES MORE AGGRESSIVE

During the eleventh century, a general expansionary movement began to manifest itself in the West, in diverse regions and in various forms. The basis for this movement must be sought in the stabilization that the West achieved from the middle of the tenth century onwards, when the disruptive invasions from central Asia and Scandinavia finally came to an end. Agricultural production and population grew steadily, so that after a few generations the existing social ties came under pressure. In western Europe, from the eleventh century, a start was made to drain peat and marshlands, clear woodlands and cultivate the ground. The most visible expression of this was the search for new areas of settlement, both in the direct vicinity of the old western European centres of habitation and further away.

The conquests that most appeal to our imagination were certainly those of the Normans, themselves descendants of Viking settlers. Some decades before the conquest of England, enterprising knights who had not achieved the success they had dreamt of in Normandy set out for southern Italy where the first bases were in Norman hands by 1029. The sons of Tancred of Hauteville were the boldest of these knights. One of them, Robert Guiscard, defeated the forces of Pope Leo IX in 1053, and even took the pope prisoner. Six years later the same pope, who needed Robert's support in his confrontation with Emperor Henry IV, recognized him as duke of Apulia and Calabria. In 1084 he rescued Pope Gregory VII from Castel Sant' Angelo in Rome, where he was besieged by the emperor. His expeditions took him as far as Serbia, where he intervened in 1081 in the contest for the imperial crown of Byzantium. His youngest brother, Roger, took Sicily from the Moors between the years 1061 and 1091. The pope gave his blessing to this offensive against Islam and even appointed Roger as his legate, a position normally filled by a prelate. This was an important precedent for the crusades in Palestine. The Norman kings built a solid kingdom based on the institutions founded by Byzantine and Arab rulers. By 1130 the newly created kingdom of Sicily included all of southern Italy and Sicily, and later even contained some of the coastal regions of Tunisia. It lasted for centuries in this form. Roger II (1130–1154) recognized the pope as his overlord and paid him an annuity, in return for which he could do as he pleased. His position was of great strategic importance for Rome in its struggles against the Muslims and Byzantium, and also as backing against the German emperors.

A part of the growing population of Western Europe sought new means of livelihood to the east in the thinly populated German Empire and in the Slavic regions beyond. It is striking that from the middle of the thirteenth century this *Drang nach Osten*, which in fact was nothing less than the occupation of land, was presented as a crusade against the pagan Slavs and Balts. Christian enterprises in Palestine had come to a standstill, and part of the West's drive for expansion was directed at the European frontiers of Christianity in Iberia, central Europe and the Celtic periphery of the British islands.

The active resumption of trading relationships from the West was another form of the same expansionary movement. By the ninth and tenth centuries, when there were still frequent Arab raids along the coasts of the western Mediterranean Sea, Amalfi traders profited from their contacts with the surrounding Muslim regions. They withdrew from the purely nominal rule of the Byzantine Empire and developed close ties with the Fatimid Empire in Egypt. A rare document from 996 shows that at that time there were about two hundred traders from Amalfi in Cairo. They supplied wood and iron for shipbuilding, and bought as many luxury goods as possible that the highly developed Arab market economy had to offer. In the middle of the eleventh century, a Persian traveller observed Christian ships in the Syrian port of Tripoli, from where they would set sail to other Islamic harbours. Muslims who wished to sail from the Maghreb (the western lands of Islam) to the Levant (Syria and Palestine) would from then onwards do so on Christian ships.

Venice was another centre for the expansion of commercial links between Italy and the eastern Mediterranean Sea. The city still formally recognized the supremacy of Byzantium, which, in 1082, responding to the Norman advance into the Balkans, gave Venice exclusive free-trade privileges without any levies and duties. Until the eleventh century there was a lively slave trade in people who had been captured during raids in the Slav regions of central Europe and the Balkans. This trade decreased as those areas became converted to Christianity, and was replaced and diversified by trade in other products. For Byzantium, threatened as it was on every side, the support of the Venetian fleet was of strategic importance. For their part, the Venetians profited from the vast material and cultural wealth that Byzantium still could provide.

It is very likely that Sicily's trade with Egypt and Syria continued under Norman rule. In the western Mediterranean, the ports of Pisa and Genoa carried out a successful naval attack in 1088 on the pirates' nest at Mahdiya in Tunisia. The pope gave his blessing in retrospect to this undertaking, motivated in the first place by economic reasons but also part of the increasingly aggressive attitude of the Catholic Church towards the Muslims. It is striking that, in all these regions, westerners took the initiative in the contacts with the much earlier developed East, and this in the period preceding the crusades. Religious differences were no barrier at all to close commercial ties.

Everything indicates that it was this very intensification of the contacts that offered the West opportunities for growth, based on the adoption of more highly developed and varied products, technology and other cultural features. Through their commercial activities, the Italians in particular learned to deal with other cultures, new products and the advanced trading methods that were commonplace in Constantinople, Tripoli, Alexandria and Cairo. Indirectly they gained entry to large and distant markets, which, in turn, gave them a head start on other Western Europeans. They were able to set themselves up as the great intermediaries between East and West, a position they would hold until the sixteenth century. The expansionary westerners showed greater dynamism and drive, and they were more open to innovation, all of which enabled them to overtake their stronger rivals in the long run.

Shifting centres of gravity

The period from the ninth century to the eleventh formed the apex of political, economic and cultural developments, both in the Byzantine Empire and the diverse Muslim kingdoms. For more than half a century after the death of Basil II in 1025 the Byzantine Empire was plagued by the misgovernment of a series of weak emperors, at the very time that strong new adversaries appeared on its borders. The Byzantines managed to check the Pechenegs, yet another nomadic people who had entered the Lower Danube region, but they were powerless to the threat from the Normans in southern Italy and the Seljuk Turks in Asia Minor. The greater part of all the regions they had conquered with their blood, sweat and tears during the tenth century was lost in the course of just a few years. The disastrous year of 1071 was symbolic of the course of events: this was the year of Manzikert (see p. 189), the same year that the Normans took Bari in the West. The two events marked the loss of Byzantine power in South Italy and the largest part of Asia Minor.

The strong emperors of the Comnenus dynasty, which came to power in Constantinople in 1081, could not rectify this loss of territory, but they did succeed in preventing further erosion of Byzantine possessions in Asia Minor. Alexius I Comnenus (1081–1118) exploited the long-term presence of the first western crusade army in the region. It led to the Byzantines again having all the coastal regions of Asia Minor firmly under their control.

As a result of the developments sketched above, the Byzantine Empire underwent a power-shifting process from the centre to local potentates from the eleventh century onwards. Great landowners ruled over several village communities and thousands of slaves. The emperors had to rely on their cooperation to collect the taxes in their areas, in exchange for which they kept a part for themselves. Other elements of state power also fell into their hands, including the administration of justice, maintaining order, the conscription and command of troops. The landowners thus became real warlords who tried to make their position hereditary. Independent peasants were forced out of existence by the heavy tax burden, which they could escape only by seeking the protection of the warlords – on whom they then became directly dependent and to whom they had to make payments. Imperial power was thus gradually eroded. The highly developed bureaucracy proved to be no match for the warlords, who were of course indispensable for warding off the constant attacks from nomadic peoples. The use of mercenaries (usually 'Franks', by which all Western Europeans were meant, sometimes Turks as well) did not bring long-term relief to the emperors, as so much money was needed to pay them and their forces often proved untrustworthy. Like so many other empires, Byzantium collapsed under a combination of internal erosion and external pressure.

The other major power in the eastern Mediterranean was the Fatimid Empire in Egypt, which had emerged within a short time of its establishment in 969 as the dynamic centre of the Muslim world. The new capital, Cairo, grew into one of the most important markets in the Near East, attracting cotton from Nubia, slaves from black Africa and wood from Calabria, Kabylia and the Taurus mountains. Caravans of thousands of camels brought supplies to Cairo from black Africa, which was forced by military action to pay tribute in the form of slaves. This flow of humanity to the Mediterranean region has been estimated at 20,000 people per year – men for the army and heavy labour, women for household tasks. This slave trade continued from the ninth century to the twentieth and most certainly contributed to the demographic stagnation and dislocation of social ties in black Africa. In the Near East, wood, needed particularly for shipbuilding and as fuel for ovens, was the most strategically scarce raw material. The major powers fought each other continually for control of wooded regions. High-quality, traditionally made products fed a rich export trade. The prominent Jewish community in Cairo specialized in glass-making and in dyeing fine linens and cottons. They formed an important link in these industries, which according to surviving letters and bills must have included 265 different crafts.

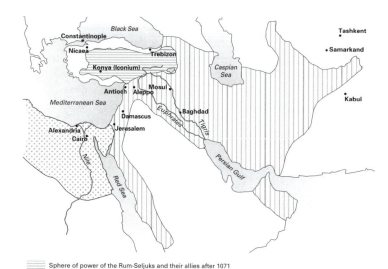

Sphere of power of the Rum-Seljuks and their allies after 1071

Muslim empire of the Great Seljuks

Caliphate of the Fatimids

Map 10.1 The empires of the Fatimids and the Seljuk Turks after 1071

Besides military power and economic prosperity the Fatimid Empire radiated a high degree of cultural activity. This was reflected in its own architectural style for mosques and palaces, decorated with coloured enamel tiles. The caliph's palace contained a library of 18,000 volumes, including 1,200 copies of the *Universal history* of al-Tabarî (d. 923). Caliph al-Hakim (996–1021) founded a great Shi'ite school near the al-Azhar Mosque, with the purpose of spreading the moral principles of the Koran. His religious fanaticism led to new tensions and divisions, and it was under his rule that the Holy Sepulchre in Jerusalem was destroyed. At the end of the eleventh century a fierce power struggle flared up in Cairo between Turks, Berbers and black ethnic groups in the army.

Largely responsible for the shifting balance of power in the Near East during the eleventh century, the Oghuz, a nomadic Turkic people recently converted to Islam, usually known as Turkmen, underwent a period of tremendous expansion. Their leaders, the Seljuks, made a pact with the Iranian aristocracy, who were anxious to restore political unity and religious orthodoxy. After 1038 they were in effective control in Baghdad, and in 1055 the caliph made the Seljuk leader sultan and 'king of the East and the West'. Hence the caliphate of Baghdad is more properly called the 'empire of the Great-Seljuks'. Syria and Palestine also fell into their hands, only the ports remaining under Fatimid rule. In about the same period another group of Seljuks, under the pretext of waging a holy war, started to raid the upland plains of Anatolia to the detriment of the Armenian and Byzantine regions. In 1071 they so thoroughly destroyed the imperial army at Manzikert that all Asia Minor came under Seljuk control, after which it was known as the empire of the Rum Seljuks (Rum meaning 'Roman').

The Seljuks encouraged religious orthodoxy in the areas they conquered. Between 1071 and 1092 their rule was characterized by laborious efforts to establish some degree of state authority, not an easy undertaking for a nomadic people unfamiliar with abstract power constructions of this sort. After the death of Malikshâh, who had built a peaceful organization in the Great Seljuk Empire, differences and rivalries between family members led to its collapse. On the Catholic side, the ferocity of the Seljuk conquests was given as a decisive reason for launching the crusades. Yet it must be remembered that Christians were by no means the only victims of the admittedly violent Turkmen. More intolerance was directed against radical Shi'ites than against Christians, and it was the representatives of the Byzantine Orthodox Church rather than other Christians who were unacceptable to the new rulers. With a few exceptions, all the Christian monasteries were allowed to remain. Even the Greek Patriarch kept his position in Jerusalem. Evidence from different sources shows that pilgrims from the West were also allowed to visit Palestine under the Turkish rule. The St John's Hospital and two monasteries near the Holy Sepulchre, founded for pilgrims by merchants from Amalfi in 1080, continued to function as usual. The sources contain no evidence of Christians being persecuted or of systematic desecration of Christianity's holy places by the Turks.

When the crusaders invaded Syria in 1096 they thus found themselves in a situation where the opposition was not on a par with them. The two great powers, Byzantium and the Fatimid Empire, were weakened and divided. The Seljuk Turks, the conquerors of the preceding decades, were now entangled in a dynastic struggle. They dominated Baghdad and, after 1071, the sultan of the Rum Seljuks installed a permanent residence in Nicaea and later in Konya/Iconium. Others hired their military might for their own strategic purposes. The Near East, already extremely complex and rarely stable, found itself in a new, very unsettled constellation as a result of western intervention. During the first half of the twelfth century this brought about a weakening of the Muslim empires, which was to the advantage of the Byzantine Empire and the Latin crusader states in Syria.

The multicultural East

It is important to remember that in origin Islam did not aim at being a religion essentially different from Judaism or Christianity. In theory the Muslims recognized the beliefs of the two other 'peoples of the Book', on the understanding that they did not claim to possess the undistorted, definitive version of the message.

This makes it easier for us to understand the Muslim attitude towards peoples of other faiths in the lands over which they ruled. In principle they allowed everyone to choose between Islam and their own faith: should they choose the latter, then they were expected to recognize the political supremacy of Islam and not to dispute it. On payment of a special tax, non-Muslims could enjoy the traditional Arabic contractual hospitality, *dhimma*, which guaranteed their personal safety and that of their goods and religious services. At the time this was certainly a progressive and exceptionally tolerant attitude through which some 200,000 Arabs succeeded in ruling more than ten million people of different cultures and, in the course of time, in gradually assimilating large numbers of them.

In the region where the crusaders directed their attacks, there certainly was no clear-cut evidence for a religious situation of dominant Muslims and subjected Christians. No less important than the religious differences between Muslims, Jews and Christians, and within Islam itself, between Sunnis and Shi'ites, were the ethnic, linguistic and cultural differences. The general picture is one of a great variety of peoples, led through clans whose authority was based partly on a specific religious conviction.

In Syria, in which the Muslims also included Palestine, the crusaders encountered mostly Shi'ites in the north and Sunnis in the south, each with their own rulers. There were diverse other cultures, too, such as the Druses who recognized the Fatimid caliphate. Another Shi'ite sect, with the ominous name of *hashîshiyûn* or hashish-drinkers, lived in the north of Iran and Syria. Because murder was their most important method of fighting the Sunni Turks, the name of these *hashîshiyûn* became 'assassins' in the French of the crusaders.

Among the Christian communities in the East, in addition to ethnic and linguistic differences, there was a diversity of religious currents from the early centuries that had been pronounced heterodox in the West, but which had survived in a fossilized form under Islamic rule. They included the Nestorians, Maronites stemming from the Monothelite tradition, and three Monophysitic Churches: the Armenian, the Jacobite (with a liturgy in Syrian) and the Egyptian-Coptic; there also were orthodoxies following the patriarchate of Constantinople or of Antioch, Jerusalem or Alexandria. Obviously, in this region of very divergent communities, the Catholic Church in Rome had no authority at all.

The Jews lived in small scattered communities, especially in the towns. They looked upon the Islamic rulers as their protectors from the heavy handed Byzantine or, in Iberia, Visigothic rulers. This view was also shared by many Christian communities who had welcomed the Muslims as their liberators from an exacting imperium. There was no segregation or ghetto forming. On the contrary, from the ninth to the eleventh centuries the Jews flourished economically and culturally throughout the Arab world.

There is thus every reason to look for the motives for the crusades not in the East but in the West, the more so since as far as we can tell from surviving texts any knowledge of Islam and the situation in Palestine was demonstrably lacking. The crusades, then, can be interpreted as a form of Western expansionism on both religious and political grounds. Thanks to the unbroken tradition of pilgrimages to Jerusalem and the economic relationships between Italy and the Near East, which had been in existence long before, it was possible to consolidate the effects of this expansion.

The impulse for the crusades

It was above all bishops and archbishops from France and Spain who took part in the council gathered at Clermont on 24 November 1095. On the agenda was the matter of the excommunication of Philip I, king of France, who had repudiated his queen and refused to end his affair with the wife of one of his barons. Pope Urban II also inveighed strongly against the lay investiture of bishops and the acts of violence and injustice committed by knights contrary to the Peace of God alliances supported by the Church. It is in this light that his call for a crusade – addressed to the knights at the end of the council – should be seen. The pope urged them to devote their forces rather to the defence of their brothers in faith in the East, who had become the victims of the infidels' violence. He said that he had received requests for help from the Christians in the East, referring here to letters sent by Emperor Alexius Comnenus to himself and the count of Flanders (in 1091), and by the emperor's sister to diverse western leaders asking for mercenary troops. The pope appealed to those attending the Council to help the Byzantine Empire. The canons of the council record that those warriors of the faith who went to Jerusalem without thought of vainglory or material gain, but only with the intention of visiting the Holy Sepulchre, would be granted plenary indulgence; that is to say, a full remission of punishment in the hereafter for sins committed in life (see Chapter 15).

In addition to the undoubtedly sincere religious motivations to promote the Christian faith and the purity of the Church, the pope also would have had political considerations in mind. The request for military support from the Byzantine emperor offered the western Church the chance to strengthen its position there, as it already had done in Sicily and Iberia. The aim of the expedition was certainly not the defence of the Byzantine Empire – the crusaders travelled straight through. The nomadic Seljuks were put to flight, but not eliminated. A papal vassal state in Palestine, on the Sicilian model, however, would have been an excellent result from the opportunities offered. Seen in this light, it is remarkable that the pope tied the Church hierarchy in the newly conquered regions to Rome and not to the patriarch of Constantinople.

The western invasions in the Middle East that followed Urban II's proclamation were accompanied by an intensive propaganda campaign for the greater glory of the Catholic Church and the nobles who took the cross. Practically all the surviving sources in the West relating to the crusades breathe a virulent partisanship and portray a clichéd image of the enemy, which fitted in logically with the Church's campaign to crusade. The opening verses of Psalm 79 were frequently quoted to vindicate what was to be seen as a war of liberation of the Holy Sepulchre: 'O God, the heathen are come into thine inheritance; thy holy temple have they defiled'. On earlier occasions, when Jerusalem was taken by the Muslims in the seventh century or when the Holy Sepulchre was destroyed by Caliph al-Hakim at the beginning of the eleventh century, the Catholic Church had not yet attained the moral and organizational strength it acquired in the second half of the eleventh century. The great Church Reform, the Peace of God movement, the Schism with the Orthodox Church in 1054,

the Investiture Contest and the encouragement of the Iberian *Reconquista*, all were expressions of this newly acquired self-confidence.

Neither is there any need to doubt the deeply religious motives of most crusaders. Chroniclers called the men (and some women too) who took part 'pilgrims', or even 'martyrs' or 'new apostles', the expeditions themselves 'pilgrimages' – all terms that underlined their elevated religious status and their willingness to make great sacrifices in the eyes of contemporaries. Abbot Guibert de Nogent, one of the non-participating historians of the First Crusade, linked together the concepts of holy war against the infidels – knightly virtue, earthly salvation, God's grace and religious vocation – even more explicitly than did Pope Urban II in his Clermont speech. In short, crusades were never 'simply military campaigns' but always and primarily 'acts of devotion and a means of salvation' (Madden). Crusaders were unlikely to be driven by love of gain alone: they wanted to cleanse their sins and save their souls. To that end they and their families had to make huge financial sacrifices, and they often had to face appalling hardships on their journey. Most of them eventually returned to their homeland, which also indicates that the acquisition of new land never was their prime motive.

On the other hand, the behaviour of the crusaders in the Holy Land was quite another matter. The cruelty of their actions, in particular the plundering and wholesale murder for which they were responsible – for instance, during the First Crusade in Ma'arrat al-No'man and Jerusalem, however explicable it may have been because of the irregular provisioning – filled the local population with revulsion and exposed the desire of many 'Franks' to take as much booty as quickly as possible.

Crusades, crusader states and Western colonies in the East

The proclamation of Urban II was followed by the fervent preaching of Peter the Hermit, who won over great numbers of supporters among the ordinary people. This still unstructured movement, in all its enthusiasm, proceeded to pogroms against the Jews in the towns along the Rhine, but it was entirely wiped out in its first encounter with the Turkmen. The real crusades would be led by the experienced warrior class of knights and princes. However, there was no logistic provisioning for the hordes of many thousands of fighters and followers. In the first instance, this led to plundering and fighting in Hungary until an accord was reached with the cooperation of King Kálmán of Hungary, who set up lodgings and crossing places along the Danube and founded a monastery in Jerusalem.

Most of those who took part in the First Crusade came from the north of France. The relationship between Urban II, born in the Marne region, and Emperor Henry IV was very tense because Henry still stood by the antipope he had appointed. Very little cooperation could thus be expected from the German Empire, even though Godfrey of Bouillon, of the powerful house of Boulogne and the most famous leader of the First Crusade, was, as titular duke of Lower Lorraine, technically a German lord. An important force came from Norman Sicily under the leadership of Bohemond of Taranto, elder son of Robert Guiscard, who had lost most of the territories he was meant to inherit to the Byzantines. Of all the city-ports of northern Italy only Genoa came into action immediately; its ships would ensure that the 'Franks' were provisioned. Genoese carpenters built the equipment needed for the siege of Antioch, and, together with English vessels, supplied the wood needed for the construction of siege towers and cata-pults just in time for the decisive attack on Jerusalem. In 1104 they provided valuable assistance at the capture of Acre. The Genoese, and subsequently also the Pisans, accepted rich remuneration for their services to the crusaders, above all in the shape of extensive commercial privileges and allocations of property in the conquered regions. Venetian involvement was more limited; they were most interested in keeping their rivals out of the region where they had obtained a monopoly from the emperor. In Constantinople itself they were the only foreigners who had been assigned their own quarter.

The success of the First Crusade was indeed almost a miracle. Having been ferried piecemeal over the Bosporus in the spring of 1097, the crusader army immediately gained an important victory by defeating Kilij Arslan, sultan of the Rum Seljuks, under the walls of Nicaea. Shortly afterwards it embarked on a summer-long, disastrous crossing of hot and dry Anatolia. Then, in the autumn, the tide turned again. By two strokes of luck, two important cities fell into the hands of the crusaders: first Armenian Edessa, literally given to Godfrey of Bouillon's brother, Baldwin of Boulogne, who had just come to rally Armenian support; second, Antioch, an impregnable fortress, taken by trick and treason shortly before the arrival of a large Turkish relief force. Edessa and Antioch became the centres of the first two crusader territories or states in the Near East: the County of Edessa, which would last until 1144, and the Principality of Antioch, which managed to survive until 1268 and whose first lord would be Bohemond of Taranto.

Jerusalem was taken on 15 July 1099, after a siege lasting less than five weeks. Godfrey of Bouillon had himself proclaimed 'defender of the Church and the Holy Sepulchre', bringing him much personal renown. No doubt it was good for the salvation of his soul, for he died just one year later. His brother Baldwin succeeded him and took the title 'King of Jerusalem',

△△△ Armenia Minor
⸬⸬⸬ Principality of Antioch
═══ County of Edessa
▓▓▓ County of Tripoli
||||| Kingdom of Jerusalem

Map 10.2 Crusader states in about 1150

thus relegating his dependence on the pope to the background. The crusader-kings of Jerusalem did not enjoy any supremacy over the other Latin rulers in the region. A fourth state, the County of Tripoli, was formed by Raymond of Toulouse and was a magnet for Italian traders. In 1187 it became part of the Principality of Antioch. For the first 20 years the 'Franks' fought fiercely to win the cities along the coast. Acre fell to them in 1104, Sidon and Beirut in 1110 and Tyre in 1124. The support and provisioning from Italian fleets was essential for this.

Relationships between the Byzantines and Latin Christians were fraught with difficulty, despite the undoubtedly good intentions of emperor and pope. Moreover, it was difficult to discern any feelings of mutual solidarity between the Latin rulers. After the great conquests perhaps a few hundred 'Frankish' knights and some thousands of foot-soldiers remained in the conquered regions, but in the tangle of coalitions they made to survive and prosper they did not form a homogeneous block that could challenge the Muslims or Byzantines. Every sort of combination was made, cutting straight across religious borders. From 1128 there was close cooperation between the Muslims of northern Syria and Mesopotamia in which the latter took over control of Aleppo and pushed back the Latin states of Antioch and Edessa. In southern Syria a form of peaceful co-existence grew up with impregnable Damascus.

The Latin colonization was generally limited to the towns because the westerners were relatively few in number and therefore needed the cover of robust walls to ensure their safety. They settled only sporadically in villages, under the protection of castles. The strongholds, known as *kraks*, were situated in high places and could stand firm against Muslim sieges. Later, it was mainly the religious foundations that formed a few domains where vineyards were planted and sugar-cane, indigo and grain cultivated. The 'Franks' of Syria and Palestine did not create an extensive feudal system based on the holding of land, such as existed in their countries of origin. The shortage of men compelled them to make very flexible rules of succession in favour of younger sons and daughters, making it difficult to accumulate property, while the continual struggle made everything uncertain. Knights were tied to more powerful lords by 'bezant loans', rents paid in cash; the

Plate 10.1 Krak des Chevaliers (top), raised in the County of Tripoli after the First Crusade, could house 2,000 crusaders. The architecture of the 'Gravensteen' – the castle of the counts of Flanders – at Ghent (below) would have been inspired by Krak

'bezant' was a Byzantine gold coin that was imitated locally. In this way the greater degree of monetization in the East compensated for the lesser degree of control over the land by western standards.

Besides the knights, the religious orders helped to consolidate the Latin presence in the Holy Land. In addition to new and existing monasteries and hospitals, original foundations were created that took the form of military orders (see Chapter 7). The number of knights offering their services to these new orders grew quickly, and pious gifts began flowing in. All sorts of banking practices were developed to transfer these riches from the West to the East. Pilgrims leaving for the Holy

Land could 'buy' a credit in one of the western houses of these orders, in Paris or London for example, which they could cash in the local currency once they had arrived safely in Jerusalem – an early type of traveller's cheque.

The military orders formed the largest concentrations of Latin power in the Levant. They accumulated enormous estates and fortunes, in the West as well as in the East. By the end of the twelfth century, the Templars owned some 20 strongholds north of Tripoli, one of which housed 1,700 fighting men. Besides their own heavily armed and solidly trained knights, they also took Islamic mercenaries into their service. For the latter, money apparently prevailed over faith.

The third category of Latin colonists in the East, after the knights and the military orders, was formed by Italian traders. They benefited from the military protection offered by the Latin strongholds and accepted substantial rewards for their services. An excellent example of this was the agreement the doge of Venice made with representatives of the king of Jerusalem in 1123. With an eye to the conquest of the port of Tyre, still in Islamic hands, the Venetians insisted on being given a legally autonomous commercial quarter in every town in the kingdom, and fiscal advantages, in return for their fleet's support. Should Tyre and Ascalon be taken, one-third of those towns would come to them in free and permanent possession.

BOX 10.1 LEGAL PROTECTION OF FOREIGN TRADERS

Letter from Al-Abbas, vizier of the Fatimid caliph Al-Zafir, to the archbishop and commune of Pisa, 17 February 1154:

[. . .] Your ambassador Raynerio Botaccio has come to us with letters from Archbishop Villano and from the consul and notables of the city of Pisa. In them you tell us that traders from your town, your brothers and relations whom you sent to us as a son to his father, were last year arrested and deprived of much of their merchandise, which is not fitting for such a large kingdom, far greater than any on earth. Therefore we have sent you this embassy with a splendour that you only use for the greatest occasions, with a galleon where an ordinary ship is usual, in order to arrange everything in accordance with his judgment. . . .

We have explained to your ambassador that his complaint is not based on the truth. We have been informed that our traders in Alexandria, who embarked in good faith on the same ship as your traders, were killed most treacherously. They had been told that Frankish pirates had been sighted, and therefore descended into the hull, whence one by one they were thrown into the sea. Your men then took their wives and children and property for themselves. The law and the trading agreement between us provide for the imprisonment of the guilty people and their accomplices, and that we hold your traders who are staying in our land until you have delivered the culprits to us with compensation for the families of the victims. . . . Your ambassador also complained that many of your compatriots are in our prisons. To this we have replied that we captured those Pisans while they were making war against us with the Franks, to whom they gave help and supplies. According to the treaty between us, Pisans who are found on the same ship as the Franks are treated in the same way as the Franks. . . .

After long negotiations with us and with his companions, your ambassador has promised to remain completely loyal to us and not to threaten our subjects in any way at all. They will not enter into any agreement with the Franks, nor with any of our possible enemies, on land, at sea, or in our harbours. They will not undertake any enemy action against our army, either on their own or together with others. None of your traders will bring a Frank from Syria here, disguised as a trader. . . .

Now we extend you the privilege of coming to Alexandria for gold, silver and all your business affairs and allow you to live there in your *funduq*. You may transport everything that you have for sale to all places in our empire, after payment of 12 per cent customs duty, and also take them back with you, with the exception of wood, iron and pitch which our customs purchase at the market price. . . . We hereby confirm all the privileges that were previously granted by us, and in addition grant you a *funduq* in Cairo and exemption from the duty on silver.

Text: C. Cahen, *Orient et Occident au temps des Croisades* (Paris, 1983), pp. 228–230.

The privileges that the Italians acquired from the conquerors were probably more attractive on paper than in reality. The endless years of war would have thoroughly disrupted commercial relationships – in particular those with the hinterlands of the Middle East and the Far East, the very places in which the westerners were most interested. During the first half of the twelfth century Egypt thus continued to be the most important connection. The commercial significance of the new Latin settlements in the Levant in that period should therefore not be assessed too highly. Surviving documents relating to overseas commercial transactions show how important the trading monopoly in Byzantium was to the Venetians, while Genoa concentrated more on Egypt. The Genoese also maintained intensive commercial relations with Sicily where, among other things, they bought grain and sold cloth from Flanders, and further round the western Mediterranean with Marseilles, Sardinia, Almeira, Ceuta, Bougie and Tunis. For both Venice and Genoa, the contact with the ports of the Latin East was sound but in no way dominant.

Antioch, Tyre, Acre, Cyprus and Armenia Minor were among sites of the substantial trading posts now built by the Italian cities; they demanded exclusive jurisdiction over the posts and sent their own representatives as administrators (consuls or *bayles*). On the pattern of the *funduq* in Islamic areas, these trading posts were blocks of houses or entire quarters of a town where the foreign traders stored their goods in warehouses, lived, had their churches, bath-houses, ovens, administrative and court buildings, and often even a watchtower and fence. They enjoyed full administrative and judicial autonomy and could enjoy their own culture in their own circle. In Acre, which became the capital of the kingdom after the loss of Jerusalem in 1187, the three Italian *fondachi* (the Italian corruption of *funduq*) dominated the economic life of the entire city. The Genoese, Venetians and Pisans held 6.5, 4 and 3 hectares of land there, respectively, where caravans arrived from the interior, ships moored and craftsmen and money-changers set up their establishments.

This colonization formed the steady undercurrent of western expansion, while the crusades themselves were its spectacular but not very effective phases of concentration. Although commercial relations before 1096 should not be underestimated, and those of the first decades of the twelfth century were not focused primarily on the Latin East, it cannot be denied that the crusades gave a new impulse to the commercial expansion of the West. Italian shipping was given new functions in the logistical support of fellow believers overseas, and Italian traders had fantastic opportunities to explore new markets. They had no difficulty, then, in adding eastern products to their supplies when Egypt closed its doors to them. The advancing westerners were an irritant, especially to the Byzantines, who had expected that the crusades would restore their own empire and certainly not establish Latin competition in their backyard. The Pisans and Genoese had followed the Venetian example and acquired trading rights in Constantinople. In 1182 a wave of disaffection broke out against them and they were completely annihilated.

The later crusades

The rise to power of the dynasty of Zengi, the Turkish ruler of Mosul and Aleppo in northern Iraq, provoked the Second Crusade (1146–1148) after Zengi invaded the Christian county of Edessa and conquered its capital. The crusade, now headed by the kings of Germany and France, was aimed at recapturing Edessa and attacking Damascus, but it was a failure in all possible respects – the County of Edessa was lost for good. A new threat to the remaining crusader states appeared when Zengi's son, Nur ed-Din, conquered Egypt in 1171, thus uniting Syria and Egypt. When Nur ed-Din died three years later, Saladin, his Kurdish vizier (governor) of Egypt, staged a successful *coup d'état* and was recognized as the new leader of Egypt and Syria. Subsequently, he turned a fierce power struggle over the throne of Jerusalem between several noble 'Frankish' families and their supporters to his own advantage. In 1187 Saladin crushed a crusader army at the Horns of Hattin, a dry plateau above Lake Tiberias, and shortly afterwards captured Jerusalem. Most of Palestine was lost. Saladin's empire would stay in the hands of his dynasty, known as the Ayyubids, for more than fifty years, without ever achieving a high degree of centralization.

News of Saladin's conquest of Jerusalem in 1187 is said to have caused the death of Pope Urban III. It provoked his successor into calling upon all Catholic princes to take the cross. He allowed them to collect one-tenth of the Church revenues within their realms to support their endeavour. In May 1189, Emperor Frederick Barbarossa, then aged 66, took command of a huge army in Regensburg. The kings of France and England, Philip II Augustus and Richard the Lionheart, needed two more years to set aside their rivalry before joining the advance on Palestine. Some narrative sources tell of 100,000 participants, which is of course a gross exaggeration, but even 15,000 would have been a large number and would have created enormous logistical problems. Frederick's threat to conquer the Byzantine Empire if it did not support the crusaders resulted in more than just the immediate acquiescence of the Byzantine emperor. Frederick faced the greatest difficulties in taking his army through Byzantine territory. The German troops laid waste to Thessaloniki and Adrianople. It became clear,

especially to the popes, that the Hohenstaufen could well have an interest in universal power with the restoration of a united Roman Empire. The emperor's death by drowning in 1190 pushed such an eventuality into the background for the time being, but it would reappear under Frederick II. After part of the German army had returned home following the death of Barbarossa, the remainder advanced under the leadership of his son Frederick of Swabia. This army joined the French and English troops that retook Acre in July 1191, after the English had seized the island of Cyprus from the Byzantines. Frederick of Swabia died of a contagious disease during the siege. Philip Augustus, after performing some spectacular feats of chivalry, returned home because he wanted to assert control over Vermandois, which had reverted to the crown because its heir, Count Philip of Flanders, had died in the siege of Acre. Richard twice came close to the walls of Jerusalem, but on both occasions decided to retreat because he judged an attack on the city to be unwise under the circumstances. In the end, he had to content himself with an agreement about pilgrims' access to Jerusalem. All things considered, the Third Crusade was not a great success, even if the recapture of the coastal towns of Palestine and the conquest of Cyprus assured the 'Frankish' presence in the Near East for another century.

The Fourth Crusade (1201–1204) highlighted the lack of a coordinated Western policy with regard to Palestine. The emperor of Byzantium seemed to have become the prime enemy. After his experiences with Frederick Barbarossa in 1190 he had refused to allow the crusaders to cross through his territory. Now that the crusaders were forced to go by sea, Venice had a golden opportunity to make its mark on events. The first target was to engineer a change of power in Constantinople. Before the crusaders had embarked, the Venetians decided that they would have the right to three-quarters of the booty, three-eighths of the territorial conquests and one-half of the committee to select the new emperor of Constantinople. In 1204, the crusaders took the proud capital and established their Latin Empire there, which extended over most of Greece and lasted until 1261.

The distraction of the Fourth Crusade from its real goal persuaded Pope Innocent III to suggest at the Fourth Lateran Council of 1215 that a new crusade be preached as soon as possible. Prelates from Syria were also among the participants at the Council. The date of departure was set for 1 June 1217. The massive mobilization had a modest success with the capture of the fortress on Mount Tabor, so that Acre was no longer under threat. The goal then shifted to Egypt since that was the stronghold of Muslim power in the Near East. In February 1218 the 'Franks' laid siege to the port of Damietta at the mouth of the Nile. The town was taken after 22 months, its garrison exhausted and its people starved, but in 1221 the 'Franks' had to give it up again.

The West cherished great hopes that Emperor Frederick II would join the crusade, as he had vowed to do at his coronation. Differing views on relationships with the Arab and Greek world, and tension between himself and the popes, however, made him hold back. In 1228 his fleet finally put to sea. Frederick was accompanied by just a few hundred knights; using his knowledge of the Arabic language and culture he made a peace treaty with the sultan, under the terms of which the Christian king of Jerusalem would again have authority over the city and a few places on the road to the coast. Jerusalem was again under Christian rule, with the exception of the holy places of Islam on the Temple Mount. Christian pilgrims were allowed to visit the Holy Sepulchre if they behaved with respect and discretion. The Muslims would be allowed to keep their own law. This ten-year peace was respected on both sides, but the haggling over the most holy city in Christendom and one of the most sacred places of Islam was seen as a despicable act of treason by most Christians and Muslims alike. Frederick had himself crowned king of Jerusalem in the Church of the Holy Sepulchre, demonstrating his direct link to God. This was exactly what the pope had feared and why two years earlier he had already excommunicated the emperor.

Soon after the ten-year peace came to an end a sixth crusade took place, from 1239 to1240. Because the emperor refused to take part, the crusade was led by Thibaut IV of Champagne, king of Navarre, and Richard of Cornwall, count of Poitou. Once again their military successes were little more than the retaking of former positions. The role of diplomacy increasingly supplemented that of force. The Christians held their ground by allying themselves to one of the rival Muslim princes, in particular trying to play Syria and Egypt against each other. Their game was completely disrupted in 1243 when a huge army of the expelled Ayyubid ruler of Syria, as-Salih, and his allies from northern Iran advanced through the Bekaa valley into Jerusalem, murdering even in the Church of the Holy Sepulchre. In October 1244 the Christian army lost many thousands of men. The Latin Empire had received a blow from which it never recovered.

Louis IX of France now took control, embarking for Cyprus in 1248. By May 1249 he had assembled an international crusader army of more than 2,500 knights, 5,000 archers and 15,000 other troops. Once again their target was the Nile delta. Damietta fell into their hands quickly, but then the crusader army was decimated by scurvy and hunger. In April 1250 Louis decided to return to Damietta. He was suffering from dysentery, and was captured by the Egyptians along with thousands of his men. The ransom demanded was equivalent to the French crown's income for a whole year. Under pressure, the Templars agreed to make the first payment. When the Christian prisoners were not released in accordance with the agreement, Louis decided to head for Jaffa. During his four-year stay in Palestine he made peace between the Latin rulers and contributed to the consolidation of places threatened by the sultan of Egypt. The exceptional financial and human effort had brought nothing but disappointment to France. Louis' second crusade was even more disastrous, ending with his death in Tunis in 1270 where he had sought an operational base for his army, weakened through sickness. King Edward I of England carried on to Acre. The idea of crusading had not yet disappeared, but when the Christians were forced to evacuate Acre, the last Latin city, in 1291 there was no longer any effective reaction from the West.

The spread of faith and colonization

For two centuries the West had sent relatively large streams of people, services and capital eastwards. It is not difficult to imagine that without this outlet the West would have suffered far greater internal tensions. The Latin Empire established in 1204 made it possible for the Venetians to build up their network of trading posts in the Aegean Sea and the Peloponnese. After

1212 Venetians went on to found a colony on Crete. The island was divided into six, on the model of the 'six parts' in their own city, and a Latin Church hierarchy was established. The Venetians took over the land and controlled it until 1669. They established sugar plantations (the name of the capital, Candia, became a generic name for candy), and later proceeded to colonize other islands, such as Euboia in the Aegean Sea, providing them with a plantation economy and slave labour. Thus, long before 1300, the trading cities of the Mediterranean already had ventured upon a colonization movement, which continued without any serious interruption until after the fifteenth century along the coast of Africa and then across the oceans. Two forms of colonization were developed: networks of trading posts along distant overseas routes and settlement colonies where slaves worked on plantations. The former were the links in the chain between regional commercial circuits offering goods of different kinds.

The Byzantine Empire was split into a number of small principalities along the south coast of the Black Sea and the Aegean coast as far as Smyrna. In the tradition of the great rivalry with Venice the Genoese supported these rulers, which enabled them to set up trading posts with monopoly rights along the Black Sea in Trebizond, in Tana on the mouth of the Don in the Sea of Azov and, above all, in Kaffa in the Crimea where they installed a consul in 1281. Through these places they could stock up on slaves and exploit the overland routes to the Mongol khanates and China, whence they brought back silk and spices. Because of the support they gave to the Orthodox emperors who regained control in Constantinople, the Genoese were allotted an important settlement in Pera, on the Golden Horn just opposite Constantinople, and also on the island of Chios. This was an enormous breakthrough for the West: economically seen, they were now masters of all the Mediterranean and a large part of the Black Sea. The Italians had eliminated the Muslims as middlemen in the trade with the Far East. In the western Mediterranean the Genoese, Pisans and Barcelonans similarly created links with the caravan routes bringing gold from Senegal, across the Sahara.

Events in the Islamic world during the thirteenth century were influenced less by the crusades than they were by Mongol invasions. First, Genghis Khan (*c.* 1167–1227) annihilated the Iranian empire of the

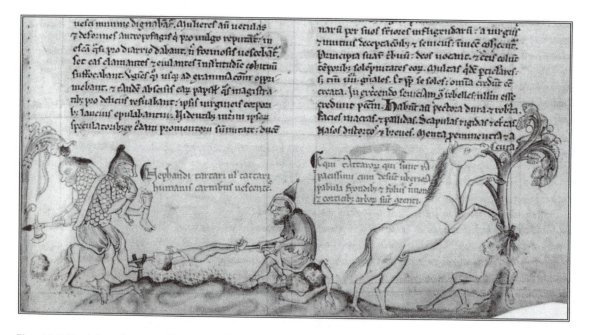

Plate 10.2 Depiction of western ideas about the Mongols

Khwarazm shahs in 1220. Then, in 1253, Genghis's grandson Hülegü, the Mongol master of Iran, invaded Iraq and Syria with a huge army. Five years later he conquered Baghdad, where he caused a horrifying bloodbath with the last caliph of the Abbasid line as one of the thousands of victims. Aleppo and Damascus followed soon after, but in 1260 the Mongols were defeated at Ayn Jalut by the army of the sultan of Egypt. The Mongols would never rule over Palestine, but their defeat also heralded the end of the last crusader states. The Christians' original hope of consolidating their crumbling positions with the help of the Mongols evaporated.

The region's new rulers were the Mamelukes, horsemen of generally Kipchak-Turkish origin who played a key role in Egyptian warfare. In 1250 a Mameluke coup had ended Ayyubid rule. Egypt, Syria and Palestine came under the rule of Mameluke generals, who bore the title of sultan. Between 1516 and 1520 their sultanate was absorbed into the Ottoman Empire.

The stagnation of the colonization of the Holy Land after the thirteenth century gave a new impulse to the movements of colonization to the continental peripheries of Europe itself. This link is clearly visible among the citizens of Bremen and Lübeck who, first in Jerusalem and later in Acre, maintained a hospital for their pilgrims. In Acre they were even allocated their own quarter. There they founded a religious order of knights whose rules were approved by Pope Innocent III in 1199. This German (or Teutonic) Order first acquired considerable property in both the East and West. After 1211 its primary focus was on the protection of Christianity on its European eastern frontier. In the meantime, in 1197, the bishop of Riga had founded another order of knights, with the telling name of 'Brethren of the Sword', specifically to suppress the pagan Latvians and Livonians. From 1230 the German bishops proclaimed a permanent crusade against the Baltic and Slavic peoples. Both military orders were given considerable political, legal and material rights to spread Christianity by force of arms through the sparsely populated regions of central and eastern Europe, and to deprive the few inhabitants of their land and liberty.

The Teutonic Order took the land on the fertile plains of the lower reaches of the Vistula and established a series of towns there between 1231 and 1237. These towns were laid out in a chequerboard pattern, and were populated with Christians from the Lower German linguistic area in the west. The native Prussian inhabitants of the region were forced to pay rents in kind to the Order. Others were set to work as serfs on the great estates where grain was cultivated in vast quantities: in the fifteenth century this grain would occasionally help to reduce the food shortages in western Europe in years of bad harvests. This was a typical export economy, in the hands of a foreign upper class. The knights were generally recruited from among the lower, partly unfree, German nobility of service (ministerials) who could thus achieve the ideal of the *Drang nach Osten* ('Urge to go eastward'). Thousands of villages were founded in this way by groups of migrants from the west, whose own Flemish, Hollandic, Brabant or west German customary law was often recognized; their language and culture, and most noticeably such place-names as 'Flamen' and 'Holland', also left permanent traces in the regions they settled. There were analogous expansion movements elsewhere, in Iberia with the Christian Reconquest, and under the Anglo-Norman kings the English pushed deep into the border regions of the British Isles.

In this massive battle for Catholicism, religion played a mobilizing role. Yet the religious factor should not be seen as decisive in each and every respect. On both the Islamic and Christian (even the Catholic) sides there was a clear lack of solidarity. The caliphs in Baghdad did not do much for their fellow believers in Syria; their main interest was to maintain or restore their own authority. The Almohads in Iberia showed no interest in the struggle in the Levant. On the Christian side the increasingly serious clashes were particularly noticeable, of course; they led to a full-blown war between Latins and Greeks, and eventually to the decline of the Byzantine Empire. Latin princes and Latin trading cities were so busy quarrelling with each other that they missed opportunities and even brought harm upon themselves. Yet was it not these typically western divisions of power – Church, princes, traders, and multiples of the last two – that had produced a more dynamic, flexible and therefore more durable system than the orthodox dominions of Christianity or Islam? In the long run, it was the western system of autonomous spheres of power for religion, state government and market economy, including its two forms of colonization – plantation colonies and trading posts – that has become dominant in the world. Its origins lay in the events just discussed.

TAKE OFF TO A COMMERCIAL REVOLUTION

The relative autonomy of the towns with respect to the ecclesiastical, feudal or monarchic authorities was a basic condition for the 'European miracle', the

Plate 10.3 The drapery market at Bologna in the fifteenth century. Miniature from the drapers' guild register

superiority that north-west Europe established from the tenth to the nineteenth centuries over the other continents, behind which it originally lagged. Because of the relative freedom that the multitude of separate jurisdictions helped to bring about it was possible for an entrepreneurial and consumerist set of norms and values to develop in the towns. Part of it was a rational, boundless pursuit of material riches through the accumulation and reinvestment of profits from trade.

R.S. Lopez, the Italian-American economic historian, once characterized this swing as the 'commercial revolution', a breakthrough whose effects were similar to those of the Industrial Revolution. Beginning with Italy during the tenth century, he saw how trade obtained an ever-stronger hold on the production process and on the mentality and way of life in general. Far-reaching innovations in traffic and transport, commercial skills, products available, environmental frameworks and institutions were introduced. Many of them were completely new and still exist: accounting systems, credit, insurance, bills of exchange, banking, share companies, the capitalist mentality. In this, Italy played the role in the commercial revolution that England was to perform later in the Industrial Revolution.

The causes of these innovations were complex and reinforced each other. Just as demographic growth was the fundamental motor for agricultural progress, agriculture in turn formed the essential basis for the commercial revolution. The steady growth of agricultural production certainly benefited from the growing political stability at the local level. The halt to external conquests contributed to the consolidation of the growth. Italy played a pioneering role because it was supported by its contacts with those Mediterranean shores that were in the lead. The shortage of raw materials (wood, high-quality wool, minerals) forced it to explore overseas possibilities as the population increased. Internal growth and external events, economy and politics thus were all part of the explanation for the take-off of the Western European economy.

The gradual increase in agricultural productivity was certainly a precondition of commercialization, since it resulted in surpluses that could be put into circulation. In those regions that were by nature particularly suited for this, specialized products like wool, salt, minerals or wine were involved – elsewhere, ordinary foodstuffs.

Specialization took shape, and in itself contributed to trade.

In addition to the internal causes of commercialization, there were external causes. We have already referred to the reversal in the power relationships between Western Europe and surrounding cultures. There should be no doubt about the considerable extent to which this part of the continent lagged behind the Mediterranean area. In about the year 1000 the leading zones lay clearly in Byzantium and the Muslim areas. In northern Europe, southern Scandinavia – which was also in contact with Byzantium and Persia, through overland routes straight across Russia – functioned as a centre of development, although on a far more primitive level. Trade with the less developed regions provided the core areas with raw materials, primarily wood, which was always extremely scarce in the Muslim world, but also with weapons and slaves. In the periphery this trade set its own dynamics in motion. Southern Italy and Venice profited most from it. Merchants from Amalfi settled in their own district in Constantinople even before 944, and there must have been many hundreds of them in Cairo. Around 1070 they built two monasteries and a guest-house for pilgrims in Jerusalem. Three years later the Normans conquered Amalfi, cutting short its commercial growth but not the relations between Sicily and southern Italy with the East. Venice owed its ascendancy to close ties with Byzantium, its unique geographical location, salt-winning and the glass industry.

In about 1000, fleets from Pisa and Genoa cleared the Tyrrhenian Sea area of Islamic pirates and raiders. In 1015 Pisa conquered first Sardinia, then Corsica. At the time of the Reconquest of Iberia, and sometimes in coordinated actions, the Pisans and Genoese frequently captured Muslims off the east coast, but this seemed to make no difference to regular trade. On the one hand, the key role played by the fleets of the north Italian towns in transporting large armies to Palestine and Syria testifies to the level of their development. On the other, these combative seafarers took advantage of the situation by accepting substantial rewards for their services and then followed the crusaders and gained a firm foothold in the seaports of the eastern Mediterranean. In 1099, Pisan fleets won trading rights in Antioch and Laodicea. Between 1098 and 1110, the Genoese obtained concessions in Antioch, Caesarea, Arsuf, Acre, Beirut, Gibelet and Laodicea. Venice already had a firm footing in the Byzantine Empire, where its merchants had been exempt from all taxes and customs duties since 1082. In 1119 the town also established another solid bridgehead in Tyre.

If we look from the perspective of the core regions in the eastern Mediterranean in about the year 1000, and not from that of Western Europe and later history, then we would have no reason to attach any special significance to these developments. After all, the highest level of development had been concentrated in that region for 8,000 years, and it was still by far the richest in every respect. Slight shifts of core locations and territorial authority, and even the temporary supremacy of the Roman Empire, had not essentially affected the situation. That handful of barbarian 'Franks' in Palestine could never hold out against the superior strength of the enormous armies of Islam. The westerners' heavy armour did give them some advantage, but it was not suitable for use on Arab horses. Although this analysis is not wrong in itself, it does not take into account the growth effects that the intensification of commercial relationships in Italy, Catalonia, and also the hinterland of north-western Europe, would produce.

There has been much discussion about the origins of the financial capital employed by the earliest urban traders. Referring to a single description of the life of one saint, Godric, Henri Pirenne stressed the element of luck. In his view, the first merchants were rootless people, in the most literal meaning of the word, who had been forced by overpopulation to seek a new life outside the secure existence on a demesne.

Biographies of saints have provided credible information that can be compared with facts from other types of sources. The London toll tariff at the time of King Ethelred II (978–1016) records the regular presence there of *Flandrenses*, Flemish merchants, as well as folk from Liège, Huy and Nivelles – a whole century, thus, before Godric in Pirenne's story. The following incident recounted in the *Vita sancti Bavonis*, the story of the life of St Bavo, also dates from this time. A storm had destroyed the boat of a merchant, who thus ended up in Ghent totally ruined. Seeking solace in the church of the rich abbey of St Bavo, at the confluence of the Lys and the Scheldt rivers, he noticed a golden chalice on the altar. The merchant prayed to the saint, begging him to lend him the chalice so that he could restart his business. He promised to pay it back many times over should he be successful. We can assume that St Bavo agreed to this request, for some time later the merchant reappeared in the abbey church with a far greater treasure than he had taken away. The good monks noted this episode as yet another proof of the activities of their patron saint. From this story we know that Ghent around 1000 was one of the places to which merchants journeyed by boat. Their fate was uncertain: they might lose their entire fortune in a storm, and even their life, for they travelled together with their wares. With a certain amount of starting capital, however, it was possible to show a handsome profit in a short time. Comparable evidence from that time shows that Ghent held a fair each year on 1 October, the feast day of St Bavo, at which, besides the religious ceremonies and pilgrimages there was also a flourishing interregional trade among the people crowding in from far and wide.

A characteristic of this commercialization was that, in comparison to the early Middle Ages, it was no longer limited to very scarce or unique commodities in small quantities and with a very high value. Merchants no longer came only from distant leading regions such as Syria. From the thirteenth century commerce became more wholesale, and increasingly included everyday consumer articles such as cloth, which for many centuries was the source of the wealth of northern France and Flanders. This was only possible through the increase in demand and purchasing power and because the evolving methods of transport could accommodate the growth.

The transport revolution

The Roman network of roads was built primarily to enable the state to fulfil its administrative and military functions. Until then most bulk goods had to be transported by ship. In later centuries no political unit was able to build roads on a similar scale and with the same technical standards as the Romans. The modernization of country roads was limited to the small territories of the trading towns. Medieval towns grew up at traffic junctions with water courses, and in the first instance these were then extended and adapted. During the first half of the thirteenth century great efforts were made to regulate the water level in the Po valley and to link all the towns by canals. In Flanders, in the second half of the same century, Ghent, Bruges and Ypres dug canals in order to improve communications with each other and, above all, with the sea. Florence, situated on the Arno, with its extremely fluctuating water levels, elaborated a transport system to ensure its grain provision and the supply of other bulk goods. It took three days with seaworthy barges 10 metres long and 3 metres broad, and on the way a transfer to smaller boats, to get from Porto Pisano upstream to Signa, 14 kilometres from Florence. In Signa the town built warehouses and a paved road to carry the goods to their destination by four-wheeled wagons. The cost of this transport meant that in 1284 salt was 28 per cent more expensive in Florence than in Pisa.

At the end of the fourteenth century a fruitless attempt was made to cut through the 60-kilometre-wide neck of land between Lübeck and Hamburg in the hope of cutting out the journey round Jutland. Traffic over the Alps was made easier by constructing new roads over passes and improving existing ones – the St Gothard in 1237, and the Great St Bernard even earlier. The enormous investments required for such undertakings could only be recovered through the levy of tolls on the vastly increased flow of traffic.

The market price was under heavy pressure from the manifold transaction costs of goods on their way from producer to consumer. Merchants therefore sought their competitive advantage largely in the reduction of these transaction costs. Shipping took place traditionally along the coast. The Chinese already had a primitive ship's compass, which consisted of a magnetic needle stuck into a figurine of a fish or a turtle floating in a bowl of water or mounted on a short spearhead. During the twelfth century this instrument became known to European seamen, but it was not perfected until the fourteenth century, when it was mounted on an axis. The Islamic knowledge of geography was far more advanced than that of the Christian world. In the thirteenth century, through their contacts with Muslims, the Italians and Catalans learned to draw charts showing the navigational routes from harbour to harbour along visually recognizable coastlines; they were known as portolan charts.

Plate 10.4 Portolan map from a Venetian atlas of *c.* 1400. Portolan maps (medieval nautical charts) were drawn with the aid of a wind rose. They offer a detailed picture of coastlines and were used for charting the course and calculating the distance between two harbours.

An even more important discovery was the rudder, attached to the stern-post and turning on a beam, first introduced along the coast of the North Sea from which it spread to the south. The most important type of ship in the north was the cog, a fairly high, single-masted vessel with a rounded bow, 30 metres long, 7 metres broad and a draught of 3 metres, able to carry a cargo in excess of 200 tons. In the Mediterranean, the ancient tradition of the flat-bottomed galley was continued, each propelled by 100–200 oarsmen. Although it was suited to the windless and mainly calm inland seas, the galley did not have much cargo space, and was expensive because slaves or convicts were needed to row it: this made it ideal for the transport of luxury goods. To transport goods in bulk, the Italians began using the *nave* during the thirteenth century; this was rather similar to the cog, but had two masts and triangular sails. In the fourteenth century the Italians designed the *coca*, a vessel which, with its fixed rudder and square sails, bore even greater resemblance to the cog. In about 1470 the Genoese were the first to reduce its manpower and yet enlarge the cargo space to

450 tons. Thanks to this technical advantage, they were also the first to sail round Gibraltar to the North Sea and the ports of Sluis/Bruges and Southampton; the oldest reference to such traffic was found in a notarial contract of 1277.

The spirit of renewal, acceleration, enlargement and expansion that breathes through all these innovations is similarly apparent in the journeys to the Far East undertaken by members of various monastic orders after 1240. One of them, William of Rubroek, the Flemish Franciscan, wrote a detailed account of his journey in which he contrasted his own observations with the traditional geographical insights still derived from the works of Isidore of Seville. From 1232 to 1237 four Hungarian Dominican friars travelled to the Volga region in search of the allegedly Scythian roots of the Magyars. One of them, the only survivor, did indeed find this 'Magna Hungaria' in Bashkiria, the region between the Volga and the southern stretches of the Ural mountain chain where, in his probably correct opinion, a language related to Hungarian was spoken. On his return to the West this friar was the first to bring news of the upcoming Mongol invasion. Journeys of discovery to China, such as those made by the Venetian merchant family Polo between 1270 and 1290, strengthened the contacts with the new Mongolian rulers of China. Their exploring mentality would lead Western skippers to undertake voyages of discovery along the west coast of Africa in the following centuries.

Progress in organization

The merchant's major concern was to reduce the risks to which he and his wares were exposed. As long as merchants accompanied their wares they sought protection by travelling in groups that were linked by reciprocal oaths of solidarity and support. Merchant guilds and hanses basically met this need for safety. As collectives, they tried to obtain guarantees of legal protection and exemption from tolls for their members from the local governments in the relevant areas. In theory, privileges for foreign merchants meant that they enjoyed the protection of the authorities. This meant that they could apply their own jurisdiction to settle disputes among themselves, while disputes with local people would be resolved in accordance with the customs of international mercantile law. If that did not succeed, then reprisals were generally used as a means of applying pressure: a fellow-townsman or fellow-countryman of the debtor would be arrested, or his property confiscated, in the hope that his local authority would put pressure on him to settle the matter. Measures of this sort were liable to escalate quickly, so the solution to trading disputes was sometimes very complicated and could drag on for years.

This system of protection applied both to merchants who went abroad for just a few weeks and to those who were settled in colonies on a semi-permanent basis. In their contracts for the year 1197, Genoese notaries recorded 5,261 sales of cloth, for which Flemings were present as sellers in 2,046 cases, northern Frenchmen in 1,942 and Englishmen in 258. These foreigners must have been well organized to have travelled so far with their products. Some decades later, 198 foreign merchants were recorded as living in Genoa, of whom 95 were Flemish and 51 French. For their own protection, and so that local authorities could keep check on them, foreign merchants lived close to each other in a particular building or in a designated street or quarter. In Islamic seaports, Italians were allotted a *funduq*, a town district, for their accommodation and storage space. On the coast of North Africa, Venetians and Genoese had walled quarters, just as they had in Tabriz. In Bougie and Tunis, in 1261, the Barcelonans enjoyed the jurisdiction of their own consuls and had at their disposal a notary, their own shops, a bakery, an inn and a chapel. In 1228 the Venetians housed the South German merchants in their city in the *fondaco dei Tedeschi*, near the Rialto bridge; the *fondaco dei Turchi* could be found a little further along the Grand Canal.

The establishment of trading colonies demanded enduring relationships, based on trust and mutual interests on the part of hosts and foreigners alike. A permanent settlement overseas was only worth while when there was a considerable volume of profitable trade. Two different circuits were crossing in these places, such as the caravan routes from China and Persia, which the Christians met in the ports of Syria and Palestine, or the routes from South Russia, Bulgaria and modern-day Romania to Kaffa in the Crimea or Tana on the Sea of Azov.

The Italian system of trading settlements was by far the largest in medieval Europe. Starting during the twelfth century, a similar system of trading settlements was developed by North Germans in Scandinavia and along the Baltic coast, although on a more modest scale. The most important centre was the island of Gotland, off the east coast of Sweden, where Danes and North Germans from Lübeck, and later also from Westphalia, came into contact with local traders and from there engaged in trade with Novgorod (where the Germans had a settlement by about 1190), England and Flanders. Traders from different regions organized themselves for their own protection on certain routes. Similar trading organizations were formed in other places during the twelfth and thirteenth centuries – for the Anglo-Flemish trade, for example, and for the trade from Flanders, Artois and Brabant to the annual fairs in Champagne. These were private associations, formed to provide mutual assistance, that were granted privileges by the ruling powers in the areas in question. Some of these organizations were called 'guild', others 'hanse'. The best-known of them is the German Hanse, in the thirteenth century a league of older regional merchants' associations from the regions round Lübeck and Westphalia, Saxony and Prussia. In 1356 the German Hanse transformed itself into an alliance of towns. At its peak it had some 200 member towns, from Novgorod via the Scandinavian coasts to the Low Countries. It functioned until 1669 on an interregional scale to promote the trading interests of the citizens of its member towns and acted externally as a collective, public body. Merchants of the German Hanse in London stayed in the *Stahlhof*, Steelyard, close to the Thames, and in Bergen, Norway, in the *Tyske brygge*, literally 'the German harbour'. Together with Novgorod, and especially Bruges, these cities were home to the so-called *Kontors*, the main privileged locations of the Hanse outside the German Empire.

Local authorities understood that there were advantages in protecting foreign merchants from being indiscriminately plundered by robber barons. After all, their well-regulated activities stimulated the local economy and helped increase revenues from tolls, mintage and the administration of justice. Influential abbeys, towns or landowners tried to further trading activities within the areas under their jurisdiction by guaranteeing protection on the road to an annual fair, where they proclaimed the market peace, vouched for safe conducts for the visitors and levied low tolls.

Differences could be settled on the spot in a special court of law, while notaries, clerks or a local magistrate were on hand to record agreements in writing. The important abbey of Saint-Denis, a few kilometres north of Paris, protected the *foire du Lendit* in this way. In theory, the local saint's feast day was the occasion for holding a fair lasting several weeks. Merchants poured in from far and wide with everything they had to offer, but farmers and craftsmen from the region, on payment of a small levy, could also do business safely and freely with a large and varied buying public. The main advantage of the fairs was the concentration of a global supply and a broad demand. The proximity to Paris obviously contributed to the success of the Lendit fair.

The location of fairs was decided by the situation in or close to a large town, on an important trading route or in a production area. The English wool trade was concentrated in a few places in south-east England, which certainly formed a network by 1180. Individual markets, some of which were founded by an abbey or a large cattle-farmer, were associated under a joint royal privilege that assured visiting merchants of justice throughout England. The dates of the fairs in all these places were so fixed that they followed each other in a yearly cycle. In this way, merchants were able to travel from one fair to another. The cycle commenced at Stamford in Lent, around Easter it was the turn of St Ives, Boston in July, King's Lynn at the end of July, Winchester in September, Westminster in October, Northampton in November and Bury St Edmunds in December. Another fair coupled to a particular product was Schonen, on the south-western cape of Sweden. Spurred on by the merchants of Lübeck, fairs flourished in Schonen during the fourteenth century, centred around the sale of the enormous herring harvest from the Kattegat. Lübeck supplied salt for the brine from the mines in Lüneburg and was the largest customer for the herring, which were gutted and packed in barrels primarily for resale. These fairs lost their importance when the herring catch declined sharply around 1400.

It was possible to visit fairs in neighbouring regions one after the other. The other important fair cycles were those in Flanders (Lille, Ypres, Mesen, Torhout and Bruges), and especially in the county of Champagne (Lagny, Bar-sur-Aube, Provins and

Troyes; the last two held a market twice a year). The Champagne region lay fairly central on the overland route between England and Italy and was thus an excellent place for merchants from all over Europe to meet, particularly from the southern Low Countries and Lombardy. In the Lower Rhine region, a cycle was formed around the markets of Cologne, Aachen, Duisburg and Utrecht by the end of the twelfth century.

All these fair cycles allowed travelling merchants to journey in safety and do business with each other on a regular basis. Mutual trust grew out of this regularity, and credit transactions from one market to another became common. The Italians needed to use their positive balance of payments – the unit value of their supply was higher than that of the northerners – productively. They invested the hard cash surplus, preferring to make more profit than run the risk of losing it on the journey home. For this reason they extended relatively cheap credit to their customers, further strengthening their dominant

Drawn after: F. Irsigler, JUISTE REFERENTIE MOET NOG VOLGEN

Map 10.3 Fair cycles in north-western Europe in the twelfth and thirteenth centuries

position as wholesale merchants. They rapidly emerged as financiers who provided credit for nobles and princes. They had this sort of transaction recorded briefly but objectively in written bonds, payable at a particular fair in another country, sometimes to associates or business partners of the creditors. The credit transaction was thus coupled to a money exchange transaction since the repayment was made in another currency; it could also be used to complete different transactions for the creditor. Naturally, substantial rates of interest were charged for this, although they were generally not specifically recorded. Ten to 15 per cent was held as entirely reasonable for short-term commercial credit; an interest rate of up to 43.33 per cent was considered acceptable for risky loans. Only when higher rates were asked for did it become a question of usury, and the Church prescribed severe punishments for usury.

In general, fairs served distant trade and regional or local trade at the same time. For the two latter functions there were smaller fairs in a number of places, some of which specialized in a particular product, such as horses or linen. The locations, which owed their importance mainly to their situation as staging points on a route, fell into obscurity as a result of shifts in macro-economic and political circumstances. So it was that the fairs of Champagne lost their role as west European meeting places in about 1300, chiefly as a result of the further growth in the volume of trade. The shipping links along the Atlantic coast then became more efficient than the land route, and trading houses began to work through permanent representatives. On top of this, political vicissitudes around 1300 disrupted the peace of northern France, while the taxes levied by the king, who in the meantime had inherited the county of Champagne, soared sky-high. Other fairs came in their place: the duke of Burgundy promoted the fair of Chalon-sur-Saône, the duke of Savoy that of Geneva, and in 1460 the king of France lent his support to the Lyons fair in a sort of economic war. During the late medieval period of contraction (see Chapter 13) fairs would enjoy a new lease of life. In Brabant the cycle of Antwerp and Bergen-op-Zoom prepared the role that Antwerp, on the Scheldt, would assume in the sixteenth century as the western metropolis. The Deventer fairs linked the Rhineland with the Hanse and a growing Amsterdam; Frankfurt

was linked to this cycle as well as to that of Brabant, and was the gateway to the overland routes to central Europe.

Although the *Frankfurter Messe* and fairs in a few other towns still take place every year, their function as a central location for all products and payments has disappeared. There is a simple reason for this: with the further growth of commercial traffic, the short-term meetings no longer sufficed and there was a growing need for permanent markets. This is why international fairs only survived in the fifteenth and sixteenth centuries in large towns where local production and sales already formed a solid basis. Elsewhere, more modern forms of organization took over their functions. The density of the northern Italian network of towns explains why fairs never played such an important role there as in the north: the urban facilities provided a constant and comprehensive supply and demand.

Italy, thanks to the volume of its trade, which was considerably larger and more varied than in the north, made further steps in commercial organization. The general tendency was towards a division of labour between the merchant and the transporter, towards an increase in the scale of commercial enterprises and the formation of networks of permanent representatives. The trade settlements of the Italians in the Levant brought them into contact with the often more sophisticated Muslim methods. Family concerns sent their younger offspring for a number of years to the *funduqs* to learn the business. They corresponded regularly with the home office. For the spreading of risks, overseas trade required forms of cooperation between a partner on land and a captain at sea. Later on nobody invested in an entire cargo: to spread the risk of loss, parts or shares were bought in the cargo of a ship, and then in several ships or cargoes at the same time. In Genoa forms of marine insurance came into use during the thirteenth century through notarial contracts. According to various sources, and depending on the circumstances, this cost between 7 and 15 per cent of the value of the cargo on the route of a Genoese *nave* from London or Southampton to Porto Pisano at the mouth of the Arno. For journeys on the safer Mediterranean, a rate of 4 per cent was normal. In Venice, where the great merchant families exercised their authority over the town in relative harmony, the state took upon itself the collective protection of the merchant fleets by having them sail in convoys, escorted if necessary by armed galleys of the state. This reduced the cost of insurance to 1 or 1.5 per cent for journeys by galley to Alexandria.

As early as the twelfth century, companies (derived from the Latin *cum pane*, 'eating bread together') were forming in the towns of Lombardy and Tuscany, whose family core enlarged its capital by issuing shares that yielded a proportional share of the profits. All partners, together with their fortunes, had an unlimited liability for the company, which naturally presupposed a strong bond. Companies from Piacenza, Lucca, Siena, Florence and Pistoia operated collectively at the fairs in the north. Moreover, their business with the pope was a gold mine, as they channelled papal revenues from all over Christendom to the Apostolic Chamber. It suited both parties that the Italian partnerships in the north could accept Church monies and transfer them to Rome. It enabled the merchants to buy wool in England, cloth, linen or furs in Flanders and Champagne, and give the pope what they owed him – after the deduction of certain expenses, of course – from the sales of those goods in Italy, without having to move or invest one single penny themselves. It was indeed Church pennies that gave Italian merchants their working capital.

The activities of a company had to be put down in writing so that the trading operations, as they became more complex, could be run more efficiently. Shareholders wanted to have some insight into the trading results in order to calculate their profits. Commercial correspondence between partners was another symptom of this. From 1260 couriers travelled regularly between Tuscany and Champagne. A century later 17 Florentine companies together set up the *scarsella*, a private courier service linking the major trading towns of western Europe. These couriers travelled between 50 and 60 kilometres per day, depending on the state of the roads. Rapid reporting of the situation of the markets enabled the headquarters of the medieval multinationals to make the best purchases and sales. Trade representatives, known as factors or agents, kept their principals informed about exchange rates, the prices of products and political situations that might have repercussions on trade. They also advised them by letter of the contents of the cargoes they shipped, so that verification was possible on arrival or in the case of loss. In its heyday in the fourteenth century the Florentine company, Bardi, had 120 factors in its service who supplied the headquarters with a mass of information about hundreds of products in more than twenty places. The entire archive of one trading house – that of Francesco Datini from Prato, who was active between 1380 and 1410 – is still in existence, and contains many thousands of letters that his correspondents in Barcelona, Paris, Avignon, Bruges and London sent him almost every week. Datini was certainly not one of the largest merchants of his time, but his business produced a mountain of paperwork – nearly 500 account books, 300 contracts of partnership, 400 insurance policies, thousands of invoices, bills of exchange and cheques, and about 150,000 letters. The greatest businesses, such as that of the Medici family, were split into different companies for production (silk and cloth), commerce and banking. Towards the end of the fifteenth century all its branches were given an independent status so that if business was going badly in one division it would not necessarily bring the concern as a whole into difficulties.

The practice of the bill of exchange for the transfer of money emerged at the end of the thirteenth century. In place of the older declarations of debt, drawn up by a notary or town clerk, the Italian firms introduced this completely informal method of payment. There were four parties in two places, linked to each other through their regular trading relationships. The drawer gave a bill to the deliverer; this was addressed to the drawer's trading agent in another place. This drawee was invited to pay a sum of money to the party accredited, the payee, who was a partner of the deliverer. The bill was of no use to any highwayman emptying an agent's bag of letters because he was not a partner in the money transfer. Like the bonds arranged at the annual fairs, this was a combined operation: the loan of a short-term commercial credit, the exchange of currency and the transfer of money from one place to another with no coins involved. Some weeks would elapse before the drawee received the letter and could look for the person whom he must reimburse in another currency for the goods bought by his partner in another place. A price to cover the service and the use of a few weeks' credit were included in the calculation of the exchange rate.

Plate 10.5 Two scenes from a counting house

This system could only function if a number of transactions could be arranged at the same time in the framework of an extended network of enduring partnerships. The more frequent the operations and the closer the contact between representatives, the easier it became to commission an associate or partner elsewhere to settle a debt with one of the creditor's partners. In Bruges and Barcelona, a bourse, or exchange, was held every day at a set time and a set place to fix the rates of exchange. There, anyone who had a bill of exchange to redeem or pay out could decide if the time was right to do so. At the exchange, it was easy to find the necessary partners with whom the bills could be traded. In Bruges the exchange was in the middle of the merchants' quarter where the 'nations' of the Genoese and Florentine merchants had their houses, and which was also the site of the famous inn belonging to the Van der Beurse family. The great advantage for the users was that they could settle their business without a gold or silver coin changing hands, thus avoiding loss. At a time when precious metals were scarce this method of transferring money allowed an unlimited expansion of the money supply. The bill of exchange considerably simplified international payments, as long as one had sufficient reliable contacts. The northern border of this critical mass, necessary for the use of bills of exchange, was formed by the line London–Bruges–Cologne, then due south to Frankfurt and Geneva.

Paper currency existed in imperial China, and

Marco Polo was amazed that the Chinese attached value to this stamped paper. The difference with Europe was of course the unity of authority. Europe, on the other hand, found its integration through the market: Italian gold florins and ducats were eagerly accepted as a means of payment everywhere. Moreover, the commercial networks created their own paper money, the fiduciary currency circulating among the merchants in the form of bonds, cheques and bills of exchange. In addition transferable money became popular: deposits with a money changer or banker could be used as a current account from which money could be transferred by *giro* (Italian for 'by return') to a different account with the same or another banker.

The system of bookkeeping had to be improved so that the complex relations and data could be scrutinized and the chances of profit assessed. The double-entry system of bookkeeping was devised in Venice in the fourteenth century. The principle behind it was that separate accounts were kept per partner, client, associate, etc., per product and per type of transaction. Every account showed the debit, what the person owed, on the left-hand page; the credit, what the person had, was shown on the right-hand page. Every transaction was noted twice: once as a mutation in the liquid assets of the firm, and once as a mutation in its relationship with a partner. In this way the manager was able to make up the accounts of a particular partner, a product or the balance at any given moment.

Merchants had to be very well trained in arithmetic, knowledge of commodities and commercial skills. By the twelfth century, schools in the towns had broken the Church's monopoly on education as the merchants demanded practical knowledge. In Ghent, a town school already existed in 1179 with a syllabus clearly very different from that of the school run by the local religious chapter. As in the crafts, boys were given a practical training under the guidance of experienced family members. Moreover, in Italy there were textbooks containing information about a number of different places: how best to travel there, what products could be found there and their quality, what measures, weights and coins were in use, and which local customs should be respected (such as the payment of bribes to customs officers). The fourteenth-century merchant revealed a mentality that clearly saw the rational pursuit of the maximum possible profit as an aim in itself; he was inclined to reinvest a goodly portion of that profit in his business so that it would surpass that of rival firms and thus make an even greater profit. Such an attitude is called a capitalist mentality.

The development of commercial capitalism stood in sharp contrast with the teaching of the Church, which still strongly condemned the unrestrained pursuit of material gain and usury. Some theologians certainly looked for conditions that might justify the application of a moderate interest to a loan, such as the risk of damage. The theory of the 'fair price' challenged exaggerated profits, but accepted nonetheless the principle of profit in return for services rendered. Yet the preachers of the mendicant orders, in particular, gave many a merchant an uneasy conscience, leading to the introduction of God as a creditor in merchants' accounts and to many account books opening with a short prayer to God 'and the profit He may give us'. And, of course, the drawing up of a will gave usurers another opportunity to make restitution.

BOX 10.2 A FLORENTINE MERCHANT'S MANUAL

Francesco Balducci Pegolotti became a representative of the Florentine trading house of Bardi in 1310. In that capacity he reached an agreement in 1315 with the duke of Brabant at Antwerp by which the same favourable excise duties that the Germans, English and Genoese already enjoyed would also apply to the merchants of Florence. From 1317 to 1321 he acted for his firm in London, collecting papal revenues in England and transferring them to Avignon. In 1324 he obtained from the king of Cyprus the same excise privileges for the Florentines as the Pisans. In the years following, he guaranteed the collection of the papal revenues in Cyprus and their transfer to Avignon. During the long years of his stay in Famagusta, in Cyprus, he carried out detailed research into the quality of local syrups and sugar, their pure weight and their packaging.

While he was there he also collected precise information about products and routes in the Levant, Constantinople and Alexandria. After 1329 he held various positions in the ruling council of Florence. In 1347, as one of its most prominent members, he was involved in the liquidation of the now bankrupt Bardi firm.

During his journeys, Pegolotti apparently made notes on the quality of products, popular sizes, weights, coins, excise duties and commercial practices in sundry locations, which would have been useful to a merchant. Between 1338 and 1342 he compiled these into a voluminous book that he called the 'Book about the differences between countries, trading sizes, and other pieces of information for merchants from diverse parts of the world etc.'

In his book Pegolotti provides detailed conversion tables for weights and currencies, as well as information about the differences in the quality of goods available and about commercial practices in the major trading towns round the Mediterranean Sea, the Black Sea, and in France, Flanders and England. There were other practical handbooks for merchants in circulation in North Italy, all written in Italian, but Pegolotti's is one of the oldest and certainly the most comprehensive. The modern printed edition has 383 pages. It contains numerous tables and sketches.

An example in the long survey of weight conversions from Famagusta follows:

> With Bruges in Flanders.
> One Cyprus *cantaro* makes 518 pounds in Bruges.
> 80 *Ruotoli* alum in Cyprus makes a cartload or 400 pounds in Bruges.
> 40 *Cafissi* grain in Cyprus makes 1 hoet in Bruges.
> One mark of silver in Bruges, or 6 ounces, makes 6 ounces and 13 sterling in Cyprus.

In his survey of the levies on trade in Constantinople Pegolotti notes:

> Remember well that if you show respect to customs officials, their clerks and 'turkmen' [sergeants], and slip them a little something or some money, they will also behave very courteously and will tax the goods that you later bring by them lower than their real value.

Literature: Francesco Balducci Pegolotti, *La Pratica della Mercatura*, ed. A. Evans (Cambridge, Mass., 1936), pp. xvii–xxvi, 42.100.

The commercialization of the countryside

During the twelfth and thirteenth centuries consumptive demand, particularly from the booming towns, was increasingly focused on bulk goods. This was one way in which the use of money penetrated the rural economy. Another was by means of dues in cash owed by peasants to their lords. And, finally, in the countryside too, an increasing number of people could no longer live exclusively on the proceeds of their small plots of ground, and looked for a supplementary cash income as manual workers or labourers. In correlation with these three developments, and stimulated by the consolidation of territorial principalities, trade and transport improved in different ways so that transport and transaction costs were lowered.

In England, the earliest phases of the process of commercialization in the countryside to which we refer are relatively easy to follow, thanks to the excellent sources. Even before the Norman conquest of 1066, Anglo-Saxon England had a network of more than 150 places in which regularly held markets provided their lords with income – and that number does not include the probably large number of places where merchants met informally. The penetration of money into England's rural economy is also fairly well documented. So we know exactly how much money the tenants-in-chief, the most important Anglo-Norman crown vassals after 1066, received from their rich possessions. In the end, the greater part came from the peasants on the manors that constituted their tenancies. Information from a variety of eleventh- and twelfth-century sources likewise indicates the broad distribution of coins among the ordinary people: the oldest demesne accounts of Church estates already contain many cash payments by serfs; royal courts of law collected fines in cash from all sorts of people; pilgrims from all over England who visited the tombs of national saints, such as that of St Cuthbert in Durham, filled the offertory boxes with coins.

The commercialization of the rural economy in England gained momentum between about 1180 and 1330. In that period, as grain prices were beginning to rise (1240–1315), many large landowners preferred to exploit the resources on their demesnes commercially with the help of hired labour. This meant that many services of serf labour were transformed into money payments at this time. When land was developed outside existing settlements, its exploitation was no longer organized through the manorial system; dues from peasants to their lords were predominantly in the form of money payments right from the beginning. In the countryside there was a steady growth in the number of people who no longer could supply their own food needs and were dependent on the market. They constituted as much as 45 per cent of the rural population by about 1300.

The proportion of England's urban population increased between the end of the eleventh century and the beginning of the fourteenth from about 10 per cent to 15 or 20 per cent. London, the most important town in England, grew into a metropolis with 60,000 to 80,000 inhabitants by the beginning of the fourteenth century. Such a sizeable concentration of people needed a strongly commercialized agriculture in a wide surrounding area. Regional specializations were also strengthened, partly in response to the growing foreign demand for raw materials such as wool and tin. Tin ore had been mined in Cornwall since prehistoric times, but its extraction was expanded considerably in the twelfth to the fourteenth centuries; by 1300 it provided work for more than two thousand people. In other remote and thinly populated areas, the Lake District for example, the growing use of water-driven

fulling mills similarly led to specialized industrial activity outside the urban sphere in the same period.

All in all, a substantial part of England's agricultural production – according to estimates made by C.C. Dyer and R.H. Britnell, at least 25 per cent of the yields from arable production and considerably more from cattle farming – was intended for the market at the beginning of the fourteenth century. This strong commercialization of the rural economy went hand in hand with a broadening of the supply of agricultural products and an increase in and sophistication of trading networks, with market places as logical nodes. There had been markets in Anglo-Saxon England in the early Middle Ages, but their number increased enormously during the twelfth and thirteenth centuries and a certain hierarchy became evident. The 'intermediary markets' were of the greatest significance in the commercialization of the agrarian economy; every county had a couple of intermediary markets that formed the vital links between the direct agricultural producers and the more than fifty larger regional trading centres found in England around 1300, which in turn were linked to interregional and sometimes even international trade.

The transport of bulk goods of low value, such as grain, over large distances was not profitable at normal market prices because of the high costs of transport and transactions. The transportation of grain by cart in England in the thirteenth century cost 0.4 per cent of the grain's value per mile; so transport over ten miles (more than 16 kilometres) increased the costs by 4 per cent, and transport over a hundred miles by 40 per cent. This did not include the cost of the many tolls on the journey, which easily could have added another couple of per cent to the cost of the cargo.

Still, in the most densely populated regions of Europe regular interregional trade in grain appeared to be worth while. The fertile loam soil and intensive methods of agriculture made very high yields possible for the wheat harvest in Artois, even before 1300. The south–north flow of the rivers enabled the enormous surpluses – an average of 1.5 million hectolitres per annum, enough to feed 400,000 people – to be shipped down river to the towns of Brabant and Flanders, which could never have become so large without such a fertile agricultural hinterland so near by. During periods of grain shortage in the fifteenth century Flanders imported massive quantities of rye from Prussia, because the trebling of the market price made the transport worth while. From the sixteenth century onwards, this supply had a structural nature in the Low Countries.

Goods and money

Long-distance trade probably represented only a very small part of the total volume of commerce. But even if it were only 5 to 10 per cent, it could still have been indicative because it involved indispensable scarce goods, demanded the most capital and the most progressive methods, and could exert a strategic influence on the whole economy. As we already have seen in the case of annual fairs, the international and national trading circuits were linked to each other so that the *économie du pourtour* – as Fernand Braudel called the coastal trade round Europe and the Mediterranean Sea – penetrated deeply into the European economy, albeit partly indirectly.

In economic systems one often distinguishes core areas from peripheries. Between both a broad division of labour exists. Core areas show a preponderance of capital accumulation, technical and organizational ingenuity; labour is relatively expensive there; they control the flow of goods, and in addition they mainly import raw materials and basic foods and export finished products and high-quality services. Peripheries are penetrated by external undertakings that exploit their raw materials and stimulate the cultivation of specific crops in response to the needs or trading possibilities of the core. During the tenth to the twelfth centuries the ports of northern Italy worked themselves out of a peripheral position in relation to Byzantium and the Muslim regions. By 1200, Byzantium itself had become subordinate to Venice. The classification is less equivocal in regard to the world of Islam. While the West engaged in large-scale trade in varied, mostly high-quality products, it was unable to impose its own conditions upon those leading areas from which it had learned so much. In fact, Egypt and Syria retained core positions in an economic system that in essence was directed towards the east, and to which Europe just tagged on.

It has to be remembered that economic and demographic growth also occurred in China during the period from around 1000 to 1500. Thanks to the easy transport for bulk cargoes on the great rivers and the Great Canal linking the Yangzi and Huang Hi valleys, 100 million people were connected to an integrated and safe market system using a single paper currency. All these factors reduced transaction costs, as compared to Europe. From the eleventh century, wet rice cultivation on terraces made two harvests per year possible. In a sharp contrast to Europe, agrarian production increased at the same pace as urban manufacturing. A great deal of the artisanal production of silk, porcelain, cotton and iron was commercialized. Around 1100, more than half the state income was paid in cash. Along the Chinese, Indian and south-east Asian coasts, intensive trade circuits were in operation, linked to those of the Persian Gulf and the Red Sea. Indian spices were part and parcel of this trade. European expansion thus meant linkage to these higher-developed and similarly growing Asian networks.

In the twelfth century the well-known eastern spice trade still passed in its entirety through Alexandria, where there were settlements of Venetians and Genoese. The collective name 'spices' also included products with which the westerners had become familiar in the Levant, where they were cultivated or extracted. Among them were a number of medicinal herbs, sugar, dyes, coral, oils and metals. Greek wines were among the bulk goods bought by the Italians, in part for transit to north-west Europe.

Italian merchants tried to reduce their dependence on eastern suppliers by themselves making products that had not earlier existed in Europe; they introduced the cultivation of rice, cotton, sugar-cane, saffron, and the silkworm, for example. In the warm climate zones silk was not only a luxury, it was also much more pleasant to wear than wool or linen. The large demand for silk stimulated production under their own control, and this replaced some of the imports. The same applied to cotton and cane sugar, cultivated in certain Venetian colonies and also, at the end of the fifteenth century, on islands in the Atlantic, such as Madeira. Paper – which from the thirteenth century began to supplement and eventually replace parchment, which was becoming much too expensive as literacy increased – was another Chinese innovation that Europeans copied so as not to have to import it any longer. The toughest relationships existed in the areas round the Black Sea, from where slaves, hides, grain and wood were imported. Genoa, in particular, which was built right up against the mountains and did not have a natural hinterland, had to rely on massive imports of grain, first from Sicily, but if that was not sufficient then from Thrace and the Crimea.

The fact that Italians controlled contacts with the Levant meant that they were the sole distributors of Mediterranean and eastern products throughout the rest of Europe. South Germans collected the products themselves directly from Venice or Milan. Italians took them to the fairs in Champagne, and from the last quarter of the thirteenth century shipped them to Bruges, where the spice trade became one of the most important activities, just as it was at the fairs of Antwerp. What could they offer their trading partners in the East in exchange? For many centuries far less than they bought, and this led to a continuous outflow of precious metals. In 1983 E. Ashtor calculated that the balance of payments between the Levant and the West showed a deficit of 56 per cent in the fifteenth century. Expressed in pure gold, this was an annual outflow of 1,317 kilos. The West imported goods from the East to a total value of 630,000 ducats, and could barely sell 260,000 ducats worth of their own products, mostly woollen goods, linen, weapons and wood. The difference (370,000 ducats) had to be made up in liquid assets.

Europe itself had few possibilities for mining gold or silver. After the resurgence of trade much of the precious metals that had been turned into valuable jewellery and cult objects in earlier centuries was brought back into circulation as currency. The increase in trade caused the demand for silver to grow far more quickly than the supply. Frantic searches were made for deposits of silver ore, which indeed were found here and there. The yields from mines in Saxony, the Tirol, Bohemia and elsewhere, however, were not sufficient to satisfy Western Europe's hunger for money. Around 1200, the need for a valuable means of payment had already led Venice to minting far larger silver coins than the old species, the *grossi*, from which the Dutch *groot*, the German *Grosche* and equivalents in many other languages are derived. The new type of coin found general acceptance because it satisfied a need. Nevertheless, in the long term, the general reaction of the rulers was to lower the silver content of the coins, a form of depreciation. With the same amount of silver they put more money into circulation. All used protectionist measures to try to attract precious metals and keep them within their borders. However, economic laws always proved stronger than government regulations and sanctions.

Through their commercial ties with the Maghreb, Iberian and Italian merchants were able to obtain gold dust from West Africa, which reached the ports by caravan. In exchange, Christians offered textiles, copper objects, foodstuffs and general cargo trade along the north coast of Africa. In 1231, this enabled the Emperor Frederic II in Sicily to mint the first western gold coins since the seventh century, the *augustales*, which bore a portrait of him strikingly modelled on those of the Roman emperors. Since 650, only Byzantine and Arabian gold coins had been in circulation in the Christian world. When the Mongol conquests put an end to the supply of dinars (the Arabian gold coins) in 1252 the great commercial centres of Genoa and Florence turned to issuing coins of pure gold with a weight of 3.54 grams. Venice followed in 1284. These three coins, the *genovino*, *fiorino* (florin) and *ducato* (ducat), became the gold coins in standard use throughout Europe for centuries. Their stability rested on the economic domination of the cities. The fact that they were of equal weight and value was a matter of economic insight.

The evolution of the instruments of payment reflects the powerful growth of the movement of goods and services, at least until the middle of the fourteenth century. Yet the West always had to compensate the heavy negative balance of payment with the East. This was only made possible through a whole chain of relationships reaching all the way back to the gold and silver mines in Saxony, Bohemia, Slovakia and Hungary. Production flowed from those lands to Italy and the Low Countries where high-quality articles and exotic goods were bought. The Low Countries and, indirectly, England as well, were thus able to bring their negative balance of payment with Italy into equilibrium. The Hanse, too, brought silver to the Low Countries because it imported many finished products and luxury goods from there, including large quantities of textiles, French and Mediterranean wine, arts and crafts, while its own exports consisted mainly of cheap bulk goods (beer, iron, wood, hides, amber, wax and, increasingly, grain).

By the first half of the fourteenth century the English must have been well aware that wool from 9 million of their sheep was being exported to the Continent. Some of this they bought back in the form of trendy felt hats and trousers cut to the latest fashion in Bruges. At the height of the trade, between 1350 and 1360, England exported 30,000 sacks of wool per year; after 1450 that number varied between 2,000 and 11,000. Protectionism had stimulated the export of its own cloth, which rose from 10,000 to 20,000 pieces between 1355 and 1360 to 60,000 between 1480 and 1500. When the war taxation levied by the kings made English wool too expensive, merchants from the Low Countries began to look for other sources of supply. At the end of the fifteenth century, Castile sent the wool from 9 million merino sheep to Bruges, where it was transformed into richly coloured tapestries and also into cheap clothing that was shipped to Prussia in exchange for grain. So it can be seen that the European market was already well integrated during the fourteenth and fifteenth centuries, and the effects of commercialization in the advanced areas could be strongly felt in the peripheries.

Peter Spufford has estimated that the total value of maritime trade in the Mediterranean Sea was at least six times higher than in the Baltic. This superiority would not shift to the North Sea until the seventeenth century. Until then, the North Sea fulfilled a switching function between the northern and southern economic systems, a role that became increasingly pivotal as Antwerp expanded and the Atlantic routes became more important.

The volume of commercial traffic increased substantially during the late Middle Ages, shown by the size of the merchant fleets among other things. This is remarkable, considering that after 1300 the population of Europe decreased by one-third, which would presuppose a drop in demand. That in fact the very opposite happened can be explained by two factors. First, the decrease in population led to a rise in the standard of living of the survivors; they could thus afford more luxuries and foreign products (see Chapter 13). Second, the commercial expansion of previous centuries had set in motion dynamics of its own, which explored ever-new opportunities for profit and thus adapted to the changes in demand. The integration of European markets rested on inequality, complementary relationships and competition, and together these brought new constellations into being. A European dynamic had been born, unstoppable on its way to global hegemony.

FURTHER READING

Abu-Lughod, Janet L. (1989), *Before European Hegemony: The World System A.D. 1250–1350* (New York and Oxford: Oxford University Press).

Amitai-Preiss, Reuven (1995), *Mongols and Mamluks: The Mamluk–Ilkhanid War, 1260–1281* (Cambridge: Cambridge University Press).

Angold, Michael (2003), *The Fourth Crusade: Event and Context* (Harlow: Pearson Education).

Ashtor, Eliyahu (1983), *Levant Trade in the Later Middle Ages* (Princeton, N.J.: Princeton University Press).

Britnell, R.H. (1993), *The Commercialisation of English Society 1000–1500* (Cambridge: Cambridge University Press).

—— and B.M.S. Campbell (eds) (1995), *A Commercializing Economy: England 1086–1300* (Manchester: Manchester University Press).

Bronstein, Judith (2005), *The Hospitallers and the Holy Land: Financing the Latin East, 1187–1274* (Woodbridge and Rochester, N.Y.: Boydell & Brewer).

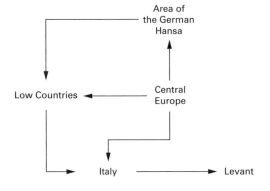

Figure 10.1 Deficits on the balance of payments between European regions in the fourteenth century

Bull, Marcus and Norman Housely (eds) (2003), *The Experience of Crusading. 1. Western Approaches* (Cambridge: Cambridge University Press).

Cahen, Claude (2001), *The Formation of Turkey: The Seljukid Sultanate of Rum, Eleventh to Fourteenth Century* (London: Longman).

Cardini, Franco (2000), *Europe and Islam. History of a Misunderstanding* (Oxford: Basil Blackwell) (orig. Italian, 2000).

Christian, David (1998), *A History of Russia, Central Asia, and Mongolia: Inner Eurasia from Prehistory to the Mongol Empire* (Malden, Mass. and Oxford: Blackwell).

Christiansen, Eric (1980), *The Northern Crusades. The Baltic and the Catholic Frontier 1100–1525* (London and Basingstoke: Macmillan).

Davis, R.H.C. (1976) *The Normans and Their Myth* (London: Thames & Hudson).

Day, John (1987), *The Medieval Market Economy* (Oxford: Blackwell).

Edbury, Peter and Jonathan Phillips (eds) (2003), *The Experience of Crusading. 2. Defining the Crusader Kingdom* (Cambridge: Cambridge University Press).

Ellenblum, Ronnie (1998), *Frankish Rural Settlement in the Latin Kingdom of Jerusalem* (Cambridge: Cambridge University Press).

Favier, Jean (1998) *Gold and Spices: The Rise of Commerce in the Middle Ages* (New York: Holmes & Meier) (orig. French, 1987).

France, John (2005), *The Crusades and the Expansion of Catholic Christendom, 1000–1714* (London and New York: Routledge).

Hillenbrand, Carole (1999), *The Crusades. Islamic Perspectives* (Edinburgh: Edinburgh University Press).

Hodgson, Marshall G.S. (2005), *The Secret Order of Assassins: The Struggle of the Early Nizari Ismailis Against the Islamic World* (Philadelphia, Pa.: University of Pennsylvania Press).

Houben, Hubert (2002), *Roger II of Sicily: A Ruler Between East and West* (Cambridge: Cambridge University Press) (orig. German, 1997).

Housley, Norman (1982), *The Italian Crusades: The Papal–Angevin Alliance and the Crusades Against Christian Lay Powers, 1254–1343* (Oxford: Clarendon).

—— (1992), *The Later Crusades, 1274–1580. From Lyons to Alcázar* (Oxford: Oxford University Press).

Hunt, E.S. (1994), *The Medieval Super-companies. A Study of the Peruzzi Company of Florence* (Cambridge: Cambridge University Press).

—— and James M. Murray (1999), *A History of Business in Medieval Europe, 1200–1550* (Cambridge: Cambridge University Press).

Jackson, Peter (2005), *The Mongols and the West, 1221–1410* (Harlow: Pearson Education).

Jacoby, David (2005), *Commercial Exchange Across the Mediterranean: Byzantium, the Crusader Levant, Egypt and Italy* (Aldershot: Ashgate) (Variorum Collected Studies).

Kedar, Benjamin Z. (1988), *Crusade and Mission: European Approaches Toward the Muslims* (Princeton, N.J.: Princeton University Press).

—— (1994), *The Franks in the Levant, 11th to 14th Centuries* (Aldershot: Ashgate) (Variorum Collected Studies).

Köprülü, Mehmed Fuad (1992), *Seljuks of Anatolia: Their History and Culture According to Local Muslim Sources* (Salt Lake City: University of Utah Press) (orig. Turkish, 1991).

Lane, Frederic (1973), *Venice: A Maritime Republic* (Baltimore, Md.: Johns Hopkins University Press).

Larner, John (1999), *Marco Polo and the Discovery of the World* (New Haven, Conn. and London: Yale University Press).

Lock, Peter (1995), *The Franks in the Aegean 1204–1500* (London and New York: Longman).

—— (2006), *The Routledge Companion to the Crusades* (London and New York: Routledge).

Lopez, Roberto S. (1976), *The Commercial Revolution of the Middle Ages, 950–1350* (Cambridge: Cambridge University Press).

Loud, Graham A. (2000), *The Age of Robert Guiscard: Southern Italy and Northern Conquest* (London and New York: Longman).

Madden, Thomas F. (1999), *A Concise History of the Crusades* (Lanham, Md.: Rowman & Littlefield).

—— (2003), *Enrico Dandolo and the Rise of Venice* (Baltimore, Md. and London: Johns Hopkins University Press).

—— (gen. ed.) (2004), *Crusades: The Illustrated History. Christendom, Islam, Pilgrimage, War* (Ann Arbor: University of Michigan Press).

Masschaele, James (1997), *Peasants, Merchants, and Markets: Inland Trade in Medieval England, 1150–1350* (New York: St Martin's Press).

Matthew, Donald (1992), *The Norman Kingdom of Sicily* (Cambridge: Cambridge University Press).

Moore, Ellen Wedemeyer (1985), *The Fairs of Medieval England. An Introductory Study* (Toronto: Pontifical Institute of Mediaeval Studies).

Morgan, David (1986), *The Mongols* (Cambridge, Mass. and Oxford: Blackwell).

North, D.C. and R.P. Thomas (1973), *The Rise of the Western World: A New Economic History* (Cambridge: Cambridge University Press).

Philipp, Thomas and Ulrich Haarmann (eds) (1998), *The Mamluks in Egyptian Politics and Society* (Cambridge: Cambridge University Press).

Riley-Smith, Jonathan (1992) *What Were the Crusades?*, 2nd edn (Basingstoke and London: Macmillan).

Roover, Raymond de (1976), *Business, Banking, and Economic Thought in Late Medieval and Early Modern Europe: Selected Studies* (Chicago, Ill.: University of Chicago Press).

Scammell, G.V. (1981), *The World Encompassed: The First European Maritime Empires, c. 800–1650* (London: Methuen).

Schildhauer, Johannes (1985), *The Hansa: History and Culture* (Leipzig: Edition Leipzig).

Spufford, Peter (1988) *Money and Its Use in Medieval Europe* (Cambridge: Cambridge University Press).

—— (2002), *Power and Profit: The Merchant in Medieval Europe* (London: Thames & Hudson).

Tyerman, Christopher (1998), *The Invention of the Crusades* (Basingstoke and London: Macmillan).

Webber, Nick (2005), *The Evolution of Norman Identity, 911–1154* (Woodbridge and Rochester, N.Y.: Boydell & Brewer).

Winter, Michael and Amalia Levanoni (eds) (2004), *The Mamluks in Egyptian and Syrian Politics and Society* (Leiden and Boston, Mass.: Brill).

CHAPTER 11

The urbanized society

No other phenomenon in European history before industrialization has had such a profound influence as the process of the growth of towns that started during the tenth century. Like most features of development undergone by Europe in the *longue durée*, this transformation appeared earlier and was more intensive in the southern and western regions of the Continent than in the North and East.

Urbanization means the development by which the urban way of life grows in importance in a society as a whole. By 'town' we mean the spatial concentration of a population that does not produce its own food; thus one that does not live primarily from agriculture, livestock-farming or fishing. In addition, a town, however small, fulfils the function of a central place for a service area: it localizes the market, government, centres of religion, and some specialized services. The supply of functions in a centre depends on the size, population density and socio-economic characteristics of its hinterland. We distinguish between the concept of urbanization and the growth of towns, by which we mean the enlargement of urban settlements.

THE PHENOMENON OF THE TOWN

The scale of towns and of urbanization

First of all we shall try to acquire some quantitative insight into the order of magnitude of urbanization. The relative growth was only possible because the total population of certain regions began to increase from the seventh century, and in general from the tenth century. In Chapter 7 we saw that in the most heavily populated areas this led to a relative overpopulation of the countryside. This was partly offset by emigration to scarcely populated regions of central Europe, and partly by urbanization. Exact figures are not available because large-scale censuses were conducted very rarely in that period. The figures below are therefore estimates based on very incomplete statistical data, and different scholars have reached different results. However, the global tendency is undisputed: the population of Europe doubled in three centuries (see Table 11.1).

Urban growth refers not only to the growing absolute population number, but also to the rising share of the town population within the total number of inhabitants of a region. Both tendencies coincided in Europe between roughly 1000 and 1300; after that the size of the towns stagnated, or even fell. Nevertheless, the share of the urban population in the whole increased (see Table 11.2). Between 1300 and 1500 the number of towns with between 10,000 and 20,000 inhabitants rose considerably. Accordingly the combined numbers of their populations grew, while the total population of Europe fell by 19 per cent, from 75 to 61 million. Thus the overall number of towns grew during the fourteenth and fifteenth centuries, while the number of inhabitants of most towns decreased. This means that even when population numbers fell, the attraction of the towns remained strong and the urban element of society weighed heavier. The tables show that by 1500 some 10 per cent of Europeans lived in towns with a population of at least 5,000. In Iberia and Italy this share was clearly above the average, namely 14 per cent. The scale of medieval towns remained relatively modest: in 1300 only Venice, Florence, Milan and Paris had (slightly) more than 100,000 inhabitants. By 1500, Florence was reduced to 40,000 inhabitants, and only around 150 towns had above 10,000. The population of the great majority – about 3,500 of the 4,000 places that enjoyed town rights – varied from a few hundred to a few thousand.

Table 11.1 Estimated population of Europe, in
millions

Year	Population
1000	38
1300	75
1450	50
1500	61

The small towns, *Kleinstädte*, were mostly situated in the land mass of the Continent, while the larger towns developed mainly along the coasts and major rivers. The reason for this was that for the supply of bulk goods such as grain, building materials and raw materials for other industries, accessibility by ship was of overriding importance. Transport by ship was many times cheaper per unit of weight than transport by land. All the big towns were of necessity ports, therefore. In 1500 the really large towns were still around the Mediterranean Sea, where, during Antiquity, Rome probably had a population of one million, and, in the early Middle Ages, Constantinople and Córdoba grew to half a million.

What was the reason for the existence of towns of such exceptional size in the Mediterranean region? The explanation must be sought in the productivity of agriculture in the region, accessibility for large ships, availability of raw materials for a large-scale export industry, and the attraction or pressure that a major town could exert on an extensive hinterland.

In Europe north of the Alps and Pyrenees only one or two metropolises had as many as 100,000 inhabitants before the sixteenth century. Antwerp, then the heart of the economic world system, was one of them. The other one was Paris, the capital city of a large kingdom, which attracted the population surplus from a wide countryside where no other important cities had been founded. A century later Amsterdam reached a new threshold (200,000), which was easily surpassed by London in the eighteenth century. These were the unique centres of the world economy in their time; they could only grow to such a size because they formed the core of an ever-expanding economic system.

The capitals of reasonably centralized states, such as Constantinople, Paris, London and ancient Rome, had a special attraction because central administrative organs could concentrate their resources there. On a far more modest scale episcopal towns and the administrative centres of territorial princes served as concentration points for the consumer expenditure of the elites and their clients. The taxes centralized there on the spot created a separate market for specific goods and services.

We can conclude that a town could never be considered without its hinterland. A town population was formed in the first instance by migration from the countryside; we know from later centuries that pre-industrial towns always had a mortality surplus, so that a town's population could only remain level or increase through immigration. The primary explanation for the growth of the towns must always be sought in the countryside.

Table 11.2 Urban population by size of towns

Population	Number of towns		Urban population × 1,000	
	in 1300	in 1500	in 1300	in 1500
>100,000	4	4	(400)	450
40,000–99,000	15	14	(750)	704
20,000–39,000	33	37	(890)	981
10,000–19,000	73	99	(950)	1,306
5,000–9,000	?	363	?	2,468
Totals	?	517	?	5,909

From an economical perspective, every town was both a market and a production centre for industries and services. In the first place, the town's inhabitants could eat only if there were sufficient food surpluses in the surrounding countryside to be sold in the town. As the town grew, food had to be brought from a wider hinterland, and the market took on interregional dimensions. Townspeople had to be productive themselves, of course, in order to buy their food and raw materials. In this way, every town was entirely dependent on its supply lines and potential markets for its own products. Hence, the more a town grew, the more its control over longer trading routes through an extensive hinterland became necessary.

Conversely, the presence of an urban market stimulated the rural economy: the demand encouraged market-oriented production, in the sense of both enlargement and diversification of the supply. Purchasing power was concentrated in the town for a variety of foodstuffs, such as meat and dairy products, as well as for the raw materials from the countryside needed for industry – wool, leather, building materials, fuel, dyes and more. The townspeople themselves contributed directly to diversification in rural production by buying up land as a safe investment, by keeping livestock in order to make certain of their own supply, and by becoming owners of peat lands, lime kilns, stone quarries or vineyards.

Some scarce goods, such as wine, certain sorts of wood, iron and stone, could be brought from much further afield. Urban demand had a profound effect on its immediate surroundings, but for specific products the effects were felt at a distance too. Sheep-farming in rural England, for example, was greatly stimulated by the demand for wool from the cloth industry in northern France and the Low Countries from the eleventh century onwards. Alums were mined in Turkey, amber collected on Prussian beaches, and pitch and tar gathered in Poland's forests to be worked in industries in the Low Countries. This created a need for long-distance transport. In this way the urban minority brought about the transformation of a considerable part of the economy's primary sector.

The interlinking of town and hinterland can be seen in the correlation between the degree of urbanization and the population density of a specific region. Where there were relatively many townspeople, the density of

population in the hinterland was also proportionately high. This is logical because only an overpopulated rural area could afford to lose people to the town, but also because the proximity of the town, with its demand and investment capital, led to an intensification of agriculture.

Jan de Vries, the American historian, has devised a sophisticated method to express in one single standard the level of urbanization in pre-industrial Europe (omitting the Balkans for source-technical reasons). It is based on three factors: (1) the absolute population numbers of towns with more than 10,000 inhabitants; (2) the distances between these towns; (3) the geographical location, expressed in a rating. For each one of the 154 towns with at least 10,000 inhabitants in about 1500 he calculated what he called an 'urban potential' at different moments in the three centuries between 1500 and 1800. By charting the measured ratings it was possible to reconstruct a geography of urbanization moving through time, one that was not determined or defined by continually changing and often random political units but by the socio-geographical reality.

In 1500 Venice scored the highest absolute rating. This is not surprising: with possibly 120,000 inhab-

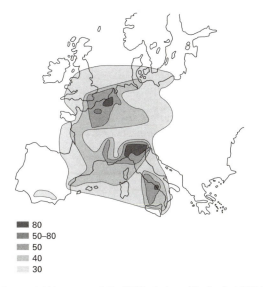

80
50–80
50
40
30

Map 11.1 Urban potential in 1500 relative to Venice (= 100%)

Source: Jan de Vries, *European Urbanization, 1500–1800*, Cambridge, Mass., 1984), p. 160

itants it was the biggest city of its time; there were several other large towns nearby, and it was a port. Three regions stand out with the highest relative ratings, namely 80 per cent of that of Venice: the Po valley including Milan, Turin and Genoa; the southern Low Countries and the Gulf of Naples. These three regions formed a large area of high consumption, emphasizing even more the enormous predominance of the extensive northern Italian belt of towns.

After these three peaks the ratings drop quickly to just above 50 per cent round Paris and 50 per cent in the great region of the Loire via London to Holland, Utrecht, Guelders and Liège; the Rhône Valley and the coastline of the Ligurian Sea also appear to have had a fairly high urban growth. Very low ratings applied in the Iberian peninsula, with the exception of the northeast and Andalusia, central and northern Europe and the Celtic periphery of the British Isles. In northern Italy and the coastal and river regions of the Low Countries one out of three inhabitants lived in a large town. In central Europe this was less than one in ten. This is a significantly marked contrast, revealing clearly the enormous regional diversity of this continent of Europe.

Of course there are some drawbacks to the method used by de Vries. In particular, the restriction to towns with a minimum of 10,000 inhabitants means that, for the Middle Ages, too many towns that functioned as real centres are ignored. De Vries made his choice in order to be able to maintain an equal measurement gauge in his long-term perspective until 1800. In the period before 1750 the thousands of towns with just a few thousand inhabitants formed points of reference in their area for economic and administrative activity. Some had a special significance for a particular branch of industry, as a fishing port or a market for an important agricultural hinterland, for example. The role of some small towns was particularly important in areas with very low levels of urbanization.

The morphology of the medieval town

Contemporaries of the medieval towns were clearly aware of their distinctive character, and in many cases archaeological remains still bear witness to their typical manifestations. Town walls, ramparts and gates marked the separation between the urban space and the surrounding country. The town community shut itself off from the environs both literally and metaphorically. Its walls protected it from attacks and invaders. The model of a town's defences was actually an enlargement of a castle's defences: walls one could walk around, battlements, watch-towers, fortified gates and drawbridges. The town community came into being in a world dominated by feudal warriors, like a foreign body that had to use the same means to defend itself.

In the early Middle Ages the old *civitates* within the former Roman Empire still retained some administrative functions as episcopal seats and thereby some urban characteristics of a town, albeit greatly reduced in comparison to the situation in the third century. Rheims, the metropolis of the province of Belgica Secunda, spread over some 30 hectares; Cologne, the capital of Germania Secunda, enclosed more than 96 hectares within its ancient walls. Many of these ancient towns were at the heart of the medieval expansion.

The oldest town communities that were formed spontaneously grew up on new locations with features very different from those of the Roman towns. Many of the Roman towns had been planned from a centralized empire with a substantial network of roads. Most of the medieval towns were unplanned, and their location was primarily determined by navigable waterways. Favourable locations were river confluences (Coblenz, Namur, Dordrecht, Ghent), river mouths (Venice, Hamburg, Danzig, Pisa, [Arne] Muiden), small islands which made a crossing easier (Paris, Strasbourg, Lille [= *insula, L'Isle*], Leiden), natural harbours (Rouen, Antwerp), fords (Bruges, Utrecht, Douai), and junctions of rivers and roads (Maastricht, Louvain).

The earliest town settlements were populated mainly by merchants and artisans. They often settled in the vicinity of an older centre of authority, such as an abbey or a fortress, as well as in geographically favourable locations. The demarcation of the spheres of influence of the established lords might involve much negotiation and not infrequent struggles, but, in the event of a threat, an existing fortification could always offer protection.

As towns continued to grow, they had to provide their own security: originally an earthen wall with a palisade and a moat, later on a wall. In Namur, which

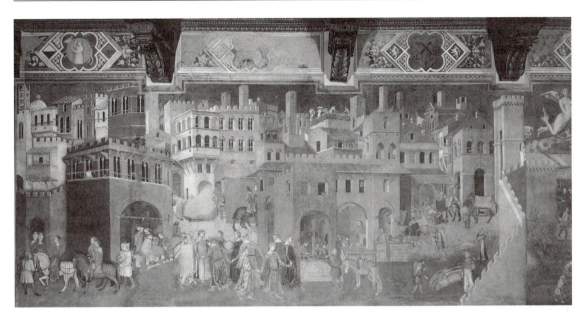

Plate 11.1 Urban scenes from the first half of the fourteenth century. Fresco of the Allegory of Good Government by Ambrogio Lorenzetti in the Palazzo Pubblico (town hall) at Siena

was a metalworking centre, the *portus* or *vicus*, as the settlement of merchants and artisans was called, was fortified as early as 937. In Cologne a wall was built round a suburb, the *Rheinvorstadt*, in 948: the name recalls that this was a settlement on the Rhine outside the walls of the ancient town. Verdun, on the Meuse, an important centre of the slave trade in the early Middle Ages, seems to have had a fortified commercial settlement before 985. In the course of the eleventh century new walls were recorded in Liège, Tournai, Bruges and Ghent. Utrecht, which played an important part in the trade on the Waal branch of the Rhine and the IJssel, was fortified in about 1122.

The size and chronology of the growth of the towns can be seen in the succession of walls, still often recognizable as concentric circles in the ground plans of city centres. Strasbourg was originally built on an island in the Ill and enclosed some 71 hectares inside its fortifications of 1220. After expansion, the walled town covered an area of 99 hectares by the beginning of the fourteenth century, and 202 hectares by 1541. The city wall of Paris, dated from the beginning of the thirteenth century, was 2.8 kilometres long on the right bank of the Seine, 2.5 kilometres on the left bank, and encompassed 253 hectares. When these fortifications

were extended at the beginning of the fourteenth century, the town covered 439 hectares. In Flanders and Brabant, towns were fairly spread out, less closely built and, above all, the buildings were not as tall as in the south. Ghent was the most extensive, with a surface area of 644 hectares, and walls of almost 13 kilometres in circumference.

Two things stand out at this point: the town communities made very considerable investments in these fortifications, for which they must have collected financial resources. The first public works, with their own book-keeping, were thus created in the name and under the control of the community. On the other hand, the increased size of the towns made it more difficult for military offensives to lay siege to them.

The morphology of the medieval town was the result of a natural process of growth that, according to the condition of the terrain, expanded concentrically out from one or more cores in all possible directions. This made the ground plans of medieval towns irregular, but either semi-circular or circular (on one or both banks of a river) in form, bisected by axes running from the central marketplace to the gates. Only those towns founded and built at one time revealed the chessboard pattern of the Roman towns: examples of these in the

Low Countries were the harbour towns of Nieuwpoort, Damme and Grevelingen, founded by the count of Flanders in the 1160s, and Schoonhoven and Leerdam in Holland. The duke of Lower Austria built Wiener Neustadt in 1194 as a bulwark against the Hungarians, financing it with the ransom that had been paid shortly before for Richard the Lionheart (see Chapter 9). As part of the policy of *Ostkolonisation*, shortly after 1200 the Germans founded a series of towns along the south coast of the Baltic Sea, among them Stralsund, Greifswald, Rostock, Danzig and Riga. Colony towns founded by the Teutonic Order in Prussia (Torun/Thorn and Elblag/Elbing on the Vistula) had a more geometrical ground plan. The general tendency, however, was one of unplanned, spontaneous development. The growth of the towns in the Middle Ages was, for the most part, an uncontrolled process that considerably disrupted the established social order.

AUTONOMY

Urban privileges

Walls were a symbol of the separate legal status of the town community. One of the characteristics of the pre-industrial town in Europe was that it enjoyed its own set of customs and laws, specifically tailored to urban society. The origin of this can be found in the sworn pact that the earliest townspeople made with each other for their mutual protection. They swore to help each other should they be attacked in the town or on a journey, and they arranged a peaceful co-existence. These *coniurationes*, literally meaning 'swearing together' or 'sworn societies', put into practice a very old legal remedy, typical of most illiterate societies and groups of people who react against the dominant order – namely, the collective oath, sworn on holy objects so that the threat of divine retribution as well as human punishment hung over the violator of the oath.

We know of these *coniurationes* from references to them in the oldest written traditions of urban privileges or in chronicles. The reciprocal solidarity of the early townsfolk would protect them from the violence inherent in the relationships of feudal power, in the face of which as individuals they were weak but

as a group strong. The close community spirit of the early townspeople is understandable: they had come together from near and far, had often escaped from dependent relationships of serfdom, and forced return to their (former) lords was still a possibility. The 'statute' of Valenciennes, originally referred to as a 'peace', came to be called a 'community' or *commune* in later charters, meaning the community of sworn burghers who enjoyed the full privileges of the town. These citizens were legally free, without any of the limitations attached to the status of serfs on a demesne: no labour tasks, no servile dues in cash or kind, no restrictions to their freedom of movement or choice of marriage partner. For this reason, the urban area was also known as the 'freedom' of the town. Town privileges were personal: they did not apply *per se* to all inhabitants of the town area but to all its burghers, wherever they might be, inside the town or elsewhere. The administrators and magistrates of a town, known as aldermen, demanded the exclusive right to the protection of and jurisdiction over their burghers. This naturally led to continual disputes over competence with other jurisdictions.

The struggle for the liberties of the towns took place in the eleventh and twelfth centuries and was often violent, because that was after all a world dominated by knights and their private warfare. The struggle between the early developed towns of Lombardy, which as communes under the leadership of their own elected consuls had won their freedom from the territorial power of the bishops in about 1100, and Frederick Barbarossa is well known. Despite his military victory over Milan, Barbarossa could not hold on to his power in the face of the league of Lombard towns, and in 1183 he was forced to recognize their autonomy under a very nominal vassalage. In the twelfth century the German kings recognized the rights to freedom of the inhabitants of the old episcopal towns along the Rhine, but there was no question of recognizing autonomous towns for a long time. About the same time the kings of France granted rights with local autonomy to several towns in the north of their kingdom, partly with an eye to strengthening the monarchy against the great feudal lords who until then held these territories in their grasp. King Louis IX explained this in so many words in his *Enseignements* ('Instructions') to his son: 'I well recollect that Paris and the good towns of my

BOX 11.1 THE 'PEACE' OF VALENCIENNES

An early example of a comprehensive town statute is the so-called 'peace' of Valenciennes, granted by Count Renaud IV of Hainault in 1114. The grant followed a whole series of enactments of town privileges in what is now northern France: Cambrai in 1077, Saint-Quentin in 1080, Beauvais around 1099, Noyon in 1108 and Laon around 1109. These first written documents generally meant no more than the recognition by the lord or bishop of an already existing situation, consisting of a 'community' or 'commune' with its own (customary) law that had been formed on the basis of a sworn association. The designation 'peace' indicated the primary concern of the citizenry: protection from the violence of the world of the knights. The peace movement that had been set in motion by the bishops and abbots of southern France shortly before 1000 had paved the way for the foundation of more specific territorial jurisdictions where peace could be established in accordance with their own, non-feudal law. Towns were thus islands of peace in the midst of a world in which legal uncertainty and lack of safety reigned.

On reaching the age of 16, every burgher of Valenciennes had to swear faithfully to observe the 'peace'. Should he refuse to do so, even after a day's grace to reconsider the matter if necessary, he was required to leave the town immediately and his house was pulled down. The community was based on compulsory mutual support and solidarity, within the walls and outside. The 'peace' formulated punishments typical for the towns, in which private revenge was replaced as far as possible by officially imposed fines. Exclusion from the 'community', later systematically worked out as banishment, was one form of punishment. Corporal punishment was imposed exclusively on strangers, described as those who did not belong to the circle of 'men of the peace'. The 'peace' aimed to replace irrational proof (trial by ordeal and the judicial duel) whenever possible by the testimony of at least two 'men of the peace' or fellow burghers. This was one of the oldest non-ecclesiastical texts in which such a procedure

was provided for. The articles below (there were 57 articles in the oldest version) shed a clear light on the burghers' concerns:

1   'It is solemnly observed and agreed in peace that every merchant who comes to the market in Valenciennes or goes from it may be secure at all times, himself and his wares, the only exception being the burghers of Douai. Whoever contravenes this and is caught in the act or charged through the evidence of two men from the peace of Valenciennes, even if he is a knight, shall firstly be required to make good the damage that he has done to the merchant and further pay a fine of sixty shillings, of which the merchant shall receive 20 and the chancellor of the peace 40. . . .

2   Any person, be he knight or not, who takes commodities or other goods, movable or not, from men of the peace of the town of Valenciennes on their way to the market at Valenciennes or elsewhere, and who is caught in the act or charged through the evidence of two men of the mentioned peace, must make amends as laid down above. . . .

3   If a person from the surrounding countryside comes to and departs from the market of Valenciennes between sunrise on a Thursday and sunrise on a Monday, his lord may not arrest him unless it is to bring him to the count's law court. . . . Should the governor or the lord maltreat the man it shall be considered a violation of the peace for which there is a fine of sixty shillings payable to the count and his chancellor. . . .

4   Should a person who is a member of the town peace be accosted or molested at a market elsewhere because of the administration of justice of the town or for another cause, then shall his accuser be charged with violation of the peace as if it had happened in our own town.'

Literature: Ph. Godding and J. Pycke, 'La paix de Valenciennes de 1114. Commentaire et édition critique', *Bulletin de la Commission royale pour la publication des anciennes lois et ordonnances de Belgique XXIX* (1981).

kingdom helped me against the barons when I was newly crowned.'

Bishops who had been lord and master in their episcopal seats since the establishment of the bishoprics were the least inclined to give up any of their rights to the urban community. The struggle was primarily about the personal freedom of all the residents of a town, a recognition that they were no longer tied to the duties and restrictions resting on them as serfs. Agreement was reached that the inhabitants of that town would acquire their freedom under law after living in a town for a period of a year and a day.

An important step in the movement towards the emancipation of the towns consisted of their claim to autonomy, the right to formulate their own customs and laws and regulations for their own community, and to exercise jurisdiction over it. This meant that the lord of the district in which the town originated had to relinquish all or part of his authority over the area. Most lords set a price for this, receiving compensation in the form of perpetual rents or levies and a share in the growing yields from the taxes and administration of the law. The results of these struggles varied from place to place, depending on the proximity and power of the town's lord and how far the size and wealth of the town commune could tip the balance. Similarly, the privileges of a town were continually subject to revision and adaptation, prompted by the evolution of society and changing power relations.

Hence the customs and law of a town consisted of an odd mixture of privileges granted in writing by various authorities in the course of centuries, and their interpretation and extensions in daily practice. In tangible form, it could be seen as a heavy chest full of solemnly sealed documents and deeds from diverse authorities – from popes, emperors and kings to local lords. Everyone had his say on specific matters and sometimes the ruler granted extensive statutes dealing primarily with criminal justice and economic rights. There did not seem to be much system to it. Because many statutes stated that the magistracy had the right to interpret the statute and to alter it if necessary, unwritten customary laws grew up alongside the written laws. This was a sort of jurisprudence based on the force of precedent. Customary law could be reconstructed only from the records of a town's juridical actions, or by appealing to the memory of old officials.

This gave rise to frequent disputes between rulers and town councils or among local officials. The situation changed only very slowly from the fourteenth century onwards with the development of a judicial hierarchy, whereby the rulers' central courts were allowed to review the verdicts of local courts of justice.

The personality of the law was nevertheless maintained throughout the *ancien régime*; it meant that a person fell under a specific judicial system either because he belonged to a privileged estate (clergy, noble, royal official) or was a burgher of a particular town or village with privileges. Law that was applied strictly territorially was extremely rare. Indeed, the stronger the economic and demographic weight of a town, the better its chance of safeguarding its juridical autonomy. Town law was therefore both territorial, in that it applied in principle to everyone inside the walls and in the surrounding district (within the town's jurisdiction), and personal, in that it applied to the burghers of the town, wherever they might be.

Public order

The administration and the judicial system of a town were always in the hands of its community of burghers. In one way or another, the richest merchants, entrepreneurs and landowners monopolized power. Town councils were generally plutocracies that used co-option to keep the power within the circle of a few families. In accordance with the statutes granted by their ruler, they exercised political as well as judicial and legislative power: this was a result of the delegation of authority by princes who united all those aspects in their own position. They generally reserved the right to appoint an officer of justice who, in their name, urged the judges to produce verdicts and carried them out. After 1170, the count of Flanders appointed *ballivi* (bailiffs) in that capacity, officials whom he recompensed with a sum of money. In other places, these officers of justice were also known as *schout, sheriff, Schuldheiss* or *amman, Ambtmann*. The combination of administrator and judge was maintained in towns all over Europe until the end of the eighteenth century.

In the town community, and its surrounding area of jurisdiction defined as town, the rule of peace, in the sense of the exclusion of the right of retaliation or taking the law into one's own hands, prevailed.

However, many conflicts were the direct continuation of the right of feuding that knights claimed as their own. Until the end of the Middle Ages, and for even longer in central Europe, all towns wrestled with the inclination of the foremost families to follow the code of the knights and fight out their differences in private wars. In the privilege accorded by Count Charles the Good of Flanders to the town of Ypres in 1116, he allowed the citizens to solve their conflicts in a more peaceful and rational manner by letting five honest men testify under oath for a plaintiff, instead of trial by combat and trial by ordeal with water or red-hot iron. Of the 28 articles of the privilege granted between 1165 and 1177 by Count Philip of Alsace to Ghent and the six other large towns of his county of Flanders, half dealt with the prevention of acts of violence; ten others were concerned with judicial procedures.

Revenge, the fighting of feuds on a purely private law basis, was the archetypal way to restore damaged status. There was no government to impose punishment, but concerned parties – entire families with their supporters – who were bound together in a reciprocal relationship. The damage suffered, even when it was only a matter of injured honour, had to be compensated for in accordance with an accepted code. In the beginning, this only applied to those who were allowed to bear arms – free men. It often happened that the parties could not reach reconciliation very quickly because revenge brought with it the risk of over-compensation, hitting back harder than was justifiable, so that the imbalance veered in the other direction. Once mediation had brought about reconciliation, with the concomitant compensations, retributions, restoration of honour, pilgrimages for the salvation of the souls of the victims and pious foundations, then the parties were expected to behave as friends, for there was no longer any reason for resentment. The Flemish town privileges of 1165–1177 did not challenge the right of the 'good men' of the town to wage a feud, these 'good men' no doubt being the elite. However, the *scabini*, the town magistrates or aldermen, did attempt to reconcile the parties and to make the agreement binding, on pain of a fine.

Neither *scabini* nor officers of justice were obliged to prosecute feud-wagers, nor could they act as criminal judges in such affairs; they were only allowed to punish any refusal to reconciliation. The parties retained the right to make their own arrangements for compensation, either by causing the other party equal damage or by obtaining financial and moral satisfaction. As long as town magistrates could not forbid and punish private feuds they were in a weak position *vis-à-vis* the most important families within their walls who very often provided the magistrates and thus had an interest in keeping the law in their own hands.

Until the fifteenth century the large powerful towns of central and northern Italy had to cope with this structural weakness in relation to their own elites. In the twelfth and thirteenth centuries, these towns were governed by consuls from their own community, each presided over by an officer of justice, the *podestà*, a professional judge who usually came from outside the city and was therefore thought to be to able to stand above parties and thus maintain the peace and cohesiveness. In this way, the communes succeeded in breaking the oligarchic regime of the *milites*. The *podestà* originally was appointed for a term of one year or six months. When he took office, he swore an oath on the statutes and administrative laws of the town, including the new laws from his predecessor that were added to the statute book at that time. In this way a strong legal tradition evolved, supported by an established written record. An education in law, such as that provided by the famous university of Bologna, gave officials, notaries and judges a basis that made it possible for them to introduce a supra-local legal culture. This high degree of judicial professionalism in the legal system was limited for a long time to the towns of northern and central Italy. From the fourteenth century onwards, the role of the *podestà* was weakened by further bureaucratization or even by the emergence of a new type of seigniorial regime.

Nevertheless, the important urban families continued to control and terrorize the towns. They were organized as clans, with a strict hierarchy of descent through the male line and surrounded by other kin and associates all of whom belonging to the elite. A third class was formed by the sergeants, paid servants. All acted in accordance with a code that resembled that of the knights, although the violence was of a more instrumental, less professional nature. The clan members were mutually bound by reciprocal loyalties. We are strongly reminded of the knightly culture when we consider the clans of the towns of Italy and Flanders, decked out in the heraldic colours of the family, exhibiting the reckless group virility as a means of affirming their honour and status and, if necessary, of showing their superior strength. The magnificent stone-built houses of these clans dominated the townscape. With their obvious ability to withstand a siege their solid construction, battlements and towers radiated strength to one and all. In the towns of northern and central Italy, with San Gimignano still a good example, all the great houses had tall towers, which had both a military and a symbolic function.

The ultimate explanation for the continuing rivalry between the clans in the Italian towns can be found in the spread of violence, and the means of committing it. As long as the *commune* (for this term, see p. 222) was not strong enough as a collective government to impose public order, the clans ruled the streets. As long as they were in charge of the town administration, nothing changed. Sometimes a superior external power could impose the peace; Count Philip of Flanders, for example, gave some small support to the town magistrates by *c*. 1170. In practice, during the thirteenth century the counts had little authority over the powerful towns, and the town administrations remained in effect privatized.

It was much the same in Italy: even the powerful Hohenstaufen emperors had to admit their impotence against the towns of Lombardy. Factions in the towns attempted to make use of the political divisions between the emperor, the pope and later also the kings of Sicily and Naples to strengthen their position through coalitions. Discord on the territorial level was advantageous to towns. The factions originally grew from the differences between the rival German ruling houses. The Hohenstaufens, whose stronghold at Waiblingen gave them the name *Ghibellini* in Italy, were the figurehead for one party, while the opposition to the emperor in the Lombard towns appealed to the house of the Guelphs. As a reaction they supported the pope.

Once they had taken root in the political culture, these opposing factions did not easily disappear: the factional problems had grown fixed through long tradition, and all other tensions were cast into this model. The dominant Guelph faction in Pistoia and Florence split into the Blacks and Whites during the fourteenth century. In this complex situation, the elites

had a mutual interest in maintaining their oligarchic power, particularly when that power was openly threatened in the fourteenth century by the claims of the artisans. Faced with such a challenge, the town authorities strengthened their legitimacy by taking on an intermediary role and presenting themselves as defenders of the common good. A number of terms were used to express the abstract ideal, linking it to the principles of Roman law: *bonum commune, utilitas publica, quod interest civitati*, the common weal, the public good. The interests of the town justified interference in certain interests and even in some legal rules. As the authorities could better appeal to such general principles in individual decisions, their actions acquired greater authority while the cohesion of the elite and the town was also enhanced. The support given to administrators by professional lawyers helped them as an institution to rise above parties. Their role as judge was decisive because it demonstrated the effectiveness and credibility of the establishment and maintenance of public order. Criminal proceedings brought by the officer of justice *ex officio* on the grounds of offences against the common good, such as breaches of the peace, placed greater demands on the authority's ability to trace offenders and build up a legitimate case against them.

The juxtaposition of the private law reconciliation procedure, in which town magistrates could act merely as intermediaries and observers of the negotiated settlement, and the public law criminal proceedings *ex officio* disappeared entirely from Western Europe between the fourteenth and sixteenth centuries. This presupposed, however, that peace, still an exceptional circumstance in the eleventh and twelfth centuries, would thenceforth be considered the normal situation. It could only be maintained effectively if a government had sufficient superior strength, based on the recognition of its use of force as the only legitimate one. The criminal ordinances issued by Emperor Charles V in 1530–1532 in the German Empire and the Low Countries formally ended toleration of the right of retaliation. In regions where government authority was weak, the Tyrol, south Italy, Sicily and Corsica, for example, the feud remained common practice for several centuries.

Public office and common good

In less politically sensitive areas, the towns were able to create public functions much more quickly. As a sworn association, the original community became a legal person, demanding and giving solidarity, an abstract concept in comparison with the personal ties of loyalty that were characteristic of feudalism. The jurisdiction of the towns had been precisely demarcated in the struggle with their former lords, with Church institutions and princes retaining their immunities inside the walls.

The construction of town walls required an enormous effort on the part of the towns. A system of taxation had to be created for the purpose, raised mainly by levies on consumer goods. The burghers knew, therefore, that they were making efforts for their own community, just as they had done for the raising of taxes or ransoms for their lords. By the late thirteenth century, management of the collective resources was already a bone of contention between the established oligarchy and the artisans, who were beginning to organize themselves into guilds and demanding accountability for how the tax money was spent. After revolts by the craft guilds in 1279 and 1280, Count Guy of Flanders forced the magistrates of his major towns to keep accounts of public income and expenditure, and thus to be accountable for their policies. This was also the time when towns formed their own militias, organized according to districts and crafts. Mustered behind their banners and clad in their colourful tunics, they gave very forceful expression to the self-awareness of the burghers.

In addition to the walls, the towns erected more buildings with a public function: the town hall, of course, but also often free-standing bell towers, the *belforts, belfries* of France and Flanders. They served diverse purposes: that of watch-tower, tolling the bells to mark public events and the start and finish of the day's work; they bore sundials or mechanical clocks; the chest containing the town's charter was kept there under lock and key. In time, the impressive tower became a symbol of the town itself. Other building works with a public function included trade halls, halls for the sale of foodstuffs, warehouses, harbours, canals, locks, bridges, roads, cranes, weigh-houses, water conduits and fountains. Moreover the town created public spaces: in the first place the markets, the primary function of the town, but also streets and squares that were the stages for public demonstrations or everyday urban life. The churches similarly served as public buildings; they were often largely financed by monies from the town community, although they were managed by the clergy and local church boards made up of laypeople. As an orderly architectural entity, the town formed a framework for the lifestyle which gave tangible and visible shape to the concept of community.

It is interesting to consider the extent of the public domain in the towns. Social care was originally in Church hands, but through foundations by citizens it came increasingly under the control of representatives of the town authorities. They supervised the management of their property and also laid down regulations; their three-way relationship with private donors and religious charitable care was much respected. This was also true of hospitals, whose management was left to the religious orders, and of poor relief, which rested mainly with the parishes. The care of old people, widows and orphans, in so far as it was not covered by these two categories, was in the hands of guilds and confraternities. In all these cases the town authorities exercised a supervisory function. The guardianship of the mentally ill was seen as a public-order problem, which, like the prison, was looked after by the town. Thus, in the fifteenth century, towns also employed doctors and midwives to provide help in cases of public disasters such as famines and epidemics.

In the early decades of the sixteenth century town authorities throughout Europe took on a more emphatically organizational function in order to coordinate the diverse forms of social care and to impose strict controls on it. With the new increase in population there was a keenly felt need for rationalization in times of economic depression. During the fourteenth century a number of towns had already set up one or more schools, a clear break with the traditional monopoly of the Church. The spread of the Reformation accelerated this, because now all denominations rushed to win the souls of children.

In the pre-industrial towns the tasks of the local authorities were administrative and legislative as well as judicial, as we have already seen. The separation of these powers did not take place at the local level until around 1800. In the administration of justice, the tasks were generally divided. An officer of justice (*bailli, schout, amb[t]man, Schuldheiss, sénéschal, podestà, alcalde, corregidor*, 'sheriff'), in the service of the ruler, continued to supervise the process of law: he summoned the judges, presided over them and carried out the sentence. By virtue of the town charter, the interpretation of the rules of law devolved upon the officials elected from the local community, the aldermen. They passed judgment in accordance with local town laws as established by privileges and custom.

In many towns the authorities carried out tasks – which in Italy and France were vested in notaries, in the Roman tradition, in particular the registration of private agreements and the distribution of official deeds to persons concerned. Often, the aldermen also supervised the guardianship of orphans. This was done to keep check on any quarrels between and within families, with an inheritance at stake and a feud as a likely outcome. Activities relating to commerce and industry were subject to town regulation as well, so that aldermen also acted as judges with respect to the application of the laws.

In areas of northern Italy, Flanders and the Upper Rhine, where artisans gained entry to the aldermen's bench, large councils were formed with hundreds of representatives coming from craft guilds and the well-to-do. These councils often made decisions about taxes and other matters of general policy; similar organs played a part in the selection of aldermen, often through complicated procedures. From the fourteenth century, the office of alderman was often limited to one year, with the possibility of immediate reappointment, depending on the administrative structure of the town. Almost everywhere, it was far more difficult for artisans to build a political career than for merchants or other well-to-do burghers; without exception, in both fortune and lifestyle, those who did succeed outgrew the class they were thought to represent.

The many and varied areas in which towns performed collective functions until well into the sixteenth century make it clear that they, or at least the larger ones, formed a socially very differentiated environment with intensive human contacts. It heightened the potential for conflict perhaps, but also, undoubtedly, the creativity, enabling the towns to gain a head start in modernization on the surrounding countryside. In particular, the idea of *res publica*, republic, once again acquired a very real and original meaning in the towns

Plate 11.2 Hans Leu the Elder. View of Zürich, *c.* 1492–1496. In the water to the right is the prison tower

for the first time since the Roman era. In fact the medieval concept of a commune referred to the community that formed a collective identity and organized its affairs in a public context, in far more concrete terms than the *res publica* borrowed by scholars from the language of Antiquity. In this respect, the towns went much further than the monarchies, which found it difficult to make the distinction between the public domain and the ruler's private patrimony. Yet the fundamental constraint of the town's concept of public government was its particularism; every town enjoyed its own laws and no more wished to have them meddled with than it wished to share them. Though it started out as a right, with its liberating character dating from the time of the earliest town charters, citizenship gradually became a restrictive system of privileges that did not apply to those excluded from it, both the non-burghers inside the towns and the rural population outside.

This desire to be separate and to remain so became characteristic of urban societies all over pre-industrial Europe. If they occasionally did reach some form of mutual cooperation, then it usually happened either through the subordination of smaller towns to larger ones – such as in the Italian regional states dominated by metropolises like Florence, Milan and Venice and in the colonies controlled by Genoa and Venice – or on a very unstable basis. Citizens focused on their own immediate interests and were unwilling to share their privileges with others. Even within the towns themselves, fierce conflicts broke out between clans, classes and occupational groups. Corporative egoism was thus the outcome of the townspeople's originally egalitarian concept of community. Not until after the French Revolution was the strict territorialization of the law enforced everywhere. It is interesting to note that the terms 'burgher', 'bourgeois', 'citizen', all of which nowadays indicate state citizenship, came from the environment in which the concept of public law was re-invented in Europe: the town.

SOCIAL RELATIONSHIPS

Patrician government

In their earliest phase the towns were open, fairly egalitarian societies. The people populating the towns came from a wide variety of geographical and social backgrounds, all trying to use the favourable conditions to build up a new life. In most cases they had escaped from an unfree status in the overpopulated rural areas and were looking above all for the freedom to develop. This meant they had to be open to differences and prepared to cooperate with other people. As the landowners and feudal lords still held much authority, the townspeople had to show their unity in order to survive in an intimidating environment. This explains the strong commitment to solidarity laid down in the first town charters and the regulations of merchant guilds. Hence, also, the strengthening of community spirit by the oath compulsory on joining the sworn alliance of burghers and by collective church rituals and drinking bouts in the guilds. What is noticeable here is that this new, united society was originally one of equals who had escaped from serfdom by obtaining the rights of a citizen and living in the town for a year and a day. Freedom for them meant that they were henceforth released from countless obligations and all manner of restrictions on their movements and actions.

In the first instance, then, freedom as the release from interference in a person's actions had a negative definition. A man was free when he was no longer 'somebody's man', a position of dependence that demanded homage, obedience, services and deliveries. Looking at it from our current western expectation and acceptance of these fundamental values, it is difficult to realize what a radical effect these new developments must have had on the social order of the eleventh to thirteenth centuries. Feudal relationships, built up from diverse ties of dependence between people of unequal status, gave a vertical structure to society. There were two models for this: the patriarchal and the feudal. In the context of the family and in monastic communities, the authority of the strong but loving and merciful father held sway. The authority of the father abbot and of the *pater familias* derived from God the Father. The relationship between a liege lord and his vassal or between the lord of a demesne and his serf was similarly based on inequality, although it could be dressed up as feelings of loyalty and protection. Alongside this the alternative of horizontal social ties now came into existence in the towns, where people of equal status promised each other support and solidarity. The inspiration for this may have been in part religious, for the Church considered all the faithful as equal before God. Religious fraternities were an expression of this. What seems to us to be decisive, however, were the circumstances which, in a new and unstructured situation, offered everyone in towns the same opportunities provided that there was mutual solidarity.

In some towns, this general egalitarian tendency clashed with the private rights of already existing groups. The original inhabitants were in a better position than newcomers to guarantee certain privileges for themselves; for example, exemption from payment of a tax on the land upon which the town was built. As time went by and the population increased, these old distinctions faded away.

New social differences were created as the town community increased in size. It is a sociological law that certain relationships that are efficient in a group of a particular size fail to operate in a much larger one. In practice, this means that in the small early communes, where everyone had sworn an oath of mutual assistance to each other and knew each other, the ties of fellowship were strong, but that they weakened when there was a large increase in the number of fellow citizens. Social differentiation similarly resulted from the differences in economic activity. More capital and business sense was needed for long-distance commerce than for baking bread and spinning yarn, for example, while the chances of profit from such commercial activities were considerably larger than from crafts, because the scale of operation was bigger and the profit margins greater. In addition, for their supply of raw materials and the sale of their products, many artisans depended on middlemen who profited from their wider knowledge of the market and their interregional contacts.

It is clear that over several generations merchants were able to emerge as a new social elite. This superiority was no longer based on physical force or lack of legal freedoms. It was founded on the economic dependence of artisans as compared with merchants.

After all, it was the merchants who supplied the wool imported from England to the cloth industry, and the dyes from the Mediterranean area bought from the Italians. It was the merchants who as entrepreneurs coordinated the production process and delivered the semi-finished articles to the various specialized artisans for completion. And, finally, it was these same merchant-entrepreneurs who were responsible for exporting the finished products. In this way, all the artisans in their workshops were dependent on the orders and price-fixing of the merchants.

The new elite had enough capital at its disposal to buy up freehold land in the town. The phenomenal rise in the value of the land resulting from urban development formed a new source of wealth, and possibly also of prestige, for whoever could build a big stone house with towers, battlements and embrasures in the heart of the old town was indeed a real seigneur. Such a lord looked beyond the town walls for even greater status by copying the lifestyle of the nobility. He travelled on horseback, so that he was literally higher than the ordinary people, and surrounded himself with a retinue of squires and servants decked out in the colourful livery of his family. He bought property, if possible a feudal benefice with seigneurial rights and the prestigious obligation to serve the prince in his wars, on horseback and with a number of followers. He used a personal seal, assumed a coat of arms, and even dreamed of a noble title, or at least of marrying his children to aristocratic heirs. The noble lifestyle, which actually dated back to the stylized forms of medieval chivalry, continued to exercise a great attraction for socially climbing burghers until the nineteenth century. In northern and central Italy, the integration between the merchant elite and the old landed nobility took place more quickly than it did further north, because the towns radiated their domination over the countryside so rapidly that landowners also moved into the towns. Elsewhere the aristocracy entrenched themselves in castles and strongholds in the country.

Merchant guilds, or hanses, thus formed the core of the new social elite in most of the mercantile towns. In the oldest surviving statutes of these associations – such as that of the confraternity of Valenciennes, dating from between 1051 and 1070 – membership was still completely open, and most attention was given to religious ceremonies, to mutual assistance on the journeys undertaken in armed groups to distant markets, and to pacifying disorderly behaviour and fights that might occur during the drinking bouts. In contemporary regulations of the merchant guilds of Saint-Omer and Arras in northern France, particular attention was given to maintaining order and setting standards of behaviour during the meetings and binges. Charitable gifts of wine were also prescribed for the clergy, the poor and the lepers of the town. During the thirteenth century these regulations paid little attention to the behaviour of the guild brethren; that particular problem seems to have been solved in the course of a few generations. A new problem emerged, however – that of keeping the artisans out. Merchant guilds now acquired an exclusive character whereby the less wealthy, perhaps also the less well-behaved, and certainly the less powerful citizens were excluded from what would henceforth be a club for top people.

So between 1050 and 1250 a process of group forming and civilization (from the Latin *civis*, burgher) took place in the towns. In the initial phase, this was directed towards all future burghers, but during the process of growth the original core closed ranks to newcomers and the less well off. The explanation for this process of closure and exclusion is twofold. It was about numbers: firm solidarity does not work above a critical limit; and about saturation: after the original, immense possibilities for growth, as competition became fiercer the longer-established burghers tried to keep the privileges they had won for themselves and their children. Since commercial activities had produced the largest fortunes, this meant that the merchants set themselves up as an elite that formally differentiated itself from the other burghers. An extreme example of this was the Council of Venice in 1297: the names of a thousand notable families were entered in a Golden Book; in the course of the centuries many families died out and fewer and fewer survived, but no new ones were admitted to the Golden Book until the end of the Republic, conquered by the French in 1796.

The basis of the new social differentiation was economic: the possession of capital generated through commerce and then reinvested in it. The fact that the profits from trade were invested partly in land in the town, monumental stone houses and later also in property did not alter the essential difference between the new town elite and the feudal aristocracy. The ownership of land had, after all, formed the basis of the wealth and dominant position of the feudal aristocracy. In every town, the urban elite had its own name. In Ghent the members were *viri hereditarii*, hereditary men, meaning that they owned land in the town. In Paris the elite organized itself into a guild of merchants who controlled the river trade; they elected the *prévot des marchands* and four aldermen who, in addition to holding certain powers in the city, issued economic regulations and administered justice. In Bruges, the London Hanse, the association of merchants engaging in trade with England, formed the heart of the town's government; in Florence and Louvain, meanwhile, it was important to be a member of one of the guilds of cloth merchants, and in Deventer of the merchant guild.

To cover this variety of names and criteria, modern historians have borrowed the word 'patriciate' from ancient Roman history and use it to refer to the new urban elite of wealthy merchants. A distinctive feature is that, from the original solidarity between the core of sworn men and the commune, this elite came to monopolize the administration of the towns. The patricians thus became the dominant group, not only economically but also politically. They naturally used the authority of their functions to serve their own interests, which increasingly diverged from those of the town community as a whole and more and more took on a clearly class character.

During the second half of the thirteenth century there were uprisings in several towns, caused by popular anger at a falling economy or new taxes. It was not the worst off who stood to benefit from these revolts, however, but the newly rich. Until then, they had been excluded from power, but, by placing themselves at the head of a popular movement, they were able to force a breakthrough. An uprising in Florence in 1293 broke the power monopoly of the *magnati*, the patriciate. In Genoa the old aristocracy offered more resistance and it was not until 1339 that a popular revolt brought Simon Boccanegra to power; representatives of the craftspeople won a quarter of the seats on the council. Yet all these shifts of power took place inside the urban upper class. Those who were excluded from it made use of the *popolo*, the middle classes, to seize power. In Flanders the liberation movement against the French occupation broke the patrician monopoly in 1302. The majority of the aldermen's seats were awarded to the artisans: in Ghent, as many as 20 out of the 26. In the German Empire the 'council families', as they were called, meaning the old patriciate, generally retained their authority or even their monopoly. In Nuremberg, Zurich and Strasbourg, their position was not threatened until the nineteenth century, and in Lübeck revolts at the beginning of the fifteenth century were crushed. Only in Cologne and a few other towns along the upper reaches of the Rhine (Worms, Speyer, Freiburg, Basle) did the artisans triumph. The extent to which town authorities could be forced open to allow in new generations of merchants and artisans depended on the relationships of numbers and power inside a town, and on the opportunities to form a coalition, which occurred more often than not. As was the case with the acquisition of town privileges, the result varied considerably from region to region and often also from town to town.

Urban society

The concentration of thousands, or even tens of thousands, of inhabitants within a town's walls, made life there extremely vulnerable, a consequence of the often unhygienic living conditions. The spread of leprosy during the twelfth and thirteenth centuries was certainly connected to this. Moreover, the supply of food – grain in particular – was precarious. There were famines throughout western Europe in 1125, and again in 1195 and 1196. In these cases, chronicles describe how people's stomachs were swollen from undernourishment, how bread prices increased tenfold or even twentyfold in a short time, and the mass of starving people dying on the streets in search of food and alms. The large concentrations of people dependent on grain supplies from their hinterland heightened the vulnerability of the towns to natural fluctuations in harvest yields resulting from changing weather conditions. While farmers could attribute the failure of a harvest to the will of God, town-dwellers saw that the price of bread in times of scarcity rose more sharply than seemed to be justified by the dwindling supply. They also saw, or suspected, that large religious institutions, grain dealers and comfortably off burghers had well-filled grain lofts that they kept for their own use,

or that they sent only small quantities of grain to the market in order to fetch the highest prices. Human actions were visible in the events that threatened the existence of the poor townspeople.

The artisans were also affected by changing situations in the international markets for their raw materials and finished products. It was not difficult to realize that the middlemen made more profit from their labour than they themselves did, and that interruptions in trade as a result of wars or boycotts were the work of humans. Unlike the farming communities, a more rational insight into the causes of life's uncertainties developed in the towns where there was direct evidence of human behaviour. So a specifically burgher mentality grew up, different from that of the chivalric or religious environments or of the farming communities. Once other people had been identified as the authors of a specific problem, then rational actions would bring change far sooner than any appeal to supernatural powers.

The French medievalist, Jacques le Goff, has strikingly illustrated the pragmatic mentality of the medieval town by pointing to the change in the awareness of time. In the country, nature, with its cycle of seasons and the unequal division of light and darkness, determined the rhythm of life. The farmer arranged his daily activities according to the position of the sun and moon, and the seasons. There was the church, whose bells tolled in the rhythm of the services and feast days. In the towns nature and church had far less influence on the rhythm of life. The town bell towered above the churches, and rang out the working day. Mechanical clocks appeared in the late thirteenth century. They divided the day into hours of equal length, determined by the people themselves. Time was no longer in God's hands.

This more businesslike world-view fostered the idea that the reality was not a God-given order that could not or should not be challenged, as the theologians had maintained. If society was the work of humans then it could also be changed by humans. A challenge to the established social order was then no longer blasphemous. It can even be assumed that the fervent preaching of the mendicant orders, in particular the Franciscans, against amassing worldly wealth and supporting the ideal of poverty in imitation of Christ, had contributed to the fact that the urban proletariat now became more articulate, condemned exploitation by 'the rich' and started to make demands (see also Chapter 12).

The question of how an urban society was structured can be approached from both a legal and a socio-economic point of view. Legally speaking, there were a number of categories of townspeople, each of which fell under its own statutory laws. Many of them were unable to fulfil the financial conditions for citizenship, but remained in the town to carry out low-paid work. This group formed a mobile mass that could react quickly to fluctuations in the economy and moved to where the opportunities seemed most favourable. There were also diverse categories that did not enjoy civic rights because they had a different legal status; they included members of a prince's court, the clergy, nobles with their retinue, foreigners, Jews and Muslims.

In the regions of the Iberian peninsula that had been recovered by Christians, there were countless Muslims and people of a mixed religious background who would be systematically persecuted under Philip II and in 1609 were deported *en masse* to North Africa. They worked mainly on the land and were unflatteringly known as *mudéjares*, 'tamed animals' in Arabic. There were large numbers of Jews, too, particularly in the Mediterranean towns. The 25,000 Jews of Catalonia represented almost a seventh of the urban population

there. In Carpentras it was one-tenth. Among them were not only merchants and moneylenders but also doctors and scholars. They lived in their own neighbourhoods, known as *juiverie, juderie* or *calls*, depending on the local language. Legally they enjoyed the protection of the king or prince; in return for payment of a sum of money to him, they were his 'servants'.

In the cities of central Europe, such as Prague and Cracow, diverse ethnic, religious or social categories lived inside the same agglomeration in separate, adjacent townships, with their own institutions and often also their own walls, town hall, market square, and more. There was greater integration in the West. In Italy and Iberia, slavery continued to exist throughout the Middle Ages, particularly for members of the household staff. Slaves were also used to a limited extent on the Italian sugar plantations in Cyprus and Crete and for salt production on Ibiza. The slave markets were most lively round the Black Sea, where Caucasians, Tartars, Russians and Balkan Slavs were bought and sold; in Andalusia, the trade was in blacks from Guinea and Muslims from the reconquered parts of Mallorca and Valencia.

From a socio-economic viewpoint, the populations of the towns could be distinguished in economic sections, categories of well-being, and so forth. Some insight is possible through statistical data, thanks to

Table 11.3 Percentual division of occupations in Florence, Pisa, and the small towns of Tuscany

	Florence	Pisa	Small towns
Agriculture	0.3	6.0	32.7
Selling of food	4.7	5.9	1.9
Cloth	16.3	7.0	2.1
Other textiles	4.7	3.4	0.5
Paper	0.1	0.2	0.2
Leather, skins	5.7	9.3	2.6
Spices	1.2	2.0	0.7
Metalworking	2.8	3.2	1.9
Wood, masonry, etc.	4.0	5.0	1.1
Service industries	16.3	13.5	7.1
Unknown	43.9	44.6	49.3
Total number of households	9,722	1,714	6,262

Source: D. Herlihy and C. Klapisch-Zuber, *Tuscans and their Families* (New Haven and London 1985), p. 127.

the rich documentation of the towns of Tuscany (see Table 11.3). The social structure according to occupation appears to have been more varied in the large towns than in the small. In other words, there were more different and more specialized occupations in a town like Florence than in the small towns of the region. The larger the town, the smaller the proportion of people there who lived from agriculture, and the larger the proportion who lived from the service sector.

Craft specialization in one sector was only profitable on a large scale: in Florence the textile sector represented 21 per cent of the workforce; in Ghent, around the year 1356, as much as 63 per cent of a total population of 64,000; in Pisa only 10.4 per cent, and in small Tuscan towns barely 2.6 per cent.

The capital resources of the members of diverse occupational groups varied enormously: the wealth of the Florentine bankers was on average 83 times larger than that of a transport worker, that of a wool merchant about 31 times greater, and of a spice merchant ten times. Among the artisans themselves there was a considerable difference in status between the specialized occupations that required a certain amount of capital and skill, the ordinary skilled trades and the jobs requiring no skills at all. The greatest differences were found at the top of the social pyramid.

The thousands of small towns of late medieval Europe still had an agrarian character. One can understand why Louis IX instructed the city council of Bourges in 1262 to 'drive all the roaming pigs out of the town because they are completely ruining it'. On the other hand, certain commercial activities were responsible for a large share of the employment opportunities, particularly in towns with more than 10,000 inhabitants.

Craft guilds

In the larger towns, artisans were organized into occupational groups from the thirteenth century onwards. For some specialized activities, such as goldsmiths, basket weavers or leather workers, this involved living in the same street. For expensive products, the central location was critical because of the basic price and the proximity of customers. For other, sometimes polluting, activities the availability of sufficient flowing water and the actual distance from the town centre to limit environmental damage were deciding factors. This applied to tanners in particular, while fullers and brewers were dependent on clean water. For reasons of hygiene and also to facilitate quality control, town authorities concentrated the vendors of fresh foodstuffs in one street or market hall. There is still a very large meat hall in Ghent dating from the fourteenth century, Brussels has its *Beenhouwersstraat* (Butchers' Street), and vegetable, fish and cattle markets are familiar everywhere.

In the earliest stages, in Milan before 1068 and in Florence, the members of the local aristocracy and the merchants seem to have taken the initiative to organize the artisans, in order to have a better grip on them. In time, town militias would be formed on the same basis. The merchant guilds were in control of production in various English towns by the beginning of the twelfth century, and in Cambridge, for example, as early as the eleventh. In a number of French towns, Toulouse for example, some craft guilds were already recognized by the authorities in the twelfth century; notably these were in the sectors for food and leather-working, most sensitive to deterioration and environmental pollution. The members of these guilds were obliged to take an oath promising to obey the regulations. During the thirteenth century artisans formed religious and charitable fraternities in Catalonia and Flanders, as the first urban merchants had done two centuries earlier. The aim was mutual assistance and religious services, with a view to counteracting the uncertainties of life. The uncertainties of life for artisans, unlike merchants, had less to do with long-distance travel but were connected to the poverty caused by sickness, disablement, unemployment and widowhood. During the fourteenth and fifteenth centuries large fraternities and craft guilds founded homes for their aged and needy members. In the town communities, such charitable organizations, based on mutual self-help, took on the functions which in rural communities were fulfilled by the family. Households in the towns were smaller, however, so that the need for institutionalized services increased.

Organization on the basis of neighbourhood and religious and charitable functions formed the common cove of the European craft guilds system. In addition, the interests of the authorities and the artisans, and the instability of political struggles, shaped the institutional expansion in very divergent ways. Control of production and of the artisans themselves was a strong motive for the town authorities to give a certain organizational form to the corporations. Price controls and the hallmark of product quality were in the interests of traders and consumers alike. Even in the period of exclusive patrician rule, therefore, craft guilds received legal recognition as monopolistic occupational groups: only members of the guilds were allowed to practise a particular craft, and training was arranged by the artisans themselves.

Town authorities laid down regulations for working hours and technical matters to guarantee the standards of quality and to combat unfair competition between fellow artisans. For a prescribed number of years (often 2–4, 8–10 in many cases in Paris in 1268, sometimes as many as 12) an apprentice lived and worked with a recognized master artisan, and so learned the trade in practice. A workplace thus had a decidedly family character, contributing to the close ties between the master artisans and the lower ranks. When the apprenticeship was completed, the apprentice became a journeyman, a skilled worker in the employ of a master. In some cases, recorded from the thirteenth century onwards, the journeyman could then qualify as a master after submitting a 'masterpiece' to the guild masters as proof of his professional skill. To be recognized as a master artisan a man was required to be a burgher of the town, to pay an entrance fee, to provide a banquet and to have his own workshop and tools. Here, there was a class distinction between master and journeyman, because a master owned his own production means. Just as in the thirteenth century the merchant guilds became more exclusive as the competition became stiffer, so in a period of a small market the legal and material requirements to become a master worked as a barrier the established masters could use to protect their own positions against newcomers. This happened particularly during the demographic decline of the fourteenth century. The right of entry was made considerably more expensive for members from outside the town or from the country, and cheaper for the sons of existing masters. There was thus a tendency for a craft to become hereditary, especially in those sectors where the potential markets decreased. In the German Empire, where most towns were relatively small and the chivalric ethic still largely determined the pattern

of values, many *Zünfte* (craft guilds) set the requirement of 'honourable' conduct as a condition of entry: 'honour' there was concerned with the exclusion of unmarried cohabitants or people of Slavic origin. Among those professions considered *unehrliche* or lacking honour, and thus not permitted to form guilds, were those of executioner, gravedigger, barber and bathhouse master.

Under the rule of the patricians, the merchants–entrepreneurs–administrators exerted close control over the craft guilds. They had an interest in social and economic regulations and tolerated the charitable and religious activities of guilds. For entrepreneurs, these had the useful effect that the artisans held themselves in reserve when there was not much work. In the large towns with a predominant textile industry, there were many thousands of workers in the same objective circumstances. The masters in the sector could hardly act as small independent entrepreneurs because the raw materials remained the property of the merchant-entrepreneurs during the production process. Even though their primary aims may have been charitable and religious, and even though they were strictly controlled by the patricians, the existence of craft organizations nevertheless provided a framework within which artisans could share experiences and invent alternatives. This explains the fact that in the typical textile towns of Douai, Ypres and Ghent the earliest collective actions of workers organized into guilds took place in periods of recession or other encroachments on their standard of living. In 1274, the weavers and fullers of Ghent deserted their town in protest against bad working conditions. The entrepreneurs reacted to this by making an agreement with employers in other towns not to employ strikers, an early form of lockout. In 1302, another strike broke out in Ghent among all the *artes mechanicae*, the artisans who worked with equipment, in reaction to the increased taxes imposed by the patrician authorities. By 1300, the social contrasts had become sharpened in all the large towns partly because the economic downturn interrupted the powerful growth of the preceding centuries, making incomes insecure, while entrepreneurs tried as far as possible to transfer their risks to the artisans.

In some towns, upheavals resulted in some artisans winning a certain degree of autonomy and a political voice. Control of a craft guild was then no longer in the hands of patricians but of members elected from their own circle. The guilds themselves had gained the right to exercise authority over their members, impose and collect fines and issue regulations. In Florence the most prosperous artisans (*arti maggiori*) were represented in the town government in 1293; later, in the fourteenth century, a number of the more modest *arti* (craft guilds) were also included. Whoever was then finally allowed to converse with the old aristocracy in the Palazzo del Comune belonged to what we would call the labour aristocracy: small, independent entrepreneurs and merchants who were only too keen to forget their modest origins and, like the old patricians, enjoy the respect accorded to the seniors. The breakthrough of the artisans in Flanders was more radical and more general than elsewhere because, in 1302, their militias had played a decisive part in reversing the French occupation of the county at the Battle of the Golden Spurs at Courtrai. This was the first time that an army of urban foot soldiers, mustered for the occasion, defeated a king's army of knights. Even though the townsfolk may have been helped by the marshy terrain, their victory made a great impression on their contemporaries, and they capitalized on it by appropriating political and social rights for themselves. In some cases not only masters but journeymen as well could be elected to be governor of their guild (the fullers of Bruges in 1303, in Oudenaarde and Courtrai in 1305), or their voice was heard indirectly (the weavers, fullers and shearers of Saint-Omer in 1306). This revolution in Flanders was imitated in neighbouring regions, so that artisans in Liège, Middelburg, Dordrecht and Utrecht won a considerable share of political power and were able to hold on to it for centuries.

What could artisans do with the political and social power they had won in this fashion? In the first place, they could defend their standard of living when their purchasing power was eroded as a result of the devaluation of the coinage during the fourteenth century. They placed restrictions on the combination of wholesale trade and entrepreneurship. This enabled the weavers, who technically controlled the entire production process in the textile sector and formed by far the largest occupational group in towns like Ghent and Leiden, to work their way up to become small entrepreneurs (drapers) and employ other specialized workers, such as dyers, fullers and shearers, on a piecework basis. From that moment, however, like all free entrepreneurs, they were faced with a recession all over Europe, so that the margins to improve the lot of their workers became narrowed. In villages and those areas where there were no craft guilds or where the craft guilds had little power, wages remained low. This made them attractive to entrepreneurs, who therefore shifted their activities to those areas. It was easy for them to do this because in the common *Verlagsystem* – 'putting out' as it is known in English – the burden of the costs of the means of production, the workplaces and tools in particular, was largely shouldered by the artisans themselves. Under this system, an entrepreneur brought the raw materials or semi-finished articles to the cheapest workers – those in rural areas. The de-industrialization of the once-leading areas and the industrialization of low-wage areas took place on a large scale during the fourteenth century. The rural areas of Flanders and England and the towns of Brabant and Holland eagerly took over a large share of the cloth production that had become too expensive in the old Flemish centres.

The response of the craft guilds worsened the situation: they sought salvation in a restrictive protectionism and the exclusion of newcomers. In this way, the established workers used legal and economic discrimination, and even force, to try to hold on to their share of the market. They took prohibitive measures against imitations and imports in the vain hope of thereby salvaging their own position. In the crafts for which the markets became increasingly weak, the hereditary position of master was even laid down in the statutes. In the long run, market forces proved stronger than regulations, and the old textile centres could only survive in a slimmed-down form by focusing on refined, high-quality and even fashionable products, of which the famed Flemish tapestries were the glorious masterpieces. In the rural areas and newer centres, aiming at the production of cheaper textiles, the small scale made it impossible to impose the labour sharing and specialization that was normal in the large towns and, partly as a result of this, to achieve a similar quality.

During the Middle Ages there were no craft guilds specifically for women, yet many women followed a skilled occupation and even took the lead in some occupations, such as spinning and selling foodstuffs in the marketplace. In general women were under someone's guardianship: of their father, uncle or brother as long as they were unmarried, of their husband, or of a priest (male, of course) if they were in a convent. Only widowhood could emancipate them. An artisan's widow who had been accustomed to work with him in his workplace or shop could carry on the business as an equal and, in that capacity, could enjoy all the rights of a guild member. As long as they did not remarry, widows in 's-Hertogenbosch could acquire the title of master in the dyers' guild and in Breda in the victuallers' or grocers' guild. Around 1470 there was even some rivalry among the fullers of Leiden between women and the apprentices who found that the women were taking the bread out of their mouths. There were also, however, specifically female occupations, that of midwife being the most obvious. To become a recognized midwife, one had to follow a traditional practical training under a 'master' midwife, after which a skills test gave entry to the profession and membership of the guild, often the guild of surgeons.

As entry to the craft guilds became more difficult for newcomers, the journeymen began to look for alternatives. In some towns they organized themselves in separate journeymen's associations (*compagnonnages, Gesellenverbände*), which in time also received recognition. In the towns of the Holy Roman Empire, the custom of young, 15- to 22-year-old journeymen travelling around the country for long periods of time became common during the second half of the fourteenth century: *die Wanderschaft der fahrenden Gesellen*. In the inns a specific etiquette developed for these young men, who were finding their way about a broad labour market. Town authorities, however, tried to impose all sorts of restrictions on their self-organization. These young Germans went by the dozens to work in Italian towns, driven by the lack of prospects in their home towns and their desire to be independent. Furthermore, countless unskilled workers remained outside the organizational framework of the craft guilds. Employment for them was often as uncertain as it was flexible: if there was a large construction project somewhere, a dike to be reinforced or a military expedition undertaken, then hundreds of labourers were required. Farmers needed temporary workers at harvest time. Out of sheer necessity unskilled labourers moved around to wherever they could earn a living. As they had to be very mobile and could not organize themselves in any town, their position remained weak.

The system of guilds, or corporatism, was originally a form of social organization endowed with varied powers and rights; it would continue to exist in France until 1792 and elsewhere until the nineteenth century. In general it can still be seen that the organization per occupational group of apprentices, journeymen and masters had far-reaching consequences for the nature of social differences in the late Middle Ages. Craft guilds formed the framework for their members' way of life, within which they saw not only the expression of their social, political and economic rights and responsibilities but through which they also took part in town festivities or organized their own Church celebrations or secular rites. Furthermore, they could count on support in times of need. The craft guilds built imposing guildhalls in which they held their meetings and stored the banners that the members carried in processions and battles. Artisans thus identified themselves very closely with their guilds. Inside this framework they focused their hopes of social promotion, of becoming masters, and ultimately of achieving positions of authority in the guild or even in the town itself.

Such vertical organization per occupational group could mean that social conflicts were not defined in terms of class distinctions (capital versus labour) but rather according to rivalries between the sectors. This fact, as well as the entire working of craft guilds, leads us to the conclusion that this form of organization, in spite of all the conflicts that it brought, contributed in the long term to the social stability of the larger towns of Europe during the *ancien régime*.

NETWORKS OF TOWNS

Not all towns had commerce as their primary function: a number of them came into being or were founded to provide services to a cathedral or some other administrative centre. Iberian towns derived their great freedoms from the Reconquest, led by the kings, and thus functioned as bases of conquest and occupation. During the Middle Ages, towns with such one-sided functions were usually relatively small, like the archiepiscopal seats of Canterbury, Sens and Esztergom.

What is striking is that the largest commercial metropolises enjoyed a wide degree of autonomy with respect to their surrounding states until well into the eighteenth century. They were often situated in small states where they exerted considerable influence on government. They were able to expand this position of relative autonomy if their own development took place before royal power had been consolidated, particularly in coastal areas. Moreover, metropolises were concerned primarily with matters that were not of interest to rulers, such as the safety of traffic routes, the protection of travelling merchants, negotiating business agreements with diverse partners and providing efficient regulations for conciliation and jurisdiction. Neither the feudal lords nor their ecclesiastical advisors knew much about such matters, so that it was merchants directly involved who developed the relevant institutional rules and even put them into effect, in some cases with the formal seal of a neighbouring prince.

A good example is Barcelona, which developed its network during the thirteenth century, chiefly in the western Mediterranean, with settlements in the Balearics, Sardinia and Sicily and consulates in Tunis, Bougie and Oran. Its primary aim was to organize markets and ensure the safety of trading routes and the protection of its own citizens abroad. For this purpose, concessions were made with local rulers, including those in Islamic areas.

Groups of towns employed a variety of means to arrange their own protection in a world that, with the fragmentation of effective authority, had become extremely unsafe for travellers. Because good traffic links with their hinterland and other markets were essential for these towns, the safety of the roads was a continual concern. Small feudal lords found it very tempting to exploit their control over a particular area through which a strategic route passed by threatening travelling merchants with robbery and violence if they refused to pay the toll demanded. In the best case, tolls were the going price for what in a positive sense was called protection: if the toll was paid then the merchant could be certain of safe passage. The amount of the toll was often a subject of controversy, for it was difficult to rule out arbitrariness on the part of either the ruler or his toll collector.

A vital traffic axis such as the Rhine was strewn with local rulers who profited from the busy river traffic. From the thirteenth to the fifteenth centuries it was common for towns in this region and in Alsace and Swabia to join together to seek protection from assaults on their safety or that of their citizens and their commercial traffic. In a number of cases they were even able to involve some feudal lords in their alliance or, in exchange for financial support, were given guarantees or rights from the German king or emperor. The first major alliance of the Rhine towns dated from 1254, when the Interregnum (the period between 1254 and 1273 when there was no king generally recognized in Germany) created problems in the field of public order. By forming a sworn alliance that placed them directly under the protection of Christ, the towns tried above all to maintain peace, to resolve conflicts by legal means or by arbitration, to organize the joint prosecution of peace-breakers and to limit the tolls on rivers and roads. These agenda points were clearly in conflict with the activities of noblemen, yet the movement did succeed in persuading a number of archbishops and bishops, the count palatine of the Rhine and a few counts and lords to join the alliance. Just as the *pax Dei* (Peace of God) movement had done earlier, the alliance thus took upon itself a task that was in essence the province of the king – namely, maintaining peace and justice in the public interest and stopping the nobility from feuding and taking the law into their own hands. Such alliances between towns did not last long, however, and their rare joint military actions met with only limited success.

What did unite towns was their trade. But towns also had to support and safeguard a flow of people and goods to and from the surrounding rural areas to provide for their livelihood. Food supplies generally had to come from the immediate vicinity, making market regulations necessary to ensure that there would be no shortages. Many residents invested their capital in land outside the town, often to develop market-oriented produce but not infrequently with the proviso that their income would take the form of produce in kind by which they might avoid the fluctuations of the food market. At the same time every town made efforts to protect its own production by prohibiting similar activities in its vicinity.

Relationships between the towns were even less idyllic and were strictly defined by their mutual dependency in a hierarchy of markets. Larger towns exercised as stifling an hegemony over smaller ones as they did over the rural areas. The larger towns also fulfilled specialized functions in a particular region. As we have seen above in the case of Florence, these were only profitable in large centres where they could attract enough customers from a wide hinterland. The region that relied on this sort of specialized function of a town is called its service area. It has been possible to reconstruct a whole hierarchy of towns and villages that fulfilled central functions for their own service areas at different levels. It involved markets for labour, specialized services and goods. Broadly speaking, geographers have ascertained that, in theory, central locations spread following concentric models, resembling crystals. In reality, specific characteristics of the landscape, such as a coast, mountain range or river influenced this pattern. A hierarchy of markets to three or four levels was nevertheless a common phenomenon. This insight helps us to understand the diverse forms of interdependence, known as a network, that existed between town and country and between towns of unlike size within the same system.

The most sharply crystallized relationships were found in the most urbanized region – that of northern and central Italy. During the fifteenth and sixteenth centuries, regional states were formed here, spurred on by the largest towns, Venice, Florence, Genoa and Milan, which then waged a fierce competition for hegemony in the region. The conquest and subjection of Pisa by Florence in 1406 meant that Florence finally gained control over a harbour. Its *contado* gradually expanded to a territory of about 12,000 square kilometres. Between 1404 and 1428, Venice captured a huge area in the Po valley, measuring some 30,000 square kilometres and reaching to within 20 kilometres of Milan. The subordinate towns came under an administration appointed by the capital. The capital's law courts enjoyed precedence throughout the entire countryside, the *contado*; in legal matters townspeople received preferential treatment over country dwellers, rural goods were taxed more heavily than those from the town, town guilds enjoyed more privileges than the country artisans, and urban landownership penetrated deeply into the country. In this way political hegemony numbed market relationships, which still offered more scope to the larger centres than to the small. The

northern and central Italian regional states demonstrated yet another model of a socio-economic and political order, which was stabilized in 1454 through the Peace of Lodi. This political system came into being without, and sometimes even in defiance of, monarchal activities.

Different political systems were thus made possible through the dynamism of the towns; the Italian system, with its overseas and domestic components, was able to develop freely, with the greatest demographic and economic concentrations of the late Middle Ages and relatively few monarchs nearby. Even the invasions of French armies in 1494, followed by those of the Empire, which caused heavy damage to the land during the first half of the sixteenth century, essentially could not affect this system of regional states; at most it was reduced to a series of virtually autonomous vassal states. Elsewhere the relationships of power were less emphatically to the advantage of (large) towns, and other configurations were formed in which monarchic states would exercise stricter control.

In certain parts of Europe, where the formation of feudal and monarchic power did not take place early and did not penetrate deeply, towns thus developed their own political and social structures in order to look after their vital common interests. Using the maintenance of the peace as a pretext, they arranged to protect their trade and to pasture their cattle independently, locally and along the routes linking them. Where they enjoyed superiority, they formed hegemonic market systems of colonial dimensions. As the kingdoms and territorial principalities expanded their territory and power, they naturally came into contact with the power systems that urban networks had already built up in some areas. Conflicts of competence and open power struggles arose between them, yet various forms of cooperation also proved to be possible. What is clear is that the urban communities gave the history of Europe a unique character.

FURTHER READING

Barron, Caroline M. (2004), *London in the Later Middle Ages: Government and People, 1200–1500* (Oxford and New York: Oxford University Press).

Black, Anthony (1984), *Guilds and Civil Society in European Political Thought From the Twelfth Century to the Present* (London and New York: Methuen).

Boffey, Julia and Pamela King (eds) (1995), *London and Europe in the Later Middle Ages* (Turnhout: Brepols).

Dean, Trevor and Chris Wickham (eds) (2003), *City and Countryside in Late Medieval and Renaissance Italy: Essays Presented to Philip Jones* (London: Hambledon).

Edwards, John (1982), *Christian Córdoba: The City and Its Region in the Late Middle Ages* (Cambridge: Cambridge University Press).

Ennen, Edith (1979), *The Medieval Town* (Amsterdam: Elsevier) (orig. German, 1972).

Epstein, Steven A. (1991), *Wage Labor and Guilds in Medieval Europe* (Chapel Hill: University of North Carolina Press).

Epstein, S.R. (ed.) (2004) *Town and Country in Europe, 1300–1800* (Cambridge: Cambridge University Press).

Farmer, Sharon A. (2002), *Surviving Poverty in Medieval Paris: Gender, Ideology, and the Daily Lives of the Poor* (Ithaca, N.Y. and London: Cornell University Press).

Frugoni, Chiara and Arsenio Frugoni (2005), *A Day in a Medieval City* (Chicago, Ill.: University of Chicago Press) (orig. Italian, 1997).

Goldthwaite, Richard A. (1980), *The Building of Renaissance Florence. A Social and Economic History* (Baltimore, Md.: Johns Hopkins University Press).

Hall, Derek (2002), *Burgess, Merchant and Priest: The Medieval Scottish Town* (Edinburgh: Birlinn Publishers).

Hanawalt, Barbara and Kathryn L. Reyerson (eds) (1994), *City and Spectacle in Medieval Europe* (Minneapolis: University of Minnesota Press).

Hilton, Rodney (1992), *English and French Towns in Feudal Society* (Cambridge: Cambridge University Press).

Hohenberg, P.M. and L.H. Lees (1995), *The Making of Urban Europe, 1000–1994*, 2nd edn (Cambridge, Mass.: Harvard University Press).

Huffman, Joseph P. (1998), *Family, Commerce and Religion in London and Cologne. Anglo-German Emigrants, c.1000–c.1300* (Cambridge: Cambridge University Press).

Le Goff, Jacques (1980), *Time, Work, and Culture in the Middle Ages* (Chicago, Ill.: University of Chicago Press) (orig. French, 1979).

Lilley, Keith D. (2002), *Urban Life in the Middle Ages, 1000–1450* (Basingstoke and New York: Palgrave).

Miller, Edward and John Hatcher (1995), *Medieval England: Towns, Commerce and Crafts 1086–1348*, 2nd edn (London: Longman).

Nicholas, D.M. (1987), *The Metamorphosis of a Medieval City: Ghent in the Age of the Arteveldes, 1302–1390* (Lincoln: University of Nebraska Press).

—— (1997), *The Growth of the Medieval City from Late Antiquity to the Early Fourteenth Century* (London and New York: Longman).

—— (1997), *The Later Medieval City 1300–1500* (London and New York: Longman).

—— (2003), *Urban Europe, 1100–1700* (Basingstoke: Palgrave Macmillan).

Palliser, David M. (2006), *Towns and Local Communities in Medieval and Early Modern England* (Aldershot: Ashgate).

Pounds, Norman (2005), *The Medieval Town and Social Change* (Westport, Conn.: Greenwood Press).

Reynolds, Susan (1977), *An Introduction to the History of English Medieval Towns* (Oxford: Clarendon).

Vance, James E. Jr (1990), *The Continuing City: Urban Morphology in Western Civilization* (Baltimore, Md.: Johns Hopkins University Press).

Verhulst, Adriaan (1999) *The Rise of Cities in North-West Europe* (Cambridge: Cambridge University Press).

Vries, Jan de (1984) *European Urbanization, 1500–1800* (Cambridge, Mass.: Harvard University Press and London: Methuen).

Webb, Diana (1996), *Patrons and Defenders: The Saints in the Italian City State* (London and New York: I.B. Tauris).

CHAPTER 12

Thinking about man and the world

A GREEK LEGACY: THE MEDIEVAL VIEW OF THE WORLD AND MANKIND

The intellectual achievements of the Middle Ages were considerable, but should not conceal the fact that the scholarly view of the world and of mankind remained in essence unchanged between Antiquity and the early modern period. C.S. Lewis, the literary historian, who first drew attention to this in his now classic work *The Discarded Image* (1964), traced the roots of this 'medieval model of the universe' back to the great Greek philosophers of the fourth century BC, Plato (427–347) and Aristotle (384–322). Because the most important additions to this model also came from Greece (Ptolemy and Galen, both of whom lived in the second century AD), we can safely say that the learned medieval view of the natural order was a Graeco-pagan legacy and not Judaeo-Christian. There were also essential differences of course. In the medieval Christian view the world was finite and not eternal, as the Greeks believed, and the medieval view of the world was firmly anchored in the belief in one God, while that of the Greeks was embedded in polytheism.

The Greek legacy could only endure because the medieval intellectual elite was involved in a permanent dialogue, as it were, with Antiquity. In some periods this dialogue was carried on with exceptional vigour. We can speak, then, of a renaissance, a term closely linked to another concept – that of humanism (see Chapter 1). The three most significant renaissances traditionally distinguished – the Carolingian, that of the twelfth century and the Italian – form the pivotal points of this chapter, which further focuses on developments in intellectual formation and higher learning. After all this was the only route along which the ancient concepts about mankind and the world, mingled with Christian ideas, could be reproduced and carried forward through the centuries.

Universe, earth, man, spirit

In the Greek model of the cosmos the earth was the immovable centre of the universe; around it there moved, in concentric order, ten transparent convex spaces or spheres, beginning with those of the seven known planets, in which the sun and the moon were included. Beyond the sphere of the furthest planet, Saturn, began that of the fixed stars (*stellatum*); beyond that lay the vaguer circles of 'the chrystalline', presented as a thin mass of water encircling the entire firmament, and that of the *primum mobile*, the first of the spheres to show movement and to pass that movement on to the lower spheres. It was not the stars and planets themselves, then, but the spheres within which they had their set place that made slow orbits round the earth. Beyond the *primum mobile* extended the immovable *empyreum*, in the medieval Christian concept the location of heaven. Although the earth then formed the centre of the universe, nevertheless it was fully understood that it was insignificant on the cosmic scale. One estimate showed that a complete revolution of the stellar sphere round the earth took 36,000 years. An English chap-book (popular book) from the fourteenth century calculated that a journey from the earth to the *stellatum* would take 8,000 years, at an average travelling time of 40 miles per day. It is nothing compared to the actual 100,000 light years that separate earth from the end of our galaxy, but still a vast distance for the medieval imagination of man.

It was presumed that the stars, the planets and the earth, just like the spheres in which they revolved, were spherical in shape – the idea of a flat earth was not completely discarded but never found favour in intellectual circles. Planets were seen as animate, often even as intelligent bodies that influenced life on earth. It was the task of astrology to discover and determine that influence. Astrology in the Middle Ages, just as in Antiquity, was accepted as a source of rational knowledge, although those elements that were clearly contrary to Christian orthodoxy were forbidden by the Church, among them 'reading the future' from the stars and the worship of heavenly bodies. It was seriously believed that the planets had an influence on the formation of metals and on people's physical and mental state, to mention just two totally different matters. Doctors and apothecaries in particular made frequent use of astrological knowledge, but kings and princes of the Church had their court and personal astrologers too.

There was a fundamental difference between the sublunary or terrestrial world and the world outside: only the earth was imperfect, everything above it was incorruptible. The perfect 'fifth element', ether (*aether* or *quintessens*), only existed in the 'world outside'. The terrestrial world consisted of four elements that formed the building blocks of all earthly matter: earth, air, fire and water. Each element was 'caused' by a combination of two of the four 'primary qualities': hot, cold, wet and dry.

Two images dominated in the concept of earthly geography (see Plate 1.1) The first was that the earth was composed of five ring-shaped zones, three of which – two at the poles and one wide band on either side of the Equator – were uninhabitable because of either extreme cold or extreme heat. Only the two temperate zones – one in the northern, the other in the southern hemisphere – were inhabited. The antipodes dwelt in the southern hemisphere, but they could never meet the inhabitants of the northern hemisphere as it was impossible to penetrate the hot zone. Some Christian writers found this problematic because the Bible stated that all the people who lived on earth after the flood were descendants of Noah, and all the peoples of the earth should sooner or later be able to receive the word of God. The second dominant image was that of the division of the northern land mass into three continents, Europe, Africa and Asia, separated from each other by three broad stretches of water: the Mediterranean Sea (Europe–Africa), the Don and the Black Sea (Europe–Asia) and the Nile (Asia–Africa).

For the Christian Middle Ages, the geometric centre, not only of the northern continents but of the entire earth, was Jerusalem. This geographical representation formed the basis of different types of what are known as O-T maps (a T-shaped arrangement of three continents on a circular ground plan with Jerusalem in the middle). A far more accurate mapping of the (inhabited) world came in sight when the Venetians brought Ptolemy's standard geographical work, the *Geography*, from Constantinople shortly after 1200. This work propagated and indicated the use of degrees of latitude and longitude, showing how the curved surface of the earth should be reproduced in a flat depiction. However, a Latin translation of this work was not produced until 1400. In a sense, this was tragic because respect for Ptolemy's great authority impeded any substantial new improvement in cartography resulting from the journeys of discovery.

At the heart of the ancient view of mankind was the remarkable idea that the general condition of the human body was determined in the first place by the four primary qualities and thereafter by all sorts of other external influences. This is known as the interference theory and dates back to Aristotle, but it was given its classical representation only in the work of the great Greek doctor, Galen of Pergamum (*c.* 129–200). Galen saw the body as a microcosm or, more accurately, as a reduced reflection of the sublunary realm. Just as four different combinations of the four primary qualities formed the four elements of matter, so on the scale of the human body they formed the four humours or bodily fluids: hot and wet made blood, hot and dry made yellow bile or choler (*cholera* in Greek), cold and wet made phlegm (*flegma* in Greek), cold and dry made black bile or melancholy (Greek, *melancholia*). All individuals had their own mixture of four fluids, which determined their *complexio* or 'temperament'. So, in addition to more or less 'melancholic' and 'choleric' types, there were also 'phlegmatic' and 'sanguine' ones. 'Temperament' had not only a particular exterior and a particular physical state, it also generated specific character traits. To complicate matters even further it was believed that other factors, preferably divisible by four, could influence the *complexio* and thus the state of health of an individual; these factors included the four divisions of the day, the four seasons, the four points of the compass and the four gustatory qualities (salty, sour, bitter, sweet). Should a person fall ill, physically or mentally, then the foremost task of the attending physician was to diagnose how, under the influence of certain factors, the patient's specific mixture of humours had been disturbed; the treatment could then be adapted accordingly, aimed at restoring the body's balance. In addition, the physician had to take into account the patient's sex or age, or the part of the day or the season in which he administered his medicine.

Humans were not the only living beings in the universe. Medieval people were thoroughly aware of the essential difference between plants, animals and human beings. Only the latter were endowed with an *anima rationalis* (a soul that was able to reason), with intellectual insight, linguistic ability and a conscious will. The originally Platonic conviction that the rational soul worked only through divine enlightenment – in Christian terms, through the intervention of the Holy Ghost – was widespread.

Mankind shared the terrestrial area not only with plants and animals but also with angelic beings (Latin *genii*, cf. Arabic *djini*), who dwelt in the air between the earth and the ether. The invisible good spirit who, in the ancient view, guided every individual and was 'witness and keeper' of a person's life, in the New Testament took on a Christian shape as the 'guardian angel', who protected every human being day and night from the tricks and guiles of devils. The latter in turn had emerged from the evil spirits of Antiquity. Most angels dwelt in the perfect heaven; they were purely etherial beings. The medieval image of them drew much from the work of Pseudo-Dionysius, an anonymous Christian writer from the beginning of the sixth century, wrongly identified with Dionysius the Areopagite, who was an Athenian convert of St Paul. Writings by Pseudo-Dionysius surfaced round 750 in Frankish Gaul, where Dionysius had come to be equated with St Denis, the legendary first bishop of Paris. In one of his works, Pseudo-Dionysius divided the angels into nine, hierarchically ordered 'choirs'. This arrangement came to form the basis of a real devotion to angels and a serious doctrine dealing with angels (angelology) in medieval thought, traces of which (cherubim, archangels) survive today.

THE HEAVY BURDEN OF *AUCTORITAS*

Praised by one of his pupils as the 'most abundant source of Letters to be found in France', Bernard of Chartres is credited with the famous statement, 'We are like dwarves on the shoulders of giants, so that we can see more than they can, and at a greater distance, not by virtue of any sharpness of sight on our part, or any physical distinction, but because we are carried high and raised up by their giant size.' Such a metaphor testifies to both profound respect and great self-confidence, and that is precisely the feeling that must have been in the air *c.* 1100 when Bernard made his statement. The reverse of the image is also true. When Bernard was alive, most of the giants had been dead for a thousand years or more, but the weight of their authority continued to press no less heavily upon intellectual enquiry. From that perspective it was the dwarves who carried the giants as a heavy burden with them.

Great awe for the authority of the past often has been considered to be a fundamental characteristic of medieval thought and scholarship. While that is certainly true, it is also important to define the relationship between respect for authority and scholarship in the Middle Ages more precisely. The practice of scholarship, then as now, always has entailed that new research is embedded into existing authoritative pronouncements – otherwise footnotes and literature lists would be unnecessary. The age of the pronouncements is not important; important is that they still matter, and can be fully and fundamentally discussed. However, the meaning of medieval Latin '*auctoritas*' was essentially different: a text with *auctoritas* in principle revealed an irrefutable 'truth'. The only discussion possible was whether an author or a text possessed *auctoritas*. Moreover, the authority of a writer was not reflected in all his books. Not all the works of the most authoritative Father of the Church, St Augustine, for example, did carry the weight of *auctoritas*. It was also realized, especially after the twelfth century, that the revelation of the 'truth' in authoritative texts depended first on the quality of the textual tradition and second on the text's interpretation by the reader/user. And interpretations did vary. 'An authority has a wax nose; it can be turned in different directions (*in diversum sensum*)', wrote Alan of Lille at the end of the twelfth century with a certain sense of humour, for Latin *sensus* could mean both 'direction' and 'meaning'.

In spite of the burden of *auctoritas* medieval intellectuals thus had some, admittedly limited, room to manoeuvre. Throughout the Middle Ages the authority of the Bible and the dogmas of the Catholic Church prevailed as an absolute precondition and an unavoidable point of reference for every form of intellectual effort. This is why the leaders of the early Church had viewed the Graeco-Roman heritage with such mixed feelings: should it be plundered and diverted to their own use, as Augustine thought, or should it be contemptuously ignored? Fortunately Augustine's authority proved unassailable on this point.

BOX 12.1 ADVANCES IN MEDICINE? HUMAN DISSECTION AND SURGERY IN THE MIDDLE AGES

During the Middle Ages the practice of the medical and paramedical professions was as many-hued as it was obscure. At one extreme were the better-educated doctors, who were university-trained from the thirteenth century onwards. At the other extreme was 'folk medicine', based entirely on experience, which was handed-down and practised by a disordered army of amateurs and charlatans who promised to cure their needy patients with magic spells, numerical formulas, little prayers, tarot cards or their own home-made potions, prescriptions and pills. Between the two extremes there was a growing army of surgeons, apothecaries and herbalists (*herbarii*), especially in the towns, all organized into recognized guilds; in their wake came yet other artisans and tradesmen who were involved with medical treatments on the side, such as the barbers who let blood, pulled teeth and performed minor operations ('prodding' a cataract, for example), bathhouse managers and masseurs who specialized in setting broken limbs, and midwives who, in an emergency, carried out life-threatening caesarian sections.

The fact that university-educated doctors were not visibly more successful in their treatment of patients explains why they never managed to gain a far-reaching monopoly over medical practice or to control it by other means. This again was due to the lack of progress in the medical study in the medieval universities. Just as nowadays, the study consisted of a theoretical and a practical part. Pathology, governed as it was by the ancient Greek theory of

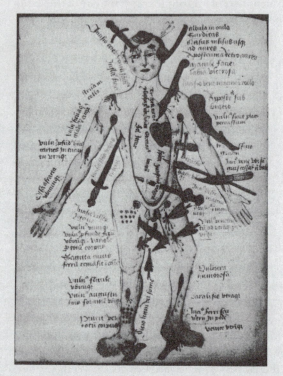

'Man with wounds', from the surgical manual *Surgical Treatment for Blows, Stab and Gunshot Wounds*

humours, was central to the theoretical part. The tripartite division of the practical part into dietetics, pharmacy and surgery was borrowed from the same tradition. The increasing emphasis on the theoretical aspects of the study of medicine, influenced by the great success of Aristotelian natural philosophy in the thirteenth century, was crippling for the advance of practical surgery and, moreover, heightened tensions between university-educated doctors (often called *fysici*, later *doctores medicinae*), and traditionally trained surgeons, apothecaries and herbalists. The physicians believed that the latter did not have the theoretical knowledge to make accurate diagnoses. Yet both groups joined forces in their fight against real quacks and charlatans.

Real progress in one branch of medicine, surgery, seemed to become possible when dissection of the human corpse, which had met much resistance and aversion in both ancient Graeco-Roman and Arab-Islamic medical science, became tolerated in the Latin-Christian West. The earliest reports of dissection date from the first half of the twelfth century, and, despite regular protests from the Church, secular authorities did allow it from that time onwards. Yet this did not immediately deepen the knowledge of human anatomy and physiology. Again the main reason for this seems to be the authoritative way of thinking: when dissecting corpses, academically educated doctors were in fact only looking for confirmation of what they believed they knew already from the textbooks of Galen and Avicenna. There was nothing resembling systematic anatomical and physiological research, and the gradual advances in surgery seem to have been made outside the circuit of academic medicine.

Research in Italy has shown that the dissection of human corpses took place within four different contexts. First, in surgery practicals used in medical training at the universities. From the end of the thirteenth century new manuals were written specially for this purpose by famous academic surgeons from Italy and France, such as Lanfranc of Milan, Henri de Mondeville and Guy de Chauliac. Second, in the exercise of their profession, physicians who were curious and wanted to know what their patients had died from opened up their bodies. This could be called real autopsy. It sometimes happened at the express wish of the patients themselves, or their relatives, who hoped thus to avoid dying from the same sickness; in other cases, family members were opposed to any such *post mortem* examination. Third, in the context of forensic autopsy. Dissection then took place at the request of a court of law wanting to establish the cause of a victim's death, and hoping for clues about the perpetrator and the weapon used. The fourth context was that of the disposal of the dead. In the Middle Ages, bodies of important people were embalmed in a number of ways; the brains and internal organs were removed as a first step in the procedure. In the case of saints, it was hoped that dissection would reveal external signs of their saintliness, like the form of a cross that was clearly visible on the heart of St Clara of Montefalco (d. 1308), cut open by her sister nuns. In addition, if people had died far from home, but their relatives wanted to bury them nearby, it was easier to trasport mere bones than complete bodies. To this end a body would be cut up and boiled. Occasionally, the heart would be kept separate.

The bodies of executed criminals were normally made available for scientific dissection; not so much to make the sentence tougher but because often the criminals were strangers and there was therefore little danger of hurting their bereaved relatives. By the end of the fifteenth century, for the same reason, the bodies of people who had died in hospitals without any family were increasingly used for dissection. At that time there was an enormous increase in the demand for corpses because of the sudden broadening of surgical education. It was only then that the study of human anatomy reached a higher level. This is evident from the new generation of high-quality surgical manuals appearing rapidly one after the other in the second half of the sixteenth century – among them those of Jacopo Berengario da Carpi, Niccolò Massa, and especially that of Andreas Vesalius of Brabant who taught in Padua. Painters and sculptors were often present at dissections in Italian universities; their efforts to emulate Antiquity's great works of art made them particularly interested in human anatomy. The brilliant sketchbooks of Leonardo da Vinci reveal how this custom bore fruit.

It seemed that nothing could quench the passion of university teachers, students and visual artists for anatomical and physiological research. The great Vesalius was famed for the enthusiasm with which he seized upon bodies, sometimes, it was said, of people who were not yet truly dead. Cases are known from Italy in which the courts handed over criminals, sentenced to death, directly to surgeons, who could then kill them before making a start on dissection. Occasionally the dissection devotees went too far in the eyes of their contemporaries. In his *Life of the Artists*, Giorgio Vasari recounts a story of the sculptor Silvio Cosini from Fiesole, rather reminiscent of the movie *Silence of the Lambs*; after a dissection he had the complete skin of a criminal made into a coat, convinced that if he wore it the dead bandit's physical strength would be transferred to him. This sort of story, whether true or not, led to a growing opposition to human dissection in the middle of the sixteenth century.

Literature: Heinrich Schipperges, *Der Garten der Gesundheit, Medizin im Mittelalter* (Munich, 1987). Nancy G. Siraisi, *Medieval and Early Renaissance Medicine: An Introduction to Knowledge and Practice* (Chicago, 1990). Luis García-Ballester *et al.* (eds), *Practical Medicine from Salerno to the Black Death* (Cambridge, 1994). Katherine Park, 'The criminal and the saintly body: autopsy and dissection in Renaissance Italy', *Renaissance Quarterly* 47 (1994), pp. 1–33. *Illustration*: Schipperges, p. 115.

The higher education programme of late Antiquity in the early Middle Ages

Scholarship became a rare commodity during the early Middle Ages, but insofar as opportunities for intellectual formation and higher education continued to exist in monasteries or in *civitates*, they were grafted onto the classical Roman syllabuses. At the heart of this was the study of *artes liberales* ('free arts' or 'free skills'), a broad spectrum of disciplines standardized by Marcus Terentius Varro (116–27 BC). Varro distinguished nine arts: grammar, dialectics or logic, rhetoric, geometry, arithmetic, astronomy, harmonics, medicine and architecture. Over the centuries medicine and architecture were reclassified as 'mechanical' arts, so that by late Antiquity seven liberal arts remained, whereby 'liberal' (free) referred to the fact that their practice was free from manual labour. It implied that the practitioner of the liberal arts was both a free man and well off. From the Carolingian period the seven liberal arts were usually divided into two groups: the *trivium*, the collective name for the linguistic arts, those connected with the spoken and written word, and the *quadrivium*, the collective name for the four mathematical disciplines. During the early Middle Ages education in the seven 'liberal arts' was supplemented by training in the *ethica*, ethics or moral philosophy. The arts and ethics together represented the whole field of learning (*scientia* or *philosophia* in medieval Latin) at that time.

There were, of course, textbooks for these higher studies. For ethics there was the adaptation of Seneca's moral advice to Emperor Nero made by Bishop Martin of Braga (*c.* 515–580). For education in the liberal arts, by far the most used was the encyclopaedia of Martianus Capella, a contemporary and compatriot of Augustine, although some objected to the fact that Martianus was pagan. Augustine, along with practically every scholar in the centuries after him with whose names we are still familiar, Boethius and Cassidorus in Ostrogothic Italy, Isidore of Seville in Visigothic Spain, Gregory of Tours in Merovingian Gaul, drew extensively on this source in the didactic treatises that they themselves wrote concerning the arts. Isidore (*c.* 570–636) dealt with the seven liberal arts in the beginning of his *Etymologiae*, an encyclopaedic text in 20 books that, with the help of word definitions, attempted to give a systematic overview of all the knowledge available at the time. For the whole of the Middle Ages, the *Etymologiae* enjoyed an enormous popularity, apparent from the more than a thousand manuscripts of this vast work still in existence. Even though the Roman study of the arts remained at the heart of all higher education in the Middle Ages, it served a different purpose than in Antiquity: to provide the resources and develop the intellectual skills necessary for the 'real work' towards which every intellectual effort should be directed: the study of the Bible, of the great Fathers of the Church and of other important canonical texts such as the creeds and confessions of faith established in Church councils. For therein was every truth worth knowing. Much of the meaning lay hidden, however, and could only be exposed with support from the liberal arts. This was why Augustine cherished the pious hope that every Christian would receive at least an elementary education.

In reality, the number of young people who had access to any form of intellectual education was drastically reduced in the early Middle Ages. Education was only available for a small circle of young people destined for a life in a monastery or in the secular clergy. There were only two places where an education could be acquired in the early Middle Ages: in the schools attached to the cathedrals and in the monasteries, although it is unlikely that each and every cathedral and abbey had its own school. Moreover, the repeated calls to improve education, heard at councils until into the twelfth and thirteenth centuries, strongly suggest that in many schools little more than elementary grammar and Bible studies were taught; there was certainly no question of generally available full education in the liberal arts. The few schools that did flourish in the early Middle Ages often existed in perhaps unlikely places, such as Anglo-Saxon England. These produced a number of the most prominent intellectuals of the early Middle Ages, the greatest of whom was the Venerable Bede (673–735). Bede spent most of his life in the abbeys of Wearmouth and Jarrow on the east coast of the kingdom of Northumbria. Among his principal works are a history of Anglo-Saxon England (*Historia ecclesiastica gentis Anglorum*, 'Ecclesiastical History of the English People'), written in classical style, and a survey of the natural sciences (*De natura rerum*, 'On the Nature of Things'). The latter, though based on Isidore of Seville, nevertheless went further because, unlike Isidore, Bede had direct access to the best-known encyclopaedia of natural science from Roman Antiquity, the *Historia Naturalis* of Pliny the Elder (d. AD 79).

THE CAROLINGIAN RENAISSANCE

On the Continent the limited formation of *literati* – those people who had access to ancient and early Christian knowledge and who therefore had to be able to read and write Latin – received a new impulse under the Carolingians. Even though Charlemagne never was what some scholars have described as an 'exalted inspector of elementary schools' (De Jong)

who launched a literacy campaign, his support for wider accessibility to elementary education, as expressed in the great reform capitulary *Admonitio Generalis* (General Exhortation), was real enough. It championed a broadening of education and a general moral-religious revival. Texts from the time referred to the *emendatio populi christiani*, the improvement of the Christian people. This revival, and the reforms to the Church and monasteries connected with it, transformed the worldly ruler – in the Roman-Byzantine and also the Arab-Islamic tradition – into the principal guardian of the religious community. Among his primary tasks was that of furthering *pietas* ('piety'), a life which was acceptable to God and which would lead his subjects along the narrow path to salvation in the world to come.

There was, of course, a wide gulf between such lofty ideals and their realization. Certainly for ordinary laymen the *emendatio* offensive did not mean much. The members of the tiny intellectual elite were encouraged to write Latin in the classical literary manner so that they could better understand the Bible and Church Fathers and not make technical mistakes in the Church liturgy. This brings us to the heart of the Carolingian renaissance, which we should see first and foremost as a humanistic movement in the strict sense of the term. The collecting and copying of manuscripts of ancient texts, which formed a substantial part of it, was of exceptional significance for western culture. The oldest surviving version of most ancient literary texts dating from the Roman period can be found in a Carolingian manuscript. In other words, if the Carolingians had not taken the trouble to collect and copy the material, probably several times over, then knowledge of the famous works of Cicero, Virgil, Ovid, Julius Caesar, Tacitus, Seneca and countless others would have been lost for ever. Some historians even suggest that for this reason alone 'the true renaissance was the Carolingian renaissance' (Mostert).

Nonetheless, the Carolingian renaissance was a 'movement' carried by a very small circle of people. At its heart was a select and colourful company of learned confidants of the king, men who were attached to the court schools for varying lengths of time and who generally ended up as bishops or abbots in the great imperial monasteries. At the time of Charlemagne, the greatest living scholar was considered to be the

Anglo-Saxon, Alcuin of York. He is generally thought to have been the ideological designer of Charlemagne's imperial ambitions. Alcuin ended his brilliant career as abbot of the Abbey of St Martin at Tours, where, at the request of the emperor, he produced a completely revise standard version of the Vulgate. In 787 Charlemagne welcomed another foreign scholar into his service, the Spaniard Theodulf, to formulate a suitable response to the iconoclastic views of the emperor in Byzantium. Later, he was appointed bishop of Orléans. Hildebald's career went in reverse order. He was bishop of Cologne before he became arch-chaplain, that is to say, head of the royal chapel, which made him the king's chancellor and an important royal counsellor. This intellectual inner circle also had laymen among its members, such as Einhard, Charlemagne's master builder and biographer, and Angilbert, who lived with, though did not marry, Charlemagne's daughter Berta. He was the prop and stay of her half-brother, Pippin, and his poetic talents earned him the nickname of 'Homer'. Under Louis the Pious and his sons, Hrabanus Maurus, Alcuin's pupil, was for a long time the uncrowned king of the intellectual elite. He in turn educated several talented young men who continued the humanistic tradition in the ninth century, such as Walafrid Strabo, tutor of Charles the Bald and later abbot of Reichenau.

The Carolingian renaissance did not introduce any changes to the educational curriculum. Logic and the disciplines of the quadrivium were particularly neglected, with the exception of the arithmetics needed for calendar calculations, and the rare experts in these fields were looked on as half-magicians. John Scotus Eriugena ('John, the Irish-born Scot'), the court scholar and close friend of Charles the Bald, was said to have become a star that roamed the firmament after his death. He was one of the few western scholars who still knew Greek in his time. Scotus translated several works by Pseudo-Dionysius the Areopagite from Greek, which became very popular and strengthened the Neoplatonic tradition in Catholic philosophy. Gerbert of Aurillac, a young man of simple origins who received an education in the liberal arts in the Spanish March, became a legend in his lifetime. He attached great importance to the mathematical subjects of the quadrivium, which as a result of Arabic influences were

taught there to a far higher level than elsewhere in the West. He created a sensation by using scale models and figures that were displayed in the front of the class on large pieces of parchment sewn together – the earliest known use of a flip-chart. His familiarity with instruments like the abacus and the astrolabe gave him the mystique of a wizard, while to his enemies he was a 'servant of Satan'. He became spiritual advisor of the German king/emperor Otto III (983–1002) and architect of his policy for the *renovatio imperii Romani* ('renewal of the Roman Empire'). Otto appointed him archbishop of Ravenna and later pope (Silvester II, 999–1003).

THE TWELFTH-CENTURY RENAISSANCE: AN INTELLECTUAL REVOLUTION?

The term 'twelfth-century renaissance' itself predates the publication of Jakob Burckhardt's *Die Kultur der Renaissance in Italien* (1860). But it only really became accepted in 1927 with the publication of *The Renaissance of the Twelfth Century* by the American medievalist Charles Homer Haskins as a sort of delayed reaction to Burckhardt. Contradicting the title of his own book, Haskins painted the elite culture of the twelfth century not so much as a rebirth of Antiquity but as a magnificent revival of literary and intellectual life, the result of a 'general quickening of the spirit'. Many attempts have since been made to give a more exact explanation of the concept 'twelfth-century renaissance'. Some have seen it as a sort of Italian renaissance, taking place three centuries earlier, whose glorious epicentre was France, not Italy, but which otherwise shared the same main features: a flowering of humanism and a clear recognition of human individuality. Others have given the twelfth-century renaissance a character of its own by embedding it in the exceptional economic and social dynamics of the years between about 1000 and 1200. The crusades, the colonization movements, the growth of international trade, rapid urbanization and increasing geographical and social mobility formed the background to a new 'spiritual hunger' (Chenu), to a new openness of mind and self-awareness, to a drive for intellectual renewal and superiority, even to a real belief in progress.

These two approaches meet on a number of points. First of all, they share the opinion that a revolutionary new view of nature, and thus in fact of 'the world', was revealed in twelfth-century thinking. Magical and purely symbolic interpretations of natural phenomena were at last abandoned, and the monastic ideal of spurning the world was put into perspective. Following in Plato's footsteps, scholars now began to discern some 'order' in nature, which naturally reflected the boundless goodness and wisdom of its creator. Moreover, the natural order and its laws, such as the principle of causality, could be understood rationally because humans themselves, the only creatures endowed with the power of reason, held a central place in that order. Any study of the natural order had to begin with sensory experience that would stimulate reason. Visible for the first time was a plea for both empirical-inductive and logical-deductive approaches in (natural) scientific research. The third method, the mathematical, was also used more.

A major difference between the twelfth-century renaissance and the Italian renaissance of the late Middle Ages is that in the later period the humanists never succeeded in dominating higher, or university, education, while in the twelfth century the *scholae* ('schools'), the forerunners of the universities, were at the very centre of the new humanistic ideas and methods. This close link was aptly expressed in the term 'scholasticism', which broadly refers to the education in the *scholae*. In addition, twelfth-century scholasticism has acquired a narrower, technical meaning in the sense of a particular analytic method based on Aristotelian logic, but adopted in every academic discipline, both in teaching and in the production of text books.

Literati, collectors and translators

Before we look at the developments in the *scholae*, we must point out that the twelfth-century renaissance also had a strong humanistic orientation in a narrow sense. Many intellectuals known from the twelfth century were first and foremost literati, collectors of ancient texts, and also writers who, with visible pleasure but varied results, produced their own literary works in the classical style and following classical models. Far more Latin literary texts have survived from the

eleventh and twelfth centuries than from the two preceding or two succeeding centuries. Some of them are considered among the high points of medieval Latin literature. What is remarkable about this literature is that for the first time since late Antiquity it displays a thorough familiarity with ancient non-Christian themes and mythological conceptions.

Such dazzling literary activity also revealed a diligent search for ancient, non-literary texts. The Graeco-Roman legacy still was not fully exploited, particularly in what we would now call the natural sciences, mathematics and logic. We already have mentioned one important reason for this: most elementary texts in these fields were written in Greek, which, with few exceptions, no longer was mastered by western intellectuals in the early Middle Ages. Renewed acquaintance with ancient Greek learning depended, therefore, on an increase in translating. At the end of the eleventh century there were two major channels: the Byzantine world and the Arabic world. The great conquests of the first century following the establishment of Islam in the Middle East and North Africa brought the Arabs into contact with the achievements of ancient Greek philosophy. These were avidly absorbed, and then expanded in different fields. Far earlier than in the West, the Arabic world showed a serious interest in exact sciences such as mathematics, astronomy and medicine.

During the eleventh century, Spain and Sicily served as conduits for Arabic knowledge to the West. The conquest in 1085 of Toledo, the centre of Moorish culture, and the establishment of Norman power in Sicily at about the same time, were strong stimuli to the intellectual encounter between East and West. The Christian elite's hunger for new knowledge overcame its aversion to Islam, and some openly admired the scientific achievements of the infidel. One of them, the Englishman Adelard of Bath (*c.* 1070–1150), scoured the Mediterranean in his search for Arabic knowledge, which he equated with independent and critical rational thought and considered far superior to slavishly following '*auctoritas*'. He was the first to translate the complete text of two elementary mathematical treatises, Euclid's *Elements* and the *Algebra* of al-Khwarizmi (d. *c.* 850), the bane of every schoolchild even today. It is thanks to al-Khwarizmi that we use 'arabic' numerals for counting, although we should not forget that the Arabs brought this notation from India.

The most productive of the translators was an Italian, Gerard of Cremona, who in the middle of the twelfth century spent some time in Toledo translating between 70 and 100 Greek and Arab treatises from Arabic into Latin. In addition to Aristotle's *Analytica Posteriora*, a cornerstone of the 'new logic', these included *Technè*, Galen's principal medical work and Ptolemy's astronomical compilation *The Great Treatise*, better known under its Arabic name *Almagest* – works which were of the greatest importance for the further support and refinement of the western view of man and the world.

Translations made directly from Greek did became available not much later, thanks to the efforts of Italians from cities with large commercial interests in the eastern Mediterranean, such as Venice and Pisa. Already before the middle of the twelfth century James of Venice had translated most of Aristotle's logical treatises from the Greek. These direct translations were important because Arabic – a non-Indo-European 'intermediate language' – often corrupted the quality of the original Greek versions. The Fourth Crusade and the establishment of the Latin Empire (1204–1261) gave a further powerful spur to the translation and collection of Greek texts, because Greece came under western rule for more than half a century and western scholars had unfettered access to the treasures of Greek libraries. The Flemish Dominican, William of Moerbeke (*c.* 1215–1286), was one of those who took advantage of the situation. After he had been appointed bishop of Corinth, he found the time and opportunity to translate some 50 works from Greek into Latin, including almost all the works of Aristotle and Archimedes. In the same period, Michael Scot (*c.* 1175–*c.* 1232), who also acted as Emperor Frederick II's court astrologer, alchemist and personal physician in Sicily, provided translations, all from Arabic, of Aristotle's *Metaphysics*, as well as of several major commentaries on Aristotle by the Andalusian philosopher Ibn Rushd (1126–1198), generally known in the West as Averroës.

The revival of Aristotle

It was Gerbert of Aurillac who, around the turn of the first millennium, had presided over the marvellous Aristotelian revival in the medieval *scholae*. As we have seen, Gerbert was a teacher in heart and soul, who did everything possible to improve the quality of the liberal arts curriculum. Two matters are worth recording in connection with the development of scholasticism. First, Gerbert introduced the *disputatio* or oral debate as a didactic art in his teaching of rhetoric. Second, he made more room in the curriculum for lessons in logic, or dialectics, in order to improve his pupils' debating skills. Their knowledge, first developed by Aristotle, had never been entirely lost during the early Middle Ages, mainly due to Anicius Boethius (*c.* 480–524), a statesman and philosopher in Ostrogothic Italy. Boethius translated Aristotle's elementary treatises on logic, together with an introduction by Porphyrius, the Neoplatonist (end of third century AD), into Latin,

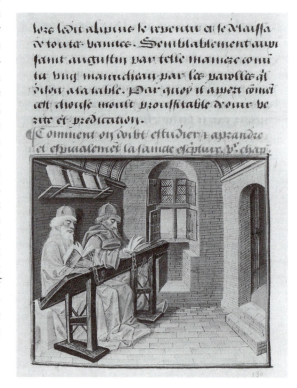

Plate 12.1 The consultation of books on a chain in a medieval library

and added his own commentaries about the theory of argumentation. However, very little of this had permeated the early medieval discipline of dialectics until Gerbert of Aurillac made the case for the reintroduction of what later came to be known as 'old logic'. From the beginning of the twelfth century Boethius' translations of Aristotle's more advanced and much fuller treatises on logic were rescued from oblivion, constituting what we refer to as the 'new logic'. Only one work was still missing, the *Analytica Posteriora*, which eventually was translated first from the Arabic and soon afterwards (*c.* 1150) from the Greek. Aristotle's complete works on logic, sometimes called *Organon* or 'Instrument', were available to the West once again.

But Aristotle's influence extended beyond his works on logic. The great Greek philosopher had also written extensively on natural phenomena, metaphysics and ethics. This entire corpus was translated into Latin between about 1150 and 1250, both from the Arabic and from the Greek. In the Arab world Aristotle was considered to be *the* philosopher, just as he was in the Christian West. Arabic scholars such as Averroës wrote major commentaries to Aristotle's psychological and metaphysical works, which soon became compulsory reading in the universities of Western Europe. The study of Aristotle came to dominate higher learning, as is demonstrated by the number of manuscripts of his work that have survived in medieval Latin, some 2,000 of them, a number that is approached only by Galen's medical texts. Aristotle thus became the uncrowned leader in the establishment of a new academic paradigm, which we refer to as scholastic rationalism.

The influence of the new logic

The enormous importance of the revival of dialectics/logic as a fully developed academic discipline must not be underestimated. In a world with very little insight into the workings of natural phenomena, at least not at the level of physical laws and chemical processes, and in which there were few impulses to expand that insight, dialectics – the art of logical reasoning – provided the best possible intellectual anchor to bring order into what must have seemed infinitely varied and complex. In that light the scientific work of the first generation of intellectuals, who combined their extraordinary knowledge of authoritative Christian texts with a sound training in the 'new' Aristotelian logic, radiated an almost shameless optimism and self-confidence. They thought that all of life could be understood by using logic to make a systematic record of the relationships between man and nature and, above all, between humankind and God. The real motive was the growing realization that the traditional authorities (the Bible and Church Fathers) were in themselves too often contradictory. Many scholars were convinced that inconsistencies could only be confronted and then eradicated by careful and logical analysis of texts. This presented them for the first time with the fundamental epistemological question: to what extent does language, processed into written texts, represent perceptual, 'objective' reality?

From the polemic between Berengarius and Lanfranc about the essence of the eucharist (see Box 12.2) it appears that Aristotelian logic was given an entirely new dimension when it was applied to matters of Christian dogma. The value of this application was contentious from the outset. Its supporters believed that God and the divine became more approachable through a process of rational thought. Opponents such as Peter Damian (1007–1072), one of the leaders of the Gregorian reform movement, were equally firm in their conviction that the possibilities of reason were limited in that respect, that the dogmas of the Holy Church were threatened by rationalism or that God could only be found by a mystic path, that of non-rational contemplation. In the middle of the twelfth century, these contrasting views were personified in Bernard of Clairvaux and the famous logician and theologian, Peter Abelard. Mindful of Abelard's maxim, 'we can only come to [rational] inquiry through doubt and only through inquiry can we reach the truth', Bernard was blistering in his attacks: 'Be done! Away with the mere thought that the Christian faith knows any of the limits suggested by those academics who doubt everything and know nothing. I am certain of one sentence of Paul, "For I know him whom I have believed" (II Tim. 1:12). And I know for certain that I cannot be brought into confusion.'

But there was no stopping the advance of the new approach. The ultimate confidence in what human reason could achieve was the rational proof of God's existence dating from this time, such as those made by

BOX 12.2 'THIS IS MY BODY': LEARNED DISCUSSION ABOUT TRANSUBSTANTIATION IN THE EUCHARIST

One of the most renowned debates of early scholasticism concerned the real meaning of the sacrament of the Eucharist. It brought Berengarius, a teacher at the cathedral school of Tours, into conflict with Lanfranc of Pavia, abbot of the Norman monastery of Le Bec and, from 1066 until his death in 1089, archbishop of Canterbury. The question was what exactly takes place during Mass in the ritual commemoration of the Last Supper, when the priest, while breaking bread and drinking wine, speaks the words, 'This is my body' and 'This is my blood'? Nobody could contend that the host had outwardly changed from bread into human flesh or the wine into human blood, yet nobody dared to deny that Christ really was present after the consecration of the bread and wine. Both Berengarius and Lanfranc, therefore, saw the sacrament of the Eucharist as a *figura* or *similitudo*, a symbolically charged metaphor. But in Lanfranc's interpretation the metaphor contained a mysterious manifestation of the 'naked truth', and pointed directly to a higher spiritual reality. Bread and wine do not turn into actual flesh and blood, but are experienced as such through the consecration. Berengarius found this absurd: for him, the words spoken at the consecration were a linguistic designation (*significatio*) of the living body of Christ. Only through linguistic and dialectical study of that application of meaning (*significare*) would it perhaps be possible to reveal the deeper truth of the Eucharist.

What is interesting is that both opponents used two fundamental concepts of Aristotelian logic, *substantia* and *accidentia*. Aristotle had introduced these concepts in order to be able to make a distinction between what we would now call the essential, tangible substrate of an object (*substantia*) and its inessential, external features or characteristics (*accidentia*). Lanfranc's contention was that the change of bread and wine was indeed essential (of substance) but not outwardly visible (accidental) – hence his solution has been called 'trans-substantiation'. According to the logic of Aristotle, such transformation was impossible. Hence it could take place only because God had intervened miraculously during the consecration of the host and sacramental wine, briefly suspending the laws of nature. Berengarius refuted this interpretation on logical grounds, and also produced the linguistic argument that in the formula, 'This is my body', 'This' could only refer to the host, which at that selfsame moment was raised on high by the celebrant. Clever as it was, Berengarius' interpretation did not survive because at the Fourth Lateran Council (1215) the doctrine of transubstantiation became official dogma.

St Anselm of Aosta (1033–1109), who followed Lanfranc first as abbot of Le Bec and later as archbishop of Canterbury. Anselm constructed a number of proofs for the existence of God a posteriori, meaning proofs that are derived from the visible result of God's intervention in the world – the creation. Of greater philosophical interest, however, is his proof a priori, known as *ratio Anselmi* ('Anselm's reasoning'), which has occupied the minds of great philosophers over the centuries, among them Immanuel Kant and Bertrand Russell. In fact what Anselm did was to attempt to prove the validity of Seneca's definition of God, 'God is the best and most sublime that man can imagine'. As was proper, Anselm examined this definition in light of a biblical quotation, from the fourteenth psalm which opens with the words, 'The fool hath said in his heart, There is no God'. Anselm propounded that even a fool would understand the words 'something that is the greatest that man can imagine'. If those words had any meaning then 'the greatest that man can imagine' must really exist; should that not be the case, and should 'the greatest' be merely a figment of the imagination, then man would still be able to think of something even greater than 'the greatest that man can imagine'; namely, the greatest that does exist in reality, outside the mind. For Anselm, of course, this 'greatest' could be no other than God. But it must be remembered that he expressly stated that this was a matter of faith, for that is one of the two contextual restrictions that precludes the loss of logical consistency in Anselm's proof. The other is the Neoplatonic idea that everything that of necessity exists both inside and outside the intellect is of a higher order of being than something that only does so potentially, such as most things in the natural world. For Anselm, the 'fool' in the psalm was the unbeliever. One of Anselm's maxims, taken from the Old Testament book of Isaiah, was *credo ut intelligam*, 'I believe in order that I may understand'. However powerful an instrument human reason might be, Anselm found that deeper insight was not possible without first believing. His other famous dictum, *fides quaerens intellectum*, 'faith seeking support in reason', stresses the crucial importance of faith. The difference in nuance between these two maxims expresses perfectly the contradictory feelings of devout men like Anselm who struggled with the relationship between faith and reason.

The man who finally made Aristotelian logic a cornerstone of scholastic rationalism was the Breton, Peter Abelard (1079–1142). As a young man he acquired a great reputation in Paris, first as a freely established teacher of dialectics, later as a teacher of theology at the cathedral school of Notre-Dame. His treatise *Sic et non* (literally 'Yes and No', meaning 'For and Against') shows his approach as a logician and is particularly interesting from a methodological point of view. For the first time the scholastic method of working can be seen in action. The text consists of 158 theological topics, *quaestiones*; each one opens with a question, after which the pros and cons of the possible answers are weighed up systematically and using the technique of logical analysis, before drawing a balanced conclusion. This treatment of *quaestiones disputatae* ('matters in dispute') became an increasingly fixed component of higher education in the course of the twelfth century. At the same time, too, scholastic textbooks started to follow the same template. There were fewer works in other genres, such as compendiums, encyclopaedic works or single tracts.

Nowadays we do not find this very surprising, but we should not forget that, until then, intellectuals were much burdened with *auctoritas* and by modern standards did not have a very critical approach to their source texts. Numerous errors and contradictions in

the body of authoritative texts came to light through Abelard's methodical approach. Known by friend and foe alike as 'our Aristotle' and as *peripateticus palatinus* (literally, 'Aristotle's pupil from Le Pallet [Abelard's birthplace]', but also meaning 'the paladin of Aristotle' or 'the vagrant from Le Pallet'), the Breton scholar even surpassed his Greek master. Aristotelian logic was aimed exclusively at establishing whether a process of reasoning was valid or not by testing the consistency of the connection between the propositions on which it rested. Abelard gave this procedure an important additional value by checking any possible differences of meaning depending on the context between similar terms used in the propositions. His aim was most certainly not to cast doubt upon the deeper truth of the texts that were so authoritative for Christian faith, but to critically examine the versions of the text in which they survived.

In addition to being a competent logician, Abelard was, to say the least, a colourful figure, as brilliant as he was arrogant, a man who 'made enemies with the dedication of a stamp-collector' (Brooke). 'Truly, the man takes pleasure in disputing everything, be it matters of faith or matters of the world', sighed one of his many critics with a mixture of dislike and admiration. It comes as no surprise, therefore, that Abelard's theological views were twice condemned by the Church, the second time at the Synod of Sens in 1140. Abelard was declared a heretic and sentenced to eternal silence. It was Bernard of Clairvaux who voiced the accusations at the synod, closing his speech with the words, 'Peter Abelard, from now on stick to your schoolboys and your young ladies'. This was a malicious reference to the event which brought Abelard more fame during his lifetime than his philosophical works – the turbulent relationship he had earlier with Heloise, niece of a canon of the Notre Dame in Paris. When she became pregnant he married her in secret and was emasculated by Heloise's enraged relatives. Both Heloise and Abelard then retired to a convent. We know of this from Abelard's frank autobiography, *Historia calamitatum* ('The Story of my Calamities') and from the passionate, but above all devout, letters that the now separated couple wrote to each other. Although their authenticity sometimes has been questioned, these documents are proof of the existence of a great sensitivity that was directed not only towards

God and the saints but also towards personal introspection and interpersonal relationships. In this connection another tract by Abelard, *Scito te ipsum* ('Know thyself', a reference to a saying from a Greek oracle and also the motto of the Roman emperor-philosopher, Marcus Aurelius), is considered a milestone. For the first time in Western Christian thought it is clearly contended that in judging sins the intention of the sinner should weigh more heavily than the nature of the sin. For Abelard, morality was thus always internal and personal. External penance without internal repentance and recovery of one's own moral integrity was completely meaningless. These ideas resonated with contemporary spirituality (see Chapter 8), with the revival of theological interest in the matter of predestination and with the greater emphasis put on admission of sin and repentance in the confessional. At the same time, they reveal the existence of a realization that human individuals are complex, self-conscious and responsible personalities who have interior lives and who are equipped with diverse and unique characteristics.

Natural philosophy and metaphysics

The second aspect of the Aristotelian revival was formed by the rediscovery of Aristotle's numerous *libri naturales* and his works on metaphysics and ethics. The former included works on physics, cosmology, meteorology, zoology and on sleep, dreams and memory. The term 'metaphysics' refers originally to the place allocated to Aristotle's treatment of what he called 'being as being' in the later editions of his works, coming after the works on physics ('metaphysics' means literally 'behind' or 'after physics'). Metaphysics is the philosophical search for the foundations of 'being', separate from sensory experience. Some commentators of Aristotle argued for a close connection between metaphysical and theological studies, others for the very opposite. Aristotle's contribution to ethics includes a broad moral guideline, known as the *Ethica Nicomachaea*, presumed to have been written for his son Nicomachos. It stood as a model for the second and most elaborate part of the *Summa Theologiae* of Thomas Aquinas.

Renewed acquaintance with this part of Aristotle's work also led to radical changes in higher education.

Eventually, these took the form of superimposing the three so-called philosophies on the traditional arts curriculum: rational philiosophy (comprising the Logica Nova), 'natural philosophy', including both Aristotelian physics and metaphysics, and moral philosophy (supplementing existing ethics with Aristotle). Of these three, natural philosophy needs a little explanation, because rendering it as 'physics' could easily create wrong associations. Natural philosophy was aimed at the rational investigation of the four ways or modalities by which 'natural bodies' (objects in nature) could change (e.g. movement or change of place) in conjunction with the four basic 'causes' or principles of movement or change in the universe (e.g. finality). As such, the study of natural philosophy comprised the entire fields of cosmology and astronomy, as well as physics, biology and psychology.

Among the early critics of Aristotles' increasingly firm hold on the arts curriculum was John of Salisbury (*c.* 1115–1180), who studied logic under Abelard before entering upon a long career as a diplomat in Rome, as a secretary to various archbishops of Canterbury, and finally as bishop of Chartres. In one of his chief works, the *Metalogicon* ('In defense of the *artes logicales*' – another name for the disciplines of the trivium), John complained of what he considered the excessive attention given in the arts curriculum to Aristotelian logic, at the expense of the other two subjects of the trivium, grammar and rhetoric. He saw this as an undesirable consequence because he believed that human superiority ultimately rested upon the power of the word. Linguistic competence was thus what mattered, an argument that anticipated the educational programme of the humanists in the fifteenth century. In the centuries after 1200 there was more widespread criticism of Aristotle, which led to repeated crises in scholarship. But the Aristotelians would not give way. Scholastic rationalism continued to dominate higher education until the eighteenth century.

The formation of universities

We have seen that the only centres of intellectual advancement during the early Middle Ages were the schools attached to cathedrals and monasteries. Looked at in that light, the formation of the universities can be seen as a liberation movement, gradually detaching higher education from the monopoly of monks and bishops. Exactly how this happened is not clear, but it is useful to mention three very different backgrounds. First, there was a tendency in the great *scholae* or *studia* for teachers or students, or both together, to organize themselves into corporations in order to look after their own interests. The common medieval Latin term for this type of corporation was *universitas*, which could very well be translated as 'guild'. Second, the growing demand for higher learning led to a broadening of the supply of education. Outside the scope of the liberal arts, specialized *scholae* began to appear for the study of medicine and written law; that is, Roman Justinian law or Church canonical law. The special teaching of the Bible and Church Fathers, which traditionally had topped off a liberal arts education, gradually developed into a separate and complete theological study. In those towns where there was more than one *schola*, this diversification in higher education led quite naturally to their working together, so that the first large schools with a number of faculties or branches came into being. Third, following the resolution of the Third Lateran Council in 1179, the Church relinquished its monopoly on education when it compelled the bishops to yield their exclusive rights to issue licences to teach

'everywhere' (*licentiae ubique docendi*) to recognized schools in their dioceses.

The teaching establishment that we now know as a university evolved gradually from all these developments, although it is difficult to say exactly when this happened. Nor did the liberation of higher education sketched above take place without a struggle. From the beginning, of course, the *scholae* were assured of the not insignificant support of the popes and of many rulers who made higher education the spearhead of their policy to improve the quality of their administration. There was fierce opposition, however, both from bishops and the monastic world. In Paris, for example, the chancellor or bishop's secretary disputed the infringement of his unique authority to grant the *licentia docendi* for many years. That the share of the monastic schools in higher education decreased was partly the fault of the monks themselves, for they had been severely critical of the direction in which higher education was moving. The new order of the Cistercians, in particular, had voiced dissatisfaction, and their comments were forceful. We have already mentioned how Bernard of Clairvaux hurled abuse at Abelard, calling him a danger to society and a heathen and a monster. Since canon law forbade the Cistercians to attend a school outside the monastery, they ran the

Map 12.1 European universities in the late Middle Ages

risk of becoming intellectually isolated by not responding to the new direction that the arts study was taking. The new mendicant orders, especially the Dominicans, recognized this problem and solved it by founding their own schools, with their own teachers, in large towns like Paris and Cologne. In this way, they could keep in touch with what was happening in the world of science. These schools were intended primarily for members of their orders, but very soon opened their door to other interested students. The example set by the mendicant orders was copied in time by other religious orders, including the Cistercians.

The process of trial and error, of support and opposition in the realm of administration and organization can be best explained in the light of developments in the two most important centres of higher learning in Western Europe: Paris and Bologna. In twelfth-century Paris there were schools in the neighbourhood of Notre-Dame (the old cathedral school) and near several abbeys on the left bank of the Seine, such as those of Saint-Victor and Mont-Sainte-Geneviève. Even before 1150 Paris was a mecca for young people; by 1200 it had between 3,000 and 4,000 students, perhaps 10 per cent of the town's population. There were nearly 150 *magistri* teaching there, more than a hundred in the arts, 20 each in the faculties of medicine and law, and eight in the faculty of theology. They had joined together to form a guild of teachers, first referred to in 1208. The influx of students caused all sorts of problems, varying from the organization of teaching programmes and the form that lectures should take to strained relationships between town and gown. All parties concerned (Church and secular authorities, townspeople, teachers and students) realized that matters concerning higher education required better regulation. This did actually happen around 1200, for in that year the combined schools of Paris were granted a royal charter recognizing their administrative autonomy. It also contained two other provisions of immense importance. First, the *scolares* (teachers and students) were placed under special royal protection from physical violence and damage to property. Second, they were placed under Church law: only the trial of very serious crimes would be heard in the royal court of law. This in fact put the *scolares* on an equal footing with the clergy, if they were not already clerics. This measure would have far-reaching consequences,

for it became the norm for all recognized universities of Europe when the pope confirmed the Paris privilege in 1231. It meant that members of university communities everywhere stood outside the secular system of justice and enjoyed clerical status.

The background to the University of Bologna's foundation was very different and had its origins in the training of lawyers unrelated to the Church. The Roman custom of recording business transactions between private individuals in writing had never disappeared in Italy. It was done by professional scribes, *notai* (Latin *notarii*, whence 'notary'), who were trained in the use of the correct, legally valid notation. The revival of the study of Roman Justinian law in the second half of the eleventh century gave a powerful stimulus to notarial training. Since Roman law was imperial law, the development of these notarial schools into a university was closely connected to imperial intervention, evident in the events of the Diet of Roncaglia in 1158. Frederick Barbarossa, consciously imitating Justinian, was assisted by four renowned lawyers from Bologna when he negotiated with the towns of northern Italy the matter of the *regalia*, 'the rights reserved for the king', which were set down in formulas taken from Roman law (even if Roman law did not know regalia as such). This was not surprising, for some years earlier Frederick had given the schools in Bologna a privilege under the far-sighted motto that 'the world [would be] controlled and enlightened by knowledge'.

Originally every teacher in Bologna formed a guild with his regular students. By 1200 the number of guilds was restricted to two student guilds, one for Italians and one for non-Italians. Teachers were excluded from membership. These student guilds rapidly grew into powerful organizations that, if necessary, would enforce demands made to the teachers or Bologna's commune government by shutting everything down through strikes or threatening to leave the town and continue their studies elsewhere. One of these threats was actually carried out, and the academic exodus led to the foundation of the University of Padua in 1222. The University of Cambridge was also established at about the same time after a similar secession, in this case from Oxford. The legal schools of Bologna enjoyed a fine reputation and were tacitly recognized as a university at about the same time.

Besides the great universities of Paris and Bologna, which evolved gradually from existing schools, the thirteenth century saw the foundation of universities 'out of nothing', often on royal initiative and always with royal or papal approval. The oldest known institutions of this sort were the universities of Salamanca in Castile (1218) and Naples (1224). Around 75 universities were created in this manner between 1200 and 1500. Some were small and specialized (such as the medical school at Salerno and the legal school in Orléans), others large and broadly based (Paris and Oxford). Between 1350 and 1500 it is estimated that a total of 750,000 students registered at universities – all male; women were not allowed.

One would expect the new universities to have been built mainly in urbanized districts, but this was only partly so. There were two important universities in England, for example, at a time when there were scarcely any large towns. Moreover, both were founded in relatively small, albeit old, towns (Oxford and Cambridge), and not in one of the few centres of importance that did exist (London or Winchester). On the other hand, the relatively densely populated Low Countries did not have a university until 1425. It was established not in Flanders but at Louvain, in Brabant. The German Empire, by no means a backward region in the twelfth and thirteenth centuries, was devoid of a university for a long time. The oldest was at Prague, in Bohemia (1348), followed in the second half of the fourteenth century by Vienna, Erfurt, Heidelberg and Cologne, although Cologne already had two illustrious *studia* for higher learning long before – the cathedral school and the school of the Dominican order, founded in 1248.

UNIVERSITY SCHOLARSHIP AND THE INTELLECTUAL CRISIS AT THE END OF THE THIRTEENTH CENTURY

University scholarship in action

University studies in the Middle Ages took a long time. Seven years was originally prescribed for an education in the liberal arts: four years for the baccalaureate (bachelor: BA) and then another three years to obtain the title of *magister artium* (master of [liberal] arts: MA)

with the teaching qualification, *licentia docendi*, attached to it. The higher studies were equally long – certainly theology, which normally took at least ten years. Since most students studied the arts before embarking upon advanced study, although this was not compulsory everywhere, those who stayed spent a considerable part of their lives at university. They probably formed a fairly small group, however, as most students dropped out after a couple of years or settled for the baccalaureate. Twelfth-century satirical texts may tell a different tale, but for a long time even a baccalaureate would have offered considerable prospects for a good position in society. There was a continual demand for academically educated administrators in the swelling bureaucracies of European kingdoms: the University of Naples was established with the explicit purpose of satisfying that demand. The labour market for these trained administrators worsened after 1300.

While Aristotle dominated the liberal arts curriculum, his works made accessible for students in manuals like the *Summulae logicales* ('Small handbooks for logic') by Peter of Spain (later to become Pope John XXI, 1276–1277) and innumerable commentaries on the natural arts, in theological training everything revolved round the study of the Bible and Church Fathers. For the first time, useful aids to Bible study were produced, facilitating systematic access to the text, such as a standard division of the text into chapters and verses, subject indexes and concordances. In the intellectual tradition of the early Middle Ages the Bible had of course been annotated countless times in the form of extensive treatises and commentaries and short marginal notes or glosses. Collections of these glosses had been made, but their quality was improved with the compilation of the *Glossa Ordinaria* ('Standard Gloss'), for a long time attributed to Walafrid Strabo but actually begun only in 1100 by Anselm of Laon and completed some years later by Gilbert of Poitiers and Peter Lombard. In about the middle of the twelfth century the latter produced an extensive collection of the teachings of the Church Fathers concerning Christian dogmas, all treated in accordance with the new format of logical argumentation. This compendium, the *Quattuor libri sententiarum* ('Four Books of Sentences'), rapidly achieved the status of the standard university textbook. A new handbook of biblical history, an historical interpretation of the Bible in common use in the late Middle Ages, dates from the same period. It was the *Historia Scholastica* by Peter Comestor ('Peter the Eater'), a compatriot of Peter Lombard and chancellor to his successor as bishop of Paris, Maurice de Sully.

The bibles for the study of law were the *Corpus iuris civilis*, of course, and the greatly enlarged and complex corpus of canonical texts, such as council decisions and papal decrees. Gratian, an Italian monk, brought some order to this chaos with the publication of his *Concordantia discordantium canonum* ('The Harmonization of Contradictory Laws'), which soon became known as the *Decretum Gratiani*. It dominated the study of Church law to such an extent that graduates often were referred to as 'decretists'. The most important medieval addition to this corpus, the *Liber Extra*, was completed in 1234. To simplify the study of Roman law, Accursius, a leading Bolognese jurist in the middle of the thirteenth century, compiled a *glossa ordinaria* ('standard gloss'), a systematic overview of nearly 100,000 glosses to Justinian's *Corpus iuris civilis* produced over the years in the law schools of Bologna. And, finally, the works of Hippocrates, Galen and several Arabic scholars, including Avicenna (Ibn Sina, 980–1039) and Constantinus Africanus (*c.* 1010–1087), dominated the study of medicine.

The course of an academic career in the early days of the medieval university is well illustrated by the life of the great theologian, Thomas Aquinas (1224–1274). He was a descendant of a high noble family near Monte Cassino, where he was sent at an early age to prepare for a career in the Church. Between 1239 and 1244 he studied the arts at the recently founded University of Naples and then, very much against the will of his family, he entered the Dominican order. There, his intellectual gifts were immediately recognized and he was sent to Paris and Cologne. Thomas immersed himself in the works of Aristotle and studied theology under one of the greatest minds of the thirteenth century, Albertus Magnus. As an advanced student in Cologne, Thomas held the function of *cursor biblicus*, which meant that he had to teach elementary Bible studies to new theological students. At the age of 27 he became a *baccalaureus* (young for the time) and began his study to become a master in theology.

As *baccalaureus* he also gave instruction in Peter Lombard's *Sententiae* and assisted the *magister residens* (professor with a tenured chair) in holding disputes. Finally, in 1255, Thomas himself became a *magister in Sacra Pagina*, professor of biblical studies (i.e. theology).

The main teaching tasks of a *magister* consisted of giving lectures (*lectiones*) and holding disputes. A dispute, as we have seen, required the treatment of a topic (*quaestio*) to be elaborated in accordance with the scholastic dialectical method. A distinction was made here between the *quastiones disputatae*, on more-or-less set subjects (often lasting for more than one day) and the *quaestiones quodlibetales* – free disputes in which the students could suggest their own topics. To underpin his lectures, Thomas wrote a number of treatises in *quaestio* form, one of which was the *Summa Theologiae*, intended for those embarking on theology. He also put down in writing the 253 *quaestiones disputatae*, which he had conducted and for which there was great demand amongst his audience. At the beginning of the fourteenth century this collection, in 46 loose quires, could be rented for copying at the price of four silver coins. Every *baccalaureus* had to determine a dispute as part of the final examination, for which in addition to the collections of *quaestiones* published by teachers, other handbooks were on sale to help in their preparation.

When, despite his young age, Thomas received his master's degree his order appointed him to one of the two chairs of theology held by the Dominicans at the University of Paris. Even then the number of chairs per faculty was limited. In 1255 the faculty of theology had 12 chairs, half of which were allocated to the secular clergy, two to the Dominicans, one to the Franciscans, and the remaining three to the (regular) canons of the Paris cathedral chapter. This division was the result of heated discussions on the place of the new mendicant orders, which always met with vehement and lengthy opposition because the secular masters felt their livelihood was threatened. Soon afterwards, the number of chairs was enlarged in favour of other orders, both existing and new. Chairs were not normally occupied for life. Secular masters usually gave them up after a few years and moved on to important administrative posts. It was the custom of regular masters, at least those from the mendicant orders, to change to a new post every two or three years. Thomas Aquinas thus taught in Paris from 1255 to 1259, then moved to Naples, Orvieto, Rome and Viterbo (where the popes often held their court), returned to Paris (1269–1272), and ended his career in Naples at the university where he had started his studies. During that time, Thomas penned or dictated, often simultaneously, many pages of superlative Latin prose, in quantities of which most modern scholars can only dream. No wonder that his inspiration was extinguished so soon. In December 1273, Thomas, then aged 48, told his secretary, 'I cannot go on. It is as if everything I have written is made of straw.' He died at the abbey of Fossanuova a few months later.

After persistent pressure of the Dominicans Thomas Aquinas was canonized a saint in 1323. Within his own order Thomas's works had already for a long time been compulsory reading in the study of theology. Outside the order they were in fact less valued than it was made to appear at the end of the nineteenth century, when Aquinas was made the showpiece of the Catholic emancipation movement and was given the reputation of having reconciled faith and reason. Besides this being the motto of William of Conches (1080–1145), a much earlier theologian, the borderline between reason and faith in Thomas's works is actually extremely subtle. On the one hand, not only Aristotelian nature but also the existence of God can be understood through reason, while on the other no revealed article of faith is self-evidently rational. Every insight into God depends on divine grace. But those who are allowed to share the grace may then make use of reason to deduce less profound articles of faith from more substantial ones. Among non-theologians, Aquinas is still widely recognized today for his sharp analytical ability, the clarity of his style and his deep psychological insight.

University scholarship in crisis

The opposition Thomas Aquinas aroused during his lifetime was connected with the growing resistance to the dominance of Aristotle in the university curriculum. Friction came to a head during the 'second round' of the Aristotelian revival, because his non-logic works on metaphysics, on the soul and natural philosophy contained views that were seemingly irreconcilable with the Catholic faith. Aristotle thought, in Averroës' explanation, that the world and the universe were 'eternal', that they had no beginning and no end, and that after a person's physical death his immortal soul would lose its individuality. Both these ideas are clearly incompatible with Judaeo-Christian concepts of creation and resurrection, and it was for this reason that not only Christian theologians but also Jewish thinkers at this time, such as Moses Maimonides in Cairo (1135–1204), struggled with Aristotle's philosophy.

Particularly in Paris, latent anti-Aristotelianism led to an intriguing discussion about the limits of human reason. The most important spokesman of the anti-Aristotelians was Giovanni Fidanza, better known as Bonaventura (1221–1274), a gifted preacher who taught theology in Paris around 1270 and who later became general (or head) of the Franciscan order. Bonaventura did not reject the work of Aristotle in principle. On the contrary, he happily used it in his own writings; but he was opposed to its excessive use in theological education, realizing that Aristotle only offered limited possibilities to reach a deeper knowledge of God. According to Bonaventura, this knowledge could only be reached by a mystical path and necessitated a burning desire for God and a blind faith in divine grace that would rise above every call upon reason.

Yet, it is not right to see the adherents of Aristotle as reckless rationalists. Certainly the masters in the liberal arts resolutely stuck to their viewpoint that the arts curriculum was separated from the study of theology and so could never cause a conflict between Aristotle and Christian dogmatics, for the simple reason that it was not up to them to express an opinion on matters of faith. This point of view is important – not because it made an implicit division between reason and faith, for that had already been made on previous occasions, but because that division was now considered to be a meaningful demarcation in the exercise of scholarship. The best liberal arts masters, such as Siger of Brabant and Boethius of Dacia (a Dane), made every effort to gain as much as possible from Aristotle without bringing their faith into discussion. After 1270 this led to a bitter clash.

Boethius of Dacia defended himself by acknowledging, loudly and clearly, that 'there are many things in faith that cannot be shown by reason'; but that was no help at all. Radical Aristotelianism in the Paris faculty of arts was given an official episcopal reprimand twice in as many years through the publication of theses that every scholar was expected to reject under penalty of excommunication. The list published in March 1277 contained no fewer than 219 of such propositions, 60 of which could be traced back to the works of Siger and Boethius. Some months earlier, Siger of Brabant and two associates had been summoned to appear before the Inquisition. Wisely, they failed to turn up and fled to Italy.

William of Ockham

The uproar caused by the condemnations of 1277, and the deep intellectual crisis that they exposed at the University of Paris in particular, had died down by about 1300. The way was thus cleared for a new generation of philosophers and theologians, the best of whom could measure up to Thomas Aquinas. This group surely included the Englishman, William of Ockham (before 1287–1349), a Franciscan who, in the 1320s, made a name for himself in London and Oxford as a teacher of theology, although he never took a Master's degree in that discipline. This we know from his contemporaries' appreciative nickname, *venerabilis inceptor* ('venerable candidate'). Ockham's university career was thwarted by John Lutterell, the Oxford chancellor, who suspected him of unorthodoxy. For this Ockham was required to answer to a papal court in Avignon, where he waited for his trial for many years under a form of house arrest. While the pope's attention was increasingly focused on another controversial issue in which the Franciscans were also involved, the question of poverty, Ockham fled in 1328 with Michael of Cesena, the general of the order, to the court of Emperor Louis of Bavaria in Munich, where he died of the plague in 1349.

Ockham and the debate about *universalia*

The originality and greatness of Ockham's thought is best illustrated by his treatment of what is known as the question of universals, a problem that vexed almost every medieval philosopher and theologian. Put simply, the problem relates to the status of universals,

terms that 'group' or categorize all that is particular, or that indicate their qualities or properties, for example 'dog' (noun) or 'red' (adjective). Are there only particular dogs and red things, or do the species of dog and the colour red possess some extra-mental or mind-independent reality – that is, real existence outside the human mind – as distinct from particular things? Normally the second position is called 'realistic' and the first 'nominalistic'. In its purest and most extreme form the realistic standpoint goes back to Plato, who was convinced that an immaterial parallel world exists outside, and strictly separated from, our physical world: the world of the Forms, eternal, pure and perfect exemplars that 'cause' the transitory and inconstant things of the material world without them ever becoming more than just weak and imperfect reflections of the Forms. According to Plato, man recollects or recognizes the Forms in individual things because sensory experience of them reminds the observer of the immaterial world of the Forms, which is also the place where the soul originates. Platonic realism came to influence Christian thought through Neoplatonism (and Saint Augustine), in particular. God was seen as the creator of the world, who before creation had thought out everything in his mind. Thus, concrete reality was in essence an imperfect reflection of the perfect ideas (Forms) in God's mind.

This was not the path taken to approach the problem of the status of universals, however. The problem was seen as a matter of logic, and Aristotle reigned supreme in the study of logic. Aristotle had rejected Plato's theory of the Forms. He did indeed attribute reality to the Forms, which he called Essences, but he denied their transcendent existence; that is to say, their being outside concrete, physical things. In other words, the Essences were enclosed within – and only within – the natural world. The human mind is able to discern Essences because of its ability to make comparisons. While in Plato's view any particular dog, say, any 'Fido', participates in the perfect form of 'dog' in an imperfect manner, for Aristotle Fido embodies or 'realizes' the Essence of 'dog'; conversely, the Essence of 'dog' exists as a sort of sum total of characteristics that concrete specimens (Fidos) must fulfil in order to be called 'dog'. In Aristotle's view this means that Essences can exist solely if they can be said of something or can be 'predicated of several'; as it is termed in

Aristotelian logic: it must be possible to say of something or someone, 'is a dog' or 'is red' in order to accept the existence of the Essence of 'the dog' or of 'redness'. It also means that Aristotle was convinced that the categories into which he divided and classified the physical world were not just intellectual, intra-mental schemes but representations of the natural order that had extra-mental existence.

Aristotle's view, which is called 'moderately realistic' because it believes in the real existence of Essences without placing them in an extra-material world, was also accepted by Boethius, who was the first to bring up the question of the universals in the Middle Ages. It did not become the subject of proper learned discussion until the end of the eleventh century, when Roscelin of Compiègne (where he was a *scholaster* or teacher) defended an extreme nominalistic standpoint – which, alas, we only know from references in the writings of his opponents. As far as we can tell, Roscelin radically rejected any form of realism by postulating that universals can never be anything more than verbal expressions, the uttering of the word (*flatus vocis* in Latin) by which they are named: thus they do not correspond to any extra-mental reality but are merely linguistic constructs, names (Latin *nomina*, whence nominalism). Roscelin found himself in great trouble when he launched this idea in connection with the dogma of the Holy Trinity and concluded that either there must be three separate godheads or the doctrine of the Trinity could not be elucidated through logic.

Roscelin's reputation was ruined, but everything seems to indicate that he did not stand alone and that, before 1100, there were heated discussions in the cathedral schools of northern France between the supporters and opponents of Roscelin's view of universals. There is a lovely story from Lille, where the universals dispute had reached such a pitch by the end of the eleventh century that it was decided to put the matter to a deaf-mute fortune-teller of high repute in the town. A canon explained the matter in sign language. The fortune-teller understood at once and firmly took the side of the realists. His foresight proved to be somewhat limited, for nominalism would eventually triumph in a large part of the university world, though it was a long time before that came about. In his debate with Roscelin, Abelard formulated a moderate-realistic compromise that was widely

followed in the twelfth and thirteenth centuries, and which we also find in Thomas Aquinas and Bonaventura among others. Abelard sat rather on the fence by presenting universals as mental abstractions. Universals are enclosed in separate things, but possess a higher mental reality through the human mind's ability to make abstractions. Nor did Abelard express an opinion over the question whether or not universals as intra-mental, intellectual abstractions also represented categories or classes in the extra-mental, physical reality, as Aristotle thought. Apart from that, his concept was very close to that of Aristotle – a remarkable fact because Abelard did not have direct knowledge of the *Metaphysics*, in which Aristotle had revealed his ideas about universals but which was not known in the West until shortly after Abelard's death in 1142.

Abelard's standpoint of moderate realism was generally accepted by western philosophers and further refined by John Duns Scotus (*c.* 1270–1308), who denied that universals as such had any real existence; they started to do so only when they acquired 'thisness' (*haecceitas* in Latin); that is to say, when they were concretized in a particular thing. Consequently, for Duns Scotus the relation between universal and particular was of a formal rather than a 'real' nature. This idea provided an important starting-point for William of Ockham's handling of the question of universals. Ockham distinguished between 'difference' and 'diversity'; the latter, belonging to the realm of extra-mental reality, generated the former, confined to the realm of the mind. In other words, Ockham came to the conclusion that Abelard did not dare to draw: only particular things in an endless variety exist in extra-mental reality. Conversely, universals are in no way substantial but only products of the mind, needed to bring order into the extra-mental world. Therefore, in Ockham's moderately nominalistic view, universals are ontologically *intentiones animae* ('intentions of the mind'), which can refer both to particulars in extra-mental reality ('Fido is a dog') and to categories produced by the mind ('A dog is a species'). Semantically, both 'intentions' are merely *signa* ('natural signs'), while the logical status of universals is thus none other than that of subject and predicate terms incorporated in propositions. In other words, 'Fido is a dog' does not refer to a general category (or biological species) that exists in reality, but 'is a dog' is a predicate that points to a wider predicate ('is a living being'). Science for Ockham was not directly concerned with extra-mental, physical reality itself, not with study of the physical world, but first and foremost with the validity – or not – of statements about particular things that are contained in propositions with the help of the human ability to understand: *solae propositiones sciuntur* ('only propositions can be known', i.e. 'can provide scientific knowledge').

Ockham's theology

In addition to being an innovative logician who reinforced the linguistic turn medieval philosophy was taking, Ockham was an exceptional theologian. For him, theology was not a science based on rational proofs supported by logic or by natural philosophy, nor did it allow him any certain statements about God. The only thing that he knew with any certainty was that God was perfectly transcendent and autonomous. God was powerful in the sense that no power could compel him. His freedom of action was circumscribed only by the requirements of internal consistency and order: even God could not do anything that lacked order or that at the same time was the opposite of what was happening. The creation was no more and no less than the contingent product of a choice made by God out of infinitely many options, but within the two limitations he had set for himself.

In Ockham's eyes only faith could lead to insight into the sort of higher truths that were indispensable for achieving eternal salvation – not because such truths were possibly irrational but because human reason was restricted. Faith could not be achieved solely by study, theological or other; an essential part of it was instilled (*infusa* in Latin) as it were through the grace-giving sacrament of Holy Baptism. With this proposition, Ockham openly stood against the rationalists. Reason and faith should be separate in principle, as should science and theology. Science should be directed towards reason and the 'natural' forms of proof that reason could reach, while theology should be directed towards faith, and faith towards divine revelation.

Ockham's impact on higher education in the late Middle Ages must not be underestimated. Based on his innovative approach, schools were formed soon after his death, which caused a general split in the arts curricula of the late medieval universities. The new way (*via moderna*) was also called the nominalistic or Ockhamist (*doctrina* or *scientia okamica*) school (although Ockham never was a radical nominalist); the old way (*via antica*), on the other hand, referred to the school that continued to adhere to the (moderate) realism that had dominated liberal arts education before William of Ockham, and which was particularly associated with the writings of Thomas Aquinas and John Duns Scotus. The difference between these two schools of thought dominated the university arts curriculum until well into the sixteenth century. Universities made it quite clear whether they followed the *via moderna* or the *via antica*, or both, but obviously a lot depended on the personal preferences of individual teachers. The University of Erfurt in Germany, for example, traditionally followed the *via antica*, but when the young Martin Luther studied the arts there, Jodocus Trutfetter, the resident professor, taught the *via moderna*.

It is difficult to explain briefly what the two streams precisely stood for. The direction a student followed depended largely on the material to be studied, and this was selected by the master. Which author's commentaries or other works would be examined? *Via moderna* masters were often only partly or superficially acquainted with Ockham's writings and twisted many of his views. That even happened with teachers who attempted to follow his teachings faithfully, such as John Buridan (*c.* 1292–1358), a successful Flemish teacher of the arts in Paris and author of a much-used logics textbook. Buridan knew Ockham's works well and let it be clearly known that he was an Ockhamist, but he searched for rational proofs for articles of faith in spite of Ockham's explicit advice against this.

Aristotle criticized

More significant, however, was the fact that the advance of the *via moderna* in late medieval universities went hand in hand with an increasingly critical attitude towards Aristotle until in the fifteenth and sixteenth centuries undermining Aristotle's authority 'had become fashionable in certain circles and was something of a literary topos' (de Rijk). Yet all criticism

Plate 12.2 A professor – imagined as Aristotle himself – lecturing *ex cathedra* before an audience of masters in the liberal arts (left) and masters in the mechanical arts (right). Flemish miniature from Peter of Abano's *Expositio problematum Aristotelis, c.* 1500

did not lead to the rejection of the Greek view of man and the world. The main reason is that fundamental criticism of Aristotle was not yet accompanied by a paradigmatic shift in the study of the natural sciences. In general, thinking about physical phenomena continued to be based on rational analysis, supported by technical logic, from a very limited body of empirical evidence; analysis was not supported by collecting more data, nor by exact measurements or systematically repeated experiments, nor by translating the results into mathematical formulae. For that matter, Arabic scientific thinking went no further than its Christian counterpart.

Did scholasticism at its zenith not result in any scientific progress at all then? Indeed it did. The new 'naturalism' of the twelfth century resulted in a cautious attempt to control nature, to make it useful to humankind, but interest in it was eventually directed towards applicable technology in particular, such as building works, rather than towards fundamental empirical study. Among the exceptions to this trend, the English Franciscans, Robert Grosseteste (*c.* 1170–1253) and Roger Bacon, his eccentric pupil, ought to be mentioned. Grosseteste, who first taught arts and then theology at Oxford from about 1220, and later became bishop of Lincoln, could read Greek and was influenced by both Plato and Aristotle. He wrote on a

wide range of scientific problems. He developed his own method to study physical phenomena, making intensive use of hypotheses (Grosseteste is perhaps the spiritual father of the scientific hypothesis), experiments and mathematical descriptions. He applied this method in his ground-breaking study of the refraction of light in rainbows that would later be refined by Bacon and the German Dominican, Dietrich of Freiburg. It is true that the theory did not correspond on all points with current theory, but Grosseteste and his followers proved that in barely 50 years it was possible to make great advances in the physical sciences with the help of experiments and mathematics.

Scholars of such outstanding ability and with the wide interests of Grosseteste and Bacon were exceptional, even at the University of Paris. John Buridan thoroughly rejected Aristotle's impetus theory concerning the velocity of a body that is accelerated in a non-natural way. This led again to a substantiated claim by Buridan's best pupil, Nicolas Oresme (*c.* 1320–1382), that the earth revolved on its own axis, a view that, although not expressed for the first time, contradicted the Aristotelian model of the universe with earth as its motionless centre.

Yet, all in all, these experimental physicists remained a marginal group within the arts faculties. They did not manage to form a school. This revealed a flaw in university education that had crept in with the custom that young intellectuals could undertake a theological study only after they had completed the arts course. It meant that theologians intervened constantly in debates on questions of natural philosophy, and that they knew what they were talking about. This theological monitoring slowed the development of natural philosophy towards a natural science focused less on metaphysical and theological problems and more on observation, experimentation and measurements related to purely physical phenomena.

Such factors may help to explain why the unique breeding ground that was established with the foundation of universities for a fairly autonomous scholarship in the European Middle Ages did not lead to a scientific revolution until the seventeenth century. Before that time, the Greek model of the universe, which had reigned supreme for almost two thousand years, was challenged far less from the bulwarks of science than from the adventurous world beyond. Two of the most important discoveries of the thirteenth century, the mechanical clock and spectacles, were developed, as far as we know, outside the university. And it was merchants and navigators – helped by such practical inventions as the astrolabe (probably of Hellenistic origin, but vastly improved in the eleventh century), the magnetic compass (twelfth century), the double compasses, and the calculation of coordinates (eleventh century) – who made it clear that many Aristotelian laws were simply incorrect. It explains the joke circulating in the middle of the sixteenth century that you could learn more from the Portuguese in one day than you could from the Greeks and Romans in a hundred years.

THE HUMANISM OF THE LATE MIDDLE AGES

Studia humanitatis and the new humanism in Italy

While scholasticism was reaching its zenith in the course of the fourteenth century, an entirely new educational curriculum was being propagated in Italy. Contemporaries spoke of the *studia humanitatis*. Instead of the strong accent the scholastic liberal arts course put on technical logic, natural philosophy, and metaphysics in the Aristotelian tradition, the *studia humanitatis* programme was constructed around five disciplines – grammar, rhetoric, history (not then a separate discipline), knowledge of poetry and moral philosophy (meaning philosophy focused on ethical, non-metaphysical or theological questions). The basic texts for the subjects were by classical, primarily non-Christian, Roman writers. Favourite genres became discursive dialogues and speeches.

The new programme certainly did not take the world of higher learning by storm. Quite the contrary, it never even gained a firm foothold in the arts curriculum beyond humanistic adaptations of the traditional trivium subjects of grammar and rhetoric. It is better, therefore, to refer to an intellectual sub-culture, first established in Italy where the scholastic tradition in the universities was relatively weak and where empathy with Roman antiquity still was strongly felt. From

there, this sub-culture gradually spread over the Alps, where it was linked more closely to the intellectual debate about reforms in the Catholic Church than in Italy. Although in the long term the *studia humanitatis* would not triumph in the university syllabus they were successful at a lower level; that is, in the Latin schools founded in large towns all over late medieval Europe to educate children from the upper echelons of the bourgeoisie, but not necessarily to prepare them for a university education.

At first sight the demand for the *studia humanitatis* appears to have been a plea for a reactionary, not revolutionary, shift of emphasis in intellectual formation, a return to the arts programmes from before the Aristotelian revival. In reality, a substantial change in mentality lay behind it. The new humanists wanted above all to expand the practical value of higher education that they felt was lacking in scholastic learning. In addition to a direct focus on the human condition, the new humanists' revolt against scholasticism therefore reflects a new sort of 'utilitarian thinking' that was emerging among the urban elites and higher middle classes. In contrast to our own times, this way of thinking did not aim to extend individual material well-being but to develop those character traits which enabled individuals to make sensible moral, business and, above all, political decisions in a pragmatic way. In the communes of northern and central Italy, where the new mentality first took root, both the degree of civic participation and the amount of informal organization were far greater than in western society today. For that reason, we ought to be wary of putting too much stress on the individualistic and secularizing trends in the new humanism, as was done particularly by nineteenth-century historians like Jakob Burckhardt. On the contrary, direct involvement of the better-off in local political life furthered a feeling of collective responsibility and a natural readiness to do one's best for the public good. Neither was this endeavour seen as primarily secular, as 'opposed to Christian piety'; rather, 'it was regarded as its complement' (Rüegg).

Cicero replaced Aristotle as the great classical example for the new humanists. No other figure in the ancient world so effectively combined high public morality with unrestrained political activity as he did. Cicero's writings also taught that eloquent expression or rhetoric was an important skill through which to achieve moral wisdom, because only clarity of expression in the written and spoken word could lead to the correct formulation of that wisdom.

The renewed interest in Antiquity's literary treasures led to important methodological innovations in textual criticism. For the first time the authenticity of a text was questioned through a systematic study of such textual characteristics as the writer's style and vocabulary, supplemented by a number of exterior features. In addition, context-bound interpretation was given a wider range than was common since Abelard's time. It was realized that what a writer intended to say at a certain place in the text could not be determined solely by a semantic analysis of the vocabulary. In a philological study of a text, the complete text had to be used as well as its author's other works or works by others writing at the same time, or other possibly relevant historical information. The new philological criticism, the prelude to modern scientific philology, was thus both comparative and historical in nature. It achieved resounding results, including the definitive exposure of the *Donatio Constantini* as a forgery by the papal secretary, Lorenzo Valla, and the German humanist and cardinal, Nicholas of Kues. It helped the new humanists to reject the medieval Christian idea that their own time was the depressing lowest point, the very nadir of world history. Without breaking with the inevitable scheme of Christian salvation history they began to take more heed of history's vagaries – which true leaders should try to surmount or bend to their will. But the new, historical textual criticism had much wider advantages, for even if the Greek model of the universe did not give way as yet, the conditions for its undermining were enhanced by the availability of more and better versions of the original texts in which the model was couched.

It is impossible to imagine the flowering and enormous growth of the humanistic education programme without a new stress on the study of Latin. The new humanists were convinced that Latin was the only vehicle worthy of expounding their ideals. They were horrified by the 'barbaric' Latin of the scholastics, which admittedly was contorted by the need to give modern Latin equivalents to the very complex and often obscure terminology of Aristotle's Greek and which often resulted in rather ugly neologisms. But even the sophisticated Latin of the twelfth-century men of letters was not good enough. It was a source of pride for the new humanists to master Latin so perfectly that it was indistinguishable from the best literary Latin from classical Antiquity. The choice of material or genres was also based on classical models, not always to the satisfaction of the modern reader, who can perhaps recognize the ingenuity but not the pleasure of interminable imitations of the great epic poems of Virgil or Lucan, of incomprehensible mythological images in rigid metric verse, or of bombastic letters and speeches inspired by Cicero or Seneca. No wonder then that of the works of the most illustrious of the earliest humanists, Petrarch and Boccaccio, only those written in Italian (which were also very much appreciated in their own time) are read nowadays, and their far more numerous and extensive works in classical Latin have been all but forgotten.

Petrarch (Francesco Petrarca) was surely the most remarkable of the pair. The son of a lawyer from the neighbourhood of Arezzo, he settled in Avignon where the papal court was in residence and made influential friends there who helped him obtain his first position in the household of the renowned Colonna family. As a cleric in lower orders he enjoyed the income from various ecclesiastical benefices in Tuscany and Lombardy, which he fulfilled nominally. Petrarch soon became known as an orator and poet and was perhaps the first writer since classical Antiquity to achieve celebrity status. The high point of his career undoubtedly occurred in 1341, on the Campidoglio (the Capitoline Hill of ancient Rome), where, after his poetic abilities were tested by King Robert of Naples, he was crowned with the laurel wreath, the symbol of the writer's glory. Thereafter Petrarch became the eloquent advocate of the popes' return to Rome and lent his half-hearted support to the 'revolution' of Cola di Rienzo, the parvenu tradesman who seized power in Rome in 1347 in the belief that he could restore Rome to its former glory. Meanwhile, Petrarch journeyed from one princely court to another in an Italy torn by political strife, trying to put his talents as an orator and diplomat to use. He died in the summer of 1374 at his house in the hills above Padua while reading a book – the most beautiful death a poet and a scholar can imagine. The *Canzoniere*, a collection of 366 poems in Italian, is considered to be his most important literary legacy.

Petrarch's friend and kindred spirit, the Florentine Giovanni Boccaccio (1313–1375), died not long afterwards. He is best known as the author of the *Decameron*, a collection of short stories written in the vernacular, but like Petrarch he was a passionate Latinist, philologist and collector of manuscripts of classical literature. The two shared a profound admiration for the works of Dante Alighieri (1265–1321), who in no way can be considered a humanist; rather, he was more of an exponent of the scholastic tradition. The Florentine magistrates gave Boccaccio the first teaching commission to lecture in public on Dante's masterpiece, the *Divina Commedia*. Even more important, however, was that he made Florence the heart of the new humanistic movement. It is telling that the two most prominent spiritual heirs of Petrarch and Boccaccio, Coluccio Salutati and Leonardo Bruni of Arezzo, were both chancellor or town secretary in Florence. Salutati was the first humanist to use the *studia humanitatis* for political gain, for he employed his rhetorical gifts as a mighty weapon in Florence's struggle with Milan in 1401 and 1402. His reflective prose works show strong secular leanings and a genuine dislike of ivory-tower intellectuals and religious contemplation. 'Must I call someone learned', he wrote in a letter, 'who knows everything the human intellect can grasp about heavenly and divine matters but who never looks at himself? Who has never done anything useful for his friends, his family, his parents or his town?' This sophisticated attitude was not immediately representative of the intellectual climate in which the new humanism took root. Petrarch, for example, favoured a withdrawn, contemplative existence, a sort of Christian version of the Roman ideal of *otium*, and he looked to Augustine as his spiritual guide even more than to Seneca and Cicero – a preference shared by many later humanists.

Intellectual life in Florence during the fifteenth century, then, was not dominated entirely by the moral humanism strongly oriented towards public service that Salutati and Bruni propagated. No less popular among the elite in the second half of the fifteenth century was the so-called 'Florentine Platonism', an esoteric brew of original ideas of Plato, widely known by then as his works had been translated from Greek, mixed with a dash of Neoplatonism and a good measure of magical and occult humbug taken from the Jewish Kabbala and the ancient Greek cult of Hermes Trismegistos. The result resembled some of today's New Age philosophies, for Florentine Platonism had a strongly egocentric and apolitical slant. A typical product of this thinking was the work on the dignity of man by Giovanni Pico della Mirandola (1463–1494), published posthumously. It defends the extremely voluntaristic view that the human individual, with no limitations to his own free will, creates his own personality. Visual pointers to the ideas of this philosophical current can be seen in the early paintings of Sandro Botticelli (1444–1510).

The work of Niccolò Machiavelli (1469–1527) was less high-brow and more akin to the early political-moral humanism of around 1400, but it lacked the optimistic view of human nature and human potentialities that was so characteristic of early moral humanism and Florentine Platonism. One of the aphorisms of Machiavelli, also a chancellor of Florence but relieved of his office in 1512 after the political comeback of the Medici, is that 'People only do good when they are compelled to'. Humans were by nature evil and their actions were determined by self-interest, by a desire for gain and glory, by opportunism and hypocrisy. To be sure, human nature could not be changed; what could be manipulated and re-formed, though, was 'character', constituting that part of man's disposition that was dependent on circumstances and free will. People did indeed have free will, but they could only determine half their fate, the other half being in the hands of fortune. A good ruler was one who succeeded best in adapting to historical circumstances either by trying to master fortune or by presenting the state's interest as the self-interest of (the majority of) its subjects or by bending his subjects' characters on serving the common good of the state rather than his will. Machiavelli was rather ambiguous about the best possible type of government; while in one of his principal works, *The Prince* (*Il Principe*), he argues in favour of monarchy, in the other, *Discourses on Livy*, he seems to prefer a republic with a mixed, aristocratic–popular regime. Machiavelli's ideas about the limits of force that a state may use are best known from *The Prince*, a mirror of princes tinged with

Aristotelian ideas on psychological motivation of human action. It evokes two kinds of comments. First, a good prince is never a tyrant, but on the other hand allows himself to be guided by his subjects' preferences only if expedient. When necessary – that is to say, when laws did not work properly – he should be prepared to take an uncompromising and unambiguous stand, combining the strength of a lion with the cunning of a fox. The man whom Machiavelli believed to possess all the desired qualities, and who was held up as an example to the reader of *Il Principe*, was Cesare Borgia. The son of Pope Alexander VI, Cesare was an unscrupulous scoundrel but also a gifted strategist. Nonetheless, in Machiavelli's eyes he was the embodiment of the right character of a forceful 'prince', being a combination of *virtù* (personal ability), *ingegno* (emotional disposition) and *fantasia* (power of imagination) – all three keywords of the Italian Renaissance to describe the individual.

Second, if in *The Prince* the idea of an amoral *raison d'état* is expounded for the first time, in which the actors are allowed almost unlimited latitude and freedom of action, it must be made clear that Machiavelli only approved of amoral actions (which could also imply immoral actions) if they served the public interest of the state. Good Christian that he was, Machiavelli strongly condemned immoral actions motivated by the individual's self-interest.

We will only briefly discuss the relationship between Italian humanism and the visual art of the Italian Renaissance, which nonetheless played an important role in the debate about the unique nature of this period of Italian history. At a cursory glance the link with humanism is plain and uncomplicated. Just as in the study of letters, so too in the language of forms, geometrical proportions, and the solving of problems of perspective in architecture, sculpture and painting there was a conscious and direct return to the models of Antiquity. The watershed between 'old' and 'new' art came in the 1420s, when Filippo Brunelleschi completed the dome of the cathedral church in Florence, when Donatello made his first free-standing sculptures of human figures in a natural pose (known as the *contrapposto*), and when the painter Masaccio applied the technique of vanishing-point or optical perspective and made considerable efforts to ensure that his figures were anatomically correct. As their technical mastery

grew so did their social ambitions. Artists were no longer content with being seen as craftsmen, practitioners of the *artes mechanicae*, they wanted to be considered as scholars, practitioners of the *artes liberales*. The techniques and constructs applied and the elaboration of subjects and motifs surely demanded more than just a superficial knowledge of different disciplines of the trivium and quadrivium. This claim was honoured only in part. On the one hand, leading artists like Leonardo da Vinci (1452–1519) and Michelangelo Buonarotti (1475–1564) were considered 'universal', even divinely inspired geniuses (and this was reflected in the level of their fees); on the other hand, Leonardo was frustrated throughout his life that he never was accepted by the learned humanists as one of their own.

Unlike the new humanism, the new Italian visual arts did not travel north of the Alps until relatively late, with a few exceptions such as Albrecht Dürer (1471–1528), the South German graphic artist and painter. A unique and distinctive realistic style of painting and sculpture developed in north-western Europe during the fifteenth century, finding its most sublime expression in the works of the Flemish painters, Jan van Eyck and Rogier van der Weyden.

The literature of the Italian Renaissance reveals a curious mixture of typically medieval and typically ancient genres. The former is illustrated by the epic poetry of Matteo Maria Boiardo (1441–1494) and Ludovico Ariosto (1474–1533), dealing with events happening in Charlemagne's time, and the latter by the bucolic and pastoral verse of Jacopo Sannazzaro (1455–1530). Such examples reveal, once again, that there was a great variety of forms, not all of which meant a conscious break with the 'dark Middle Ages'.

The new humanism outside Italy

The influence of the new humanism outside of Italy was originally found in comparable, densely urbanized regions such as southern Germany and the Low Countries, but it has now become clear that the intellectual elite elsewhere – England, France, Spain and Poland – also came into contact with the programme of the *studia humanitatis* at an early stage. The networks that existed between universities and the personal connections between intellectuals, kept up by travels to Italy (the *iter Italicum* as part of the intellectual formation of aristocrats), by correspondence, by employment and by diplomatic missions, apparently were far more important than strictly socio-geographical structures. Peter Luder (1415–1472), the German humanist who as a young man travelled to Italy several times to study, is a good example. He discovered the *studia humanitatis* and transferred his enthusiasm to his students and colleagues in the many universities of the German Empire at which he taught. The most important northern humanist was undoubtedly Rudolf Agricola (1444–1485), who studied in Pavia and Ferrara for more than ten years before taking an official position in Groningen in the northern Low Countries, from where he originated. Among his writings is a textbook inspired by humanistic thought, *De inventione dialectica*, which was widely used for teaching philosophy in the sixteenth century. Agricola argued that the humanistic ideal of a pragmatic search for plausible solutions to everyday questions was worth more than all the speculation about things that could not be experienced to which scholastic dialectics was devoted.

Through men like Luder and Agricola the new humanism permeated the circles of higher education and the governments of towns and principalities outside Italy, though it also encountered objections. The propagation of ancient 'pagan' virtues aroused

Map 12.2 The beginning of the art of printing: places where printers were established in about 1470

particular suspicion in conservative clerical circles, and for this reason the humanists failed to get university curricula adapted to their educational ideals, even though they certainly tried often enough in the German Empire during the second half of the fifteenth century. From time to time their efforts procured the appointment of a humanistic teacher to lecture in rhetoric or classical poetry. Martin Luther was closely connected to one of the attempts at reform which bore some fruit. Luther was not a humanist in the strict sense – he was not interested in pre-Christian Latin or Greek literature – but he had an intense dislike for the scholastic teaching of philosophy and theology. In his view, the teaching of theology should be based solely on the Bible, and good teaching of the Bible benefited from humanism's new historical-philological methods. With that thought Luther was able to persuade the governing body of the still young University of Wittenberg to make far-reaching changes in the syllabus. His brilliant young friend, Philip Melanchthon, who taught there, threw himself wholeheartedly into carrying these changes through.

Other northern humanists shared Luther's attempts to use the *studia humanitatis* to implement necessary reforms in the Church, and they, too, saw the establishment of a historical-philologically sound new text of the Bible as the first desideratum. The most famous of them was Desiderius Erasmus of Rotterdam (*c.* 1467–1536). His religious ideals, which he referred to as the 'philosophy of Christ', were greatly influenced by his upbringing in the spirit of the *Devotio Moderna* (see Chapter 15). Erasmus found that the basis of faith could never be learned theology; it was a personal and unbounded trust in God, driven by internal experience and complemented by a morally pure life. He found the Church's outward show of minor importance, and in *Praise of Folly*, a work still popular today, he used his most feared weapon, satire, to poke fun at the carnivalesque features of Catholic religious life of the time and at the greed and tyranny of prelates and monks. Yet Erasmus never wanted to break with the Church of Rome. He was more in favour of a rebirth than a reformation of Christianity, and that was precisely where he differed with Luther, from whom he openly distanced himself in 1520.

Education was at the heart of the rebirth of faith envisaged by Erasmus, education aimed at the moral improvement of individual believers in the spirit of early Christianity, and not at rejecting the Church's doctrines and institutions. Erasmus wrote a sort of moral guideline specially for the purpose entitled *Enchiridion militis Christi* ('Handbook of a Christian Knight'), advocating knowledge and prayer as weapons to be used in the fight against vice and sin.

Erasmus and Luther belonged to the earliest generation of intellectuals who were able to disseminate their views through a revolutionary new medium, the printing press. Erasmus was the very first to recognize its enormous potential: 23 editions of his *Enchiridion* appeared between 1515 and 1521. He could often be found in the offices and workshops of the Swiss and northern Italian printers who published his works, and, without ever having held a public office of any significance, Erasmus achieved the status of a best-selling writer and cultural megastar. At the height of his fame, around 1515, his name was on the lips of every intellectual of importance in Europe.

FURTHER READING

Benson, Robert L. and Giles Constable (eds) (1982), *Renaissance and Renewal in the Twelfth Century* (Oxford: Clarendon).

Brundage, James A. (1995), *Medieval Canon Law* (London and New York: Longman).

Carabine, Deirdre (2000), *John Scottus Eriugena* (New York and Oxford: Oxford University Press).

Clanchy, M.T. (1997), *Abelard: A Medieval Life* (Oxford: Blackwell).

Colish, Marcia L. (1994), *Peter Lombard*, 2 vols (Leiden: Brill).

—— (1997), *Medieval Foundations of the Western Intellectual Tradition, 400–1400*, (New Haven, Conn. and London: Yale University Press).

Cook, William R. and Ronald B. Herzman (2004), *The Medieval World View: An Introduction*, 2nd edn (New York and Oxford: Oxford University Press).

Courtenay, William J. (1987), *Schools and Scholars in Fourteenth-century England* (Princeton, N.J.: Princeton University Press).

—— and Jürgen Miethke (with David B. Priest) (eds) (2000), *Universities and Schooling in Medieval Society* (Leiden: Brill).

Cowdrey, H.E.J. (2003), *Lanfranc: Scholar, Monk, and Archbishop* (Oxford: Oxford University Press).

Crosby, Alfred W. (1997), *The Measure of Reality. Quantification and Western Society, 1250–1600* (Cambridge: Cambridge University Press).

Dales, Richard C. (1992), *The Intellectual Life of Western Europe in the Middle Ages* (Leiden: Brill).

Edson, Evelyn (1997), *Mapping Time and Space. How Medieval Mapmakers Viewed Their World* (London: British Library).

—— and E. Savage-Smith (2004), *Medieval Views of the Cosmos* (Chicago: University of Chicago Press).

Eisenstein, Elisabeth L. (1979), *The Printing Press As an Agent of Change: Communications and Cultural Transformations in Early-modern Europe*, 2 vols (Cambridge: Cambridge University Press).

Ferruolo, Stephen (1985), *The Origins of the University: The Schools of Paris and Their Critics, 1100–1215* (Stanford, Calif.: Stanford University Press).

French, Roger (2003), *Medicine before Science: The Rational and Learned Doctor from the Middle Ages to the Enlightenment* (Cambridge: Cambridge University Press).

Gimpel, Jean (1976), *The Medieval Machine: The Industrial Revolution of the Middle Ages* (New York: Holt, Rinehart & Winston) (orig. French, 1975).

Grant, Edward (1996), *The Foundations of Science in the Middle Ages. Their Religious, Institutional and Intellectual Contexts* (Cambridge: Cambridge University Press).

Grendler, Paul F. (2002), *The Universities of the Italian Renaissance* (Baltmore, Md. and London: Johns Hopkins University Press).

Halkin, Léon-E. (1994), *Erasmus: A Critical Biography* (Oxford: Blackwell) (orig. French, 1987).

Harvey, P.D.A. (1991), *Medieval Maps* (London: British Library).

Hollander, Robert (2001), *Dante: A Life in Works* (New Haven, Conn. and London: Yale University Press).

Jaeger, C. Stephen (2000), *The Envy of Angels. Cathedral Schools and Social Ideals in Medieval Europe, 950–1200* (Philadelphia, Pa.: University of Pennsylvania Press).

Kline, Naomi Reed (2001), *Maps of Medieval Thought: The Hereford Paradigm* (Woodbridge: Boydell).

Leff, Gordon (1975), *William of Ockham: The Metamorphosis of Scholastic Discourse* (Lanham, Md.: Rowman & Littlefield).

Lewis, C.S. (1964), *The Discarded Image: An Introduction to Medieval and Renaissance Literature* (Cambridge: Cambridge University Press).

Long, Pamela O. (2001), *Openness, Secrecy, Authorship: Technical Arts and the Culture of Knowledge from Antiquity to the Renaissance* (Baltimore, Md. and London: Johns Hopkins University Press).

—— (2003), *Technology and Society in the Medieval Centuries: Byzantium, Islam and the West, 500–1300* (Washington DC: American Historical Association).

McGrade, Arthur Stephen (2002), *The Political Thought of William Ockham: Personal and Institutional Principles*, 2nd edn (Cambridge: Cambridge University Press).

McKitterick, Rosamond (1990), *The Uses of Literacy in Early Medieval Europe* (Cambridge: Cambridge University Press).

Mann, Nicholas (1984), *Petrarch* (Oxford and New York: Oxford University Press).

Marenbon, John (1983), *Early Medieval Philosophy (450–1150): An Introduction* (London: Routledge & Kegan Paul).

—— (1987), *Later Medieval Philosophy (1150–1350): An Introduction* (London: Routledge & Kegan Paul).

—— (1997), *The Philosophy of Peter Abelard* (Cambridge: Cambridge University Press).

—— (2003), *Boethius* (Oxford and New York: Oxford University Press).

Martin, John Jeffries (ed.) (2002), *The Renaissance: Italy and Abroad* (London and New York: Routledge).

Matthews, Gareth B. (1998), *The Augustinian Tradition* (Berkeley and London: University of California Press).

Nauert, Charles J. Jr. (1995), *Humanism and the Culture of Renaissance Europe* (Cambridge: Cambridge University Press).

O'Boyle, Cornelius (1998), *The Art of Medicine: Medical Teaching at the University of Paris, 1250–1400* (Leiden: Brill).

Pedersen, Olaf (1997), *The First Universities.* Studium Generale *and the Origins of University Education in Europe* (Cambridge: Cambridge University Press).

Ridder-Symoens, Hilde de (ed.) (1992), *A History of the University in Europe. Vol 1. Universities in the Middle Ages* (Cambridge: Cambridge University Press).

Rosemann, Philipp W. (2004), *Peter Lombard* (Oxford and New York: Oxford University Press).

Schoek, Richard J. (1990–1993), *Erasmus of Europe*, 2 vols (Edinburgh: Edinburgh University Press).

Simek, Rudolf (1996), *Heaven and Earth in the Middle Ages: The Physical World Before Columbus* (Woodbridge: Boydell) (orig. German, 1992).

Siraisi, Nancy G. (1990), *Medieval and Early Renaissance Medicine: An Introduction to Knowledge and Practice* (Chicago, Ill.: University of Chicago Press).

—— (2000), *Medicine and the Italian Universities, 1250–1600* (Leiden: Brill).

Southern, R.W. (1990), *Saint Anselm: A Portrait in a Landscape* (Cambridge: Cambridge University Press).

—— (1995–2001), *Scholastic Humanism and the Unification of Europe*, 2 vols (Oxford: Blackwell).

Stock, Brian (1983), *The Implications of Literacy. Written Language and Models of Interpretation in the Eleventh and Twelfth Century* (Princeton, N.J.: Princeton University Press).

Swanson, R.N. (1999), *The Twelfth-century Renaissance* (Manchester and New York: Manchester University Press).

Tracy, James D. (1996), *Erasmus of the Low Countries* (Berkeley: University of California Press).

Trinkaus, Charles (1979) *The Poet as Philosopher: Petrarch and the Formation of Renaissance Consciousness* (New Haven, Conn. and London: Yale University Press).

—— (1983), *The Scope of Renaissance Humanism* (Ann Arbor: University of Michigan Press).

Watt, W. Montgomery (1972), *The Influence of Islam on Medieval Europe* (Edinburgh: Edinburgh University Press).

Weisheipl, James A. (1975), *Friar Thomas d'Aquino. His Life, Thought, and Works* (Oxford: Blackwell).

—— (1980), *Thomas d'Aquino and Albert His Teacher* (Toronto: Pontifical Institute of Mediaeval Studies).

Zupko, Jack (2003), *John Buridan: Portrait of a Fourteenth-Century Arts Master* (Notre Dame, Ill.: University of Notre Dame Press).

CHAPTER 13

Between crisis and contraction

Population, economy and society in the late Middle Ages

WAR, FAMINE AND PESTILENCE

In the fifth chapter of the last book of the Bible, the enigmatic Revelation of John of Patmos, there is a reference to a scroll 'written within and on the back, sealed with seven seals'. The scroll is held in the right hand of God, who is sitting on his throne in heaven. It announces the seven disasters that the Lord has in store for mankind at the end of the world. An angel speaks with a great voice saying, 'Who is worthy to open the book, and to loose the seals thereof?' Only one creature felt called to do this, a lamb with seven horns and seven eyes – a mystical symbol for Christ himself, who had been crucified (slaughtered like a lamb) and risen from the dead. The lamb broke open the first four seals and each time a horse and rider appeared. When the fourth seal was opened the horse was a 'pale horse' and the name of its rider was Death, and a crowd of dead people from the abode of the dead followed him. And they 'were given authority over the fourth part of the earth, to kill with sword, and with famine, and with death, and by the wild beasts of the earth'. This image of apocalyptic terror, of an army of skeletons sowing death and destruction through war, famine and pestilence (*bellum, fames et pestis*), was often found in the literature and visual arts of the late Middle Ages. It is not difficult to understand the reason for this: between the beginning of the fourteenth and the middle of the fifteenth centuries, Europe, with terrifying frequency, was struck by the disasters foretold in the fourth seal (only the wild beasts were lacking).

Famines and subsistence crises

In the pre-industrial period, food shortages were a regularly recurring nightmare for large groups of people. No wonder that the popular culture of the late Middle Ages fantasized over a land of plenty, Cockaigne, an 'extraordinary out-door restaurant with unusually good service', as Mullett described it, where the roast chickens flew through the air and a dessert of ice-cooled strawberries made dreamers' mouths water. In many cases, the first action of rebellious peasants

Plate 13.1 Fifteenth-century evocation of the pest procession in Rome in 590, led by Pope Gregory the Great, to implore God's saving intervention. Miniature from the *Très riches Heures du Duc de Berry*, 1416–before 1489

was to plunder the storerooms and wine cellars of rich aristocrats and abbeys.

Yet real famines, with widespread mortality as a direct result of undernourishment, occurred relatively seldom even during the late Middle Ages. The greatest killer was without any doubt the notorious famine of 1315–1317, caused by a series of serious harvest failures in three successive seasons in north-western Europe due to exceptionally bad weather. To make matters worse, the same meteorological conditions caused a heavy death toll among cattle and sheep. To be able to appreciate the magnitude of the disaster, we must remember that the low average yields of medieval agriculture meant that the grain harvested was consumed in the year following the harvest: storage for a longer period was out of the question.

The consequences of the situation are easy to surmise. Worst hit were the urban populations that were entirely dependent on the market for their food supply. Grain prices soared to unprecedented heights – in Hainault at the height of the famine wheat was between 25 and 30 times more expensive than during normal years. Moderate wage increases could not keep up with such rising prices. But there were shortages in the countryside too, and even peasants went hungry. After a while, many of them could no longer pay their rents and were obliged to sell their land and their farms for next to nothing, or to borrow money at an exorbitant rate. Even the great landowners suffered. They were able to ask high prices for any grain they could still bring to the market, but the quantities available were far lower; and – especially in the case of ecclesiastical landowners – falling incomes contrasted sharply with rising expenses necessitated by the enormous increase in the demand for charity.

Government intervention in removing the negative effects of grain shortages was characteristic of the strong ruling authority developing in the states at this time. In England the king and diverse town governments took steps to control prices and prosecute hoarders and speculators. Great effort was made to import as much grain as possible from English possessions in south-western France, which had been spared the poor harvests. But powerful government also showed its darker side in these circumstances. During those calamitous years, Edward II continued to raise taxes for the war against the Scots. His French counterpart

used hunger as a weapon in the struggle against the rebellious Flemings, hindering the export of grain to Flanders in all manner of ways. In France and the Holy Roman Empire food riots and heretical sects were suppressed by force.

Chronicles and other written sources dating from the time show how the protracted grain shortage of 1315–1317 threatened the lives of large groups of people. The symptoms of serious undernourishment were clearly described. Horrifying stories circulated of emaciated people, their stomachs swollen from hunger edema, grazing like cows or resorting to cannibalism. Eating unusual or rotten foods led to epidemics of diarrhoea or ergotism. Ergotism, which was known during the Middle Ages as St Anthony's Fire, was caused by eating rye poisoned by fungi. Precisely how many people died during the famine is not known, but the best estimates suggest an extra mortality of about seventy per thousand (7 per cent) in the stricken regions for 1316 alone, which is about twice the normal rate in late medieval populations. The long-term effects are difficult to guess at. On the one hand, famines have very little effect on marital productivity (fertility) and it is not unlikely that the Great Famine was followed by a small baby boom. On the other, there is a view that the children who survived the famine, but who had been seriously undernourished for a long period of time, formed a generation with many 'weak specimens' that 30 years later were particularly susceptible to disease. This view, still recently advanced by the American medievalist W.C. Jordan, is nevertheless difficult to defend, for it would imply that the Black Death should have had fewer victims in southern Europe (which was not stricken by the famine of 1315–1317) than in the north; and this certainly was not the case.

The exceptional situation of serious harvest failure in two successive years occurred again in the north-west in 1437 and 1438, although this time the effects were less severe. Southern Europe, too, had its catastrophic years. There was famine in Catalonia, for example, in 1333 and 1334, in Tuscany in 1346 and 1347, the years immediately preceding the Black Death. But the failure of just one harvest was enough to cause problems, making the formation of reserves uncertain; this happened about once every ten years in pre-industrial agriculture with its low yields and absence of any effective defence against vermin and diseased crops. Such disruption is generally referred to by modern scholars as 'subsistence crisis', a term usually related to the disastrous effects of harvest failures on market prices. The assumption is that differences in the size of the harvest were reflected and magnified

BOX 13.1 THE TRIUMPH OF DEATH

One of the most remarkable architectural spaces created in the Middle Ages was the 'square' or 'field of miracles' (*Piazza* or *Prato dei Miracoli*) in the centre of Pisa in Tuscany. Three separate buildings were constructed there during the eleventh and twelfth centuries, all in pure white stone: the cathedral church, the round baptistery (*baptisterium*) and the bell tower (*campanile*) – the world-famous 'leaning tower of Pisa'. A graveyard was laid out on the north side of the square at an early date and incorporated sometime after 1278 into a monumental new building: the *camposanto* (literally 'holy field'). This was a square construction that looked from the inside like a cloister around a central open space, the original burial ground, containing earth brought from Golgotha, the hill outside Jerusalem upon which Christ died on the cross. At some date after 1330 the inside walls of the ambulatory were decorated with frescos painted by the first of the Tuscan artists, including Benozzo Gozzoli. One of the frescos was known as 'The Triumph of Death'. The theme of the fresco was a traditional story – three young men, in the prime of life and enjoying the pleasures of the hunt, were suddenly confronted with three corpses in various states of decomposition in which they recognized themselves. The death theme was enlivened by the young men's female companions, a hermit who displayed a biblical text about the futility of worldly pleasures, a skeleton flying overhead, and an aerial battle between angels and devils fighting for the souls of the dead.

For a long time it was believed that 'The Triumph of Death' was painted soon after 1348, when Pisa was stricken by the Black Death. Nowadays an earlier date, about 1330, has been assumed and the painting has been connected with either the visit to Pisa of Emperor Louis of Bavaria in 1328 or the preaching activities of the Dominicans in Pisa; the scene on the fresco apparently was borrowed from a

passage in the collection of saints' lives by the Pisan friar Domenico Cavalca. There is also disagreement about the artist. It used to be thought that Francesco Traini, a Pisan, was the painter, but a more detailed study has suggested other possible artists, in particular the Florentine, Buffalmacco.

Many of the frescos were severely damaged during the twentieth century by local youths playing football in the *camposanto* and by the American bombardment of German positions during the Second World War. Fortunately, the frescos were known in detail from old engravings and photographs, which were used in the recent, successful restoration.

Literature: *The Dictionary of Art*, 34 vols (London and New York, 1966), SVV 'Pisa' and 'Masters, anonymous 1, Master of the Triumph of the Death'. *Camposanto monumentale di Pisa. Affreschi e sinopie*, Guiseppe Ramalli (pres.) (Pisa, 1960). Joseph Polzer, 'Aspects of the Fourteenth-century Iconography of Death and the Plague', in *The Black Death. The Impact of the Fourteenth-Century Plague*, ed. Daniel Williman (Binghampton, 1982), pp. 107–130.

in the market. The inordinate profits of middlemen played a part in this, as did three other mechanisms.

First, even in the late Middle Ages only a small part of the grain harvest was intended for the market, with the result that there was much greater fluctuation in the annual market supply than in the size of the annual harvest. Second, large price fluctuations attracted shifts in consumer preferences that were contrary to economic laws. If grain suddenly rose in price then ordinary consumers paradoxically seemed inclined to spend as much of their income as possible on grain, in order to have something to eat; this increased the demand for grain and the price rose even higher, while demand for other goods and services fell. Through this mechanism every major increase in the price of grain resulted in a general depression as one branch after another was dragged into an avalanche of declines in spending. Third, market prices – at least in the spring – were partly determined by the expectations of the forthcoming harvest. If the crops in the field looked bad, and shortages could thus be expected on the market, then grain prices started to climb, and vice versa.

Because of highly imperfect highways, means of transport and trading networks, there were significant regional differences in the price of grain. Nevertheless, in the late Middle Ages, price fluctuations throughout north-western Europe remained more or less equal as a result of growing market integration. In other words, if grain was expensive in Paris it was also expensive in Cologne. This did not mean, however, that the price in Paris was the same as in Cologne. The price could vary considerably, depending on how far the large towns were from the production areas supplying them and the actual volume of the supplies. Market integration could only help to remove extreme imbalances in supply, because the volume of the international grain trade was still far too small to remove them entirely. At the beginning of the fourteenth century there was no regular commercial contact between western Europe and the grain-producing areas of the Baltic, which were later to be so important. Nevertheless, subsistence crises in the late Middle Ages were in all probability less serious than before, thanks to international trade and the increasing degree of commercialization in agriculture.

The mystery of the Black Death and its echo epidemics

The Black Death is the name traditionally given to the great epidemic that raged throughout Europe between 1347 and 1351 and which, according to a cautious estimate, cost the lives of more than one-third of the total population of about 75 million in 1300. This earned the Black Death the reputation of being one of the most fatal disasters ever to affect mankind. The disease has long been thought to have been the plague, caused by the bacterial strain *Yersinia pestis*, named after the Swiss physician Alexandre Yersin, a student of Louis Pasteur. During an outbreak in Hong Kong in 1894 Yersin succeeded in identifying and describing the bacillus that wrought the havoc. He immediately claimed that he had discovered the evil culprit behind the medieval pandemics of the sixth and fourteenth centuries, and until recently no historian ever seriously doubted this claim. It is only in the last decade that received opinion on the identity of the Black Death has been challenged and is still discussed by historians as well as epidemiologists. The historian Samuel Cohn recently argued that there are more inconsistencies than similarities between medieval descriptions of the disease and the medical symptoms of bubonic plague as they are known from modern observation; neither do data on virulence and spread patterns coincide. There are several other possible diseases under discussion, ranging from a fast-spreading type of influenza to a mixture of infectious diseases, including bubonic plague. Whatever the outcome of the new debate, however, the fact remains that the disease that hit medieval Europe around the middle of the fourteenth century must be considered one of the most disastrous epidemics to have swept the continent in the last thousand years.

The Black Death was brought from the Crimea to the Mediterranean region at the end of 1347. From that moment, its triumphant progress through Europe can be closely followed. By the next summer it reached Paris, the heart of medieval Europe, and southern England shortly afterwards. From there it spread northward through the British Isles and Scandinavia, and eastward to the Low Countries, the Holy Roman Empire and Eastern Europe. By the end of 1350 the Black Death reached Russia after a long roundabout

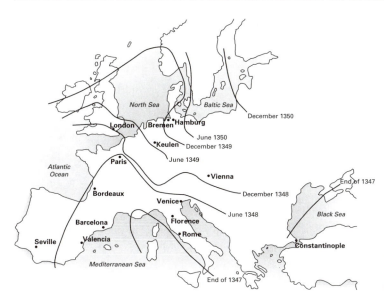

Map 13.1 The spread of the Black Death

Source: P. Zeigler, *The Black Death*, Harmondsworth (1970), pp. 106–107.

journey. Curiously enough, thinly populated regions like Norway and remote island groups such as the Faeroes, Shetlands, Orkneys and Hebrides were hit as hard as the densely populated metropolises of Constantinople, Cairo and Florence. On the other hand, entire regions, such as Bohemia, and a number of major towns are known to have suffered relatively little. As far as the former are concerned, there must have been an ecological reason (Bohemia, for instance, did not have the niches suitable for foreign rat populations). The towns that were spared owed this above all to sensible government. Although medieval doctors had not the slightest idea about the bacterial origins of diseases, nor of how they spread, they did realize that they could be highly contagious and therefore that it was best to keep the disease at a distance. This could be done in two ways: a town could be isolated from the outside world by strictly controlling the traffic entering, and within the town itself, houses, streets or certain quarters where disease had broken out could be completely closed off. These methods were applied successfully in Milan, a city with a population of 100,000, which the Visconti family ruled with an iron hand. It is estimated that no more than 15 per cent of the population of Milan died during the epidemic. The magistracy of Nuremberg went a step further, for Nuremberg experienced virtually no extra mortality because of its hygienic regulations, which seem almost

modern and which were not introduced specifically in connection with the epidemic. The roads were paved and the streets were swept; the inhabitants were expected to dispose of their own household refuse; the town had 14 public bathhouses, which were carefully supervised and were frequented by local civil servants who received a salary bonus in the form of bath money. In later outbreaks other towns introduced similar policies. Eventually, Venice set up a well-organized system of quarantine, although the first experiment was set up in Ragusa (modern Dubrovnik) in 1377. During the fifteenth century, quarantine even became compulsory in Venice. The measure meant that everyone who wanted to visit the city during periods of contagious disease had first to stay on an island in the lagoon for 40 days (quarantine means 'a period of 40 days'); whoever was alive and well after the 40 days was allowed to enter Venice.

Despite quarantines and hygienic regulations, the Black Death struck mercilessly and repeatedly, in 1361, 1362, 1369 and from 1400 to 1402, and on other occasions in the hundred years after 1350. Between 10 and 20 per cent of the population of Europe succumbed in every echo epidemic. After 1402 the length of time between epidemics increased, and they were less widespread. Nevertheless, the frequency with which the sickness reared its head continued to hinder demographic recovery, the more so because it sometimes appeared together with other apocalyptic horrors. This was the case, for example, in the years 1437 and 1438, when disease and famine stalked the land together. In Normandy, where much research has been done, the population decreased by one-third at that time. Nor should we forget that various diseases could take on epidemic forms in more or less the same period. Although the vague descriptions found in sources do not always permit a proper medical diagnosis, we do know that, besides the possible plague, various forms of typhus, diphtheria, dysentery (from which King John Lackland of England died), malaria (the cause of the death of several German kings in Italy) and occasionally influenza proved fatal to many of their victims.

The damage and suffering of war

It is difficult to calculate the demographic effects of wars on the late Middle Ages. Compared with wars in our own time even protracted conflicts such as the Hundred Years War did not directly cause many civilian casualties, until the French king, Charles VIII, set a depressing new standard during his invasion of Italy in 1494. Actual hostilities were limited to a number of years, armies were relatively small when compared to those in later centuries, and the theatre of war changed constantly. It is true that large battles did claim the lives of thousands of soldiers; a relatively high number. For this reason there was a high mortality rate among the nobles who took an active part in war during the late Middle Ages. For common people, however, the consequences were more indirect and long term. Troops on campaign or people escaping from the violence of war increased the risk of contagious diseases spreading. In those areas through which armies crossed or where mercenaries remained once the campaign was over in the hope of finding new employment, there was no end to the misery, for all was pillaged and ravaged relentlessly. This would have affected the fertility rate more than mortality. Yet the war-stricken population of France recovered from the economic depression of the late Middle Ages sooner than that of England, which was spared the violence of war until 1455.

THEORIES ON DEMOGRAPHIC DECLINE AND ECONOMIC DEVELOPMENT

There is not the slightest doubt that the size of the population during the fourteenth century decreased markedly all over Europe, from the principality of Kiev in the east to the kingdom of Portugal in the southwest. There are no exact figures, but it is generally assumed that the population of Europe around 1450 was approximately two-thirds of what it had been in 1300. It then made a hesitant recovery, with considerable regional differences. In 1520 England still only had about half the estimated number of inhabitants it had at the end of the thirteenth century; that number was not reached until about 1600. Demographic recovery started earlier in France, and the population size of about 1300 would again have been reached by 1550. In certain strongly urbanized regions, such as Flanders and Holland, the population level of 1300 was probably reached even before the end of the fifteenth century; but others, among them Tuscany, would only approach the estimated population density of the thirteenth century in the course of the nineteenth century.

This difference in the phases of demographic recovery is certainly not linked to large regional discrepancies in the mortality rate. We should relate it then to differences in marital fertility, and through that to features of the economic structure or development, and to cultural differences. For England that link points to the relatively high labour participation of women in the century after the Black Death, which had a negative influence on fertility. Cultural factors may well have played a role in Tuscany, where it no longer was customary for widows who were still of childbearing age to remarry. That, too, helped keep the fertility rate low in a period of high mortality.

The link with economic developments is more complicated. For obvious reasons, the late medieval dramatic demographic decline inspired various interpretations. The currently most respected view, and the one that has thus acquired the status of an academic paradigm or widely accepted model, is the following. Around 1300 Europe was relatively overpopulated, a demographic crisis that precipitated a long phase of economic stagnation. In this manner the Middle Ages fits perfectly into the image of a pre-industrial, mainly agrarian society governed by a cyclical alternation of secular trends – in other words, of protracted, sluggish phases of expansion and contraction. This complex explanation is usually termed 'Neomalthusian', because it goes back ultimately to the ideas of the British 'classic economist' Thomas Robert Malthus. Between the 1930s and 1970s it was propagated in the work of prominent socio-economic historians such as Wilhelm Abel, Michael Postan, Bernard Slicher van Bath and Emmanuel Le Roy Ladurie. We shall now review the key factors in these interpretations.

Europe 1300: a society under pressure?

In his influential *Essay on the Principle of Population* of 1798 Malthus put forward the theory that each population tends to grow more quickly than does the amount of food that it can itself produce. Sooner or later, population growth is thus restructured to remove the tensions between population pressure and food production. This can happen favourably, by means of what Malthus called 'preventive checks', or unfavourably through 'positive checks': favourably, by limiting the number of children (that is, the number of births: a fall in the birth rate), which in pre-industrial Europe implied lowering marital fertility; unfavourably as a consequence of disease, famine and violence in an over-full world (increased mortality).

David Ricardo, a contemporary of Malthus, provided an explanation for Malthus's position by referring to two economic laws. The first, known as the 'law of diminishing returns', predicted that the addition of increasing amounts of labour to a constant area of land would very soon lead to a drop in labour productivity (yield per worker deployed). Expansion of agricultural production through the cultivation of new land would not help either when there was continuing population growth because, according to Ricardo's ground rent theory, the best land would be the first to be cultivated. As population pressure made it necessary to exploit less suitable land so land productivity (yield per unit of area) decreased as well.

Ricardo realized that technological developments could counteract a reduction in productivity, but he believed that the chances of that happening were limited, and that over time technology would always be outdone by nature. This is one of the points on which the Neomalthusian view was criticized at an early stage by Neomarxist historians. According to them, insufficient investment was made in technological development in medieval agriculture because of the weight and compulsive, non-economic nature of burdening peasants with all kinds of charges (surplus extraction). That is why regional variations in surplus extraction caused population growth to lead to tensions in one region earlier than in another.

Despite objections of this sort, the Neomalthusian view of demographic developments during the first half of the fourteenth century is still generally accepted, even by its Neomarxist critics. There appear to be enough indications of growing demographic pressure towards the end of the thirteenth century. Regulated agriculture had penetrated agro-ecological marginal regions, such as the Alps and the Scottish Highlands. In more densely populated areas the pieces of land

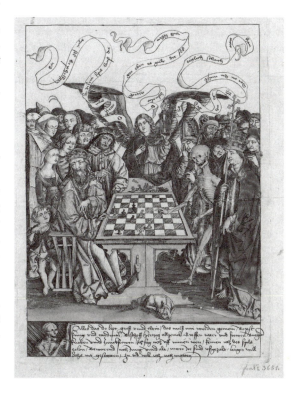

Plate 13.2 Chess game with Death. Coloured engraving, German, *c.* 1480–1490

owned by peasants were radically split up, the communal use of pasture, wood and wasteland came under pressure, and the rate of urbanization flagged. Colonization and land reclamation came to a standstill. Each of these indications on its own does not say much, but together they support the picture of a relatively overpopulated Europe. It is impossible to say whether the tensions between population growth and means of subsistence would ever have resulted in a Malthusian discharge, for the Black Death intervened as a macabre killjoy. The deadly epidemic was a completely exogenous factor, not a positive check in the Malthusian sense raised by internal circumstances. The same is also true of the Great Famine of 1315–1317, the severity of which was the result of exceptionally bad weather conditions.

The agrarian crisis of the late Middle Ages

This brings us to the next component of the Neomalthusian view of the economic history of the late Middle Ages that raises questions. It rests on two suppositions. First, the demographic devastation caused by the Black Death and its echo epidemics set in motion a deflationary economic spiral that struck the agricultural sector in particular extremely hard. Second, this economic crisis was an impediment to rapid population recovery because of its negative effects on marriage patterns and marriage fertility, and thus on the birth rate.

Symptoms

There is absolutely no doubt that the drastic reduction in population numbers after 1350 had far-reaching consequences for economic developments in the late medieval countryside. In the first place, there was a change in the land/labour ratio, the relationship between the acreage available for cultivation and the number of people working on that land. This led to agricultural land being used more extensively, or even being entirely neglected if it was in an unfavourable location or of poor quality. A typical late medieval phenomenon was that of 'deserted land', which often resulted in entire villages being abandoned. In the Holy Roman Empire 40,000 out of a total of 170,000 settlements, almost a quarter, were lost! To be sure

there may have been other reasons behind the loss of these villages (administrative or military, for example), but there is no doubt at all that the need for farming land decreased. It led everywhere to a radical fall in the rents and sale prices of farmland.

A second consequence was linked directly to the first. The severe decline in the size of the population pushed down the price of grain, the basic foodstuff. This was less logical than it may seem – certainly in view of the relative urbanization of late medieval society, which made more people dependent on agricultural production. The reasoning is that the decrease in the size of the population made it possible to concentrate grain production on the most suitable land so that the average yields per unit of area rose. Perhaps the first of these things did happen, but the second one certainly did not because the fields were worked less intensively than previously as a result of the shortage of labour. There was, then, a different, three-part reason for the falling market prices of grain. First, despite falling land productivity, labour productivity in agriculture, and thus production per consumer, probably remained at the same level (see Table 13.1, calculated using a hypothetical example). Second, because land was cheap, many smallholders succeeded in acquiring enough land to avoid being dependent on the market for buying grain. Third, the shortage of labour caused wages to rise. This favourable development in wages in relation to prices led to an improvement in the standard of living of those groups who were largely or entirely dependent on wage income. The improvement

Table 13.1 Hypothetical development of grain production and agrarian productivity between 1300 and 1450, given a general population decline of 35 per cent and a degree of urbanization increase from 10–15 per cent (index: 1300 = 100)

	1300	1450
(1) Acreage of arable land	100	75
(2) Labour force	100	55
(3) Yields in grain	100	65
(4) Land productivity	100	85
(5) Labour productivity	100	120
(6) Number of consumers	100	65
(7) Production per consumer	100	100

was reflected in greater consumption, not of bread but of more expensive foodstuffs such as meat, fish and dairy products. This structural change in consumer preferences can partially explain the tendency towards low grain prices. But it was only a tendency. We have seen that the market prices of grain could fluctuate under the influence of great variations in the size of the harvests from one year to another, and that crises of subsistence occurred just as often in the late Middle Ages as in the periods before or after.

Solutions

The new scarcity and price relations that came into existence after the Black Death did not have the same effect on every social group involved in agricultural production. Those hardest hit were the traditional large landowners, the nobility and the monasteries in particular. Falling incomes, either from surpluses which they brought to market or from rents or leases in cash or kind, contrasted with soaring wage costs and the rising expenses of non-agricultural goods. In sum, this group found itself 'trapped in the blades of a negative price scissors', to use the words of the German agricultural historian Wilhelm Abel. In such circumstances many landowners felt forced to capitalize on parts of their land. Others, private individuals rather than (ecclesiastical) institutions, tried either to 'marry money' or find an alternative source of income in the growing official, diplomatic or military apparatuses of kings and princes.

Less drastic solutions allowed large landowners to keep their position intact and sometimes even to strengthen it. One such way included every attempt to counter market forces by keeping wages low, obstructing the free movement of labour or increasing all sorts of traditional payments in spite of their inalterable character. Such solutions were applied under pressure in Catalonia, but not often in north-western Europe where lords attempted to placate peasants by offering them favourable levies and leases or dangling the prospect of improvements in their legal status before them. In England, the two reactions followed each other: landlords first used legal means to compel people to work and to fix a maximum wage. This solution was probably initiated by the Commons in Parliament, the representatives of the lower nobility and the prosperous middle class; neither group could compete with the wealthy higher nobility and ecclesiastical landowners who simply used force if they found it necessary. The earliest of these legal measures was the Ordinance of Labourers issued by Edward III on 18 June 1349 when the Black Death caused havoc in England. Special judges, the justices of labourers, were appointed to enforce the ordinance. Less than two years later, a more systematic law dealing with the same issue was introduced: the Statute of Labourers. Several stricter measures followed, among them the petition 'against rebellious peasants', passed by the Commons in 1377. England was not alone in taking such steps. Similar measures were taken elsewhere in the same period, including France (for the Paris region), Castile and Austria.

When the passage of laws to ensure that agricultural labour remained affordable proved ineffective, many English landlords abandoned the direct exploitation of their estates. It often meant that they leased out the demesne parts or *réserves* (the parts of manors reserved for the lord) and made written contracts, known as copyholds, with their bondsmen for the possession of their holdings in a form of hereditary lease. This in fact finally brought an end to serfdom in England. The Catalan peasants were equally successful in their resistance to the reactionary attitude of their landlords, albeit over a longer period.

Those landlords who continued to exploit their land and turned to the market had to make sure that they profited from altered price relations. Not all agricultural products showed the same tendency to drop in price. As a result of the changes in consumer preferences and the expansion of urban industries, the prices of animal products (wool, beef, leather and butter in particular), luxury foods (wine and fruit) and any variety of crops that could be used as raw materials in urban industries (flax, hemp, barley for brewing, vegetable dyes and flavourings) were generally far more stable than the price of corn. Because the cultivation of cash crops was extremely labour-intensive, this provided a solution for smaller peasants who did not have to hire labourers.

Large landowners profited more by specializing in extensive forms of pastoral farming, which required plenty of land but not much labour. There was a phenomenal growth in sheep farming during the Middle

Plate 13.3 Danse macabre: from minstrel to bishop, everybody is involved in the dance of death. Early fifteenth-century fresco in the church of La Ferté-Loupière (France, Dept. of Yonne)

Ages, especially in the more sparsely populated regions of England and Castile. It has been said that from the late Middle Ages sheep changed from being a 'peasant's animal' to a 'lord's animal', but this had been the case in the coastal regions of Flanders for many centuries.

By the beginning of the fourteenth century, England had already exported the wool of an estimated 8 million sheep; many larger landlords switched to sheep-farming in the second half of the fifteenth century when domestic cloth production started booming, greatly increasing the demand for wool. English land-lords soon found themselves clashing with peasants, who traditionally had grazing rights allowing sheep to use the vast tracts of wasteland. This heralded the breakthrough of the enclosure movement, whereby the landlords enclosed grazing lands and shut them off to common use. In the kingdoms of Naples and Castile, the growing number of sheep led to increased transhumance, the seasonal migration of livestock between the higher-lying summer pastures and the plains and valleys. This, too, caused all sorts of prob-lems. In an effort to deal with them, sheep-owners sometimes organized themselves into associations,

the best known of which is the *Mesta* in Castile. Dominated from the beginning by noble landowners and knightly orders, by 1360 this 'brotherhood' had kept a total of one million sheep; by the middle of the fifteenth century that number had increased to three million, and by 1500 to five million.

In addition to a more extensive land use, the appli-cation of labour-saving techniques sometimes brought relief because they kept wages down while the capital investment needed was not exceptionally large. Two of these innovations were developed in Flanders: the light plough, which needed fewer horses and labourers, and the reaping hook, or short scythe, which replaced the sickle for harvesting. It was possible to work far more quickly with the reaping hook and also to harvest more straw, used as a roofing material and in the preparation of manure.

And what of the peasants themselves, the direct agricultural producers? In order to assess what hap-pened to them it is best to divide them into three groups: a middle class, which had just enough land to support itself; above that, a (small) group of peasants with substantial holdings who regularly produced

surpluses for the market and who employed labourers; and, at the bottom, a broad underlayer of smallholders and people without any land at all, dependent more or less entirely on irregular or seasonal wages. As wages were relatively high at the time, the late Middle Ages was generally a favourable period for this last group. They often had to find extra income from non-agricultural or para-agricultural sources. Urban traders and entrepreneurs found it attractive to move some aspects of cloth production, such as spinning and weaving, to the countryside where the wages were lower than in the towns with their guilds and collective protests against excessive exploitation. In some parts of fifteenth-century Flanders and England, completely new centres for the production of cheap woollen cloth emerged, such as Hondschoote and Poperinge in West Flanders or Castle Combe in Wiltshire. In the vicinity of Ghent, large numbers of smallholders specialized in the labour-intensive cultivation of flax. After the harvest, they added extra income by combing, retting and spinning the raw flax themselves. Only then was the flax thread sent to the linen weavers as a semi-manufactured product.

The integration of non-agrarian activities into the rural economy is not necessarily limited to the textile industry only. In the County of Holland, small-scale farming was combined with a medley of non-agricultural activities: shipbuilding, shipping and fishery, peat and salt extraction, reed cutting and brick-making. Also, there was always a great demand for wage work in the construction and maintenance of dikes, ditches and sluices. As a result, more than half the rural population of Holland had become heavily dependent for its income on wage earnings by 1500. The same proportion has been mentioned in connection with East Anglia, where wages were usually earned by labour on large farms in the region. In those parts of England rich in minerals (coal, tin, copper, lead), such as Durham, Devon and Cornwall, the exploitation of smallholdings was often combined with work in the mines.

The middle group of peasants, in possession of its own land, always remained a vulnerable group because it had difficulty in building up financial reserves. These peasants were not only unable to profit from the low price of land but were particularly vulnerable to damage from war or natural disasters such as failed harvests, storms and floods for they had no resources on which to fall back; moreover, they were also easy prey for large farmers and landowners. Their pitiful situation worsened in many parts of western Europe when their tax burden increased rapidly after the fifteenth century.

The prospects for the third group, that of large farmers, were better in this respect. They were able to create a financial buffer and, through diversification, could gear production to market demand better than those peasants whose primary occupation was simply to subsist. Certainly some peasants ended up in the grip of the negative price scissor, but not to such an extent as the great landowners. The peasants had a far more modest pattern of consumption and they could keep the costs of hired labour to a minimum by getting members of their family to help or by taking in farmhands and helpers as boarders or paying them in kind. In this way, many better-off peasants managed to enlarge their fortunes and invest their savings in cheap land. The trend continued during the period of renewed expansion, starting around 1450. A class of prosperous large farmers then emerged in England, the yeomen, whose social status was just below that of the lower nobility or gentry.

ECONOMIC CRISIS OR CONTRACTION?

Many authors who have studied the economic history of the late Middle Ages use the terms 'crisis' and 'contraction' rather indiscriminately, which we think is wrong. We have preferred to typify the period as a whole as a phase of contraction, and not as a crisis. Demographic shrinkage is not disputed, nor the resulting fall in the total production of goods. To what extent and why this situation was detrimental for certain forms of income has been discussed above. Thus only for those people whose income was affected might it be possible to speak of an agricultural 'crisis'. It is clear that not all social groups who could lay claim to income from agriculture found themselves in a crisis situation.

Approaching the question from other angles, we can put the alleged late medieval crisis even further into perspective. Wage-earners – first and foremost urban groups – saw a considerable increase in their real earnings, and thus in their standard of living. Not without reason, the fifteenth century has often been referred to as 'the golden age of the labourer', and the improvement, in addition to free time, would have been reflected in the purchase of more expensive

foodstuffs and products of industry. This development stimulated the production of and trade in goods of mass consumption, perhaps for the first time in European history. Much research still needs to be done in this field, but there are clear indications that, by and large and despite the horrors of chronic crises of existence, late medieval people were better fed, better clothed and better housed than their forefathers. This can be deduced from certain economic-institutional developments, as well as from an archaeological and art-historical study of the material culture. During the late Middle Ages, economic institutions such as markets increasingly were given a primarily regional function. Hundreds of new fairs were introduced, for example. The largest and most important – at Lyons, Frankfurt-am-Main, Vienna, Nuremberg, Cracow and Bergen-op-Zoom – became part of dynamic new cycles of annual fairs with an international character. They were just the tip of the iceberg, however, showing that more and more small places were linked up with trading networks, enabling people of modest means to buy simple goods from other places. By the same token, these same people could try to find bigger or more distant markets for their local produce. Information from Flanders shows how well they succeeded in this: cheap woollen materials produced in the new rural textile centres found their way to Russia as early as the fifteenth century. It is therefore generally accepted that the total volume of trade was far larger in 1500 than it had been at the end of the period of expansion two centuries earlier.

Even in this 'optimistic' scenario, however, cyclical movements and regional differences in tempo still must be taken into consideration. Regions that did well at a relatively early date, such as Castile and southern Germany, formed a contrast with those that only got underway later, such as Normandy and England.

CHARACTERISTICS OF LATE MEDIEVAL SOCIETY

Openness and closure

With its frequent epidemics, the late Middle Ages was a period of intermittent dynamism. Apart from the social and psychological disruptions, which at times must have been unimaginable, the lottery of death – it was impossible to predict who would die or who would survive – led to radical rearrangements of capital. No wonder that the ancient theme of vicissitudes of fortune enjoyed such popularity. That was true of another new motif as well, the dance of death, the procession of rich and poor, young and old, man and wife, led by death (often depicted as a skeleton holding a scythe), which was intended to make all mortals realize that death was no respecter of persons and could carry anyone off, at any time.

If the mortality crises undeniably furthered geographical and social mobility, paradoxically enough they also advanced the tendency to social closure. The paradox is admirably illustrated by the development of the late medieval English nobility. Under the influence of the Hundred Years War in particular, the nobility was considerably enlarged through the recognition of two additional noble 'ranks', those of (e)squire and gentleman. The number of nobles tripled. This new nobility then became increasingly exclusive. Taxation was the background to this development: when the crown taxed the nobility it had to be clear who belonged to the group.

Even after enlargement, therefore, the English nobility remained a select group, comprising no more than 1.6 per cent of the taxable population at the middle of the fifteenth century. Table 13.2, with an overview of the English nobility in 1436, clearly shows the enormous differences in income within the nobility,

especially within the highest category of nobles, the peers. The richest peer in England in that year was Richard, duke of York, who had a taxable income of £3,230. This was more than fifty times greater than the £60 listed for Lord Clinton, the least well-off peer in the tax records. Further, the records also show that Clinton's income was 'only' 12 times the minimum annual income of £5 necessary to be counted a gentleman.

The nobility was never hermetically sealed off, however – had that happened it would have soon died out everywhere! One road open to it was to embrace people who were closest to the nobility in wealth and lifestyle: in England the ownership of extensive property largely determined entry; in the Low Countries it was often the possession of seigneurial rights. Vice versa, nobility and knighthood excluded members who were no longer able to maintain their position, whatever the reason. More or less fixed mechanisms were in place to regulate this: one important criterion to exclude an individual was whether he himself performed farm work or other forms of manual labour.

A similar paradox applies to urban settings. On the one hand, urbanization increased rather than decreased during the late Middle Ages. Moreover, the expectation of life was shorter in the towns than in the country. For both reasons, there always was a steady flow of migrants into the towns resulting in greater flexibility and mobility of labour, which in the large and

Table 13.2 Stratification of the nobility in England according to income tax demands in 1436. The total number of taxpayers was about 450,000.

Category	No.	Range	
		Taxable annual income (£)	Average annual income (£)
Peers	50	60–3,230	865
Knights (knightly class)	933	40–600	88
Esquires	1,200	20–39	24
(Larger) freeholders	1,600	10–19	[14.5]
(Ordinary) gentlemen	c. 3,400	5–10	[7.5]

Source: Calculated from S.H. Rigby, *English Society in the later Middle Ages. Class, Status and Gender* (Basingstoke and London, 1995), p. 190

medium-sized towns led to the formation of a highly mobile, almost 'floating' underclass of people who did not have the formal status of burgher, were employed on a daily basis or not at all and who thus lived from hand to mouth. On the other hand, the increasing organization and regulation of labour and production in the crafts, the retail trade and the services reinforced the tendency to exclusion. This was in fact a protracted development that went back to the period of expansion and would not reach its peak until after the Middle Ages. In the late medieval economic circumstances, the result was that a structural labour shortage coincided with a process of exclusion and protectionism amongst the labour elite.

This entire development fits in with the more general tendency in Western European society during the later Middle Ages and the early modern period towards social compartmentalization and the formation of what Max Weber called 'status groups'. By this he meant groups that were clearly separate from each other socially and sometimes even legally, and reinforced that separation by their way of life and their own codes of behaviour. The origin of this tendency to classification must be sought in the twelfth century, when all sorts of new urban groups and associations had to find their places in a social order that, according to medieval social ideology (cf. Chapter 7), had to be firmly and hierarchically constructed and able to function organically. As reality became increasingly complex, however, the social order showed symptoms of emancipation and mobility that were difficult to reconcile with this ideology. The listings and plans of social groups from that time betray the need felt for an appointed place; all segments of society had to be absolutely certain concerning what was expected of them, by which external signs they could be recognized, the sort of behaviour fitting for their members, and so on. All sorts of social categories were even provided with 'typical' virtues and vices. Moral group assessments of this sort were imprinted through the so-called *sermones ad status*, literally meaning 'sermons addressed to the [social] orders'. The tendency was articulated even further during the late Middle Ages. One famous literary witness of the extreme 'boxes mentality' of this period was Geoffrey Chaucer's verse narrative, the *Canterbury Tales*; this story of the journey of a pilgrimage to the shrine of Thomas Becket at

Canterbury formed a perfect frame for an ironic parade of individuals, each of which represented a recognizable social type.

The position of women

What influence did the socio-economic climate of the late Middle Ages have on the position of women in society? The answer to this question must begin with the observation that virtually no one during the period ever got beyond the essentially ambiguous attitude that has in fact been characteristic of the entire history of Christian European culture from ancient times right up to the present. The misogynous undercurrent within it went far back in time, to Greek philosophers like Aristotle, and was reinforced in late ancient Christian theology. Along the way the negative image of women became firmly embedded in medical, sexological, sociological, theological and legal views. According to those views, not only were women inferior to men in a physical respect, they were also less intelligent and less inhibited emotionally. Nevertheless, Christianity set a positive counter-current in motion by admitting women from the outset to the heart of the gallery of Christian saints, beginning with the Virgin Mary, mother of Christ. This counter-current was reinforced under the influence of the new religious and courtly sentiments that came to the fore from the eleventh century onwards and by changes in the Church's ideas on marriage. A Christian marriage could only be founded on the agreement of both marriage partners, and mutual affection between spouses became the canonical basis of a good marriage.

But all this brought little change in the prevailing negative attitude towards women in medieval society. Through their lesser 'nature', women had an essentially different function than men. They had no place in public life, and had no business there. In both the public and private spheres they were subject to the authority of men: fathers, brothers or uncles and eventually mostly husbands, who controlled their marriage portions and had the unwritten right to take harsh measures to keep wayward women under control.

Outside the private sphere, women had only limited rights. They could not hold public office – except for that of abbess, as well as the temporal rulership positions such as queen, duchess or countess, often connected with considerable genuine power. Ordinary women, on the other hand, could act independently on their own behalf or on behalf of another, without the aid of a male 'guardian', or appear before ecclesiastical or secular courts only in very precisely described, exceptional cases. Their legal liability was thus also limited, which had its advantages of course: in emergencies women could always call on their legal incapacity.

From a socio-economic point of view, there was less inequality between men and women in the lower classes than in the upper classes. In the lower classes, a woman normally was actively involved in income-earning, there was little property or capital for men to manage, and men had few or no public (administrative or judicial) responsibilities that gave them a sense of superiority. The relative degree of autonomy allowed to women who were active in trade or the retail business in towns was particularly remarkable. In Flanders, every generally recognized *coopvrouw*, a female merchant, was allowed to carry on business on her own account and at her own risk, whatever her civil status. We have seen something of the position of women in craft guilds in Chapter 11. Most working women, however, were employed on the fringes of the economy and not in association with guilds. They often performed undervalued tasks in the textile trade, such as spinning, combing, knotting and knitting, or they peddled foodstuffs on the street, sold cheap cloth or ran a junk shop. Many women worked as domestic servants, while others cared for the sick – clearly risky but therefore better paid.

From a purely legal viewpoint, widows were the best off. As long as they did not remarry, widows had far more control over their own affairs than did married women. For economic reasons, however, many women could not afford to permanently escape 'a man's rod', in the words of the Antwerp poetess Anna Bijns (1493–1575), and thus they remarried unless there were strong cultural prejudices against remarriage, as was the case in the Mediterranean area. Not without reason widows were placed under the special protection of the Church as *personae miserabiles* even into the fourteenth century. Only the well-off widow, with sufficient means to carry on or possibly rent out the business of her deceased husband, could gain recognition as a full master (or mistress) within a craft guild. It is also noticeable how many widows were among the creditors mentioned in countless loan letters dating from the late Middle Ages.

BOX 13.2 A WOMAN FIGHTS BACK WITH THE PEN: THE LIFE AND WORKS OF CHRISTINE DE PIZAN (1364–*c.* 1430)

Perhaps the most remarkable example of a successful widow in the late Middle Ages was Christine of Pisa (Christine de Pizan) (1364–*c.* 1430), daughter of the Venetian court astrologer to the French king, Charles V. After the death of her husband Étienne de Castel, a royal secretary, Christine became a public figure with an extensive literary *oeuvre* consisting of poems in the lyrical, courtly style, biographies and didactic works. The *Livre de la cité des dames* ('Book of the City of Ladies') and *Epistres sur le Rommant de la Rose* ('Letters about the *Roman de la Rose*') are considered her most important works. The first, completed in 1405, was a very free translation into French of *De claris mulieribus* ('Concerning Famous Women'), a poetical work written in Latin by Giovanni Boccaccio. While Boccaccio had included only the biographies of exemplary women from pagan Antiquity, not considering it fitting to describe the saintly lives of Christian women in the same context, Christine had no hesitation in doing just that. And after a comparative enumeration of virtues that were mirrored in the lives of those famous women from the past, she proffered a philosophical defence against the misogynous mainstream of medieval intellectual thought. The city of ladies was built under the supervision of Reason, Rectitude and Justice; its citizens had proved that they contributed at least as much as men did to the formation of an ordered Christian society. Women were different from men, but it was not possible that they were less perfect creations of God, and for that reason their natural weaknesses were amply compensated for by positive characteristics. In Christine's view, the withholding of a proper education from women was the main reason for their seeming inferiority.

The same themes were dealt with in the *Epistres*, though in a less veiled way, for in this polemic Christine took the side of female honour and honesty against the uncomplimentary treatment of women in the immensely popular *Roman de la Rose*. The interminable *Roman* was an allegorical treatment of courtly love. It was begun around 1240 by the northern French knight, Guillaume de Loris, and continued in much more satirical, and anti-female vein by Jean de Meung, a poet of bourgeois origins, a quarter of a century later. Christine's criticism provoked heated public discussions about the value of the *Roman*, in which she could count on the support of the famous preacher and chancellor of the University of Paris, Jean Gerson, who called Christine 'a woman like a man' (*femina ista virilis*).

On her own, Christine de Pizan was of course no more a proof of the existence of wide support for the emancipation of women than was Joan of Arc, the Maid of Orléans whom Christine praised in one of her poems. Moreover, Christine's works were traditional in form and, above all, encouraged conventional marital virtues and female codes of conduct. Nonetheless, they had an emancipatory tenor, especially because they propagated the idea, previously defended only by Abelard, that women too may have *auctoritas*, and that they deserve a full and valued place within the community. In this connection Christine also urged that elementary education be made available to women.

Literature: Maureen Quilligan, *The Allegory of Female Authority: Christine de Pizan's 'Cité des dames'* (Ithaca, N.Y., 1991); *Une femme de lettres au Moyen Age. Etudes autour de Christine de Pizan*, Liliane Dulac and Bernard Ribémont (eds) (Orléans, 1995); Alcuin Blamires, *The Case for Women in Medieval Culture* (Oxford, 1997).

Whether the position of women improved or worsened during the late Middle Ages is a much discussed matter. One theory broadly suggests that women's chances in life were much improved in the late Middle Ages in comparison with the early period. Their negotiating position on the 'marriage market' had weakened, however, because they had become far less scarce. Such demographic reasoning may appear rather far-fetched, but the idea of a relative surplus of women in the late Middle Ages is by no means absurd, as long as it is applied only to towns. Comparatively large numbers of women lived in towns. Wealthier households generally had many live-in female servants. Older widows from the countryside often moved within the protection of the town walls if they could afford to do so. For similar reasons the towns housed many women's convents. Towns then were places where there were concentrations of women without them necessarily forming an economic or social problem for urban society, a perspective suggested in German historiography in particular. The supposed excess of unmarried women, all of whom secretly desired a husband, was often ridiculed in the satirical literature of the time. It also provided a fertile breeding ground for another, by no means harmless, phenomenon: the demonization of single, elderly women. The stereotype of the ill-tempered old woman who used magic spells to cause harm had been around for much longer – there was a continued demand for practitioners of magic throughout the entire Middle Ages – but now a new element was added, one which was particularly dangerous for those concerned: that malicious people could make a pact with the devil. This demonization of women who were wrongly suspected of practising magic had a variety of backgrounds. The ubiquitous presence of death and decay certainly contributed to it, as did the 'boxed-in mentality' discussed on p. 284 and the growing moralism in public life through which more and more emphasis was laid on the moral reputation of individuals – and the reputation of single women was easily besmirched. And, finally, the gradual professionalization of medical and pharmaceutical care and the rise of a professional 'care sector' (again, mainly in the towns) would have played a part as they tried to submerge all forms of popular medicine and magic, which came to be seen in an increasingly bad light. In short, by the end of the Middle Ages there were clear signs of a religious-psychological climate of fear and rejection that would end in the great witch hunts of the early modern period.

SOCIAL CONTRASTS AND SOCIAL CONFLICTS

Contrasts between town and country

In addition to the old antithesis between peasants and aristocratic lords, the rise of the towns created a new contrast, one between town and country, between farmers and townspeople, between a rustic and a civic culture. It seemed to be a logical consequence of the tendency of the towns to dominate the surrounding countryside politically, militarily and economically. That tendency was reinforced in the late Middle Ages in those parts of Europe with an increased degree of urbanization.

Late medieval urban imperialism caused the distinct, multidimensional interrelation between town and country to widen rather than to narrow the social and cultural gulf between country people and town dwellers. In 1525, Wolfgang Königstein, a canon of Frankfurt, could refer to the Peasants' War that had just broken out (see pp. 288–289) as an 'uffruer von ein folk, genannt die bauern' (a 'revolt of a people, known as the peasants'), as if he were talking about the Huns or the Mongols. A revealing remark. The urban elite had a profound dislike of everything rustic, and this dislike was translated into stereotypes that sometimes merely repeated the old aristocratic prejudices against peasants and sometimes reflected new ones. Peasants were seen as clumsy, churlish, dirty and stupid, lacking any sense of proportion and self-control either in eating and drinking or in dealing with conflicts. An Italian proverb summed it up: 'la città buon' huomeni de' fare, la villa buone bestie' ('the task of the town is to make good people, and of the village to make good beasts'). In the eyes of literary historians the 'burgher culture' was rooted in the positive view that contrasted with the negative characteristics of rustic life. If we are to use the term 'burgher culture' we must remember that it refers exclusively to the culture of the urban elite. In the late Middle Ages the established middle class had embarked upon what the French historian Robert

Map 13.2 Targets of the Peasant's Revolt, 1381

Source: A. Goodman, 'The Peasant's Revolt of 1381', in Angus Mackay and David Ditchburn (eds), *Atlas of Medieval Europe* (London and New York, 1997), p. 227

Muchembled) has called a 'civilizing offensive'. This was a reaction against both the noisy nobility abhorrent of manual labour and the common folk, particularly the peasants in the countryside. The offensive did not take place in social isolation. There was continual social interaction between the nobility and the patriciate in the towns, which not only led to marriages and political or economical unions but also brought about a cultural blending.

A new 'culture of revolt'?

Throughout the Middle Ages internal peace and order was cruelly broken from time to time by the violent discharges of social tensions that were hidden behind the ideal of harmony in an organically functioning society professed by the clerical elite. The late Middle Ages were no exception in this respect. There were a number of large uprisings in both the country and the urban sphere, but it is not known if there were more or fewer than in the period before or after. It appears that three factors seem to have promoted rebellion. First, the structural shortage of labour was the cause of tensions between serfs and lords, and between employers and employees. Sometimes these tensions revolved around the abolition of personal freedom and the limits to mobility, sometimes around wage levels or political representation. The rapid growth in fiscal demands imposed by rulers upon their subjects at this time formed a second factor. This teething trouble of the early modern state was without doubt one of the major reasons for revolt. Finally, the call for Church reformation, punctuated with widespread anticlerical feelings and linked with a desire for far-reaching social change, fuelled some major revolts such as that of the Hussites in Bohemia and the Peasants' War in Germany in 1525.

The French Jacquerie in 1358, the English Peasants' Revolt in 1381, the German Peasants' War in 1525 and the Catalan *remensas* movement – which was not limited to just one year (and for that reason alone was rather different) – are all classic examples of peasant uprisings in the late Middle Ages. The Jacquerie – the name is derived from the traditional nickname for a French peasant, Jacques Bonhomme ('Jack Goodfellow') – was first and foremost an outpouring of anger at the nobility, who were considered responsible for the depression in the countryside resulting from low grain prices, the growing tax burden and a wage freeze. To make matters worse the countryside was being ravaged by disbanded mercenaries of the French army, which had suffered a humiliating defeat by the English at Poitiers in 1356 – yet another reason for bitterness. The ferocious insurrection, in which the peasants raved like mad dogs, according to the anti-peasant chronicler Jean Froissart, was crushed swiftly and bloodily.

The immediate cause of the great Peasants' Revolt of 1381 was what many peasants believed was an unreasonable increase in the poll tax, a tax introduced a few years earlier and levied on every individual. Rebellious peasants from Kent and Essex marched on London where the governing council around the young king, Richard II (1377–1399), deferred military action. Led by Wat Tyler, the peasants forced their way into the city and razed the Savoy, the palace belonging to the duke of Lancaster, the unpopular regent and uncle to the king. At Mile End, not far outside the city walls, the rebels handed their demands over to the king in person. Although the king appeared willing to make concessions, the peasants stormed the Tower of London, the royal fortress. At a second meeting outside the city walls, this time at Smithfield, the mayor of London struck Wat Tyler dead as the latter, in the king's face, rinsed his mouth with water and then ordered a mug of beer. The king succeeded in regaining control over London, and severe repressions followed. The petitions of Mile End and Smithfield give a good idea of what the rebels actually wanted, and why – especially outside London – the great abbeys formed the target of the peasants' aggression. The most important demands were the definitive abolition of serfdom to which many peasants in south-east England were still subject, the repeal of the labour laws limiting wage increases passed after the Black Death, participation of common people in the government of the country and the dismantling of the worldly riches of the Church in England. The last point was less radical than it may appear, in view of John Wyclif's ideas on Church reformation that were circulating at the time – and to which the hated duke of Lancaster was reputed to be sympathetic.

There were several causes for the great Peasants' War that blazed through southern and central Germany (including parts of present-day Austria and Switzerland) in 1525. Many peasants in the area were still serfs, weighed down by the heavy burdens attached to their personal status. Moreover, everyone, free or unfree, was faced with the spread of local lordships, for these areas were swarming with the so-called *reichsunmittelbare*, minor lords holding the title of count, abbot or knight. Subject only to the purely nominal authority of the German king/emperor, these lords had autonomous rule over territories the size of a few villages where they were often important landowners or landlords as well. It was this combination of lordships that caused such antagonism.

The rebellion of the south German peasantry was remarkable in that it involved not only public violence but also a propaganda offensive of an almost apologetic nature. The hotbed of the revolt was Upper Swabia, where the peasant communities printed their tersely formulated demands and spread them as a manifesto. The so-called 'Twelve Articles of Memmingen' were so well known that they served as a model for countless other 'article letters'. The demands were concrete and succinct, varying from a village's right to choose its own pastor to the abolition of serf taxes, curtailment of the tithe levy, the autonomous right to decide over the use of common woods, meadows and waters, and the guarantee that justice in local courts would be administered in accordance with local customs and not following the statutes mixed with Roman law that many lords had prescribed for their subjects on their own authority.

The new medium of the printing press in particular ensured that the uprising spread like wildfire. Some historians, Peter Blickle among them, believe that it took on the characteristics of a revolution solely because of this medium, for it was only in this way that the radical ideas about social renewal hinted at in the 'article letters' could be so widely disseminated and discussed. This social renewal had two aspects. On the one hand, the insurgents demanded a voice for the common people, the *gemeine Mann*. By this they did not mean every Tom, Dick and Harry, but the more substantial peasants and craftsmen who owned their farmhouse or workplace, the rural equivalent of the 'citizens' in Marsilius of Padua's *Defensor Pacis*. In this respect the revolt was more conservative than revolutionary. On the other hand, there was a revolutionary zeal, grafted onto the ideals of the Reformation. What the peasants envisaged was a drastically improved society in which the common good would be defined in evangelical terms and no longer derived from the interests of the lords; a society, too, in which divine justice and not the arbitrary rulings of the lords would be the guiding principle of regulation and justice.

The leaders of the Reformation did not always welcome the socio-religious ideals of the discontented peasants. After initial hesitation, Luther decidedly rejected the 'rebels'. Yet others, such as Thomas Müntzer in Thüringia and Michael Gaismair in Tirol, sided wholeheartedly with the peasants. Gaismair, a 'tireless advocate of the Christianization of the state and society' (Blickle), wanted to turn Tirol into a radically egalitarian society modelled on the Old Testament. Müntzer was a frustrated disciple of Luther, a substitute pastor in a village in Saxony with

no hope of a glittering career in the Catholic Church. Müntzer's theological views were influenced by mysticism, but he was increasingly prone to apocalyptic delusions to which he bore witness in a violent vocabulary where the keywords were 'purify' and 'destruction'. The end of the world was at hand, but a thousand-year reign of evangelical purity before the Last Judgment was in the offing. It would emerge after a terrible struggle in which countless true believers would die a martyr's death. On the battlefield of Frankenhausen it became clear whom Müntzer had preordained for that martyrdom: the 8,000 Thüringian peasants who, singing psalms and brandishing cudgels and pitchforks, were sent to face the trained lancers of the Landgrave of Hessen.

At Frankenhausen the German princes sent out a horrifying signal of what was in store for the subjects who failed to obey them. Nearly 100,000 peasants perished on the battlegrounds and execution sites of Thüringia, Hessen, Franconia and Swabia in 1525 and 1526. Many German historians consider the failure of the Peasants' War a decisive moment in German history, for two reasons. The first was that the development towards territorial principalities with a semi-sovereign status that had begun under the Hohenstaufens was from now on irreversible. The noble and ecclesiastical owners of local lordships were the great losers, not the peasants. The second reason was that it was out of the question that central and southern Germany would switch to the Reformation.

Finally, the earlier Catalan *remensas* movement, which began during the third quarter of the fourteenth century, evolved from persistent protests by the peasantry of Catalonia against the policy of the spiritual and temporal lords to end the popular practice of allowing peasants to buy off all seigneurial obligations (the sources speak of *payese de remensa*, literally 'peasants of redemption', hence *remensa*). In addition to this, the resettlement policy of the owners of large estates who took on migrants from beyond the Pyrenees met with widespread resistance. Curiously enough the Catalan peasants were supported in their fight by lawyers who believed that, in the case of the *remensas*, the lords were acting contrary to natural law – peasants, too, were by nature free! Even the king of Aragon shared this view. In spite of such powerful allies, however, the peasants had to wait until 1486 for satisfaction when, after a long struggle, most of their demands were acceded to in the Compromise of Guadalupe.

The pre-eminent example of urban rebellion took place in Florence in the summer of 1378. The so-called revolt of the *ciompi* was in fact the outburst of the disaffection that had smouldered for a long time among the lower craftsmen and workers (*sottoposti* in Italian, meaning 'lowly placed') in the textile industry, an estimated 13,000, most of them without their own means of production. These true proletarians were named after the largest group among them, the *ciompi* ('pals'). The *sottoposti* were not organized into guilds and thus had no political influence, because members of the town council were chosen from among the merchants and craft guilds. The *sottoposti* were powerless against the arbitrary decisions of officials when it came to taxation and against every form of exploitation by the great entrepreneurs. The fiasco of an expensive war against the pope was the last straw. The *ciompi* took to the streets and forced three new craft guilds to be established. The place given to the three new guilds in the various organs of public administration was negligible, however, and their leaders, one of whom was the wool-carder Michele di Lando, were hedged in and rapidly neutralized. The *ciompi* felt betrayed by their comrades, and the result was a revolt-in-a-revolt, the rising of the *popolo di Dio* ('God's people'). Michele di Lando refused to back down and led the bloody reprisals in person. The *ciompi* revolt lost its momentum soon afterwards, although relationships in the governing council of Florence did not return to normal until 1382.

Most of the late medieval social revolts underlined the differences between town and country (mentioned on p. 287), for a real coalition between peasant rebels and urban rebels occurred only occasionally, although at times there was a feeling of mutual sympathy or inspiration. In Germany, for example, there were riots in several towns in 1525, these being clearly inspired by the peasants' rebellion. Yet none of them led to joint action, or even to a joint programme of action. The Flemish revolt, which took place from 1323 to 1328, was the only exception. The basis for the revolt was the serious complaints made by the well-organized peasant communities in the district round Bruges about the unfairness and corruption of the country nobility and village notables when taxes were levied. Later the peasants' hatred was directed at the lords in general, including the great abbeys with their rich estates and revenues from tithes. The aristocrats reacted as they usually did, answering violence with more violence. What the third and politically most important social party – the major towns – would do in the struggle was important for the outcome of the conflict. This party was guided by its dislike of the pro-French sentiments of the young count, Louis of Nevers, but was split by internal rivalries: Bruges joined the rebels, while Ghent remained loyal.

At first the revolt was successful. Supported where necessary by Bruges militias, the peasant armies had a number of impressive military victories in what is now West Flanders. In Courtrai and Ypres, the peasants could count on massive help from the local people at the crucial moment. They even captured Count Louis of Nevers. But without the cooperation of Ghent, and with the eventual intervention of Philip VI of France, who according to feudal law was obliged to come to the aid of his vassal, the insurgents were broken. When the uprising threatened to radicalize again, the king mustered a formidable army of knights on the Flemish border in the summer of 1328. The peasants were defeated at Cassel.

In recent years there has been a trend to see the great social upheavals of the late Middle Ages as the resistance of peasants and craftsmen to beneficiaries and employers who did not participate in the process of primary production. Yet, without wishing to detract from the importance of the socio-economic motives that were undoubtedly very real, we do not want to use the term 'class struggle' in the classic Marxist sense. First of all, most rebellions showed remarkably little social homogeneity – this was equally true of the peasants' movements such as the Jacquerie, the Peasants' Revolt and the *Bauernkrieg*, and of the *ciompi* revolt in Florence. There always seem to have been considerable differences in the economic position and well-being of the insurgents. Second, class interests were mixed with other binding social ties of a more vertical nature, cutting across classes. In this context we can consider factions or parties, clientage-like networks or religious groupings. Third, there was no consistent revolution-ary ideology reflecting class-consciousness, an essential ingredient of class struggle in the Marxist sense. Most of the late medieval uprisings studied so far did not seem to have been aimed at overthrowing the existing social order. The only serious exceptions were the rising of the Hussites in the 1420s (see p. 331) and the Peasants' War in 1525. In these cases, the rebels pressed for a new, biblically inspired society of autonomous peasant and town republics.

Contrary to what one might think, peasant uprisings were generally better organized than urban revolts. This proves once again how strong and self-assured village communities had become by then. The peasants of the Jacquerie in the Île de France were probably the only ones not to operate out of their own village communities, hence their rapid defeat. The Flemish, English, Catalan and German peasants, in the other uprisings mentioned, were most emphatically based in village communities. It also meant that rebellious peasants were not just desperados, driven by hunger and poverty; on the contrary, many of them, starting with their leaders, belonged invariably to such village elites as rich peasants, smiths, inn keepers and local bailiffs or judges.

A WORLD OF UBIQUITOUS POVERTY

Because of technological and economic underdevelop-ment and the regular occurrence of subsistence crises allied to it, as well as the lack of anything at all approaching our modern system of social security, the medieval world was one filled with undisguised, grind-ing poverty. As is the case with other forms of human suffering, poverty is a phenomenon that is less easy for historians to understand than may appear at first sight. This is so because poverty never is a clear and unequivocal concept. Even if we were to start from the seemingly simple definition that the poor are in every case people who cannot or can only barely obtain the minimum biological necessities of life, it would still be impossible to get a true impression of the extent of poverty in the Middle Ages from the sources available. In those sources roughly three sorts of 'poor' appear:

1 Poor people, in the sense of the fiscally poor, meaning permanent residents of villages and towns, whose capital resources were too small to have to pay taxes. Taxation records from various parts of the Low Countries in the fourteenth and fifteenth centuries show that they would have formed between 20 and 30 per cent of the total population.

2 Poor people in the sense of people who could be considered eligible for poor relief, meaning occasional support from municipal or religious and charitable institutions. Such support was usually in the form of food rations, sometimes with other basic necessities such as shoes, clothing and fuel.

3 Poor people in the sense of marginal people who did not have any resources of their own and lived on the fringes of society. They would include Third World-like armies of vagrants, beggars and prostitutes with no fixed places of residence and no fixed income.

These three categories overlapped only partly. Not every one who received poor relief was fiscally poor and, conversely, the fiscally poor were not necessarily on poor relief; the marginals were by definition not fiscally poor, nor were they considered for certain types of poor relief.

Institutionalized care for the poor as it existed in the late Middle Ages first started at the end of the twelfth century. Before then it had been a matter for the convents and bishops who at specified times doled out food and clothing to paupers waiting at the gates. New religious sentiments ensured that laypeople became increasingly involved in poor relief, resulting in the creation of two types of facility. The first of these consisted of hospitals and hospices. Hospitals were originally institutions for the care of the sick, aged, travellers on a journey and the poor. In large towns the care became more specialized in the thirteenth century, but the sick and the poor were often housed in the same institute. The oldest urban hospitals came into being as an initiative of the bishops. In time they were often staffed by religious orders specially trained for this purpose, such as the brothers of the Holy Ghost and the Trinitarians. Many hospitals were partly financed through legacies and gifts – often with the condition that the donor or legator would enjoy a pension for life.

The second type of facility was formed by local 'poor tables' or 'tables of the Holy Ghost', forms of poor relief supported by the local community and organized in the parishes. This arrangement was always closely connected with the parish church and was intended for the needy of the particular parish only. These were mostly the 'housebound' poor, people who were either structurally poor, such as elderly widows, or people who had only occasional or insufficient work – people who could not find work in the winter, for example. Research into care for the urban poor in the Netherlands in the fifteenth century shows that relief was very meagre and, even more alarming, tended to shrink just when demand was greatest. The main reasons for this were the lack of funds and too many

Plate 13.4 Food aid to the poor of Bruges. Decorative edging in a charter of 1354

overheads. The situation was especially disastrous when the economy remained weak for a prolonged period of time. Poor tables then had less chance to replenish their coffers from legacies, gifts and such, while the number of the poor could rise alarmingly and with frightening speed. Those afflicted could only hope that emergency measures set in place by religious institutions or rich individuals would offer some help.

Although poverty was so general and widespread it was not always viewed in the same way throughout the Middle Ages. In that sense the great economic, political and religious changes in the years after 1000 form a watershed. Before that time poverty left the aristocratic elite totally cold, to put it bluntly; the Christian duty of charity was left to the clergy and the monks to fulfil.

In the years following 1000 two different movements in the attitude to poverty can be seen, and they were diametrically opposed to each other. On the one hand there was an awareness brought about by the new religiosity that, for two reasons, the poor were in principle 'good'. First, they were – in imitation of Christ and his apostles – living examples of how Christians should actually live: they were the real *domini omnium rerum ecclesiarum* ('lords of all ecclesiastical matters'). Second, through their presence they offered to everyone who could not live such an authentically Christian life the opportunity to relieve the troubled soul by means of 'good works' (alms-giving) and thus to shorten the length of time spent in Purgatory. On the other hand, the commercialization of the economy, aimed at financial gain, gradually created a – still recognizable – mentality in which (manual) labour was regarded in an extremely positive light and poverty was seen as the direct consequence of an unwillingness to work, thus as something for which many indigents had only themselves to blame.

During the late Middle Ages these contradictory views became sharper for several reasons. The demographic contraction caused a structural shortage of labour, which easily gave the impression that there was work for everyone who could and would work. By contrast, among the increasingly widespread and louder calls for reformation in the Church there were bitter complaints that too many Christians, above all the Catholic clergy, allowed themselves to be governed by the sin of greed (*avaritia*) and showed no interest in the Christian duty of charity. In this 'clash of two value systems' (Mullett) poverty was defended loudly and publicly by socially conscious preachers from the mendicant orders. They appear in the sources as champions of a truly 'moral revolution', by which the old aristocratic gift-exchange economy with its conditional grants would have to make way for a real 'alms economy', based on voluntary and unconditional giving, which in fact was no more than restitution by the rich of what belonged to the poor. The observant Franciscan, St Bernardine of Siena (1380–1444), did not shrink from using apocalyptic threats against the rich in his sermons, which also were interspersed with communist ideas even before the concept existed:

> The poor call for alms and only the dogs react . . . You, rich people, who have so much wheat lying in your warehouses that you cannot even keep it clean so that the stuff rots and is eaten by worms and starlings, while the poor suffer the pangs of hunger – what do you think God will do with you? I tell you that your surpluses belong not to you but to your poor neighbours.

His no less celebrated compatriot, the Dominican, Girolamo Savonarola (1452–1498), aired similar ideas by pleading for economic, though not political, rights for the poor. Not only did he preach, he also took action. He breathed new life into the *monti di pietà* in Florence, the credit banks where the needy could borrow money at a low rate of interest. He also agitated for a tax on the extravagance and luxury in which the rich Florentines lived at the time of the Italian Renaissance; if the Dominican had had his way, the famous museums of Florence would not now be stuffed full of the works of art that we so admire today. With the demagogic arsenal of a modern American televangelist, he brought his audience of believers to deeds of collective self-mortification bordering on mass hysteria. In a solemn public meeting his wealthy followers went so far as to throw their sumptuous luxuries – from jewels and cosmetics to playing cards and perfumes – onto a great 'bonfire of vanities', while Savanarola, director-like, did his utmost to give the whole show a feeling of mutual solidarity and social harmony. Not long afterwards, during the traditional carnival, he persuaded well-to-do young men to dress in rags

and go begging for the poor. In the end Savonarola's activities sowed more hatred than harmony, even resulting in the formation of anti-Savonarola groups in Florence.

The other value system found eloquent supporters in humanistic circles. Poggio Bracciolini (1380–1459), for many years attached to the papal Curia as a secretary and thereafter chancellor of Florence, was the first publicly to put the sin of avarice into perspective, even though he was himself a cleric. He considered the desire to acquire more and more as something productive. 'Money', wrote Poggio, 'is a necessary good for the state, and for that reason people who love money are the foundation of the state.' Several great humanists from the beginning of the sixteenth century, men like Erasmus, Juan Luis Vives and Thomas More, spoke disapprovingly of begging and believed that everyone who was able to work had the moral duty to do so. These sentiments, inspired by classical texts, echoed the ideas behind acts of legislation in the years following the Black Death and repeated numerous times in the century thereafter. Poverty, unemployment and vagrancy were always knowingly put in the same category. The poor were all idlers and layabouts, lazy scum who needed a heavy hand to make them improve their ways. This view gradually became more firmly fixed in the mentality of the upper levels of society as the early modern period advanced, and the poor were increasingly stigmatized. Poor relief was more and more seen as a minimum provision, to be used solely to lighten the needs of the poor in their own community who really could not be blamed for the situation they found themselves in.

FURTHER READING

Bartlett, Robert (2004), *The Hanged Man. A Story of Miracle, Memory, and Colonialism in the Middle Ages* (Princeton, N.J. and Oxford: Princeton University Press).

Benedictow, Ole J. (2004), *The Black Death 1346–1353: The Complete History* (Woodbridge and Rochester, N.Y.: Boydell & Brewer).

Biller, Peter (2001), *The Measure of Multitude: Population in Medieval Thought* (Oxford: Oxford University Press).

Blamires, Alcuin (1997) *The Case for Women in Medieval Culture* (Oxford: Clarendon).

Blickle, Peter (1985), *The Revolution of 1525: The German Peasants' War from a New Perspective*, 2nd edn (Baltimore, Md.: Johns Hopkins University Press) (orig.German, 1975).

—— (1998), *From the Communal Reformation to the Revolution of the Common Man* (Leiden: Brill) (trans. from the 3rd German edn, 1993).

Campbell, Bruce M.S. (ed.) (1991), *Before the Black Death: Studies in the 'Crisis' of the Early Fourteenth Century* (Manchester: Manchester University Press).

Cantor, Norman F. (2001), *In the Wake of the Plague: The Black Death and the World it Made* (New York and London: Free Press/Simon & Schuster).

Cohn, Samuel K. Jr (1999), *Creating the Florentine State: Peasants and Rebellion 1348–1434* (Cambridge: Cambridge University Press).

—— (2002), *The Black Death Transformed: Disease and Culture in Early Renaissance Europe* (London and New York: Arnold/Oxford University Press).

Coss, Peter (2003), *The Origins of the English Gentry* (Cambridge: Cambridge University Press).

Denton, Jeffrey Howard (ed.) (1999) *Orders and Hierarchies in Late Medieval and Renaissance Europe* (Basingstoke: Palgrave Macmillan).

Dyer, Christopher (1998), *Standards of Living in the Later Middle Ages. Social Change in England, c.1200–1520*, 2nd edn (Cambridge: Cambridge University Press).

Epstein, Stephan R. (1992), *An Island for Itself: Economic Development and Social Change in Late Medieval Sicily* (Cambridge: Cambridge University Press).

Epstein, Steven A. (2001), *Speaking of Slavery: Color, Ethnicity, and Human Bondage in Italy* (Ithaca, N.Y. and London: Cornell University Press).

Goldberg, P.J.P. (1992) *Women, Work and Life-Cycle in a Medieval Economy: Women in York and Yorkshire* (Oxford: Clarendon).

Hatcher, John (1977), *Plague, Population and the English Economy 1348–1530* (London and Basingstoke: Macmillan).

Herlihy, David and Christiane Klapisch-Zuber (1985), *Tuscans and Their Families* (New Haven, Conn.: Yale University Press) (orig. French, 1978).

Hilton, Rodney (2003), *Bond Men Made Free. Medieval Peasant Movements and the English Rising of 1381*, 2nd edn (London and New York: Routledge).

Housley, Norman (2002), *Religious Warfare in Europe, 1400–1536* (Oxford and New York: Oxford University Press).

Howell, Martha C. (1998), *The Marriage Exchange: Property, Social Place, and Gender in Cities of the Low Countries, 1300–1550* (Chicago, Ill.: University of Chicago Press).

Jordan, William Chester (1996), *The Great Famine. Northern Europe in the Early Fourteenth Century* (Princeton, N.J.: Princeton University Press).

Kaye, Joel (1998), *Economy and Nature in the Fourteenth Century. Money, Market Exchange, and the Emergence of Scientific Thought* (Cambridge: Cambridge University Press).

Langholm, Odd (1992), *Economics in the Medieval Schools: Wealth, Exchange, Value, Money, and Usury According to the Paris Theological Tradition 1200–1350* (Leiden: Brill).

—— (2003), *The Merchant in the Confessional: Trade and Price in the Pre-Reformation Penitential Handbooks* (Leiden: Brill).

Le Roy Ladurie, Emmanuel (1978), *Montaillou: The Promised Land of Error* (New York: George Braziler) (orig. French, 1975).

Martines, Lauro (2006), *Fire in the City: Savonarola and the Struggle for the Soul of Renaissance Florence* (New York and Oxford: Oxford University Press).

Mate, Mavis E. (1998), *Daughters, Wives and Widows after the Black Death. Women in Sussex, 1350–1535* (Woodbridge: Boydell).

Meyerson, Mark D. (2004), *Jews in an Iberian Frontier Kingdom: Society, Economy and Politics in Morvedre, 1248–1391* (Leiden and Boston, Mass.: Brill).

—— (2004), *A Jewish Renaissance in Fifteenth-Century Spain* (Princeton, N.J.: Princeton University Press).

Mollat, Michel (1987) *The Poor in the Middle Ages: An Essay in Social History* (New Haven, Conn.: Yale University Press) (orig. French, 1979).

—— and Philippe Wolff (1973), *The Popular Revolutions of the Late Middle Ages* (London: Allen & Unwin) (orig. French, 1970).

Montanari, Massimo (1996), *The Culture of Food* (Oxford: Blackwell) (orig. Italian, 1993).

Mormando, Franco (1999), *The Preacher's Demons:*

Bernardino of Siena and the Social Underworld of Early Renaissance Italy (Chicago, Ill.: University of Chicago Press).

Mullett, Michael (1987), *Popular Culture and Popular Protest in Late Medieval and Early Modern Europe* (London: Croom Helm).

Nirenberg, David (1996), *Communities of Violence. Persecution of Minorities in the Middle Ages* (Princeton, N.J.: Princeton University Press).

Platt, Colin (1996) *King Death: The Black Death and Its Aftermath in Late Medieval England* (London: UCL Press).

Pleij, Herman (2001), *Dreaming of Cockaigne. Medieval Phantasies of the Perfect Life* (New York: Columbia University Press).

Polecritti, Cynthia L. (2000), *Preaching Peace in Renaissance Italy: Bernardino of Siena and His Audience* (Baltimore, Md.: Catholic University of America Press).

Rigby, S.H. (1995), *English Society in the Later Middle Ages: Class, Status and Gender* (Basingstoke and London: Macmillan).

Schofield, Philipp R. (2003), *Peasant and Community in Medieval England, 1200–1500* (Basingstoke and New York: Palgrave Macmillan).

Shahar, Shulamith (2003), *The Fourth Estate: A History of Women in the Middle Ages*, 2nd edn (London and New York: Routledge).

TeBrake, William H. (1993), *A Plague of Insurrection. Popular Politics and Peasant Revolt in Flanders, 1323–1328* (Philadelphia, Pa.: University of Pennsylvania Press).

Vivanco, Laura (2004), *Death in Fifteenth-Century Castile: Ideologies of the Elites* (Woodbridge and Rochester, N.Y.: Boydell & Brewer)

Willard, Charity Cannon (1984), *Christine de Pizan: Her Life and Works* (New York: Persea Books).

Wright, Nicholas (1998), *Knights and Peasants. The Hundred Years War in the French Countryside* (Woodbridge: Boydell).

CHAPTER 14

The consolidation of states

FROM PRINCIPALITY TO STATE

Types of sovereign government

By about 1500 the sovereign political units in Europe showed great diversity in size, form of government and internal structure. Depending on the nature of the expansive power dominant in a region it is possible to distinguish a whole range of types of public authority. They are listed here in ascending order of extent, with scholarly judgement determining where the dividing line between states and other embodiments of public authority are drawn. If, with Charles Tilly, we define a state as a relatively centralized organization, differentiated from others, claiming to control a well-defined, mostly continuous territory, having at its disposal superior means of physical force, then the late medieval and early modern history of Europe saw the long-lasting co-existence of the following types of states and inter- and supra-state-like structures, all exercising some form of sovereign public authority:

- free peasant communities joined in a loose federation (East Friesland, Graubünden);
- autonomous towns with a more or less extensive agrarian hinterland (German free imperial cities such as Nuremberg and Hamburg; Genoa, Novgorod, Ragusa/Dubrovnik);
- local lordships that may at some point have been elevated to a higher status such as a duchy or principality (Mechelen, Salins, Liechtenstein, Monaco, San Marino, Andorra);
- federations of autonomous towns and peasant communities (Swiss Confederation, Friesland);
- leagues of towns, sometimes including feudal lords (the German Hanse, the Swabian League);
- regional states dominated by one large city that subordinated other towns, lordships and communities to it (Venice, Florence, Milan);
- ecclesiastical principalities (Utrecht, Liège, Cologne, Münster, the states of the German Order in Prussia and the states of the Maltese Order);
- effectively autonomous (secular) territorial principalities (the duchies of Brittany, Saxony and Ferrara, and the County of Toulouse before 1271);
- personal unions of territorial principalities in which each of the constituent entities kept its own institutions, but the prince determined a common policy (Hainault, Holland and Zeeland under the houses of Hainault and Bavaria; the Low Countries under the houses of Burgundy and Habsburg; Jülich, Marck and Berg);
- kingdoms (England, France, Portugal, Scotland, Sweden);
- personal unions of one or more kingdoms and/or territorial principalities (Poland–Lithuania; Bohemia–Moravia–Lausitz; the Crown of Aragon, comprising Aragon–Catalonia–Mallorca–Valencia (1412), later also Sicily, Naples, and Sardinia, all united in 1479 with the Crown of León–Castile; Denmark–Sweden–Norway in the Union of Kalmar (1397–1523);
- empires (Holy Roman Empire, Ottoman Empire).

Sovereignty, understood as a power not recognizing any higher authority, was not seen as entirely exclusive, as it was to become in the nineteenth century. It could very well have been located at different levels simultaneously. The emperor clearly did not recognize any higher authority, but even if the dukes, counts, prince-bishops and the 'free imperial cities' paid homage to him it did not prevent them from exercising public authority as practically autonomous polities. This diversity of political constellations came into being as the result of complex interactions, and it continues to change. It is more important to observe the reality of the exercise of power than the claims and titles. After 1250, the German emperorship meant little more than the theoretical authority enjoyed by the holder of that supreme temporal office and the resources that he had at his disposal as a territorial prince, his *Hausmacht*. Except for the imperial court, the *Reichskammergericht*, founded in 1495 but operational only much later and limited in its jurisdiction by the fierce opposition of the larger principalities, there were no central institutions, no capital city, no general taxation at the level of the Empire. Real state power in the Empire was to be found at the level of the principalities and free cities. In the first quarter of the fourteenth century the annual revenue of the city of Florence was equal to that of the kingdom of Naples and the pope in Avignon, and half as much as that of the king of France, who in his turn was still surpassed by Genoa. No wonder that such cities built a state around themselves.

In the kingdom of Castile the crown exercised jurisdiction over just 55 per cent of the population. The remaining 45 per cent fell under a variety of noble and ecclesiastical landowners who enjoyed immunity

Plate 14.1 The royal body presented as an allegory of the state. French miniature from the *Avis aus Roys*, Paris(?), *c.* 1369

and levied taxes, raised armies and administered justice on their own behalf. The contrasts between crown, nobility and towns were less sharp there than in other parts of Europe. During the Reconquest, the crown established towns in the reconquered areas and gave them many freedoms, with the aim of attracting Christian immigrants to replace the Muslims who had fled. The same town governments, which generally consisted of *hidalgos* (knights), were given extensive grants of land in the surrounding areas. Seville was an extreme case: this large, wealthy town was reconquered in 1248 and was granted 9,000 square kilometres of land. Crown, knighthood, town and country showed a certain degree of unity of interests, while elsewhere they were often in direct conflict. The process of development through which large state units were formed explains many of the peculiarities of each constellation. Castile and Aragon were united under the same royal couple in 1469 by dynastic union (Ferdinand of Aragon–Sicily and Isabella of Castile–León, the 'Catholic kings') and have been inherited jointly since then, with each retaining its own identity and institutions. In fact, this pattern may be considered as fairly general: unification at the top mostly did not change the pre-existing institutions and traditions. Technical problems of communication and mobility hampered the centralization of power and the ability of the centre to penetrate into regional and local communities. During the late Middle Ages and the early modern period, monarchies tended to expand their control over larger territories, incorporating and annexing smaller or weaker competitors. Even then, however, earlier structures remained very tangible, even if new rulers imposed certain exigencies upon them.

On the geographical outskirts of medieval Europe there were still anomalies: from the autonomous mini-'kingdoms' of Ireland and the farmer aristocracy of Iceland (tied to Norway after 1262 anyway) in the West, to the Russian confederation (to be discussed at the end of this chapter) in the East.

State-making through warfare

When one thinks of late medieval political history, the first event that springs to mind is the Hundred Years War. The causes of this titanic struggle between the two most powerful kingdoms of the time, France and

England, were twofold. First, there was the matter of Aquitaine, the last continental remnant of the once-glorious Angevin Empire still held by the English. The fact that the king of England held Aquitaine in fief from the king of France became a matter of discord between the two lands; sooner or later it was bound to lead to war. Second, the king of England, Edward III (1327–1377) attempted to claim the French throne after the house of Capet died out in 1328. His claim was based on descent through the female line (King Philip IV, the Fair, of France was his maternal grandfather). However, the *pairs de France*, the French high aristocracy, rejected the idea of the dynastic union of France and England, raising the argument that the French monarchy could only be inherited through the male line. They chose the side of Philip, a son of Charles of Valois (a brother of Philip the Fair), who was crowned Philip VI (1328–1350). In 1337, both issues came together when Philip seized Guienne (the coastal region of Aquitaine from the Garonne to the Pyrenees), whereupon Edward pressed ahead with his title and set out to conquer, proclaiming himself king of France.

The first stage of the ensuing Hundred Years War (1337–1453) was convincingly to the advantage of the English. Their army consisted of professional mercenary soldiers whom they could pay well, thanks to an efficient tax system. The French army of knights suffered dramatic defeats at Crécy in 1346 and ten years later at Poitiers. Here, the Black Prince, the heir to the English throne, captured the French king, John the Good, for whom an enormous ransom had to be paid. In 1358 the craftsmen of Paris rose in revolt against the pressure of high taxation and the economic slump resulting from the war. In this disastrous period the Estates General were summoned to approve emergency taxes. The peace of 1360 ratified a considerable expansion of the English possessions in central France, which now became sovereign, in exchange for the renunciation of the English claim to the French throne. The successful struggle had provided the English nobility with exceptional opportunities to enrich themselves.

The war caused a profound economic crisis in France, partly a result of a series of devaluations of coinage meant to cover some of the costs of the war. When the conquests came to an end tensions mounted

in England too. The Lancastrian king, Henry IV (1399–1413), engineered the deposition and execution of his cousin and predecessor Richard II (1377–1399), and attempted to legitimize his usurpation by relaunching the offensive in France. He achieved many successes at a time when the rivalries among the dukes over the insane king, Charles VI (1380–1422), plunged France into civil war (Armagnacs versus Burgundians). After the disastrous French defeat at Agincourt in 1415, Normandy and Paris fell into the hands of the English. At the Treaty of Troyes in 1420, Charles VI disinherited his legitimate son, the dauphin Charles, in favour of Henry V of England, whom he married to his daughter Catherine and recognized as his heir. The kingdom of France was now at rock bottom. After the death of Charles VI, the authority of the dauphin, still a minor, was recognized only south of the Loire: the north-west was in the hands of the English; the north-east in the hands of the dukes of Burgundy, who had extended their position in the Low Countries significantly.

The final phase of the Hundred Years War was heralded by the remarkable appearance of Joan of Arc, a young woman of peasant origins who claimed to hear divine voices that called on her to liberate France. By taking over leadership of the army, she broke through two privileges – one of the men and one of the nobility, who by tradition held the command. In 1429 she relieved Orléans and had the dauphin crowned in the cathedral of Rheims as Charles VII (1422/1429–1461). The French regained self-confidence, this being expressed in various forms of national sentiments and underpinned by the introduction of fixed royal taxes. The systematic recovery gave the king considerable prestige and new means of exercising power. In 1435, at Arras, he made a separate treaty with Duke Philip of Burgundy to whom important territories and rights were ceded, thus ensuring that the English lost their most important ally. In turn, it was the English who found themselves in trouble: changes in political fortunes brought their intense economic relations with the Low Countries under pressure. By 1453 the English had lost all of their French possessions except the port of Calais. Almost immediately the control of the English crown became a matter of contention between the two branches of the house of Plantagenet, York and Lancaster, and the baron factions that formed

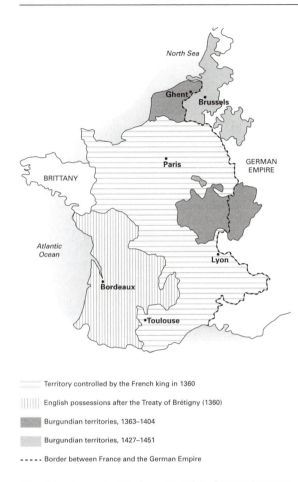

North Sea

Ghent
Brussels

Paris

BRITTANY

GERMAN
EMPIRE

Atlantic
Ocean

Lyon

Bordeaux

Toulouse

—— Territory controlled by the French king in 1360

|||||| English possessions after the Treaty of Brétigny (1360)

▓ Burgundian territories, 1363–1404

░ Burgundian territories, 1427–1451

- - - - Border between France and the German Empire

Map 14.1 France and the formation of the Burgundian state during the Hundred Years War

around them, and tensions started to build up. They boiled over in the Wars of the Roses (1455–1485), so called after the white and red roses of the Yorkist and Lancastrian coats of arms. The wars were devastating for the baronage rather than for English society as a whole, and only ended after three decades with the general recognition of Henry VII (1485–1509). He had prevailed on the battlefield and was also acceptable as a compromise candidate because, as the descendent of an eminent Welsh dynasty, the Tudors, he was linked to the houses of both York and Lancaster.

In the long term the Anglo-French dynastic struggle exhausted both sides, of course, although agricultural production was disrupted more severely in France simply because that was where the fighting occurred.

Institutionally seen, the French monarchy, as the saviour of the country, emerged from the struggle stronger, at the expense of the Estates General, which were practically never summoned again after that, and of the dukes. In England, the crown's efforts brought neither fame nor fortune, and parliament and the barons continued to be formidable adversaries.

The Holy Roman Empire: balance of powers

From a historical point of view it may be of no great importance to know which house ruled the Holy Roman Empire after the Interregnum ended. For contemporaries, however, it did matter, because the Holy Roman emperor still enjoyed enormous prestige. In the late Middle Ages the emperorship certainly was not something to be scrambled for. In fact, for most of the time between 1273 and 1519 the emperors came from only two families: the Austrian Habsburgs and the House of Luxemburg; moreover, the longest-lasting exception, Louis IV of Bavaria (1314–1347), was closely related to the Habsburgs. The election of the German king had always been the preserve of the highest-ranking princes of Germany, but the number of electors was finally constitutionally restricted to seven in the Golden Bull of 1356. Of these seven, three were ecclesiastical princes, the archbishops of Mainz, Trier, and Cologne, and four were secular princes – the duke of Saxony, the count Palatine of the Rhine, the margrave of Brandenburg, and the king of Bohemia. Bohemia had been incorporated into the German Empire in 1158, together with Moravia, and recognized as a kingdom. The Golden Bull also confirmed a rule that had been introduced some years before, namely; that the German king, once elected, was automatically entitled to the title of Roman emperor without the need of papal approval or coronation. But this did little to change the actual authority of the emperor, which remained largely theoretical if only because anything resembling a centralized imperial bureaucracy was lacking. What power the emperors had depended entirely on the territorial principalities in their possession: notably the dukedom of Austria for the Habsburgs and the kingdom of Bohemia for the Luxemburg emperors. From that perspective, the German emperors were truly *primi inter pares*, the highest ranking of many dozens of dukes, margraves, counts and prince-bishops of all those autonomous principalities that, together with numerous independent urban and rural communes, made up 'Germany' until 1806.

The authority claimed by the emperors over northern and central Italy had stumbled against the powerful resistance of the Lombard towns as early as the twelfth century. Long after the house of Hohenstaufen had disappeared (1254/1266), the rivalry between popes and emperors formed a pattern of factions that set one political group against another, right down to the local level. Initially the autonomous communal city republic had emerged as the predominant type of government in this part of Italy. But here, as elsewhere in the Empire, the future would be in territorial principalities. Few of them were still fiefs held from the emperor. The main exception was the vast duchy of Savoy-Piedmont, united since 1418, which stretched along both sides of the western Alps. Most of the old city republics, however, turned into *signorie* or dictatorships, established all over northern and central Italy (including the papal territories) from the middle of the thirteenth century by powerful Ghibelline leaders or, more often, by *condottieri* or mercenary captains in the service of cities. The most famous of these new lords acquired presumptuous titles such as 'duke' or 'marquis' and succeeded in establishing dynasties that sometimes remained in power for centuries. The Visconti family controlled Milan until 1450, followed by the Sforzas, while the Scaligeri ruled in Verona, the d'Este family in Ferrara, the Gonzagas in Mantua, the Malatestas in Rimini, and the Montefeltros in Urbino. This pattern of ruling *signorie* was resisted by Venice, Genoa and Siena, which maintained their republican forms of government run by councils. After a long struggle, Florence was forced to abandon its republican ambitions when it finally gave way in 1512 to the *signoria* of the Medici family, who had in fact governed the republic since 1434.

In the first half of the fifteenth century, some of the major cities conquered large territories in order to protect their economic interests and strengthen their positions in the ongoing competition, especially Venice, Milan and Florence (see Chapter 11). Venice gradually expanded its dependent territory, known as the *Terraferma*, the largest of the regional states, which

survived until its conquest by Napoleon in 1796. The northern and central Italian regional states demonstrated a model of a socio-economic and political order, which was stabilized in 1454 through the Peace of Lodi. This political system came into being without, and sometimes even in defiance of, monarchal activities. Thanks to the game of coalitions, the continual struggles between the largest of these regional states made it possible for some smaller units such as Ferrara, Mantua, Lucca, Siena and Urbino to survive. Even the invasions of French armies in 1494, followed by those of the Habsburgs, which caused heavy damage to the land during the first half of the sixteenth century, essentially could not affect this system of regional states; at most it was reduced to a series of virtually autonomous vassal states.

If further political unity appeared to be out of reach, a most remarkable balance of power came into being in the form of the Italian League of 1455. This was in fact a pact of non-aggression made between the five major Italian powers – Venice, Milan, Florence, the Papal State and the kingdom of Naples and Sicily – which felt threatened by increasing Ottoman and French pressures. The League would hold for more than twenty-five years. The resulting relatively stable situation in the second half of the fifteenth century was disrupted by the invasions of the French kings, Charles VIII in 1494 and Louis XII in 1499, who laid claim to the crown of Naples and the duchy of Milan. This set in motion a vast system of international alliances in which the Habsburgs played a major part. As a result, Italy became the main battleground of Europe for 50 years, though this did not lead to any essential change in the pattern of the regional division of power in Italy until the nineteenth century.

After the collapse of Hohenstaufens, southern Italy continued to be governed by a monarchy, at first under the house of Anjou, which enjoyed the support of the popes. During the Sicilian Vespers, a popular rising against the French occupation that broke out in 1282, the king of Aragon, Peter III, occupied the island of Sicily on the basis of a dubious claim to the succession. The Angevins stood firm in the kingdom of Naples until 1442, when Aragon took the crown there as well. As a result of the personal union between Castile and Aragon after 1516, southern Italy came under Spanish-Habsburg rule for a long period of time.

Iberia: kings and *cortes*

Quite understandably, state formation in Spain was affected dramatically by the progressive Reconquest – which in reality was as often a matter of negotiation with Muslim leaders as it was of military victory – and the vital issue of repopulation that followed in its wake. But the results were quite different in the two largest Christian kingdoms, Castile and Aragon, both of which contained several previously independent kingdoms, such as León and Valencia respectively. To start with, there was a difference in the non-feudal versus feudal character of their respective constitutions. Whereas feudo-vassalic ties remained normative in structuring power relations in Aragon, neither military service nor the exercise of public authority became feudalized in Castile: the Castilian kings did not give any estates or lordships in fief or benefice in return for any public services. Paradoxically, the unmediated relationship between king and subjects in Castile set in motion a long-term tendency to absolutist royal power. In Aragon, on the other hand, a contractual relationship remained intact between the king and the greater number of his subjects, with mutual obligations to be fulfilled. It fuelled a tendency that has been termed 'pactism' between Crown and 'people', whereby the exercise of royal power was conditional to the king's recognition of the customs and privileges of his subjects, also and especially against possible intrusions by feudal lords. Another major difference between Castile and the various kingdoms along the Iberian east coast and the Balearic Islands under the Crown of Aragon, was the density of mighty commercial cities in this part of the mainland.

Pactism took shape first and foremost within the scope of representative assemblies (parliaments), called *cortes* in Spain. From early on in Aragon, all the monarch's major decisions, especially those relating to finance and taxation, were submitted to the *cortes* for approval. In addition the king was obliged to answer all grievances brought forward by the *cortes*, and there was no royal interference whatsoever with the appointment of representatives of the third estate. The ability of the Castilian *cortes* to curb royal power, already evident before 1190, was clearly on the increase in the second half of the fourteenth century when a war of succession broke out between King Peter the Cruel and his illegitimate half-brother, Henry of Trastámara; because the English and French supported opposite parties in this struggle Castile became a side theatre of the Hundred Years War. Soon afterwards, however, there was a return to absolutism, partly as a reaction to the growing Aragonese influence in Castile during the first half of the fifteenth century.

The political differences between Castile and Aragon were the result of a major contrast in economic and social structures. Simplifying enormously, one could characterize Castile as a land of grain, olives and sheep, dominated by large landowners, whereas Aragon was the heart of an overseas commercial empire that encompassed not only Catalonia but also the Balearic Islands (reconquered around 1230), Sicily (from 1282), Sardinia, and even stretches of Greece. Consequently, the Castilian *cortes* were dominated by the nobility, the Aragonese *cortes* by the rich merchant class, praised by one of its eulogists, friar Francesc Eiximenes (*c.* 1340–1409), as 'the treasure of the commonweal, the food of the poor, the mainstay of good business'.

The interests of the merchant elites of Barcelona and Valencia, Aragon's two most important cities, were jealously guarded by their representatives in the *cortes* and by the *consulados del mar* ('consulates of the sea'); these were powerful guilds that came into existence around the middle of the thirteenth century and received important jurisdictional autonomy by the end of the fourteenth, making them virtually independent of the royal courts of justice. Aragon's fortunes started to wane around 1400, however, when the Castilians and Portuguese excluded Catalan sailors from the Atlantic trade, while in the Mediterranean, Aragon experienced increasing commercial and military competition from the Genoese.

Scandinavian dynastic unions

Scandinavian politics in the late Middle Ages were governed by the establishment of a number of personal unions that bound the Scandinavian kingdoms together. In 1319, Norway and Sweden were unified under the same Swedish royal dynasty. Denmark was drawn in some decades later. In 1387/1388, Margrete, the youngest daughter of Waldemar Atterdag, the Danish king, and widow of King Håkon of Norway, was formally recognized as 'almighty lady and husband and guardian' of the kingdoms of Denmark, Norway, and finally also Sweden, after the death of her only son Oluf, a minor. This was one of the rare occasions in medieval history when a woman was officially proclaimed head of state in her own right, not acting on behalf of one of her children. However, Margrete's appointment was not an admission of political indecisiveness or weakness but the logical outcome of her self-assured action as mother-regent to her minor son in the preceding years. After his death she did not act simply as a transitional figure, but rather revealed herself as the ruling monarch in all but name. Her unusual strength and power, as well as cunning and ruthlessness, in that male-dominated world can be illustrated by her handling of two major issues. First, rather than trying to produce another heir herself, Margrete adopted her great-nephew, Bogeslav of Pommern, who on that occasion received the Christian-Scandinavian name of Erik, and pushed through his designation as the royal heir. This was all the more remarkable since in both Denmark and Sweden kingship had always remained dependent on election; only in Norway was rightful hereditary succession sufficient. Second, Margrete's appointment had not gone uncontested in Sweden because Oluf had never ruled there, whereas the actual king, Albrecht of Mecklenburg, was alive and well and had no intention of stepping down voluntarily. Worse still, Albrecht had equally good claims to the thrones of Norway and Denmark. But Margrete was not a person to allow anything or anyone to stand in her way, so this meant war. A stalemate was reached when Albrecht was taken captive after a lost battle, while his German followers could not be driven from the important town of Stockholm. After years of violent hostilities, in which piracy, sponsored by the Mecklenburg princes, alternated with attempts at arbitration by the Hanseatic League, which was keen to keep trading routes safe, both parties were prepared to compromise. Even before the terms of this treaty were completed, however, Margrete had her adopted son Erik crowned king of Denmark, Norway and Sweden in one ceremony at the royal castle of Kalmar in July 1397. At the same time, a document was drawn up, but never sealed, setting out the terms of this 'Union of Kalmar'. The essence of it was that the three kingdoms would

never again be separated, while at the same time each would be governed according to its own laws. Real power remained in the hands of Queen Margrete, who died in office in 1412. King Erik had far more difficulty than his stepmother did in fending off growing German influence in Scandinavian affairs. For instance, his introduction around 1425 of the so-called Sound Tolls, a tariff on all Baltic shipping trade, ensured the permanent enmity and meddling of the Hanseatic League. Nor did he succeed in producing any offspring. Only because of substantial juggling with the rules of inheritance was it possible for the Union of Kalmar to remain intact after Erik's death. After a bloody civil war, Sweden went its own way in 1523, but Norway remained united with Denmark until 1814.

Central Europe and the Baltic

In the fourteenth century three of the venerable royal dynasties that had ruled huge stretches of eastern Europe since the tenth century died out in the direct male line: first, the Hungarian Árpáds in 1301, followed shortly afterwards in 1306 by the Bohemian Premyslids, while the last king of Poland from the house of Piast died in 1370. All three were succeeded by prominent Western European dynasties that were linked by marriage: the house of Anjou in Hungary and Poland, the house of Luxemburg in Bohemia. This course of events can be 'blamed' in part on changes in succession rules. Traditionally, the royal dynasties that ruled in central and eastern Europe applied a form of collateral succession whereby a king or prince was succeeded after his death by the oldest living male relative of the same generation – usually a younger brother of the deceased. Gradually however, descendant succession in the male line – succession by son or grandson – as was common in the West, came to be customary, considerably increasing the risk of dynastic extinction.

After a period of severe crisis, which had turned the kingdom into a bleak shadow of its eleventh-century grandeur, Poland enjoyed a revival under the last Piast kings, Wladislaw the Short (1320–1333) and his son Casimir III the Great (1333–1370). Even so there were territorial losses. Most of the old Polish dukedoms of Silesia were taken over by Bohemia and only regained after the Second World War, while Pomerelia, the rich rye-producing plains along the Vistula, with important towns such as Torun/Thorn and the harbour of Gdansk/Danzig, was annexed to the Prussian lands of the Teutonic Order. At the same time, relative peace in the north and west gave Casimir the opportunity to expand Polish territory in the east (Mazovia) and south (Ruthenia, which included Polish Galicia). This is often seen as a turning point in Polish history, because 'it firmly turned Poland's face to the east' (Knoll). Besides, Polish expansionism to the east could always count on papal support, mainly because it could be seen as an extra defence against the non-Catholic world: together with its most loyal ally, Hungary, Poland extended and reinforced the Catholic barrier against pagans (Lithuanians, Mongols) and Christian schismatics (the Greek Orthodox Russians).

When the last king of the old Magyar dynasty of Árpád died in 1301 Hungary had grown into a most remarkable society that already in the Middle Ages held the reputation of welcoming immigrants from all quarters. Hungary did indeed have a very ethnically mixed population, including substantial non-Christian minorities. Because of very low population density, medieval Hungary preserved for a long time a 'cellular' character, in which the *status aparte* and privileges of each group of *hospites* ('guests' or 'foreign settlers') was recognized. The Cuman was certainly the largest of the non-Christian minorities. It originated in the thirteenth century when, after the Mongol invasions of the western steppes, a substantial number of Cuman or Kipchak-Turk nomads were allowed to settle in Hungary in return for cavalry service against the Mongol threat. In the end, the Cuman minority may have constituted up to 8 per cent of the Hungarian population; indeed, the penultimate Árpád ruler of Hungary, László IV (1272–1290), was half-Cuman.

Hungary in László's time was much larger than the present-day state of the same name. After the beginning of the twelfth century it comprised Croatia and its Dalmatian coast, whereas the possession of Bosnia was constantly disputed between Hungary and the kingdom of Serbia. Only after Hungary came under Angevin rule (1310–1387) did it lose its hold on its Balkan–Slav territories. The accession to power of the house of Anjou was not without problems. The first

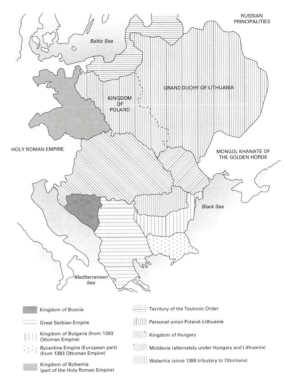

Map 14.2 Central Europe, c. 1375

Angevin king, Charles-Robert, sweetly shortened to Carobert, a grandson of an Árpád princess, had to be crowned three times in ten years before he was finally generally accepted. But Carobert succeeded in turning anarchy into order and stability, and the long reign of his son Louis (1342–1382), 'Lajos' in Hungarian, radiated ambition – Alexander the Great, no less, became his favourite role model. He gave shape to this ambition in the construction of sumptuous palaces and costly military expeditions into southern Italy, the Dalmatian coast, the Balkans or to the north, in support of his Polish ally. More than by taxes, the costs of his expeditions were defrayed by the huge share the king could take from the revenues of several new gold and silver mines that had been discovered in northern Hungary. Although attempts to put his younger brother, Andrew, on the throne of Naples were shattered, Louis himself became king of Poland in 1370. But for all his ambitions, the days of the illustrious House of Anjou in East Europe were numbered: Louis died in 1382 without leaving a son and a *coup d'état* by the Neapolitan branch of the dynasty failed. Now the way was clear for Sigismund of Luxemburg, a younger son of the emperor Charles IV and married to Louis' daughter Maria, to take over – after having paid the staggering amount of 565,000 gold florins. Even then it would take Sigismund, who assumed the crown in 1387, another 15 years to smooth over the fierce opposition of the Hungarian nobility to the 'Czech swine'. Thereafter, his power and prestige began to rise, especially after he was elected emperor of the Holy Roman Empire in 1410.

When Sigismund died in 1437, after a long reign, Hungarian history repeated itself: since there was no living male heir the kingdom became the plaything of the great dynasties of the age, in this case those of the Austrian Habsburgs and the Polish/Lithuanian Jagiellons. In the end, however, it would be a noble Hungarian family, the Hunyadi, that took the prize. This was all thanks to János Hunyadi who made a meteoric rise to power in the first half of the fifteenth century, starting as a rather obscure member of the lesser nobility and ending around 1450 as the most powerful magnate in Hungary and the owner of a fortune beyond belief – his landed possessions alone would have comprised about 2.3 million hectares of land and included countless villages, towns and fortresses. However, what contributed most to the enhancement of Hunyadi's position, as well as to his virtuous reputation, which has remained untarnished right up to the present day, were his relative successes as a military leader in the hopeless struggle against the Ottomans. It is a tale of lost but legendary battles, such as Kosovo's famous Field of the Blackbirds in 1448 – the second battle on that spot – where Hunyadi stood shoulder to shoulder with Vlad ('the impaler') Dracula, the governor of Wallachia. Even if it did not bring victory, it eventually brought the Hunyadi the Hungarian crown, which in 1458 was placed on the head of János's younger son, Mathias Corvinus ('raven-like') (1458–1490), who, like his father, would attain legendary status. Mathias was in every respect 'made of the stuff of a great Renaissance prince' (Molnár): a great patron of the arts, a politician capable of reform and change, a talented diplomat, a dauntless warrior. Supported by his so-called 'black army' of 20,000 soldiers of fortune Corvinus was able not only to keep the Ottomans at bay but also to form a serious

military threat to Bohemia and Austria. Nevertheless, despite Corvinus's efforts to curb private violence, for example, Hungary remained a weak state by Western European standards, simply because even he proved unable to extend the royal domain, that part of Hungary's territory in which the king could exercise direct lordship and display royal power to the full.

Perhaps most astonishing in the later medieval history of central and eastern Europe was the rapid rise of the grand duchy of Baltic Lithuania. In western eyes 'Lithuania' was no more than a vague indication of the vast forests that stretched beyond the Neman river, a 'wild east' filled with pagan savages, lurking in nebulous marshes and dark woods, and giving themselves over to hideous rites. The second part of this idea was fantasy. In reality, Lithuania emerges from later medieval sources – not unlike medieval Russia – as a loose confederacy of numerous small lordships under the nominal leadership of princes who, at least as early as the thirteenth century, styled themselves 'grand dukes [of Aukstaitija/Upper Lithuania]'. Further unity and some degree of centralization were reached under the grand ducal dynasty of the Gediminids, so called after Gediminas, the younger of two brothers who successively ruled Lithuania between 1295 and 1342. They succeeded in consolidating Lithuanian power in a period when the brunt of Teutonic Order aggression had shifted from Prussia and Livonia, now conquered, towards the only area left in Europe that was not yet Christian and therefore formed the potential spoils of legitimate crusade. To that end the Order repeatedly recruited western princes, such as the son of the count of Hainault and Holland, who with substantial followings of knights came to 'hunt pagans' on *Litauenreisen* during wintertime – the only season when it was possible for armies to approach the impenetrable forests and marshes of western Lithuania.

The Gediminids stood their ground, however, and they continued to adhere to their native polytheistic religion. Even if there was a clear Christian presence in Lithuania from the thirteenth century on (friars were active as missionaries and the wives of many noblemen were Christians), the grand dukes only converted officially in 1387. This was the only occasion in medieval Europe when Christianity played no part in the formation of a state. Even so, Lithuania only reached the zenith of success after its conversion. Under grand duke Vytautas the Great (1392–1430) it grew into the most powerful principality in eastern Europe and in area the largest state of late medieval Europe.

The extension of Lithuanian power from the late thirteenth century onwards – through military strength, clever marriages and forceful alliances – was set in motion by commercial interests and land hunger. It happened largely at the expense of the western and central Russian principalities of what is now north-west Russia (the Pskov district), White Russia and Ukraine – including the original Rus' capital of Kiev, first captured in 1323 and then again in 1362. In due time Lithuanian imperialism even threatened the stronger Russian principalities farther to the east (Novgorod and Moscow), as well as the western fringes of the Golden Horde, the Mongolian power base in the vast steppe area to the north of the Black Sea and the Caspian Sea. Not until the beginning of the sixteenth century did the Lithuanian Empire start to crumble under Russian (Muscovite) pressure; the important town of Smolensk fell into Russian hands in 1514, for example. By that time, a long-lasting involvement in Russian affairs had left a deep and enduring Slav mark on Lithuanian society and culture.

On the frontier with Poland the Gediminids were not very successful; as we saw, they lost the long struggle over Ruthenia. Expectations rose sharply again when, in 1386, Grand Duke Jagiello married Jadwiga, daughter of Louis of Anjou and heiress to the kingdom of Poland. But this first personal union of Poland and Lithuania did not lead to any real political association, since Jagiello soon had to cede the actual lordship over Lithuania to his cousin Vytautas. Only much later, in 1447, was a longer-lasting personal union of Poland and Lithuania effected, after Grand Duke Casimir (1440–1492) was recognized as king of Poland. Short as the first union had been, this second union was a happy one, but after Casimir's death the two kingdoms were once again separated and divided between his two sons. The Gediminid dynasty remained in power in Lithuania until 1572.

The remarkable expansion of Lithuania is difficult to understand if one is not prepared to believe that this was a well-organized, state-like society with a strong army and capable of mustering considerable resources.

Such an impression is confirmed by the rare historical documents, which reveal many features of an early state under construction. Although the grand-ducal dynasty still had to rely heavily on its possession of land, organized in large estates, the Lithuanian nobility owed military service and was involved in public administration. In addition, trade was taxed in exchange for efficient protection of traders and trade routes. Military organization had a high level of sophistication. Military strategy was aimed at avoiding pitched battles with clearly stronger enemies, such as the Teutonic knights and their allies. The Lithuanians preferred to counter them by making use of guerrilla tactics adapted to the difficult terrain, operating in relatively small but swiftly moving intervention forces built round a core of light cavalry, constructing fortresses, by excellent military intelligence work and the use of diplomatic skills, and by impeding enemy efforts to consolidate any military victory. Clearly there were substantial differences in political development with the most advanced principalities of the West, but they were not as profound as has too often been suggested.

DRIVING FORCES IN THE FORMATION OF STATES

Dynasties, territories, institutions, peoples

Princes were constantly devising strategies to acquire new lands without much effort, either through marriage and succession, or possibly through purchase or as security. The formula of the double marriage, by which a male and a female descendant of one dynasty were married to a female and male descendant of another dynasty, was designed to tie the bonds between two houses as tightly as possibly. Bavaria and Burgundy were united in this way in 1386, so that later Hainault, Holland and Zeeland (a Bavarian possession) came under the same ruler as Burgundian Flanders and Brabant. In 1496 there was a double marriage between Spain and Habsburg, laying the foundations of the European empire of Charles V. By 1500 similar dynastic strategies had made the number of truly independent political units in Europe considerably smaller than three centuries previously. During the competition most 'winners' became larger and more powerful. The constant efforts of princes and feudal lords to expand their territories and the revenues they provided formed a driving force in this process. The continuity of competent rulers in a dynasty, the space for expansion and the presence of internal and external cores of power, which would possibly act as a counterweight to the established prince, played a large part in systems that were focused so strongly on the person of the ruler.

Heraldic symbols, public ceremonial, mottos, emblems and genealogical histories strengthened the ties between princes and their subjects. Something as abstract as a state, the contours of which were not yet settled, only penetrated the collective consciousness very slowly. The differences between the Scots and the Irish on the one hand and the English on the other were fed by the repeated efforts made by the English to dominate. The centuries-long war between the English and the French similarly strengthened national sentiments on both sides of the Channel. The Czechs derived a strong sense of nationality from their opposition to continuing German expansion.

Dynastic ambitions and opportunities, however, cannot explain everything. Much depended on the society in the territory involved. During the late Middle Ages society was no longer composed almost solely of peasants, serfs or otherwise; there was, as we have seen, considerable differentiation through the development of the towns, communities of free peasants, the commercialization and sometimes even the industrialization of the countryside. Their interaction gave shape to the states that were formed out of the power struggle, in relation both to their territory and to their internal organization. The enlarged scale of the competing units, the broadening of the resources at their disposal, in particular the increase in the power of military destruction, made conflicts more drastic. The numbers of those fighting in wars increased, they caused greater and more lasting damage to the economy, and they created more victims. As state violence increased, subjects began to offer fiercer resistance as they became more conscious of their rights and organized themselves better.

It is obvious that late medieval states emerged in ways that never could have been so willed or planned. They were the results of the trials of strength between countless conflicting ambitions, interests and opposing forces. In many cases, wars did not produce the results intended by the aggressors, but nevertheless they left deep marks. The Hundred Years War made a significant contribution to the formation of French and English national consciousness. At the same time it created political affinities that steered relations between the kings and their subjects in both lands for many centuries to come, in particular the resounding voice of the English parliament in contrast with the virtual elimination of the French Estates General. The path trodden by a society in its confrontations between its members and with its rulers and neighbours gradually gave shape to the institutions that together formed the state; likewise it was imprinted in the collective memory of the communities concerned, which through their common fortunes imperceptibly formed a national loyalty in addition to a local and dynastic one.

One of the characteristic state structures of the late Middle Ages was the development of a civil service apparatus, which expressed public authority in a more abstract sense and also more effectively than before. The king's person and his relations with powerful vassals were no longer the sole determinants of the fortunes of a state. Kings were bound by laws and institutions and in many cases by representation. They were obliged to create an official hierarchy that would tie them to rules and procedures. The exercise of power became more complex and less personal.

War

The American historical sociologist Charles Tilly once observed that 'wars made states and states made war', by which he meant that states, both for the demarcation of their territories and the growth of their institutions, were the product of continual competition between diverse political units. Conversely, the largest part of the resources – financial, material and services – that states had at their disposal was destined to make preparations for war, to wage it and to pay for it. Indeed, it was precisely during those long periods of warfare that the state apparatuses managed to increase the tax burden on their subjects considerably and thus to enlarge the state resources. From the end of the thirteenth century onwards, rulers increasingly financed their wars by contracting debts that had to be paid back afterwards with substantial interest. Interest groups played an important role in this development: because they could profit from it or expected rewards from their state at war, they steered the decision process towards war. It is clear that the nobility, for whom armed conflict was not only a matter of honour but also gave them the opportunity to acquire land, take home booty or gain the favour of the king, continued to be a driving force behind the casual acceptance with which war was seen as a fixed part of continuing political competition.

Of course the great economic and demographic changes between the tenth and the thirteenth centuries were not without consequences for the art of war. During the thirteenth century more archers appeared on the battlefield, while foot soldiers were frequently hired from Wales. That was when the longbow and the crossbow came into use. In the course of the century these archers were often deployed as auxiliary troops, but by 1300 they were increasingly fighting for themselves. The Swiss peasants who defeated the Habsburg army of knights in 1291 and 1315 made history. On a much larger scale Flemish craftsmen and peasants cut the army of knights of the French king to pieces at the Battle of the Golden Spurs in 1302. Such victories were a sign of the new power relations resulting from the growth of urban populations. In 1302 the Flemish force, 11,000 strong, fought 7,500 French – one-third of whom were heavily armed horsemen. Horses and equipment, and the attendants who were indispensable to them, were extremely expensive investments; considerable practice was needed to acquire the combative skills, moreover, and only the aristocracy could afford this. The Scots who defeated the English at Bannockburn in 1314 also fought for the most part on foot, armed with bows, pikes, and striking and stabbing weapons. They slashed away without fear or favour, clearly driven by a desire for liberation from what they saw as foreign domination.

The Lombard towns dominated neighbouring countrysides by mobilizing the remnants of feudalism. Warlords took troops into their personal service in exchange for payment and hired themselves out with their companies to the highest bidder. The phenomenon of the *condottiere*, a commander of a mercenary company, was closely connected to the rivalry between the small but rich regional states of northern and cen-

Plate 14.2 Monstrelet, Chronique: Battle of Agincourt

tral Italy. The foot soldiers in either paid or obligatory service were given more importance in the armies of the princes. The Welsh archers contributed to the loss of 1,500 French knights at Crécy in 1346. The knights had certainly had their day with the arrival of the cannon in the 1330s.

When the towns built their walls they adopted the principle of the fortified castle on a larger scale. The assailant was vulnerable, the defender was protected as long as his supplies lasted. The long circumference of the towns made an effective blockade difficult, requiring a large number of troops over a long period of time, which often exhausted the financial resources of the besiegers. From the last decades of the fourteenth century, however, the cannon turned the towns' former advantage in siege warfare into a disadvantage. Town walls had been designed to face battering rams, not the force of cannon balls. They were built high to resist projectiles from catapults and siege towers: it was difficult to breach the walls with trebuchets – at most the gates and parapets were damaged. When they were shot at by cannon, however, the walls became particularly vulnerable, especially if they were high. The effectiveness of cannon on the battlefield was limited by their enormous weight, slowness, and lack of accuracy and reach until the sixteenth century. But from the end of the fourteenth century towns and castles were no longer safe from an army equipped with gunpowder artillery.

During the fifteenth century there was thus a discrepancy in military resources that gave the besiegers a considerable advantage as long as they could afford the high price of cannon. The new technique played into the hands of the largest competitors who were able to pay for the expensive innovations and the technically trained personnel to operate them. Besides, they could make far more effective use of them than the defenders could. Princes now saw the possibility of dealing a definitive blow against their most formidable rivals, local and regional rulers. Rebellions in France, the Low Countries and northern Germany often gave princes the excuse to use their military supremacy to restrict the autonomy of large towns. The most spectacular example of this was the capture of Constantinople by the Ottomans in 1453: the legendary high walls, which had withstood every siege since the sixth century, were shot to pieces by the Turkish artillery. In northern and central Italy there were few territorial monarchs apart from the pope who could afford to make use of the new military technology on a significant scale, so the advantage fell to the largest towns, which were thus able to enlarge the regions they controlled. Venice was the most successful: faced with losing part of its colonial empire to the Ottomans, it assured its domestic safety and prosperity by taking control of the Po valley.

On the battlefields, offensive action again gained the advantage at this time, providing military logistics adapted to new challenges. To offer some resistance to the massive power of foot soldiers, the most progressive princes turned their infantry into mobile phalanxes equipped with extremely long pikes. These were used to bring the enemy cavalry to a halt and force them back, or could lead the attack on the enemy infantry. The cavalry now was literally sidelined to the flanks, where it could carry out intermittent attacks. The initiative for this modern plan came from France, where for the first time in 1439 Charles VII was allocated

money to establish a standing army. In contrast to feudal practice, when the vassals were called up in the good season for campaigns of a limited length (40 days, for example), war had become a year-round business that required trained troops to be available permanently. The French king now took between 20,000 and 25,000 officers and men into permanent paid service as *gens d'armes*, who used a combination of different weapons. The initiative coincided with the final offensive of the Hundred Years War and contributed to the definitive expulsion of the English.

As more subjects became involved in the business of war, and negotiations had to be undertaken with the parliament or assemblies of towns and estates for providing troops and subsidies, the necessity to justify these efforts grew. Religion was an obvious legitimization. It was the justification for the merciless war of extermination against the Languedoc Cathars, which reached its most brutal stage with the dreadful massacre at Montségur in 1244, giving Louis IX, the Saint, the opportunity to bring the County of Toulouse under his direct authority. Further, because the papal client, Charles of Anjou, had lost his kingdom of Sicily to Peter III of Aragon during the Sicilian Vespers of 1282, the pope urged his nephew, Philip III of France, to undertake what he called a 'crusade against Aragon'. Alas, this time God did not take the side of these crusaders, and the campaign of 1285 cost the king his life. In addition, the war against Bohemian independence was waged by successive German kings, Wenceslas and Sigismund, between 1411 and 1436 under the motto of a crusade against the heretical Hussites, the followers of the Church reformer, Jan Hus.

Kings could also use the link to a saint as a legitimization of their wars. The cult of a national saint was one means of achieving this: in France, for example, the saints Denis, the first bishop of Paris whose name resounded in the battle-cry 'Montjoie Saint-Denis', Michael, and (after 1297) Louis IX. Military heroes had the privilege of being buried alongside the kings in the mausoleum of Saint-Denis, which also housed the *oriflamme*, the banner carried during the king's campaigns. As leaders of a war of liberation against foreign invaders, the kings of France could plead that they served a higher good than did the great territorial princes. In this way the king's war could be presented as the only one in the general interests of the kingdom, the only lawful and sacred one. The defence of the *patria*, fatherland, presented as a mystic body by analogy with the body of Christ, was worth a courageous death, as the propaganda in fifteenth-century texts increasingly proclaimed. The kings stopped at nothing to give an exclusive justification to their wars, while those of the territorial princes under them were demoted to mere private conflicts, sometimes even to rebellions against the lawful authority.

STATE INSTITUTIONS AND SOCIAL ORDER

Superior means of force was an essential condition for the long-term exercise of power, but not enough in itself. If large groups of subjects did not accept the legitimacy of the government imposed upon them, then it provoked internal resistance that forced up the costs of control for those in power, damaged their claims to provide protection for all subjects in their region, and made their government vulnerable to coalitions between domestic and foreign foes. If we accept that in addition to a healthy dose of aggression every human community shows a fundamental need for peace and stability, then we can expect to see subjects and rulers make some attempt to reach long-term arrangements. Such arrangements inevitably were concerned with life's basic needs – the distribution of scarce goods, the establishment and maintenance of a degree of social order and giving some purpose to life.

Supreme law courts

Kings and territorial princes attempted to establish their higher authority over the traditional forms of dispensing justice, but until the end of the eighteenth century they always had to take into account the large variety of legal systems and local customs within their territories. As the territories expanded, so did this variety. In general, they tried hard to reduce the autonomous action of foreign courts outside their own territories, especially ecclesiastical ones.

Princes made every effort to give their own laws precedence over local customs and privileges and to apply them to all subjects within their territories, thus

to give their administration of justice the highest validity – if not a monopoly. Such a process was anything but easy, in view of the conflicting interests. In England the law courts of the king enjoyed priority over all other courts as early as the twelfth century; in the course of the thirteenth century three central courts of justice emerged, among them the King's Bench, which, apart from handling pleas to the crown, had the exclusive right to try serious crimes. The French king found it far more difficult to reserve for himself certain 'royal cases' such as counterfeiting, *lèse-majesté* and appeals. The Parliament of Paris, which Louis IX had established around 1250 as the highest court of justice in the kingdom, had an increasing number of cases to deal with as confidence in the judges' independence grew.

The success of the princes' higher administration of justice over the many competing legal circles was based on several factors, above all on pure power relationships. Powerful local lords and rich towns offered effective opposition until well into the eighteenth century. Venice allowed all subordinate towns in the *Terraferma* to retain their own privileges and institutions, but made them subject to its political authority and fiscal discrimination. For the peasants, Venetian supremacy meant liberation from the class-based justice of the burghers in the smaller towns. Elsewhere, too, the possibility of appealing to a higher court of law offered new opportunities for parties who were economically or politically weak in relation to the main lords or towns. The princes tried to place their justice above local and regional law courts, and at the same time applied more general procedures and principles, often borrowed from learned law or jurisprudence. For instance, from the end of the fourteenth century Castilian peasants increasingly appealed to the crown to act as arbitrator in complaints against their exploitation by aristocratic landowners. To deal with the growing number of cases, royal judges (*alcaldes*) were appointed and a central court of justice, the *Audiencia*, was installed. In the long term the justice administered by the crowns of both Castile and Aragon strengthened the position of the peasants, and also that of the king as the highest guarantor of justice.

Both canon and Roman law, which from the twelfth century spread from Bologna and was studied intensively in the emergent universities, contained many elements that were of particular use to the princes in their efforts to justify their centralizing activities. The surviving Roman law was the Byzantine record from the middle of the sixth century (see Chapter 2), and had a strongly centralistic and absolutist slant, with principles such as 'the prince is above the law' and 'what pleases the prince has the force of law'. Emperor Frederick Barbarossa made much use of these quotations after he defeated Milan in 1162, as did the king of Castile, much later, in the fifteenth century. In the thirteenth century lawyers close to the kings of France used formulas of the same type to justify decrees in which they claimed to serve the 'common interest'. This usage also aroused opposition, however – for example, at the English court, which did not wish to consider itself subordinate to the emperor. Henry Bracton, a priest who served as judge on the King's Bench in the middle of the thirteenth century, wrote a treatise on the laws and customs of England, based on a collection of 2,000 judgments. He defended the superiority of the English jury system and natural law, for in his view Roman law favoured the king's interest. English law, on the other hand, defends the interests of the people, Bracton said. Outside England, Roman law certainly formed one of the basic subjects in the training of lawyers. Their thinking and their use of administrative language was permeated with concepts, such as that of *res publica*, *la chose publique*, which, even without an exact equivalent at the time, sharpened state thinking and highlighted the distinction between public and private law.

Attempts to codify the law applying at the level of kingdoms were exceptional in the Middle Ages. One attempt was made in Castile, soon after the kingdom had experienced considerable growth at the expense of the Muslims: the *Fuero Real* of the early 1250s, another, the *Siete Partidas*, in the 1260s. In similar circumstances of rapid territorial expansion a royal law code was produced in Poland in 1347. The breakthrough in the systematic recording of law did not occur until the sixteenth century, in a generally painstaking assessment of the many regional and national customary laws. In France the royal order in the middle of the fifteenth century to provide an official, authorized record of the countless regional customary laws was carried out with painful slowness. A century later most of them had been published in

the north and in central France; but not in the south, however, despite its much stronger Roman tradition. A real codification, a systematic collection and homogenization on the authority of the central government, never came about. Local judges continued to enjoy considerable freedom in the administration of justice.

The influence of canon law was felt in the administrative and judicial practices of the young states even earlier than Roman law. The rational investigation of the facts by a judge before a person was charged, in contrast to the early medieval customs of accusation and single combat, was modelled on the Church's *inquisitio*, the judicial inquiry. In 1215 the Fourth Lateran Council condemned trial by ordeal as a means of obtaining evidence because it was irrational and the outcome was often questionable. In the twelfth and thirteenth centuries both Church and secular authorities had progressed so far that they shunned the unpredictability of a trial by a publicly proclaimed ordeal and supported a more rational method of investigation.

It is of fundamental significance for western thought that in the young universities law (Roman and canon law) was recognized as a separate discipline, independent of theology. Even if the universities were under ecclesiastical authority they still provided the opportunity for the development of non-dogmatic, rational juridical thinking, free of religious precepts, unlike the Islamic schools for example. The technique of interpreting legal texts made continual renewal and adaptation to the changing reality possible. In this way the principles of Roman law were also absorbed in new jurisprudence.

University trained lawyers were given key positions in all public administrations, inside and outside the state. In Italy and southern France they played a major part in the public urban life from the thirteenth century – in town government, the administrations of territorial and ecclesiastical authorities, and as advocates and notaries. Courts and law-making bodies were increasingly often staffed with academically trained lawyers. Their activities contributed to the wider introduction of laws into public life, including principles from jurisprudence that protected individual interests from governments, in particular the defence of private property, testamentary disposition, the freedom of contracting parties and the protection of widows and orphans. The concept of the corporate legal entity, *universitas*, made its way into the towns and communities in their associated and constituent organs, such as guilds. Like so many other matters, the spread of modern, rational legal thinking was closely connected to the urban environment, as well as, and in contrast to, that of the great royal courts. From a social point of view, the university study of law paved the way to social upward mobility for burghers who could use their technical knowledge in the Church or in a secular career, especially in the towns and at the courts of kings and princes. As a result the powerful position of the knights crumbled. In those parts of Germany and central and northern Europe that had been characterized by a continuously strong nobility and feudal relationships for a very long period, the new rational forms of law penetrated only partially and very slowly. Not until the sixteenth century were university trained lawyers of middle-class origins appointed to key positions throughout the Empire.

The administration of justice played a larger part in social reality than did the legislation of princes. Local regulations were much closer to everyday life and could be more easily enforced by a combination of social control and common interest. In this respect, the situation in England was rather different from that on the Continent – on the one hand because of the long tradition of trial by a jury of laymen, and on the other because of the early (from the twelfth century) development of a system of professional royal courts of law with extensive powers. Common law, the growing part of customary law that was administered by royal judges according to uniform procedures only minimally influenced by jurisprudence and attaching much importance to legal precedent, remained intact in England, which meant that in fact it was the courts that made the law. Nor should we believe that the legislation of the French kings simply reflected the wishes, *le bon plaisir*, of the sovereign: the great majority of royal ordinances came into being in response to requests, via petitions from pressure groups. A petition was investigated thoroughly and, once it became a written record, the final formulation of a government act still needed the agreement of diverse officials and of the highest college of law, the *Parlement de Paris*. Bureaucratic checks were a hindrance to arbitrary decisions as early as the fourteenth century.

The interests of parties looking for justice stimulated the growth of the royal administration of justice. It was, after all, independent and provided the additional possibility of appeal. The central courts were formed through the specialization and splitting off of separate chambers and councils from a prince's original court council. As more lawsuits were brought before the crown, there was a growing need for the enlargement and specialization of the highest judicial organs. Their purpose was to function as courts of appeal for all the lower courts in the territory, sometimes thus passing over old privileges that had been granted to towns and lordships. Where principalities were combined, as in the German Empire, this resulted in the formation of three levels of courts in a local, regional and central hierarchy. Finally, the prince himself continued to exercise his sovereign judicial power and retained his right to grant pardons, and thus to annul every judicial process.

The establishment of the *Reichskammergericht*, the imperial high court, in 1495, itself the successor of the *Reichshofgericht* installed by Frederick II in 1235, offered opportunities for appeal throughout the German Empire, at least in theory. The weakness of the Empire was exposed, however, when the emperor was immediately compelled to allow powerful territorial princes exemption for their subjects, because the princes set up their own territorial central courts. The regionalism was evident in France as well, where 'parlements', in this particular context meaning law courts, were set up in districts with a strong tradition of autonomy. In Languedoc, for example, the king allowed the regional oligarchy of clientages to continue to administer financial affairs in exchange for their recognition of the political and cultural hegemony of the state. The monarchy was able to adapt to this regional diversity and imposed its own model as far as the circumstances allowed. It was a matter of pacification inside the borders and creaming off resources for defence or imperialistic aims.

Bureaucratization

As early as the twelfth century the emerging monarchies felt the need to surround themselves with growing numbers of experts in administrative matters. The growth into the *Beamtenstaat*, a civil service state, can best be seen as a concentric development, beginning in the household of a territorial prince or king. The most elementary functions grew into differentiated court offices, whose structures remained fairly generally applied until the seventeenth century. To draw up and publish their written documents, the earliest princes called upon the services of nearby clerics, the only people who could read or write, and primarily so in Latin. This was common practice everywhere. As a result of help requested from the clerics by the illiterate ruffians who were the feudal lords to formulate their administrative activities, judicial pronouncements and agreements, Church Latin also became the administrative language of the early states all over Europe.

England was far ahead of the rest of Europe in matters of administrative and judicial organization. This was the result of the strong unifying organization in Anglo-Saxon England and the fact that after 1066 the Normans had to keep a tight grip on the land they had conquered. In the second half of the twelfth century two separate courts become recognizable, in two fields that required specific expertise: first, the Exchequer, the treasury, where the king's financial officers had to justify their accounts, and then the Court of Common Pleas or Common Bench, the central royal court of law for dealing with civil suits. This development can be seen as a general European tendency, and took place at diverse times and to varying degrees depending on the social evolution of a particular region: progressive specialization and bureaucratization resulting from the splitting off of great crown vassals from an originally unitary council. Advisory functions were expanded and made permanent in separate institutions sustained by officials. In the papal Curia, secretaries of state appeared at the head of separate departments during the fifteenth century.

Around the middle of the thirteenth century, vernacular languages started to appear in official documents on the European continent. In England, old English has been used for this purpose since the ninth century. This change in the language used was connected to the growing role played by burghers in government, which helped to some extent to bridge the traditional gap between the knightly and urban worlds. One important result of this opening up of government circles to the vernacular and to officials

of bourgeois origin was that all aspects of national government were made accessible to the subjects, in contrast to the situation in the Catholic Church or the Chinese Empire. Government was no longer shrouded in a foreign, esoteric language and culture, keeping it remote from the people. Prince, officials and representatives of the people could now talk to one another directly, hence the term 'parliament'. We should bear in mind that every linguistic area contained a number of regional languages, that High German would have been considered a foreign language by speakers of Low German, for example, just as *langue d'oil* differed from *langue d'oc* and many other regional languages such as Breton and Frisian. In the Norman tradition, the English court continued to use French in certain official functions until the sixteenth century, which of course was connected to its claims to the French throne. In England, Latin never held an exclusive position in administration as it did on the Continent. Use of the official language gained in social importance as government and judiciary increasingly relied on written procedures. On several occasions during the fourteenth and fifteenth centuries, representatives of the Estates protested successfully against the use of a foreign language by their rulers: German in Bohemia or French in the Burgundian Low Countries. Administrative centres narrowed the gap with their subjects by using the vernacular, so that their language acquired a wider area of circulation than others, albeit often only in official documents.

Nevertheless, the lead enjoyed by the Church in the written culture of the West left its traces in the clerical status of the heads of the royal secretariats, the chancellors. After 1070 the counts of Flanders invariably recruited the provosts of the St Donatian chapter in Bruges to serve as their chancellors. The chancellors of the German kings were generally bishops, or were made bishops soon after their appointment. It was not until 1424 that a layman became chancellor in Germany. Between 1280 and 1332 all the French chancellors were incumbents of the rich bishopric of Laon. In the fourteenth century, the Avignon popes promoted several French chancellors to cardinal; one of them would even become pope. In 1390, the chancellor of the king of Navarre received the red hat of a cardinal. In France, however, secularization set in from the middle of the fourteenth century onwards:

chancellors now were laymen and, by 1500, only 8 per cent of the royal secretaries were clerics.

Clerics had more to offer the princes than just their original monopoly of expertise. It was important that their ecclesiastical dignity provided them with their own substantial incomes, making them cheap employees for the princes. The Church freely granted dispensation to its clerics to enter such service, doubtless motivated by feelings of charity and concern for the good government of the faithful. As a result of providing such services the Church was in an excellent position to look after its own interests, directly and discreetly. No wonder that the overwhelming majority of all surviving pre-1300 documents deal with Church property. On the other hand, it was important that the princes could rely on the support of the Church, which was after all the largest landowner and very influential. Again, because of the celibacy rule, clerics were less inclined than temporal lords to put family and personal interests first. In theory they had no sons to step into their shoes, and could be returned to their spiritual duties without any problem when they were advanced in years, or after a conflict.

In addition to the chancery and various functions such as councillor, diplomacy was a field of activity much favoured by the clerics. Their internationally standardized education and knowledge of Latin were obvious reasons for this, together with the inviolability of their legal position and the trust radiating from their clerical status. Most diplomatic delegations then contained clerics whose number and rank were determined by the importance a government wanted to attach to the mission. The institution of bilateral resident embassies grew out of the complicated Italian relationships during the fifteenth century. Around 1500, the western monarchies gradually started to adopt this form of regular mutual communication. At that time the Habsburg dynasty saw its sphere of interests suddenly expand enormously with the prospect of inheriting the Spanish Empire, making the need for permanent lines of communication between the various princely courts very acute.

Clerical expertise in the fields of administration, literacy and diplomacy was less obvious in the field of finance. Clerics usually left the management of their own domains in the hands of secular stewards, who generally had to account to them in writing. During the second half of the thirteenth century northern Italian financial specialists made their appearance in the princely courts of north-western Europe, no doubt in the pursuit of their activities as financiers and moneylenders. They held high positions in the service of princes as receivers, treasurers, tax farmers or mint masters until about the middle of the fourteenth century. In those capacities they rationalized the management of the rapidly growing princely finances, doubtless safeguarding their own interests at the same time. Towards the end of the fourteenth century, the reaction against foreign officials, coupled with the growth of domestic expertise, pushed the Italian financiers from the official, executive level to that of councillor.

An example of the numerical evolution of royal bureaucracy can be found in the central administration in France: at the beginning of the fourteenth century it had eight master accountants, 19 by 1484; ten notaries worked in the chancery in 1286, 59 in 1361, 79 in 1418 and 120 by the early sixteenth century. Around 1200, the king of England had 15 messengers in his service and in 1350 about 60, enabling the sheriffs of the counties to receive mail from the capital every week. After that there was an enormous acceleration in bureaucratization: by 1515 the French state in its entirety employed more than four thousand officials. In England there were probably fewer state officials per head of population, partly because several functions, such as that of justice of the peace, were unsalaried.

Taxation

The collection of taxes required a widely ramified network of collectors, which kings and territorial princes could not build up easily, inevitably because all fiscal immunities, such as seigneuries, church domains and towns, insisted upon maintaining their autonomy. They preferred to hand in a total amount for their whole area, so that they could keep the collection and thus the control over the tax-bearing capacity of the population in their own hands. The system of levying customs in the ports enabled the English kings to install their own collectors there: these duties were new crown rights mainly involving foreign buyers. The introduction of general and permanent royal taxation, under the pressure of the Hundred Years War, gave the French king the opportunity to keep the collection of those taxes largely in his own hands. In Castile, too, the expansion of the crown's powers by conquest at the expense of the Muslims gave it the right to appoint the *regidores* as collectors in the towns. In other parts of Europe, however, the monarchies encountered great difficulty in centralizing the collection of taxes by their own officials over the whole territory.

In those regions where there were enough silver coins in circulation, the kings could generate a new form of revenue: levies in cash. From 1091, the crusades in Castile formed a reason for the introduction of a permanent tax for both Christians and Muslims. The holy war was the justification for this, with compensation in the form of land grants after the conquest at its basis. The threat of invasion was a second excuse for introducing general taxation. In order to offer some resistance to a new wave of Viking attacks, Danegeld, which had been levied at the time of the first invasions, was reintroduced in England in 991, but now on a permanent footing. It remained, under the name of *heregeld* after the Danes seized power and under the Norman conquerors until the 1160s. It was based on a fixed assessment per area of land and was paid in silver coin, of which many more were minted during this period. *Heregeld* can thus be considered the oldest regular state tax in Europe.

Other general taxes were introduced in England far earlier than on the Continent. In 1185, at the pope's dogged insistence, a tithe (10 per cent) was levied on personal property and incomes in preparation for the Third Crusade. It was a fiscal success, which is all the more remarkable because a similar attempt in France not only ran up against the immunities of the great territorial princes, who were powerful enough to refuse to cooperate, but also against the fundamental objection that the king by his own authority did not have the right to levy taxes on personal property or incomes. Soon afterwards the principle of the proportional tax on personal property was again applied in England, until the excesses of John Lackland led to the clauses against arbitrary taxation in the Magna Carta in 1215. In the long term, however, taxation proved to be the most successful method to enable the English crown to centralize its power.

In 1275 the English parliament approved indirect taxes for the first time. They mainly affected the export of wool. These taxes would form a permanent source of income for the crown and at the same time function as a political weapon against buyers on the Continent, notably the Italians, Flemings and northern Germans. Parliament continued to determine the conditions of the tax, so a public discussion about great economic and political questions took place. When general taxation, both direct and indirect, was placed on a permanent footing in the thirteenth century, its level and frequency were determined by the rhythms of the war. Taxes were not levied during periods of peace with Scotland (1297–1306) and truces with France (1360–1369). By contrast, the intensive warfare of 1294–1298 and the beginning of the Hundred Years War caused explosive growth in the burden of taxation. The war enabled princes to ask for extra money and support from their subjects on the pretext of defending the country, which was after all the concern of every subject. The terms 'necessity' and 'self-defence' were brought out by learned advisors when the excuse of the crusades could no longer be used. But which land had to be defended, and who was the aggressor? In 1297 the barons found that Edward's attack on Flanders could no longer be described as national defence, but his campaigns in Aquitaine, Wales and Scotland did not attract such a protest.

From 1292 onwards the *ayudas* (literally, 'bids for help') rapidly followed each other in the lands under the Aragonese crown, as a result of the royal wars. The principle was that, outside the circumstances when as highest lord he could count on the services of his vassals, a prince must ask his free subjects for help. This meant negotiating with subjects, who could then set their conditions and wrest benefits or more autonomy from the prince. The conquest of Sardinia in 1326, the war against the Muslims and Genoese ten years later, the launching of an armada of 20 galleys to the Straits of Gibraltar in 1340, the conquest of Mallorca in 1342 – all formed a legitimate reason. The lengthy wars against Castile in the middle of the fourteenth century made the levying of taxes on all subjects permanent. In 1363 the *Cortes Generales* of Valencia, Aragon, Catalonia and Mallorca agreed to introduce a tax on the production of cloth and the export of merchandise.

On the French side, the war also naturally demanded new fiscal resources. From 1295 onwards, Philip IV regularly summoned regional assemblies in Languedoc and made urgent requests for money, using the legal argument of 'the right of the state'. Initially this produced little result: in 1293 the tax income of the Italian city of Genoa alone was more than three-and-a-half times the amount flowing annually into King Philip's coffers. The English crown was far more successful than the French in drastically increasing its revenues in a short time. Expressed in tonnes of fine silver, Edward III received 32 tonnes in 1336, 66 in 1337 and 92 in 1339. Loans then accounted for more than half the receipts; this was only possible if enough moneylenders were prepared to extend credit to the king. The French king's income was no more than 53 tonnes in 1339 and 56 in 1340. Clearly, at the beginning of the Hundred Years War the English, with their surprise attack, had an enormous advantage over the French, who could not react adequately militarily, and certainly not logistically or financially. The disastrous course of the first phase of the war led to immense fiscal demands from the French crown, which was then obliged to make promises and concessions to the States General. But the monarchy came off best, because it was granted permanent indirect taxes. It started in 1355 with the *gabelle*, a tax on salt, and a levy of one-thirtieth of the value of merchandise; this ratio was raised to one-twentieth in 1435. The great opportunity came in 1440 with the introduction of a permanent annual tallage, *taille*, to be collected by officials of the king. Unlike the English parliament, the French States General and regional assemblies thus allowed themselves to be marginalized as a political body by surrendering the right to approve the tax every year. In the long run, this had enormous consequences, leading to the supremacy of the crown in France as opposed to the supremacy of parliament in England.

'Money is the sinew of war', wrote Cicero; by implication, it was also the touchstone of the relationships between those who made the decisions about war and lesser mortals. The more a prince was tempted to wage war, the more taxes he had to impose on or demand of his subjects. As soon as his wishes rose above what a lord might expect his vassals to accomplish, he had to ask for an exceptional voluntary contribution or aid. Princes made a habit of this from the thirteenth century onwards, and they also made use of each other to justify their call for self-defence or the just demand. Every war of aggression could be presented somehow or other as legitimate self-defence. Now that princes asked for increasingly large taxes increasingly often, the governments of towns and other representative bodies saw opportunities to negotiate about conditions for possible agreement. This development was one of extreme importance, which came to an end in many countries – France, but also Poland, Hungary, Sweden and Denmark – between the fifteenth and seventeenth centuries. The ability of princes to gain access to a tax system that could function independently of the approval of people's representatives played an essential role in this development.

The possibility for raising taxes again and again depended on the type of economy prevailing in a particular country. In England and Catalonia it was clear in the thirteenth and fourteenth centuries, respectively, that taxes could be levied on exports. An export-oriented economy could thus form the basis for a fiscal system that taxed not its own subjects but the foreign buyers. This functioned especially well when a 'unique selling point' was at stake, such as English wool, oriental spices and wines. Even then, however, the level of taxation might put the competitiveness of a country's export trade at risk. Where the possibility of an export tax did not exist, the only recourse was to tax the subjects, with the risk of rebellion when the burden was felt to be unfair. There was a delicate relationship between increasing fiscal demands and strengthening opposition to them from people's representatives. In France and most other states, the princes were able to force the representative institutions into a modest, almost ritual role in the course of the fifteenth century. In other regions, however, such institutions put up an effective resistance to this encroachment upon their rights, and thus the rights of the subjects also, especially when the allocation of the distribution of taxes were involved.

In the Low Countries, as in Aragon, most regions cherished an ancient tradition, chiefly borne by the main towns, of having a say in their own affairs. Through tough negotiations at every request for a tax, they were able to get a large number of their own demands met and thus played a part in deciding policies. If a prince asked for money for a war of conquest, which did not seem necessary or desirable to them, they did not pay up. They actively opposed higher tariffs for princely tolls because they would damage their vital commercial interests. This is not surprising when one considers that the duke of Burgundy received 13,000 pounds in 1445 from his toll at Gravelines (on the border of Flanders near Calais, the 'staple' where all English wool for the Low Countries was imported), while his entire county of Namur brought in an income of only about 8,000 pounds. For the same reasons, and also to ensure that their own voice would not be silenced, the great towns of Flanders offered unyielding and effective opposition to their duke's plan to introduce a permanent salt tax in 1447 after following France's example.

On five occasions during the first half of the sixteenth century the towns of the County of Holland successfully opposed the plans of the Habsburg government to put a tax on grain exports. This was of vital interest to them because the grain trade formed the basis of Holland's international economy. In 1542, when the government tried to impose a number of indirect taxes, such as the 'hundredth penny' (1 per cent) on exports and the 'tenth penny' (10 per cent) on commercial profits, again following foreign precedents, there was such vehement opposition that within three years the plans were abandoned. As in England, and even more so in the Swiss Confederation, the supervision of the tax system by representative bodies put a brake on the increase of the tax burden to a level far above the capacity of the subjects. The ordinary burgher was closer to economic reality than the princes and their advisors, who displayed aristocratic contempt for it.

During the fifteenth and sixteenth centuries the Low Countries brought in a volume of tax that grew far more strongly than the population, economic growth and inflation. The region may at that time have been the nucleus of the world economy, but the amount the state creamed off, in spite of active representation on behalf of the people, attacked the very roots of its prosperity. The state's annual income rose by 69 per cent between 1445 and 1531–1534, two periods of peace. The share of taxes in relation to traditional demesne revenues of the princes climbed from 38 per cent to 80 per cent. Such a flexible tax levy was only imaginable in a very wealthy land, but at the same time it was the quickest way to rob that land of its economic assets.

State budgets swelled under the growing pressure of the costs of wars, financed to a large extent by loans. But these loans meant there would be an additional tax increase in the long term. In the middle of the fourteenth century and the early fifteenth, the city-state of Florence was engaged in a series of wars against the Papal States, Milan and Pisa. At the beginning of the period the republic's expenditure was 40,000 florins, but the wars cost 2.5, 7.5 and 4.5 million florins respectively. The difference had to be found in tax increases and in loans, for which the interest found its way into the pockets of the financiers, but was paid for by taxes on the everyday consumer goods of ordinary people. Government debts thus enriched the wealthy at the expense of simple taxpayers.

If we look at fiscality as a means of exercising power then we are struck by the direct and continuing relationship between war and taxation. Wars stimulated new and higher taxation, and even active representative institutions could not really offer resistance. Princes were not guided by macro-economic considerations. They really could not know what results their activities might bring because there was no reliable statistical information available about their own finances or those of their subjects. Time and again the unplanned expenses for the purpose of war threw state finances into confusion. Once a conflict had broken out, expenses could not be kept under control because only victory counted in a war, not economic efficiency. Therefore a lot of money had to be spent, borrowed against high rates of interest, the repayment of which would have a snowball effect and continue to burden expenditure for decades thereafter. Only the states that seemed to be creditworthy could actually obtain credit. In other words, a well-functioning tax system increased the chances of obtaining credit, which then threatened the equilibrium of that system.

The economic system thus made a twofold difference in a state's chances of obtaining money: in a commercialized economy, surpluses could be syphoned off far more easily through indirect taxes, regardless of the level at which they were levied, than in an agrarian subsistence economy. Moreover, credit was cheaper and more easily available in a commercialized economy, making a rapid expansion of liquid assets

Plate 14.3 Opening of the English parliament in April 1523 during the rule of Henry VIII

possible, while the agrarian economy was mainly limited to the sluggish, restricted and barely flexible yields from the demesnes. One result of this was that from the thirteenth century onwards a state's military opportunities were more and more determined by its access to the money market. The more commercialized regions could then achieve military superiority simply because they were able to hire as many soldiers as they needed. These mercenaries came predominantly from periphery regions that still had agricultural economies, such as Wales, Scotland, central France, Castile, the Swiss Confederation and central Germany. It is thus quite conceivable that the agricultural regions not only produced fewer resources with which to resist the supremacy of the core regions but that their own populations often also supplied the troops that would subject them.

The subjects

The initiative for the continual competition for more concentrated means of power, which led to the formation of increasingly large and strongly equipped states, naturally emanated from those persons and bodies that were already ahead in the power stakes: feudal lords, large landowners, princes, princes of the Church, urban oligarchies. Yet the outcome of this centuries-long struggle was not decided solely by these elites. The people who were subordinated to more powerful states did not just sit and watch: communities formed their own political systems, which for a long time were a weighty factor in the contest. The feudal lords, who were no match for their mightier rivals, sometimes formed alliances against their rulers and even sought the support of their natural opponents in the towns or ecclesiastical institutions. In short, the formation of stronger concentrations of power provoked counter-reactions in which losing parties formed coalitions that could turn the tide at the first sign of a ruler's weakness. This dialectical process created forms of representation and resistance that would make a unique contribution to world history: the system of parliamentary government.

The recognition of a ruler, just like a feudal contract, took the form of a reciprocal oath of loyalty in which first the future ruler promised to protect the rights of his subjects and the Church, and then his vassals and other representatives of his subjects swore an oath of faithful service to him. It was on the basis of this statutory extension of the feudal oath of homage, subject to the sanctions of breach of contract, that the vassals and the privileged urban communities freely decided to accept a territorial lord and to hold him to the obligations he had assumed.

The appointment of a legitimate successor was a recurring problem, a consequence of the high mortality rate among the hardened warriors; disagreement generally arose because of the variety of legal rules for succession and complex family ramifications. Rules of succession, such as the right of the first-born (primogeniture) and the admission (England, Castile, Low Countries) or exclusion (France, German Empire, Aragon) of women, were pointers to the choice in theory but did not guarantee an unequivocal or good solution. Problems arose in one out of every two successions because there were several contenders with equally valid claims, or because the successor was a minor, incompetent or female. Even in those countries where a woman could succeed, there were always arguments about her husband and his claims. In those circumstances, the subjects who were called to recognize a new ruler had the opportunity to assert their preference and to lay down conditions for their agreement. This applied even more strongly in those regions where the kingship was by definition arranged by election – namely, in the German Empire and its originally vassal kingdoms of Bohemia, Hungary and Poland, as well as in Sweden. Until the Habsburgs made the kingship hereditary in practice after 1438 the election contest always stirred up intense rivalry among the most important princely houses, so that the kingship itself remained weak. The heavily debated succession to Emperor Maximilian I led his grandson Charles V to accept a whole series of conditions and restrictions to his power in 1519.

From the twelfth century onwards evidence throughout Europe points to the representatives of different estates, including burghers, being involved in the recognition of a ruler and the formulation of the basic rules of his government. Not in France, however: until 1328, the succession in the Capetian dynasty was problem-free, and when that house died out only the 12 peers, six bishops and six dukes decided that their preference was for Philip of Valois rather than Edward III of England, as he was a 'natural prince'. Philip was indeed a member of a male line that had been born and bred indigenously in the country since time immemorial.

In 1135 Alfonso VII had himself proclaimed emperor of Spain before a solemn assembly made up of important spiritual dignitaries and great barons and 'judges', by which it is possible that the elected representatives of the towns could be meant. This was certainly the case in 1187 when the governments of 50 towns took part in the meeting of the royal council of Castile, which affirmed Berenguela's right to the succession and her contract of marriage to Conrad of Hohenstaufen. One year later, after a much-disputed succession to the throne, Alfonso IX of León promised before 'the archbishops, bishops, religious orders, counts and other nobles of the kingdom together with elected burghers of the towns' to respect the good customs and only to make decisions about war and

peace after discussions with 'the bishops, nobles and good men'. The assembly in turn swore allegiance and to maintain the law and peace in the kingdom. In the neighbouring kingdom of Aragon the *cortes* (assembly of the estates) met regularly from the mid-twelfth century onwards, with more than a hundred members, some of them from the towns. The *cortes* dealt with political questions such as the maintenance of order, administration of justice, taxation and the minting of coinage. A general *cortes*, in 1214, consisting of 'barons, knights, burghers and vassals from the castles and villages', swore allegiance to the under-age king, James, in return for financial and judicial advantages. When the dynasty was in crisis, as happened in Castile–León between 1275 and 1325, the *cortes* formulated their grievances about a variety of matters in the kingdom and thus brought their influence to bear on the government to choose a rival claimant to the throne. The far-reaching rights that Spanish noblemen and towns had won in connection with the Reconquest gave them a stronger basis in their dealings with the crown than that of their colleagues elsewhere in Europe. In Aragon, where feudal institutions were fully developed, this tendency was even more outspoken than in Castile, where feudalism was largely absent in the structuring of power relations.

In Flanders representatives of nobility and large towns had gone a step further as early as 1128. They demanded public reparation for all the injustices committed by William of Normandy, a count who had been forced on them by their liege lord, Louis VI of France, and who, within no time at all, had violated all the privileges he had granted and sworn to at his investiture. They proposed laying their disputes before a special court of law, composed of eminent men from each of the three estates. Should they decide that the count had indeed contravened the rights of his subjects and continually refused to make good the violations, then they would depose the perjured count and seek a more suitable candidate. The proposed meeting never took place because Count William took up arms, in the ancient tradition of chivalry, and was by chance killed. This was the first time that the principle that the oath of homage bound a prince to the agreed legal relations was formulated and that the feudal right of resistance was applied to the government of his entire land. Consequently, in the event of violation, he lost the allegiance not only of his vassals but of all his subjects too, and therefore also his office (see p. 167). It would be further applied in Brabant in 1420 and in the Low Countries as a whole on the 'abjuration' of Philip II of Spain (1580–1581), and, via the English revolutions of the seventeenth century, would later be found as the impeachment process in the American constitution. In essence, the famous Magna Carta of 1215 was also a list of complaints that King John's vassals addressed to him for breaching the feudal law. London was the only city mentioned. The deposition and execution of Edward II in 1327 and Richard II in 1399 were supported by similar procedures carried out in parliament, although they were often poisoned by rivalries between the great families.

In urbanized regions, burghers did not wait until their princes had dynastic problems to introduce consultative structures on a regional and interregional scale. In this way they could take care of their own commercial interests with all the implications for coinage, administration of justice and safety. If these interests were damaged by their own or foreign princes, then burghers brought their grievances and requests to them as a collective body, compelling their compliance sometimes by means of financial concessions and, if necessary, through boycotts or reprisals. Since overseas and overland trading routes crossed several jurisdictions, governments of trading towns operated in associations far beyond the territorial ones. As long as princes showed no interest in economic politics, which was true of most of them until the fifteenth century, traders enjoyed much freedom in this. The attempts at territorialization and the expansion of the apparatus of state set them on a collision course with the princes. Typical points of friction were the harmful effects of dynastic wars on commercial relations, toll collections, the arrest of foreign merchants by a prince's officers of justice and devaluation of the currency.

With their associations, privileges, merchants' guilds and their own legal systems trading towns had created solid structures that to a large extent functioned independently of the monarchy. They could not be brushed aside easily by the new state apparatuses: after all, they had a great deal of specialist knowledge and contacts and were not inclined to give them up for nothing. Governments were thus obliged to negotiate with the urban representative organizations with a long tradition of autonomous representation. That was where the money was. The moment when their governments were incorporated into tighter state structures formed an excellent occasion for this. Hence the emphatic role they played in purely political events, such as succession crises in regions like Aragon, Flanders and Brabant.

The survival of effectively functioning representative institutions depended both on external pressure and the social, economic and political structures of the regions concerned. The parliament in England owed its exceptional continuity (despite some interruptions of several years at the end of the fifteenth century) to the solid anchorage of its representation in the counties and boroughs, where the tradition of the subjects' participation went back to the time of the Anglo-Saxon kings. Even the most centralized states could not completely eliminate the traditionally strong regional systems of representation. All the newly incorporated territories kept their traditional rights: for example, in France the Normans received their charter in 1315, Lorraine as late as 1766. Also in France, the state assemblies of Burgundy and of Languedoc functioned until the end of the eighteenth century, the *ancien régime*. This was also the case in the southern Low Countries under Habsburg rule.

In their origins, representative institutions were a reflection of the power relations in a particular region. Like all human institutions, however, they had a tendency to ossify and become oligarchic. Established groups were primarily concerned with their own interests, sometimes even to the detriment of other categories. They took up a corporate position, as representatives of a specific group whose interests they served exclusively, without regard for the interests of their neighbours or members of other estates. So, after the fifteenth century, representatives of the towns certainly could no longer be considered as members of a dynamic commercial bourgeoisie: in many cases they were so accustomed to the consultative structure that they became local clients of the monarchy, in the 'pactist' system previously described. This was certainly the case in the lands held by the crowns of Aragon and Castile when the revolts of the *Germanías* and the *Comuneros* broke out between 1519 and 1523. The revolts began as a political resistance by the urban knighthood. They were dissatisfied with the years of bad government, exacerbated by exorbitant claims made by the followers of the young king and future emperor Charles (V) of Habsburg. When the revolts radicalized further and were joined by the members of crafts guilds and peasants, they were savagely repressed by royal troops.

A great deal depended then on how representative the representatives really were. In the towns, if the representatives were purely private individuals with an eye on a noble title then they ran the risk of their subjects sending a petition directly to the king or, even worse, being brought down by revolts. Their role as intermediary between the centre and periphery in the state then took a terrible blow. Two sorts of factors increased the pressure on such 'representatives' from the fifteenth century onwards: the expansion of monarchal authority limited their room for manoeuvre, and the escalation of war continually raised the fiscal and military expectations of the crown. Both these trends appeared at the same time, although the extreme lack of financial resources for the war compelled the state to give in and make concessions to the local elites.

Balance of powers

In the competition described above there were naturally more losers than winners. Among the losers in the process of state formation were countless local lords and territorial princes whose lands were swallowed up by more competitive units. In this we can see an increased efficiency within the same type of dominion. It was a different matter for the cultural losers, like the Welsh, Irish and Bohemians whose languages were banned from Church services, government and the law; Muslims, who became second-class citizens in Castile, Portugal and the lands under the crown of Aragon; and Christians in the Balkans after the Ottoman conquests. The German upper class in the central European and Baltic towns and in the rural areas of Prussia was shameless in its discrimination against the Slav population. A great deal of urban autonomy was lost in the process of strengthening state power, because princes gained a tight hold on the composition of town government, the exercise of judicial powers and financial expenditure. There was naturally no question of independent military activity in the context of the state. Insurgency was repressed by superior strength.

Yet the fourteenth century was rife with rebellion. Massive peasant revolts broke out in west Flanders (1323–1328), the Jacquerie in central France (1358), in England (1381) and in large parts of the German Empire (1524–1526), as we saw in Chapter 13. In every case the revolt received the support of the proletariat of a large town (Bruges, Paris, London and Mainz, respectively), which made it an even more serious threat to the established order. Opposition to the increased taxation imposed by the states to finance their wars was among the motives behind these rebellions.

However strong the concentration of people and capital in the towns, they were compelled to relinquish a large measure of their autonomy to the monarchies because, apart from northern and central Italy, the states gradually came to have more means of exercising power at their disposal. If the budgets of towns like Ghent and Louvain were more or less equal to the budgets of the count of Flanders and the duke of Brabant, respectively, in the fourteenth century, the territorial expansion and the systematic tax levies gave the princes the advantage. The towns seldom managed to cooperate effectively for any length of time to form a counterbalance. Unions of German towns in regions like Swabia, Alsace and the Upper Rhine, which contemplated protecting certain common interests of their burghers from the feudal powers, suffered from a lack of genuine solidarity. Even in the German Hanse, the great urban league, most of the time the interests of the regional groupings were deeply divergent, often even diametrically opposed. This made truly coordinated action only possible in exceptional circumstances. Certainly, the members would not support each other in purely political conflicts with nearby princes.

The strengthening of state power was thus a predominant pattern of the late Middle Ages. States continually occupied more territory, they concentrated a greater superiority of means of violence in relation to other power cores in society, and they built an apparatus of officials to maintain the law and collect the taxes. This image applied particularly to England, Poland, France and Spain.

In the German Empire several territorial princes consolidated their positions at the expense of smaller contestants and towns, but the continually changing coalitions among the dozens of units prevented any real concentration from taking place. The Empire as a whole lost substantial areas because of the lack of cohesion in its periphery. The imperial principalities in the Low Countries were combined into an exceptionally powerful complex under the Burgundian-Habsburg dynasty. Alsace, Lotharingia (Lorraine), Franche-Comté, Dauphiné and Provence came into the French sphere of influence. The Swiss Confederation detached itself gradually, and in 1501 formally, from the Empire. Under the rule of Emperor Charles IV in 1373, after whom the famous bridge in Prague was named, the kingdom of Bohemia succeeded in stringing together vast areas of land that stretched from Brandenburg through Lausitz, Silesia, Moravia, Austria, Styria, Carinthia as far as the Tirol. The Habsburg dynasty eventually supplanted the Luxemburg house and, in 1526, brought all those regions back *heim ins Reich* through tactical marriages. In the same year, most of Hungary fell to the Ottoman Empire, which had conquered the entire Balkan region between 1355 and 1470, causing a massive exodus of Christians.

The enlargement of the monarchic states' power did not take place solely at the expense of local and territorial lords and princes and the towns. The Church also lost ground at every level during the fourteenth and fifteenth centuries. The ideal of the crusade was degraded in the thirteenth century to a purely political, internal-European weapon and disappeared into the realm of fiction. The popes' universalistic claims stranded finally on French opposition, leading to a profound territorialization of the Church, which came to depend on temporal rulers and began to serve their interests more directly. Church property was thenceforth taxed regularly. Towns and states took over a growing number of functions that the Church had previously considered its own. Secular courts of law ruled on matters of marriage and heresy, the organization of poor relief and health care came increasingly into lay hands; care of the poor and the sick, which had been given its original form by the cloisters and parochial bodies, was now controlled by laypeople. Papal moral authority was diminished through the increasingly magnanimous application of the principle of granting indulgences (a reduction of punishment in the hereafter for sins committed on earth) and dispensations for illegitimate birth and the marriage

of close relatives. As it became clear that it was increasingly possible to buy such favours, those who could afford to used them purely instrumentally. The general tendency was towards secularization: a growing number of matters were no longer dealt with in a religious dimension but on a purely human or material level. Although the role of the Church was in no way played out, the Church had lost its supremacy and even its independence in relation to the stronger secular rulers.

It must be clear from the foregoing that in 1500 (just as in 1800) there still was no question of a single type of state in Europe. Expansion in the German Empire and Italy was curbed by the balances of power existing between the countless political units. Incorporation into larger units rarely meant the abrogation of customary law and institutions. The stronger states could rely on a modern commercialized economy in which greater quantities of more flexible resources were available than in a traditional agrarian economy, such as that of Poland or Denmark. In Italy the commercial middle class ruled the cities directly during the so-called 'communal period', but, from the mid-fourteenth century onwards, the tendency towards investment in land and seigniorial rights underpinned the tendency towards the formation of *signorie*, or even outright monarchic rule. Commercial capital was not tied to a particular place or a particular territory. Should the lack of safety, non-repayment of royal debts, heavy tax burden or excessively high wages create unattractive conditions for investors in search of profits, then they sought refuge elsewhere and the local economy collapsed. Princes could not control capitalists, and since they could not exist without their credit they had to allow them freedom in their activities. This mixed model would offer the best chances for the future.

CONTRASTS. NEW EMPIRES IN THE EAST: RIURIKID RUSSIA AND THE OTTOMAN EMPIRE

Riurikid Russia

When speaking of medieval Russia we in fact refer to a confederation of principalities that emerged from the original Rus' or Viking principality around Kiev (see

Chapter 5). Typically for Eastern Europe, only male descendants of the quasi-legendary first Scandinavian ruler of Kiev, Riurik, could qualify for lording over one of the changing number of territorial units that were formed over the centuries in a combined process of territorial expansion, subdivision and loss. Hence the common denomination for medieval Russia is Riurikid Russia, which lasted uninterruptedly until 1598 when Feodor, the feeble-minded son of Tsar Ivan the Terrible, died without leaving any heirs. By that time, the original tradition of collateral succession per generation, explained on p. 302, had long been replaced by vertical succession in the male line. A certain measure of unity between the Riurikid principalities was maintained by the recognition of their dynastic leader as grand prince 'of All Rus', a title first connected to the lordship of Kiev, later of Vladimir in the Suzdal area, east of Moscow. This reallocation of the titular base of the grand principality was significant for the gradual north-eastward shift of actual power in Riurikid Russia, a tendency further stressed after many of the western principalities became subject to Lithuania and the remainder came under Mongolian suzerainty. The latter development was the consequence of the conquest of the western steppe lands of central Asia by the Mongolian army of Chinggis Khan's grandson, Batu, who established an iron dominion over the entire area west of the Urals. This dominion, known as the Golden Horde, located its headquarters in the city of Sarai, near the mouth of the Volga, and was to last until the early fifteenth century. For the Russian principalities, even those that in due time were conquered by the Lithuanians, the Golden Horde hegemony meant that no prince could rule without a formal and written Mongolian consent (so-called *iarlyks* or 'permits to rule'), and that all were obliged to pay tribute to their Mongol masters in the form of money, goods or soldiers. Understandably, some Riurikid princes were more cooperative than others, but from a historical point of view cooperation paid off, because during the Golden Horde period the most trusted Riurikid allies of the Mongol khans emerged as the most powerful rulers of Russia: these were the princes of Moscow, until that moment an insignificant town.

A key factor in the rise of Moscow, apart from its unstinting allegiance to the Mongols, was its control of the southern trade routes from Novgorod. Novgorod was by far the most important commercial centre of Riurikid Russia: the axis in all trade between the Baltic on the one hand, and the Black Sea area, with its connections to the Italian and Byzantine markets of the Mediterranean, the souks of the Muslim Middle East and the great silk route to China. Novgorod was also the capital of a vast northern territory, extending from the Gulf of Finland to the shores of the arctic White Sea, and an eldorado for such prized forest products as squirrel furs, wood, honey and wax. Within the Russian confederation Novgorod had succeeded in taking an autonomous position; often it functioned essentially as an autonomous, quite oligarchic, city-state. During the fourteenth century, however, pressure on this autonomy started to build up, from both Muscovite and Lithuanian sides, until finally, in 1478, Novgorod was incorporated into the new Muscovite state, which was followed by large-scale confiscation and reassignment of landed property. In that crucial period, the Muscovite principality, as well as the title of Grand Prince of Vladimir, was already firmly in the hands of the Danilovich branch of the Riurikid dynasty, the first to have switched to vertical succession. The Danilovich took their name from Danil, a younger son of the more famous prince of Moscow, Alexander 'Nevsky' who, around 1240, halted Swedish and German expansionist ambitions in the Novgorod area. But it would take another two centuries, until after Mongolian dominance had declined and Lithuanian imperialism had lost its momentum, before the grand princes of Moscow could realize their own territorial ambitions. Around the middle of the sixteenth century the Muscovite-Russian empire stretched from the Ob river in the north-east to within a short distance of the Sea of Azov in the south. A new superpower had been born, and the world would soon be made aware of this. After the fall of Constantinople in 1453, Moscow set itself up as its successor and as new leader of the Orthodox Church. Grand Prince Ivan III (1462–1505) married the Byzantine princess Sofia Paleologa. From the 1520s onwards, claims were elaborated into a full-blown 'Third Rome theory'. It was in 1547 that Ivan 'the Terrible' was the first to be crowned with the title 'tsar' (caesar) of Russia as if he were the rightful heir and successor to the Roman emperors. His capital, Moscow, may have been a pale reflection of Constantinople at the pinnacle of its glory, but it definitely was a booming city, with probably well over 100,000 inhabitants at the beginning of the sixteenth century – certainly three times as many as Novgorod at the time.

Danilovich Moscow developed all the characteristics of an early modern state that have been discussed in this chapter: there was some form of centralized, bureaucratic government with a high level of written documentation to support taxation and public administration; there was a clear jurisdictional hierarchy (with the grand prince himself acting as supreme judge); territorial principalities were replaced by provinces and rural districts led by appointed governors and district chiefs, who had their own small staffs of subordinate officials; for special tasks, special officials were centrally appointed. General taxes were levied and the army was gradually modernized by centralizing recruitment and command, by assigning to the tsar greater control over military resources, and by reducing the importance of the private military retinues of princes and boyars. The core of the Muscovite army consisted of professional soldiers who, from Ivan III onwards, were increasingly rewarded with (confiscated) lands.

The most remarkable feature of the Muscovite political system, however, was undoubtedly its idea of loyalty to the state, according to which the entire elite was assumed to be ministerial in the literal sense of being a 'servant' of the grand prince or tsar. In addition, a service hierarchy was devised and each member of the political elite had his place assigned via an intricate ranking system with meritocratic features, the so-called *mestnichestvo*. All members of the high nobility of *boyars* and *okol'nichii* were appointed by the tsar; they occupied most court offices, while the tsar's council or *duma* consisted of 10–15 of the highest-ranking noblemen. This high nobility was partly recruited from old Riurikid princely families, partly also from untitled aristocratic families.

The formation of the Ottoman Empire

In spite of the largely symbolic importance of the taking of Constantinople by the Turks on 29 May 1453, it marked the end of the East Roman or Byzantine Empire more than it heralded the dawn of a new empire. Indeed the first steps in the formation of the

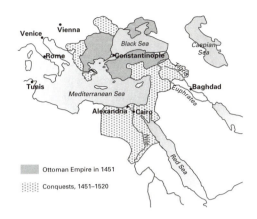

Map 14.3 The rise of the Ottoman Empire

Ottoman Empire, which would dominate large parts of Europe, Asia and Africa until 1918, can be situated in the early fourteenth century. The principality of the renowned Osman was located in north-west Anatolia. It was one of the many Turkish states created after the defeat of the Mongols by the Turkish Mamelukes in 1260, who ruled Syria, Egypt and the Red Sea coast of Arabia. These were the regions that were then annexed by the Ottomans.

The Ottomans first extended their power along the Dardanelles and the whole south coast of the Sea of Marmara, an area that had previously been of strategic importance for the Byzantine Empire as well. In 1326 they established their capital in Bursa, whence they could control access to Constantinople from both Anatolia and the West. Around 1350 their armies operated on European soil in the service of the Byzantine emperor. They profited from this when they took Gallipoli on the European side of the Straits in 1354 and then Adrianople in Bulgaria in 1361; five years later they made Adrianople their capital. Together with the north of Anatolia, the Balkans would be their most important area of expansion in the fourteenth century. The victory over the Serbian princes at the infamous Field of the Blackbirds in Kosovo took place in 1389. In 1393 the Ottomans took control of Bulgaria, Macedonia and Thessaly. The crusade of 1396, under the leadership of the Hungarian king Sigismund, resulted in a crushing defeat for the Christians at Nicopolis on the Danube; Walachia, north of the Danube, became a Turkish vassal state.

The secret of the Ottomans' success lay in the fact that while their state and army were tightly organized, their numerous opponents were divided and weakened. For religious and political reasons the centuries-long battle waged by the Byzantines in the Balkans, for the most part with mercenary armies, benefited nobody. From the fourteenth century onwards the region suffered severely from epidemics of plague. The native population was certainly no more hostile to the Ottoman Turks than to the Greeks, the more so since there had been a substantial Turkish settlement in Bulgaria during the fourteenth century.

The Mongol advance under Timur Lenk in 1402 brought a halt to Ottoman expansion for some 20 years. After their retreat Anatolia broke up again into a string of principalities until a reorganization from Bursa under Mourad II (1421–1451) made a new wave of conquests possible, first in Anatolia and then in the Balkans. Despite their fierce resistance the Hungarians and Albanians suffered resounding defeats in 1444 and 1448, which paved the way for the incorporation of Serbia, Albania and Morea (the Peloponnese) into the Ottoman Empire. Deprived of its hinterland and surrounded by Turkish galleys, Constantinople could offer no more resistance in 1453 once enemy artillery had breached its ancient walls. Caffa, the last Genoese trading colony on the Black Sea, fell into Turkish hands in 1475, but the Venetians would fight for their settlements on the islands and along the coasts of the Adriatic and Aegean for years to come. After taking the Mameluke regions, with the holy places of Islam in 1517, the Ottomans mounted a new offensive in the direction of central Europe. The king of Hungary was killed at the Battle of Mohács in 1526, and Bosnia and the greater part of Hungary fell into Ottoman hands, those of sultan and caliph Suleiman II.

The systematic Ottoman conquests over two centuries had a spectacular result – the creation of an Islamic imperium that extended over an immense area and lasted for five centuries. Tight military organization was the key to this success. The sultans recruited a permanent, personal guard of foot soldiers, the janissaries (from the Turkish *yeni cheri*, meaning 'new troops'). As remuneration cavalrymen were given the right to levy taxes in a particular region, but this concession was only enough to maintain a small number of men and was strictly controlled. The sultans recruited important officials from the servants, often slaves, at their court, who would remain loyal and did not immediately form a warrior aristocracy. The sultan and his household manifested themselves as religious leaders who kept a careful watch on every aspect of religious life and imposed a sort of state church. Their wars were thus holy wars. In that light, and with their strong dynastic approach, the Ottomans succeeded in bridging the traditional differences between Sunnis and Shi'ites. They were also able to involve subjected populations in government and war, through which their loyalty was assured. Mosques and Koranic schools were established everywhere, but the subjected peoples were free to choose their religion. The sultan's successor was chosen from among the children of the harem ladies, most of whom were slaves and often from Georgia.

The entire system of warfare and state bureaucracy was only possible because the Ottoman Empire made use of the existing traditions of government in the region and, if necessary, gave them a new religious and personal stimulus. The Ottomans profited from their empire's flourishing economy. The imposed internal pacification and assured external peace brought about tax yields that were higher than during the previous centuries of constant mutual conflict.

Why, we may ask, did the many attempts at the formation of an empire in western and central Europe fail? A comparison with the formation of the Ottoman and Russian Empires reveals the following differences:

- Christianity, the dominant religion in the West from the fifth century, was exclusivist: Islam was tolerant, thus removing one reason for opposition;
- in many cases Christianity was rooted in Western Europe earlier than the kingdoms: the Ottoman Empire grew in an already Islamized context, but in its expansion Islam and political authority were imposed together;
- the European component of the Ottoman Empire was established by highly motivated and centrally guided warriors, with a religious point of view: in Western Europe kingdoms developed far more laboriously and with much greater heterogeneity, only partially in connection with Christianity;
- the formation of the kingdoms in the West took

place over several centuries from a multiplicity of expansive cores that, as they grew, also formed a counterweight to each other: the Ottoman Empire imposed its system from outside as a superior power in every respect in less than two centuries;

- Western European states were formed in a protracted process of the centralization of functions, in which the concentration of resources was always inadequate: from its beginnings the Ottoman Empire was able to direct a strongly concentrated flow of funds to its conquests and to recompense its office-holders; this prevented a decentralization of power, at least during the period of expansion.

The conditions that formed the basis of the two developments were so completely different that it seems pointless to speculate on the chances of success for the formation of an empire in the West.

FURTHER READING

Allmand, Chrisopher (1988), *The Hundred Years War. England and France At War c.1300–c.1450* (Cambridge: Cambridge University Press).

—— (1992), *Henry V* (Berkeley: University of California Press).

Arnold, Benjamin (1991), *Princes and Territories in Medieval Germany* (Cambridge: Cambridge University Press).

Bartusis, Mark C. (1992), *The Late Byzantine Army. Arms and Society, 1204–1453* (Philadelphia, Pa.: Pennsylvania State University Press).

Bean, J.M.W. (1989), *From Lord to Patron: Lordship in Late Medieval England* (Manchester: Manchester University Press).

Blockmans, Wim and Walter Prevenier (1999), *The Promised Lands: The Low Countries under Burgundian Rule, 1369–1530* (Philadelphia, Pa.: University of Pennsylvania Press) (orig. Dutch, 1997).

Brand, Paul (2003), *Kings, Barons, and Justices: The Making and Enforcement of Legislation in Thirteenth-century England* (Cambridge: Cambridge University Press).

Brown, A.L. (1989), *The Governance of Late-Medieval England, 1272–1461* (Stanford, Calif.: Stanford University Press).

Brown, Michael (2004), *The Wars of Scotland, 1214–1371* (Edinburgh and New York: Edinburgh University Press/Columbia University Press).

Burleigh, Michael (1984), *Prussian Society and the German Order: An Aristocratic Corporation in Crisis, c.1410–1466* (Cambridge: Cambridge University Press).

Burns, J.H. (1992), *Lordship, Kingdom and Empire: The Idea of Monarchy 1400–1525* (Oxford: Clarendon).

Carpenter, Christine (1997), *The Wars of the Roses: Politics and the Constitution in England, c.1477–1509* (Cambridge: Cambridge University Press).

Connell, William J. and Andrea Zorzi (eds) (2000), *Florentine Tuscany: Structures and Practices of Power* (Cambridge: Cambridge University Press).

DeVries, Kelly (1996), *Infantry Warfare in the Early Fourteenth Century: Disipline, Tactics and Technology* (Woodbridge: Boydell).

Engel, Pal (2005), *The Realm of St. Stephen: A History of Medieval Hungary*, 2nd edn (London and New York: I.B. Tauris).

Etting, Vivian (2004), *Queen Margrete I (1353–1412) and the Founding of the Nordic Union* (Leiden: Brill).

Franklin, Simon and Jonathan Shepard (1996), *The Emergence of Rus, 750–1200* (London and New York: Longman)

Given-Wilson, Chris (1987), *The English Nobility in the Late Middle Ages. The Fourteenth-Century Political Community* (London and New York: Routledge).

Gomes, Rita Costa (2003), *The Making of a Court Society: Kings and Nobles in Late Medieval Portugal* (Cambridge: Cambridge University Press).

Guenée, Bernard (1985), *States and Rulers in Later Medieval Europe* (Oxford: Blackwell) (orig. French, 1971).

Harriss, Gerald (2005), *Shaping the Nation: England 1360–1461* (New York and Oxford: Oxford University Press).

Heer, Friedrich (1995), *The Holy Roman Empire* (London: Phoenix Press) (orig. German, 1967).

Horrox, Rosemary (1989), *Richard III: A Study of Service* (Cambridge: Cambridge University Press).

Imber, Colin (1990), *The Ottoman Empire 1300–1481* (Istanbul: ISIS Press).

—— (2002), *The Ottoman Empire, 1300–1650* (Basingstoke: Palgrave Macmillan).

Inalcik, Halil (1973), *The Ottoman Empire: The Classical Age 1300–1600* (London: Weidenfeld & Nicolson) (orig. Turkish).

—— (1997), *An Economic and Social History of the Ottoman Empire. Volume 1: 1300–1600* (Cambridge: Cambridge University Press).

Kaeuper, Richard W. (1988), *War, Justice and Public Order: England and France in the Later Middle Ages* (Oxford: Clarendon).

Kafadar, Cemal (1995), *Between Two Worlds: The Construction of the Ottoman State* (Berkeley: University of California Press).

Kelly, Samantha (2003), *The New Solomon: Robert of Naples (1309–1343) and Fourteenth-century Kingship* (Leiden and Boston, Mass. Boston: Brill).

Kirshner, Julius (ed.) (1995), *The Origins of the State in Italy 1300–1600* (Chicago and London: University of Chicago Press).

Knecht, Robert (2004), *The Valois Kings of France, 1328–1589* (Basingstoke: Palgrave Macmillan).

Knoll, Paul W. (1972), *The Rise of the Polish Monarchy: Piast Poland in East central Europe, 1320–1370* (Chicago, Ill. and London: Chicago University Press).

Le Roy Ladurie, Emmanuel (1994), *The Royal French State 1460–1610* (Oxford: Blackwell) (orig. French, 1987).

Martin, Janet L.B. (1995), *Medieval Russia, 980–1584* (Cambridge: Cambridge University Press).

Martines, Lauro (2002), *Power and Imagination. City-States in Renaissance Italy*, 2nd edn (London: Pimlico).

McFarlane, Kenneth Bruce (1981), *England in the Fifteenth Century: Collected Essays*, Introduction G.L. Harriss (London: Hambledon Press).

Nicol, D.M. (1993), *The Last Centuries of Byzantium, 1261–1453*, 2nd edn (Cambridge: Cambridge University Press).

Ormrod, W.M. (1990), *The Reign of Edward III: Crown and Political Society in England 1327–1377* (New Haven, Conn. and London: Yale University Press).

—— (1995), *Political Life in Medieval England, 1300–1450* (Basingstoke and New York: Macmillan/St Martin's Press).

Ostrowski, Donald (1998), *Muscovy and the Mongols: Cross-cultural Influences on the Steppe Frontier, 1304–1589* (Cambridge: Cambridge University Press).

Pernoud, Régine and Marie-Véronique Clin (2000), *Joan of Arc: Her Story*, 2nd edn (London: Weidenfeld & Nicolson).

Potter, David (1995), *A History of France, 1460–1560: The Emergence of a Nation-State* (New York and Oxford: Oxford University Press).

Prestwich, Michael (1997), *Edward I* (New Haven, Conn. and London: Yale University Press).

—— (2003), *The Three Edwards: War and State in England 1272–1377*, 2nd edn (London and New York: Routledge).

Raban, Sandra (2000), *England under Edward I and Edward II, 1259–1327* (Oxford and Malden, Mass.: Blackwell).

Rose, Susan and Margaret L. Kekewich (2004), *Britain, France and the Empire, 1350–1500* (Basingstoke: Palgrave Macmillan).

Rowell, S.C. (1994), *Lithuania Ascending: A Pagan Empire within East-Central Europe, 1295–1345* (Cambridge: Cambridge University Press).

Saul, Nigel (1997) *Richard II* (New Haven, Conn. and London: Yale University Press).

Strayer, Joseph R. (1980), *The Reign of Philip the Fair* (Princeton, N.J.: Princeton University Press).

Sugar, Peter F. (1977), *Southeastern Europe under Ottoman rule, 1354–1804* (Seattle and London: University of Washington Press).

Tilly, Charles (1990), *Coercion, Capital and European States, 990–1990* (Cambridge, Mass.: Blackwell).

Tuck, Anthony (1999), *Crown and Nobility: England 1272–1461*, 2nd edn (Oxford: Blackwell).

Vale, Malcolm (1981), *War and Chivalry: Warfare and Aristocratic Culture in England, France and Burgundy at the End of the Middle Ages* (London: Duckworth).

—— (2001), *The Princely Court: Medieval Courts and Culture in North-West Europe (1270–1380)* (Oxford and New York: Oxford University Press).

Vaughan, Richard (2004), *Philip the Good: The Apogee of Burgundy*, 2nd edn (Woodbridge: Boydell).

—— (2004), *Charles the Bold: The Last Valois Duke of Burgundy*, 2nd edn (Woodbridge: Boydell).

—— (2005), *Philip the Bold: The Foundation of the Burgundian State*, 2nd edn (Woodbridge: Boydell).

—— (2005), *John the Fearless: The Growth of Burgundian Power*, 2nd edn (Woodbridge: Boydell).

Vernier, Richard (2003), *The Flower of Chivalry: Bertrand du Guesclin and the Hundred Years War* (Woodbridge and Rochester, N.Y.: Boydell & Brewer).

Wheeler, Bonnie and Charles T. Woods (eds) (1996), *Fresh Verdicts on Joan of Arc* (New York: Garland).

Wolffe, B.P. (1981), *Henry VI* (London: Eyre Methuen).

Wood, Charles T. (1988), *Joan of Arc and Richard III: Sex, Saints and Government in the Middle Ages* (New York and Oxford: Oxford University Press).

CHAPTER 15

Crisis in the church and the reorientation of the faithful, 1250–1500

WHO LEADS CHRISTENDOM?

Towards the end of the thirteenth century it gradually became clear that the hierocratic aspirations of the popes would finally have to give way to a new type of caesaropapism, the formation of 'national churches' on which kings or other secular rulers had a strong hold. The history of the years around 1300 teaches us that the pope in Rome had not properly understood the signs of the times. We are indebted to his misunderstanding for some of the most fascinating politico-ideological documents of the Middle Ages, as the final act of the struggle between emperor and pope and between pope and French king was played out to the accompaniment of an unprecedented polemic barrage. The starting signal came in 1294 when pope Celestine V abdicated after a pontificate of barely five months; the contest ended with the death of Emperor Louis of Bavaria in 1347.

In the entire history of the papacy there has never been such a difference in personality of two successive popes as there was between Celestine V (1294) and Boniface VIII (1294–1303). Both have been called a living anachronism, yet for totally different reasons. Celestine, an unworldly hermit, emerged as a compromise candidate whom nobody really wanted when the papal throne had been vacant for a long period. Once he had become pope, so shocked was he by the moral laxity of the world he had entered that he could not retire quickly enough from his new dignity. Some reports say that a certain amount of pressure was brought to bear on him by his successor, Cardinal Benedetto Caetani, a brilliant lawyer who ascended the papal throne under the name of Boniface VIII. Soon afterwards, the man of the world that Boniface had been became a man who wanted to be exalted above that world. And for the last time, a pope thundered

from the Lateran that the highest power in the world belonged to him and him alone. Through his papal bulls and his legates he interfered in the high politics of temporal princes from Sicily to Denmark, only to be rebuffed everywhere.

Boniface's aggression was directed mainly at the French king, Philip IV, the Fair, questioning his right to levy taxes on the French clergy and to try them in secular courts of law. Tensions mounted, resulting in the publication of a series of radical bulls, the last of which, *Unam Sanctam* (1302), competes with the *Dictatus Papae* (1075), issued by Gregory VII, for the prize of being the most extreme formulation ever of papal claims to temporal power. Philip the Fair, who suspected the pope of conspiring against him with the king of Aragon, decided to remove the Holy Father from the scene by constructing a charge of heresy against him and then having him kidnapped from Italy. The last part of the plan failed, although a Franco-Italian commando unit under the leadership of Philip's confidant, Guillaume de Nogaret, did manage to take Boniface prisoner in his summer residence at Anagni. The pope was released a day later, but died soon after his traumatic and humiliating arrest.

A combination of events led to the removal of the papal court to Avignon in 1309. Avignon was then part of the county of Provence, a principality in the German Empire held in fief from the German king by the kings of Naples (of the French House of Anjou), and not yet French. The popes, who were to remain in Avignon until 1377, bought the town from the Angevins in 1348. Shortly afterwards, they obtained full suzerainty over both town and the surrounding county of Venais from the emperor. The decision of Pope Clement V to move to Provence was connected with the denouement of the Boniface VIII affair. Clement was anxious to prevent the French king at all costs from going ahead

Plate 15.1 Rogier van der Weyden, 'The Sacraments of Baptism, Confirmation and Penance'. Left panel of the *Altar of the Sacraments*, ordered in 1441 by the Bishop of Tournai, Jean Chevrot, for his private chapel

order had established its headquarters in Paris and successfully entered the banking business. The French crown was one of its largest debtors. Philip IV and his advisors were mightily envious and looked for ways to destroy the order and confiscate its French possessions. In a sinister portent of the witch-hunts of early modern times, and of the Stalinist state terror of the 1930s, between 1307 and 1312 the Templars were 'unmasked' as a band of heretics and blasphemers given to homosexual practices and diabolic rituals. Many of them died as the result of terrible tortures or were burned at the stake.

During his pontificate Clement V was not only confronted with this new form of 'state realism', he also witnessed the deathbed of imperial universalism. It began in 1310 when the King of the Romans, Henry VII of Luxemburg, crossed the Alps with a small armed force to have himself crowned emperor and to impose his authority on the communes of northern and central Italy. The original enthusiasm of those who hoped that a powerful Roman king would put an end to the political schisms in Italy rapidly faded away when Henry acted particularly harshly against the Lombard towns that refused to open their gates to him. At a tumultuous meeting, where he literally had to fight his way in, Henry was crowned emperor in Rome in 1312. He died the following year *en route* to southern Italy to take the kingdom of Naples.

The journey made to Italy in 1327 by his successor, Louis of Bavaria, was even more audacious. The pope had kept himself fairly aloof in 1311 and 1312, but now, from his palace in Avignon, he turned against the Roman king. In defiance, Louis had himself crowned emperor in Rome by the city's governor, Sciarra Colonna, who was not a prelate. It was a curious episode, stirring up memories from an already distant past. The pope laid an interdict on the Holy City and excommunicated the emperor; pope and emperor accused each other of heresy, and the emperor had an antipope elected. Louis of Bavaria returned to Germany in 1330 without having accomplished very much in Italy.

with his plan of having Boniface posthumously declared a heretic. He found it completely unacceptable that someone who had been invested with the keys of St Peter would ever be called an enemy of the faith, but he paid an outrageous price for Philip's acquiescence: he agreed to the persecution and eventual condemnation of the Knights Templar. After the fall of the last Christian bulwark in Palestine at the end of the thirteenth century this extremely wealthy military

New ideas on the relationship between spiritual and secular power

The confrontations between Philip the Fair and Boniface VIII and of Louis of Bavaria and John XXII (1316–1334) were conflicts between irreconcilable aspirations and also between powerful and obstinate personalities. All received the support of eminent intellectuals, most of them Italians, who were well able to cloak the actions in ideology. For this reason the first three decades of the fourteenth century are a goldmine for those with an interest in the history of political thought.

The papal position was stated most clearly by Jacopo Cappucci of Viterbo, Edigio Colonna of Rome (Aegidius Romanus), who is seen as the ideological brain behind Boniface VIII, and Augustinus Triumphus of Ancona. Steven Ozment, the American religious historian, once compared them to 'legal beavers' who 'labored methodically to construct a protective dam against the surging tide of secular power'. There was not much new to record, however. The most important of their hierocratic arguments were by now very well known: the pope, as Christ's only representative on earth, did not have to justify himself to any human authority. Equally, the pope could call every secular ruler to account, for papal power was higher than, and the source of, all secular power. It was best for the pope to leave the exercise of temporal power in the hands of princes, because sometimes it was necessary to use force. But the pope could certainly be involved in the drawing up of important policies. What was new was that the old arguments were underpinned by reasoning borrowed from Aristotle.

The position of the French king, Philip the Fair, was subtly defended by Jean Quidort, a theologian at the University of Paris and thus also known as John of Paris. In his dualistic proposition he did not limit himself simply to repeating the doctrine of the two swords postulated by Pope Gelasius (see Chapter 4). He denied the clergy, pope included, every form of *dominium*, which in the legal jargon of the time meant every authority that brought with it the exercise of force or rights of ownership. In this view the pope, as holder of a Church office, could have no direct control over Church property; he could only administer it, for the real owner was the legal entity, the Church of Rome. The implication was that the pope should not intervene in any way with the affairs of secular authority; the pope should only be heard when princes contravened the laws of the Holy Church. Quidort recognized that spiritual power was indeed superior to temporal power, but only on a higher, metaphysical level. In the real world pope and secular princes were autonomous and supreme, each in his own well-defined sphere.

Louis of Bavaria could count on the formidable intellectual support of Marsilius of Padua (*c.*1275–1342), a physician who taught at the *artes* faculty in Paris and was in the service of the Visconti family, the pro-German rulers of Milan. Once it had been discovered that he was the author of *Defensor Pacis* ('The Defender of the Peace'), which had been circulating since 1324, he fled to the Bavarian court in Munich. He accompanied Louis on his journey to Rome, where he was responsible for the coronation ceremony and the pro-imperial propaganda around it. *Defensor Pacis* is undoubtedly one of the most original politico-theoretical treatises of the entire Middle Ages. Marsilius suggested that the basis of all authority in the world rests on the people or, more specifically, on *universitas civium*, the community of established, and thus enfranchised, male 'citizens'. In addition to his views on the sovereignty of the people, not all of them quite new, he also held ideas about the relationship between temporal power and spiritual authority that were nothing short of revolutionary and, in the eyes of the Church, heretical. They were inspired by Marsilius' deep conviction that the interference of prelates, in particular the pope, in the exercise of secular power was the major cause of the disruption of peace in the (Christian) world. And since the conditions for achieving eternal salvation could only be created in a society where peace reigned, every form of secular power must be denied to the clerical estate. Good government meant taking care of the material and physical well-being of citizens; the care of their souls was a matter of concern for the individual believer. The role of the Church should be limited to the moral and spiritual education of the faithful and the administration of the sacraments.

By extending the principle of the sovereignty of the people over the Church, Marsilius blazed a second revolutionary trail. He argued that only the communion of the faithful (*universitas fidelium*) could be the fount of law-making and the exercise of authority within the Church, including, for instance, the excommunication of heretics, which in Marsilius' view was only an option when they threatened civil harmony. For practical reasons, this fundamental competence could best be delegated to the civil authorities and not to the clerics, for the clergy should not hold any coercive power in the world. This also applied to general Church councils, which represented the community of the faithful at the highest level, but which should then leave secular princes to convert their pronouncements into enforceable laws. As if this was not enough, Marsilius delivered the *coup de grâce* to the Church hierarchy by pronouncing that Christ had not made any distinction in rank when he established the priesthood, so the pope was no higher than a village priest, let alone the holder of *plenitudo potestatis*! Moreover, the Church should not have any worldly possessions, for Christ and the apostles had had none either.

Marsilius borrowed this view from the spiritual Franciscans who, after a century of varying success in their struggle to gain control inside the Franciscan order and the acceptance of the Church authorities outside, were silenced in 1323 when Pope John XXII declared the idea of the absolute poverty of Christ and the apostles to be heretical. Interestingly enough, the Franciscans, in their defence, were the first to advance explicitly a theory of papal infallibility. They pointed out that in 1279 Pope Nicholas III had endorsed the doctrine of apostolic poverty, so John XXII was not allowed to teach to the contrary because every pope was 'infallible' in his doctrinal judgements. But at the time all this was to no avail – papal infallibility in doctrinal matters would not become the official teaching of the Catholic Church until 1870 – and several Franciscan leaders fled to Munich, which was rapidly becoming a meeting place for radical dissidents. Among them was William of Ockham, who shared many of Marsilius' ideas about the strict division of temporal and spiritual power.

Radical as the ideas of Marsilius and Ockham were, they could never have caused a reformation before the Reformation. Not that Marsilius and Ockham aimed to do so. The English theologian John Wyclif (*c.*1325–1384), who worked at the University of Oxford and frequented the courts of Edward III and Richard II of England, came closer to such reformation. He developed pronounced views on the role of faith and the place of the Church in the world. He saw the visible Catholic Church as an artificial, unworthy shell sheltering the true Church, the invisible community of the faithful, which included only those who had been chosen by divine preordination. Since in earthly life it is not known who the chosen are, the visible Church must continue to exist, for want of anything better. That is why reforms were needed so urgently. The reforms should deal with three points. The first of these shows how much Wyclif as well was influenced by the spiritual Franciscans, for he believed that the visible Church should have no *dominium*; that is, no possessions and no worldly power. In Wyclif's view, *dominium* was always the result of divine grace, so that lawful *dominium* could only rest on those whom God had chosen and who already lived in a state of grace on earth. As it was impossible to identify this elite body, Wyclif considered it best that Church property and rights should be confiscated by the king and managed by him. No wonder that Wyclif had many supporters in royal circles! Second, Wyclif believed that the whole truth of the faith lay enclosed in the Bible; every individual believer could thus have access to this truth, all the more so because Wyclif argued for a literal interpretation of the Bible and not the allegorical exegesis that was customary in the Middle Ages. The third point followed on from this: clerics were in fact superfluous as 'middlemen' in the mediation of the truth, especially those who did not themselves live in the spirit of the Gospel.

As we have said, Wyclif could count on the protection of the highest circles, but he also had many followers in the lower ranks of society. And yet there was no 'reformation before the Reformation' in England. The main reason was that Wyclif's supporters, the Lollards, radicalized very soon after his death and lost the support of the elite. Matters were different in Bohemia where Wyclif's works had been a great influence on Jan Hus, a dissident theologian at the University of Prague who linked his ideas on the reformation of the Church with an anti-German Czech nationalism. After the death of Hus at the stake in 1415 it looked for a long time as if Bohemia would break away from both the German Empire and the Catholic Church. It was not until 1434 that the German emperor, Sigismund, and moderate forces in Bohemia reached a compromise that prevented this from happening.

THE POPES IN AVIGNON AND THE BUREAUCRATIZATION OF THE CURIA

The Avignon papacy has long had a negative reputation amongst modern historians, which it does not deserve. With the loss of its universalistic pretensions, the Catholic Church certainly lost much of the moral and spiritual leadership within Christian Europe. On the other hand, the Avignon popes were very successful in developing another thirteenth-century legacy: the attempts to centralize the exercise of papal authority within the Church. This process led inevitably to the strengthening of the bureaucracy in the Curia, the

Plate 15.2 Pulpit by Michelozzo on the outside wall of the Cathedral of Santo Stefano at Prato

papal court, together with the consolidation of the position of the pope himself. The four permanent departments of the Curia established in the thirteenth century – chancery, *Camera Apostolica*, *Penitentiaria* and *Audientia* – were expanded and given new sections or wider powers if necessary. In the fourteenth century the chancery or secretariat consisted of seven offices, each one with its own precisely defined tasks, which gave the treatment of incoming and outgoing documents an almost Prussian perfection. The enormous growth in chancery output was obviously closely connected with the expansion of the activities of the departments of finance and justice. It became necessary to split one of the papal law courts, the Audientia, into two colleges.

The basis for enlarging the financial scope of the Curia was laid during the papacy of Innocent III. He was the first pope to impose taxes on the clergy throughout Latin Christendom for 'urgent matters' such as crusades. In that way the popes became less dependent on their Italian possessions and occasional princely subsidies. A second new source of income, the collection of which was perfected during the Avignon papacy, was formed by the revenues from the granting of lower Church offices and the incomes attached to them (*beneficia*). Before the thirteenth century the popes had seldom intervened in appointments – only in exceptional circumstances or when conflicts arose. This changed gradually, and in the bull *Licet ecclesiarum* issued in 1265 Pope Clement IV laid down the basis in canon law for unrestrained papal intervention. The bull proclaimed that, as the holder of supreme authority in the Church, the pope could dispose of all ecclesiastical offices and their related benefices. Of course, this did not bring an immediate end to the existing practices of canonical election that had been accepted since the investiture controversy. The popes could not afford to trample on the rights of others, but they systematically began to increase the number of occasions when their intervention was accepted. Their efforts reached a climax during the Avignon period. Pope John XXII, for example, issued some 3,000 dispositions relating to benefices in the first year of his pontificate, sometimes in the form of appointments in contested cases ('provisions'), sometimes in the form of firm allocations known as 'reservations', and sometimes in the form of promises concerning benefices that were expected to become free in a short time (hence 'expectancies'). Not surprisingly, all these papal dispositions had to be paid for. Added to other new as well as existing sources of income, these proceeds from dispositions raised papal revenue during the Avignon period to between 166,000 and 481,000 gold florins per year. This did not make the popes as rich as the kings of France, England or Naples, but it certainly put them in the same league. No wonder that one of John's successors, Clement VI (1342–1352), had no trouble in finding the revenue to construct the magnificent new Palais des Papes.

Clearly the whole machinery could only work with the assistance of a well-oiled bureaucratic apparatus. All together, the Curia employed between 5,000 and 6,000 people in 1350, more than double the number of a century earlier. This included the household staff and those involved with guard duties, but excluded the personal staffs of individual cardinals, which also comprised dozens of members, for the cardinals administered justice in a private capacity and were jointly responsible for the management of their revenues.

THE GREAT SCHISM AND THE CONCILIAR MOVEMENT

Despite the fact that the papacy and the papal Curia became strongly Gallicized during the Avignon period, almost all the popes continued to work towards a return to Rome. Peace in Italy was one of the conditions for this. In 1319 Pope John XXII sent a legate to Italy, accompanied by a small armed force that would be complemented with mercenary troops on the spot, with instructions to get things organized in the papal territories; but the legate, Cardinal Bertrand du Poujet, was not always very adroit. The mission of Cardinal Gil Albornoz, archbishop of Toledo and a tough veteran from the latter days of the Reconquest, reached Italy in 1350 and met with greater success, but Albornoz got caught up in the web of Italian politics. So it was that the popes did not return to Rome until Gregory XI (1370–1378). He arrived there in January 1377 only to die the following year.

Nobody could have foreseen the events that followed. The cardinals voted for an apparently risk-free candidate, tried and tested in papal administration, but soon backtracked on their choice, probably fearing that the new pope would drastically reduce their influence in the Curia. To make matters worse, they then chose an antipope who took up residence in the papal palace in Avignon while their first choice stayed in Rome. The Great Schism was a fact, although it was impossible then to surmise that this split within the Church – by no means the first! – would last for nearly forty years, from 1378 until 1417. The Schism immediately posed a major problem because the whole of Latin Christian Europe had to choose one of the two popes. Not surprisingly, the main dividing lines in the field of international political power determined the composition of the two spheres of papal authority, or obediences: France and its allies (Naples, the great Spanish kingdoms, Scotland) chose Avignon; England, the German Empire, the Scandinavian kingdoms, Poland, Hungary and Portugal supported Rome. The obediences were by no means fixed; states changed sides as circumstances dictated.

From the very beginning, many on both sides made efforts to bring the Schism to an end. Since neither of the popes could oust the other by force of arms, nor was prepared to abdicate or submit to arbitration, a general council was suggested after some time as being the appropriate means of ending the sordid discord within the Church. The idea of allowing a general council to pass judgment on a pope was not in itself new. We have seen how in the first half of the fourteenth century ideas about the role of general councils began to form a fixed part of the discourse on the relation between Church and state, as an almost natural counterweight to the growing centralism of the papacy.

Conciliarism developed further the longer the Great Schism lasted. It acquired, however, another, less divisive basis. Two French theologians appeared as its most eloquent exponents: Pierre d'Ailly (1350–1420), a gifted and versatile scholar, who was attached for many years to the University of Paris, was then bishop successively of Le Puy and Cambrai and was finally elevated to the purple in 1411, and Jean Gerson (1363–1429), a fellow-teacher from Paris. The basis of their conciliar thinking was that a general council could make a judgment over the pope, and indeed had the duty to do so if the pope 'strayed from the faith' and threatened the continued existence of the Church –

which a schism naturally did. This opinion could still be supported with canon law. The more radical view that a pope was subordinate to a general council, whatever the circumstances, never prevailed.

The first attempt to put conciliar thinking into practice ended in a fiasco in 1409. The general council organized shortly thereafter by the German emperor, Sigismund, proved an unqualified success, however. The Council of Constance (1414–1418) was the largest Church assembly in the Middle Ages; its sessions were public and attracted a steady stream of princes, nobles, members of the lower clergy and students; and all the ecclesiastics present were allowed to vote. The sitting popes were forced to resign and a new pope, Martin V (1417–1431), was elected and immediately accepted practically everywhere. At long last the Great Schism was at an end.

It seemed as if the way was clear now for conciliar thinking to be transformed into a constitutional element in Church organization. At Constance it had been decided to hold general Church councils at regular intervals, as had been the custom of the early Christian Church as well as in the twelfth and thirteenth centuries. For a while it looked as if this would indeed become standard practice. But things started to go wrong in the second council taking place after Constance, the Council of Basle in 1431. This was due mainly to the lack of cooperation by Pope Eugene IV (1431–1447), who refused to be browbeaten by the headstrong prelates; he felt far superior to them. At the end of 1437 he moved the meeting to Ferrara, a clever manoeuvre, dividing those attending the council. The majority, including the most important spokesman for the conciliar movement at the time, Nicholas of Kues (1401–1465), made the best of the situation and joined the pope. Only a rump group of radicals remained in Basle, where they became rapidly marginalized. Bereft of significant support, the assembly finally adjourned in 1449. In hindsight the removal to Ferrara can be seen as a turning point – the beginning of the end of conciliarism as a mainstream movement within the Church, although it should be borne in mind that it persisted until at least the middle of the sixteenth century.

All things considered, two factors can be held responsible for the failure of conciliarism. In the first place, the conciliarists failed to create an institution or apparatus that would give their programme a firm basis and which would have looked after their interests between councils. Second, their criticism focused too much on the position of the pope inside the Church and too little on reforms in other segments of the Church.

The collapse of the conciliar movement opened the way to a powerful recovery of the papacy, but a high price had to be paid for the Great Schism and the conciliar period. It was precisely during this very critical phase that the forces opposing papal centralism had grown stronger. England and France, kingdoms constantly in need of money as a result of the Hundred Years War, were determined to prevent any drainage of ecclesiastical revenues to Rome. Their stance led to the formation of what have rightly been called 'national Churches', like the so-called Gallican Church in France, where as early as 1438 the king was able to re-establish his influence over the appointment of bishops, abbots and provosts.

Elsewhere, although the control exercised by kings and other rulers over the clerics was perhaps less strong, a new balance was found between papal and princely authority over Church and clergy within the boundaries of territorial principalities. The Renaissance popes fully understood this and even created a similar new power base by finally consolidating their Italian possessions into the Papal State. The success of their policy was mirrored in the pomp of their court as well as in the new splendour they gave to Rome. The downside of this arrangement, however, was that after giving up the ideal of universal and unified Christendom under uncontested papal leadership, the head of the Catholic Church also surrendered the famous 'freedom of the Church', which had been so desperately fought for in the eleventh and twelfth centuries.

RELIGIOUS LIFE IN THE LATE MIDDLE AGES

The rich religious life of the late Middle Ages has fascinated many generations of historians. While some have looked primarily for the roots of the Reformation, others have stressed the very continuity with the past: religious sentiments underwent deep-seated change in the eleventh and twelfth centuries; the fourteenth and fifteenth just continued the trends that had then been set in motion. At first glance, the evidence for the continuity view appears to be stronger, but this ignores two matters. First, it was not the forms in which religion found its expression as much as their profusion and the intensity of the faith experience that require some explanation. Second, the Reformation did not just happen: its prehistory must be placed in the late Middle Ages. We would only like to shift the emphasis. In the past, every critical attitude to wrongs in the Catholic Church, every expression of moral and religious reflection, was seen as heralding the Reformation. Nowadays, the generally accepted view is that from the very beginning the reformers blamed the Church for demanding too much of the faithful rather than too little, and that criticism was rarely accompanied by a complete rejection of the Church, its ideology, institution and rituals. This fits in better with the image of a bipolar pluriformity in late medieval religious life. Between the two extremes of a piety directed towards the internalization of religious values and personal contact with the divine (introspective extreme) on the one hand, and, on the other, a popular faith accompanied by a great deal of external show (extrovert extreme), lay a broad grey area, full of rich forms of expression and offering something for everyone. One common element was the obsession with dying and death, which is hardly surprising in view of the high mortality of the period. It meant that the lists of souls to be remembered in prayer grew ever longer, and that religious poetry, songs, sermons, paintings and sculptures were full of motifs that made the reader, hearer or viewer grimly aware of the constant proximity of death.

Never before had Christian religious life shown such a wealth of 'Roman' opulence, never before had individual involvement in religion been so great, and never before had there been such wide public support for the works of the Church. The Church had apparently succeeded more than ever in reaching the faithful and in getting its most important religious and moral messages through to a broad spectrum of the people.

Observantism and the new secular movements

Calls for reformation inside monasticism were heard from time to time through the entire Middle Ages. Apparent weaknesses in the observance of the strict monastic rules provoked a reaction aimed at a return to basic principles. These reactionary aspirations became known as observantism (from *observare*, 'to comply with'). From the second half of the fourteenth century monasticism was characterized by a new wave

Plate 15.3 Purgatory. Detail from a miniature in the *Très riches Heures du Duc de Berry*, fifteenth century

of observantism, which made itself felt in every order – even those, such as the mendicant orders, that had not been long in existence. It was accompanied by a peculiar form of separateness, in which observant communities did not break with the order to which they belonged but differentiated themselves from the non-observant monasteries within the order. Observant monasteries united in congregations that made communal agreements about the practical interpretation of the monastic rules and carried out checks on their enforcement.

In addition to purifying monastic life such efforts bore fruit in other ways. There existed in the late Middle Ages, even more than before, a basis for criticism of monasticism in secular society, just as there was for anticlericalism in general. Early signs of this criticism are found in satirical works – in Boccaccio's *Decameron*, for example, Franciscans are systematically portrayed as libertines and debauchees. The number of entrants to some orders began to fall noticeably, and the size of gifts of money and goods decreased drastically. Observantism was able to reverse this negative trend to some extent. Orders such as the Carthusians, who followed their rule without any need for correction, were richly rewarded, with the result that the Carthusians flourished in the fifteenth century as never before. The years between about 1350 and 1500 saw the establishment of countless new convents, and even the foundation of several new orders with long-forgotten names such as Bridgettines, Colettines, Hieronymites, Jesuati (not to be confused with the later Jesuits) and Theatines. In urban areas especially, this gave rise to a richly varied monastic landscape. The County of Holland had just a handful of monasteries in 1350, but within a century this number had risen to more than two hundred. It should be remembered that all these new initiatives were only made possible through the financial support of prosperous laymen and secular clerics.

Some of these benefactors found that just giving donations was not enough, and they decided to live a regulated religious life themselves. Again the parallel with the twelfth and thirteenth centuries springs to mind. At that time the pressure to lead an authentically Christian life resulted in the foundation of new religious orders and the formation of groups of laypeople who led a religious life, following a rule, but did not

take a monastic vow or withdraw from life in the world – such as the Beguines and the third orders of the Franciscans and Dominicans. The Beguines met with exceptional and continuing success in the southern Low Countries and the adjacent Rhineland. In the former more than two hundred beguinages and convents were founded between 1230 and 1320, each with an average of 15 members, while 167 beguinages are known to have existed in the Rhineland city of Cologne alone from about the middle of the thirteenth century until the end of the fourteenth. The Beguines settled on the edges of the towns in small houses built in enclosed courtyards with their own chapels or churches. They were supervised by a mistress or prioress and had rules for internal order. There were domestic quarters and larger buildings for communal activities. The Beguines supported themselves with

Plate 15.4 Thomas a Kempis at work in his study. Fifteenth-century miniature

their spinning and embroidery, often coming into conflict with the craft guilds, which accused them of unfair competition.

Overijssel in the Low Countries, part of the prince-bishopric of Utrecht, produced the classic example of both tendencies in the late Middle Ages. Geert Groote (1340–1384), the son of a cloth merchant from Deventer, studied in Paris and then lived comfortably on the Church benefices, which he held as a canon in minor orders, before repenting of his ways in about 1370. He gave up his livings and started to follow a strictly moral and devout way of life that he propagated in sermons fiercely attacking the laxity of many clergy. His example led to the formation of both a pious lay movement with its own houses, the Brothers and Sisters of the Common Life, and an observant association of convents of Augustine canons known as the Congregation of Windesheim. Both spread far beyond the IJssel region, in particular towards the Rhine basin. These exponents of what is known as Modern Devotion saw their most important mission as writing, translating, copying or condensing texts into the vernacular, to help the individual reader in his devotions. The most popular texts were passages from the Bible, prayers and edifying works, produced in simple, cheap books on a large scale.

If Geert Groote and his followers sometimes bordered on the unacceptable in the eyes of the Church authorities, another movement of critical laypeople and clerics, which started in England at about the same time and originated among a few priests close to John Wyclif, certainly went too far. A central belief of these Lollards (meaning 'mumblers') was the idea borrowed from Wyclif that within the Church there was a direct relationship between God and the faithful that had no need of the intervention of clerics, sacraments or even of saints. The Lollards laboured for an English translation of the Bible, the only source of Christian truth, and for Bible exegesis through sermons in the vernacular. The English-language Bible and other key texts were duplicated on a scale and at a speed that would only be exceeded with the discovery of printing. In this way, the Lollards clearly helped to promote literacy in England.

As the movement received increasing support from members of the lower clergy and self-educated laypeople so it became more radical. A virulent anti-clericalism, expressed in fiery songs, began to predominate. After a revolt against the king the movement was forced underground and many Lollards met their end at the stake or on the gallows. It continued in south-eastern England until the Reformation, however, chiefly because the Lollards could count on the continued sympathy of educated craftsmen and, in time, ecclesiastical authorities became rather half-hearted in pursuing them.

Devotion and mysticism

One of the fundamental differences between the movement of Geert Groote and the Lollards was the dislike expressed by the English movement for a new sort of piety that had a central role in the former. The original Congregation of Windesheim called the religious and moral awakening inspired by Geert Groote the 'Modern Devotion'. 'Devotion' was undoubtedly a key idea in the religious life of the late Middle Ages, but it is a rather vague concept and difficult to explain. We have indicated earlier (Chapter 8) that an essential part of the religious revival in the centuries after 1000 consisted of a renewal of the spiritual tradition in the Christian perception of faith. The Modern Devotion continued and strengthened this tradition. It was focused on a strongly individual, inner spirituality and experience of God brought about through prayer and meditation. Seen from that perspective, Church rituals, above all the celebration of the Mass, had first and foremost the task of priming an interior, rebirth-like transformation within the devout believer. An exaggerated emphasis on ostentatious display, on the other hand, would only hinder spiritual worship, as would an excessive attachment to physical and material things. It was simplicity and silence, patience and penitence, austerity and restraint that were aimed for, the inner eye always turned towards the eternal light at the end of this world's vale of tears, which could only be reached by following Christ's example.

The advantage of the new devotion was that it was accessible to laypeople who were motivated but had no intellectual training. At the same time it sent out a hidden threat to the established Church order, for if an individual believer could effect his own salvation by focusing his life on God, what was the point of the clergy and Church institutions? This was why the

Catholic Church always had an ambivalent attitude towards lay devotion, encouraging it on the one hand, yet regarding the forms in which it was expressed with suspicion and, in the long term, pursuing them aggressively.

The late Middle Ages produced a great variety of new spiritual and pietistic currents and movements. Most of them were modelled on the monastic example. This is evident from the rules that their sympathizers prescribed: unconditional obedience to the confessor, regular confession after intensive examination of one's conscience, frequent fasting, sexual abstinence and suchlike – all religious and moral precepts borrowed directly from the monastic observantism of the eleventh and twelfth centuries. There were clear differences in emphasis, however. In the Modern Devotion, for example, the search for God lay along the path of active practice of virtue rather than passive contemplation.

Mysticism was a substantially different form of spirituality that flourished in the late Middle Ages. It can be described as a spiritual attempt to achieve intuitive and emotional, often even ecstatic, union of the innermost soul with God. Often this attempt is described in terms of a mental journey along a difficult path, which leads in stages of increasing detachment from the transient world to the Divine. Within later medieval mysticism we can distinguish between a more intellectual current, directly inspired by fifth-century Christian Neoplatonism, and a non-intellectual trend, in which pure willpower, visions and an exaggerated affection for the suffering Christ were central. A group of German Dominican theologians at the end of the thirteenth and beginning of the fourteenth centuries, the best known of whom is Meister Eckhart (c. 1260–1328), was typical of the first current, while the Cistercian Bernard of Clairvaux was the kingpin of the second. Useful as this distinction may be, it is worth stressing that in practice both currents could easily flow across to each other; one needs only to point to the close contacts between the Dominican order and the Beguine movement in the German Rhineland, each of which represents a different mystic current. This mystical 'cross-over' certainly contributed to growing suspicions about the Catholic orthodoxy of a trained theologian like Meister Eckhart, who was also active in pastoral care. At the end of his life he was tried before a tribunal of the Inquisition. However, the new spiritual movement of Modern Devotion also tended to treat the concepts of mysticism with circumspection. Few or no traces can be found in its most important manifesto, *Imitation of Christ* by Thomas a Kempis (1380–1471), one of the most widely read works in the Catholic world.

Within non-intellectual spirituality and mysticism the suffering Christ was of particular appeal to devout women. According to the American historian, Caroline Walker Bynum, this was the result of a subtle manipulation of the medieval symbols for masculinity and femininity at a deeper psychological level. Because typically feminine qualities such as physical weakness and kindness were ascribed to men like Christ and St Francis in order to demonstrate how they had shown their humility by laying aside their male 'strength', religious women found it easy to identify with them; their special physical affinity with Christ made them complete people so to speak, equal to or even better than men. This is a curious counterpart to a topos of the later courtly literature, in which women managed to overcome the weakness of their sex by warrior-like behaviour.

New forms of devotion created new types of saints, indeed often women, whose *vitae* (biographies and autobiographies) combined topoi and well-known themes from monastic saints' lives, especially from the eleventh and twelfth centuries, with not particularly subtle, populistic descriptions of the most extreme forms of mortification and self-effacement, of ruthless penitence, spiritual agony, quasi-erotic adoration and endless prayer, all of which, according to Richard Kieckhefer, not only disturbed and shocked their readers but were also intended to achieve that very effect. In the late Middle Ages religious spirituality, which had existed from the early days of Christianity, reached unprecedented, dramatic levels of fervour and intensity.

The religious perception of ordinary believers

The introverted aspect of late medieval religious perceptions was the realm of just a small minority of highly motivated believers, both clerical and lay. Most believers gave expression to their faith through externals. This extrovert aspect of religious life was carefully orchestrated and controlled by the Church and clergy, who had to take into account what mattered to the people. This interaction can be described by the use of a well-known analysis model from communications theory, in which the two-way traffic between sender and receiver is central (cf. Swanson). The sender (the Church) had to make use of feedback procedures to find out whether the message (the faith) had reached the receiver (the believer) properly. Should this not be the case, then the sender had to correct itself, either by adapting the form in which the message was shaped or by improving the channels of communication through which the message was transmitted. This approach not only allows greater attention to be given to what the Church was thinking and wanting 'officially', but also and especially to the 'translation switch' it had to make in order to instil the convictions and moral behaviour it desired, as well as to the 'demand' made by the faithful and to the forms in which the faithful eventually made manifest their beliefs, their experience of the faith.

To reach the people the Church had above all to keep the message simple. Only a few of the faithful were able to read even the Bible in its entirety; most were only acquainted with selected parts of it through readings during the Mass or sermons, while we should remember that the Mass was said entirely in Latin. The Christian message therefore had to be as succinct and simple as possible. It boiled down to five components:

1   Knowledge of the creed (credo, 'I believe'), a short statement of the essential articles of the faith. The most usual creeds were those established at the Council of Nicaea in 325 and the Fourth Lateran Council in 1215. Every believer was required to be able to say the creed before confession and communion.

2   Knowledge of the most important prayers: the 'Our Father' and 'Hail Mary' were already standard prayers in the late Middle Ages. Well-to-do believers had special prayer books or 'books of hours' made for their own use. Examples from the thirteenth century are still in existence, some of them illustrated with beautiful miniatures.

3   Knowledge of the most important moral precepts of Christianity – the Ten Commandments from the Old Testament and the three theological virtues (faith, hope and charity) from the New, with the four cardinal virtues from ancient philosophy (prudence, justice, fortitude and temperance) making up the seven capital virtues that were mirrored by the seven cardinal or deadly sins.

4   Some knowledge of the seven grace-giving sacraments (see Chapter 4).

5   Some knowledge of eschatology, the complex ideas on life after death. Central to this was the presentation of Purgatory, the temporary residence of the souls of Christians who had not been purged of their sins on earth. People were quite convinced that the length of the unpleasant stay in Purgatory could be shortened by indulgences (see Box 15.1), prayer, the practice of the seven works of charity or love (feeding the hungry, caring for the sick, etc.) and the works of spiritual comfort (such as granting forgiveness), of which there were also seven.

The people most clearly indicated to deliver this message were the parish clergy, especially since the ordinary faithful probably went to church more often during the late Middle Ages than before. It is questionable whether the clergy were adequately prepared for their task: for a long time perhaps only a limited number were up to it. Most of them had no more than an elementary education. The situation clearly improved in all respects during the late Middle Ages: some historians even speak of a 'pastoral revolution'. A hint of a changing approach could already be seen in the strong emphasis given to pastoral theology in twelfth-century education at the famous monastic school of St Victor in Paris, although there was no real progress until the Fourth Lateran Council of 1215. The council fathers decided upon a package of measures to raise the level of knowledge and the moral standards of parish clergy. In addition, the bishops were urged to instruct the clerics under their supervision by teaching and preaching. Later, the first written instructions for spiritual care appeared, and by the end of the Middle Ages substantial numbers of parish clergy had probably been to university. At the same time bishops took greater pains with their periodical visitations to the parish clerics, which often revealed

Plate 15.5 A small house altar of the so-called 'Enclosed Garden' (*hortus conclusus*) type, *c.* 1500. At the bottom it says: 'Time is short, death is quick/Beware of sin and you will do well/O, how many delights will await you/where a thousand years is but one day.'

grievous shortcomings in their capabilities or lifestyle. The bishops thus went some way to counter the virulent anti-clerical criticism that, as we have seen, regularly raised its head in the late Middle Ages. Apart from the usual complaints about poor education, suspect morality and simony, criticism was directed chiefly towards a fault that resulted from the papal policy on benefices – pluralism ('stacking up' benefices) and the absenteeism inherent to it (a cleric could only be in one place at one time). This contemporary criticism is shared by modern Church historians, who condemned the institution of the benefice as 'the rock upon which late-medieval attempts at church-wide reform were shipwrecked' (Oakley).

From the thirteenth century onwards, parish clergy had always been helped in carrying out their duties by preachers from the mendicant orders, a situation that did not always please them as shared tasks meant shared incomes. Top preachers, Bernardino of Siena of the Franciscan order, and the Dominicans Vincent Ferrer (*c.* 1350–1419) and Girolamo Savonarola (d. 1498), for example, attracted enormous audiences for their sermons, or even weeks of sermons, especially during Lent, the period of fasting preceding Easter, when they might produce a lengthy sermon with a different theme every day for 40 days. Ferrer, a Spaniard, was nicknamed 'the angel of the Last Judgment' because he constantly threatened his hearers with hell and

BOX 15.1 INDULGENCES AND THE INDULGENCE TRADE

Among the odder expressions of Catholic belief is the granting of indulgences, defined in canon law as 'the remission of temporal punishment for sin, in response to certain prayers or good works'. The indulgence (Latin, *indulgentia*) relates to the penitence part of the Christian ritual of confession and penance, not to the guilt part, which for a person who has received the sacrament of confession was dealt with in the absolution ('remission [of guilt]') granted by the confessor. It is its non-sacramental nature that makes the indulgence theologically suspect and canonically problematic. While the sacraments are recognized instruments to achieve divine grace, the indulgence is presented as yet another means of grace that in fact has never acquired the status of a sacrament. The granting of an indulgence was always an exclusive right of popes, who saw themselves as the keepers of some heavenly 'treasury of satisfactions', from which they could draw as they would wish. It was also the popes themselves – Alexander II in 1063 and Urban II in 1095 – who first 'launched' the indulgence as a new grace-giving instrument with a collective purpose: anyone who was ready to take up arms against the Moors in defence of the Holy Sepulchre could be sure of a 'plenary' indulgence, a general remission of all temporal punishment for all sins. Indulgences gradually became more institutionalized: this happened with the crusade indulgence, for example, at the Fourth Lateran Council in 1215. In time the number of occasions at which indulgences could be earned was expanded, first to include certain forms of church attendance and the giving of alms or financial aid to build a new church, and later also intense and frequent prayer. After a while, and despite official Church opposition, the idea spread among the faithful that the bereaved could earn indulgences for their deceased relatives by remembering them frequently and at length in their prayers.

The abstract idea of the punishment indulgence soon came to be presented in sermons as a reduction of the time spent by sinners in Purgatory, the place where the souls of the departed suffer for a time until they are purged of their sins. Inflation inevitably set in, and the number of purgatory-free days soon reached astronomical levels. This illustrates how the system of indulgences gradually became commercialized. As early as the twelfth century, itinerant indulgence-preachers, commonly called pardoners, licensed by the pope, would preach a sermon and then hand out letters of indulgence in exchange for generous donations to all sorts of vague good works; the indulgence stated exactly how much remission the bearer could count on. With the advent of printing came the sale of indulgence prints, devout *Andachtsbilder* produced in large numbers, bearing a simple prayer and noting an indulgence.

From early on there was opposition to such developments in the indulgence system, also from the new mendicant orders that had to live on preaching and alms – the Dominican Albertus Magnus, for example, railed against every form of trade in indulgences. In the run-up to the Reformation, such criticisms reached storm force and indulgences became one of the primary targets of the original reformers, above all because they were such a familiar phenomenon to every believer. The pardoners ran an increasing risk of being physically attacked, especially when reformation of the Catholic Church was under discussion, as it was during the *Bauernkrieg* in Germany in 1525.

Literature: *Lexicon für Theologie und Kirche*, Band I (Freiburg, 1993), S.V.V. 'Ablass', 'Ablassbilder' and 'Ablassprediger'; J. van Herwaarden, 'Middeleeuwse aflaten en Nederlandse devotie', in *De Nederlanden in de late Middeleeuwen*, D.E.H. de Boer and J.W. Marsilje (eds) (Utrecht, 1987), pp. 31–68.

damnation. It was not all innocent, however. With his inflammatory sermons, Ferrer earns a considerable share of the blame for the terrible persecution of Spanish Jews in 1391.

Preachers had a number of resources to help them when they were preparing their sermons. These included the first catechisms, which appeared after the Fourth Lateran Council, the *Legenda Aurea* ('Golden Legend'), an extensive collection of saints' lives, compiled around 1265 by the Genoese Dominican, Jacopo of Voragine; and the *A, B, C des simples gens*, by Jean Gerson, which became very popular in the fifteenth century. The larger churches, of course, supplied plenty of visual support in the form of paintings, sculptures, carvings and stained-glass windows, while liturgy was further adapted to satisfy both the spiritual sensibilities of the passionate believers and the theatrical expectations of the masses. The invention of printing made it possible for the first time to spread devotional and moralizing texts and prints among the ordinary faithful on a large scale.

Of course, we cannot know exactly what was retained from the message spread through sermons and other channels. We have indicated (Chapters 4 and 8) the survival of many superstitions that often had their roots in pre-Christian practices. Some religious historians continue to insist that the Christian faith of ordinary people in the late Middle Ages was a mixture of Christian, pre-Christian and magical elements. The Church tolerated that to some extent. What else could it do when even popes consulted astrologers and priests sprinkled holy water and were convinced that devils and angels (demons) really did exist? Be that as it may, the religious life of the masses, with the traditional worship of saints at its centre, creates a rich, vital impression. Devotion to Christ and the Virgin Mary grew up during the eleventh century and gained in popularity. Christ's suffering was commemorated in several Church festivals – among them Corpus Christi or the 'body of Christ', the day of the Sacred Heart and the day of the Holy Cross – and supported by the so-called *Andachtsbilder* (literally: 'pictures that focus attention'), what we might nowadays consider rather repulsive pictures of Christ's sufferings, sometimes even with instruments of torture, which were intended to stimulate empathy and inner reflection on the meaning of the crucifixion. In the worship of Mary, it was the virginity of the Mother of God that most appealed to the faithful. This led to the increased popularity of other holy virgins, who were preferably martyrs too, such as the saints Catherine, Barbara and Lucia and – every boy's dream – Ursula and the 11,000 virgins from Cologne. More in general one can speak of a 'feminization' of holiness in the later Middle Ages. Of the numerous local and regional saints who until the thirteenth century were acclaimed as saints by the faithful themselves or by the parish clergy, an increasing number were females. The popes clamped down on the unrestrained growth of the whole business by making canonization, preceded by a critical examination with a real 'devil's advocate', the prerogative of the pope, a step that effectively curbed the proliferation of saints.

The pilgrimage was a direct extension of the veneration of saints. In addition to its devotional aims it could have a penitentiary purpose – the pilgrimage as a punishment imposed by an ecclesiastical or secular court. By the late Middle Ages the pilgrimage also began to show holiday-like symptoms. Top destinations such as Jerusalem, Rome and Santiago de Compostela were joined by others: Rocamadour in the Dordogne, Canterbury and Mont-Saint-Michel. The miraculous images of some saints, most generally Mary, became centres for religious confraternities that exploited the veneration and spent the proceeds on charitable works. Good examples are the Compagnia della Madonna di Orsanmichele in Florence and the Illustere-Lieve-Vrouwenbroederschap in 's-Hertogenbosch/Bois-le-Duc (of which the painter Hieronymus Bosch was a member). Large cities like Florence and Ghent had dozens of such confraternities, but they were also to be found in smaller towns and even in villages. Sometimes they were primarily connected to the cult of a saint, sometimes associated with a craft guild or a particular age-group or social class. The richest of them had their own meeting-house and chapel, but most simply had an altar in a side aisle of a church. Their activities and numbers of members varied greatly. There were special confraternities of penitents who held collective flagellation sessions as well as simple prayer and choral societies. The most common activities included the funeral arrangements and memorial services for deceased members, sometimes financial support for widows and orphans and participation in local processions at which religious or morality plays often were enacted – another new medium through which the Christian message could be relayed in a simplified form to a broad public.

The sixteenth-century reformers directed their criticism towards the outward display and superficial nature of this lay devotion, the most important aim of which seemed to be to gain as much quantifiable credit ('addition-devotion') as possible with God and the saints, while the inner state of the believer scarcely seemed to matter. On the other hand, the Catholic Church was more successful in taking its message directly to the ordinary faithful in the late Middle Ages than before. Through the variety of its institutions and rituals the Church offered the faithful a solid framework and support that gave meaning to their existence and provided them with mental and material succour in time of need. Had these ordinary believers not been so mobilized or their awareness so kindled, and without the critical approach to various aspects of Catholic life, which was indeed the result, Luther, Zwingli and Calvin would never have found ground where their ideas could take root.

FURTHER READING

Black, Anthony (1992), *Political Thought in Europe 1250–1450* (Cambridge: Cambridge University Press).

—— (2003), *Church, State and Community: Historical and Comparative Perspectives* (Aldershot and Burlington, Vt: Ashgate) (Variorum Collected Studies).

Bossy, John (1985), *Christianity in the West, 1400–1700* (Oxford: Oxford University Press).

Chareyron, Nicole (2005), *Pilgrims to Jerusalem in the Middle Ages* (New York: Columbia University Press).

Cohn, Samuel K. Jr. (1992), *The Cult of Remembrance and the Black Death: Six Renaissance Cities in central Italy* (Baltimore, Md.: Johns Hopkins University Press).

Collins, Amanda (2002), *Greater than Emperor: Cola di Rienzo (ca.1313–54) and the World of Fourteenth-century Rome* (Ann Arbor: University of Michigan Press).

Elliott, Dyan (2004), *Proving Woman: Female Spirituality and Inquisitional Culture in the Later Middle Ages* (Princeton, N.J.: Princeton University Press).

Fudge, Thomas A. (1998), *The Magnificent Ride: The First Reformation in Hussite Bohemia* (Aldershot: Ashgate).

Garnett, George (2006), *Marsilius of Padua and 'the Truth of History'* (Oxford and New York: Oxford University Press).

Heft, James (1986), *John XXII and Papal Teaching Authority* (Lewiston, N.Y.: Edwin Mellen Press).

Herwaarden, Jan van (2003), *Between Saint James and Erasmus. Studies in Late-Medieval Religious Life: Devotion and Pilgrimage in the Netherlands* (Leiden and Boston, Mass.: Brill).

Jansen, Katherine Ludwig (2000), *The Making of the Magdalen: Preaching and Popular Devotion in the Later Middle Ages* (Princeton, N.J.: Princeton University Press).

Jordan, William Chester (2005), *Unceasing Strife, Unending Fear: Jacques de Thérines and the Freedom of the Church in the Age of the Last Capetians* (Princeton, N.J.: Princeton University Press).

Kamerick, Kathleen (2002), *Popular Piety and Art in the Late Middle Ages: Image Worship and Idolatry in England, 1350–1500* (Basingstoke: Palgrave Macmillan).

Kenny, Anthony (1985), *Wyclif* (Oxford: Oxford University Press).

—— (ed.) (1986) *Wyclif in His Times* (Oxford: Clarendon).

Kieckhefer, Richard (1976), *European Witch Trials: Their Foundations in Popular and Learned Culture* (Berkely: University of California Press).

—— (1984), *Unquiet Souls: Fourteenth-Century Saints and Their Religious Milieu* (Chicago, Ill. and London: University of Chicago Press).

Lahey, Stephen E. (2003), *Philosophy and Politics in the Thought of John Wyclif* (Cambridge: Cambridge University Press).

Lerner, R.E. (1972), *The Heresy of the Free Spirit in the Later Middle Ages* (Berkeley: University of California Press).

Linder, Amnon (2003), *Raising Arms: Liturgy in the*

Struggle to Liberate Jerusalem in the Late Middle Ages (Turnhout: Brepols).

MacCulloch, Diarmaid (2003), *The Reformation: A History* (London: Penguin Group).

MacDonald, A.A., H.N.B. Ridderbos and R.M. Schlusemann (eds) (1998), *The Broken Body: Passion Devotion in Late-Medieval Culture* (Groningen: Forsten).

McGinn, Bernard (1994–), *The Presence of God: A History of Western Mysticism*, 6 vols, of which 4 have been published to date (2006), (New York: Crossroad).

—— (2001), *The Mystical Thought of Meister Eckhart: The Man from Whom God Hid Nothing* (New York: Crossroad).

—— (2005), *The Harvest of Mysticism in Medieval Germany (1300–1500)* (New York: Crossroad).

—— (ed.) (1994), *Meister Eckhart and the Beguine Mystics: Hadewijch of Brabant, Mechteld of Magdeburg and Marguerite Porete* (New York: Continuum).

Mansfield, Mary C. (2005), *The Humiliation of Sinners: Public Penance in Thirteenth-Century France* (Ithaca, N.Y.: Cornell University Press).

Marks, Richard (2004), *Image and Devotion in Late Medieval England* (Stroud: Sutton).

Menache, Sophia (1998), *Clement V* (Cambridge: Cambridge University Press).

Musto, Ronald G. (2003), *Apocalypse in Rome: Cola di Rienzo and the Politics of the New Age* (Berkeley and London: University of California Press).

Murdoch, Brian (2003), *The Medieval Popular Bible. Expansions of Genesis in the Middle Ages* (Rochester, N.Y. and Woodbridge: Boydell & Brewer).

Nieuwenhove, Rik van (2003), *Jan van Ruusbroec: Mystical Theologian of the Trinity* (Notre Dame, Ind.: University of Notre Dame Press).

Nixon, Virginia (2004), *Mary's Mother: Saint Anne in Late Medieval Europe* (University Park, Pa.: Penn State Press).

Oakley, Francis (1979) *The Western Church in the Later Middle Ages* (Ithaca, N.Y.: Cornell University Press).

—— (1984), *Natural Law, Conciliarism and Consent in the Late Middle Ages. Studies in Ecclesiastical and Intellectual History* (London: Variorum Reprints) (Collected Studies).

—— (2003), *The Conciliarist Tradition: Constitutionalism in the Catholic Church, 1300–1870* (Oxford and New York: Oxford University Press).

Oberman, Heiko A. (1986), *The Dawn of the Reformation: Essays in Late Medieval and Early Reformation Thought* (Edinburgh: T&T Clark).

Ozment, Steven (1980), *The Age of Reform, 1250–1550: An Intellectual and Religious History of Late Medieval and Reformation Europe* (New Haven, Conn.: Yale University Press).

Palmer, Robert C. (2002), *Selling the Church: The English Parish in Law, Commerce, and Religion, 1350–1550* (Chapel Hill and London: University of North Carolina Press).

Post, R.R. (1968), *The Modern Devotion: Confrontation with Reformation and Humanism* (Leiden: Brill) (orig. Dutch, 1940).

Renouard, Yves (1970), *The Avignon Papacy, 1305–1403* (London: Faber) (orig. French, 1969).

Rex, Richard (2002), *The Lollards* (Basingstoke and New York: Palgrave).

Rosenthal, Joel (1972), *The Purchase of Paradise. Gift Giving and the Aristocracy, 1307–1485* (London: Routledge & Kegan Paul).

Rubin, Miri (1991), *Corpus Christi: The Eucharist in Late Medieval Culture* (Cambridge: Cambridge University Press).

Saak, Eric L. (2002), *High Way to Heaven: The Augustinian Platform between Reform and Reformation, 1292–1524* (Leiden: Brill).

Simons, Walter (2001), *Cities of Ladies. Beguine Communities in the Medieval Low Countries, 1200–1565* (Philadelphia, Pa.: University of Pennsylvania Press).

Somerset, Fiona, Jill C. Havens and Derrick G. Pitard (eds) (2003), *Lollards and Their Influence in Late Medieval England* (Woodbridge and Rochester, N.Y.: Boydell & Brewer).

Stephens, Walter (2002), *Demon Lovers: Witchcraft, Sex, and the Crisis of Belief* (Chicago, Ill. and London: University of Chicago Press).

Swanson, R.N. (1995), *Religion and Devotion in Europe, c.1215–c.1515* (Cambridge: Cambridge University Press).

Tierney, Brian (1998), *Foundations of the Conciliar Theory: The Contribution of the Medieval Canonists from Gratian to the Great Schism*, 2nd edn (Leiden: Brill).

Vauchez, André (1993), *The Laity in the Middle Ages: Religious Beliefs and Devotional Practices* (Notre Dame, Ind.: University of Notre Dame Press) (orig. French, 1987).

—— (1997), *Sainthood in the Later Middle Ages* (Cambridge: Cambridge University Press) (orig. French, 1981).

Waters, Claire (2004), *Angels and Earthly Creatures: Preaching, Performance, and Gender in the Later Middle Ages* (Philadelphia, Pa.: University of Pennsylvania Press).

CHAPTER 16

New times?

As we saw in the introductory chapter it is difficult to draw a sharp line between the 'Middle Ages' and 'early modern' times. No general 'historical' switch took place around any of the well-known symbolic dates (1453, 1492, 1498, 1517, let alone 1500). Each one of them dealt with one particular aspect of the reality of the time (Ottoman expansion, the journeys of discovery and colonization, the Reformation). Moreover, at least until the French Revolution the basic structures of the Middle Ages remained intact: a mainly agrarian, class-based hierarchical society, built on a monarchal and locally particularistic foundation. Rather than engage in a pointless controversy about the demarcation of an era, we have chosen, as we did with the transition from late Antiquity, to indicate the perspective of the historians who either believe they can detect the new very early on or those who continue to see the old for a long time. In reality, of course, both tendencies existed side by side in a relationship of creative tension.

Fernand Braudel, the renowned French historian, introduced the concept of the 'long sixteenth century', which he placed between 1450 and 1650. It was a time of growth, expansion and innovation throughout almost all Europe. His view is supported by demographic and economic indicators: despite the sporadic outbursts of plague epidemics, their effect was less disastrous than between 1347 and 1450, and the population of Europe grew again. If the recurring epidemics had caused it to drop from 75 million to 50 million in about 1450, then by 1500 it had recovered to a total that – depending on the estimate and whether or not Russia and the Balkans are counted – lay somewhere between 61 and 82 million, and by 1600 had reached between 78 and 106 million – more than ever before. People had learnt to cope with contagious disease and could thus keep it better under control.

The population growth was made possible primarily through further introduction of intensive methods of agriculture, which had previously only been applied in the most advanced areas. Substantial growth in shipping capacity also facilitated the regular export of large quantities of grain to densely populated regions: 6,000 hectolitres of grain were exported from Danzig/Gdansk to the West in 1470, 30,000 in 1490 and 120,000 in 1560. The total volume of grain exported from Prussia between 1562 and 1569 is estimated at an average of 218 million litres per year, sufficient to cover the demand for bread for 650,000 people.

A generalization such as typifying the 'long sixteenth century' as a growth phase of course ignores regional differences, which were very considerable even in the twentieth century. The Balkans and Hungary suffered terribly under the Ottoman wars of conquest. After 1494 there was a grave crisis in northern and central Italy as the great powers continued to wage their wars there. It was one of the causes of the shift of the economic leadership – Italy had been the undisputed leader since the growth phase at the beginning of the eleventh century – to the North Sea area, to Antwerp in particular. Should one share Braudel's view of the unity of the period between 1450 and 1650, the economic perspective is crucial. We shall summarize here some of the trends discernible in the fifteenth and first half of the sixteenth centuries that resulted directly from developments during the late Middle Ages.

ACCELERATION

From the perspective of the Middle Ages the innovations of the late fifteenth and sixteenth centuries can be better described as progressive accelerations than as radical breaks. This is even true of the invention of printing. From the thirteenth century, government, trade, the Church, education and literature made increasing use of the written word. At the same time there was a swing to the use of the vernacular languages for all these purposes, so that much larger segments of the population took part in the culture of writing. Parchment soon became a scarce item, reserved for luxury books. Cheaper paper made the continued growth of literacy possible. In the Low Countries, the religious reform movement of the Modern Devotion, which rapidly won large numbers of followers in the last decades of the fourteenth century, is a typical example. Among its aims was the dissemination of pious literature in the Dutch language in the form of cheap pamphlets that could be read by everyone 'in a corner', as Geert Groote expressed it.

Growing demand for the written word explains the search for methods to reproduce it more quickly and on a larger scale. When Gutenberg printed his first Bible in Mainz in 1456, he set in motion a process that would quickly be imitated and improved. There is no doubt that printing was a considerable help in spreading new political, religious and scientific ideas. Yet it was not technology that was initially responsible for this media revolution, but the strongly increasing demand for devotional literature for quiet personal reading that met the need for a more individual perception of religion. Uwe Neddermeyer has calculated that in the German Empire, including most of the Low Countries, the production of handwritten books twice increased tenfold during the late Middle Ages: from 20,000 annually in 1370 to 200,000 by 1460, and to 2 million around 1500. No wonder that efforts were made to find more efficient methods of production.

Overseas colonization expanded around the Mediterranean, Baltic and Irish seas from the twelfth century. European travellers started searching for overland routes to the Far East from the mid-thirteenth century, and soon afterwards for sea routes as well. Europeans showed themselves to be expansive in relation to the peripheral areas, even if at first these areas represented cultures that were superior in every respect, such as that of the Muslims. The voyages of discovery along the coast of Africa and later across the oceans were the logical consequence of the dynamic that had been growing for centuries, although it must be recognized that Columbus and Vasco da Gama gave

an impetus to qualitative leaps. For several decades, however, these discoveries had only marginal effects on the European economy. The economic growth of the sixteenth and seventeenth centuries did not imply a breakthrough to a totally different system, only the highest state of pre-industrial society. Nor should it be assumed that at this time Europe had achieved a higher level of economic, cultural and political development than China, Japan or the princely states of India. Until industrialization, Western Europe was no more than one of the world's more highly developed agricultural societies. At most it took more initiatives towards other continents, but whether this was a sign of development or of relative need is still a matter of debate.

European voyages of discovery obviously and quickly changed western views of the world. Geographical insights, as visualized in maps, grew on the basis of wider knowledge and experience of the seafarers. The atlases published in Antwerp by Abraham Ortelius in 1570 and Gerard Mercator between 1585 and 1589 took many of their new facts and insights from the descriptions of coasts that had been collected gradually and handed on piecemeal by generations of sailors. In this way people's view of their planet grew in a few generations into the globe that we know today.

Chapter 12 described how fourteenth- and fifteenth-century Italian humanists refined their knowledge of ancient sources, brought the study of classical languages and literature to a higher level and, above all, how they forged an educational concept from them. The 'Latin school' was the dominant pedagogic model until the 1960s, propagating its own methods as fundamentally innovative. Both the Counter-Reformation schools, notably those run by the Jesuits, and the grammar schools and high schools in Protestant countries were powerful forces in spreading this image of a fundamental renaissance. But both systems made the mistake of overestimating themselves. There was interest in and admiration for the culture of Antiquity throughout the Middle Ages. Although the late medieval humanists examined more and older manuscripts of ancient and early Christian texts and became more critical in their search for sources, it was not until the nineteenth century that scientific philology actually reached a level that still meets current standards. That being said, without the assiduous copying by diligent medieval monks, the translations of Iberian scholars and the curiosity of Franciscans and Dominicans, a substantial part of the writings of Antiquity would never have been preserved for us.

Medieval methods and concepts were still followed at the universities, despite the work of the Italian humanists. Medical education was based on the ancient Greeks' teachings of the four humours or body fluids until the seventeenth century, and was far removed from the sickbed, while theology focused on the authority of teachers from Antiquity. In 1543 the founder of modern anatomy, Andreas Vesalius of Brussels, published a massive and richly illustrated empirical study of the human anatomy, pointing out the mistakes in Galen's second-century theory. He dissected bodies in front of his students, confronting them with these empirical observations and Galen's outdated ideas. He met with so much opposition from supporters of traditional teachings that he had to resign from the universities of Louvain, Padua and Pisa where he taught consecutively. Innovative as Vesalius' findings were, he was part of a surgical tradition that was active at the universities of Paris and Montpellier at about 1300.

In 1920 no less a scholar than Max Weber advanced the proposition that commercial capitalism's rational pursuit of profit could only truly flourish in those lands where the Protestant ethic of austerity held sway. By this he meant that commercial capitalism could not have existed in the Middle Ages. Nevertheless, it must be remembered here, too, that after a more thorough study of medieval commercial and other sources the modern specialists are in unanimous agreement that merchants and entrepreneurs in the Italian, southern French, Catalan and Flemish cities in particular consistently displayed a 'capitalist mentality' from the twelfth century onwards: they made rationalized efforts to make as much profit as possible, which was then reinvested in the business to make it grow. Other considerations, religious or ethical, for example, were subordinated to their pursuit of profit. Forms of vertical integration and of partnerships based on shareholdings were seen in growing numbers since the thirteenth century. Here, too, we must remember that the great sixteenth-century capitalist firms, such as the Fuggers and Welsers of Augsburg, were larger than their medieval predecessors, but essentially no different.

Just like book production, colonization, car-tography, surgery and commercial capitalism, the Reformation was not a fundamentally new phenomenon. Luther was more conservative in many respects, in his political and social principles, for example, than the so-called heretics among the thirteenth-century Cathars or John Wyclif. Criticism of the clergy echoed through the works of John of Leeuwen, the 'good cook' of the priory of Groenendaal in the Sonian Forest just south of Brussels between 1355 and 1370, no less sharply than in Erasmus. Geert Groote was inspired by John of Ruusbroec, the first prior of Groenendaal, who, with his emphasis on simplicity, austerity and sincere personal devotion, joined a long line of reformers in a call for Church reformation that had been made at regular intervals since the tenth century. Some were given their place within the Church, sometimes after difficult negotiations, concessions and secessions, such as Francis of Assisi and his followers. Others, especially those who exposed the socio-political order, such as the Cathars, Lollards and Hussites, and the Lutherans and Anabaptists in the sixteenth century, were condemned as heretics and burned without mercy.

The criticisms levelled by early sixteenth-century reformers closely resembled those made by the critics of previous centuries. They spoke out against the love of luxury and the worldly conduct of the clergy, against the purely formal character of Church ritual. They pleaded for the Bible and private reading matter in the vernacular, and for the role of the individual conscience. The great differences between the situation during the first half of the sixteenth century and the situations during those earlier movements for reform lay in the combination of a Church lacking moral authority and incapable of incorporating criticism positively, the strong interrelation between the authority of the state and the hierarchy of the Church, and the enormous spread of reformist thinking, made possible by the printing press. Evidently, the effects of the sixteenth-century Reformation were more lasting than those of the earlier reform movements that had sown the seed.

Finally, 'early modern' times are often associated with the age of the 'modern state'. Even when a precise description of this term is adhered to, in the sense of a centralized government organization that showed itself to be an effective supreme power in its own territory, early examples can be seen – England from the twelfth century – as well as late developers, in particular Castile and Poland in the seventeenth and eighteenth centuries. Here, too, we must emphasize that the differences were those of degree and not of fundamental importance, and there were considerable variations between the regions in every period. Expansion did indeed take place in the prominent monarchies of the West from the twelfth century onwards, in a development that was not always direct but was continuous in the long term.

The territories of France, England, the Spanish kingdoms, the principalities of the Low Countries and the Italian regional states expanded steadily and their resources grew more than proportionally. Their destructive power far exceeded that of lesser princes, local lords or towns, who were thus fatally deprived of their power. The autonomy of local bodies and their political voice in the form of parliaments and state assemblies suffered. This again was a process that was set in motion in the central Middle Ages, sometimes accelerating, sometimes encountering setbacks. The so-called medieval particularist state model, based on the autonomous rights of local communities and regions, existed until the end of the eighteenth century in Europe's most progressive states – the United Provinces, northern Italy and Switzerland. Monarchal states became larger and stronger as a result of constant and continual fighting between each other, especially between the Habsburg Empire, France and England. The threat of Ottoman expansion was ever present, especially for the Habsburgs.

THE MEDIEVAL ROOTS OF MODERN CULTURE

In conclusion, we would like to examine which characteristics of our own culture can be traced back directly to medieval origins. Many fundamental characteristics of what Europe is today evolved out of developments occurring during the Middle Ages.

Europe is characterized by its cultural diversity: the multiplicity of peoples, languages and customs form the basis of a consciousness that in certain periods has been fanned into an aggressive nationalism. During the early Middle Ages, linguistic areas were consolidated as the result of migration and acculturation. This diversity now forms a marked contrast with continents where, despite a great variety of cultures, a common language and a set of common values provide an integrating framework. Such a culture was provided in China by the Empire, in Islamic regions by the religion and the Arabic language. This unifying cultural pattern was completely absent in Europe. The Catholic Church provided something of the sort, and Latin – the language of the Church – also operated as a universal language for scholarship and government until the thirteenth century, functioning in Europe rather as Mandarin did in China. But the Church failed in its ambition to become a universal power. Political fragmentation formed a barrier to cultural homogenization, gradually even reinforcing the national identity.

Throughout the ages, the Church has been an exceptionally influential cultural institution. It was the most important medium for the transfer of the classical culture, to which it added specifically Christian values that in many cases were diametrically opposed to those of Antiquity. In principle the Church defended every human soul and was thus obligated to oppose slavery, indentureship, arbitrary killing. It defended, again in theory, spiritual values over material values, poverty over riches, the weak over the mighty, and it encouraged charity and love of one's neighbour. However much and however often these principles may have been set aside, reformers and zealots could still receive the message and pass it on. The Church was the oldest and most all-encompassing medieval institution and, in the long term, was thus able to assert its message in relative independence. Slavery disappeared among European Christians in the course of the Middle Ages. Rulers could no longer apply violence indiscriminately: sooner or later they would have to render account to the clerics. The institutional division between Church and secular power, which had grown gradually out of the realities of the Late Roman Empire and had been shaped by the doctrine of the two swords, was unprecedented in world history. It allowed breakthroughs in Europe that had either never taken place elsewhere or never produced such long-lasting results: autonomous forms of rationality in the fields of religion, government, economic activity and scientific thought. The secular and spiritual spheres were separate in most parts of the Islamic world also, for many periods, enabling astonishing progress to be made. The essential difference here, however, was in the absence of a hierarchical estate of clerics. In the Aztec or Chinese cultures, for example, where these spheres continued to be united in a theocracy, innovations in one particular area could be curbed for the sake of considerations of another nature.

During the Middle Ages feudalism gradually took shape as a system of feudo-vassalic relations aimed at a controlled distribution of lordship and at warranting military power. It was a strong, intensive and direct form of exercising power, reaching from the suzerain downwards to the local level. Strictly organized and carefully managed, lordships and principalities were created out of small units through a process of continuous competition and struggle. This was followed by the elimination of weaker rivals and the expansion of the surviving entities, forming the basis of monarchal states. It is impossible to imagine European history without the basic units upon which it was built: political fragmentation was added to the cultural diversity. The two categories – peoples and states – did not overlap each other, for they had grown out of differing dynamics. Despite the strong trend towards homogenization during the last few hundred years, most European states are still made up of more than one ethnic group. Diversity of cultures and states, with all the concomitant tensions, conflicts and creativity, has been the European characteristic par excellence. A coordinated empire had no chance of surviving here because of the cohesiveness of the older political and cultural patterns. Empires with real power could not last for long in the West. In later centuries the Ottoman, Habsburg and Russian empires were only able to survive in the less progressive and more thinly populated parts of the Continent. They all disintegrated after the First World War, in part under pressures from national cultures dating from the Middle Ages.

The multiplicity of political and cultural entities was an impediment to the monolithic exercise of power, a situation that was reinforced by the separate organization of Church and state. In Europe there was no single central authority that could intervene in every field of human activity throughout a very extensive territory, as there was in China for example. The relatively short distances made it possible for dissidents and other persecuted people to move to other areas of authority. Inside the monarchic states, central authority again encountered large areas that governed themselves to a large extent. Religious institutions and noble lords held considerable domains where states were unable to exercise direct control. Towns continued to enjoy a great degree of self-government and could administer their own laws. This autonomy forced rulers to consult with influential subjects and their representatives, from which constitutional constraints on the monarchy grew up and a parliamentary tradition could develop. No single European prince could function as an absolute ruler during the Middle Ages; he was accountable both to his confessor and to subjects who had their own means of exercising power. Europe was therefore the only continent in which representative institutions came into being that could control the purse strings on behalf of specific categories of subjects – the estates: clergy, nobles, burghers, free peasants – and at crucial moments had the power to curb the arbitrary designs of princes.

A civic culture grew up in towns, which, together with chivalric culture, gave shape to the pattern of values and the imagination of Europeans for many centuries. There are substantial differences between them. The culture of chivalry valued bravery and skill with weapons, valorous deeds, brilliant physical accomplishments, selfless assistance to widows, orphans, clerics and other people in need, willingness to serve one's lord and the Christian faith actively, generosity in sharing booty and gifts with followers, indifference to material gain. In the romanticized version this grew into the cult of courtly love, a literary form that survives in today's popular literature.

The burgher culture, on the other hand, was characterized by its businesslike attitude, the desire for material gain but also the ability to deal with and learn from other cultures and other social categories. The inhabitants of great seaports, in particular, were very open in their outlook. Townspeople had to fight for their place in a world that was controlled by landed aristocracy and were therefore more ready to make compromises. The calculation of risk, not physical conflict, offered the means of success. Certain elements from chivalric culture gradually filtered through into civic culture via the patrician elite. Yet what distinguished the burghers was that they allowed neither

Church nor princes nor aristocrats to impose their laws on them, even though they were anxious to do business with all of them. This was the context for the emergence of commercial capitalism, which became the driving force behind the western economy.

The Middle Ages saw the creation of universities, centres that reproduced and commented upon the knowledge acquired from ancient authorities. It was at the universities that efforts were made to harmonize Christian doctrines with ideas from pagan Antiquity that were considered valuable. Here, too, the initial impetus was given to test ancient theories against Arabic knowledge and personal observations. In theory, universities were under papal authority. In practice this meant that they enjoyed far-reaching independence from the clergy and temporal rulers in the immediate vicinity. The weakening of the papacy during the late Middle Ages allowed critical intellectuals to emerge and develop, who formulated new ideological foundations attuned to the radically changing social realities.

The Christian West originally grew up completely aware that it trailed behind its great neighbours, the Byzantine Empire and the Arabic world. The relationship with the latter was often discordant, but it never prevented intensive commercial dealings or frequent cultural exchanges. The close contact enabled the West to borrow much and to evolve further, gradually becoming emancipated. As the Ottoman Empire swept the Byzantine Empire off the map it formed an enormous military and cultural challenge for the West. This friction dominated the sixteenth and seventeenth centuries in Hungary and the Mediterranean. Here again we thus encounter continuity with the Middle Ages. Europe evolved during the distinctive centuries of the Middle Ages into an entity that has made a radical contribution to world history.

Index

The index was composed with the assistance of Jan de Putter MA. Not included are names of places or concepts that occur more than 25 times in the text, so one will look in vain for 'England' or 'taxes'. Generally, only names of emperors, kings and popes are provided with the years of their rule. Geographical names on maps are included in the index only when they also occur in the text. References to modern authors are marked with an asterisk (*).

Related titles from Routledge

Introduction to Early Medieval Western Europe 300-900
The sword, the plough and the book

Matthew Innes

Surveying the period of European history from the years 300 to 900, this comprehensive textbook is the first to combine the last twenty-five years of research in an accessible manner for undergraduate students. It is unique in linking an account of the historical background of the period with discussion of the social, economic, cultural and political structures of the society within it. With its synthesis and interpretations of otherwise unavailable primary research, this text is ideal for students of late antique or early medieval history, and provides researchers and postgraduate students with an invaluable source of information.

ISBN: 978-0-415-21506-0 (hb)
ISBN: 978-0-415-21507-7 (pb)

Available at all good bookshops
For ordering and further information please visit:
www.routledge.com

Related titles from Routledge

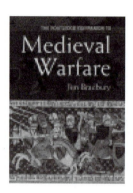

The Routledge Companion to Medieval Warfare
Jim Bradbury

'This work of reference in useful ... [it] has some very useful and
well-set-out material ... [a] very good handbook.' *History*

This comprehensive volume provides easily-accessible factual material on all
major areas of warfare in the medieval west. The whole geographical area of
medieval Europe, including Eastern Europe, is covered, including essential
elements from outside Europe such as Byzantine warfare, nomadic horde
invasions and the Crusades.

Progressing chronologically, the work is presented in themed, illustrated sections, with a narrative
outline offering a brief introduction to the area. Within each chronological section, Jim Bradbury
presents clear and informative pieces on battles, sieges, and generals.

ISBN: 978-0-415-22126-9 (hb)
ISBN: 978-0-415-41395-4 (pb)

Available at all good bookshops
For ordering and further information please visit:
www.routledge.com

Related titles from Routledge

The Two Cities: Medieval Europe, 1050–1320

Malcolm Barber

'Meets every conceivable need and effectively renders redundant all earlier textbooks on the high Middle Ages ... in short, the book is excellent in every respect.' *History Today*

First published to wide critical acclaim in 1992, *The Two Cities* has become an essential text for students of medieval history. For the second edition, the author has thoroughly revised each chapter, bringing the material up to date and taking the historiography of the past decade into account.

The Two Cities covers a colourful period from the schism between the eastern and western churches to the death of Dante. It encompasses the Crusades, the expansionist force of the Normans, major developments in the way kings, emperors and Popes exercised their powers, a great flourishing of art and architecture and the foundation of the very first universities. Running through it is the defining characteristic of the high Middle Ages - the delicate relationship between the spiritual and secular worlds, the two 'cities' of the title.

This survey provides all the facts and background information that students need, and is defined into straightforward thematic chapters. It makes extensive use of primary sources, and makes new trends in research accessible to students. Its fresh approach gives students the most rounded, lively and integrated view of the high Middle Ages available.

ISBN: 978-0-415-17414-5 (hb)
ISBN: 978-0-415-17415-2 (pb)

Available at all good bookshops
For ordering and further information please visit:
www.routledge.com

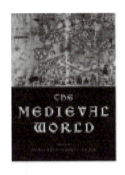